Ancient Curious and Famous Wills

Ancient Curious and Famous Wills

By
Virgil M. Harris

MEMBER OF THE SAINT LOUIS BAR, LECTURER ON WILLS IN THE
SAINT LOUIS UNIVERSITY INSTITUTE OF LAW, TRUST OFFICER
OF THE MERCANTILE TRUST COMPANY OF SAINT LOUIS,
MISSOURI, AND AUTHOR OF " THE TRUST COMPANY
OF TO-DAY," ETC.

" The boast of heraldry, the pomp of power,
And all that beauty, all that wealth e'er gave,
Await alike the inevitable hour :
The paths of glory lead but to the grave."

BeardBooks
Washington, D.C.

Boston :

Little, Brown, and Company

1911

Copyright, 1911, by Little, Brown, and Company

Reprinted 2000 by Beard Books, Washington, D.C.

ISBN 1-58798-071-1

ANCIENT, CURIOUS AND FAMOUS WILLS

"A truce to jesting; let me have a confessor to confess me, and a notary to make my will."

TO THE LATE

HONORABLE JACOB KLEIN

OF

SAINT LOUIS, MISSOURI

WHOSE LONG AND USEFUL CAREER AT THE BAR

AND WHOSE STERLING CHARACTER, LEARNING AND WISDOM

ENTITLE HIS NAME TO A PLACE IN THE GALAXY

OF GREAT AMERICAN LAWYERS

THIS BOOK

IS AFFECTIONATELY INSCRIBED

PREFACE

"Let's choose executors, and talk of wills;
And yet not so, — for what can we bequeath,
Save our deposed bodies to the ground?"

AN addition to the fifteen millions of books of which the world is now possessed demands an explanation, if not an apology.

In my experience as a lecturer on the Law of Wills, and in the practical administration of estates controlled by wills, in which I have been engaged for many years, it has been a subject of surprise to me that no one in America has seriously undertaken the collection of curious and famous wills. It has occurred to me that I might discharge the duty which every lawyer owes to his profession by making such a collection. The subject is very comprehensive, and the material required has been obtained, in most instances, from the original records of Probate and Court Registers in various parts of the world, by exhaustive research in libraries at home and abroad, and by reference to magazine and newspaper files.

It has been my effort to select from this collection the wills which appeared most interesting and entertaining. I recognize quite fully the wisdom of Lord Coke's remark, that

"Wills, and the construction of them, do more perplex a man than any other learning; and to make a certain construction of them exceedeth *jurisprudentum artem.*"

Perplexity has likewise beset me in an attempt to classify the wills in this work and place them under convenient and appropriate headings.

It must not be forgotten that while all men may make wills, and should do so, yet all men have *not* done so. It is a remarkable trait in human character that wills are for the most part postponed, and that many men of wealth and distinction die without them. So great a man as Abraham Lincoln left no will, though he had a considerable estate. General Grant also died intestate, but his estate was small. It is to be regretted that men fail to perform the duty of making their wills, as history and experience demonstrate that this neglect has often resulted in a disastrous train of consequences.

The subject of Wills is not so prosaic as might be supposed; in fact, there are few subjects of more general interest. Wills reflect, as a mirror, the customs and habits of the times when written, as well as the characters of the writers.

Our earthly possessions are, after all, but life-holdings, and the grace with which we part with them at the end of life's journey shows the heart in its least disguised form. The moment of will-writing is a solemn one. The insight we get into the character of the testator is genuine and unvarnished. Property does not always bring with it comfort and happiness, and those who have to deal with wills find that it is frequently as difficult to dispose of one's possessions as it is to acquire them.

In this work, it has been deemed inadvisable to cite many authorities. The author has experienced too much embarrassment in his researches to ask others to follow in his footsteps. The wills found in these pages have been conscientiously copied and compared; in many cases, they have been obtained in places not easily accessible to the average reader. A number of wills set forth have been abridged, where found to be too voluminous in their entirety; and, in some instances, parts which were not of general interest have been omitted.

The wills have not been created by the author, but have been taken from trustworthy sources; some of them have appeared in English works, but very few in American publications.

I desire to acknowledge my obligations for material assistance, particularly to the late Hon. Jacob Klein of Saint Louis, Mr. John Marshall Gest of Philadelphia, Mr. Daniel Remsen of New York, Messrs. Harper & Brothers of New York, the Editors of the "Green Bag" of Boston and other legal publications, and to the valuable works of Mr. Proffatt, Mr. Tegg, Julia Clara Byrne, Mr. Nicholas and Mr. Nichols.

VIRGIL M. HARRIS.

SAINT LOUIS, MISSOURI,
March 1, 1911.

CONTENTS

	PAGE
INTRODUCTION	xi

CHAPTER I
THE IMPORTANCE OF THE LAST WILL AND TESTAMENT . 1

CHAPTER II
ANCIENT WILLS 10

CHAPTER III
WILLS IN FICTION AND POETRY 49

CHAPTER IV
CURIOUS WILLS 73
  1. Relating to Husbands, Wives, and Children . . 73
  2. Relating to Animals 90
  3. Relating to Charity 102
  4. Relating to Burial 122
  5. Miscellaneous 158

CHAPTER V
TESTAMENTARY AND KINDRED MISCELLANY . . . 203

CHAPTER VI
WILLS OF FAMOUS FOREIGNERS 249

CHAPTER VII
WILLS OF FAMOUS AMERICANS 324

INDEX 455

INTRODUCTION

*"The Moving Finger writes; and, having writ,
Moves on: nor all your Piety nor Wit
Shall lure it back to cancel half a Line,
Nor all your Tears wash out a Word of it."*

THE history of wills and their study, as reflecting the character of the makers, and in throwing, as they do, a strong light on the customs and manners of the times in which they were written, are subjects profoundly interesting both to the lawyer and to the layman.

Lord Rosebery, in an address on the character of Byron, said:

"I will go a step further, and affirm that we have something to be grateful for even in the weaknesses of men. . . . We grope blindly along the catacombs of the world, we climb the dark ladder of life, we feel our way to futurity, but we can scarcely see an inch around or before us; we stumble and falter and fall, our hands and knees are bruised and sore, and we look up for light and guidance. . . . And, at the end, man is reaped — the product, not of good alone, but of evil; not of joy alone, but of sorrow — perhaps mellowed and ripened, perhaps stricken and withered and sour. How, then, shall we judge any one?"

Can we not judge a man by his will? Does not such an instrument reflect his character, his nature, and his eccentricities? A writer on the subject of Wills says:

"So surely as the berry indicates the soundness of the root, the flower of the bulb, so does man's last will tell of the goodness or foulness of the heart which conceived it. The cankered root sends up only a sickly germ, which brings forth no fruit in due season; whilst the wine that maketh glad the heart of man, the oil which maketh him a cheerful countenance, and the bread that strengthens his heart, have burst from roots which mildew has never marred, nor worm fretted."

Testamentary dispositions of property in some form are of very ancient origin; even in the Biblical period we find the statement in Genesis to the effect that Jacob gave to Joseph a portion above his brethren. Solon is said to have introduced wills into Greece, and there is good reason to believe that wills were known in Egypt ages before they were used in Europe. Charles Dufresne Du Cange, a most learned philological writer who died at Paris in 1688, mentions wills written on bark or wood in the seventh century. There are historians who gravely and learnedly assert that Adam made a will; that Noah also left one; and that Job likewise made testamentary disposition of his all. Roman wills were sealed, after they had been securely fastened and other precautions taken against forgery: the poet Horace explains how wills were drawn and secured, and Cicero also refers to the same subject. Anglo-Saxon wills were made in triplicate, and consigned to separate custodians. Tacitus records that wills were not recognized by the ancient Germans. In France, at an early date, the clergy were intrusted with the duty of looking after wills and the disposition of property under them. In England, wills were known before the Conquest, though subsequently, for a time, their use was forbidden by law.

The works of Barnabé Brisson, published in 1583 at Paris, are excellent sources for information on the subject of ancient wills. In fact, both in England and in France, authors of the highest learning and ability have done much for history and literature in the matter of collecting wills, ancient and modern.

Our form of testamentary disposition comes to us from the Roman law. In the present age, both in England and in the United States, a full and absolute disposition of property is permitted, subject to certain conditions, which are hereinafter noticed. That this general right to dispose of earthly possessions is exercised with many strange vagaries, and for objects showing many eccentricities, yet withal, in most cases, with much benevolence and generosity of nature, the following pages will fully attest. The disposition of property by will does not show that the good men do is "oft interred with their bones," but rather that the world has yet a good conscience in benefactions, and that humanity broadens and grows kindlier with the years. It may be observed that the mean and hateful traits of human nature are more frequently shown by heirs and legatees than by testators. It is true that the "ruling passion strong in death" shows itself in wills, and many testators evince a strong desire to take with them to the next world the substance collected in their dusty lives; but the law has placed hindrances, and, as Pope says:

INTRODUCTION

> "The laws of God as well as of the land
> Forbid a perpetuity to stand."

There are on file in the office of the Register of Wills in Washington City a number of wills of famous Americans; a copy of the will of Washington is there, as well as the wills of several other presidents; also, there are to be seen those of many statesmen and other eminent persons: likewise, in London, in the Registry of Wills, there are on file the original wills of great men, which the British nation has jealously guarded; all nations are interested in them, and they could not be allowed to perish. Those who desire it may in London see the will of the painter Vandyck, of Doctor Johnson, of Lord Nelson, of William Pitt, of Edmund Burke, of Izaak Walton, of the Duke of Wellington, and, greatest of all, that of William Shakespeare. The last, being of unusual interest, has been exceptionally treated, and the three folio pages of which it consists are placed under an air-tight frame made of polished oak and plate glass. The will of the Great Napoleon was to be seen for many years at old Doctors' Commons, but it was restored to the French nation in compliance with the request of the Emperor Louis Napoleon.

A chapter with the title, "The Importance of the Last Will and Testament," containing general suggestions as to the preparation of wills, has been introduced into this work, with the belief that it may prove useful to some readers; likewise a chapter on "Testamentary and Kindred Miscellany," which embraces subjects closely akin to those under consideration, and which it is hoped may not prove uninteresting.

The collecting of interesting and unusual wills is by no means an easy undertaking: the information as to their location and contents, even those of famous men, is surprisingly limited; digesting and arranging them has been a tedious but interesting task. It will be seen by the collection submitted, that all avenues of information have been sought and critically examined. If some minor errors have crept in, the indulgence of the reader is asked for a work largely on original lines, and one which covers a wide field of investigation, research, and comparison.

ANCIENT, CURIOUS, AND FAMOUS WILLS

CHAPTER I

THE IMPORTANCE OF THE LAST WILL AND TESTAMENT

"To put off making your Will until the hand of death is upon you evinces either cowardice or a shameful neglect of your temporal concerns."

It has been thought appropriate, within a brief space, to introduce into this work some general observations on the importance and preparation of wills. For that purpose, the following address, under the title given this chapter, recently delivered before the Missouri Bankers' Association, has been selected. It will be seen that the subject-matter is general in character, and this monograph has been favorably received by the legal profession and the legal and financial journals of the United States.

"No doubt most of my audience will regard my subject a lifeless, if not a commonplace one. Yet it is of daily and vital importance to bankers and business men generally, and it is to be regretted that there exist so many inaccurate impressions regarding wills.

"The *North American Review* in a recent editorial said, 'The writing of a will is a serious and formal matter, and into one a man puts his deliberate and well-reflected intentions. This makes a will stupendously revealing, and to read one over is to come very close to the spirit of the man who wrote: to know his treasures, to understand his feeling toward men, and to measure his fitness for adventures among seraphic and angelic beings. The words a man desires to have read when he lies dumb, the gifts he leaves, the grace with which he gives, all these lay bare the spirit, the heart of disposition, as few other things can. For a will is that which is to live after one, and it is written knowing that no wound inflicted can be remedied, no neglect repaired. How egotism, or miserliness, or conceit, or self-satisfaction can shine out in a will! How little exalting it is in most cases to read wills, and how often they turn us back to the authoritative statement, that it is easier for a camel to pass through the eye of a needle.'

"The power to dispose of property by a written will in the form known to us does not appear in any of the primitive systems of law, except in Egypt; yet testamentary dispositions in some form have come down to us from the earliest times. In the year 1902, the French government sent out a commission to make archæological investigations in Persia. At the city of Susa, they uncovered a stone on which was written the laws of Hammurabi, who reigned twenty-three hundred years before Christ, or one thousand years before Moses received the Ten Commandments on Mount Sinai. This code was translated by Professor Robert Francis Harper, of the Chicago University, and furnishes one of the most remarkable and readable books which has ever come into my hands; it treats of the laws of money, banking, inheritance, weights and measures, divorce, dower, crimes, and, singularly enough, some of its provisions are present-day law. There is, however, no mention of wills.

"In fact, the will, as we know it, is a Roman invention. Free liberty of disposition by will is by no means universal at this time. Complete freedom in this respect is the exception rather than the rule. Homesteads generally, estates of dower and curtesy frequently, as well as other portions of an estate, are not the subject of devise or bequest.

"There never was a fitter application of Pope's line, 'A little learning is a dangerous thing,' than in the preparation of wills; and it is a most astounding fact that men who have lived prudently, who have been conservative and successful in business, who have accumulated large wealth, who have been buffeted by every wave of misfortune, will attempt, by their own hands or through incompetent agents, to write their wills. It is always a hazardous undertaking, unless the instrument is of the simplest character. If one's child is sick, a doctor is called; if a man's roof is defective, a carpenter is sent for; if a horse throws a shoe, the animal goes to the blacksmith; yet, when it comes to the making of a will, perhaps the most solemn and consequential act of a man's life, the testator takes his pen, and frequently without aid or counsel does that which experience and our court records fully demonstrate he is incompetent to do.

"Mr. Daniel S. Remsen, of New York, an author of high repute on the preparation of wills, says that fully fifty per cent of wills contain some obscurity or omission. With this statement I find myself in complete accord. I believe that nearly half the wills written are open to attack and a large portion of them fatally defective. I have never seen more than a dozen perfectly drawn wills, gauged by the standards of perfect clearness, precision and legality.

"As stated by Mr. Remsen, ' A will is an ex-parte document and is written from one point of view; it is the expression of the wishes of the testator regarding the work of a lifetime; upon its legality depends the future happiness and welfare of the persons and objects most dear to the testator; and whether viewed from a property or a family standpoint, it is often the most important document a man of large or small means is ever called upon to prepare.'

"How many are there, in this audience of a thousand bankers, who can tell me the manner in which, under the laws of descent and distribution, is to be divided an estate consisting of five thousand dollars in cash, and real estate of the value of five thousand dollars, the testator leaving a wife and two children?

"Unfortunately the idea prevails that a will is a very simple instrument to prepare. Nothing in business life can be further from the truth; on the contrary, a will may be, and usually is, the most intricate of all legal documents. This is always true where there are gifts or devises depending upon contingencies, or where trusts are created. A deed or a contract may be changed; not so with a will, after the death of the maker. Therefore, foresight in its preparation is imperative.

"There is a well-marked legal distinction between the words, heirs, devisees, legatees, distributees, and legal representatives. Each of these terms has a clear and well-defined signification. One who has the preparation of wills must deal with the law against perpetuities. An estate cannot be tied up for a longer period than ' a life or lives in being and twenty-one years thereafter.' This is the general law of our country. The law of dower and curtesy is by no means simple. The law of vested and contingent remainders is a most intricate subject and requires years of legal study to comprehend, and cannot be simplified. The creation of life estates and trusts demands the most careful inquiry. There are spendthrift provisions which are easier to break than to prepare. The statute of uses cuts an important figure in testaments. The provisions with reference to the powers of executors and trustees are very comprehensive and must be framed with great care and precision. The subject of joint tenants, and tenants by the entirety, frequently requires the most profound consideration in the interpretation of wills.

"I recently saw a decision of one of our highest courts, where a testator gave a large sum of money by will to his wife 'to hold, possess and enjoy during her natural life'; at her death, the fund was to go to a certain college. The widow promptly set about to 'enjoy' the fund by spending it; the court held, and properly, that she had a right to do so, and that the college got nothing. The will was improperly drawn. Had it been stated that she might 'enjoy the income,' a different result would have followed.

"A few months ago I saw a will in which an estate of one million dollars was disposed of: the testator under the will divided the estate into ten parts, but overlooked the disposition of one of these parts; the omitted part passed under the general laws of inheritance, doubtless contrary to the wishes of the testator.

"There came under my observation not long ago a will drawn in Michigan: the testator owned property in Michigan and also in Missouri and South Carolina. The will had but two witnesses; it was effective in Michigan and Missouri, but in South Carolina, where three witnesses are required, it was inoperative.

"Within the last few days, I examined the will of one of our most gifted and eloquent United States senators, now deceased; an ample provision for his wife was followed by this clause: 'The acceptance by my wife of the provisions for her benefit, contained in this will, shall bar all claim by her for dower in any real estate heretofore or hereafter conveyed by me to any one.' This attempted exclusion of the wife's dower was well-nigh meaningless: his intent was to preclude her right of dower in any real estate owned by him at the time of his death; but he said 'conveyed by me to any one'; all real estate possessed by him at the time of his death was subject to dower and not excluded, because it had not been conveyed.

"A will was lately presented to me where the testator left a large estate, — one-third to his wife, one-third to a son, and one-third to a grandson; the wife predeceased the testator. The question arose as to what became of the one-third given to the wife.

"Generally speaking, under a bequest or devise to a 'child, grandchild or other relative,' the property passes to the lineal descendants of these, in the event the legatee or devisee dies before the testator; but it is otherwise as to all other persons: as to them, the devise or gift lapses; even the children of stepchildren would not take under these conditions.

"It is said 'a will has no brother,' meaning that no two are alike. The general rules of construction are too numerous and complex for a discussion here. Technical words are presumed to be used in their technical sense, unless a clear intention to use them in another is apparent from the context. Our courts are always busy in an endeavor to ascertain the intentions of testators. The truth is, few men write accurately and precisely. The proper use and selection of words in the construction of wills is a very grave duty.

"A general outline of the framework of a will may be stated as follows:

"(a) A will should revoke all former wills; if this is not done, the last will may be taken in connection with others. If the testator is unmarried, he should state that fact. His statement does not make it true, but it may serve a very excellent purpose in thwarting the claims of designing persons.

"(b) There may be a provision for funeral expenses, and suggestions with regard to a burial place and a monument.

"(c) A provision for the payment of debts should be made, and the executor given full power to pay debts and to sell and convey any portion of the estate.

"(d) A provision should be made for bequests and legacies to relatives and friends, and for charitable purposes.

"(e) Suitable provisions for the wife and children should be made.

"(f) Adequate provisions should be inserted for trust features; these are operative only after the probate administration is ended, unless otherwise directed, and they should be full, definite and clear.

"(g) There should be a residuary clause which catches up and disposes of any portion of the estate not already disposed of, including lapsed legacies and devises.

"(h) The executor should be named.

"(i) The date and signature.

"(j) Finally, the attestation.

"To me it is incomprehensible that nine men out of ten who make their wills, seek to hamper and restrain the remarriage of their widows; neither the age of the husband nor of the wife seems to deter a testator in this direction: on the other hand, I have never seen but one such restriction in the will of a married woman; and this spirit of faith and trust, in a comparative view of the sexes, is, I believe, quite as marked in the daily walks of life, notwithstanding the lines of Saxe which run:

> 'Men dying make their wills, but wives
> Escape a work so sad;
> Why should they make what all their lives,
> The gentle dames have had?'

"It may be said that a condition subsequent in general restraint of the marriage of a person who has never married, annexed to a gift, is contrary to public policy and void.

"A man should make his will when he is in a normal and healthy condition; it should be done timely and deliberately. A prominent legal writer says: 'It is astounding how frequently from indolence, procrastination, or superstition, men will postpone this needful act until the last. Some, like old Euclio in Pope, with the ruling passion strong in death, cannot endure the thought of parting with their possessions, even post mortem, and die intestate. Few testators know their own minds, and a deathbed will is as sorry a substitute for a carefully prepared instrument, as a deathbed repentance is for a well-ordered life.' A sick man or a very aged man, as a rule, is not in a condition to judge fairly of the affairs of human life. He is apt to be unconsciously influenced and misled, or even coerced. He may be diverted from the natural channels of affection, right and justice. Frequently the result is disastrous litigation, the breaking of domestic ties, and the exposure of family skeletons.

"Lord Coke said a long time ago, 'Few men, pinched with the messengers of death, have a disposing memory.' 'Such a will, he adds, 'is sometimes in haste and commonly by slender advice and is subject to so many questions in this eagle-eyed world. And it is some blemish or touch to a man well esteemed for his wisdom and discretion all his life, to leave a troubled estate behind him, amongst his wife, children or kindred, after his death.'

"A man may work out his religion from within and for himself, but when it comes to writing a will, the advice of a good, level-headed friend cannot be overestimated.

"The will, unlike other instruments, is usually not open to criticism, and in my opinion, the testator will act wisely, who takes into his confidence some trusted friend who has good judgment and just ideas, whether he be a lawyer or a layman: this would be a poor world indeed, if such were not to be found.

"Statistics show that out of every hundred persons dying in modern times, sixty-five per cent leave no estate at all, and this is true in the most prosperous and wealthy portions of the United States. Out of the hundred mentioned, about thirty-five leave estates, but less than ten per cent leave estates exceeding five thousand dollars.

"Gifts through wills to charitable, educational and kindred institutions, in recent years, have been larger than during any other period in the history of this country. In the year 1909 the value of such gifts exceeded a hundred million dollars, according to the best statistics obtainable; yet it is much to be regretted, that testators who have been blessed with fortunes, do not leave more to charitable and public uses. Very little, if any regret would be expressed by beneficiaries under wills, if testators would set aside a few hundred or a few thousand dollars for such objects: a fountain in one's native town, a scholarship, a hospital, or a park or plot of ground where the aged might rest, children play, and birds sing. Such gifts show noble natures, and all communities are proud to remember and honor the donors.

"Although the laws of our States differ somewhat in the matter of descent and in the rules as to the construction and requirements of wills, it may be stated that it is not generally necessary to mention or provide for any other persons than children or their descendants.

"The French author, Balzac, regarded by many critics as one of the keenest observers of the impulses that actuate human life, has one of his characters, a lawyer, say : 'There are in modern society three men who can never think well of the world, the priest, the doctor and the man of law; and they wear black robes, perhaps because they are in mourning for every virtue and every illusion; the most hapless of these is the lawyer; he sees the same evil feelings repeated again and again; nothing can correct them; our offices are sewers which can never be cleansed; I have known wills burned; I have seen mothers robbing their children; wives kill their husbands; I could not tell you all I have seen, for I have seen crimes against which justice is impotent. In short, all the horrors that romancers suppose they have invented are still below the truth.'

"Whether this conclusion is correct or not, the fact is, that the law seals the lips of the priest, the doctor and the lawyer. The human heart is never completely revealed; there is always a nook or a corner that is closed to the world. But the lawyer does know human nature; and, take it all in all, I do not believe there is any class of men more outspoken, and who do more in the long run to uphold our rights, our morals and our liberties, than lawyers. The lawyer will tell you to have your will written and to have it well written; he will tell you that human nature is strongly marked in wills; he will tell you that his profession knows no more complicated and perplexing a document to prepare than a will; he will tell you that wills are frequently destroyed by unauthorized hands; he will tell you that when a provision is made by will which gives less than that which is allowed by law, that that provision will be attacked; he will tell you that wills are filed in probate in nearly every instance before the dust has adjusted itself on the grave of the testator; he will tell you, if candid, that lawyers are, in a measure, responsible for poorly written wills.

"No lawyer should be asked to write a will cheaply or hastily; the testator who has no proper appreciation of this service, and who drives a bargain for ten dollars, for that which is worth a hundred or more, usually gets about what he pays for.

"In law, as in other professions, ability and experience are essential to perfect work; when you seek a lawyer to write your will, see that he has these qualifications.

"Witnesses to wills should never be interested in the instrument. If the testator is aged, the witnesses should be those well acquainted with him; in fact, this is always a good rule, whether the testator be old or young; this precaution may prevent much trouble and complication, and it has the sanction of our highest courts.

"There is a class of gifts to which I wish to call your attention, and I refer to gifts *causa mortis*. A gift *causa mortis* is a gift of personal property by a person about to die and in view of death. If there is an actual or constructive delivery of the property, the gift is good, notwithstanding the law of wills. The gift, however, must be absolute and the giver must die of that sickness.

"In making provision for children in wills, the corpus or principal fund is not infrequently to be turned over to them on arriving at legal age. According to my observation, the age of thirty is much preferable. It is not possible for any young man or woman at the end of minority to be possessed of much wisdom with reference to the care of property. Worldly knowledge is not congenital, and we have high authority that 'in youth and beauty, wisdom is but rare.'

"Even you and I, my friends, have picked up some business knowledge since we passed the line of twenty-one.

"I cannot too highly recommend trust provisions in wills, where it is sought to make allowances to children or others; the use of the income for a time or for life, instead of an absolute gift of the principal, has in many cases a most beneficial result. In the selection of an executor, my judgment is that it is better to have one than two, and unless that one is a corporation of high standing and ample capital, I would always require a bond. This works no hardship, for bonds are readily obtainable by reputable persons.

"A codicil is a supplemental will. Its object may be to explain, modify, add to or take from a will. It should be written with care and precision and its execution is attended with the same formalities as the will itself.

"A well-known author on wills says:

"'In short, a will may be a man's monument or his folly. Prudence, therefore, demands that the testator plan wisely, and frame his testamentary provisions with great care. That is, he should, if possible, use such words that his plan shall not be misunderstood and shall be carried into effect without dispute or litigation, for unlike instruments between living persons, it is only after the testator is dead and cannot explain his meaning that his will can take effect, or be open to dispute.'

"I recommend that of each will there be made a copy; the original should be placed in one safe place, and the copy in another. This very much lessens the chance of its being destroyed or falling into bad hands."

CHAPTER II

ANCIENT WILLS

"For we brought nothing into the world, and it is certain we can carry nothing out."

WILL OF ADAM

THE Mussulman claims that our forefather, Adam, left a will, and that seventy legions of angels brought him sheets of paper and quill pens, nicely nibbed, all the way from Paradise, and that the Archangel Gabriel set his seal as a witness.

It may be added, however, that the authenticity of this will has not been established.

WILL OF NOAH

It is claimed that Noah left a will, but of course this is an apocrypha. It is said that he divided his landed possessions, the globe, into three shares, one for each son. America was not included in this division for obvious reasons.

WILL OF JOB

There exists a very curious and ancient testament of Job, which was discovered and published by Cardinal Mai in 1839; it relates many details which we may look for in vain in the Canonical Book. In it Job's faithful wife, when reduced to the utmost poverty, sold the hair of her head to procure bread for her husband.

WILL OF JACOB

Jacob, the third of the Hebrew Patriarchs, died in Egypt at the age of 147, but was buried by his sons in the Cave of Machpelah at Hebron, in Palestine, the traditional burial place of the Prophets and other Biblical characters of their time.

It can be stated that the very earliest reference to an actual testamentary disposition is by the words of this Patriarch:

"And Israel said unto Joseph, Behold, I die; but God shall be with you and bring you again unto the land of your fathers."

"Moreover, I have given to thee one portion above thy brethren, which I took out of the hand of the Amorite with my sword and with my bow."

"And Jacob called unto his sons, and said, Gather yourselves together, that I may tell you that which shall befall you in the last days."

In the 48th and 49th chapters of Genesis are these words of the dying Patriarch; and here is found not only the disposition of a "portion" to Joseph, but the character of each son is shown, the virtue or fault of each is described, to each a symbolic emblem is assigned, and to each a future is prophesied.

Here is a will, in fact, and in prophecy.

WILL OF TELEMACHUS

Homer cites this will, made in favor of Piræus, to whom Telemachus bequeaths all the presents that had been made to him by Menelaus, lest they fall into the hands of his enemies; but he adds, "In case I should slay *them* and survive, you are then to restore them to me in my palace, a task as joyous to you to accomplish as to myself to profit by." Perhaps, however, this may be objected to as proceeding from fabulous history. In Biblical tradition, however, we find very early evidence of oral bequests.

WILL OF EUDAMIDAS

To Lucian we are indebted for the noble, touching, and certainly eccentric will of Eudamidas of Corinth.

This philosophical individual, who was extremely poor, was on terms of close and intimate friendship — friendship in the full and true acceptation of the term — with Arethæus and Charixenes of Sycion. Finding himself on his deathbed, he made a will, which, while exciting only the ridicule of the thoughtless or the worldly-wise, calls for respect and admiration in the breasts of those who know the value of real cordiality, and can appreciate his simple confidence in its sincerity.

"I bequeath to Arethæus my mother to support; and I pray him to have a tender care of her declining years.

"I bequeath to Charixenes my daughter to marry, and to give her to that end the best portion he can afford.

"Should either happen to die I beg the other to undertake both charges."

When this will, continues the narrator, was read in the public square (this being the accepted mode of proceeding at that time), all those who were aware of the poor circumstances of the testator; but were incapable of recognizing the ties which linked him to his friends, turned these unusual clauses into a joke; and there was not one who did not go away laughing and observing: "Arethæus and Charixenes will be lucky fellows if they accept their legacies, and he's no fool to have made himself their heir, though he be dead and they living."

But these honest legatees no sooner learned what was expected of them by their deceased friend than they hastened to put his wishes into execution.

Charixenes, however, only survived Eudamidas five days; and then Arethæus, acting in exact conformity with the will he had undertaken to execute, assumed the share bequeathed to his co-executor. He supported the mother of Eudamidas; and in due time found a suitable husband for his daughter. Of five talents of which his fortune consisted, he gave her two, and two others to his own daughter, and celebrated the two marriages on the same day.

THE OLDEST WRITTEN WILL

William Matthew Flinders Petrie, the famous English Egyptologist, unearthed not many years ago at Kahun a will which was forty-five hundred years old; there seems no reason to question either the authenticity or antiquity of the document. The will therefore antedates all other known written wills by nearly two thousand years. That excellent authority, the *Irish Law Times*, speaks of the will so entertainingly that its comments are here reproduced:

"The document is so curiously modern in form that it might almost be granted probate to-day. But, in any case, it may be assumed that it marks one of the earliest epochs of legal history, and curiously illustrates the continuity of legal methods. The value, socially, legally and historically, of a will that dates back to patriarchal times is evident.

"It consists of a settlement made by one Sekhenren in the year 44, second month of Pert, day 19, — that is, it is estimated, the 44th of Amenemhat III., or 2550 B.C., in favor of his brother, a priest of Osiris, of all his property and goods; and of another document, which bears date from the time of Amenemhat IV., or 2548 B.C. This latter instrument is, in form, nothing more nor less than a will, by which, in phraseology that might well be used to-day, the testator settles upon his wife, Teta, all the property given him by his brother, for life, but forbids in categorical terms to pull down the houses 'which my brother built for me,' although it empowers her to give them to any of her children that she pleases. A 'lieutenant' Siou is to act as guardian of the infant children.

"This remarkable instrument is witnessed by two scribes, with an attestation clause that might almost have been drafted yesterday. The papyrus is a valuable contribution to the study of ancient law, and shows, with a graphic realism, what a pitch of civilization the ancient Egyptians had reached, — at least from a lawyer's point of view. It has hitherto been believed that, in the infancy of the human race, wills were practically unknown. There probably never was a time when testaments, in some form or other, did not exist; but, in the earliest ages, it has so far been assumed that they were never written, but were nuncupatory, or delivered orally, probably at the deathbed of the testator. Among the Hindus to this day the law of succession hinges upon the due solemnization of fixed ceremonies at the dead man's funeral, not upon any written will. And it is because early wills were verbal only that their history is so obscure. It has been asserted that among the barbarian races the bare conception of a will was unknown; that we must search for the infancy of testamentary dispositions in the early Roman law. Indeed, until the ecclesiastical power assumed the prerogative of intervening at every break in the succession of the family, wills did not come into vogue in the West. But Mr. Petrie's papyrus seems to show that the system of settlement or disposition by deed or will was long antecedently practised in the East."

WILL OF SENNACHERIB

(681 B.C.)

The will of the Assyrian monarch is the next earliest written will which can be cited. It was found in the royal library of Konyunjik, where we read that to his favorite son, Esarhaddon, not being yet heir-presumptive, he bequeaths "certain bracelets, coronets, and other precious objects of gold, ivory, and precious stones, deposited for safe-keeping in the temple of Nebo."

Sennacherib was assassinated in the year 681 B.C. by two of his sons; he was succeeded by Esarhaddon.

The Will of Plato
(348 b.c.)

We give this will, handed down to us by Diogenes Laertius, being of interest, not from anything it contains, but curious, whether from its antiquity or as an illustration of the very simple form employed by the Greeks three hundred and fifty years before the Christian era. Of its intrinsic value as coming from the mind and the hand of Plato we need say nothing.

"These things hath Plato left and bequeathed: The farm of Hephæstiades bounded, etc. It is forbidden to sell or alienate it; but it shall belong to my son Adimantes, who shall enjoy the sole proprietorship thereof. I give him likewise the farm of Hereusiades, situated, etc. It is the one I acquired by purchase.

"Further, I give to my son Adimantes, three mines in cash, a silver vase weighing one hundred and sixty-five drachmæ, a cup of the same metal weighing sixty-five, a ring and pendant in gold weighing together four drachmæ, with three mines due to me from Euclid the gem-engraver.

"I free from slavery, Diana; but for Tychon, Bietas, Dionysius, and Apolloniades, I will they continue the slaves of my son Adimantes, to whom I bequeath also all my chattels as specified in an inventory held and possessed by Demetrius.

"I have no debts; and I appoint as executors and administrators of these bequests Speusippus, Demetrius, Hegias, Eurymedon, Callimachus, and Thrasippus."

Such is the will of the grand old philosopher; and we may suppose that by those simpler minds, even the date was considered unnecessary, as we find none appended to this document.

Will of Aristotle
(322 b.c.)

The will of this famous Peripatetic philosopher is like that of Plato, more remarkable for its antiquity and the interest attaching to the testator than for its contents. He was sixty-eight years of age at the time of his death, and according to his biographer, Timotheus of Athens, he cannot have been very attractive in his personal appearance. He had small eyes, a cracked voice, and thin limbs; but he was always well dressed and wore rings on his fingers; we are also told that he shaved his chin. The document in question begins thus:

"Greeting. Aristotle disposes as follows of what belongs to him. In case death should surprise me, Antipater will undertake to execute generally my last wishes and is to have the administration of everything.

"Until Nicanor can take the management of my affairs, Aristomenes, Timarchas, Hipparchus, and Theophrastus will, with his consent, assist him to take care of my property, as much on behalf of my children, as on behalf of Herpylis. As soon as my daughter shall be marriageable she is to be given Nicanor; and in case, which I do not think likely, she should die before her marriage or before she has children, Nicanor is to inherit all that I possess, and to dispose of my slaves and all the rest as he pleases.

"Nicanor will then take charge of my son Nicomachus, and of my daughter, so that they may want nothing; and he will act towards them as a father and a brother.

"Should Nicanor die before marrying my daughter, or having married her should he leave no children, he must decide what is to be done after his death.

"If, then, Theophrastus should wish to take my daughter to his home, he will enter into all the rights I give to Nicanor; or if not, the curators will dispose of my children as they shall consider for the best.

"I recommend to their guardians, and to Nicanor, to remember for my sake the affection Herpylis has always borne me, taking care of me and of my affairs. If after my death she should wish to marry, they will see that she does not marry any one below my condition. In that case, besides the presents she has already received, she is to have a talent of silver, three slaves besides the one she has, and the youth Pyrrhæus. If she wishes to live at Calchis, she can have the suite of rooms communicating with the garden; if at Stagyra, she can occupy the house of my fathers, and the curators will suitably furnish whichever of these residences she may select.

"Nicanor will take care that Myrex is sent back to his parents in a respectable and suitable way, with all that I have belonging to him.

"I give Ambracis her liberty, and assign to her, as a marriage portion, 500 drachmæ or five mines and a slave.

"I bequeath to Thala, besides the bought slave she has, a young female slave and 1000 drachmæ.

"As regards Simo, besides the money already given him to buy another slave, let one more be bought for him or let him have the value in money.

"Tacho is to have his freedom when my daughter marries. Philo, and Olympias with his son, shall also be made free at the same period. The children of my slaves shall pass into the service of my heirs, and, when they become adults, they shall be freed if they have deserved it.

"Let the statues I have ordered be finished and placed as I have instructed Gryllo, viz. those of Nicanor, Proxenes, and the mother of Nicanor; also that of Arimnestes to serve as a monument for him as he left no children.

"Also let the Ceres, belonging to my mother, be placed in the Nemea. Let the bones of my wife, Pythias, be placed in my tomb, even as she desired. I further wish the four stone animals, promised by me as votive offerings for the preservation of Nicanor, to be placed at Stagyra to Jupiter and Minerva. They are to be four cubits high."

WILL OF VIRGIL
(10 B.C.)

A singular trait in the character of this great poet was that which appeared by the clause in his will which ordered the Æneid to be burnt: "Ut rem emendatam imperfectamque." Tucca and Varus, however, his executors and friends, and, we may add also, the friends of literature and of the civilized world, assured him Augustus would never consent to this barbarous behest. On this he bequeathed to them his Mss., but on the express condition that if he should die before he had time to revise and finish them, and they should think proper to publish them, they should change nothing and should leave the imperfect and incomplete verses just as they were.

He ordered his body to be "carried to Naples, and there interred near the road to Puzzuoli, by the second milestone." The epitaph which was engraved on it was written by himself:

> Mantua me genuit, Calabri rapuere, tenet nunc
> Parthenope: cecini pascua, rura, duces.

He divided his property, which was considerable, between Valerius Proculus, his half-brother, to whom he left half; Augustus, to whom he gave a quarter; Mecænas, who got a twelfth; and the rest to Varus.

WILL OF AUGUSTUS
(13 A.D.)

Augustus Cæsar made his will under the consulate of Silius and Plancus in the year A.D. 13, and one year and four months before his death.

It is much to be regretted that this important and interesting document should not have reached our times in its entirety; nevertheless, by collating the passages relating to it by several historians, we arrive at a consid˄rable portion of it.

When Augustus had made his will, he deposited it, according to custom and the example of his uncle Julius Cæsar, in the sacred Temple of Vesta, under the care of the most ancient of the priestesses. The act was in two parts, and was written, partly by his own hand and partly under dictation to his two freedmen, Polybius and Hilarion. It was accompanied by four other portions sealed with the same seal.

As soon as Augustus was dead, Tiberius commanded that the first day of the meeting of the Senate should be consecrated to his memory; whereon the Vestals solemnly brought the will and the four appendices belonging to it, which were opened, and they then proceeded to the verification of the will; then Polybius, the freedman before mentioned, was charged to read it aloud.

The first lines were thus conceived:

"Since Heaven has taken from me my two grandchildren, Caïus and Lucilius, I declare Tiberius my successor, and I transmit to him all my rights. . . ."

He then passes to the disposal of his goods; he appoints as his heirs the above-named Tiberius and Livia, the former to receive two-thirds, the latter one-third; he then desires they should bear his name, or rather, as says Tacitus, he desires Livia to assume the title of Augusta.

In case of the death of Tiberius and Livia he replaces them by appointing one-third to Drusus, son of Tiberius, and the rest to Germanicus and his three sons.

In short, he substitutes to these, as a third arrangement, his relatives; that is to say, his grandchildren and great-grandchildren, and they defaulting, his friends, *amicos complures.*

He leaves "to the Roman people," *quadringentos sestertium.*

Item: to the Latin tribes, *tricies quinquies sestertium.*

Item: to the soldiers of his body-guards, per head, *i.e.* to each pretorian soldier, *millia nummorum*.

Item: to those of the municipal guard, the urban cohorts, *quingenos nummos*.

Item: to the soldiers of the legion, *trecentos nummos*.

But he orders all these military legacies to be paid at once, having taken the precaution to put by the sums required for this object.

As to the other legacies to different private individuals, and of which the majority of the amounts exceeded twenty sesterces, he allows a period of a year after his death for the payment of them, and he excuses himself for their smallness on the plea of the moderate amount of his fortune.

"I leave, in all, to my heirs, no more than one hundred and fifty million sesterces, although I have received by testamentary donations more than five milliards of sesterces, but I have employed the whole of this in the service of the State, as well as my two paternal patrimonies (that of Caïus Octavius, his own father, and that of Julius Cæsar, his adoptive father), and my other family inheritances."

By another clause of his testament Augustus leaves a small legacy to his daughter Julia, but he does not recall her from exile; he even forbids that her ashes, and those of the second Julia, his granddaughter, as debauched as her mother, should be placed in the tomb of the Cæsars.

Augustus also ordered that if there were any children living of those who had left him their money, such money should be restored to those children, but only on their attaining their majority, and together with the arrears of revenue; and he was accustomed to say that a father of a family only deprived his children of the inheritance they were entitled to when the prince was a tyrant.

When the Senate had verified and confirmed this will by a *senatus consultum*, they presented to the conscript-fathers the four rolls above mentioned; they were partly written by the emperor's own hand. It was Drusus who made the Senate acquainted with their contents.

In the first, Augustus prescribed the order that was to be observed at his interment.

The second was a journal of his most memorable actions, destined to be engraved on bronze and placed on the façade of his mausoleum. An ancient marble, found in the excavations of the city of Ancyra in the sixteenth century, has preserved to us a portion of this journal; and this monument, mutilated as it is, becomes precious from the certainty it gives us as to the dates of certain events in the history of Augustus.

The third contained a statement of the forces of the empire, of the troops then constituting the standing army, of the sums contained in the public treasury and in that of the emperor, of the tributes and imposts still due, and of the expenses required in times of peace and in times of war.

The fourth was a collection of instructions, addressed equally to Tiberius and to the republic, to maintain both the splendor and the tranquillity of the empire. Among other counsels he advised them to choose only wise, discreet, and virtuous men for the administration of every department of the state; he added at the same time that it was dangerous to confide to any single individual the entire authority, for then it might be feared that the power of the monarch might degenerate into tyranny, and that its ruin might involve that of the state and precipitate the Romans into irretrievable misfortunes. He recommended, above all, to those who should follow him in the cares of the government, not to preoccupy themselves about extending the limits of the empire by new conquests, but rather to apply themselves to the maintenance and good government of what they already held.

The remainder of these councils was simply the summary of the policy he had himself pursued during his reign.

These books as well as his will were approved and indorsed by the Senate. They then decreed him a costly and magnificent funeral; his corpse, or rather its image in wax, was laid upon an ivory bed, incrusted with massive gold and draped with a tissue of purple silk woven with gold; the procession, of the same extent as a triumphal progress, traversed the streets of Rome with great pomp. It halted twice; on the first occasion Drusus pronounced the funeral oration over the body; on the second Tiberius spoke another, which has been preserved, and may be considered a model of eloquence.

When the procession arrived at the Campus Martius the body was enclosed in a bier, and placed on a funeral pile to which the centurions set fire; while the clouds of smoke and flame were ascending to the sky an eagle suddenly appeared in the midst of them and took its flight to heaven, in the midst of the acclamations of the assembled people, who declared that the bird sacred to

Jupiter was carrying the emperor's soul aloft to the bosom of the king of the gods.

WILL OF A PIG

This is a very ancient document. Mr. S. Baring-Gould in his unique work "Curiosities of Olden Times," says of it:

"S. Jerome speaks of it, saying, that in his time (fourth century) children were wont to sing it at school amidst shouts of laughter. Alexander Brassicanus, who died in 1539, was the first to publish it. He found it in a Ms. at Mayence. Later, G. Fabricius gave a corrected edition of it from another Ms. found at Memel and since then it has been in the hands of the learned."

With slight modifications, the will runs as follows:

"I, M. Grunnius Corcotta Porcellus, have made my testament, which, as I can't write myself, I have dictated."

Says Magirus, the cook: "Come along, thou who turnest the house topsy-turvy, spoiler of the pavement, O fugitive Porcellus! I am resolved to slaughter thee to-day."

Says Corcotta Porcellus: "If ever I have done thee any wrong, if I have sinned in any way, if I have smashed any wee pots with my feet, O Master Cook, grant pardon to thy suppliant!"

Says the cook Magirus: "Halloo, boy! go bring me a carving-knife out of the kitchen, that I may make a bloody Porcellus of him."

Porcellus is caught by the servants, and brought out to execution on the xvi before the Lucernine Kalends, just when young colewort sprouts are in plenty, Clybaratus and Piperatus being Consuls.

Now when he saw that he was about to die, he begged hard of the cook an hour's grace, just to write his will. He called together his relations, that he might leave them some of his victuals; and he said:

" I will and bequeath to my papa, Verrinus Lardinus, 30 bush. of acorns.

" I will and bequeath to my mamma, Veturina Scrofa, 40 bush. of Laconian corn.

" I will and bequeath to my sister, Quirona, at whose nuptials I may not be present, 30 bush. of barley.

" Of my mortal remains, I will and bequeath my bristles to the cobblers, my teeth to squabblers, my ears to the deaf, my tongue to lawyers and chatterboxes, my entrails to tripemen, my hams to gluttons, my stomach to little boys, my tail to little girls, my muscles to effeminate parties, my heels to runners and hunters, my claws to thieves; and, to a certain cook, whom I won't mention by name, I bequeath the cord and stick which I brought with me from my oak grove to the sty, in hopes that he may take the cord and hang himself with it.

"I will that a monument be erected to me, inscribed with this, in golden letters:

"M. GRUNNIUS CORCOTTA PORCELLUS, who lived 999 years, — six months more, and he would have been 1000 years old.

"Friends dear to me whilst I lived, I pray you to have a kindness towards my body, and embalm it well with good condiments, such as almonds, pepper and honey, that my name may be named through ages to come.

"O my masters and my comrades, who have assisted at the drawing up of this testament, order it to be signed.

(Signed)   LUCANICUS.   CELSANUS.
               PERGILLUS.   LARDIO.
               MYSTIALICUS.   OFFELLICUS.
                               CYMATUS."

WILLS OF THE EARL OF MELLENT AND OTHERS

(1118)

Robert, the famous Earl of Mellent and Leicester, one of the early crusaders in the Holy Land, died in 1118, in the abbey of Preaux, where his body was buried; but his heart, by his own order, was conveyed to the hospital at Brackley, to be there preserved in salt. Isabella, daughter of William E. Marshall, Earl of Pembroke, who died at Berkhampstead in 1239, ordered her heart to be sent in a silver cup to her brother, then Abbot of Tewkesbury, to be there buried before the high altar. The heart of John Baliol, Lord of Barnard Castle, who died in 1269, was, by his widow's desire, enclosed in an ivory casket, richly enamelled with silver. There are many bequests of hearts on record other than the above.

WILL OF SALADIN

(1193)

Interesting to record is the last will and testament of the celebrated Saladin, born in 1136; he died in 1193, after filling the two continents of Europe and Asia with his fame.

Sultan of Egypt, he conquered Syria, Arabia, Persia, Mesopotamia, and took possession of Jerusalem in 1187. His conquests suffice to enable us to judge of the extent of his power and wealth; at his death, however, he showed that no one was more intimately convinced of the utter hollowness of the riches and greatness of the world and the vanity of its disputes.

He ordered, by his will, first, that considerable sums should be distributed to Mussulmans, Jews, and Christians, in order that the priests of the three religions might implore the mercy of God for him; next he commanded that the shirt or tunic he should be wearing at the time of his death should be carried on the end of a spear throughout the whole camp, and at the head of his army, and that the soldier who bore it should pause at intervals and say aloud, "Behold all that remains of the Emperor Saladin! Of all the states he had conquered; of all the provinces he had subdued; of the boundless treasures he had amassed; of the countless wealth he possessed, he retained in dying, nothing but this shroud!" To this we may add:

> ". . . Behold his origin and end!
> Milk and a swathe at first, his whole demand;
> His whole domain, at last, a turf or stone,
> To whom, between, a world had seemed too small."

WILL OF WILLIAM DE BEAUCHAMP
(1268)

"Will of William de Beauchamp, dated at Wauberge, upon the morrow after the Epiphany, anno 1268, 53 Henry III. My body to be buried in the Church of the Friars-Minors at Worcester. I Will that a horse, completely harnessed with all military caparisons, precede my corpse; to a priest to sing mass daily in my Chapel without the city of Worcester, near unto that house of Friars which I gave for the health of my soul, and for the souls of Isabel my wife, Isabel de Mortimer, and all the faithful deceased, all my rent of the fee of Richard Bruli, in Wiche and Winchester, with supply of what should be too short out of my own proper goods; to Walter, my son, signed with the cross, for a pilgrimage to the Holy Land on my behalf and of Isabel, his mother, two hundred marks; to Joane, my daughter, a canopy, some time belonging to St. Wolstan, and a book of Lancelot, which I have lent them; to Isabel, my daughter, a silver cup; to

Sibill, my daughter, all the money due to me from my son William, towards her marriage, and XL marks more, with the land which I bought in Britlamton, to enjoy it until she be married, and no longer; to Sarah, my daughter, one hundred marks for her marriage; to William, my eldest son, the cup and horns of St. Hugh; to my daughter the Countess, his wife, a ring with a ruby in it; to Sir Roger de Mortimer and Sir Bartholomew de Suley a ring each; to the Friars-Minors of Worcester forty shillings; to the Friars-Minors of Gloucester one mark; to the Friars-Carmelites there one mark; to the Hospital of St. Wolstan at Worcester one mark; to the Hospital of St. Oswald there ten shillings; to the Canons of Doddeford one mark; to the Church and Nuns of Cokehill x marks; to Isabel, my wife, ten marks; to the Church and Nuns of Westwood one mark; to the Church and Nuns without Worcester one mark; to every Anchorite in Worcester and the parts adjacent four shillings; to the Church of Salewarp, a house and garden near the parsonage, to find a lamp to burn continually therein to the honor of God, the Blessed Virgin, St. Katherine, and Saint Margaret; and I appoint my eldest son William Earl of Warwick, Sir Roger Mortimer, Sir Bartholomew de Sudley, and the Abbots of Evesham and of Great Malverne, my executors."

WILL OF WILLIAM DE BEAUCHAMP, EARL OF WARWICK

(1296)

"Will of William De Beauchamp, Earl of Warwick, dated Holy Rood Day, 1296, 25 Edward I. being in perfect health. My body to be buried in the quire of the Friars-Minors, commonly called the Gray-friars at Worcester, if I die within the compass of the four English Seas; otherwise, then in the house of the Friars-Minors nearest to the place in which I may happen to die, and my heart to be buried wheresoever the Countess, my dear consort, may herself resolve to be interred; to the place where I may be buried two great horses, viz., those to the which shall carry my armour at my funeral, for the solemnizing of which I bequeath two hundred pounds; to the maintenance of two soldiers in the Holy Land, one hundred pounds; to Maud my wife, all my silver vessels, with the cross, wherein is contained part of the wood of the very cross whereon our Saviour died; likewise the vestments of my Chapel, to make use of during her life; but afterwards the best suit to belong to Guy, my eldest son; the second best to my Chapel of Hanslape; and the third best to my Chapel at Hanley; to Guy, my son, a gold ring with a ruby in it, together with my blesing; to my said wife a cup, which the Bishop of Worcester gave me, and all my other cups, with my lesser sort of jewels and rings, to distribute for the health of my soul, where she may think best; to my two daughters, nuns at Shouldham, fifty marks."

WILL OF EDWARD I

(1307)

This will seems entitled to find a place among those which may be regarded as abnormal, and when we come to the record of it in the simple and *naïf* style of that matchless old chronicler Froissard, we are irresistibly tempted to make a transcript of the few lines which in describing it carry us back to the days of that turbulent and brilliant monarch.

"Le bon roy," he writes, "trépassa en la cité de Warvich. Et quend il mourut il fit appeler son aisné fils (Edouard II. qui après luy fust roy) pardeuant ses barons, et luy fit iurer sur les saincts, qu'aussitost qu'il seroit trespassé il le feroit bouilleir dans une chaudière, tant que la chair se departiroit des os: et après ferait mettre la chair en terre et garderoit les os: et toutes les fois que les Escoçois de rebelleroient contre luy, il semondroit ses gens et porteroit avesques luy les os de son père. Car il tenoit fermement que tant qu'il auroit ses os avesques luy les Escoçois n'auraient poinct de victoire contre luy. Lequel n'accomplit mie ce qu'il auait iuré: ains fit rapporter son père à Londres et là enseuelir; dont luy meschent."

WILL OF GUY DE BEAUCHAMP, EARL OF WARWICK

(1315)

"Will of Guy de Beauchamp, Earl of Warwick, dated at Warwick Castle, Monday next after the Feast of St. James the Apostle, 1315. My body to be buried in the Abbey of Bordsley, without any funeral pomp; to Alice, my wife, a proportion of plate, with a crystal cup and half my bedding, and also all the vestments and books belonging to my Chapel; the other half of my beds, rings, and jewels, I bequeath to my two daughters; to Maud, my daughter, a crystal cup; to Elizabeth, my daughter, the marriage of Astley's heir; to Thomas, my son, my best coat of mail, helmet,

ANCIENT, CURIOUS, AND FAMOUS WILLS

and suit of harness, with all that belongs thereto; to John, my son, my second coat of mail, helmet, and harness; and I Will that all the rest of my armour, bows, and other warlike implements, shall remain in Warwick Castle for my heir."

DUKES OF LANCASTER

(1360)

Henry, Duke of Lancaster, who died in 1360, thus begins the second clause of his will: "Item: we will *that our body be not buried* for three weeks after the departure of our soul."

(1399)

John, Duke of Lancaster, better known as John of Gaunt, directs as follows in his will: "If I die out of London I desire that, the night my body arrives there, it be carried direct to the Friars Carmelites, in Fleet Street, and the next day be taken straight to St. Paul's, and *that it be not buried for forty days*, during which I charge my executors that there be no embalming of my corpse."

WILL OF SIR ROBERT LAUNDE

(1367)

"Will of Sir Robert Launde, alias Atte Launde, Knt., Citizen of London, on our Lady's Eve, 1367. My body to be buried in the quire of St. Mary's, of the Charterhouse in London; to Christian, my wife; to Ada Launde, my mother; to Robert Watfield, late my servant, c *l.*; to Rose Pomfret, my sister, of Berdfield, CXL *l.*; to Richard, her son, and William, her brother; to Margaret Biernes, their sister; to Margaret, her sister, married to Aksted; to Agnes, my niece, at Hallewell; to the high altar of Hempsted, in Essex; to the poor there, by gift of Robert Watfield; to Joane Launde, of Cambridgeshire; to my noble Lady the Countess of Norfolk; to John Southcot, to find him at school; to the building of the cross in Cheapside; and I appoint Sir John Philpot, Knt., overseer of this my Will."

WILL OF LADY JOAN DE COBHAM

(1369)

"Will of Joan De Cobham, of Starburghe. August 13, 1369. My body to be buried in the church-yard of St. Mary Overhere, in Southwark, before the church door, where the image of the blessed Virgin sitteth on high over that door: and I Will that a plain marble stone be laid over my body.

"I Will that VII thousand masses be said for my soul by the Canons of Tunbrugge and Tanfugge, and the four Orders of Friars in London, viz., the Friars-Preachers, Minors, Augustines, and Carmelites, who for so doing shall have xxix *l*. iii *s*. iv *d*. Also I Will that on my funeral day twelve poor persons, clothed in black gowns and hoods, shall carry twelve torches; I bequeath to the Church of Lyngefeld a frontore with the arms of Berkeley and Cobham standing on white and purple; to Reginald, my son, a ring with a diamond; to Sir Henry Grey and Dame Joan, his wife, and to that Joane my daughter; to Joane, daughter to that Joane. I Will that my house in Southwark be sold to pay my Lord's debts, and to found prayers in the parish church of Langele-Borell for the souls of Sir John de la Mare, Knt., some time lord there, Sir Reginald Cobham, Sir Thomas Berkeley, and for the souls of my benefactors. If Reginald, my son, or any other of my heirs, shall appropriate that church for the maintenance of two priests to celebrate divine service there for ever, as it was intended and conditioned by the said Sir John de la Mare when he sold that lordship of Langele, with that of Lye, to my husband, in the presence of the Lord Berkeley, my father, then I Will that my Executors shall enfeoffe the said Reginald, or his heirs, in my water-mill at Edulme Bridge, and in my house at Southwark, for ever; to Sir John Cobham; to John de Cobham, of Devonshire."

THE WILL OF PETRARCH

(1370)

To the cultivated reader everything relating to a man who may be considered the phenomenon of his age must be interesting. The document we subjoin is especially valuable as supplying the key to a mind which has drawn to itself our warmest sympathies, and whose written thoughts are among the most attaching bequests of poetry.

The will of the poet-philosopher of Vaucluse is dated "pridiè nonas Aprilis, 1370," four years before his death, when he was sixty-six years of age, having been born at Arezzo, 20th of July, 1304.

He prefaces it with moral reflections on the certainty of death, but the uncertainty of its summons, and the necessity of putting one's affairs in order. He then proceeds to state that what he possesses is of so little value that he is in some sort ashamed to make a will; "sed," adds he, "divitum atque inopium curæ, de rebus licet imparibus, pares sunt."

After recommending his soul to Jesus Christ and imploring the succor of Mary, of St. Michael, and all the Saints, he orders very expressly that he may be buried without any sort of pomp, — "absque omni pompa et cum summa humilitate et abjectione, quanta esse potest, . . ." and renders his heir and his friends responsible for the execution of this clause. He claims no tears, as useless to the departed, but begs the prayers of the survivors, of which he has need.

Not knowing where he may be at the time of his death, he designates in different cities the spot he would choose for his burial, naming Padua, Venice, Milan, Rome, and Parma, and leaves a legacy of 200 gold ducats to the church at Padua, and 20 to the church in which he shall be interred.

Among special bequests is one to the Governor of Padua, of a very fine picture of the Virgin Mary — "opus Joctii, pictoris egregii" — which had sent been him from Florence by his friend Michael Navis. "In beholding this painting," he says, "pulchritudinem ignorantes, non intelligunt; magistri autem, artis, stupent."

He desires that all the horses he may possess at the time of his decease may be divided between his two friends, Bonzanello and Lorbardo, and acknowledges a debt to the latter of 334 gold ducats and 16 sous, which he nevertheless hopes to pay before his death.

He bequeaths to the same Lorbardo his small round goblet of silver-gilt that he may drink as much water as he likes, knowing that he prefers water to wine.

To the Sacristan, Giovanni Bocheta, he gives his large breviary, which cost him 100 livres at Venice; but desires that after the death of the Sacristan the volume may be deposited in the sacristy of the church for the use of all priests attached to that church and who will pray for him to God and the Virgin Mary.

He leaves to Giovanni di Certaldo, otherwise Boccaccio, — (*verecundi admodùm tanto viro, tam modicum*, says he), — 200 gold florins of Florence, to purchase him a winter robe suitable for his studious vigils. The words "*tanto viro*" are significant of the great esteem in which he held the genius of Boccaccio.

To Tomaso Bambasia, of Ferrara, he leaves his lute, which he describes as "good" — *leutum meum bonum* — but for singing the praises of the Lord, and by no means *pro vanitate seculi fugacis*.

To Johannes *de Horologio* — to whom he gives the title of "*physicum*" — he bequeaths 50 gold ducats to buy a ring which he will wear on his finger in memory of the testator.

As for his servants, he gives first to Bartolomeo di Siena, surnamed Pancaldus, a sum of 20 ducats, but on condition that he will not gamble with it. To Litius, he gives the same, etc.

In fine, he institutes as his heir and residuary legatee, Francesco di Borsano, residing at Milan. He names "a small property he has near Vaucluse" of which he desires to make a hospital for the poor, and if this could not be done he devises it to the son of Raymond de Clermont, surnamed Moneto. There are other unimportant clauses, after which comes the date, signature, and names of witnesses; he adds to it, however, a request to his heir to write as soon as possible after his death to his brother — a Carthusian in a convent at Marseilles (*in conventu de Materino*) — and to propose to either pay down to him a sum of 100 gold florins or an annuity of ten, as he might please. The whole terminates with these words: *Ego Franciscus Petrarca scripsi, qui testamentum aliud fecissem, si essem dives, ut vulgus insanum putat.*

Curious and suggestive as is this relic, the illustrious reformer of philosophy, eloquence, poetry, and — shall we not even add — of love, has left a yet more engaging clew to his grand character, not only in his simple and almost *naïf* "Epistle to Posterity," but in a third paper consisting of the private memorandum written in the fly-leaf of his Virgil, evidently the outpouring of his heart and intended for no human eye. The concluding lines are touching in the extreme. What, indeed, can be more sublime than the lifelong devotedness of such a soul as Petrarch's to the noblest and most beautiful, because the most disinterested, of sentiments — an all-absorbing and unaltered, yet pure and passionless, affection, and though surviving its object, losing none of its intensity!

". . . This loss," he says, writing of the death of Laura, "always present to my memory, will continually remind me that there is no state here below worthy to be called happy, and that it is time I should renounce the world since the dearest tie that linked me to it is snapped. I hope, by the help of Heaven, this resignation may become possible. My mind, in reverting to the past, will find that the solicitudes which occupied it were vain; the hope it cherished delusive; that the plans it formed were never to be realized, and could only lead to disappointment and distress."

Petrarch was found dead in his library, his head resting on an open book, on the 18th July, 1374. He was within two days of seventy.

WILL OF SIR WALTER MANNEY
(1371)

"Will of Sir Walter, Lord of Manney, Knight, London, St. Andrew's Day, 1371. My body to be buried at God's pleasure, but if it may be in the midst of the Quire of the Carthusians, called Our Lady, near West Smithfield, in the suburbs of London, of my foundation, but without any great pomp; and I Will that my Executors cause twenty masses to be said for my soul, and that every poor person coming to my funeral shall have a penny, to pray for me and the remission of my sins; to Mary, my sister a nun, x pounds; to my two bastard daughters, nuns, viz., to Mialosel and Malplesant, the one cc franks, the other c franks; to Cishbert, my cousin; to Margaret Mareschall, my dear wife, my plate which I bought of Robert Francis; also a girdle of gold, and a hook for a mantle, and likewise a garter of gold, with all my girdles and knives, all my beds and dossers in my wardrobe, excepting my folding bed, paly of blue and red, which I bequeath to my daughter of Pembroke; and I Will also that my said wife have all the goods which I purchased of Lord Segrave and the Countess Marshal. Also I Will that a tomb of alabaster, with my image as a knight, and my arms thereon, shall be made for me, like unto that of Sir John Beauchamp in Paul's, in London. I Will that prayers be said for me, and for Alice de Henalt, Countess Marshal. And whereas the King oweth me an old debt of a thousand pounds, by bills of his wardrobe, I Will that, if it can be obtained, it shall be given to the Prior and Monks of the Charter-house. And whereas there is due to me from the Prince, from the time he had been Prince of Wales, the sum of c marks per annum, for my salary as Governor of Hardelagh Castle, I bequeath one half thereof to the said Prior and Monks of the Charter-house before mentioned, and the other half to the executors of my Will. To my wife, and my daughter Pembroke, fifteen M florins of gold, and five 'vesseux estutes ph,' which Duke Albert oweth me by obligation; to Sir Guy Bryan, Knt., my best chains, whom I also appoint my Executor."

Will of Edward, Prince of Wales

(1376)

"In the name, &c., We, Edward, eldest son of the King of England and France, Prince of Wales, Duke of Cornwall, and Earl of Chester, the 7th June, 1376, in our apartment in the Palace of our Lord and Father the King at Westminster, being of good and sound memory, &c. We bequeath to the altar of Our Lady's chapel at Canterbury two basons with our arms, and a large gilt chalice enamelled with the arms of Warren. To our son Richard the bed which the King our father gave us. To Sir Roger de Clarendon a silk bed. To Sir Robert de Walsham, our Confessor, a large bed of red camora, with our arms embroidered at each corner; also embroidered with the arms of Hereford. To Mons. Alayne Cheyne our bed of camora powdered with blue eagles. And we bequeath all our goods and chattels, jewels, &c., for the payment of our funeral and debts; after which we Will that our executors pay certain legacies to our poor servants. All annuities which we have given to our Knights, Esquires, and other our followers, in reward for their services, we desire to be fully paid. And we charge our son Richard, on our blessing, that he fulfil our bequests to them. And we appoint our very dear and beloved brother of Spain, Duke of Lancaster; the Reverend Fathers in God, William Bishop of Winchester, John Bishop of Bath; William Bishop of Asaph; our Confessor, Sir Robert de Walsham; Hugh de Segrave, Steward of our Lands; Aleyn Stokes; and John Fordham, our executors. In testimony of which we have put to this our last Will our privy seal, &c."

"Published by John Ormesheved, Clerk, in the year 1376, in the presence of John Bishop of Hereford, Domini Lewis Clifford, Nicholas Bonde, and Nicholas de Scharnesford, Knights, and William de Walsham, Clerk; and of many other Knights, Clerks, and Esquires. Proved 4 idus June, 1376."

Will of Lady Alice West

(1395)

Some wills, although they cannot be called curious, are highly interesting, and excite great curiosity in the reader. For instance, Lady Alice West, widow of Sir Thomas West who fought at the Battle of Crecy, and an ancestress of the De la Warr family, by her will, dated July 15, 1395, and proved on September 1 following, bequeaths to "Johane my doughter, my sone is wyf, a masse book, and alle the bokes that I have of latyn, englisch, and frencsh, out take the forsayd matyns book that is bequeth to Thomas my sone." Who can help wondering what books, and particularly what English books, this good old lady had at a period five years before the death of Chaucer, and nearly eighty years before the first book was printed in England? Perhaps two of them were Robert of Gloucester's "Rhyming Chronicles of England," and Robert Langland's "The Vision of Piers Ploughman."

WILL OF LADY ALICE WYNDSORE
(1400)

" Will of Alice, widow of William Wyndsore, Knight, at Upmynster, on the Assumption of the Virgin Mary, August 15th, 1400, 1 Henry IV. My body to be buried in the parish Church of Upmynster on the north side before the altar of our Lady the Virgin; to the said Church one of my best oxen for a mortuary; for wax to burn about my body forty shillings; for ornaments to the said Church ten marks; for repairing the highways near the town forty shillings; I Will that ten marks be distributed to the poor on the day of my sepulture; to the Chaplain six marks; to John Pelham, Sacrist of that Church, three shillings and four pence; to Joane, my younger daughter, my manor of Gaynes, in Upmynster; to Jane and Joane, my daughters, all my other manors and advowsons which John Wyndsore, or others, have, by his consent, usurped, the which I desire my heirs and executors to recover and see them parted between my daughters, for that I say, on the pain of my soul, he hath no right there nor never had; my manor of Compton Murdac; to the poor of Upminster xx shillings. And I appoint Joane, my youngest daughter; John Kent, Mercer of London, my Executors; and Sir John Cusson, Knight, and Robert de Litton, Esquire, Overseers of this my Will."

WILL OF LADY JOANE HUNGERFORD
(1411)

"Will of Joane Lady Hungerford, February 1, 1411. My body to be buried in the Chapel of St. Anne, in the Parish Church of Farleigh, Hungerford, next to the grave of my husband. I Will that, with all possible speed after my decease, my executors cause three thousand masses to be said for my soul, and for the souls of all the faithful deceased. Also I desire on my burial day that twelve torches and two tapers burn about my body, and that twelve poor women, holding the said torches, be cloathed in russet, with linen hoods, and having stockings and shoes suitable. I Will that ten pounds be bestowed to buy black cloth for the cloathing of my sons and daughters, as likewise for the sons and daughters of all my domestic servants. I Will that the two hundred marks now in the hands of my son, Sir Walter Hungerford, be given to found a perpetual chantry of one chaplain, to celebrate divine service in the Chapel of St. Anne, in the north part of the said Church of Farleigh, for the health of my soul, and the soul of my husband, and for the souls of all our ancestors forever; to Katherine, the wife of my said son Walter, my black mantle furred with minever, and to Thomas his son a green bed, embroidered with one greyhound."

WILL OF RICHARD BERNE

(1461)

"Will of Richard Berne, of Canterbury, 28th April, 1461. My body to be buried in the aisle before the cross, in the south part of St. Paul's, at Canterbury. To the rebuilding of the bell tower of the monastery of St. Augustine ix *l*. to be paid as soon as the said work shall be begun; to the prisoners of the Castle of Canterbury and of Westgate vi *s*. viii *d*. each; to the Prioress of the Church of St. Sepulchre, towards the works of her Church, xiii *s*. iv *d*.; to the repair of the highway leading towards Sandwich, by St. Martin's Hill and the Fishpoole, x *l*.; towards the repair of the highway in the Winecheape, between Bircholle's Place and St. James's Hospital, x *l*.; to Joan, my wife, my furniture and my best cart, and my five horses fit to draw it, with all their harness; to the building of the new bell tower of Tenterden vi *s*. viii *d*."

THE WILL OF THOMAS WINDSOR, ESQ.

(1479)

"Item. I Will that I have brennying (burning) at my burying and funeral service four tapers and twenty-two torches of wax, every taper to contain the weight of ten pounds and every torch sixteen pounds, which I Will that twenty-four very poor men and well disposed shall hold, as well at the time of my burying as at my *monethe's minde* (month's remembrance).

"Item. I Will that after my *monethe's minde* done, the said four tapers be delivered to the church-wardens, &c.

"And that there be 100 children within the age of 16 years, to be at my *monethe's minde* to pray for my soul . . . that against my *monethe's minde* the candles bren (burn) before the rude in the Parish Church.

"Also that at my *monethe's minde* my executors provide 20 priests to sing *plucebo dirige*, &c."

The Will of Sir Richard Hamerton, Knt.

(1480)

This will be found interesting from the characteristic style and quaint orthography in which it is penned; the detail, too, is eminently suggestive of a simplicity in the individual mind of the testator as well as of the social tone of the times, much at variance with the more complicated habits of our own day. Sir Richard, it must be remarked, was " the head of one of the most ancient and illustrious of the Craven families, the representatives of which still flourish and count up to more than twenty generations of Hamerton's."

"Richard Hamerton, knyghte, in my hole mynde and witt. To be beryed in the kirke of Preston in Craven, in the chapell of Our Ladye and Seignt Anne, in the southe syde of the saide kirke, wherein a chauntery is founded for a prest in perpetuite to syng for Lawrence Hamerton, esquier, and me, the said Richard Hamerton, knyghte, our wyffes, our childre, and all our ancestres.

"Item: I gyff in the name of my mortuary my beste hors, with my sadell, bridell, and othre thingis pertenying to the same.

"Item: I bequeth to the abbot and convent of the monastery of Sallay a standing maser covered and gilted, to pray for me.

"Item: I bequeth to my son William my best whyte cupp of sylver standing.

"Item: To my son Sir Stephen my salet gilted, ij basyns, ij lavers, ij chafours, ij pottes, vj doublers, xij dysshes, and vj sausers, according to my fader will, as apperith folowyng: *i.e.* to the saide Sir Stephen and to the heires male of his body; and for defaute, then to Raner Hamerton, son of John Hamerton, broder to the saide Sir Stephen; then to Roger Hamerton, broder to the saide Raner; then to William Hamerton, broder to the saide Sir Stephen; and for defaute I wille that the saide sylver plate shalle remayne to the abbot and convente of the monastery of Sallay for evermore; for which the saide abbot and convente and ther successoures shall praye for the saules of the said Lawrence Hamerton and Isabell his wyffe, and me, the saide Richarde and Dame Elizabeth my wyffe, our childre saules, and all our auncestres, and for those saules whose bodyes we wer most behalden unto in ther lyffes, and for all Cristen saules.

"Item: I bequeth to my saide son, Sr. Stephen, the tabel in the chapell, wt. all thingis belongyng the same, a ladell, ij brasse pottes of the grettest, ij garingsshe of pewder vessell, a chargiom, a handreth of yern iiij fete, iiij lange spyttes of yren. To my nevewe, John Hamerton, my grete countour in the hall. To my nese, his wyffe, a standing cuppe of sylver dim gilt.

"To my broder James ij oxen, and also my wyffe hath given to hym ij whyes.

"To Raner Hamerton a horse of ij yeres olde ambulyng, another of the same age that ambulys to Roger Hamerton.

"To Cristofer Jakson, a stot and xiij s. iiij d. of money. To Richard Clerk a don hors and xiij s. iiij d.

"To John Rayngill, a stot and whye. To Thomas Kay a stot of ij yeres olde. To William Iveson a styrk.

"To William Fisshe a whye styrk. To Robert Coke a styrk and a whye. To Majory Stowte a whye of age. To William Standen an oxe.

"Item: I bequeth to a priest xij mark to syng ij yeres for my saule, and my wyffe, and all Cristen saules. To iiij orders of Freres iiij l. To the Prior and Convent of the Monastery of Bolton xl s. I bekueth x marke to be distribute emonge my pore tennantes and neghtburs. I bequeth x marc to be distribute emonge pore falkes at the daye of my burying. I ordene and mak my wyffe, Dame Elizabeth, my sones, Sir Stephen and William Hamerton, myn executors. I bequeth ij stottes to William Scarburgh. To Richard Hamerton, my broder James son, a fylle of iij yere. To my wyffe a wayne wt. vj oxen. To my son William an othir wayne and vj oxen. To John Ellis the yonger a mair.

"Testibus Ricardo Parisshe, Ablate de Sallay, et Willelmo Scarburgh generoso."

WILL OF "ARLOTTO, THE PARSON"

(1483)

"Arlotto, the Parson," who is described as an Italian priest of "infinite jest and most excellent fancy," who died in 1483, left among his testamentary documents a wish that the following words should be placed upon his tomb: "This sepulchre was made by the parson Arlotto, for himself and for any other man who may desire to enter therein." These words remained upon his tomb until they were obliterated by time.

WILL OF JOHN TURVYLE

(1500)

In a will written about the year 1500, that of John Turvyle, of Newhall, Leicestershire, "Squyer," there is a bequest to William, his "son and heire apparant," of "a bason and an ewer of silver, warnyng and chargyng him, on my blessyng, and as he will answere afore God at the day of dome, that he shall bequeith them after his decesse to his son and heire apparant, and so under this manner and condicion the forsayd basyn and ewer of silver to go from heire to heire while the world endureth." Which seems to show that the modern system of making particular articles heirlooms to go with the estates, so that they should be kept in the family, had not then been invented.

WILL OF ALICE LOVE

(1506)

A specimen of a lady's will gives some idea of the costumes and fashions of the day, and the store placed upon their wardrobes, which were not so easily replenished as they are now:

"In the name of God, amen — the 6th daye of the moneth of Octobre in the yere of our Lord God a thousand fyve hundred and sixe, I, Alice Love, the wife of Gyles Love of Rye, by the speciall license of my said husband, asked and opteyned [*What does the modern woman think of this?*], bequeath my parapharnalle — that is to seye, myn apparaill to my body belonging. First, I bequeith my sowle unto Almighty God, to our blessed Lady and to alle Saynts, my body to be buried in the chirch yarde of Rye nigh my husband's Thomas Oxenbridge. [*It will be seen that Gyles Love was this Lady's second husband.*] Item, to my moder my graye furred gowne with a long trayne; also a gowne clothe of russet, not made.

Item, to my suster Mercy my best violet gowne furred with shanks. Item, to Margarette Philip my best wolstede kyrtill. Also I gyve to my suster Mercy my dymysent with peerles and a corse of gold. Item, to Thomas Oxenbridge my best gilt gyrdell that my husband Thomas Oxenbridge bought me to my wedding. Item, to Robert Oxenbridge a rede powdred corse, with a good harness, and to everiche of them a paire of bedys of rede corall. Item, to Besse Love my best crymsyn gowne, also her moder's best girdell and her best bedys. Also to my suster Elizabeth Duke a long girdell gilt with a golden corse."

WILL OF CHRISTOPHER COLUMBUS

(1506)

There seems to be much confusion as to the will of Columbus, although, in 1498, he made one, and it is known to have existed in 1530; but it is asserted that it was unsigned, and, moreover, that it was nullified by a later will he made in 1502, but which also is not to be found at the present time.

The only authentic will of his, therefore, that has descended to us is that preserved at Genoa, but which can only be called a codicil.

It is written on the fly-leaf of a book of "Hours," richly bound and adorned, which Columbus had received from Pope Alexander VI., and to which he attached the greatest value; indeed, this is apparent, from the fact that it is the first object of which he disposes in this same codicil:

Codicillus more militari Christopheri Colombi.

Cum SS Alexander, PP. VI., me hoc devatissimo precum libello honoravit, summum mihi præbente solatium in captivitatibus, præliis et adversitatibus meis, volo ut post mortem meam pro memoria tradatur amantissimæ meæ patriæ republicæ Genuensi; et ob beneficia in eadem urbe recepta volo ex stabilibus in Italia redditibus erigi ibidem novum hospitale, ac pro pauperum in patria meliori substentatione, deficientique linea mea masculina in admiraltu meo Indiarum et annexis juxta privilegiis dicti regis insuccessorem declaro et substituo eamdem rempublicam Sancti Georgii.

Datum Valledoliti, 4 Maii, 1506.

S.
S. A. S.
X. M. V.
XPOFERENS.

The initial letters which precede the signature of the Christian name of Columbus (altered, however, into Christo-*ferens*) have never been explained, any more than the two eagles which also precede it; this spelling, however, need throw no doubt on its authenticity, as it is identical with the signatures of two letters, dated respectively 1502 and 1504, addressed to the Ambassador, Nicolas Oderigo.

WILL OF HENRY VII
(1510)

Henry VII. desires in his will that "our executors and supervisors and executors of our testament have a special respect, in our funeral, to the laud and praising of God, the health of our soul, and somewhat to our dignity royal, but avoiding damnable pomp and outrageous superfluities."

WILL OF ERASMUS
(1536)

The town of Bâle possesses together with the will of Erasmus, the ring, seal, sword, knife, pen, and the portrait by Holbein of that great and celebrated man.

The will was drawn up in Latin, five months prior to his decease, 12th February, 1536; we subjoin a literal translation of this interesting document.

"In the name of the Holy Trinity,

"I, Dediderius Erasmus of Rotterdam, honoured with the flattering diplomas of the Emperor, the Sovereign Pontiff, and renowned magistrate of the celebrated city of Bâle, declare that this act, written in my own hand, contains my last wishes; and I desire that they may be ratified and confirmed in every particular, annulling all previous dispositions that I may have made.

"Certain as I am that I have no legitimate heir (Erasmus was a natural son, and was never married), I appoint as my universal heir, the very honourable Boniface Amerbach; and I name as my testamentary executors Jerôme Froben and Nicholas Biscop, brother-in-law of Froben.

"I have already sold my library to Jean de Lasco, a Pole, as may be seen by an act passed between us, and signed by both; but my books are only to be delivered to him when he shall have handed over two hundred florins to my heir; and in case he should have destroyed the act above named, or should die before me, my heir is at liberty to dispose of my books as he may please.

"I bequeath and give to Louis Ber my gold watch; to Beatus Rhenanus a golden spoon, and a fork of the same metal; to Pietro Veteri one hundred and fifty gold crowns; to Philip Montanus the same sum; to my servant Lambert — should he still be in my service at the time of my death — two hundred gold florins, unless I should give them to him during my life; to Jehan de Brisgaw my scent-bottle of silver; to Paul Voltzius one hundred gold florins; to Sigismund Gelenius five hundred ducats; to Jehan Erasmus Froben, two rings, of which one has no stone, the other a green (?) stone called by the French *turquoise*.

"I bequeath and give to Jerôme Froben all my garments and all my furniture; *i.e.* all that composes it, whether in woollen or linen for the former, in wood or other material for the latter. I give him besides, my goblet marked with the arms of the Cardinal de Mayence. I give to his wife my ring, bearing the effigy of a woman looking behind her.

"I give to Nicholas Biscop, my cup with its cover, on the foot of which there are verses engraved; and to Justine, his wife, two gold rings of which one has a diamond, the other a small turquoise. I give to Conrad Goclenius my silver cup, surmounted by a figure of Fortune. If one of my legatees should come to die, I leave the legacy thus lapsed at the disposition of my heir.

"My said heir is to have, besides the objects already devised to him, all that shall remain of my *tazzas*, rings, and other similar articles, including the medals bearing the effigy of the King of Poland, Severin Boner, etc.; and all the double and quadruple ducats. He is to have the money I have deposited with Conrad Goclenius that he may dispose of it in Brabant, as I have recommended to him. If there should be anything of mine still remaining with Erasmus Schet, he is to demand it of him. He will employ this money and any other sums remaining over, according to the advice of the executors, in distributing alms to the poor, whom age or infirmity has rendered impotent, also for marrying young girls or assisting young people, who may show an industrious disposition, to start in the world.

"Such is the act of my last will, written by own proper hand, and sealed with my own private seal belonging to my ring, and representing the god Terminus. Let all faith be accorded to it. Given at Bale, in the house of Jerôme Froben, 12th February, 1536."

WILL OF KATHERINE OF ARAGON
(1536)

"In the name of the Father, of the Son, and of the Holy Ghost, Amen. I, Katherine, &c. supplicate and desire King Henry VIII. my good Lord, that it please him of his grace, and in alms, and for the service of God, to let me have the goods which I do hold, as well in gold and silver as other things, and also the same that is due to me in money for the time passed, to the intent that I may pay my debts and recompense my servants for the good service they have done unto me, and the same I desire as effectuously as I may, for the necessity wherein I am ready to die and to yield my soul unto God.

"First, I supplicate that my body be buried in a Convent of Observant Friars. Item, that for my soul may be said c masses. Item, that some personage go to our Lady of Walsingham, in pilgrimage, and in going by the way dole xx nobles. Item, I appoint to Mistress Darell xx £ for her marriage. Item, I ordain that the collar of gold which I brought out of Spain be to my daughter. I ordain to Mistress Blanche x £ sterling. Item, I ordain to Mistress Margery, and to Mistress Whiller, to each of them x £ sterling. Item, I ordain to Mistress Mary, my physician's wife, and to Mistress Isabel, daughter of Mistress Margery, to each of them xl £ sterling. Item, I ordain to my physician the year's coming wages. Item, I ordain to Francisco Philippe all that I owe unto him, and besides that xl £ sterling. Item, I ordain to Mr. John, mine apothecary, his wages for the year coming, and besides that all that is due unto him. Item, I ordain that Mr. Whiller be paid of expense about the making of my gown, and besides that of xx £ sterling. Item, I give to Philip, to Anthony, and to Bastian, to every of them xx £ sterling. Item, I ordain to the little maidens x £ to every of them. Item, I ordain that my goldsmith be paid of his wages for the year coming, and besides all that is due to him hitherto. Item, I ordain that my launderer be paid of that is due unto her, and besides that of her wages for the year coming. Item, I ordain to the Sabell of Vergas xx £ sterling. Item, to my ghostly father his wages for the year coming. Item, it may please the King my good Lord, that the house ornaments of the church to be made of my gowns, which he holdeth, for to serve the convent thereat I shall be buried. And the furs of the same I give for my daughter."

Katherine was the youngest daughter of Ferdinand of Aragon

and Isabella of Castile. She was born about 1483 and died in 1536. On November 14, 1501, she was married to Arthur, Prince of Wales, then about fifteen years of age, the eldest son of King Henry VII., who died about five months later. The King, unwilling to return her dowry, forced her to marry his remaining son, Henry, who was created Prince of Wales, February 18, 1503, succeeding to the throne as Henry VIII. on April 21st, 1509. On the 24th of June in the same year, they were crowned at Westminster. Her only child, Mary, was born on February 15, 1518, and succeeded her half-brother, King Edward VI., as Queen of England July 6, 1553. The history of this unfortunate, but worthy queen, is too well known to need further comment.

WILL OF SIR WILLIAM PELHAM, KNT.

(1538)

"In the name of God. Amen. 26th Oct., the yeare of our Lord God a thousande fyve hundred thirty and eight. I, William Pelham, Knt., in the countie of Sussex, being hole in mynde and of good memory, doth make and ordeign my last will and testament in manner and fourme followinge:

"First: I bequeth my soule to Almighty God my Creator, and to all the Company of Hevyn; and my body to be buried in the Chauncel of Laughton.

"Item: I bequeth vi. *l.* xiii *s.* ii *d.* for twenty sermons to be preached in Laughton, and in the parishes thereabouts.

"Item: I will that my three sonnes, William, Francis, and Edwarde, shall have twenty poundes sterlinge by the yere during their lvyes, owte of my lands, to be divided equally between them into three parts, and my wyffe to have the same, twenty poundes, every yere during the tyme of their nonage, towards their fyndinge, forthwith after my deth.

"Item: I bequeth a thousande marks sterlinge to be levyed upon my woods, to the marriage of my fyve daughters, that is to say: Bryget, Margaret, Mary, Anne, and Jane, and to be equally between them.

"Item: I bequeth to John Devynyshe, my best geldinge.

"The residue of all my goodes, debts, stuffe, and substance, I geve unto Mary my wyffe, whom I make myn executrix of this my last will.

"These being witnesses, Mary my wiffe, Nicholas my sonne and his wyffe, John Devynyshe, gentilman, Sir Robert Fourde Preest, with many other."

WILL OF MARTIN LUTHER

(1542)

There seems to be considerable obscurity about the authenticity of this document. The learned Dutchman, M. Van Proet (who gives as *his* authority the Dutch translation of the "History of the Reformation"), says that "the will of Luther is to be found in its entirety in the eighth volume of the works of Luther (Altenburg edition); that the original, on parchment, was formerly in the hands of Carpzovius, and that that original, signed by Melancthon, Crucigerus, and Bugenhagenius (or Pomeranus) differed in some places from the printed copy."

Seckendorff of Bâle, in his Commentary, lib. iii. sects. 36 and 135, p. 651, speaks thus of it, and it will be seen that Luther does not err on the side of modesty:

" *De Testamento Lutheri.* — Testatus est, ut exemplar, tom. viii. Altenb. fol. 846, relatum ostendit, anno 1542, die Euphemiæ (16 Septembris), uxoris potissimum gratiâ, cui testamentum perhibet probitatis, fidelitatis et honestatis, et quòd ab eâ semper amatus et omnibus officiis cultus sit; nec fecunditatem tacet, quòd quinque liberos tum viventes ediderit. (Observatum est ex litteris Pontani post mortem Lutheri ad electorum scriptis, quòd uxor Lutheri animum paulò elatiorem et imperiosum habuisse visa sit, et quòd tenax in victu domestico sumptuosa tamen fuerit in ædificia, imprimis in prædium illud Zeüsldorff quod ei in hâc dispositione suâ dotali nomine Lutherus assignaverat. Sed tolerabiles illi nævi fuerunt, nec ab omnibus immunem eam judicavit ipse Lutherus, licèt eam tenere amaret. . . .) Non tam conditionem adjecit iis quæ uxori destinaverat, quàm fiduciam testatus est: quòd uxor, si ad secunda vota transiret (id quod ipsius voluntati et divinæ providentiæ prorsus committit), omnia cum liberis divisura sit. Liberos verò mavult à matre quàm hanc ab illis dependere, exemplis se territum dicens, quàm iniquè sæpè liberi tractent. Denique omissâ omni solemnitate legali confidere se ait, majorem fidem se mereri quàm notarium quemque.

"Notus sum," inquit "in cœlo, in terrâ, et in inferno, et auctoritatem ad hoc sufficientem habeo ut mihi solo credatur, cùm Deus mihi homini licèt damnabili et misera peccatori, ex paternâ misericordiâ Evangelium filii sui crediderit, dederitque ut in eo verax et fidelis fuerim, ita ut multi in mundo illud per me acceperint, et me pro doctore veritatis agnoverint, spreto banno papæ, Cæsaris, regum, principum et sacerdotum, imo omnium dæmonium odio: Quidni igitur ad dispositionem hanc in re exiguâ sufficiat, si adsit manus meæ testimonium et dici possit, hæc scripsit D. Martinus Lutherus, notarius Dei et testis Evangelii ejus.

"Additæ tamen sunt subscriptiones Melancthonis, Crucigeri et Pomerani, sed alio tempore.

"Elector vero Saxoniæ rogatus à vidua diplomate domino judica hoc anno (10 April) dato, testamentum Lutheri conservavit, jubens ut illud etsi solemnitates à legibus requisitæ abessent validum haberetur et observaretur. . . ."

Our readers will doubtless remember that this curious and characteristic fragment has been quoted by Robertson, in a note to his history of Charles Quint, vol. v.

Some time ago the Evangelical Church in Hungary believed itself possessed of the original last will and testament of the great Protestant reformer, Martin Luther. The genuineness of the document was, in fact, attested as undoubted by a special commission appointed to determine that question. The members of this body, however, did not consist of historical scholars, but chiefly of noted members of Parliament. Accordingly, before long it was shown, upon the evidence of Professor Rancke's researches, that the only real testament of Luther — that written with his own hand — is, as a matter of fact, in the Heidelberg Library, and is there kept in a glass case for the inspection of visitors. It has also been satisfactorily proved that the will in the possession of the Hungarian Evangelicals, though written in a hand exactly like Luther's, is not his, but the work of one of his disciples, Henterus, who introduced the reformation into Transylvania; he made a true copy, even to the very handwriting, of the last will and testament of his master.

Will of Hans Holbein

(1543)

Hans Holbein, the younger, belonged to a celebrated family of German painters. His great paintings are scattered throughout the galleries of the world; his last years were spent in England, where he gained both success and fame. He died in London, of the plague, in 1543. His will, written shortly before his death, was found in the archives of St. Paul's Cathedral in 1861 and bears evidence of having been written in haste, as it probably was.

It reads as follows:

"In the name of God the Father, Sonne, and Holy Ghoste, I, Johan Holbeine, servante of the King's Majistie, make this my testamente and will, to wyt, that alle my goodes shall be sold, and also my horse; and I will that my debtes be payd to wyt: furste to Mr. Anthony the kynges servant of Greenwiche, ye summe of ten poundes thirtien shyllinges and sewyne pence sterlinge.

"And, moreover, I will that he shal be contented for all other thynges between him and me.

"Item: I do owe unto Mr. John of Anwarpe, Goldsmythe, saxe pounds sterling, which I will alsoe shalle be payde unto hyme with the fyrste.

"Item: I bequeathe for the kypyng of my two chylder, which be atte nurse, for every monthe, seyvene shellinges, and sexpence styrlynge.

" In wytnes I have sealed and sealed thys my testamente, thys sexthe daye of October, in the yeare of our Lorde MIVCXLIIJ.

"Wytnes, Anthony Snetcher, Armerer, Mr. John of Anwarpe, aforesaid, Goldsmythe, Obrycke Obynger, Merchante and Harry Maynaert, Paynter."

WILL OF KING HENRY VIII
(1547)

The greatest testamentary powers ever conferred on an English king were given to Henry VIII. by 25 Henry VIII. c. 7, empowering him to limit and appoint the succession to the Crown by will, in default of children by Jane Seymour.

This will of Henry VIII. is to be found in full in Nicolas's "Testamenta Vetusta," a collection of famous wills, a work of great excellence, prepared in 1825. There are also to be found the Wills of Henry II., Henry III., Henry IV., Henry V., Henry VI., and Henry VII., as are those of other Kings and Queens of England.

WILL OF RABELAIS
(1553)

The will of this ingenious satirist is adorned (or disfigured) by a very characteristic clause: "I have no available property, I owe a great deal; the rest I give to the poor."

We cannot affirm that this bull, worthy of an Irishman, is well authenticated, any more than Rabelais's facetious reply to the messenger of Cardinal du Belay, whom he sent to see how he fared in his last illness: "Je vais chercher un grand peutêtre; tirez le rideau, la farce est jouée."

Will of Mary Queen of Scots
(1587)

Mary Stuart was beheaded in 1587. Her will is to be found in a collection entitled: "Pièces fugitives pour servir à l'Histoire de France, avec des notes historiques, par M. le Baron d'Aubais," 1759. This work is in 5 vols. 4to, and the will is in the second.

It is prefaced by a short note explanatory of the attendant circumstances, viz. that it was written by the ill-fated queen on the eve of her execution, and after she had been curtly, unceremoniously, and unexpectedly informed it was to take place at eight the following morning. The writing out of this, and of an extremely touching letter to her brother-in-law, Henri III., occupied her until two o'clock in the morning, when she bathed, selected and put on her costliest dress, head-dress, and costume, distributed her little store of ready money and jewels to her attendants, retired to her oratory and prepared herself for death. All this is minutely related, also the manner of her death; for to the last moment the queen was unaware whether she were to be beheaded standing or with her head on the block. It was, however, to be by the latter mode; and the headsman proved so inexperienced, and his weapon so clumsy, that the operation was only completed after three blows.

Mary's will is written in French, and is word for word as follows:

"Au nom du Père, du Fils, et du Sainct Esprit:

"Je, Marie, par la grâce de Dieu royne d'Ecosse, douairière de France etc.: Estant preste à mourir, et n'ayant moyen de faire mon testament, j'ay mis ces articles par escrit, lesquels j'entens et veulx avoir meme force que si ilz étaient mis en forme.

"Protestant, premier de mourir en la foi chatolique apostolique romaine.

"Premier, je veulx qui'il soit faict un service complet pour mon ame a l'église Sainct Denys en France, et l'autre a Sainct Pierre de Reims, où tous mes serviteurs ce trouveront en la manière qu'il sera ordonné a ceulx a qui j'en donne la charge issi dessouts nommez.

"Plus, qu'un obit annuel soit fondé pour prier pour mon ame à perpetuité, à lieu et en la maniere qui sera advisé le plus commode.

"Pour a quoy fournir je veulx que mes maysons de Fontaynebeleau soient vendues, esperant que au surplus le roy m'aydera, comme par mon memoyre je le requiers.

"Je veulx que ma terre de Jespagn demeure a mon cousin de Guise pour une de ses filles, si elle venoit a estre mariée en ces quartiers; je quitteray la moitié des arerages qui me sont deus, ou une partie, a condition que l'autre soit payée, pour estre par mes executeurs employée en aumosne annuelle.

"Pour a quoi mieulx provoir, les papiers seront recherchez et delivrez selon l'affination pour en faire poursuite.

"Je veulx aussi que l'argens que ce retirera de mon procès de secondat, soit distribué comme s'en suit.

"Premier, a la descharge du poiement de mes dettes et mandemens si aprez nommez, qui me seront ja paiez, premier, les deux mille esqus de Courle que je veulx luy estre payez sans nulle contradiction, comme estantz en faveur de mariage sans que nous au aultre luy en puisse rien demander, quelque obligation qu'il en aye d'autant qu'elle n'est que feincte é que l'argent estoit à moy é non emprunté, lequel je ne fis que luy montray, é lé depuis retiré, et me on pris avecque le reste à Chasteley, lequel je lui donne si il le peut recovrer, comme il a esté promis pour payement ces quatre mille franks promis, pour payement ces quatre mille franks promis par mort, et mille pour marier une siene sœur, et m'ayant demandé le reste pour ses despans en prison; quant a l'assignation de pareille somme a nous, elle n'est pas d'obligation, et pour ce a toujours esté mon intention que elle fust la dernière payée et encore en cas qu'il fasse aparoir n'avoir faict contre la condition pour la quelle je les luy avoist donnéz au temoignasge de mes serviteurs.

"Pour la partie de douze cens esquus que il m'a faict alleuer par lui empruntée pour mon service de Beauregard, jusques à six sens esqus et de Gervays trois cents, et le reste je ne sais d'ou, it faut qu'il les repoye de son argent et que j'en soyes quitte é l'assignation cassée, car je n'en ay rien resceu, mais est le fond en ces coffres, si ce n'estoit que ils en soient payez par dela; comme que ce soit; it faut que cett partie me revienne bonne, n'ayant rien receu, et si elle estoit payée je doits avoir recours sur son lieu, é de plus, je veulx que Pasquier compte les deniers que il a despandus é receus par le commandement de nous, par les mains des serviteurs de M. de Chasteauneuf, l'ambassadeur de France.

"Plus, je veulx que mes comptes soyent ouys é mon tresorier payé.

"Plus, que les gages et parties de mes gens tant de l'année passée que de la presente, soyent tous payez avant toute autre choze, tant gages que pensions, parmis les pensions les pensions de Jean et de Courle, jusques a ce que l'on sasche ce qui en doit advenir et ce qu'ils auront meritez de moy pour pensions si ce n'est que la fame de Courle soyt en nécessité, ou luy maltraicté pour moy; des gages de Jean de mesme.

"Je veulx que les deux mille quatre cens franks que j'ay donnais a Jène Kenedi luy soyent payez en argent, comme il estoit porté en son premier don, é quoy fesant la pension de Willi Guillaulme Douglas me reviendra, laquelle je donne a Fontenoy pour ces services é despens non recompansez.

"Je veulx que les quatre mille esqus de ce banquier soyent sollisitez é repayez, duquel j'ay oublié le nom; mais l'evesque de Glascou s'en resoviendra assez; é si l'assignation premiére venoit à manquer, je veulx qu'il leur en soyt donné une sur les premiers deniers de secondat.

"Les dix mille franks que l'ambassadeur avoyt receux pour moy, je veulx qu'ilz soyent employez entre mes serviteurs qui s'en vont à present à scavoir, premier, deux mille franks à Elizabeth Courle; deux mille franks à Basten Pages; deux mille à Marie Pages, ma filleule; mille à Gourgon; mille à Gervays.

"Plus, sur les aultres deniers de mon revenu, à Beauregard, mille franks; à Monthay, mille franks.

"E reste de Secondat et de toutes mes casualitez, je veulx estre employez sinq cens franks à la misericorde des enfans de Reims; à mes escoliers, deux mille franks; aux quatre mandians, la somme qu'il sera nécessaire; à mes executeurs, selon les moyens qui ce trouveront, sinq cens franks aux hospitaulx.

"A l'esquier de cuisine Martin, je donne mille franks; mille franks à Hambel, e le laisse à mon cousin de Guise, son parein, a le mettre en quelque lieu en son service.

"Je laysse sinq cens franks à Robin Hamilton et prie mon filz le prendre, é Monsieur de Glascou faulte de luy, ou l'evesque de Rosse.

"Je laysse à Didier son grefe sous la faveur du roy.

"Je donne sinq cens franks à Jean Landere, é prie mon cousin de Guise ou d'Humaine (pour du Maine) le prendre en leur service, é a Messieurs de Glascou et de Rosse qu'ils ayent soing de le voir

ANCIENT, CURIOUS, AND FAMOUS WILLS

preveu; je veulx que son père soyt payé de ces gages, et luy laysse sinq cens franks.

"Je veulx que mille franks soyent payez à Gourgeon, pour argent et aultres chozes qu'ils m'a fournies en ma nécessité.

"E je veulx que si Bourgoin accompli le voiage du vœu qu'il a faict pour moy à S. Nicolas, que quinze franks lui soyent livrés à cet effet. Je laysse selon mon peu de moyen six mille franks à l'evesque de Glascou, troys mille à celuy de Rosse. E je laysse la donaison des alsualities et droicts seigneriaux recelez à mon filleul, filz de M. Duruisseau.

"Je donne troys cens franks à Laurents, plus troys cens franks à Suzanne, é laysse dix mille franks entre les quatre parties, qui ont esté respondant pour moy é au solliciteur parmy.

"Je veulx que l'argent provenant des meubles que j'ay ordonnez estre vendus à Londres soyt pour defroyer le voyage de mes gens jusques en France.

"Ma cosche je la laysse pour mener mes filles, é les chevaulx pour les vendre ou aultrement en faire leur commoditez.

"Il y a environ cent esqus des gages des années passées deus à Bourgoin, que je veulx luy estre payez.

"Je laysse deux mille franks à Meluin, mon maystre d'hostel.

"Je ordonne pour principal executeur de ma volonté mon cousin le Duc de Guise, é aprez luy l'Archevesque de Glascou, l'evesque de Rosse, et M. Duruisseau, mon chancelier.

"J'entends que sans faulte le preau jouisse de ces deux prependes.

"Je recommande Marie Pages, ma filleule, à ma cousine Madame de Guise, é la prie de prendre en son service; é ma tante de S. Pierre fayre mettre Montbraye en quelque bon lieu, ou la retenir en service pour l'honneur de Dieu.

"Faict ce jourd'hui 7 Feubrier, mil sinq cens octante é sept.

"MARIE R."

WILL OF ALESSANDRO TASSONI

(1635)

Tassoni was an Italian diplomat, poet and critic; he was born at Modena in 1565 of an old patrician family. His greatest work was the publication, "The Stolen Bucket." The following are excerpts from his will:

"I leave my soul — the most precious thing I possess — to its first great cause, the invisible, ineffable, eternal.

"As for my body, destined as it is to corruption, my own

desire would have been that it should be burned; but that being contrary to the custom of the religion in which I was born, I beg those in whose house I should die — for I have none of my own — to bury me by preference in consecrated ground; or if I should be found dead, without any other roof over me than the vault of heaven, I entreat the charitable neighbors or passers-by to render me this last service.

"My wish would be that my funeral should only employ one priest, that there should be simply the small cross and a single candle, and that as regards expense no more shall be incurred than will pay for a sack to stuff my remains into, and a porter to carry it.

"I give twelve gold crowns to the parish, because I cannot carry them away."

CHAPTER III

WILLS IN FICTION AND POETRY

"This brief abridgment of my will I make,
My soul and body to the skies and ground."

ON WILL-MAKING

AN excellent treatise on the foibles of testators and the motives which prompt devises, legacies and bequests, is to be found in the work of William Hazlitt, "Table Talk or Original Essays," under the title, "On Will-making," a portion of which is here subjoined. The fame of the author and the merit of the essay justify its introduction.

"Few things show the human character in a more ridiculous light than the circumstance of will-making. It is the latest opportunity we have of exercising the natural perversity of the disposition, and we take care to make a good use of it. We husband it with jealousy, put it off as long as we can, and then use every precaution that the world shall be no gainer by our deaths. This last act of our lives seldom belies the former tenor of them, for stupidity, caprice, and unmeaning spite. All that we seem to think of is to manage matters so (in settling accounts with those who are so unmannerly as to survive us) as to do as little good and to plague and disappoint as many people as possible."

* * * * * * *

"The art of will-making chiefly consists in baffling the importunity of expectation. I do not so much find fault with this when it is done as a punishment and oblique satire on servility and selfishness. It is in that case *Diamond cut Diamond* — a trial of skill between the legacy-hunter and the legacy-maker, which shall fool the other. The cringing toad-eater, the officious tale-bearer, is perhaps well paid for years of obsequious attendance with a bare mention and a mourning-ring; nor can I think that Gil Blas' library was not quite as much as the coxcombry of his pretensions deserved. There are some admirable scenes in Ben Jonson's

'Volpone,' shewing the humours of a legacy-hunter, and the different ways of fobbing him off with excuses and assurances of not being forgotten. Yet it is hardly right after all, to encourage this kind of pitiful, bare-faced intercourse, without meaning to pay for it; as the coquette has no right to jilt the lovers she has trifled with. Flattery and submission are marketable commodities like any other, have their price, and ought scarcely to be obtained under false pretences. If we see through and despise the wretched creature that attempts to impose on our credulity, we can at any time dispense with his services; if we are soothed by this mockery of respect and friendship, why not pay him like any other drudge, or as we satisfy the actor who performs a part in a play by our particular desire? But often these premeditated disappointments are as unjust as they are cruel, and are marked with circumstances of indignity, in proportion to the worth of the object. The suspecting, the taking it for granted that your name is down in the will, is sufficient provocation to have it struck out; the hinting at an obligation, the consciousness of it on the part of the testator, will make him determined to avoid the formal acknowledgment of it, at any expense. The disinheriting of relations is mostly for venial offences, not for base actions: we punish out of pique, to revenge some case in which we have been disappointed of our wills, some act of disobedience to what had no reasonable ground to go upon; and we are obstinate in adhering to our resolution, as it was sudden and rash, and doubly bent on asserting our authority in what we have least right to interfere in. It is the wound inflicted upon our self-love, not the stain upon the character of the thoughtless offender, that calls for condign punishment. Crimes, vices may go unchecked, or unnoticed: but it is the laughing at our weaknesses, or thwarting our humours, that is never to be forgotten. It is not the errors of others, but our own miscalculations, on which we wreak our lasting vengeance. It is ourselves that we cannot forgive."

* * * * * *

"An old man is twice a child: the dying man becomes the property of his family. He has no choice left, and his voluntary power is merged in old saws and prescriptive usages. The property we have derived from our kindred reverts tacitly to them: and not to let it take its course, is a sort of violence done to nature as well as custom. The idea of property, of something in common, does not mix cordially with friendship, but is inseparable from near relationship. We owe a return in kind, where we feel no obligation for a favour; and consign our possessions to our next of kin as mechanically as we lean our heads on the pillow, and go out of the world in the same state of stupid amazement that we came into it! ... Cetera desunt."

Human nature is ever the same: William Hazlitt wrote the above lines one hundred years ago, and yet as we read them, there appears an emphasized truth in the sentiment contained in a verse from "Mortality," a composition by William Knox, which was the favorite poem of Abraham Lincoln:

"For we are the same our fathers have been,
We see the same sights that our fathers have seen;
We drink the same stream, and view the same sun,
And run the same course our fathers have run."

It is said of Hazlitt that his domestic life was infelicitous; that he had a temperament which was erratic and self-tormenting and estranged him from his friends, even for a time from Charles Lamb. He died on September 18, 1830, with Lamb at his bedside, and though disappointed and harassed by anxiety and suffering as he had been, yet his last words were: "I've had a happy life." How many of us would have said as much!

WILLS OF THE NOVELIST

The *Green Bag* says:

"Where would the novelist of the period be without the disinheriting will, the manipulated will, the secreted will, and all kinds of wills in every style of obliteration and in every stage of destruction? Why, he would be nearly as bereft of staple stock in trade as if he had lost the lovelorn maiden, the tender-hearted soldier, or the grand old hall of our ancestors. Even writers of a higher grade find it convenient to make use of such machinery to help make the story go."

OLD NOIRTIER'S WILL

Romancers and writers of fiction have taken much interest in, and considerable liberty with, wills; for instance, old Noirtier, a character in the "Count of Monte Cristo," the great novel by Dumas, wrote his will. He was paralyzed, and his only means of communication was by the eye: to shut the eye, meant "yes":

to wink the eye, meant "no." His granddaughter had no trouble when the notaries appeared in convincing them that her grandparent knew exactly what he was doing; so, in spite of opposition and in the presence of seven witnesses, the will was executed; and as no signature was required under the French law, the act was legally accomplished.

Dr. Jekyll's Will

Then there was the famous will in "Dr. Jekyll and Mr. Hyde": the very worthy lawyer, Mr. Utterson, who was "lean, long, dusty, dreary and, somehow, lovable," refused to write this will, wherein Dr. Jekyll left his possessions to his friend and benefactor, Edward Hyde. Mr. Hyde was also to be the possessor of this property if Dr. Jekyll should disappear for a period exceeding three calendar months, the same to be free from burden or obligation, beyond the payment of a few small sums to members of the Doctor's household.

The Will of Lord Monmouth

In "Coningsby," by Disraeli, the reading of Lord Monmouth's will is a feature. The document is lengthy, and numerous codicils have been added from time to time, involving many modifications. The last codicil of all, however, was the most startling, for under it all former dispositions were upset.

Mr. Casaubon's Will

In George Eliot's "Middlemarch," we find the will of Mr. Casaubon. This gentleman had married a girl, Dorothea Brooke, who was very much younger than himself. By his will, he very properly gave her all his property. However, on reflection, and for reasons best known to himself, he added a codicil and placed the legacy given to his wife, upon the condition that she did not marry one Ladislaw.

It would further appear that until the reading of this codicil, it had not occurred to Dorothea that Ladislaw might be a possible lover; but he became one, and the very suggestion of the testator caused the defeat of the latter's wishes.

Anthony Trollope's "Orley Farm"

Our author tells us of a forgery of a codicil by the second wife of the testator: a son by a first wife is cut off, and the farm is left to a son by the second wife. This codicil is in the handwriting of the widow, witnessed by an attorney whose daughter received a handsome legacy, the other witnesses being a clerk and a maidservant. The widow swears that the codicil was drawn at the attorney's dictation, in the husband's hearing, and that she was present when it was signed by all the parties. The witnesses gave evidence as to the due execution of the codicil. The instrument was admitted to probate. It developed, however, that there was another paper, a dissolution of partnership, signed on the same day by the same witnesses. The result was, that the charming widow was found guilty of perjury.

MR. MEESON'S WILL

The following description of this famous will is taken from the *Green Bag*:

"In 'Mr. Meeson's Will,' Rider Haggard tells of a fiendish publisher and a lone island and a tattooed will. It is the particular delight of this issuer of books, though he largely sends forth works of a religious cast, to crush all the originality out of his authors and turn them into literary hacks, so that they may become dreary drudges in his vast establishment, sinking even their names in numbers, and losing every atom of individuality and every symptom of spirit. He makes a shamelessly cruel contract with the heroine, who writes novels; and the hero, his nephew, protests and is driven out of the concern. But he is driven into love with the reciprocating maker of manuscript. Then the heroine embarks for distant lands; and it happens, to the great good fortune of the inventor of the story, that the publisher sails on board the same vessel. The vessel is wrecked and these two are cast on a desert island, where they manage to get along after the style of 'Robinson Crusoe' with variations. But the publisher, upset in body and mind by these experiences, dies, pursued by ghastly visions of the suffering authors he has driven to desperation.

"Yet these very visions make him see the error of his ways, and prompt him to do justice. It is plain to him that he must set all things right by making a will in favor of the nephew whom he had disinherited. But how to carry out the plan on this spot is the question. At last a happy thought strikes the lady. The will shall be tattoed across her shoulders, and this is done, though she endures no end of agony, and faints away when the job is over.

"Of course she is rescued by a passing vessel, rejoins her lover, and seeks to establish his rights. For this purpose the will must be probated, and the law requires the original will to be filed in the office. But the Registrar, touched by 'Beauty in distress,' allows a photograph of the will to be filed. The will is contested by the other heirs, but after an exciting trial, described at length in the story, victory perches on the shoulders of the lady.

"This is the real climax of the story, but we are carried on through the ringing of the marriage bells, to learn that they lived happy ever after."

HIS REQUEST DISREGARDED

Horace Walpole writes that a certain testator who was apprehensive that his will would not be upheld, prefaced that document with these words:

"In the name of God, Amen! I am of sound mind. This is my last will and testament, and I desire the courts not to trouble themselves to make another for me."

His request seems not to have been taken in his favor, for the courts did make another will for him.

In ancient Greece, it was quite usual to introduce into wills the most formidable imprecations on those who should attempt to violate the wishes of the testator; in modern times pecuniary penalties, instead of curses, are more in favor with distrustful will-makers.

JEROME ON WILLS

Mr. Jerome K. Jerome, after months of study, inspired by a determination to get to the bottom of Stage law, mentions among the few points on which he is at all clear, the following:

That if a man dies without leaving a will, then all his property goes to the nearest villain.

But that if a man dies and leaves a will, then all his property goes to whoever can get possession of that will.

MUST NOT REMARRY

"Iris," in one of Pinero's plays of the same name, is a beautiful young widow of twenty-one. She finds herself much hampered by the terms of her husband's will, which deprives her of its benefits if she remarries. Such a provision is in law perfectly legal and its use much indulged in by dying husbands, but whether wisely or justly is a matter of serious doubt.

ANCIENT, CURIOUS, AND FAMOUS WILLS

"THE THUNDERBOLT"

Pinero's latest play, "The Thunderbolt," is a study of the manners and respectability of the middle-class of England. The play was not received with favor in London, but has been granted a hearing by the "New Theatre" of New York, and by competent judges is said to be the masterpiece of its author.

The play is based on a stolen will: the first act shows a family gathered around the bier of Edward Mortimore, who had accumulated wealth in the brewing of beer, which, during his life, was regarded by his family as rather a disreputable business. There is absent from the gathering, only one interested person, and that is an illegitimate daughter, Helen Thornhill, who is an art student in Paris. Helen arrives and is much surprised that her father has not remembered her, for the announcement is made that he left no will; and she wishes that "every ill that's conceivable" should come upon the heads of those who will inherit. It quickly develops, however, that the father did leave a will, in these words:

"I leave everything I die possessed of to Helen Thornhill, spinster, absolutely, and she is to be my sole executrix."

A confession discloses the fact that the will has been destroyed by Phyllis, wife of Thaddeus, a brother of the testator. Helen refuses to bring disgrace on the family by a prosecution, and a compromise is effected, by which she receives a substantial portion of the estate.

DICKENS A WILL-MAKER

Dickens was a great will-maker. We know that if Dick Swiveller had been a steadier youth he would have inherited more than one hundred and fifty pounds a year from his Aunt Rebecca. The loyal-hearted lover, Mr. Barkis, made Peggotty his residuary legatee. The litigation in Jarndyce v. Jarndyce arose out of a disputed will. The various wills left by old Harmon in "Our Mutual Friend" bring about no end of complications, there being at least three wills in existence at one time, and each one believed by the person discovering it to be the final will.

Mr. George W. E. Russell says that perhaps Dickens's best piece of will-making is given in the case of Mr. Spenlow, who, being a practitioner in Doctors' Commons, spoke about his own will with "a serenity, a tranquillity, a calm sunset air" which quite affected David Copperfield; and then shattered all poor David's hopes by dying intestate.

Perplexities of Poor Cecilia

All the perplexities and distresses of poor Cecilia, in Frances Burney's "Memoirs of an Heiress," grew out of a clause in her uncle's will, imposing the condition that if she married, her husband should take her family name of Beverly. Poor Cecilia! What doubts and difficulties beset her by reason of this unfortunate provision; and too, it gives the authoress an excellent opportunity to harrow up the reader on account of these delicate uncertainties and distresses.

Olivia's Will

It was suggested to Olivia in "Twelfth Night," that her graces would go to the grave and no copy be held; she responds:

"O, Sir, I will not be so hard hearted; I will give out divers schedules of my beauty; It shall be inventoried, and every particle and utensil labelled to my will; as, item, two lips indifferent red; item, two gray eyes with lids to them; item, one neck, one chin, and so forth."

Portia and Nerissa

In the "Merchant of Venice" Portia is much concerned over the will of her father with reference to the caskets:

"*Portia.* But this reasoning is not in the fashion to choose me a husband. — O me! the word choose! I may neither choose whom I would, nor refuse whom I dislike; so is the will of a living daughter curbed by the will of a dead father. — Is it not hard, Nerissa, that I cannot choose one, nor refuse none?

"*Nerissa.* Your father was ever virtuous, and holy men at their death have good inspirations; therefore, the lottery, that he hath devised in these three chests of gold, silver, and lead (whereof who chooses his meaning, chooses you) will, no doubt, never be chosen by any rightly, but one whom you shall rightly love. But what warmth is there in your affection towards any of these princely suitors that are already come?"

Will of Nicholas Gimcrack

The will of Nicholas Gimcrack, Esq., is a curious document, and reflects the mind of the worthy virtuoso, and in it his various follies, littlenesses and quaint humors are contained in an orderly and distinct fashion. This will appears in the *Tatler*, Vol. IV, No. 216, and is here written, minus certain parts which are of no great concern:

ANCIENT, CURIOUS, AND FAMOUS WILLS

"THE WILL OF A VIRTUOSO

"I Nicholas Gimcrack, being in sound Health of Mind, but in great Weakness of Body, do by this my Last Will and Testament bequeath my worldly Goods and Chattels in Manner follows:

"Imprimis, To my dear Wife,
One Box of Butterflies,
One Drawer of Shells,
A Female Skeleton,
A dried Cockatrice.

"Item, To my Daughter Elizabeth,
My Receipt for preserving dead Caterpillars,
As also my preparations of Winter May-Dew, and Embrio Pickle.

"Item, To my little Daughter Fanny,
Three Crocodiles' Eggs.
And upon the Birth of her first Child, if she marries with her Mother's Consent,
The Nest of a Humming-Bird.

"Item, To my eldest Brother, as an Acknowledgment for the Lands he has vested in my Son Charles, I bequeath
My last Year's Collection of Grasshoppers.

"Item, To his Daughter, Susanna, being his only Child, I bequeath my English Weeds pasted on Royal Paper,
With my large Folio of Indian Cabbage.

* * * * * * *

"Having fully provided for my Nephew Isaac, by making over to him some years since
A Horned Scarabæus,
The Skin of a Rattle-Snake, and
The Mummy of an Egyptian King,
I make no further Provision for him in this my Will.

"My eldest son John having spoken disrespectfully of his little sister, whom I keep by me in Spirits of Wine, and in many other instances behaved himself undutifully towards me, I do disinherit, and wholly cut off from any Part of this my Personal Estate, by giving him a single Cockle-Shell.

"To my Second Son Charles, I give and bequeath all my Flowers, Plants, Minerals, Mosses, Shells, Pebbles, Fossils, Beetles, Butterflies, Caterpillars, Grasshoppers, and Vermin, not above specified: As also all my Monsters, both wet and dry, making the said Charles whole and sole Executor of this my Last Will and Testament, he paying or causing to be paid the aforesaid Legacies within the space of Six Months after my Decease. And I do hereby revoke all other Wills whatsoever by me formerly made."

EUSTACE BUDGELL

Pope was an excellent satirist; he writes:

"Let Budgell charge lone Grub Street on my quill,
And write whate'er he please, — except my will."

Eustace Budgell was born at St. Thomas near Exeter, England, in 1685, and died in 1737. He was an essayist and miscellaneous writer, and a friend and kinsman of Joseph Addison, who was for a time Secretary of State for Ireland: he accompanied Addison to Ireland as Clerk, and later became under Secretary of State: he was, however, forced to resign his post, and returned to England.

Budgell is said to have lost a fortune in the notorious scheme known to history as the "South Sea Bubble." He published the *Bee*, a periodical which brought him into considerable notoriety. He studied law and was called to the bar, but attained little success. By the will of Dr. Matthew Tindal, who died in 1733, he was left a legacy of 2000 Guineas: it was claimed that Budgell himself inserted this legacy in the will, which was successfully disputed by the heirs to the Tindal Estate: his prospects and future being ruined, he fell into disgrace and debt, and determined upon self-destruction. Accordingly, 1737, he took a boat at Summerset Stairs, after filling his pockets with stones, and drowned himself in the Thames. On his desk was found a slip of paper on which were written these words:

"What Cato did and Addison approved cannot be wrong."

WILL OF A CHILD

In "Little Women," by Louisa M. Alcott, we find Amy's will, and it is a pretty reflection of the sweet and ingenuous spirit of a child. And humanity would be the happier for it if we could take with us into maturer years, the open hand and the self-forgetfulness of childhood.

Amy decided to follow the example of her Aunt March in will-making, though it cost her many a pang to part with her little treasures. Here is the paper Laurie was asked to read:

ANCIENT, CURIOUS, AND FAMOUS WILLS

"MY LAST WILL AND TESTAMENT

"I, Amy Curtis March, being in my sane mind, do give and bequeethe all my earthly property — viz. to wit : — namely

"To my father, my best pictures, sketches, maps, and works of art, including frames. Also my $100, to do what he likes with.

"To my mother, all my clothes, except the blue apron with pockets, — also my likeness, and my medal, with much love.

"To my dear sister Margaret, I give my turquoise ring (if I get it), also my green box with the doves on it, also my piece of real lace for her neck, and my sketch of her as a memorial of her 'little girl.'

"To Jo I leave my breast-pin, the one mended with sealing wax, also my bronze inkstand — she lost the cover — and my most precious plaster rabbit, because I am sorry I burnt up her story.

"To Beth (if she lives after me) I give my dolls and the little bureau, my fan, my linen collars and my new slippers if she can wear them being thin when she gets well. And I herewith also leave her my regret that I ever made fun of old Joanna.

"To my friend and neighbor Theodore Laurence I bequeethe my paper marshay portfolio, my clay model of a horse though he did say it hadn't any neck. Also in return for his great kindness in the hour of affliction any one of my artistic works he likes, Noter Dame is the best.

"To our venerable benefactor Mr. Laurence I leave my purple box with a looking glass in the cover which will be nice for his pens and remind him of the departed girl who thanks him for his favors to her family, specially Beth.

"I wish my favorite playmate Kitty Bryant to have the blue silk apron and my gold-bead ring with a kiss.

"To Hannah I give the bandbox she wanted and all the patchwork I leave hoping she 'will remember me, when it you see.'

"And now having disposed of my most valuable property I hope all will be satisfied and not blame the dead. I forgive every one, and trust we may all meet when the trump shall sound. Amen.

"To this will and testament I set my hand and seal on this 20th day of Nov. Anni Domino 1861.
"AMY CURTIS MARCH.

"*Witnesses:* { ESTELLE VALNOR,
THEODORE LAURENCE.

"Postscript : I wish all my curls cut off, and given round to my friends. I forgot it; but I want it done, though it will spoil my looks."

The Will of Don Quixote

"I feel, good sirs," said Don Quixote, "that death advances fast upon me. Let us then be serious, and bring me a confessor, and a notary to draw up my will, for a man in my state must not trifle with his soul. Let the notary be sent for, I beseech you, while my friend here, the priest, is taking my confession."

The priest, having listened to his dying friend's confession, came out of the room and told them that the good Alonzo Quixano was near his end, and certainly in his right senses; he therefore advised them to go in, as it was full time that his will should be made. These tidings gave a terrible stab to the overcharged hearts of the two ladies and his faithful squire, whose eyes overflowed with weeping, and whose bosoms had well-nigh burst with a thousand sighs and groans; for, indeed, it must be owned, as we have somewhere observed, that whether in the character of Alonzo Quixano the Good, or in the capacity of Don Quixote de la Mancha, the poor gentleman had always exhibited marks of a peaceable temper and agreeable demeanor, for which he was beloved, not only by his own family, but also by all those who had the pleasure of his acquaintance.

The notary entering the apartment with the rest of the company, wrote the preamble of the will, in which Don Quixote disposed of his soul in all the necessary Christian forms; then proceeding to the legacies, he said:

"Item: Whereas, Sancho Panza, whom, in my madness, I made my squire, has in his hands a certain sum of money for my use; and, as divers accounts, disbursements, and pecuniary transactions have passed between us, it is my will that he shall not be charged or brought to account for the said money; but, if there be any overplus after he has deducted the payment of what I owe him, the said overplus, which must be a mere trifle, shall be his own, and much good may it do him; and as, during my disorder, I contributed to his being made governor of an island, I would now, while I enjoy my perfect senses, confer upon him, were it in my power, a whole kingdom, which he richly deserves for the innocency of his heart and the fidelity of his service."

Then turning to the disconsolate squire, "Forgive me, friend," said he, "for having been the cause of thy appearing in the eye of the world a madman like myself, by drawing thee into my erroneous notions concerning the existence and adventures of knights-errant."

"Gentlemen," said Don Quixote, "let us proceed fair and softly. I was mad, I am now sane; I was Don Quixote de la Mancha; I am now, as formerly styled, Alonzo Quixano the Good. And may my repentance and sincerity restore me to the esteem you once had for me. Now let the notary proceed.

"Item: I bequeath to Antonia Quixano, my niece, here present, all my estate, real and personal, after the payment of all my debts and legacies; and the first to be discharged shall be the wages due to my housekeeper for the time she has been in my service, and twenty ducats besides for a suit of mourning.

"I appoint for my executors signor the priest and signor bachelor Sampson Carrasco, here present.

"Item: It is also my will that, if Antonia Quixano, my niece, should be inclined to marry, it shall be only with a man who, upon the strictest inquiry, shall be found to know nothing of books of chivalry; and, in case it appear that he is acquainted with such books, and that my niece, notwithstanding, will and doth marry him, then shall she forfeit all I have bequeathed her, which my executors may dispose of in pious uses as they think proper.

"And, finally, I beseech the said gentlemen, my executors, that if haply they should come to the knowledge of the author of a certain history dispersed abroad, entitled, 'The Second Part of the Achievements of Don Quixote de la Mancha,' that they will, in my name, most earnestly entreat him to forgive me for having been the innocent cause of his writing such a number of absurdities as that performance contains; for I quit this life with some scruples of conscience arising from that consideration."

The will being thus concluded, he was seized with a fainting-fit, and stretched himself at full length in the bed, so that all the company were alarmed and ran to his assistance. During three days which he lived after the will was signed and sealed, he frequently fainted, and the whole family was in confusion. Nevertheless, the niece ate her victuals, the housekeeper drank to the repose of his soul, and even Sancho cherished his little carcass; for the prospect of succession either dispels or moderates that affliction which an heir ought to feel at the death of the testator.

At last Don Quixote expired, after having received all the sacraments, and in the strongest terms, pathetically enforced, expressed his abomination against all books of chivalry; and the notary observed, that in all the books of that kind which he had perused, he had never read of any knight-errant who died quietly in his bed as a good Christian, like Don Quixote; who, amidst the tears and lamentations of all present, gave up the ghost, or, in other words, departed this life. The curate was no sooner certified of his decease, than he desired the notary to make out a testimonial, declaring that Alonzo Quixano the Good, commonly called Don Quixote de la Mancha, had taken his departure from this life, and died of a natural death; that no other author, different from Cid Hamet Benengeli, should falsely pretend to raise him from the dead, and write endless histories of his achievements.

This was the end of that extraordinary gentleman of La Mancha, whose birthplace Cid Hamet was careful to conceal, that all the towns and villages of that province might contend for the honor of having produced him, as did the seven cities of Greece for the glory of giving birth to Homer. The lamentations of Sancho, the niece and the housekeeper, are not here given, nor the new epitaphs on the tomb of the deceased knight, except the following one, composed by Sampson Carrasco:

"A doughty gentleman lies here,
A stranger all his life to fear;
Nor in his death could Death prevail,
In that last hour, to make him quail.

"He for the world but little cared;
And at his feats the world was scared;
A crazy man his life he passed,
But in his senses died at last."

WILLS IN POETRY OR RHYME

The disposition of one's worldly possessions by a testamentary document in poetry or rhyme, appears incongruous, yet there are numerous documents of this nature: a brief, but striking example of such, by an attorney named Smithers who resided in London, follows:

"As to all my wordly goods, now or to be in store,
I give them to my beloved wife, and hers forevermore.
I give all freely; I no limit fix;
This is my will, and she's executrix."

WILL OF MOTHER HUBBARD'S DOG

"This wonderful dog
Was Dame Hubbard's delight;
He could dance, he could sing,
He could read, he could write.

"She went to the druggist
To get him a pill;
And when she came back,
He was writing his will.

"So she gave him rich dainties
Whenever he fed;
And put up a monument
When he was dead."

On Tremont Street, in the busy heart of Boston, is the beautiful little "burying ground," called the "Granary"; Paul Revere, John Quincy Adams, John Hancock, and other distinguished citizens of New England rest here under trees which have shaded their graves for more than a century. There is also shown the visitor the grave of "Mother Goose," the alleged author of the Mother Goose Rhymes. It may be iconoclastic to shatter a legend, but the truth is, the Mother Goose Rhymes had been jingling for a century and more before this good lady was born; it appears that in ancient times, the goose was a famous story-teller for children, and the Goose Melodies are an adaptation from the French. The monument in the "Granary" is erected to Mary Goose, wife of Isaac Goose; it would seem that her claim to fame rests entirely upon her recitation of the Hubbard Melodies to such an extent that her son-in-law, Thomas Fleet, who was a printer, issued a special edition for her.

Piers Plowman

Piers Plowman, in the fourteenth century, thus made his will:

"And I wish ere I wend, now to write out my will.
In God's name, amen! lo! I make it myself.
May God have my soul who hath saved and deserved it,
Let the kirk have my carrion and keep well my bones."

Will of Paul Scarron

The will of Paul Scarron, which he chose to write in verse, is not a particularly attractive production. It consists of about two hundred lines; the following may be taken as a specimen:

" Premièrement je donne et je lègue
A ma femme, qui n'est point bègue,
Pouvoir de se remarier,

De crainte d'un plus grand désordre.
Mais pour moi je crois que cet ordre,
De ma dernière volonté
Sera celui le mieux exécuté."

As is well known, Scarron was a French author and playwright. In 1652 he married the beautiful Francine d'Aubigne, afterward Madame de Maintenon. He died on October 6, 1660.

François Villon

François Villon is an unique character in history, romance and poetry. He died about 1484. "The Poems of Master François Villon of Paris done into English Verse by John Payne," contain his two chief compositions entitled, "The Lesser Testament," and "The Greater Testament": they are satires of considerable merit and length, and a verse from the first and two from the last will suffice to show their character and his style.

From the first:

"Item, my gloves and silken hood
My friend Jacques Cardon, I declare,
Shall have in fair free gift for good;
Also the acorns willows bear
And every day a capon fair
Or goose; likewise a tenfold vat
Of chalk-white wine, besides a pair
Of lawsuits, lest he wax too fat."

From the last:

"The Register of Wills from me
Shall have no quid nor quod, I trow:
But every penny of his fee
To Tricot, the young priest, shall go;
To whose expense gladly eno'
I'd drink, though it my nightcap cost:
If but he knew the dice to throw,
Of Perette's Den I'd make him host."

"EPITAPH

"Here lies and slumbers in this place
One whom Love wreaked his ire upon:
A scholar, poor of goods and grace,
That hight of old François Villon:

Acre or furrow had he none.
'Tis known his all he gave away;
Bread, tables, tressels, all are gone.
Gallants, of him this Roundel say."

WILL OF SIR THOMAS DENNY

Thomas Denny (son and heir of Sir Edmond Denny of England, one of the King's Exchequer), 10th May, 1527, wrote his will in manner following:

". . . My body to be buried in the parish church of Cheshunt, where I dwell, and I will that a stone be laid on me, and that a picture of Death be made in the stone, with scrolls in his hand bearing this writing thereon:

"As I am so shalle ye be,
Pray for me of yr Charity,
With a Paternoster and an Ave,
For the rest of the soul of Thomas Denny."

Then follow sundry bequests and legacies.

IN LATIN VERSE

There is on record the following history of a versified will. It is that of François Joseph Terrasse Desbillons, born at Châteauneuf, in Berry, in 1711, who became a Jesuit, and, after the suppression of the order in France, principal of the College of Mannheim. He was so remarkable for the elegance and purity with which he wrote in Latin that he obtained the sobriquet of "The last of the Romans." Owing, perhaps, to this facility, he wrote his will in Latin verse. The sight of it in this singular form somewhat startled his executors; but as all the necessary formalities had been observed, no difficulty occurred, and it was carried out in entire conformity with his wishes, without any interference on the part of the law.

A WILL IN RHYME

Another poetic will, that of John Hedges, late of Finchley, Middlesex, was proved in an English court on July 5, 1737, and is worthy of a place among quaint and eccentric wills. It reads as follows:

"This fifth of May,
Being airy and gay,

To trip not inclined,
But of vigorous mind,
And my body in health,
I'll dispose of my wealth;
And of all I'm to leave
On this side the grave,
To some one or other,
I think to my brother.

"But because I presaw
That my brother-in-law
I did not take care,
Would come in for a share,
Which I noways intended,
Till their manners were mended —
And of that there's no sign.

"I do therefore enjoin,
And strictly command,
As witness my hand,
That nought I have got
Be brought to hotch-pot.

"And I give and devise,
Much as in me lies,
To the son of my mother,
My own dear brother,
To have and to hold
All my silver and gold,
As the affectionate pledges
Of his brother,
"JOHN HEDGES."

WILL OF WILLIAM HICKINGTON

William Hickington, who died in the year 1770, wrote his will in rhyme, as follows:

"This is my last will,
I insist on it still;
To sneer on and welcome,
And e'en laugh your fill.

ANCIENT, CURIOUS, AND FAMOUS WILLS

> I, William Hickington,
> Poet of Pocklington,
> Do give and bequeath,
> As free as I breathe,
> To thee, Mary Jarum,
> The Queen of my Harum,
> My cash and my cattle,
> With every chattel,
> To have and to hold,
> Come heat or come cold,
> *Sans* hindrance or strife,
> Though thou art not my wife.
> As witness my hand,
> Just here as I stand,
> The twelfth of July,
> In the year Seventy.
> "WM. HICKINGTON."

This will was admitted to probate at the Deanery Court in the City of York, England, 1770.

WILL OF WILL JACKETT

This will was proved at Doctors' Commons, London, on July 17, 1789, and runs as follows:

> "I give and bequeath,
>   When I'm laid underneath,
> To my two loving sisters most dear,
>   The whole of my store,
>   Were it twice as much more,
> Which God's goodness has given me here.
>
> "And that none may prevent
>   This my will and intent,
> Or occasion the least of law-racket,
>   With a solemn appeal
>   I confirm, sign, and seal
> This the true act and deed of Will Jackett."

Mr. William Jackett, it appears, was a faithful and trustworthy as well as a thrifty fellow, for he remained for thirty years in the service of Messrs. Fuller and Vaughan as manager of their business. He resided in the parish of St. Mary, Islington.

Will of an Irish Schoolmaster

The following is the will of Pat O'Kelly, an Irish schoolmaster, who wrote, on the leaf of a copybook which he had just finished ruling (thus exemplifying the ruling passion strong in death), the lines here transcribed:

> "I, having neither kith nor kin,
> Bequeath all I have named herein
> To Harriet my dearest wife,
> To have and hold as hers for life.
> While in good health, and sound in mind,
> This codicil I've undersigned."

Rather Sacrilegious

The spirit of sacrilege is shown in an old quatrain to be found in the books:

> "In the name of God, Amen:
> My featherbed to my wife, Jen;
> Also my carpenter's saw and hammer;
> Until she marries; then, God damn her!"

Will of William Ruffell, Esq.

William Ruffell of Shimpling, Suffolk, England, was a gentleman of an ancient and highly respectable family; he is said to have been a good specimen of an old-fashioned gentleman farmer. His will, which was written in 1803, is as follows:

> "As this life must soon end, and my frame will decay,
> And my soul to some far-distant clime wing its way,
> Ere that time arrives, now I free am from cares,
> I thus wish to settle my worldly affairs,
> A course right and proper men of sense will agree.
> I am now strong and hearty, my age forty-three;
> I make this my last will, as I think 'tis quite time,
> It conveys all I wish, though 'tis written in rhyme.
> To employ an attorney I ne'er was inclin'd,
> They are pests to society, sharks of mankind.
> To avoid that base tribe my own will I now draw,
> May I ever escape coming under their paw.
> To Ezra Dalton, my nephew, I give all my land,
> With the old Gothic cottage that thereon doth stand;

'Tis near Shimpling great road, in which I now dwell,
It looks like a chapel or hermit's old cell,
With my furniture, plate, and linen likewise,
And securities, money, with what may arise.
'Tis my wish and desire that he should enjoy these,
And pray let him take even my skin, if he please.
To my loving, kind sister I give and bequeath,
For her tender regard, when this world I shall leave,
If she choose to accept it, my rump-bone may take,
And tip it with silver, a whistle to make.
My brother-in-law is a strange-tempered dog;
He's as fierce as a tiger, in manners a hog;
A petty tyrant at home, his frowns how they dread;
Two ideas at once never entered his head.
So proud and so covetous, moreover so mean,
I dislike to look at him, the fellow is so lean.
He ne'er behaved well, and, though very unwilling,
Yet I feel that I must cut him off with a shilling.
My executors, too, should be men of good fame;
I appoint Edmund Ruffell, of Cockfield, by name;
In his old easy chair, with short pipe and snuff,
What matter his whims, he is honest enough;
With Samuel Seely, of Alpheton Lion,
I like his strong beer, and his word can rely on.
When Death's iron hand gives the last fatal blow,
And my shattered old frame in the dust must lie low,
Without funeral pomp let my remains be conveyed
To Brent Eleigh churchyard, near my father be laid.
This, written with my own hand, there can be no appeal,
I now therefore at once set my hand and my seal,
As being my last will; I to this fully agree,
This eighteenth day of March, eighteen hundred and three."

Two English Wills

The following is a copy of the will of the late Mr. Joshua West, of the Six Clerks' Office, Chancery Lane, dated December 13, 1804:

"Perhaps I died not worth a groat;
But should I die worth something more,
Then I give that, and my best coat,
And all my manuscripts in store,

To those who shall the goodness have
To cause my poor remains to rest
Within a decent shell and grave.
This is the will of Joshua West.
"JOSHUA WEST."

"Witnessed R. MILLS.
J. A. BERRY.
John BAINES."

Mr. West died possessed of property, and some valuable manuscripts, which were conveyed by the above will.

The following will in rhyme was written by William Hunnis, a gentleman of the chapel under Edward VI., and afterwards Chapel Master to Queen Elizabeth:

"To God my soule I do bequeathe, because it is his owen,
My body to be layd in grave, where to my friends best knowen;
Executors I will none make, thereby great stryfe may grow,
Because the goods that I shall leave wyll not pay all I owe."

WILL OF JAMES BIGSBY

The following is a curious testamentary paper of a North Essex laborer, who resided at Manningtree, England:

"As I feel very queer my will I now make;
Write it down, Joseph Finch, and make no mistake.
I wish to leave all things fair and right, do you see,
And my relatives satisfy. Now, listen to me.
The first in my will is Lydia my wife,
Who to me proved a comfort three years of my life;
The second my poor aged mother I say,
With whom I have quarrelled on many a day,
For which I've been sorry, and also am still;
I wish to give her a place in my will.
The third that I mention is my dear little child;
When I think of her, Joseph, I feel almost wild.
Uncle Sam Bigsby, I must think of him too,
Peradventure he will say that I scarcely can do.
And poor Uncle Gregory, I must leave him a part,
If it is nothing else but the back of the cart.
And for you, my executor, I will do what I can,
For acting towards me like an honest young man.

"Now, to my wife I bequeath greater part of my store;
First thing is the bedstead before the front door;
The next is the chair standing by the fireside,
The fender and irons she cleaned with much pride.
I also bequeath to Lydia my wife
A box in the cupboard, a sword, a gun, and knife,
And the harmless old pistol without any lock,
Which no man can fire off, for 'tis minus a cock.
The cups and the saucers I leave her also,
And a book called 'The History of Poor Little Mo,'
With the kettle, the boiler, and old frying-pan,
A shovel, a mud-scoop, a pail, and a pan.
And remember, I firmly declare my protest
That my poor aged mother shall have my oak chest
And the broken whip under it. Do you hear what I say?
Write all these things down without any delay.
And my dear little child, I must think of her too.
Friend Joseph, I am dying, what shall I do?
I give her my banyan, my cap, and my hose,
My big monkey-jacket, my shirt, and my shoes;
And to Uncle Sam Bigsby, I bequeath my high boots,
The pickaxe and mattock with which I stubbed roots.
And poor Uncle Gregory, with the whole of my heart,
I give for a bedstead the back of the cart.
And to you, my executor, last in my will,
I bequeath a few trifles to pay off your bill.
I give you my shot-belt, my dog, and my nets,
And the rest of my goods sell to pay off my debts.
      "JOSEPH FINCH, Executor;
"Dated FEBRUARY 4th, 1839."

FROM MISSOURI

Under the spell of the Muse, Joseph Johnson Cassiday, a well-known farmer of Jasper County, Missouri, prepared his will in rhyme; for several years this document answered the purposes of the testator; just prior to his death, however, in March, 1910, more serious thoughts seem to have come over him, and Mr. Cassiday executed a different will, the last being done in the usual prose form. The will in rhyme is given below:

"I, Joseph Johnson Cassiday,
Being sound of mind and memory,
Do hereby publish my intent,
This my will and testament,
That all my just debts first be paid,
Expense for burial and funeral made,
And all expenses made of late,
Out of my personal and real estate.
I do bequeath, devise and give,
As long as she, my wife, shall live,
Lot six in the original town of Lever,
To her assigns and heirs forever.
To my adopted daughter Marie,
I do devise and give in fee,
The southeast quarter of section seven
Township nine and range eleven.
To my two sons Josephus and Reach,
I do devise one dollar each.
The residue of my estate,
I do bequeath to Mary Kate,
And I hereby appoint her for,
My last will, executor.
This eighteenth day of May was done,
In the year of our Lord, Nineteen One."

CHAPTER IV

CURIOUS WILLS

"Most men are within a finger's breadth of being mad; for if a man walk with his middle finger pointing out, folk will think him mad, but not so if it be his forefinger."

"Where be your Gibes now? Your Gambols? Your songs? Your flashes of merriment, that were wont to set the table on a roar?"

1

HUSBANDS, WIVES, AND CHILDREN

"Men should be careful lest they cause women to weep, for God counts their tears."

AN editorial on "Testamentary Habits and Peculiar Wills," appeared in the *Western Reserve Law Journal* some time ago. Its excellence merits a reproduction in part:

"The laws of human nature underlie all systems of jurisprudence. Positive law is evolved out of long periods of human phenomena. The general systems of law are the composite products of innumerable generations of men. These accepted codes are supposed to embody the survivals of an immemorial struggle between right and wrong, and the highest sentiments of justice, and the clearest perfection of reason of all ages. But it is a remarkable fact that one-half of all the property in the world, in the succession of generations, is transmitted and controlled by the supreme purpose and disposition of individual men and women. The tenure of property is not always held, nor is it transmitted, according to legislative enactments or judicial law. Under the testamentary privilege secured by law the unenlightened mind often becomes the legislature which frames and promulgates the rule of descent which fixes the destiny of millions of property. The perfect freedom and untrammelled modes of expression, secured in the will-making privilege, results in the manifestation of the most normal and spontaneous spirit of the individual.

"For genuine and authentic repositories of human idiosyncrasies and whimsical peculiarities, as well as lofty sentiments and noble thoughts on high themes, there is nothing comparable with the last will and testament. There are several reasons for the existence of this fact.

" 1st. The will is usually the product of grave thought and deliberation. It is the matured disposition of the individual testator, framed and published in the exercise of one of the highest and best appreciated rights granted by society to the individual. The will is also the outgrowth of the individual's sense of duty involved in sacred domestic and family obligations and relationships.

" 2d. The right to make the will confers the privilege coveted by both men and women to speak into the universal ear 'the last word.' The sum of man's moral sense, and his exact ethical tone, is not infrequently concentrated in his last will.

" 3d. In the ages of the world, when the agitation of religious beliefs was most prevalent, men were prone to give a summary of their opinions upon religion in their wills. The rites and ceremonies of sepulchre are often prescribed; the belief in immortality is often expressed in these sacred documents. The vanities and foibles, the whims and caprices, the eccentricities and prejudices, all leave their exact mould and expression in this important instrument. The cynic adopts this means of giving a parting blow to the unfriendly and unsympathizing world. It is said that the mould and fashion of the human form was so preserved in ancient Egypt by the embalmer's art that the peculiar physiognomy of the Pharaohs is discovered after three thousand years of burial. This art of preservation has been lost. But in the numerous receptacles for recorded wills in Europe and America are found the mummified intellectual and spiritual remains of past generations as clearly and positively embalmed as are the bodies of the Pharaohs.

"It is interesting to note the influence of long-established customs upon the social habits of people. The present habitat of the will-making people is continental Europe. This fact is susceptible of easy explanation. The jurisprudence of the continent is founded on Roman law. Sir Henry Sumner Maine has well said: 'To the Romans belong preëminently the credit of inventing the will, the institution which, next to the contract, has exercised the greatest influence in transforming human society. . . . To the Roman no evil seems to have been a heavier visitation than the forfeiture of testamentary privilege; no curse seems to have been bitterer than that imprecated upon an enemy 'that he might die without a will.' "

* * * * * * *

"The odd freaks, vagaries and vanities of men thus find permanent lodgment in testamentary remains. While these features of the will at first appear to defy classification, yet by careful examination, extending over long periods, the manifestation of unvarying habits of mind, and the existence of constant and controlling instincts and motives, are readily discovered.

"These natures of ours, when freely dealing with the subject of property, and exhibiting solemn sentiments upon duty and destiny, unconsciously yield to fundamental laws of uniform operation; and these testamentary memorials may be made to furnish much curious instruction upon psychological and sociological subjects."

DUTY OF HUSBANDS TO MAKE WILLS

The following article from the pen of Harriette M. Johnston-Wood, of the New York bar, appeared in *Harper's Weekly* in the issue of September 24, 1910; there is much in it which should appeal to the sense of justice and manhood of the husbands, brothers and sons of our country. The barbaric treatment of women with reference to property rights should no longer find a place in the laws of a country which boasts of its enlightenment and freedom as does the United States. It is gratifying to record that a more liberal policy is fast being adopted by the law-making bodies of our States.

Our author says:

"It has been our custom for a number of years to pass our summer vacation on the banks of Lake Seneca, where one of us was born. Here our paternal grandparents came when the country was yet a wilderness, and here they lived and died. Their wedding journey from Rensselaerwick was made in a covered wagon, in which they brought their worldly possessions, some chairs, a table, a bed, a stove, some dishes and cooking utensils. A half-dozen sheep and a cow brought up the rear of this caravan. Here they cleared the ground and built a house. Grandmother dyed and carded and spun into yarn and wove into cloth the wool from the sheep, from which she knitted the socks and mittens and made the clothing. From the flax which grew wild thereabouts she made the household linen. No small tasks were these when eventually nine children came to demand care and protection. Once a year a perambulating shoemaker came through the country, and then this small army was shod, with boots and shoes in reserve sufficient to last until his return. By and by a frame house was built, a luxury in those days; property was accumulated.

"To whom did it belong?

"In justice and equity it belonged to both parents. Each had borne the burden; each should share in the reward. But the law said no. The wife's services belong to the husband, and their joint earnings belong to him, only the husband must support the wife. The wife owned nothing. Truly a munificent compensation for fifty years of service such as this!

"Did grandfather support grandmother? Were grandmother's services less valuable than grandfather's? By what righteous authority did everything belong to grandfather? — he being allowed to give or will away everything, except the use of one-third of the real estate, which grandmother might have after his death, but for her lifetime only. It was barely possible that grandmother might have liked to give or will something to her children on her own account. When she had earned it, by years of toil as hard as his, why should she not have been allowed to gratify this altogether worthy ambition?

"Forty years ago a boy and a girl married. He had nothing. She had saved five hundred dollars teaching school. They bought a farm, paying her five hundred dollars down, and taking a mortgage for the balance. Title was taken in the husband's name. They worked together for forty years. He died, leaving no will. There were no children. Under the law of the State the property went to his brothers and sisters, all old, all well-to-do. The personalty amounted to very little. The wife's dower, the use of one-third during her life, amounts to less than $200 a year, and this is her sole support in her old age.

"In that section of the country women can get one dollar a day for at least half the year working in fruit, tying grape-vines, putting handles on baskets, picking berries, cherries, and currants, and packing grapes, peaches and plums. Household service is always at a premium, as no one there will go out to do that kind of work. They are the descendants of the old settlers and are proud. The married women work in the fruit in the daytime, and perform their household duties at night. This means baking and cooking and stewing, and washing and ironing and mending for the hired men as well as the family. Incidentally they raise children. No one person could be hired to do this work. They do it for love, but we believe there is no insurmountable obstacle in the way of getting

ANCIENT, CURIOUS, AND FAMOUS WILLS

both love and justice; we believe that love and injustice are irreconcilable, — and if we *must* choose between them, my advice is to exact justice and take a chance on love.

"To wife's services, 40 years at $3 per week (worth $5), allowing for clothing, which she makes herself and which seldom equals and rarely exceeds $30 a year, about . . $30,000
To $500 and interest, 40 years, about 6,000
Total $36,000

"Would the whole estate have been more than this wife was entitled to?

"A bride was presented by her uncle with $2000, with which the thrifty bridegroom bought sheep. It proved a profitable investment, and in time they were well-to-do. At the expiration of fifty years of matrimony and mutual toil (which included the rearing of six children) the husband died. By his last will and testament he gave to his beloved wife two thousand dollars in cash, or her dower interest in his real estate. The wife took the cash. Her original two thousand dollars for fifty years then amounted to about $60,000.

"This shows that a wife may be considered to be a good investment.

* * * * * * *

"A clerk in a delicatessen store in a large city married a German governess. They started a similar store of their own and lived in the rear. The wife did the housework and the cooking and baking for the store, and between times waited on customers. They were frugal and prospered. After twenty years the husband died. The wife naturally thought she was entitled to the property, at least a portion of it. But the husband had made a will prior to his marriage, whereby he devised his property to his brothers and sisters."

* * * * * * *

"The staple argument of the opponents of equal laws for men and women is that wives are privileged in that they can do with their own as they like, while the husbands cannot. But is the property the husband's any more than the wife's when they accumulate it jointly? Up to the marriageable age girls earn nothing; after marriage their services belong to their husbands. Where is the opportunity to accumulate property which shall be their very own in the eyes of the law, with which they may do as they like? What provision can they make for possible incapacity and certain old age if they live?"

WILL OF A CHINAMAN

There was filed in the Surrogate's Office of Queens County, New York, on October 1, 1910, what the newspapers refer to as the queerest instrument ever recorded in New York City. The testator was John Ling, a Chinaman, of Woodbridge, New Jersey.

The original will was probated in Middlesex County, New Jersey, but as Ling was the owner of considerable real estate in Queens County, before settlement could be made an exemplified copy of the will had to be filed there.

It appears that John Ling, Jr., a son of the deceased, had taken an Irish bride, much against the will of his father. The Chinaman was enraged, and talked long and earnestly with his son upon the subject. But to no avail. The young man refused to leave his Irish bride. When the old man died, he left the following will:

"First, I leave and bequeath to John Ling, my son, the sum of $1. With the said sum of $1, or 100 cents, I wish that he would purchase a rope strong and long enough to support his Irish wife; the said sum of $1 to be paid six months after my decease by my wife, her heirs or executors.

"Secondly, I leave and bequeath to my wife, Mary Ling, all property, whether in America or England, that I may be possessed of, during her natural life; and at her death said property is to be equally divided between Samson and Mary Ling, son and daughter of John and Mary Ling; and should neither Samson nor Mary survive to come in possession of the said property now belonging to John and Mary Ling, the property is then to descend unto John Ling, the son of Joseph Ling, my nephew, now residing in Europe, with the exception of the $1 to be paid to my son, John Ling."

TWO HUNDRED DOLLARS FOR A HUSBAND

According to the *New York Sun*, an attractive young German woman of Washington, D.C., walked into a newspaper office in that city on October 11, 1910, and requested the insertion of the following advertisement:

"'Young woman, fairly wealthy, from foreign country, desires to meet at once some poor young man. Object, matrimony.'

"She gave her name as Eugenie Adams, but admitted that this was an assumed name. She said she was willing to give her prospective husband a bonus of $200. She explained that her uncle, who lived in Germany, had named her as the beneficiary in his will, provided she married in a week.

"'You see it is this way,' she explained with a German accent, 'my old uncle is very eccentric. He lives in the Fatherland, where all my people are. He has named me the beneficiary of his will if I am married by a week from to-day. I am very poor. I want the money. I plan to get married in order to obtain it. I will pay any young man $200 to marry me.

"'But I will be no trouble to him,' she continued. 'I will get a divorce from him at once and never see him again. I do not want to remain married. I only want to return to Germany at once with my marriage papers. Could a man make $200 in an easier way?'

"She declined to give the amount of the legacy she expected to obtain through her marriage."

The Result

The *St. Louis Times* in a recent editorial comments on the "Two-hundred-dollar Husband," as follows:

"We have been much interested in a story which has been telegraphed from Washington, and which relates the circumstances under which a presentable fraulein bought a husband, in order that she might inherit an estate — which was willed her on the condition that she marry within a given time.

"She appears to have wanted the estate badly, though the idea of having a husband did not appeal to her at all. Perhaps there was a ruddy faced Heine at home with whom she had danced in the old days, and who still held her heart in thrall. Be that as it may — as Laura Jean Libbey would say — she married her emergency husband in Washington only because she had to, in order to get the estate.

"She did not wish ever to see her husband again, and when a sailor appeared in response to her advertisement, she rather liked the looks of him — for the occasion at hand — but decided, wisely, that he would not do, because 'he travelled around the world, and she might see him again.' She finally decided in favor of one Harry Oliver Brown, who wore a flowing sandy mustache, and a celluloid collar, and carried a walking-stick. We should have thought the flowing sandy mustache would have been enough, though we have no objection to the celluloid collar and the walking-stick, if they be thought to possess a corroborative value.

"And so the two were married, and Mrs. Brown gave her hired husband $200 and bade him good-by and left, without even saying she would hurry back, and boarded a ship for the Fatherland, where the estate was — and, presumably, is.

"We have related this quaint fable because it seems to possess a valuable idea for those who contemplate matrimony, not because they consider themselves fitted for it in any way, but because they feel they 'have to get married' — so much the slave to public opinion are many estimable young people.

"If the thing has to be done, we commend the method of Mrs. Harry Oliver Brown. A sandy mustache, a celluloid collar, and a walking-stick can always be had for a song — and there is not a very heavy percentage of sailors."

Knew her Disposition

It is recorded of an old English farmer, that, in giving instructions for his will, he directed a legacy of one hundred pounds be given to his widow. Being informed that some distinction was usually made in case the widow married again, he doubled the sum; and when told that this was quite contrary to custom, he said, with heartfelt sympathy for his possible successor, "Aye, but him as gets her'll deserve it."

Clothes on a Hickory Limb

The will of Charles C. Dickinson, former president of the Carnegie Trust Company, who died a few months ago, contains a bequest of $4000 for the education of his son Charles, at Cornell, with the strange stipulation that the son shall forfeit this allowance if he goes "to or upon Cayuga Lake."

The lake is used by the Cornell crews and by students for canoeing and sailing.

To a nephew he leaves $2000 for educational purposes, with the same restrictions regarding Cayuga Lake.

Sarcastic Will

A British sailor requested his executors to pay to his wife one shilling, wherewith to buy hazelnuts, as she had always preferred cracking nuts to mending his stockings.

A Contrite Husband

J. Withipol of Walthamstow, Essex County, England, left his landed estates to his wife, "trusting, yea, I may say, as I think, assuring myself, that she will marry no man, for fear to meet with so evil a husband as I have been to her."

Aunt Lunky's Will

The author has sought with little success for wills which would portray the character of the negro race, although the aid of Mr. Booker T. Washington was enlisted in this behalf. One, however, is offered:

Aunt Lunky was a negro servant and resided in Jacksonville, Illinois. For several generations, she had lived with the same family and had been a party to all household duties and functions during that period: she made her will, and her savings, some two hundred and fifty dollars, she left to "little Billie." "Little Billie" was the great-grandson of her employer, and the pet of the household: in order that there might be no mistake in identifying the legatee, a picture of the baby boy was securely attached to the testament.

Will of the Duchesse de Praslin

By her will made in 1784, this testatrix, strangely enough, disinherited her own children, being falsely persuaded that her husband had substituted for them others whom he had had by an actress. She made her legatees the grandchildren of the Prince de Soubise, whom she did not even know. Her will was contested, and set aside. It contained another singular bequest — that by which she left to her husband a model of the Cheval de Bronze (the equestrian statue of Henri IV. on the Pont Neuf).

Must ever Pray

Not long ago an Italian nobleman left all his money, which amounted to about $50,000, to his wife, "to be disposed of according to her own ideas," provided she entered a religious order and spent the rest of her life praying for the repose of his soul. If she refused the conditions, the money went to the order direct, and she got nothing.

The poor woman is now fighting the will in court, and there is said to be some prospect that the estate will be divided and one-half, or at least a life interest in the income, given to her. This, however, can be done only by compromise.

The reason for this strange condition is said to have been revenge. The wife had a lover, and the husband did not discover the fact until during his last sickness, when she neglected previous precautions and he learned of her flirtations. The husband was also afraid that she would marry her lover, and is said to have told his lawyer that he would fix things so that the scoundrel could not have the benefit of his money, even if he did enjoy the affections of his wife.

A Cold World

Ellen H. Cooper, West Somerset Street, Philadelphia, died recently. Pathos and worldly wisdom are mingled in her will. She wrote the instrument with her own hand. It follows in part:

"All the money and furniture I have has been saved through my earnings and hard work, therefore, I wish my two sons, John W. Cooper and Bernard M. Cooper, to follow to the letter my wishes.

"My one real anxiety has been their future after my death. They cannot now realize what a lonely life theirs will be without home or parents, for I know, except one has money, there is no one to care what becomes of one. Therefore I have saved for one purpose, that if either, or both, live to be old and unable to work you may find a home and pay so much to be kept the rest of their lives. There will be enough left to clothe you. All I am possessed of I want put out at interest. I do not want one cent of it spent otherwise, excepting what it takes to pay my funeral expenses. Remember, dear boys, this is a cold world and I would long since have been glad to lay down my burden had it not been for my love for you."

Beautiful Sentiments to Wives

As an expression of controlling impulses and ideas, the will has ever been associated with the home and family life. Some of the purest and sweetest sentiments of the human heart are often contained in these legal muniments. They are often the permanent repositories of the loftiest feelings of conjugal and domestic affection. More than fifty per cent of the wills made bequeath the bulk of the estate, absolutely or for life, to the surviving spouse.

A beautiful expression of this holy sentiment of affection is found in the will of John Starkey, probated in 1861. This testator says: "The remainder of my wealth is vested in the affection of my dear wife, with whom I leave it, in the good hope of resuming it more pure, bright and precious, where neither moth nor rust doth corrupt, and where there are no railways or monetary panics or fluctuations of exchange, but steadfast, though progressive and unspeakable riches of glory and immortality."

The following is another example of solicitude for a devoted wife. Sharon Turner, the eminent author of the "History of the Anglo-Saxons," dying in his eightieth year, in 1847, left this testimonial to his wife, who had died before him: "It is my comfort to have remembered that I have passed with her nearly forty-nine years of unabated affection and connubial happiness, and yet she is still living, as I earnestly hope and believe, under her Saviour's care, in a superior state of being." He was anxious that her portrait, which he directed should be painted and bequeathed, should correctly represent her. He then adds: "None of the portraits of my beloved wife give any adequate representation of her beautiful face, nor of the sweet and intellectual and attractive appearance of her living features and general countenance and character."

KINDNESS TO WIDOWS

Testators in the present day frequently and ungallantly leave property to their widows only so long as they shall remain unmarried. In looking through some of the wills of the time of Henry VII., we do not find such a condition attached. There are many instances to be found, however, of the husband's affectionate care for the future comfort of his wife. To quote two or three: First, from the will of William Parker: "Also I make Master John Aggecombe, Alderman of Oxford, my overseer, to se my last will performed; and I geve to hym for his labour my best crymsyn gowne so that he be frendly to Alice my wife." In the will of Robert Offe, of Boston, Lincolnshire, after appointing Master Thomas Robynson and Master John Robynson overseers, he goes on to say: "And I besoche you, maisters both, that ye be good frends unto my wyf, and that ye will help her." William Holybrande, gentleman citizen and "tailler" of London, bequeaths to each of his executors, William Bodley and William Grove, for their labor, £5 sterling, and "to be goode and kynde to my wyfe." He appoints as overseer, "Robert Joyns, my cousin, one of the gentleman ushers of the chambre of our Sovaigne Lorde the

Kynge," and bequeaths to him £5 sterling "for his labour, and that he may help my wyfe in all her troubill, if any shall happen to her here after." He also gives and bequeaths "to Roger Delle, my servant, so that he be lovyng and gentill to my wyfe, and give a trewe accompte for such besynese as he hath reconyng of, £5 sterlinge." These three wills were all proved in 1505.

Would not be Good

In 1772, a gentleman of Surrey, England, died, and his will being opened was found to contain this peculiar clause, "Whereas, it was my misfortune to be made very uneasy by ——, my wife, for many years from our marriage, by her turbulent behavior, for she was not content to despise my admonitions, but she contrived every method to make me unhappy; she was so perverse in her nature that she would not be reclaimed, but seemed only to be born to be a plague to me; the strength of Samson, the knowledge of Homer, the prudence of Augustus, the cunning of Pyrrhus, the patience of Job, the subtlety of Hannibal and the watchfulness of Hermogenes could not have been sufficient to subdue her; for no skill or force in the world would make her good; and as we have lived separate and apart from each other for eight years, and, she having perverted her son to leave and totally abandon me, therefore, I give her a shilling."

Must remain at Home

The last will and testament of Lawrence Engler was admitted to probate September 19, 1910, at Columbus, Ohio. It disposes of an estate valued at $10,000. He was killed in a recent wreck on the Hocking Valley Railroad near Toledo.

He provides in his will that his widow and their children be given the proceeds resulting from the rent of his property and that they all must remain at home. When they leave, they forfeit all rights to the income.

So long as they live together they are to share the income, but when one leaves he loses his interest.

This arrangement is to remain during the life of all, but no provision is made for the disposal of the remainder.

The will is peculiar in another way. The testator, after its execution, took the liberty of striking out some of the provisions without having the amendments witnessed. He failed to make a codicil, but does say that he did the scratching himself.

DANGER IN MUTUAL WILLS

The wills of Mrs. Mary Louise Woeltge and Professor Albert Woeltge were filed in the Probate Court at Stamford, Connecticut, on September 20, 1910, and they reveal a somewhat unusual situation. Professor Woeltge was the first to pass away at Walpole, New Hampshire, on September 12th. His wife died there a day later. Both left wills executed April 11, 1895. Professor Woeltge left all his estate to his wife and appointed her sole executrix. Mrs. Woeltge by her will left all her property to her husband.

Professor Woeltge inserted a clause by way of explanation to his nephew, Albert A. Woeltge, and his niece, Lillie Woeltge, both of New York, of this disposition of the estate. It was, in effect, that the money by which he acquired the property disposed of in the will came most, if not all of it, from his wife or her mother.

Professor Woeltge left two letters, one addressed to his wife and the other to his niece and nephew. The letter to his wife carried a direct expression of desire that on her death all the money he left her go to the children of his brother William, "that they might know that I loved them best after you." The question arises as to who will get the property.

THE WORST OF WOMEN

Henry, Earl of Stafford, who followed the fortunes of his royal master James II., and attended him in his exile to France, married there the daughter of the Duc de Grammont, at the end of the seventeenth century. The marriage was a most unhappy one, and, after fourteen years' endurance of the disgraceful conduct of his wife, he wrote as follows in his will:

"To the worst of women, Claude Charlotte de Grammont, unfortunately my wife, guilty as she is of all crimes, I leave five-and-forty brass halfpence, which will buy a pullet for her supper. A better gift than her father can make her; for I have known when, having not the money, neither had he the credit for such a purchase; he being the worst of men, and his wife the worst of women, in all debaucheries. Had I known their characters I had never married their daughter, and made myself unhappy."

Took the Son's Part

Sir Robert Bevill, Knight, who held an official position at court under James I., was the representative of an old Hunts family, and held by entail the estates of Chesterton in that county. Dying in 1635, his will, which it appears was made within a very short time of his death, was proved, and in it occur the following clauses relative to his wife and his daughter's husband, with whom he died at enmity. These vindictive behests, be it observed, are preceded by a very devout and godly preface, bequeathing his soul "into the hands of its Maker, stedfastly believing in, and by the merits of, our Lord and Saviour Jesus Christ, to obteyne free pardon and forgiveness of al my sinnes, and at the last day to have and receive a glorious resurrection."

Immediately follows: "I give and bequeath to my son-in-law, Sir John Hewell, Baronet, tenn shillings and noe more, in respect he stroke and ceaselessly fought with mee.

"Item: I give unto my wyfe tenn shillings in respect she took her sonnes part against me, and did anymate and comfort him afterwards. These will not be forgotten." Furthermore, the testator, in resentment against his said wife — "inasmuch as she hath not only deserted mee, but hath taken into her own possession all her own goods, and hath disposed of them at her own pleasure" — declares his determination "to make no ampler provision for her."

He concludes this vindictive will by leaving all his large estates to his second son.

This will is not exactly of the class alluded to by Steele in one of his plays, where he makes one of the characters, a widow, remark, "There is no will of an husband so cheerfully obeyed as his last."

Accused of every Crime

John Parker, a bookseller, living in Old Bond Street, served his wife in the following manner, leaving her no more than fifty pounds, and in the following words:

"To one Elizabeth Parker, whom through fondness I made my wife, without regard to family, fame, or fortune, and who in return has not spared most unjustly to accuse me of every crime regarding human nature, except highway robbery, I bequeath the sum of fifty pounds."

BETWEEN THE LINES

A rich man, making his will, left legacies to all his servants except his steward, to whom he gave nothing, on the plea that, "having been in my service in that capacity twenty years I have too high an opinion of his shrewdness to suppose he has not sufficiently enriched *himself*."

MENIAL SERVICE REQUIRED

A year or two ago, a Russian gentleman, living at Odessa, bequeathed four million roubles to his four nieces, but they were to receive the money only after having worked for a year as washerwomen, chambermaids or farm servants. These conditions were carried out, and while occupying such humble positions, it is gratifying to learn that they received over eight hundred and sixty offers of marriage.

NO MUSTACHES

The will of Mr. Henry Budd, which came into force in 1862, declared against the wearing of mustaches by his sons, in the following terms: "In case my son Edward shall wear mustaches, then the devise hereinbefore contained in favour of him, his appointees, heirs, and assigns of my said estate called Pepper Park, shall be void; and I devise the same estate to my son William, his appointees, heirs, and assigns. And in case my said son William shall wear mustaches, then the devise hereinbefore contained in favour of him, his appointees, heirs, and assigns of my said estate called Twickenham Park, shall be void; and I devise the said estate to my said son Edward, his appointees, heirs, and assigns."

WILL OF WILLIAM PYM

The will of William Pym, of Woolavington, Somerset, gent., is worth citing for its originality. It bears date January 10, 1608.

After various charitable bequests, the last of which specifies the sum of twelvepence to the church at Wells, he proceeds:

"I give to Agnes, which I did a long time take for my wyfe — till shee denyd me to be her husband, all though wee were marryd with my friends' consent, her father, mother, and uncle at it; and now she swareth she will neither love mee nor evyr bee perswaded to, by preechers, nor by any other, which hath happened within these few yeres. And Toby Andrewes, the beginner, which I did see with mine own eyes when hee did more than was fitting, and this by means of others their abettors. I have lived a miserable life this six or seven yeres, and now I leve the revenge to God — and tenn pounds to buy her a gret horse, for I could not this manny yeres plese her with one gret enough."

Two years after writing this bitter record of his wrongs, William Pym, gent., gave up the ghost, and his last wishes were faithfully carried out by his two executors.

Contrary to Roosevelt's Idea

The malevolence of some men is manifested in their deaths, as well as in their lives. A certain wealthy man left this provision in his will: "Should my daughter marry and be afflicted with children, the trustees are to pay out of said legacy, Ten Thousand Dollars on the birth of the first child, to the —— Hospital; Twenty Thousand Dollars, on the second; Thirty Thousand Dollars, on the third; and an additional Ten Thousand Dollars on the birth of each fresh child, till the One Hundred and Fifty Thousand Dollars is exhausted. Should any portion of this sum be left at the end of twenty years, the balance is to be paid to her to use as she thinks fit." This item would, no doubt, interest our late President, Theodore Roosevelt.

Wife's Desertion Rewarded

A certain Glasgow doctor died some ten years ago, and left his whole estate to his sisters. In his will appeared this unusual clause: "To my wife, as a recompense for deserting me and leaving me in peace, I expect the said sister, Elizabeth, to make her a gift of ten shillings sterling, to buy her a pocket handkerchief to weep after my decease."

Would not wear the Cap

A husband left his wife sixty thousand dollars, to be increased to one hundred and twenty thousand dollars, provided she wore a widow's cap after his death. She accepted the larger amount, wore the cap for six months, and then put it off. A lawsuit followed, but the judge gave the widow a judgment and stated that the word "always" should have been inserted. Shortly after the rendition of the judgment, the widow entered into the state of matrimony.

STRANGE REQUIREMENT AS TO MARRIAGE

In 1805, Mr. Edward Hurst left a very large fortune to his only son on condition that the latter should seek out and marry a young lady, whom the father, according to his own statement, had, by acts for which he prayed forgiveness, reduced to the extremity of poverty; or failing her, her nearest unmarried female heir. The latter, by the irony of fate, turned out to be a spinster of fifty-five, who, professing herself willing to carry out her share of the imposed duty, was duly united to the young man, who had just reached his majority.

A HAPPY WIFE

Many wills have reference to the domestic felicity, or otherwise, experienced by those who executed them. As an example of the former, we may give the following passage from the testament of Lady Palmerston, an ancestress of the celebrated Premier. Referring to her husband, she says, "As I have long given you my heart and tenderest affections and fondest wishes have always been yours, so is everything else that I possess; and all that I can call mine being already yours, I have nothing to give but my heartiest thanks for the care and kindness you have at all times shown me, either in sickness or in health, for which God Almighty will, I hope, reward you in a better world." Then, for "form's sake," follow several specific bequests.

MUST WALK BAREFOOTED

A wife who domineers over her husband sometimes discovers that she has made a serious mistake. Ten years ago the London (England) newspapers reported that a publican (housekeeper) took a curious revenge on a nagging wife, whose sharp tongue had given him many bad days while he lived. When his will was read, she learned that in order to receive any property she must walk barefooted to the market-place each time the anniversary of his death came around. Holding a candle in her hand, she was there to read a paper confessing her unseemly behavior to her husband while he lived, and stating that had her tongue been shorter, her husband's days would probably have been longer. By refusing to comply with these terms she had to be satisfied with "twenty pounds a year to keep her off the parish."

ANTICIPATING THE PAST

It was Mrs. Malaprop in Sheridan's delightful comedy, "The Rivals," who declined to "anticipate the past."

Mr. John B. Luther, whose will is given below, certainly had the past in mind when the instrument was drawn; it seems clear that he desired to "anticipate the past" in so far as a provision for forgotten widows and children was concerned. The testator formerly lived in Fall River, Massachusetts, but his will was probated in San Francisco; he left an estate valued at more than $100,000.

"I do hereby declare that I am not married and that I have no children. I have noticed, however, the facility with which sworn testimony can be procured and produced in support of the claims of alleged widows and adopted children, and the frequent recurrence of such claims in recent years. I therefore make express provision in this my last will as follows: I give and bequeath to such person as shall be found, proved, and established to be my surviving wife or widow, whether the marriage be found to have taken place before or after the execution of this will, the sum of $5, and to each and every person who shall be found, proved, and established to be my child by birth, adoption, acknowledgment, or otherwise, and whether before or after the execution of this will, the sum of $5, and I declare that I do intentionally omit to make for any of the persons in this paragraph referred to any other or further provision."

2

ANIMALS

"Kind hearts are more than coronets,
And simple faith than Norman blood."

LOWER ANIMALS HAVE SOULS

The *Peoples Pulpit*, a publication issued by the "Brooklyn Tabernacle," in a recent issue under the title, "What is a Soul?" says:

"Thus we see why it is that the Scriptures speak of 'souls' in connection with the lower animals. They, as well as man, are sentient beings or creatures of intelligence, only of lower orders. They, as well as man, can see, hear, feel, taste and smell; and each can reason up to the standard of his own organism, though none can reason as abstrusely nor on as high a plane as man. This difference is not because man has a *different kind of life* from that possessed by the lower animals; for all have similar vital forces, from the same fountain or source of life, the same Creator; all sustain life in the same manner, by the digestion of similar foods, producing blood, and muscles, and bones, etc., each according to his kind or nature; and each propagates his species similarly, bestowing the *life*, originally from God, upon his posterity. They differ in shape and in mental capacity.

"Nor can it be said that while man is a *soul* (or intelligent being) beasts are without this soul-quality or intelligence, thought, feeling. On the contrary, both man and beast have soul-quality or intelligent, conscious being. Not only is this the statement of Scripture, but it is readily discernible as a fact, as soon as the real meaning of the word 'soul' is comprehended, as shown in the foregoing. To illustrate: Suppose the creation of a perfect dog; and suppose that creation had been particularly described, as was Adam's, what difference of detail could be imagined? The body of a dog created would not be a dog until the breath of life would be caused to energize that body; then it would be a *living creature* with sensibilities and powers all its own — a living soul of the lower order, called dog, as Adam, when he received life, became a *living creature* with sensibilities and powers all his own — a living soul of the highest order of flesh beings, called man."

A Heaven for Beasts

Bishop Butler and Theodore Parker offered the suggestion that there is a future for beasts, and a poem has been dedicated "To my Pony in Heaven," by Mr. Sewell of Exeter College.

Goldfish and Flowers

A certain lady left seventy pounds a year for the maintenance of three goldfish, which were to be identified as follows: "one is bigger than the other two, and these latter are to be easily recognized, as one is fat and the other lean." She also made provision for flowers to be placed upon the graves of the gold fish.

Bequest to a Fish

We have heard of lucky dogs often enough — instances of lucky fish are more rare, yet we can tell of two carps who have been testamentarily benefited. One is, or rather was, too well known to the tourist who has seen Fontainebleau, to need more than a passing mention, as he only paid the debt of nature a few years ago, having occupied the royal pond, it is said, more than a century, probably in order to bear out the proverb which gives long lives to annuitants; the other was the mute but valued friend of the Count of Mirandola, who had been in his intimacy since 1805, dwelling in an elegant antique piscina, shaded by tropical plants, in an oriel of his *salon* at Lucca, where he was still living as late as 1835, and may be there still. The count, dying in 1825, left him a handsome annuity, with special directions for his treatment.

Bequest to a Parrot

A rich and eccentric widow, whose will was proved in London some years ago, left at her death a parrot, whom, "having been her faithful companion for 24 years," she left in charge of an appointee, with an annuity of one hundred guineas, the existence and identity of the bird to be proved twice a year, and all payments to be withheld from the moment the feathered pensioner ceased to be produced.

Polly wants a Contest

In July last, at Washington, D.C., a will contest was commenced, which involves the life or death of a parrot.

It appears Mrs. Ottilie Stock left a will, by the terms of which her parrot was doomed to Oslerization by the process of chloroform. Her daughter, Elizabeth Stock, questioned the validity of the will. It seems that Elizabeth was left one dollar in money, two kitchen chairs, two pails and one broom; hence, the will contest.

Mrs. Stock, the testatrix, was the mother of one of the men who went to his death on the ill-fated battleship *Maine*, in the harbor of Havana.

What behavior induced the death sentence on Polly, is not known.

Will of Mrs. Elizabeth Hunter

This lady, a resident of London, having for many years enjoyed the society of a pet parrot, and being anxious as to the fate of her favorite after her death, bequeathed an annuity of £200, to be paid quarterly, so long as the parrot should live and its identity be satisfactorily proved. This annuity of £50 quarterly was left in the first instance to Mrs. Mary Dyer, of Park Street, Westminster, with a proviso that should that trustee die before the parrot, the sum should continue to be paid to some "respectable female who should *not* be a servant." One would think the testatrix must have had in her mind the story of Gay's cat — "Nor cruel Tom nor Susan heard!" Moreover, it was to dwell in a cage that was to cost not less than £20, and which was to be "high, long, large and roomy"; the bird also was "not to be taken out of England." This will was probated in 1813.

A Caged Annuitant

An elderly spinster, by name Caroline Hunter, wishing to provide for a favorite parrot, bequeathed the bird with a legacy of one thousand pounds to a widow, a friend of hers, giving her power to transfer both the pet and the money to any third person, provided it were to one of the female sex, who would undertake not to leave England. There was a special bequest of twenty guineas to provide a very high and handsome cage, into which the parrot was to be removed, and the executors were charged, in the event of the charge and bequest being refused by the widow, to see that the parrot was committed to the care of some trustworthy, respectable person. The will concludes: "I will and desire that whoever attempts to dispute this my last will and testament, or by any means tries to frustrate these my intentions, shall forfeit whatever I have left him, her, or them. And if any one to whom I have left legacies attempt to bring any bill or charge against me, it is my will and desire they shall forfeit whatever legacy I may have left them. I owe nothing to any one — many owe me gratitude and money, but none have paid me either."

Horses to be Shot

Frederick Christian Winslow was born in 1752; he was Councillor of State, professor of surgery, and knight of the order of Danebrog. His works on surgery have been translated into almost all the languages of Europe. He was grand-nephew of the celebrated anatomist, James Benignus Winslow. He died at Copenhagen, June 24, 1811.

His will disposes of property amounting to 37,000 crowns, but contains only one clause which can be considered singular, viz.: that which orders that his carriage-horses should be shot, lest after his death they come to be ill-treated by any person who might buy them.

Will in Favor of a Horse

Among the archives of Toulouse exists the registry of a singular will, made by a countryman of the immediate environs in 1781. This peasant, who was the owner of a considerable sum of money, besides his house and the land surrounding it, had no children, but had attached himself to a horse he always rode, though it does not seem to have been particularly comely in appearance. His affection for this animal was very constant; for, finding himself seriously ill, and having decided on making his will, he disposed of all his property in favor of the four-footed favorite in these terms: "I declare that I appoint my russet cob my universal heir, and I desire that he may belong to my nephew George."

As may be supposed, the will was contested; but, strange to say, it was ultimately confirmed. An experienced jurisconsult, by name Claude Serres, professor of "droit civil" at Montpellier, has cited the case, and gives the reason for the decision arrived at, viz.: "That the will being pronounced valid, the succession of the testator was adjudicated to the nephew whom he had designated as proprietor of the horse, because it was ruled that the simplicity of the rustic should secure to him the execution of his last will, and that, having named his nephew as legatee of the horse, he intended he should have it endowed with the bequests he had bestowed upon it."

Horses as Legatees

A curious will contest was instituted in January, 1911, in the Hungarian courts. This contest turns upon the legality of the will of an eccentric nobleman, Emile von Bizony, brother of a well-known deputy, who left all his real and personal property, amounting to about $200,000, to be used in behalf of his twelve draught horses.

As executor of his will, he named the Society for the Protection of Animals at Budapest, stipulating that the interest on his estate should be devoted to the care of his twelve draught horses, and that upon the death of one of them another aged horse was to be taken in and cared for, so that the number of twelve might always be maintained.

Herr von Bizony was sixty-five years of age, a confirmed misogynist, and at odds with all his relatives, who were naturally amazed at the contents of the will. His brother, the Deputy, Herr Alusins von Bizony, disputed the will. Negotiations were made with the above-mentioned society, and $20,000 was offered it, but refused, the society bringing an action against the Bizony family for the retention of the property.

Two Thousand Dollars for a Horse

An Irishman, James Gilwee, died in 1907 in Carondelet, a subdivision of the city of Saint Louis: by his will, filed in the Probate Court of the city of Saint Louis, he left two thousand dollars in trust, the revenue from which was to be used in the support and comfort of a favorite horse, "Tony": the children of the deceased carefully respected the wishes of their father, and the horse was shipped to Bloomington, Illinois, where corn is plentiful and meadow grass is blue, and the horse received every attention until his death, which occurred quite recently. The two thousand dollars was thereupon divided between the heirs.

Domestic Pets

Mrs. Elizabeth Balls, late of Park Lodge, Streatham, England, whose will was proved on the 5th of November, 1875, bequeathed to the Cancer Hospital, £2,000 Consols; to the Institution for the Deaf and Dumb, Old Kent Road, £1000 Consols; to the Blind Schools, Southwark, a like sum; to the Idiots' Asylum, Earlswood, £500 Consols; and to Guy's and St. Thomas's hospitals, the like sum each. She directed that her late husband's cob mare and greyhound should not be sold, but that the former should be kept in a comfortable, warm, loose box, as she had been kept since her late master's death; that she should not be put to work either in or out of harness, and that her back should not be crossed by any member of her late husband's family, but that she should be ridden by a person of light weight, not above four days a week, and not more than one hour each day, at a walking pace. For the support of this mare Mrs. Balls left £65 per annum, and for the keep and care of the greyhound £5 per annum.

Bank Stock for a Dog

The late Mrs. T. P. Roe, of Canada, bequeathed to her little dog, Frolic, the interest on four shares of Montreal Bank stock for use during his lifetime, and at his death the same was to be sold and given to the Church of St. John the Evangelist.

Dog painted by Landseer

For his faithful companion Pincher, Lord Eldon in 1838 made a testamentary provision, bequeathing him to Lady Frances Bankes, with an annuity of eight pounds during the term of his natural life, for his maintenance.

"His attachment to this animal," says Lord Campbell, "was very affecting. He used to say while he caressed him: 'Poor Pincher belonged to poor William Henry, and after I took the Sacrament with him when he was dying, he called me back as I was leaving the room and said: "Father, you will take care of poor Pincher."

"'The dog was brought home to me when all was over, and in a short time he was missed; he was immediately sought for, and it was found he had gone back and was lying on the bed beside his dead master.' He had another story about this dog which was decoyed away by a dog-stealer, and recovered by the Ex-Chancellor compounding felony with the thief. On receiving a letter signed, 'An Amateur Dog-fancier,' a negotiation was opened which led to Lord Eldon sending a servant with a five-pound note to a house in Cow Cross Street, where Pincher was found. The man being dealt with 'on honour,' freely disclosed the secrets of his trade, and in answer to a gentle reproach, replied: 'Why, what can we do? Now that Parliament has stopped our trade in procuring bodies for the surgeons, we are obliged to turn to this to get an *honest* livelihood.'

"Pincher is introduced into several portraits of his master, who said: 'Poor fellow! he has a right to be painted with me, for when my man Smith took him the other day to a law bookseller's, where there happened to be several lawyers, they all received him with great respect, and the master of the shop exclaimed: "How very like he is to *old Eldon*, particularly when he wore a wig! — but, indeed, many people say he is the handsomer chap of the two.'"

"After Lord Eldon's death, Pincher was painted by that consummate judge of the canine race, Sir Edwin Landseer, who remarked of him: 'He is a very picturesque old dog, with a wonderful look of cleverness in his face.' He has represented him listening to the ticking of a watch given to the Chancellor by George III."

ANCIENT, CURIOUS, AND FAMOUS WILLS

A Dog's Hospital

An old lady who died in Paris in December, 1876, left a singular legacy to the city of Marseilles, being 85,000 francs, for the purpose of founding within its precincts an hospital — "pour les chiens et les chevaux malheureux." M. Mertin, a notary of Paris, it was who received the will of Madame Veuve Perren, née Enouf, and who communicated its dispositions to M. Maglione, mayor of Marseilles.

Chloroform and Water for Animals

There is on file in the city of Saint Louis, Missouri, the will of Phoebe Deliah Nye, which contains, among others, these items:

"Item: I direct my Executor, immediately upon taking charge of my estate, to end the life of my faithful dog, Lily, by the application of chloroform, it being my desire to spare her from ending her days without that care which she would receive if I were living.

"Item: I direct my Trustee to establish, erect and maintain in various parts of the City of Saint Louis, Drinking Fountains and Places where both man and beast may at all times, both day and night, have fresh water to drink; convenient of access to all and free from any expense to them.

"It is my will and I direct that each and every one of such drinking places shall be so arranged that dogs and cats may drink, and that they may be permitted to do so freely; such drinking places are to be selected where they will be most needed and be most useful and in as many different places as possible, and particularly in the more congested and more frequented portions of the city.

"Item: I authorize and empower my Trustee to expend one-half of the Corpus and all of the net revenue from my estate in the establishing, erecting, and maintaining of the drinking places.

"Item: I authorize and empower my Trustee to employ such persons as in its judgment may be necessary to maintain and look after these drinking places at an expense not to exceed one-fourth of the net income and revenue from the trust estate; and to carry out my intent, my Trustee is authorized to purchase or to lease sufficient ground, upon which to establish such drinking places, and to accept donations and gifts of property, real and personal, to be added to the trust fund to be used in the same way and for the same purposes."

Chronometers and Dogs

Sir James South, the astronomer, by his will, which was proved in 1868, gave a pocket-chronometer each to the Earl of Shaftesbury, the Earl of Rosse, and Mr. A. J. Stephens, the condition in each case being that the chronometer should be carried in the pantaloon pocket of the wearer, according to the habit of the testator. Sir James South also left £30 a year to one of his female servants during the lifetime of a favorite terrier named "Tiger"; and this animal was produced in the Equity Court in 1872, when a question arose as to its existence. On behalf of the dog or its keeper, it was asked that a sum of £1000 Consols should be set apart to meet the annuity, but the Vice-Chancellor held that the rules of the court, which applied to human beings, did not extend to dogs, and said that the executor's personal undertaking for the rest of the dog's life would be sufficient.

A Lover of the Canine Race

In the *Gazetta del Popolo* of Turin, of September 2, 1874, is found the following:

"Last week was opened by Zanini, the notary public, the will of a certain L. C., who, after having made a considerable fortune by means of the journal, the *Caroccio*, disposed of it in the following manner:

"'I leave to the municipality of Casale an annuity of 1500 lire from the public debt, to be employed in rescuing all the dogs that shall fall into the hands of the civic dog-seizer (*accalappiatore*).

"'I leave to my dog Schmid a rent from the public funds of 500 lire annually, to revert after his death to the foundlings of the city.'"

Lucky Dogs

Many valuable bequests have been made to dogs, and other domestic pets. Dr. Christiano, of Venice, left sixty thousand florins for the maintenance of his three dogs, with a condition that, at their death, the sum should be added to the funds of the University of Vienna.

Sambo and Romp

A Mr. Thomas Edmett, an Englishman, died in October, 1871, having by a codicil to his will, made in 1861, bequeathed as follows: "I bequeath to my faithful servant Elizabeth Osborne, on condition that she take care of my favorite dog, an annuity of £50 for her life, to be paid to her quarterly." The annuity was given to her for her separate use, with a restraint on anticipation. The testator had at the time of making his will a favorite dog named Romp, which died before him. He, however, subsequently had another favorite dog called Sambo, which was in his possession at the time of his death. Elizabeth Osborne had taken care of Sambo as well as Romp. She claimed to be entitled to the annuity of £50 discharged from the condition of taking care of the dog.

The Vice-Chancellor held that Elizabeth Osborne was entitled to the annuity of £50 for her life. He hoped she would take care of Sambo, but he should not make the annuity contingent on her doing so.

Dog Saved his Life

A singular will was that of Mr. Berkeley, an Englishman of fortune, who died on the 5th May, 1805, at Knightsbridge. By this instrument he left a pension of twenty-five pounds to four of his dogs, having a particular affection for animals. Some one having observed to him that a portion of the sums he spent on them would be better employed in relieving his fellow-men, he replied, "Men have attempted my life, whereas it was to a dog that I own that I am alive."

And, indeed, it appeared that during a journey through France and Italy this gentleman, being attacked by brigands, had been protected and saved by his dog; the four animals he pensioned by his will were the descendants of this faithful and serviceable friend. His steward was charged to spend the whole amount on the dogs and to reserve nothing for himself; and the testator entered into the most minute particulars as to its expenditure. Feeling his end near, Mr. Berkeley desired that two arm chairs might be brought to his bedside, and his four dogs seated on them, received their last caresses, which he returned with the best of his failing strength, and died in their paws.

By an article in his will he ordered that the busts of his four dogs, descendants of the dog who saved his life, should be carved in stone and placed at the four corners of his tomb.

A Wealthy Cat

In 1892 a Paris lady left ten thousand francs to her cat. On its death, the money was to be spent on elementary schools. Recently, the death of the cat caused the money to divert to the district governing body for this purpose.

Cat, named in Will, Dead

In the will of Mrs. Sarah Titus Zabriskie, filed for probate at Newport early in September, 1910, provision was made for "Whiskers," a cat that had been Mrs. Zabriskie's pet for many years. It was provided that if Mrs. Zabriskie's daughter, who was chief beneficiary, died before "Whiskers" passed away, the cat was to be put to death painlessly by Dr. Thomas G. Sherwood, a veterinarian, of No. 107 West Thirty-seventh Street, New York.

Dr. Sherwood was not called upon, however. The animal was chloroformed a month before the will was filed. It appears "Whiskers" suffered from an incurable disease, contracted in earlier and happier years, and predeceased his mistress.

Cat and Dog Money

In a certain county in England, there is what is known as "cat and dog" money given to the poor, but which, in the first instance, was left for the support of cats and dogs. Then, too, there are the cow and bull benefactions in several English parishes, which have been left to provide cattle whose milk would go to the poor.

A Cat Menu

A remarkable will was that of a famous harpist of the seventeenth century, by name Madame Dupuis. So eccentric indeed was it considered that it gave occasion to a *cause célèbre*, and has been mentioned by various contemporary writers — among others, by Moncriff, by Mercier St. Leger and by Bayle. This testatrix died in 1677, and, if a rambling style of writing be any test of insanity, this lady ought assuredly to have been placed in durance. The document abounds in violent expressions and unchastened invective; while the singular mode of applying the very large property she has at her disposal, the vindictive retributions she conjures, and the exclamations and apostrophes into which she bursts at intervals, culminate in the final clause, which we translate faithfully as follows:

"Item: I desire my sister, Marie Bluteau, and my niece, Madame Calonge, to look to my cats. If both should survive me, thirty sous a week must be laid out upon them, in order that they may live well.

"They are to be served daily, in a clean and proper manner, with two meals of meat-soup, the same as we eat ourselves, but it is to be given them separately in two soup-plates. The bread is not to be cut up into the soup, but must be broken into squares about the size of a nut, otherwise they will refuse to eat it. A ration of meat, finely minced, is to be added to it; the whole is then to be mildly seasoned, put into a clean pan, covered close, and carefully simmered before it is dished up. If only one cat should survive, half the sum mentioned will suffice.

"Nicole-Pigeon is to take charge of my two cats, and to be very careful of them. Madame Calonge is to visit them three times a week."

A Cats' Home

A Mr. Jonathan Jackson, of Columbus, Ohio, died some thirty years ago, leaving orders to his executors to erect a cats' home, the plans and elevation of which he had drawn out with great care and thought. The building was to contain dormitories, a refectory, areas for conversation, grounds for exercise, and gently sloping roofs for climbing, with rat-holes for sport, an "auditorium" within which the inmates were to be assembled daily to listen to an accordion, which was to be played for an hour each day by an attendant, that instrument being the nearest approach to their natural voices. An infirmary, to which were to be attached a surgeon and three or four professed nurses, was to adjoin the establishment.

No mention seems to have been made of a chapel or a chaplain!

The testator gives as his reason for thus disposing of his property that " it is man's duty as lord of animals to watch over and protect the lesser and feebler, even as God watches over and protects man."

He does not, however, explain how it happens that on this principle he does not consider it his duty to protect rats from the "sporting" propensities of cats.

Lord Chesterfield's Cat

Lord Chesterfield left a sum for the support of his favorite cat, so also did one Frederic Harper, who settled one hundred pounds, invested in three per cent annuities, on his "young black cat"; the interest to be paid to his housekeeper, Mrs. Hodges, as long as the cat should remain alive. It does not appear how he provided against the substitution of any supposititious black cat for his favorite, should she have died whether of neglect or otherwise.

A Premium on Pigmanship

A wealthy tradesman, M. Thomas Heviant, died at the village of Crône-sur-Marne in 1878. In his will he made a number of singular bequests, among which was the following, which is carried out at the annual fête of the village. He ordered that among the amusements should be instituted a race with pigs, the animals to be ridden either by men or boys. The sum of 2000 francs was set apart as the prize to the lucky rider of the winning pig. The prize was not to be handed over, however, except on the condition that the winner wore deep mourning for the deceased during two years after the competition. The municipality accepted the eccentric bequest, and these singular races have been held agreeably to the terms of the will.

3

CHARITY

"... Faith, hope, charity, these three; but the greatest of these is charity."

A Perpetuity Involved

A certain gentleman of New York named Marshall had acquired a large fortune in the manufacture of cotton goods. The Lord had smiled upon him, and his wealth consequently loomed up in large proportions. He was justly proud of his material success, and, being childless and without kin on this side of the ocean, he resolved to perpetuate his name and commemorate that liberality towards charitable and religious objects, for which he had always been remarkable. His plan was to have his executors carry on his manufacturing business for the benefit of religious and charitable corporations. He left his manufacturing establishment to his executors in trust to carry on the same and divide the profits in certain proportions between the American Tract Society, the American Home Missionary Society and the American Bible Society, and the Marshall Infirmary, the latter being a hospital which he had founded. The court held, however, that there was a perpetuity involved, and directed that the estate be divided between the next of kin. The court held that the business of such religious societies was the printing of tracts and Bibles, and not the manufacture of cotton cloths. It took eight years and cost $50,000 to establish the legal meaning of the will, which was a very different meaning from that which the testator intended.

WISE WILL OF PETER BURNS

For years to come some families of Clay County, Missouri, will have occasion to remember with gratitude the wise philanthropy of a sturdy pioneer, Peter B. Burns of Liberty, who died in July, 1910; the terms of his will have just been made public. On the death of the widow half the estate, which is valued at more than $40,000, is to go to Clay County to be administered by the County Court in loans, which are not to exceed $2000 to a single individual and to bear two per cent interest; are to be secured by a mortgage on the real estate; and are to be paid off at the rate of at least $100 a year. Thus ten families at a time will constantly be given a lift toward financial independence.

The plan is based on the sensible principle of helping men to help themselves. As the help is in the shape of a loan, to be repaid, it will pauperize no one. It will go to families of small means, and it will provide an incentive to people to save enough to take advantage of the assistance offered.

NO STUDY BEFORE BREAKFAST

Countess Anna Maria Helena de Nouilles, a member of one of the historic families of France, has made a curious will which was proved in July, 1910.

She left her estate at Meads, Eastbourne, England, to found "St. Mary's Orphanage," laying down the following rules for the education of the girls:

"No competitive examinations, no study before breakfast, no study after 6 P.M., all lessons to be learned in the morning, no girl to work more than four and a half hours daily. No arithmetic, except the multiplication table for children under ten. No child with curvature of the spine to write more than five minutes a day, until thirteen. Each girl must be certified by two phrenologists as not deficient in conscientiousness and firmness. No child to be vaccinated."

Weary of Reading the Will

Nearly a hundred years ago, the Reverend Dr. Van Bunschooten departed this life and entered upon his reward: by his last will and testament, he left a legacy of $20,000 to the Dutch Reformed Church of America; the gift was accepted by that body and very properly expended for church purposes.

The testator, doubtless, with a view to posthumous fame and remembrance, made the gift on the express condition that his will should be read at all the official sessions of the Church forever. The Church has ever since been reading this document at all its official meetings.

It appears that the testament is of considerable length and much dryness, and its reading has become an irksome task: the Church has recently appealed to the courts of New York to be released from the duty of further reading the will, and it is to be hoped that the proper tribunal will determine that sufficient fidelity and honor have been shown.

Will of Pinedo, the Portuguese Jew

This remarkable Israelite, well known in Amsterdam for his enormous wealth and liberal donations, died about the middle of the eighteenth century. His will, testifying to a noble and generous nature, and disposing in the most magnanimous and tolerant spirit of the very large fortune he had made, is to be found (in Schutt's "Memorabilia Judaica," lib. iv. cap. 18) as follows:

"I bequeath to the city of Amsterdam the sum of five 'tons' of gold.

"I lend to the said city for ten years, and without interest, the sum of a million and a half of florins.

"I give to every Christian church at Amsterdam and at the Hague the sum of 10,000 florins each, and to the church in the southern quarter of Amsterdam 20,000 florins.

"I give to each Christian orphanage in the two towns the sum of 10,000 crowns.

"I give to the poor of Amsterdam forty shiploads of peat.

"I give to the orphan who shall first quit the orphanage 1000 florins, and to the one who shall succeed him 600 florins.

"I give to the synagogue at Amsterdam two and a half 'tons' of gold.

"I give to the Portuguese orphanage 30,000 crowns.

"I lend to the Government at three per cent. interest, ten 'tons' of gold on condition that the interest shall be paid to the Jews domiciled at Jerusalem: the capital to belong to the Government in perpetuity.

"I give to the German synagogue 5000 florins.

"I give to my nephew Ovis thirty-one 'tons' of gold, with all my houses and appurtenances.

"I give to my widow ten 'tons' of gold.

"I give to my other relations in equal portions 10,000 crowns.

"I give to each of my neighbours who shall assist at my funeral 100 ducats.

"I give to every unmarried person of either sex who shall be present at my burial 100 florins, and to every Christian priest in Amsterdam and at the Hague 100 crowns, and to every sacristan 50 crowns."

CHARITABLE LIGHT

John Wardall, of London, by will, dated 29th August, 1656, gave to the Grocers' Company, a tenement called the White Bear, in Walbrook, to the intent that they should yearly, within thirty days after Michaelmas, pay to the churchwardens of St. Botolph, Billingsgate, £4 to provide a good and sufficient iron and glass lantern, with a candle, for the direction of passengers to go with more security to and from the waterside all night long; the same to be fixed at the northeast corner of the parish church of St. Botolph, from the Feast Day of St. Bartholomew to Lady-day; out of which sum £1 was to be paid to the sexton for taking care of the lantern.

GRATITUDE

Charles Jones, Esq., of Lincoln's Inn, by will, dated 17th January, 1640, directed that an hospital should be built near Pullhelly for 12 poor men, and that his father first, his uncle next, and so their heirs, should fairly and justly manage and govern such hospital, which he had long resolved, and with the desire of his deceased wife, who was with his father, and their mother, his brother Griffith, his sister, his wife, himself, and other servants, mercifully preserved and brought to land in Pullhelly, from imminent and present danger of the seas by God's unspeakable love and favor; and whereas likewise he in his younger years was miraculously, by God's own hand, drawn and led from the house in Port thyn Llayn, Wales, that was instantly cast and thrown down by the moultringe of an hill near thereunto, and therein nine persons and Christians were killed by reason thereof; himself, a child of three or four years of age at the most, having newly entered the house, and in a moment returned, not thirty yards from the house, but it fell all to dust and rubbish; for these and many other of God's great mercies and loving kindness unto him, he and his deceased wife had determined of this poor hospital; for the maintenance of which hospital to be erected, he devised forever certain lands, of £50 per annum, and ordained his brother, Robert Jones, his executor.

It appears by a Latin inscription in front of the almshouses, that the benevolent intentions of the founder were entirely frustrated during the troubles of the civil war, and that the present edifice was erected by his heir, William Price, Esq., of Rhiwlas, in the year 1760.

A Light for Night Travellers

John Cooke, of St. Michael, Crooked Lane, London, by will, dated 12th September, 1662, gave to the churchwardens and vestrymen of this parish £76, to be laid out to the most profit and advantage, for various uses, and, amongst them

To the parish clerk, on condition that he should weekly, on a Saturday, sweep and make clean the aisle of the church called Fishmongers' Aisle, 6s. 8d.

For the maintenance of a lantern and candle, to be of eight in the pound at the least, to be kept and hanged out at the corner of St. Michael's Lane, next Thames Street, from Michaelmas to Ladyday, between the hours of nine and ten o'clock at night, until the hours of four or five in the morning, for affording light to passengers going through Thames Street or St. Michael's Lane, £1.

Beer for his Associates

In 1879 died at Berlin a singular character, a man of large property and a fervent follower of the sect of Gambrinus.

The *Tageblatt* states that he had made in his will some capricious dispositions as regarded his burial; so abnormal, indeed, as to call for the intervention of the police; one of his directions being that his friends were to take it in turns to roll after his hearse a barrel of beer, which they were afterwards to consume upon his grave.

He distributed his large fortune among divers charitable institutions; but to his will was appended a codicil which was not to be opened until a year after his death. This anniversary, adds the *Tageblatt*, occurred recently.

The codicil being now accessible reveals a decree creating a fund of ten thousand marks, the interest of which is to be expended in serving weekly a quarter of a tun of Bavarian beer to the frequenters of a brewery in the Prinzenstrasse, where the testator had been in the habit of spending his evenings regularly during many years — these persons being such as survived of his contemporaries. As soon as all shall be dead, the fund is to be transferred to the first foundling hospital that shall be founded in Berlin, the testator himself having been a foundling.

Travellers' Rest

George Butler, of Coleshill, Warwickshire, by will, dated September 2, 1591, gave his house at the lower end of the town of Coleshill, called the almshouse, also a house and lands in Gilson, to the uses following, viz., that the rents thereof should be employed to keep the said almshouse in repair, and buy furniture when wanting; that the feoffees, or constables, with their consent, might lodge any poor travellers that should desire it in the said almshouse; that none should be suffered to lodge there more than one night, except great cause shown; that care be taken women and men lodge not near together; that some persons be permitted to dwell there rent free, to wash the house and furniture, and to take care of the poor lodgers; that the overplus of the rent be employed to some charitable use.

Poor Maimed Soldiers

Phillip Shelley, of London, by will, dated the 6th of September, 1603, gave certain lands in Ulkerthorpe, in the county of Derby, to the Company of Goldsmiths, in trust (amongst other matters), to pay £10 per annum forever towards the relief of poor maimed soldiers, which sum is paid generally to ten pensioners of Chelsea Hospital.

Tolerance

William Wilson, of Tewkesbury, Gloucestershire, England, by his will, dated 15th of April, 1726, gave the sum of £100 South Sea Stock to the Chamber of the Corporation of Tewkesbury, upon trust, to permit the high bailiff for the time being to receive the dividends thereon, and dispose of the same, at his discretion, to poor persons of Tewkesbury, especially to such as should be visited with sickness or other calamitous accidents, without any regard to differences of political and religious opinions, the bailiff to account to the chamber for the disposal of the same, and to retain 10s. for his trouble.

A Republican Will

In August, 1874, MM. Nicolet and Colmet-d'Ange were employed to plead before the première chambre against the will of Adolphe-Théodore-Ange, du Laurens de la Barre.

The number of this gentleman's names is in itself an eccentricity; his will was another. We need not cite the whole of it, but the following was the concluding clause:

"In case I should leave no grand-nephews, I bequeath my property, after the death of Madame Duhem and Mdlle. Verdun, to the three cities of Guingamp, Morlaix, and Lannion, on condition that the revenues of the same shall be employed to give marriage portions annually, and alternately, in each such city, to five young girls of small means.

"I desire that they shall begin by Guingamp and follow with the others in regular order.

"I further request the republican members of the conseil-général of the Finisterre, to the number of five — to the absolute exclusion of Legitimists, Orleanists, Imperialists, and above all of Clericals and Communards — to find five young girls whose parents, and who also themselves, hold the same opinions as myself. If at the conseil-général there should not be found the required number of members, those there are must call upon the municipal counsellors of the above-named towns, and if they should refuse to accept, on all the municipal counsellors.

"The Breton people is dominated, enchained by old prejudices; it must be liberated from its bondage.

"I believe in an unknown God whom I invoke daily, but not in a God of human creation.

"(Signed) Adolphe-Théodore-Ange, du Laurens de la Barre.

"Guingamp, 5th October, 1872."

ANCIENT, CURIOUS, AND FAMOUS WILLS 109

A Provision for Twins

Mr. and Mrs. Henry C. Mills, of Marblehead, Massachusetts, are the first claimants under a bequest made in the will of Hon. James J. H. Gregory, which provides that the income of $1000 shall be divided each year among the parents of twins born in Marblehead. The Mills twins were born July 10, 1910, and are boys.

The will, which was probated about a month after Mr. Gregory's death in February, 1910, reads as follows:

"Having had my sympathies often aroused by reason of the extra burden and care entailed on loving mothers, poor in the things of earth, who have brought twins into the world, as an expression of that sympathy I leave in trust to my beloved town $1000, with the provision that the interest be divided on January first between all twins born in Marblehead during the previous year. In case no twins are born during a given year the interest shall be added to the principal."

Dropping Money on a Tombstone

On Good Friday, in the Churchyard of St. Bartholomew the Great, Smithfield, after divine service, one of the clergymen drops twenty-one sixpences on a tombstone, to be picked up by as many poor people, widows having the preference. The will providing for this is lost, and the distribution is now made out of the parish funds. The bequest is said to date several hundreds of years back.

Charity Sermons to commemorate National Mercies

Luke Jackson, citizen and girdler, of London, by will, dated 26th of January, 1630, reciting that he was seized in fee of certain tithes at or near Horsepool, in the county of Leicester, being about the value of £20 per annum, devised the same to certain persons on trust, yearly, to pay the clear rents and profits thereof in manner following; that is to say, two equal third parts as followeth: 40s. thereof yearly to be given for two sermons to be preached in St. Peter's church, in the town of Nottingham, on 28th of July and 5th of November, acknowledging God's mercy, and giving thanks for the deliverance of this land and people at two several times from the Invincible Armada (as it was termed) in 1588, and from the Gunpowder Plot in 1605: and the residue of the said two-thirds to be distributed amongst the poor people in the parish of St. Peter, at the discretion of his five feoffees; and the other third part of the clear profits of the said tithes as followeth, viz., 40s. for two sermons to be preached in the church of Thornton, near Horsepool, on the two above mentioned days; and the residue to be distributed amongst the poor people in the parish of Thornton, at the discretion of his feoffees.

Encouragement for Maid-servants

John Cogan, of Canterbury, England, by his will, bearing date 27th of July, 1657, recited that he had lately purchased lands and tenements in the parishes of St. Mildred and St. Mary Castle, Canterbury, and in Thanington in Kent, of the yearly value of £35, which he hoped in ten years would improve in yearly value by £10, and which he intended to dispose of for the encouragement of maid-servants, to continue in service for six or seven years together; he therefore willed and devised the sum of five pounds apiece to any such three maid-servants as should, without compulsion, dwell with any master or mistress, not being their own kindred, within the city of Canterbury, for six or seven years together, without shifting their service; and he directed that such master or mistress should give a certificate of such service, and that the wages had not exceeded fifty shillings a year, to the mayor, recorder and three or more of the aldermen of the said city for the time being; and he further directed that the overplus, after keeping the said tenements in good repair, should be employed by the said mayor, recorder and three of the said ancient aldermen for the time being, in clothing six fatherless maiden children, from the age of six to twelve years, each to have a petticoat and waistcoat of colored kersey, one pair of shoes, and one pair of stockings, on Christmas Day; and that they should go through the city of Canterbury from parish to parish, as the said overplus would extend.

Bull Baiting

George Staverton, of Wokingham, Berks, England, by will, dated May, 1661, gave out of his Staines house a yearly sum of £6 to buy a bull, which bull he gave to the poor of Wokingham town and parish, being baited, and the gift money, hide, and offal to be sold and bestowed upon the poor children in stockings of the Welsh, and shoes.

Until 1823 the baiting of the animal took place yearly on the 21st of December, in the market-place of Wokingham. In that year the Corporation determined upon discontinuing such a proceeding, which has since accordingly been omitted.

Must Attend Church

The last will and testament of Thomas Spackman, of Cliffe Pypard, Wilts, England, is as follows:

"June 5th, 1675. — I do charge my lands with twenty-one shillings by the year, and to continue for ever; viz., one shilling to the minister of the parish, to mind him of his duty in catechizing the children; twenty shillings to the poor of the parish yearly, to be given them at the church, viz. — five shillings on St. Thomas's Day, five shillings on the Annunciation of the Blessed Virgin Mary, five shillings on St. John the Baptist's and five shillings on St. Matthew's Day: my Will is, that twenty poor people do receive threepence a-piece, and that they be at the church at the beginning of prayers, or else to have no share; if the number be not twenty, then the remains to be given to those that are best deserving; and if they can, let them sing the 15th Psalm; now, if the minister be a good man, he will be careful to see this my Will performed, for the honour of the church, that at this day is almost destitute."

The land charged with this payment is in the tithing of Broad Town, and the property of William Ruddle Brown, a farmer. The sum has been for many years distributed in bread.

Fancy for Color

Henry Greene, of Melbourne, Derbyshire, England, by will, dated 22d of December, 1679, gave to his sister, Catherine Greene, during her life, all his lands in Melbourne and Newton, and after her decease to others, in trust, upon condition that the said Catherine Greene should give four green waistcoats to four poor women every year, such four green waistcoats to be lined with green galloon lace, and to be delivered to the said poor women on or before the 21st of December yearly, that they might be worn on Christmas Day.

For Paupers

Valentine Goodman, of Hallaton, Leicestershire, England, by will, dated in 1684, bequeathed £800, to be laid out in land, and the profits thereof given to the "most indigent, poorest, aged, decrepid, miserablest paupers," viz., six from Easton, four from Medbourn, four from Hallaton, and two from Blaston; and if any part of the money (was) employed for easing town levies, or not according to the intent of the testator, then he declared that the gift should cease, and the money be employed for the redemption of Turkish captives.

A Religious Task

Dr. Thomas White, of Newark, Nottinghamshire, England, Bishop of Peterborough, by his will, bearing date in 1690, gave to the poor of the parish of Newark £240, to be laid out in land, £10 of which rent he allotted to the poor yearly forever, and the surplusage, whatever it should be, to the rector, as a reward for his pains and fidelity in the distribution of the said £10 to the poor; and he directed that the distribution should be made yearly by the rector in the church porch, in the presence of the churchwardens or overseers, in the following manner, viz.: that it should be distributed the 14th of December to twenty poor families, or persons of forty years old each, by equal shares, reckoning husband and wife for one person, who should, before the receipt thereof, exactly and distinctly repeat the Lord's Prayer, the Apostles' Creed, and the Ten Commandments, without missing or changing one word therein. And if any man and wife should appear for a share in the said charity, it should not be a sufficient qualification for them that one of them made the exact rehearsal, but they should both make it, or else have no share at all in it. He also directed that no one should receive his charity twice, till all the poor of the parish should have received it once who should make the repetition aforesaid, that the advantage might spread as far as possible.

Attachment to a Family Name

John Nicholson of London, Stationer, by will, dated 28th of April, 1717, after bequeathing several specific legacies, gave all the residue of his estate in charity towards the support and maintenance of such poor persons of the Kingdom of England as should appear to be of the name of Nicholson, being Protestants; and he directed that it should be disposed of in the following manner, namely:

One hundred pounds a year to two such poor persons, men or women, of the name of Nicholson, towards their advancement in marriage; to each of them £50; always observing that no more than £50 be given to any one couple so marrying.

One hundred pounds per annum towards putting to apprentice such poor boys and girls of the name of Nicholson, or towards setting them up, as his trustees should think fit.

And one hundred pounds per annum towards the support and maintenance of such poor men and women of the name of Nicholson, as his trustees should direct; always observing that not more than £10 a year and not less than £5 a year should be given to any one person; the said sums to be paid to them at their own habitations.

He appointed William Nicholson, Lord Bishop of Carlisle; Mr. Nicholson, the Bishop's son; and three other persons of the name of Nicholson, two of whom were resident in London, trustees, and left to them the entire management of this charity and appointed them his executors.

BEQUEST TO PAY MARRIAGE FEES

Mr. Thomas Hatch, of Winkfield, Berks, England, by will, dated 3d of December, 1778, gave to the churchwardens of Winkfield £200 to be laid out in the public funds, the interest to be applied to the payment of the fees for such poor persons as are willing to marry, but cannot pay the expense.

After the payment of the marriage fees of such couples as claim it, the residue is distributed by the churchwardens in small sums of money and articles of clothing to such poor persons as they may think deserving.

WILL LEAVING A FUND TO ENDOW A ROSIÈRE

By her will, dated 6th of December, 1870, a lady of Puteaux, Madame Jeanne Cartault, bequeathed to that parish the sum of fifteen thousand francs, the interest of which was to be employed every year in providing a marriage portion for the most deserving among the poor working girls, and was to be called the Cartault foundation. The gift only to be made over to the recipient on her marriage, and the administrator to pay the amount only on the wedding-day, and in presence of the registrar. The marriage to take place on or about the 17th of January, being the wedding-day of Madame Cartault.

A clause in the will provides that the firstborn of this marriage shall, if a boy, take the name of Edmond — that of M. Cartault, and, if a girl, that of Jeanne — being the name of the testatrix.

According to these directions, on the 29th of January, 1874, took place the crowning of the first Rosière of Puteaux, in conformity with the prescriptions of the will, and with it the donation of the amount of one year's interest on the sum bequeathed — seven hundred and fifty francs.

The choice had fallen on a young woman of twenty-four, Mademoiselle Eugénie Bouillaud. Her qualifications justified the selection. She was an orphan, and from the time she was ten years of age had worked for the support of her grandparents, who lived in extreme poverty. Her mother died when she was born, and her father was killed in trying to rescue a fellow-workman from a well into which he had fallen.

The ceremony was rendered picturesque by the arrangements made to honor the occasion, but for some reason every demonstration of a religious nature was excluded. An immense tent had been erected near the mayor's house, decorated with flags and banners. The proceedings were opened with a piece of orchestral music, admirably executed by the Orpheonic band of the town. The mayor made a neat and appropriate speech, after which M. Laboulaye addressed the Rosière and the assembled spectators.

The concluding incident of the ceremony was the crowning of the young girl, whose quiet, modest demeanor well became her pale but interesting face. Her name was then inscribed on the virgin page of the *Livre d'or des Rosières de Puteaux*, and her autograph signature was written beneath it with a somewhat trembling hand.

To Promote Brotherly Love

Robert Halliday, of Eastcheap, London, by his will, dated 6th of May, 1491, gave estates in the parish of St. Leonard, Eastcheap, the rents to be applied to various purposes, and, amongst others, 5s. to the churchwardens yearly, either to make an entertainment among such persons of his home parish of St. Clement, who should be at variance with each other, in the week preceding Easter, to induce such persons to better neighborhood, and to beget brotherly love amongst them; or if none should be found in the said parish, then to make an entertainment with the said 5s. at the tavern amongst the honest parishioners of the said

ANCIENT, CURIOUS, AND FAMOUS WILLS

parish on the day of our Lord's Supper, commonly called Shere Thursday, that they may pray more fervently for the souls of certain persons named in his will.

Drinking

Edward Cooper, of Slinfold, Sussex, England, by his will, dated 10th of February, 1621, gave 20s. a year out of lands called Whitbers, in Slinfold, 15s. thereof to be bestowed by the churchwardens and overseers upon a drinking, for the use of the poor of the parish yearly, at the feast day of the Purification of the Virgin, in as good sort as they could, and the other 5s. to drink withal themselves, for their labor and pains therein.

The land is now called South Whitbreads, and the owner of the property regularly pays the sum of £1 yearly, which is distributed amongst the poor at Christmas by the churchwardens and overseers.

Encouragement to attend Divine Service

Thomas Walker, of St. James's, Bristol, England, by his will, dated 25th of April, 1666, ordered as follows: "I give and bequeath to that poor parish of St. James the sum of £200, to purchase for ever the sum of £10 8s. 0d. a year for eight poor house-keepers that are known to live in the fear of God, and to come unto the church every Lord's day, a six-penny loaf of bread every Sabbath day, after morning prayer, unto these eight poor house-keepers for ever; but for God's sake let them be no drunkards nor common swearers — no, nor that do beg in the streets from door to door, but let them be quiet people that do desire to live in the fear of God. Pray let their bread be wheaten bread, and weight as it ought to be."

Stormy Days

Thomas Williamson, of Castlerigg, Cumberland, England, by will, dated 14th of December, 1674, gave the sum of £20 to be laid out in land to be bestowed upon poor people, born within St. John's Chapelry or Castlerigg, in mutton or veal, at Martinmas yearly, when flesh might be thought cheapest, to be by them pickled or hung up and dried, that they might have something to keep them within doors upon stormy days.

Snuff and Tobacco for the Sick

Dr. F. W. Cumming left six hundred pounds to the Royal Infirmary, Edinburgh, to provide poor patients, male and female, with snuff and tobacco, giving the following reason for his unusual bequest: "I know how to feel for the suffering of those, who in addition to the irksomeness of pain and the tedium of confinement, have to endure the privation of what long habit has rendered in a great degree a necessity of life."

To toll the Bell

William Minta, of Great Gonerby, Lincolnshire, who died 8th of June, 1724, gave £5 to the poor of Gonerby, to be distributed in bread to sixteen aged people, on Good Friday, yearly, a "threepenny dole a piece," and the clerk was "to toll the bell at three o'clock, and to read the Epistle and Gospel, and sing the Lamentation of a Sinner," and to have one shilling reward.

Christmas Festivities

William Taylor, of Shropshire, England, by will, dated 6th of February, 1735, directed that Elizabeth Leigh, then owner, and the persons who subsequently should be owners of his two freehold houses, &c., situate in High Street, in the parish of St. Leonard, should yearly, for ever, on the 26th of December, give and provide a good and wholesome dinner for the poor persons, almshouse women, inhabiting the almshouse belonging to the parish of St. Leonard, in such manner as of late years has been provided for them on that day by the testator and his late brother; and they to be so entertained in the most convenient part of the house that fronted the street; and upon every default his Will was, and he ordered the sum of £10 to be paid to, and equally divided amongst, such poor persons, and the same to be chargeable upon the said houses, &c.

Gratitude for being preserved in a Battle

Ezekiel Nash, an Englishman, of Bristol, St. James', for a memorial of his thankfulness to Almighty God for his wonderful preservation in an engagement with a French frigate, March the 8th, 1762, gave by will, dated 27th of March, 1800, the sum of £100, to the churchwardens and overseers for the time being of such parish as he should be buried in, upon trust, to invest the same and apply the interest annually in manner following, viz., to the minister of the same parish, for preaching a sermon yearly, on the 8th of March, forever, one guinea; to the clerk and sexton for their attendance, 5s. each; the residue in the purchase of bread, to be distributed on the 8th of March, and the six Sundays next following, among such poor persons of the parish whom the minister, churchwardens and overseers should think fit objects to receive the same, not receiving alms or other charity.

THE GRATITUDE OF A MEMBER OF PARLIAMENT

Henry Archer, Esq., of Hale, England, in the county of Southampton, by will, dated the 5th of November, 1764, gave the sum of £500 to the poor of the borough of Warwick, in grateful remembrance of the very great honor conferred on him by the said borough (which he represented in Parliament) for thirty years and upwards, to be disposed of, and managed to the best advantage of the said poor by his brother Lord Archer, the Earl of Warwick, and Matthew Wise, Esq., and by the respective vicars, churchwardens and overseers of the poor of the parishes of St. Mary and St. Nicholas, in the said borough, for the time being.

The interest is employed in purchasing coals in the summer, and selling them to the poor at a reduced price in winter.

IN COMMEMORATION OF JOHN BUNYAN

Samuel Whitbread, Esq., of Bedford, England, by will, dated the 13th of July, 1795, gave to the trustees of the "Old Meeting," out of respect to the memory of John Bunyan, and for the relief of the poor of the congregation, five hundred pounds, to be laid out by his executors in the Three Per Cent. Consols, and the dividends to be annually applied in giving bread to the poor in quartern loaves every Sabbath morning, from October to May.

After the death of Mr. Whitbread, the sum of £500, instead of being laid out in stock, was, at the request of his son, the late Samuel Whitbread, Esq., allowed to remain in his hands on the security of his bond, conditioned for the investment of £980 Three Per Cent. Consols, being so much stock as the £500 would then purchase.

A bond, subject to the same condition, was executed about 1819 by William Henry Whitbread, Esq., eldest son of the late Samuel Whitbread, in lieu of the former bond.

The interest payable on the bond amounts to £29 8s. per annum, which is received regularly by the trustees of the Old Meeting, and is laid out by them in the purchase of quartern loaves, which are distributed at the meeting-house every Sabbath day, from May to October, among such poor persons of the congregation as the trustees select.

Dressing a Grave with Flowers

William Benson Earle, Esq., of Grateley, Hampshire, England, who died in 1796, gave three hundred guineas to the rector, churchwardens, and overseers of Grateley, in trust, to invest the same in their joint names, and expend half the interest thereof at Christmas, and the other half at Easter, in the purchase of the best ox-beef and cheese, together with potatoes or peas, or both, to be distributed in just proportions, at their discretion, among the poorest families in that parish, but nowhere else. And he requested that one guinea of the annual interest should be given yearly to the clerk of the parish, so long as he should cleanse and repair with flowers in the different seasons, as had before been done, the bed over the remains of Dame Joanna Elton, in the churchyard of Grateley.

Bread for the Poor

The Rev. Mr. Pitt, an English clergyman, directed sixty penny loaves to be given to the poor of St. Botolph's, Bishopsgate, yearly, on Whit Sunday, by eight o'clock in the morning, upon his tomb, in the burying-ground, in Old Bethlem.

Bluecoat Boys and Packets of Raisins

In accordance with the will of Peter Symonds, dated 1586, sixty of the younger boys of Christ's Hospital, London, attend divine service at the Church of Allhallows, Lombard-street, on Good Friday, and are presented each with a new penny, a bun, and a packet of raisins.

A Fixed Price for Corn and Wine

A citizen of Berne, Switzerland, left this unusual will:
"Being anxious for my fellow-citizens of Berne (who have often suffered by dearth of corn and wine), my Will is that, by the permission of Providence, they shall never for the future suffer again under the like calamity, to which end and purpose I give my estate, real and personal, to the Senate of Berne, in trust for the people;

that is to say, that they receive the produce of my estate till it shall come to the sum of (suppose two thousand pounds); that then they shall lay out the two thousand pounds in building a town house, according to a plan by me left; the lower story whereof to consist of large vaults or repositories for wine; the story above I direct to be formed into a piazza, for such persons as shall come to the market at Berne for disposing of their goods free from the injuries of the weather; above that I direct a council chamber to be erected for a committee of the Senate to meet in from time to time to adjust my accounts, and to direct such things as may be necessary for the charity; and above the council chamber as many floors for granaries as can be conveniently raised, to deposit a quantity of corn for the use of the people whenever they shall have occasion for it. And when this building shall be erected, and the expense of it discharged, I direct the Senate of Berne to receive the produce of my estate till the same shall amount to the sum (suppose of two thousand pounds); and when the price of corn shall be under the mean rate of the last ten years, one fourth part, they shall then lay out one thousand pounds in corn, and stow it in my granaries, and the same in wine, when under one fourth of the mean rate of the last ten years; and my Will is that none of the said corn or wine shall be sold until the price of corn and wine shall exceed at the common market one fourth of the mean rate for the last ten years; and then every citizen of Berne shall demand daily (and proportionally weekly) as many pounds of wheat and as many pints of wine as he has mouths in his family to consume, and no more, and that for the same he pay ready money after the mean rate that it has been at for the last ten years past, a due proportion being allowed for waste, and that to be settled by the Senate; and that each householder shall be so supplied as long as the price of corn and wine shall continue above the rate of one fourth more than the mean rate; and whatsoever increase shall be made of the capital, it shall be laid out under the same restrictions, in adding to the stock of corn and wine; which, under the blessing of God, will, I hope, in a certain time reduce these two necessary articles of life to very near a fixed price, to the glory of God and the benefit of the poor."

This legacy has existed about 300 years, and had the desired effect at Berne, and a will on the same principle has been made for purchasing fuel for the poor of Kingston-on-Thames, England.

Fish for the Poor in Lent

John Thake, of Clavering, Essex, England, by will, dated 13th of June, 1537, gave to Robert Cockerell and his heirs his house and lands called Valence, upon condition that they should forever, yearly, on Friday, the first week in Lent, give to poor people of Clavering one barrel of white herrings and a cade of red herrings (a cade is about half a barrel), always to be given by the oversight of the churchwardens and the tenants and occupiers of the lordship and parsonage of Clavering.

The owner of the farm called Valence, regularly sends to the house of the parish clerk, in Lent, a barrel of red herrings and a barrel of white, which are distributed in the church by the parish clerk and sexton, four to each married couple, two to each widow and widower, and one to each child.

Cow Charity

James Goodaker, of Woodchurch, Cheshire, England, in 1525, left a fund by will to buy twenty yoke of bullocks, which were subsequently replaced by cows, and given to the poor of Woodchurch parish: every parishioner that had a cow or cows paying yearly for each to the overseers the sum of 2s. 8d. every Friday before Whitsunday, which hire was to be a stock for the benefit of the poor forever.

The parish of Woodchurch includes ten townships, from each of which a trustee of the cow property is elected, whose duty it is to see that the animals are properly taken care of, and those persons are termed governors of the cows. There is an annual meeting, on which occasion the cows are produced and examined.

Turkeys for Parishioners

In 1691, John Hall left to the Weavers' Company a dwelling-house, with instructions to pay 10s. per annum to the churchwardens of St. Clement, Eastcheap, to provide on the Thursday night before Easter two turkeys for the parishioners, on the occasion of their annual reconciling or love-feast (settlement of quarrels or disputes).

Bread, Beer, Beef, and Broth

John Balliston, of St. Giles's, Norwich, by will, dated 17th of October, 1584, devised three tenements in St. Giles's next the

Gates to certain persons, upon condition that they should make distribution to the poor in manner following, viz. that in the week before Christmas, the week before Michaelmas, and the week after Easter, in the church of St. Giles, the minister should request the poor people, all that should receive or have need of alms, to come to church, and request them to pray for the preservation of the Prince, &c.; that the poor should place themselves four and four together, all that should be above the age of eleven years, and that every four of them should have set before them a two-penny wheat loaf, a gallon of best beer, and four pounds of beef and broth; that the minister should have fourpence for his pains on each of the three days.

The rent of £2 a year is paid to the parish for the premises, which, with other charities, is laid out in the purchase of coals.

Halfpenny Bread Charity

Robert Grainger of Godmanchester, Huntingdonshire, by his will, dated 10th of October, 1578, gave and appointed as much bread as could be made of a coomb of wheat, to be made into halfpenny loaves, and to be distributed among the poor of Godmanchester by the churchwardens, to be charged on his mansion house in Godmanchester.

The present owner of the house pays the value of four bushels of wheat, according to the average price of wheat at Huntingdon market, on the Saturday before Good Friday, to a baker, for supplying the bread, which is distributed on Good Friday.

Cuttings of Fish

Robert Harding, of London, by will, dated 20th of November, 1568, gave to the Company of Fishmongers an annuity of £3 6s. 8d. issuing out of his lands and tenements in Pudding Lane; and Simon Harding, his son, by deed, 7th of September, 1576, confirmed the same; to hold the said annuity to the wardens and commonalty and their successors, to the intent that they should pay in the Lent season £3, that is, in New Fish Street 30s. and in Old Fish Street 30s., to the use of the poor inhabiters and artificers compelled by necessity to repair thither, to buy the cuttings of fish and the refuse of fish; the residue to remain to the wardens for their labors in this behalf.

There being no poor persons of the description mentioned in the will, the annuity has been added to the fund distributed to the half-yearly poor at Christmas.

Bequest of White Peas

John Huntingtdon, of Sawston, Cambridgeshire, England, by will, dated 4th of August, 1554, devised lands and tenements to Joice his wife, and his heirs, upon condition that his heirs should yearly forever sow two acres of land, lying together in Linton field, with white peas, one coomb to be yearly bestowed upon each acre, for the relief of the people of Sawston.

Two acres, the property of Richard Huddlestone, Esq., the lord of the several manors in the parish, are annually sowed with white peas, as directed by the will, which are gathered green on a day fixed by the occupier of the land, by all the poor indiscriminately, when a complete scene of scramble and confusion ensues, attended with occasional conflicts.

Milk Tribute

Edmund Porter of Alresford, Middlesex, by will, dated 27th of May, 1558, directed that John Porter should have a house called Knapps, with the appurtenances, church fences, and caprons (which comprised thirty-one acres of land), to him and his heirs, upon condition that they should give forever the morning milk of two able milk beasts to the poor people of this parish, every Sunday yearly, from Whitsunday to Michaelmas, 3s. 4d. on Good Friday, and a like sum on Christmas Day.

This milk tribute has subsequently been commuted for a money payment, which is distributed in bread amongst the poor.

4

BURIAL

"He will awake no more; no, never more."

A Primitive Belief

There seems to have been a wide-spread primitive belief that the spirit of the departed could not rest in peace unless the obsequies were duly performed. Thus the ghost of Patroclus appeared to Achilles to request that his body might be buried in order that he might pass the gates of Hades. This belief was apparently fostered by the doctrine of the resurrection of the body.

VETERAN'S REQUEST

Robert Riedel, of Detroit, Michigan, died in June, 1910. He had fought through the Franco-Prussian War. By the terms of his will, he left to Detroit survivors of his old company, fifteen dollars with which to buy beer after they had marched to his funeral. It is said the purchase was made and duly drunk.

HIS HEART TO BE SENT HOME

There was filed in Pittsburgh, Pennsylvania, on September 24th, 1910, the will of Count Julian S. De Ovies, former Chilian Consul in Pittsburgh. He left his entire estate to his wife, Minnie, his son, Rev. Raimundo B. De Ovies, and his daughter, Edith Manselea De Ovies. One curious sentence in the will reads:

"I request that my body be cremated and my heart be sent, according to family custom, to the chapel of Santa Maria, in Luanco, Conbecejo de Gozon, Province of Austria, Spain."

WISHED A PERPENDICULAR GRAVE

A nobleman of the house of Du Châtelet, who died about 1280, left in his will a singular provision. He desired that one of the pillars in the church of Neufchâteau should be hollowed out and his body placed in it on its feet, "in order," says he, "that the vulgar may not walk about upon me." In a very different spirit was the following will.

WILL OF GUILLAUME DE CHAMPLITTE

This worthy was Sire de Pontailler and de Talmai, Viscomte de Dijon, and descended from Guillaume de Champlitte II., Viscomte de Dijon, founder of the Priory of St. Marie de Pontailler, of the order "du Val des Ecoliers." Shortly before his death in 1282, he made a will, desiring that he might be interred wearing the habit of a cordelier, and laid upon some litter. He further ordered there should be but four "chandailles," *i.e.* candles, tapers, or torches employed at his funeral. He requested also that his body should be placed under the porch of the church of the Priory of Pontailler, that passers-by might walk over it. His desire was to be laid near his father, who had likewise caused himself to be buried under the porch.

BURIED IN CAMBRIC

Lately, at Taunton, far advanced in years, Mrs. Mary Davis, an eccentric character, died. In her will she ordered that the expenses of her funeral should not exceed $1500, but that she should be buried in cambric, and that her coffin should be made of mahogany.

BEQUEATHED HIM FUNERAL EXPENSES

Mrs. Mary Thomas Piper, a wealthy widow of Kansas City, died in 1910. To Rollins Bingham, a nephew, she left $250 to be held in trust and used only for his funeral expenses. It appears that the conduct and habits of the nephew had not been pleasing to the testatrix, and she adopted this weird way of revenging herself upon one who had formerly been a favorite kinsman, but had subsequently incurred her displeasure.

This sum of $250 was left in trust in the hands of her executor to be held until the death of the nephew, and then applied to give him proper burial.

Rollins Bingham was a newspaper writer of Kansas City, Missouri, and his father was General George C. Bingham, a distinguished Missouri artist, who painted the well-known pictures, "General Order No. 11" and the "County Election." He died quite recently, shortly after the above-mentioned will was probated, and the legacy at which he scoffed was used for the purpose named.

TO INDUCE PEOPLE TO PRAY

The will of Master Robert Toste, Provost of the Collegiate Church of Wingham, dated 17th of August, 1457, recites: "My body to be buried on the uppermost step, on the north part of the high altar, where the Gospel is read in the choir on holidays in Wingham. I Will that a marble stone be laid over me, with an inscription, to induce people to pray for my soul. I bequeath part of my books to the new College of All Souls, founded by Archbishop Chicheley, part to University College, and part to the University Library of Oxford."

BURIED IN AN OLD CHEST

The Rev. Luke Imber, of Christchurch, Hants, England, one of his Majesty's Justices of the Peace for that county, who, at the age of eighty-three, married a country girl of thirteen, desired in his will that he might be buried in an old chest which he had for some time kept by him for that purpose, and that the bearers should have each of them a pair of tanned leather gloves and a new pair of shoes, which were given accordingly.

Bribing the Children

Mr. Tuke, of Wath, near Rotherham, England, who died in 1810, bequeathed one penny to every child that attended his funeral (there came from 600 to 700); 1s. to every poor woman in Wath; 10s. 6d. to the ringers to ring a peal of grandbobs, which was to strike off whilst they were putting him into his grave; to an old woman who had for eleven years tucked him up in bed, £1 1s. per annum; to his natural daughter, £4 4s. per annum; to his old and faithful servant, Joseph Pitt, £21 per annum; forty dozen penny loaves to be thrown down from the church leads on Christmas Day forever. Two handsome brass chandeliers were also bequeathed to the church, and £20 for a new set of chimes.

Hand to be Cut Off

Mysterious directions in wills are sometimes to be met with which only a knowledge of the inner family history can explain; such as the direction in the will of the late Countess of Loudoun, the half-sister of the last Marquis of Hastings: "After my death I direct my right hand to be cut off, and buried in Donnington Park, at the bend of the hill towards the Trent, with this mottoe over it, 'I byde my tyme.'" This direction was faithfully carried out by the lady's husband, and the monument can now be seen in Donnington Park, in England.

An Epitaph

There was a certain missionary who was killed in India by an attendant. His epitaph reads:

Killed by an attendant.

Well done, thou good and faithful servant.

Two Wives "Seven Foot" in Length

The will of John Wilcocks, of Chipping, Wycomb, England, 5th July, 1506. "My body to be buried in the Church of All Hallondon on Wye, before the rood. To the repair of our Lady's Chapel of my grant xxiii*s*. iv*d*., I Will that my executors pay the charge of new glazing the window in the said Chapel; also I Will that an obit be kept yearly; I Will that my executors buy a marble stone to lay on my grave, with the picture of my two wives of vii foot in length, the stone mentioning her sons Thomas and Michael Wilcocks. I appoint Walter, my son, my executor, and also Robert Ashebrooke and Robert Brampton, priests, and John Aley, my executors."

Wanted no Mourning

Theodore James Ralli, of Paris, an artist, who died at Lausanne, Switzerland, on September 26th, 1909, left personal estate in the United Kingdom valued at £8055.

The testator left to his daughter, Ina, in addition to her compulsory portion in accordance with the law of France, his automobile and the contents of his studio not otherwise bequeathed; a sum of 5000 fr. to his friend, Mr. Hawkins; 15,000 fr. to the Société des Artistes Français, the income from which is to be awarded annually as a prize to be known as The Theodore Ralli Prize; to the Fine Arts Museum in Athens, all pictures of Greek subjects and framed studies in his studio; 5000 fr. to his model if she should still be in his service at the time of his death; and the residue of his property to his brothers, Spiridon and Manati, for life, with remainder to his daughter Ina.

Appended to the will is a letter expressing his wishes in the following manner: "Let me be placed in my coffin as quickly as possible after my death, and let nobody outside the household be admitted to my death chamber before I am placed in my coffin. In a word, I do not wish anybody to attend through curiosity to see how I look. Let no photographs be made of my corpse, and let me be buried as soon as possible. For the love of God, do not weep for me. I have lived a life happy enough. The aim of my life was painting, and I gave it all of which I was capable. I might have lived twenty years more, but I could not have progressed any more, so what was the good of it? And how content I should be if no one wore any marks of mourning for me. I always had a horror of it. So, if you cannot do otherwise, wear the least of it possible."

Ashes in a Golden Receptacle

Carl Schumann, a pedlar who died in May, 1910, at the Home for the Aged in Cincinnati, Ohio, directed that his body be cremated and the ashes tossed to the winds. The will also bequeathed the sum of Fifty Dollars to the Herwegh Maennerchor Society, with instructions that after the cremation the members spend the money having a good time.

The ceremony took place at the crematory at two o'clock in the afternoon, and was conducted by Mr. A. Goldstein, the leader of the Herwegh Maennerchor. While the body was being consumed, the society sang two German songs which were Schumann's favorites.

When the body was reduced to ashes, they were gathered and placed in a golden receptacle, and as the final words were spoken, they were tossed into the air by Mr. R. Schueschner. The society then began the celebration.

Directions for Cremation

In these days cremation is recognized as a good and lawful way of disposing of our remains; but so late as 1855 it was not so, for we find Mr. William Kinsett, of London, in his will proved in October of that year, stating that, "believing in the impolicy of interring the dead amidst the living, and as an example to others, I give my body, four days after death, to the directors of the Imperial Gas Company, London, to be placed in one of their retorts and consumed to ashes, and that they be paid ten pounds by my executors for the trouble this act will impose upon them for so doing. Should a defence of fanaticism and superstition prevent their granting this my request, then my executors must submit to have my remains buried, in the plainest manner possible, in my family grave in St. John's Wood Cemetery, *to assist in poisoning the living in that neighbourhood.*"

Some time after this the matter was frequently discussed in the papers, and public opinion grew slowly in favor of the practice. But it seemed to have been generally doubted whether such a method was in accordance with law and the words in the Church Service, "Earth to earth," as in 1867 we find a testator directing his nephews to cause his body to be burned "if that can be legally done." This testamentary wish to be cremated is not confined to recent times, and there seems in the 18th century to have been no difficulty in executors carrying out the directions in this respect in the wills under which they acted. In Dodsley's "Annual Register" for 1769, under date of Sept. 26, there appears the following statement: "Last night the will of Mrs. Pratt, a widow lady, who lately died at her house in George Street, Hanover Square, was punctually fulfilled by the burning of her body to ashes in her grave in the new burying-ground adjoining to Tyburn turnpike."

Coffin covered with Calico

Judge E. Y. Terral, of Cameron, Texas, died in August, 1910. His estate was valued at eight thousand dollars. By his will, he directed that no funeral services be had over his body, that no printed notices of his death be issued, that he be buried in a coffin made from rough pine plank covered with black calico and carried in a wagon or hack to the cemetery, and that no marble slab be erected at his grave.

Cards and Wine at his Funeral

A Frenchman, who was an enthusiastic card player, left to certain of his card-playing friends a legacy of considerable size on condition that, after placing a deck of cards inside his coffin with his body, they should carry him to the grave and should stop on the way to drink a glass of wine at a small saloon, where he had passed "so many agreeable evenings at piquet."

Will of the Sieur Boby

An attempt to invalidate this will was made by the heirs of the testator seven years after his death, but the court pronounced in its favor. It is dated 1845.

It certainly exhibits many singularities, and there was no contesting the fact that the testator, who died at the age of ninety-six, had been remarkable for his eccentricities for many years. He had at one time possessed a fortune of about two and a half million dollars, and at his death left no more than $15,000; moreover, he had been placed under tutelage during the three last years of his life.

ANCIENT, CURIOUS, AND FAMOUS WILLS

Several wills were found after his death, and the singularity of some of the clauses formed a plea of imbecility on the part of those who had expected to inherit his fortune.

One of these was a legacy to an old priest, to whom, although he had in his collection many paintings of sacred subjects, he bequeathed a "Cupid nestling in a bouquet of roses" to remind him, as he said, of his youthful days.

Towards the close of his life he manifested what is in France technically known as an obituary monomania, appearing entirely preoccupied with his death, and what was to become of his remains. On this subject he expressed himself thus:

"Eight-and-forty hours after my decease I desire that a postmortem examination be made; that my heart be taken out and placed in an urn, which shall be intrusted to M. Baudoin (the undertaker). In conformity with an arrangement between him and myself, my heart is to be conveyed to a mausoleum in the department of La Mayenne, and there to be deposited as agreed."

His epitaph was written out, and in this he had allowed himself considerable margin, as he fixed the date of his death forty-five years later than it actually occurred.

The letters of announcement were all prepared:

"M. et Madame Lappey ont l'honneur de vous faire part de la perte douloureuse qu'ils viennent de faire, dans la personne de M. Boby, décédé en sa demeure rue de Louvois 10. Les convoi, service et enterrement auront lieu le . . . 1890, à midi très précis à Saint Roch."

According to *this* date he would have been one hundred and forty.

HEART AND BRAINS BEQUEATHED

Dr. Ellerby died in London in February, 1827. He was a member of the Society of Friends. He passed for being a very eccentric character, and all his habits bore the stamp of originality. In his will are to be found some singular clauses, among them the following:

"Item: I desire that immediately after my death my body shall be carried to the Anatomical Museum in Aldersgate Street, and shall be there dissected by Drs. Lawrence, Tyrell, and Wardrop, in order that the cause of my malady may be well understood.

"Item: I bequeath my heart to Mr. W., anatomist; my lungs to Mr. R.; and my brains to Mr. F., in order that they may preserve them from decomposition; and I declare that if these gentlemen shall fail faithfully to execute these my last wishes in this respect I will come — if it should be by any means possible — and torment them until they shall comply."

This threat did not much alarm the above-named parties, for it appears that they unhesitatingly renounced their several legacies.

The Earth needed for Corn

John W. Wallace, of Brooklyn, New York, died on the 28th day of December, 1909; his will contained the following novel provisions, which it is reported were literally carried out:

"I direct that my body be placed in a pine box not to cost more than five dollars; placed in an express wagon and taken to a crematory; that after cremation, the ashes shall be scattered in a field. The entire cost of the disposal of my body is not to exceed fifty dollars. My reason is, that I believe a man gets out of life all that he is entitled to, according to the amount of brain and energy he puts into it, and when he dies, should not occupy ground that may be needed for highways, or for planting corn, or for any other purpose that future generations may have for it. I believe that when I die my money, if I have any, should go to those dependent upon me, and not into expensive coffins and flowers."

Took no Chances

A horror of being buried alive so haunted Mr. R. of Chicago that on his death he left minute instructions in his will to make such a fate quite impossible in his case. His body was not to be fastened up in his coffin till thirty days after his funeral, and the vault in which the body was placed was to be kept lighted and its doors left unlocked. Provision was also made for the employment of two men — trusted employees of the deceased — who were to guard the entrance, one by day and the other by night.

Her Carriages burned and Horses Shot

Quite a number of men, both Americans and Englishmen, who have spent a great part of their lives in hunting, have wished to be buried in their hunting dress, and this desire has been shared by at least one woman. An eccentric Welsh lady, who lived at a small place called Llanrug, was buried there in 1895 in accordance with the provisions of her will, which was in keeping with the local estimate of her character. She wished to be buried in her fox-hunting clothes. The rest of her clothes and her carriages were to be burned on the day of her funeral, and all her horses — six in number, varying in value from £60 to £90 each — were to be shot on the day following the funeral. The remainder of her real and personal property to the value of £90,000 was left to her "dear husband," — a former laborer on her estate, with whom some years previously she had, on her own suggestion, contracted a marriage, — provided that he strictly and literally carried out all the orders expressed in her will.

FUNERAL COST SIX FRANCS

Some very rich men during their lives seem to enjoy the luxury of preparing at great expense the mausoleums they wish to occupy after death. M. Lalanne, a wealthy Parisian, went to the other extreme. He had a horror of anything like ostentatious funerals, and after bequeathing over a million francs to the various public institutions of his native city, he directed that his body be buried as cheaply as possible — in fact, like that of a pauper. A shabby one-horse vehicle conveyed his body to the *fosse commune* (the Potter's Field), and the total cost of the funeral was only six francs, that being the charge for the cheapest kind of funeral under the French system, in which the undertaker's business is a government monopoly.

A WOMAN HATER

Altogether unique was the whim of a rich old bachelor, who, having endured much from "attempts made by my family to put me under the yoke of matrimony," conceived and nursed such an antipathy to the fair sex as to impose upon his executors the duty of carrying out what is probably the most ungallant provision ever contained in a will. The words are as follows: "I beg that my executors will see that I am buried where there is no woman interred, either to the right or to the left of me. Should this not be practicable in the ordinary course of things, I direct that they purchase three graves, and bury me in the middle one of the three, leaving the two others unoccupied."

WITH THE SAINTS ON BARDSEY ISLAND

The late Lord Newborough, an Englishman, made the following curious provision in his will: he gave most explicit directions that, after a certain period had elapsed, his body was to be exhumed and reinterred in Bardsey Island. This island, it will be remembered, lies to the north of Cardigan Bay, and it is reputed to have had no fewer than 20,000 saints buried in its soil.

With Both Wives

Another individual desired to be buried in the space between the graves of his first and second wives; there are numerous instances of such an adjustment in American cemeteries, and wills are not uncommon which provide for such last resting places.

Too Modest for Vivisection

The Duchess of Northumberland, widow of the Protector, concluded her will as follows:

"In nowise let me be opened after I am dead; I have not used to be very bold before women, much more would I be loth to come into the hands of any living man, be he physician or surgeon."

The very reverse, we may remark, of the instructions given by Katherine of Aragon on her deathbed.

Wishes of an Infidel

In one of the wildest gorges of the Blue Ridge in western North Carolina, there lived, a few years ago, a man who was a violent infidel; when he died, it was discovered that in his will he directed that he should be buried on the summit of one of the loftiest peaks of the Blue Ridge, and that his epitaph should disclose that he died reviling Christianity. Instead of carrying out his wishes, his relatives buried him in a Christian cemetery, and on the spot where he desired to be buried, placed a large white cross.

Will of John Fane

John Fane, of Tunbridge, England, died April 6, 1488; his will runs:

"My body to be buried in the church of SS. Peter and Paul, of Tunbridge. . . . To the prior and convent of Tunbridge, to pray for my soul, xx *s.*, to the high altar of the church of Tunbridge, xx *s.*; to the structure of the rood-loft thereof, v marks. . . . To Humphrey Fane, my brother's son, a house in fee simple, with a garden at the town's end of Tunbridge."

WILL OF BAKHUYSEN THE PAINTER

Bakhuysen, born at Emden, in 1631, died at Amsterdam, in 1709, was not only a celebrated painter, but a skilful engraver, and a not inelegant poet. There appears to have been a great fund of gayety in his character, and this cheerfulness did not forsake him even in his old age, although he suffered from a lingering disease. Finding his end approaching, he ordered some of the best possible wine to be bought, and, having had it bottled, sealed the corks with his seal; he then placed in a purse seventy-eight gold coins, having lived that number of years, and by his will he invited the same number of friends — each of whom he named — to his funeral, begging them to accept his money and drink his wine with the same cordiality with which he offered it. We should mention that it is the custom in Amsterdam to present a glass of wine to guests attending at a funeral.

WILL OF HEEMSKIRK

Another Dutch painter, Martin Heemskirk, left by his will a sum to provide annually a dowry for a young girl from his native village, on condition that, on the day of the wedding, the bride and bridegroom should come and dance with the wedding-guests upon his grave. Guy Patin relates this anecdote as having occurred about the middle of the seventeenth century, and declares that the testator's prescription was faithfully carried out as long as the foundation lasted.

WILL OF FRANÇOIS, DUC DE BRETAGNE

In the will of François, first duke of Brittany, drawn up at Vannes, January 22, 1449, occurs a curious clause relating to the foundations of certain masses, and particularly the mode in which the bells were to be rung for them:

". . . The largest bell (*sain*) of the said monastery (*moustier*) to be rung by twelve strokes (*gobetiex*); one stroke distant from the other by the space commonly occupied in saying an *Ave Maria*, and the whole time of ringing to be equivalent to the time it may take to recite a *pater*, a *credo*, and a *miserere;* and for this foundation we have appointed to the said *moustier* a revenue of cc *livres*."

Equally curious, and very similarly expressed, are the wills of Pierre II., Duke of Brittany, September 5, 1457; Marguérite de Bretagne, September 22, 1469; Ysabeau of Scotland, Duke of Brittany, November 16, 1482; François II., Duke of Brittany, September 2, 1488. For these and others consult the works of Barnabé Brisson, 1585–1731.

In the Shadow of an Obelisk

An individual desired post-mortem honors in this wise: "I desire to be buried beneath the shadow of an obelisk, the style of which has been taken from ancient Egyptian civilization. I saw these wonderful monolith obelisks in Egypt, sat in their shade and sighed to have one for my monument in my far-off home in the New World." On this obelisk the following inscription was directed to be placed:

"Young man! Stop & Think!
See what has been the reward for Honesty,
Industry & Economy. In 1840 I worked on
Robert Martin's Farm near Jersey Shore for
25 cts. per day. No fortune left to me.
Lived and Died in the Faith of the Immutable
And unchangeable Laws of Nature and Nature's
God. Believed in the Gospel of Peace, Right,
and Justice.
Travelled 60,000 Miles in America, Europe,
Asia and Africa."

Will of the Duchess of Kingston

Elizabeth Chudleigh, Duchess of Kingston, was celebrated for her beauty, her eccentricities, her taste for show and dissipation, and her extraordinary propensity to indulge in masculine sports and exercises, for her travels in Italy, Germany, and Russia, and her adventures generally. She passed many years in Paris, where she resided in the Rue Coq-Héron, and died there 28th August, 1788.

Her will is altogether in accordance with the remarkable features of her character. As she was much attached to Catherine II., Empress of Russia, who reciprocated her friendship, she stipulated in her will that in case she should die at St. Petersburg she should be buried there, as it was fitting her remains should be there where her heart was. She bequeathed to the Empress a set of jewels, and to the Pope a fine brilliant; to the Countess of Salisbury she left a pair of superb earrings, because they had formerly belonged to a countess of Salisbury in the reign of Henry IV. Notwithstanding her extravagance she left a fortune of two million dollars.

WANTED A COSTLY MAUSOLEUM

Elizabeth Bastian, a New York spinster, died in June, 1910. By her will she cut off her sister and two brothers with a dollar each and left the greater part of her fortune, $65,000, to build a mausoleum in order that she might "have a splendid house to live in when dead." Her will has been attacked and her wishes may be thwarted.

The sister and brothers of the decedent, who were bequeathed one dollar each by her, recently began an action in the Surrogate's Court to set aside the probate of Miss Bastian's will on the ground that she was mentally incompetent at the time of its execution. They assert, through John Path, their lawyer, that the aged spinster was a monomanic who lived frugally that she might have a magnificent tomb in which to lie after death.

This contention, they claim, is supported by her habits in life and the provisions of her will. When alive, it is alleged, she delighted to take her friends to Woodlawn Cemetery, where she owned a $10,000 plot, and pointing to the spot would say: "There's where I'm going to live in luxury when I die."

Her will provided that a cousin with whom she lived should have $500 and his wife a like sum. Three dollars was to be distributed among her sister and brothers, "because I have been treated with abject scorn by my relatives," and $50,000 was set aside for the mausoleum. The rest of the New York estate was left in trust to the Woodlawn Cemetery Association to ornament and care for the mausoleum.

BEQUESTS OF SKULLS

Many testators have bequeathed their skulls to their friends or to public institutions.

Cartouche requested, when on the wheel, that his skull might be preserved in the Genovevan monastery at Paris, and accordingly it is to be seen to this day in the library of that building, as Eugene Aram's skull is daily seen and handled in York Castle.

Professor Morlet of Lausanne desired that his head should be sent to the anatomical museum of Berne, and he particularly requested his name should be distinctly engraven thereon, lest it should be mistaken for that of any other individual.

Professor Byrd Powell, phrenologist and physician, bequeathed to one of his lady pupils, Mrs. Kinsey of Cincinnati, his "head to be removed from his body for her use, by Mr. H. T. Kekeler." The task of decapitation was, however, performed (some weeks after the body had been relegated to the vault) by Dr. Curtis.

John Reed was gas-lighter of the Walnut Street Theatre, at Philadelphia, and filled this post for forty-four years, with a punctuality and fidelity rarely equalled; there is not on record a single representation at which he was not present. John Reed was somewhat of a character, and appears to have had his mute ambitions. As he never aspired, however, to appear on the stage in his lifetime, he imagined an ingenious device for assuming a rôle in one of Shakespeare's plays after his decease; it was *not* the ghost of Polonius, nor yet the handkerchief of Desdemona — no; it was the skull in Hamlet, and to this end he wrote a clause in his will thus: "My head to be separated from my body immediately after my death; the latter to be buried in a grave; the former, duly macerated and prepared, to be brought to the theatre, where I have served all my life, and to be employed to *represent* the skull of Yorick — and to this end I bequeath my head to the properties."

WILL OF JOHN REDMAN

The last will of John Redman, who died in 1798, citizen of the world, of Upminster, in Essex. ". . . My body to be buried in the ground in Bunhill Fields, where my grandfather, Captain John Redman, of the navy, in Queen Anne's reign, lies interred. My grave to be ten feet deep, neither gravestone, atchment (*sic*), escutcheon, mutes, nor porters at the door, to be performed at seven o'clock in the morning. . . . All my wine to be drunk on the premises, or to be shared by and between my four executors. . . . Tylehurst Lodge farm, . . . I devise to the eldest son of my second cousin, Mr. Benjamin Branfill, on condition that he, the eldest son, takes the name of Redman, or to his second or third son if the others decline it. It is hereby enjoined to the Branfills to keep the owner's apartment and land in hand to be a check on shuffling sharping tenants, who are much disposed to impoverish the land. . . . Having provided handsomely for my daughter, Mary Smith Ord, on her marriage with Craven Ord of the Cursetor's Office, London, I hereby bequeath to her children born or to be born (the eldest son excepted, whose father will provide for him), the sum of two thousand pounds to each of them at the age of one-and-twenty, for which purpose I bequeath all my valuable estates at Greensted and Ongar, late Rebotiers. . . . Holding my executors in such esteem, I desire them to pay all the legacies without the wicked swindling and base imposition of stamps that smell of blood and carnage. . . . To Mr. French of Harpur Street, . . . a set of Tom Paine's 'Rights of Man,' bound with common sense, with the answers intended by the longheads of the law, fatheads of the Church, and wiseheads of an insolent usurping aristocracy. . . . To that valuable friend of his country in the worst of times, Charles Fox, Member for Westminster, five hundred guineas. To each of the daughters of Horne Tooke, five hundred pounds."

CODICIL

"I desire and direct my executors to keep my dwelling-house on for at least a year after my decease, and also the same with my house in Essex; and I do recommend them to visit Greensted Hall at least six times in that year, and to stop from Saturday to Monday morning; to hire a light coach and an able pair of horses, set out betimes, and breakfast on the road, alternately to take one of their families, that each corner may be filled to help drink out the wine in the vault. The same to be observed in Hatton Garden. Executors to order a dinner for themselves half-score times, to consult and consider the business they have in hand, and not to spare the wine in that cellar, and the remainder at last to be divided between them and carried to their respective houses."

This will is taken from a volume published for county circulation by Philip John Budworth, M.A., J.P., and D.L., for the county of Essex, and entitled, "Memorials of the Parishes of Greensted — Budworth, Chipping Ongar, and High Laver."

WILL OF A BRUXELLOIS

A wealthy individual of Brussels, who died in July, 1824, ordered by his will that his body should be buried in the least expensive manner possible; and that the funeral service should be that known as "third-class;" but that the difference between this and a "first-class" funeral should be computed, and the sum laid out in a thousand loaves, to be distributed to the poor of his parish on the day of his funeral, and a plaquette (value $6\frac{1}{2}$ sous) to be given with each loaf.

Burial Customs in Austria

In the Austrian capital, Vienna, the undertakers have most successfully introduced the custom of dressing up the dead in satins, laces, and flowers, supplying appropriate costumes for maids, brides, wives, widows, with couches *en suite*, and decorations for the chamber of death, which is brilliantly illuminated, while the corpse, with face painted in the hues of health, lies there raised on satin pillows to receive the visits of a crowd of friends. All is done with great expedition, for the law only allows a delay of twenty-four hours between the death and burial, and all this finery has to be removed after the family and friends have done looking at it, and to be replaced by such grave-clothes as the undertaker chooses to exchange for it beneath the coffin-lid.

Buried in a Trunk

A very singular will was opened, on the 8th of October, 1877, in the office of Maître Robillart, a notary of Paris. It was that of a Sieur Benoît, formerly residing at Rue des Gravillers, and lately deceased. The last clause of it was thus worded:

"I expressly and formally desire that my remains may be enclosed for burial in my large leather trunk, instead of putting my survivors to the expense of a coffin. I am attached to that trunk, which has gone round the world with me three times."

Strange Will of Jeremy Bentham

Jeremy Bentham died in 1832. He was an English jurist, philosopher and writer of great ability. In his latter years he desired that his preserved figure might be placed in a chair at the banquet-table of his friends and disciples when they met on any great occasions of philosophy and philanthropy. He died, and his wish was carefully carried out by his favorite disciple, the late Dr. Southwood Smith, to whom he bequeathed his body in his will. Dressed in his usual clothes, wearing a gray broad-brimmed hat, and with his old hazel walking-stick, called Dapple (after a favorite old horse), the farmer-like figure of the benevolent philosopher sat in a large armchair, with a smiling, fresh-colored countenance, locked up in a mahogany case with a plate-glass front. This was his actual body preserved by some scientific process. A French artist made a wax mask. The real face was underneath it.

The body of Bentham was some years ago removed to University College, and placed in an out-of-the-way corner, and "Old Bentham" was the subject of frequent jokes among the more thoughtless of the students.

This is what Dr. Southwood Smith says on the subject:

"Jeremy Bentham," writes Dr. Southwood Smith, "left by will his body to me for dissection. I was also to deliver a public lecture over it to medical students and the public generally. The latter I did at Well Street School. After the usual anatomical demonstration a skeleton was made of the bones. I endeavoured to preserve the head untouched, merely drawing away the fluids by placing it under an air-pump over sulphuric acid. By this means the head was rendered as hard as the skulls of the New Zealanders, but all expression was gone, of course. Seeing this would not do for exhibition, I had a model made in wax by a distinguished French artist. I then had the skeleton stuffed out to fit Bentham's own clothes, and this wax likeness fitted to the trunk. The whole was then enclosed in a mahogany case with folding glass doors, seated in his armchair, and holding in his hand his favourite walking-stick, and for some years it remained in a room of my house in Finsbury Square. But I ultimately gave it to University College, where it now is."

A Capricious Bequest of Sixpences

A curious custom has existed from time almost immemorial at St. Bartholomew's the Great, Smithfield, in the churchyard, which is the oldest in the city. Its anniversary is Good Friday, on which day the incumbent is enjoined, by the will of a lady who left a foundation for the purpose, to lay down twenty-one sixpences in a row on a particular gravestone, whence they are to be picked up by as many widows, kneeling, having first attended a sermon which is to be preached on the occasion.

Letters and Portraits in her Coffin

Many persons have a singular mode of disposing of objects for which they have too great a regard to destroy, or even order them after their death to be destroyed, and as a sort of half-measure, desire that they may be buried with them. Not long since a lady died, who being fondly attached to a brother she had lost, had his portrait, in a ponderous gilt frame (which she always carried about with her when she travelled), placed in her coffin at her death.

Actuated by a similar sentiment, Mrs. Anna Margaret Birkbeck, of Inverness Terrace (who died July 2, 1877, and whose will and two codicils, dated January, 1868, were proved on 29th of July, 1877), directs that the letters of her late daughters, of her late son, and of her late husband, both before and after her marriage, be buried with her.

Will of L. Cortusio, Jurisconsultus of Padua

We are indebted to several sources for the following testamentary document: mention is made of it by the celebrated Paolo de Castro; by Scardeon, who gives it more in detail in his "Vies des Jurisconsultes de Padoue," book ii., chap. viii.; in P. Garasse's "Doctrine Curieuse," page 912; and in Dreux de Radier's "Récréations Historiques," tome i., page 232.

By his last will and testament, the testator in question, Messer Lodovico Cortusio, forbids any of his friends and relatives to weep at his funeral. He among them who shall be found so weeping shall be disinherited; while, on the other hand, he who shall laugh most heartily shall be his principal heir and universal legatee. It would have been superfluous to address to such a man Young's apostrophe —

"Lorenzo, hast thou ever weighed a sigh,
Or studied the philosophy of tears?"

It is quite evident he appreciated their value.

The testator next prohibits that his house or the church in which he is to be buried should be hung with black, desiring, on the contrary, that it shall be strewn with flowers and green branches on the day of his funeral. While his body should be borne to the church, he ordered that music should take the place of tolling bells. All the musicians (or minstrels) of the town were to be invited to his burial, however, the number was to be limited to fifty, and were to walk with the clergy, so many to precede, and so many to follow the body, and they were to make the air ring with the sound of lutes, violins, flutes, hautboys, trumpets, tambourines, and other musical instruments; the performance was to wind up with a hallelujah as for an Easter rejoicing, and for their services each was to receive the pay of half-a-crown. The body, enclosed in a bier covered with a cloth of divers colors which were to be bright and striking, was to be carried by twelve young girls habited in green, who were to sing cheerful and lively songs. To each of them the testator bequeathed a certain sum as her dowry. Young boys and girls were to accompany the procession carrying branches or palms, and were to wear on their heads crowns of flowers, while their voices were to join in chorus with those of the bearers. All the clergy belonging to the church, attended by a hundred torch-bearers, were to precede the procession, with all the monks in the town, except those whose habit was black — the express desire of the testator being either that they should wear a light-colored costume or refrain from attending, in order not to sadden the spectacle by an appearance of mourning. The executor appointed by this singular testator was solemnly charged to carry out all these directions in their fullest detail, or was to have no participation in the beneficial clauses of the will. Ludovico Cortusio died on July 17, 1418, Festival of St. Alexis. Strange to say, his wishes were conscientiously complied with. He was buried in the church of Sta. Sophia, at Padua, the ceremony having the appearance rather of a wedding than of a funeral.

WILL OF A CONJURER

An individual exercising the calling of a conjurer at Rochdale, named Clegg, made a humorous will, in which he desired that, if he should escape hanging, and should die a natural death within two miles of Shaw Chapel, his executors, of whom he named two, should assemble threescore of the truest of his friends — not to include any woman, nor yet man whose avocations compel him to wear a white cap or an apron, nor any man in the habit of taking snuff or using tobacco. Four fiddles were to attend, and the company were to make merry and to dance. For the refreshment of the guests were to be provided sixty-two spiced buns and twenty shillings' worth of the best ale.

The body, dressed in his "roast-meat" (or Sunday) clothes, was to be laid on a bier in the midst. As each guest arrived, sprigs of gorse, holly, and rosemary were to be distributed, and each was to receive a cake; then all were to make merry for a couple of hours.

The musicians were then to play, in lively time, the tune of "Britons, strike home," while glasses of gin were being handed round to the company; after this the fiddlers, repeating the said tune, were to head the cortége, the guests to follow two-and-two, the whole being closed by the curate riding upon an ass, for which service he was to receive a fee of one guinea. No one was on any account to indulge in tears; and, as soon as the coffin had been covered over, they were to repair to the public-house at which the departed had been best known, and there to eat and drink as they pleased to the amount of thirty shillings, to be defrayed by the "estate."

No Tombstone Honors

The late Jesse H. Griffen of Yorktown, New York, who was a prominent citizen of that part of the State, drew his will on a billhead. Among other provisions were these: "I desire that my corpse be put in a plain walnut coffin and carried in an ordinary spring wagon, and that no tombstone be erected where my mortal remains are deposited. I notice that people in moderate circumstances are often distressed by expensive displays at funerals, and tombstone honors are a truer indication of the vanity of survivors than of the virtues of the dead."

Will of Philippe Bouton

Philippe Bouton, *bailli* of Dijon, dying in 1515, desired by his will that fourteen girls should be found, who, being clothed in green cloth, — that hue being sacred to hope, — should attend at his obsequies, and at all the services consequent thereon. He was buried in the church of Corberon.

Will of Charles Bouton (of Poitou)

"I, Charles Bouton, Seigneur of Fay, desire by this my will and testament, that after my death the sacristans of Louhaus shall throw over my coffin a white winding-sheet, that they shall recite the psalter before carrying it into the church; that they shall have my body carried into the Church of St. Peter of Louhaus, where it shall repose one night; that on the following morning it shall be placed on a waggon, such as those used for carting manure, and borne to my chapel of Fay and deposited within its charnel-house, there to be left without any other light than that of four small tapers, each weighing half-a-pound."

This testator does not appear to have been in any way related to the Philippe Bouton cited above: he died in 1532.

WILL OF AN ENGLISH FARMER

A Hertfordshire farmer inserted in his will his written wish that "as he was about to take a thirty years' nap, his coffin might be suspended from a beam in his barn, and by no means nailed down." He, however, permitted it to be locked, provided a hole were made in the side through which the key might be pushed, so that he might let himself out when he awoke. However, as his death took place in 1720, and in 1750 he showed no signs of waking, his nephew, who inherited his property, after allowing him one year's grace, caused a hole to be dug and had the coffin put into it.

WILL OF M. HELLOIN, JUGE DE PAIX

This gentleman, well known as a magistrate, and residing on his own landed property, close to Caen, in Normandy, France, died in the month of June, 1828. He was of eccentric habits, and of the calmest and most placid disposition. Nothing was ever known to ruffle his equanimity or to disturb the repose and tranquillity of his domestic arrangements. He lived and died unmarried, and passed his life either reclining on a couch or lying in bed. Even when exercising his judicial functions he maintained this recumbent attitude; his bedroom became his audience-chamber, and he gave judgment in a horizontal position, his body lazily stretched out, and his head thrown back on a down pillow. This luxurious life, however, did not suffice to protect him from the inevitable lot of mortals; and M. Helloin, in due time, felt that his end was not far off. Under these circumstances he made his will, apparently with the intention of proving his fidelity to his traditions, for he decreed thereby that "he should be buried at night, in his bed, and in the position in which death should surprise him — viz., with his mattress, sheets, blankets, pillows — and, in short, all that constituted the belongings of a bedstead." As there was some difficulty in carrying out such a clause, an enormous pit was dug, and the deceased was lowered into his last resting-place exactly as he had died, nothing around or about him having been altered. Boards were placed above the bedstead, in order that the earth, when filled in again, should not trouble the repose of this imperturbable Quietist.

His Ashes improved the Fishing

A German gentleman, who was a member of a New York fishing club, in his will requested his fellow-fishermen, after cremating his body, to throw his ashes into the sea on the shoals of New York Bay, where he had often fished. The will was carried out to the letter. Although it cannot be asserted that the ashes attracted the fish, the fishermen related that when they again threw out their lines where they had sprinkled the remains of their deceased friend, they made an exceptionally large catch.

Buried in his Bed

The Reverend Langton Freeman, rector of Bilton, Northamptonshire, England, desired in his will that his body should be left undisturbed on the bed whereon he died till it could no longer be kept, that it was then to be carried, bed and all, decently and privately to the summer-house in his own private garden at Whilton. The bed with the body on it was then to be wrapped in a strong double winding-sheet, and to be treated in all respects as was the body of our Lord. The doors and windows of the summer-house were then to be secured, and the building planted round with evergreens and fenced with dark-blue palings. This eccentric will was conscientiously obeyed. The fence and even the trees have now disappeared, and the summer-house is in ruins. Some years ago an entrance was effected through the roof, and the deceased was found completely mummified, without any wrappers, one arm lying down by the side, the other across the chest.

Will of a New York Spinster

A spinster of New York desired that all the money she should die possessed of, might be employed in building a church in her native city, but stipulated that her remains should be mixed up in the mortar used for fixing the first stone.

Will of a Rich Jewess

A rich Jewess residing in London died in 1794. Having all her days regretted not to have passed her life in the ancient and celebrated city illustrated by the presence and the great deeds of David, Solomon, the prophets, the Maccabees, and others, she resolved that at all events her mortal remains should await there the day of their resurrection. She accordingly ordered by her will that her body should be carried from England to Jerusalem, to be buried there. Two of her coreligionists established in London were chosen by her to accompany her body and fulfil her last wishes; these gentlemen were gratified each with a legacy of four hundred pounds to pay their expenses.

Robert Fabyan

There are some extremely curious and valuable clauses in this will which would be too long to transcribe, and probably tedious to the majority of readers. It is dated 1511. Those who wish to read it in its entirety are referred to vol. ii., "Testamenta Vetusta," page 498.

We will confine ourselves to a portion of his instructions for his "little tumbe of freestone, upon the which I will be spent liij *s*. iv *d*. att the moast; and in the face of this tumbe I will be made too plates of laten, ii figurys of a man and a woman, with x men children and vi women children; and over and above the said figurys I will be made a figure of the Fader of Heven, inclosed in a sonne; and from the man figure I will be made a rolle toward the said figure of the Fader, and in hit to be graven, ' O Pater in cœlis;' and from the figure of the woman another lyke rolle, whereyn to be graven, 'Hos tecum pascere velis;' and at the feet of the said figurys I will be graven thes ix verses folowing:

"'Preterit ista dies origo secundi
An labor, an requies; sic transit gloria mundi.
Like as the day hys cours doeth consume
And the new morrow spryngith agayn as fast,
So man and woman by naturys costume
This lyfe doo pass and last in erth ar cast
In joye and sorrowe in whiche here theyr tyme did wast
Never in oon state but in co's transitorey
Soo full of chaunge is of this worlde the glory.'

"And before upon the said tumbys border I will be written these words following:

"'Tumulus Roberti Fabyan dudum pannarius ac Aldermannus London qui obiit. . . . Fevr. . . .'"

The above directions were to be followed in the event of the testator's dying and being buried "within the Citye of London," but if buried in the church of Heydon Earnon, the grave is to be much more elaborately decorated, according to instructions further given to his executors, who can have had no sinecure, for this same alderman-draper seems to have been possessed of considerable landed and other property.

We find it throughout all these earlier wills the custom to bequeath not only beds with all their furniture, but wearing apparel, which in those days were so costly as to be considered valuable heirlooms; probably also the fashion of these articles did not undergo such rapid changes as in our own day.

An Exacting and Peculiar Will

After an eventful life as soldier, linguist, "rain-maker," Deputy Commissioner of Patents, man of affairs, and wealthy patent attorney, Robert G. Dryenforth, of Washington, D.C., died July 4, 1910. His will is one of the most unusual instruments ever offered for probate in the United States: his estate is a large one and is left to an eight-year-old foster son, Robert St. George Dryenforth, subject to conditions of a remarkable character:

The lad is to get practically the entire estate — provided he conscientiously complies with all conditions — when he reaches the age of twenty-eight. Robert St. George will be busily occupied for the intervening twenty years in complying with conditions.

Here are some of them.

He must not associate with one Jennie Dryenforth or her daughter, Rose Marie Knowlton. Should he do so, the estate goes to William H., Harold and Robert Dryenforth, who are named as executors.

The above-named executors will also share the estate in the event Robert St. George thoughtlessly dies before he reaches the given age.

The boy must be trained right from the start to shy at the wiles of women. If he must marry, he must not marry beneath him.

The will says:

"I particularly request my executors to thoughtfully and well guard my beloved son from women, and sensibly, that is, gradually,

ANCIENT, CURIOUS, AND FAMOUS WILLS

through no erratic extreme, to let him be informed and know the artful and parasitical nature of most of the unfortunate sex, and to care that he does not marry beneath him."

The lad must keep his face between the covers of a book for a great portion of these twenty years. He will become a confirmed burner of the midnight oil. Here is the programme, duly mapped out in the will:

He must be prepared to enter high school at the age of fourteen.

At the age of eighteen he must be ready to enter Harvard, there to take a special course fitting him for Oxford University.

In the meantime, the boy must be taken to see one country in Europe each year.

As soon as he graduates from Oxford, the boy is to hasten back to these shores and to enter immediately the United States Military Academy, complete the course and serve the required time in the army.

After he has well and patiently performed these preliminary tasks, the young man is then required to take up the practice of law, at which profession he may while his time away until he reaches the twenty-eighth milestone. Upon that happy and long-delayed day, the executors will take an inventory, and if the stewardship of Robert St. George has been good, he will receive talents an hundred fold.

Scattered about through the will are minor restrictions, having to do with the boy's religion and habits. The lad must be reared a Protestant Episcopalian. He will have no difficulty whatever in picking his faith, his father having attended to this detail before he departed this life.

In no event is the boy to be permitted to become a Catholic, and the executors are further charged with the duty of seeing that the late Lawyer Dryenforth's remains are not interred in a Catholic cemetery nor in Arlington.

A graduating scale of allowances for the boy's maintenance also has been carefully worked out in the will. Until he is twelve years of age Robert St. George must not overdraw an account of $50 monthly. After that age, $1000 yearly is set aside for his support and education. Later, the amount is to be increased to $1500 per year, which will help some in event Robert St. George is not immediately retained by some of the big corporations as soon as he hangs out his shingle as a lawyer.

Dame Maud De Say

Dame Maud, daughter of Guy, Earl of Warwick, widow of Geoffrey, Lord Say, Admiral of the King's Fleet, died Tuesday next after the Feast of the Apostles Simon and Jude, 1369. Her will recites:

"My body to be buried in the Church of the Friars Preachers of London, near Edmond, my loving husband; to the Friars there X pounds, and I desire that no feast be made on my funeral day, but that immediately after my decease my corpse shall be carried to burial, covered only with a linen cloth, having a red cross thereon, with two tapers, one at the head and another at the feet."

A Mother's Pathetic Affection

A lady, who was a singularly affectionate mother, lost two of her children, one aged three, the other five; their remains were carried with the usual ceremonies to the family vault, but she found it impossible to part with them, and having obtained the permission of the clergyman to have them exhumed, she had the two little coffins carried back to the house, and glass lids made to them. They were kept in a room set apart for the purpose, and remained there until her death — a period of a quarter of a century. On that event they were again buried by one of her sons, a clergyman, who, having been born long after their death, used to remark: "There was not probably another clergyman who could say he had buried two people who died before he was born."

Will of Mr. Greftulke

An individual named Greftulke, who entertained a great dread of being buried alive, added to his will this clause: "I do not wish to be buried; but desire that my body be embalmed, and placed in a coffin, the lid of which shall be glazed; also I desire it be not nailed down, so that my body may not be deprived of air and light. Ultimately it may be buried, if the law permit."

This will was proved October, 1867, and signed John Louis Greftulke.

Will of Thomas Hollis

This testator, Thomas Hollis of Cusicombe, Dorsetshire, England, ordered his corpse to be buried in one of his cornfields, ten feet below the surface, and the ground to be immediately ploughed, so that no trace of the spot might remain.

ANCIENT, CURIOUS, AND FAMOUS WILLS

WILL OF MRS. MARIA REDDING

This lady's behests are sufficiently singular to be recorded here: "If," she writes, "I should die away from Branksome, I desire that my remains, after being duly placed in the usual coffins (*i.e.* first a leaden and then an elm one), be enclosed in a plain deal box, and conveyed by goods train to Poole. Let no mention be made of the contents, as the conveyance will then not be charged more for than an ordinary package. From Poole station let it be brought in a cart to Branksome tower, and it will be found the easiest way to get the coffin out of the house will be to take out one of the dining-room windows." This will was probated in 1870.

THE WILL OF THE DOWAGER COUNTESS OF SANDWICH

This will provides against those useless inventions, which only serve to aggravate the grief of the survivors, and to swell the extortionate charges of the upholsterers of death. She therefore forbids "all grotesque paraphernalia, desiring only to be buried quietly and decently, with no scarfs, hatbands, or other excuses for fraud and cheating."

HORROR OF DARKNESS

A Vienna millionnaire seemed to have a horror of darkness, for he provided that not only the vault in which his body was to be placed should be lighted by electricity, but the coffin should be similarly illumined.

WILL OF LA DUCHESSE D'OLONNE

This lady, whose life was full of eccentricities, seems to have been determined to signalize her departure from the world by the singularity of her testamentary dispositions.

She desired in her will, probated in 1776, that her body should be carried into the principality of Lux, situated in Basse Navarre, and about two hundred and fifty miles from Paris. So far there was nothing very extraordinary; but she also desired to be followed by a very long procession, which was to consist of six mourning-coaches draped with black, for the family and the ecclesiastics, and of two hundred persons bearing torches, who were to receive a crown a day. The cortège was to walk at a solemn pace, and not to make more than five leagues per day, and at every five leagues, or as near that distance as it was possible to find a convenient resting-place, a funeral service was to be celebrated before the procession started again, and every church where such service should be held was to be hung with black.

What the cost of all this ceremony amounted to may be computed by the cost of the carriages alone, the hire of which amounted to eighteen thousand francs.

By another article in her will, the duchess devises liberal donations and annuities to her servants, proportioned to their services, but at the same time she sends them into exile; for she assigns to each a fixed residence at a certain distance from Paris, so that they shall be all separated from each other, and she specifies that they can only receive such annuities in the locality appointed them, and on condition that they shall make that their residence, because, as she alleges, she does not wish them to congregate together, and talk about her affairs and her character.

She left fifteen thousand francs to the poet Robbé, whom she lodged and supported in Paris, though it is difficult to discover on what grounds she patronized a man of such mediocre merit.

Lady Nicotine

A young lady of Kentucky exhibited a depth of sentiment rarely equalled, when she directed in her will that tobacco should be planted over her grave, that the weed, nourished by her dust, might be smoked by her bereaved lovers.

Forget John Underwood

On the 6th of May, 1735, was buried at Wittesca, Mr. John Underwood, of Lexington. The body was lowered into the grave at five o'clock, and as soon as the prayers were concluded a marble tablet was fixed at the extremity of the grave, bearing this inscription:

> Non omnis moriar,
> JOHN UNDERWOOD
> May 6, 1735.

All the detail of the interment was in strict accordance with the testamentary prescriptions of the deceased, and proceeded as follows: As soon as the grave was filled up and covered with turf, the six friends who, by his desire, had attended on the occasion, sang the last stanza of the twentieth ode of the second book of Horace:

"Absint inani funere nœniæ,
Luctusque turpes et querimoniæ;
Compesce clamorem, ac sepulcri
Mitte supervacuos honores."

No bell was tolled; no relative was present; the bier was painted green, and the body was laid on it dressed in ordinary clothes; beneath the head was placed a copy of Horace, at his feet a Milton, on his right hand a small Greek Bible, with his name on the binding in gilt letters, on the left a smaller edition of Horace, with the inscription "Musis amicus, J.U.," and under his shoulders Bentley's Horace. When the ceremony was concluded, his friends returned to his house, where his sister awaited them, and all sat down to an elegant supper; after it was over, the company joined in singing the thirty-first ode of the first book of Horace:

"Quid dedicatum poscit Apollinem vates?"

Then they drank gayly for some time, but retired at eight o'clock. Mr. John Underwood bequeathed about fifty thousand dollars to his sister, on condition that she should carry out faithfully the conditions of his will. He left $50 to each of his friends, requesting them not to wear mourning; then came the singular directions, which were carried out as above, and the will concluded thus: ". . . This done, I request my friends to separate, after drinking cheerfully together, and to think no more of John Underwood."

WITHOUT POMP OR VAINGLORY

Joan, Lady Bergavenny, whose will is dated 10th of January, 1434, wills "that my body *be kept unburied* in the place where it happeneth me to die, unto the time my 'maygne' (household) be clothed in black, my hearse, my chare, and other convenable purveyance made, and then to be carried unto the place of my burying before rehearsed, with all the worship that ought to be done unto a woman of mine estate, which God knoweth well proceedeth not of no pomp or vain glory, that I am set in for my body, but for a memorial and remembrance of my soul to my kin, friends, servants, and all other. . . ."

Desired Beautiful Scenery

Lord Camelford, the famous duellist, wrote a codicil to his will, by which he desired that his body "should not be buried within city walls or the haunts of men, but should be removed to a far-distant spot, where the surrounding scenery might smile upon his remains." The Lake of St. Lampierre, in Switzerland, was the spot selected. On the borders of this lake was a sloping bank marked by three trees. The testator designated the centre one as that under which he had passed many hours meditating on the mutability of human affairs, and he requested that this might be carefully removed, his body interred beneath it, and the tree replaced. These, his last wishes, were faithfully executed.

Will of Richard-sans-Peur

This brave Duke of Normandy had prepared his tomb, many years before his death, in the Abbey of Fécamp, and ordered that his burial should be conducted with the utmost simplicity. So great was his humility that he expressed his wishes as follows: "Je veulx estre enseveli devant l'huys de l'église, afin d'être *coneulqué* (trodden under foot) de tous les entrans dans l'église." These, his last wishes, were executed; but some years after an Abbot of Fécamp, considering that "à si digne personnage plus décente sépulture appartenait," had his body exhumed and buried in front of the altar.

Fifteen Maidens with Torches

François de la Palu Varembon, Seigneur de Beaumont sur Vingeanne, in Burgundy, made, in 1456, a will by which he testifies his objection to lugubrious colors at his interment; desiring that fifteen maidens of the very poorest of his vassals, clothed in white cloth at the expense of his estate, each wearing a scarlet hood and carrying a torch of three pounds' weight, should walk in procession before the body, and that his heirs shall also wear white at his funeral and at every successive anniversary of his death. He further orders that four wax candles, of twenty-five pounds' weight each, shall be placed at the corners of his coffin.

Body carried to a Café

One September afternoon, in 1874, an empty hearse was seen standing at about four o'clock at the entrance of the salons of the

Café Riche, Rue Le Peletier. On inquiry it was found that a frequenter of this famous establishment had inserted in his will a clause to this effect:

"I desire that on the day of my burial I may be carried round by the Rue Le Peletier, to visit once more the table where I have spent so many of the pleasantest hours of my life."

As we have seen, this singular wish was respected by the survivors of the testator.

BARBER NOT WANTED

The will, dated January 9th, 1873, of Mr. Richard Christopher Carrington, late of Churt, near Farnham, Surrey, England, astronomer, who died on the previous November 27th, was proved by Mrs. Esther Clarke Carrington, the mother of the deceased, the personal estate being sworn under £20,000. The testator desired to be buried at a depth of between ten and twelve feet in the grounds surrounding his own freehold house at Churt, at an expense not exceeding £5, without any service being read over his grave, and without any memorial being erected to his memory; and he directed that after his death neither his chin be shaved nor his shirt changed. He bequeathed to the Royal Society and the Royal Astronomical Society £2000 Three Per Cent. Consolidated Bank Annuities each, both free of legacy duty.

YOUNG LADY'S PICTURESQUE FUNERAL

A somewhat unusual funeral cortège astonished the inhabitants of Brighton, England, traversing it from the west end to the railway station, one morning in the autumn of 1879. Concerning it some very romantic, highly imaginative, but somewhat incorrect rumors gained currency. The funeral was that of a young lady, named Ellen Elizabeth Parren, the daughter of William Parren, Esq., of Beckenham, in Kent, who had arrived in Brighton that day week, on a visit to her uncle, Captain Dunhill, of Brunswick Road. Though delicate, she was thought to be in her usual health; but on the following Monday she died somewhat suddenly. The deceased young lady, being a great favorite both in her own family and amongst her friends, it was decided that the obsequies should not partake of that gloomy and melancholy character which is the usually accepted mode of burial, but that it should be more inspiring and hopeful in its tone. The handsome funeral car was drawn by four grays, in the place of black horses, and the funeral coaches were represented by three landaus, each drawn by a pair of grays. The coffin, having been placed upon the car, was covered by a handsome white-and-gold pall, upon which were laid a number of beautiful wreaths of white flowers. The cortège as thus arranged left Brunswick Road, Hove, for the railway station, and then proceeded to Croydon. Here, the funeral procession having been rearranged and augmented by two other landaus drawn by pairs of grays and a number of private carriages, proceeded to Norwood Cemetery, where the remains were laid in the grave, the service being performed by two Nonconformist ministers, the Rev. Mr. Eldridge and the Rev. Mr. Jenkinson. The coffin was of polished oak, with plated silver ornaments and inscription plate, the latter having upon it the following: "Ellen Elizabeth, daughter of Wm. Parren, Esq., died August 25, 1879, aged 25."

To curtail Funeral Bills

The will of Mr. Francis Offley Martin, formerly of Lincoln's Inn, but late of 89 Onslow Gardens, one of the Charity Commissioners for England and Wales, who died on December 4th, 1878, was proved by William Smith, the sole executor, the personal estate being sworn under £7000. The testator, in his directions for his funeral, provides that no scarfs or hatbands be used or given away on the occasion either to the clergyman or any other person, as he wishes to break through the custom of running up funeral bills; and he declares that this prohibition is to extend also to gloves.

Full Dress Uniform

The late Surgeon-Major Wyatt, C.B., of the Coldstream Guards, who did good service to suffering humanity in Paris after the siege in 1871, desired in his will to be buried in the full-dress uniform of the regiment in which he had passed the greater part of his useful and honorable life. A Bible presented to him by his wife was to be placed in his coffin, and the horses used at his funeral were not to be "decorated" — plumed and draped, we presume — in any manner; the mutes and other attendants were not to wear hatbands or scarfs; each person attending his funeral was to wear in token of mourning only a black band of medium width — crape for relatives and cloth for friends; the gloves were to be black;

but each person in the procession was to wear a camellia or other white flower in his buttonhole, as it was the worthy surgeon-major's wish that the ceremony "should be as free as possible from all gloomy associations, and to be considered more as an occasion for rejoicing than for mourning." Consonant with this leading idea was the expressed wish that no kind of widow's cap or weeds should be worn by his relict, and no particle of crape should appear on the garments of his relations. Side by side with this, publication was given to a will announcing the desire of another testator to be buried with a hearse surmounted by sable ostrich-plumes, with horses duly *panachés* and caparisoned, mutes and bearers and "pages," scarfs and flowing hatbands and brazen-tipped staves, and all the rest of that elaborate panoply of woe which finds so much favor in the eyes, and affords such comfortable entries in the books, of old-established undertakers. *Quot homines, tot sententiæ*, thus every man seems to be of a different mind concerning the ordering of his funeral.

Under the Oak Trees

Sir Charles Hastings requested that his body might "not be coffined, but swathed in any coarse stuff that would hold it together, and then buried in a spot designated by him. That the ground should then be planted with acorns, so that he might render a last service to his country by contributing to nourish some good English oaks."

An Abnormal Burial

Lord Truro, of England, whose residence was at Falconhurst, on the summit of Shooter's Hill, afforded a novel example of funeral simplicity. On the demise of Lady Truro, Lord Truro having, according to her desire, placed the body in a lightly constructed box, so that the process of decay might not be arrested, buried it himself in a grave dug in the lawn fronting the house, at a spot she had selected for the purpose. The grave is about four feet deep, and a marble monument has been raised upon it.

Protected his Whiskers

Valentine Tapley, owner of the longest beard in the world, died Saturday, April 2, 1910, at his home, Spencerburg, Pike County, Missouri. He was eighty years old. It is said that when Lincoln was a candidate for the Presidency, Mr. Tapley, who was a Democrat, made a vow that if Lincoln was elected he would never cut his beard. The length of his beard was 12½ feet for several years prior to his death. This is said to be longer than any other beard known. Mr. Tapley took great pride in his whiskers, and wore them wrapped in silk and wound about his body. During the latter part of his life he was apprehensive his grave would be robbed for his whiskers, and in his will he made provision for a tomb of extra strength to guard against this. Mr. Tapley declined several offers to exhibit his beard. He was a large owner of Pike County farming land, and died wealthy.

DASTARDS AND FOOLS

In France, not long ago, died an eccentric Frenchman who declared the French to be "a nation of dastards and fools." For that reason, he devised the whole of his fortune to the people of London, and directed that his body be thrown into the sea a mile from the English coast. An attempt was made to have him adjudged insane when he made the will, but it failed.

RECIPE AND RESTITUTION

Another Frenchman directed that a new cooking recipe should be pasted on his tomb every day; and still another Frenchman, a lawyer, left fifty thousand dollars to a lunatic asylum, declaring that it was simply an act of restitution to the clients who were insane enough to employ his services.

TO THE FOUR WINDS

A queer request was made by a German who died in Pittsburgh, Pennsylvania, in 1887. By his will, he directed that his body should be cremated and the ashes forwarded to the German Consul at New York, who was to deliver them to the captain of the steamship *Elbe*. When in mid-ocean, the captain was to request a passenger to dress himself in nautical costume, and, ascending with the funeral urn to the topmast, to scatter the ashes to the four winds of heaven. And these strange directions were literally carried out.

ANCIENT, CURIOUS, AND FAMOUS WILLS 157

Their Ashes into the Mississippi River

During the last twenty-five years, the great Eads Bridge, which spans the Mississippi River at St. Louis, Missouri, has been favored as a spot by those who desired that their mortal ashes should be scattered to the winds. On more than one occasion, could have been seen unusual gatherings on the bridge, and after certain religious formalities, human ashes have been deposited in the river.

The latest ceremony of this kind occurred on Sunday, January 29, 1911: Joel Braunmiller, an eccentric old bachelor, lived alone in a large house on his farm, eight miles north of Maryville, Missouri. He died recently, and left a large estate to his brothers and sisters. The following clause was contained in his will:

"I direct that after my death, my body be shipped by express to St. Louis, Mo., and there cremated and my ashes strewn to the winds from the south side of the Eads Bridge over the river."

On the date named, Charles R. Lupton, an undertaker of St. Louis, with an urn containing the ashes of Mr. Braunmiller, leaned over the south parapet of the bridge, tipped the urn gradually, and let the ashes fall into the river. The wind, whirling about the piers and buttresses of the great bridge, caught up the ashes and flung them in every direction. When the urn had been emptied, it, too, was dropped into the river.

Mr. S. H. Kemp, Cashier of the Maryville National Bank, who was a close friend of Mr. Braunmiller, and also the executor of his will, stood close beside the undertaker to see that the ceremony was carried out according to the wishes of the deceased. There were also present relatives of the deceased, who had come from various parts of the United States.

Ruling Passion Strong in Death

The wife of Mr. Fisher Dilke, of England, brother-in-law to Sir Peter Wentworth, one of the regicide judges, was interred in the year 1660 in a very singular way.

Her husband caused her coffin to be made of the wooden palings of his barn, and bargaining hard with the sexton beat him down from " a shilling " (the usual sum) to a groat (fourpence); he avoided the expense of bearing by begging four of his friends and neighbors to discharge this office. Having assembled them he read to them a chapter of the book of Job, and then distributed to them the contents of a bottle of Burgundy and sixpennyworth of spiced cakes. As there was no ecclesiastic present, Dilke himself, who acted as chief mourner, took up the spade, and as soon as the coffin was lowered, threw earth upon it, repeating the usual words, "Dust to dust," etc., adding, "Lord, now lettest thou," etc. Then the party returned home.

5

MISCELLANEOUS

" Learn to live well, or fairly make your will;
  You've played, and loved, and eat, and drank your fill:
Walk sober off; before a sprightlier age
  Comes titt'ring on, and shoves you from the stage."

HER ADORABLE NOSE

A certain individual, one of the Vanderbilts, left to a lady a bequest in these words: "I supplicate Miss B. to accept my whole fortune, too feeble an acknowledgment of the inexpressible sensations which the contemplation of her adorable nose has produced on me."

REMEMBERED THE POLICE STATION

Not long ago a will was contested in New York, because the testatrix had bequeathed a grand piano, several oil paintings, and five pieces of Japanese pottery to a police station. The protesting heir won the case, and there was a reversion of these art treasures to the natural heirs.

ALL SMILED SWEETLY

A certain will reads, "to that amiable young lady, Miss Blank, who smiles so sweetly in the street when we meet, I give Twenty-Five Hundred Dollars." Now in the Blank family, there were six sisters; they all claimed to be "the amiable young lady," but which of them got the legacy, history sayeth not.

A SALUTATION DIRECTED

Pursuant to the will of Sir John Salter, who died in the year 1605, and who was a good benefactor to the Company, the beadles and servants of the Worshipful Company of Salters are to attend at St. Magnus' Church, London Bridge, in the first week in October, and knock upon his gravestone, with sticks or staves, three times each person, and say, "How do you do, Brother Salter? I hope you are well."

ANCIENT, CURIOUS, AND FAMOUS WILLS

No Underclothes in Winter

A crabbed old German professor, who died at Berlin in 1900, entertaining a great dislike for his sole surviving relative, left his property to him, but on the absolute condition that he should always wear white linen clothes at all seasons of the year, and should not supplement them in winter by extra undergarments.

Had $100, gave away $700,000

A singular will was that of Miss Cora Johnson, who resided in an apartment at No. 819 Beacon Street, Boston, and who died in September, 1910, at a hospital in that city. The value of her entire possessions, when inventoried, was found not to exceed $100, and she was buried by friends; yet, by her will, she created bequests and legacies amounting to $700,000; she claimed that she was entitled to a large fortune from the estate of an unnamed person living in New York.

Miss Johnson, it is claimed, never revealed the name of this person, and even her attorney, who drew her will, was not acquainted with it; all she disclosed was that she expected a large estate from a wealthy, elderly woman, who made her will in her favor and became insane, and was in a sanitarium in New York, and this will could not be changed by reason of the insanity of the testator. Evidently, she had a firm conviction that the estate must reach her, in any event.

That part of the will referring to the promised millions reads:

"Whereas it is possible that at the time of my decease I shall not be the owner of property sufficient in amount to pay the foregoing bequests, and

"Whereas I have been credibly informed and believe that there is in existence a certain will made by a person now an inhabitant of the city and state of New York by which will certain property is devised and bequeathed to me, and

"Whereas I have been credibly informed and believe that in said will it is provided, that in case I shall die before the maker of said will, the property therein bequeathed and devised to me, shall pass to and be paid over and delivered to the persons, corporations and objects which I shall in my last will name, select and appoint:

"Now, therefore, I do hereby exercise any and all powers of appointment contained in and given to me by any such will by any person if any such will there be, desiring and intending that whether or not I survive the maker of said will, the persons, corporations and institutions hereinbefore named shall be benefited in accordance with and to the extent of the terms of this instrument, either as legatees hereunder in case of my survival of the maker of said will, or as my appointees thereunder in case of my predecease."

His Earthly Happiness

An old bachelor, on dying, left the whole of his property to three ladies to whom he had proposed marriage, and who had refused him. The reason for this bequest, he stated, was that by their refusal, "to them I owe all my earthly happiness."

Must Pay For Her Drinks

Mr. Davis, of Clapham, England, left the sum of 5s. "to Mary Davis, daughter of Peter Delaport, which is sufficient to enable her to get drunk for the last time at my expense."

Imaginary Wife and Children

A Mr. George, resident of one of the British Colonies, who died possessed of a large property, contrived to puzzle the brains of his executors by imagining and inserting in his will two heirs who had no existence but in his brain. After bequeathing his worldly goods in the usual form, he named as his residuary legatees a son and daughter, whom he stated to be his children by a beautiful Circassian he had married at Plymouth in St. Peter's Church. He added that, though the lady had subsequently eloped with a parson, he bore no ill-will to the children, whom she had taken with her, but should be glad to think they would be traced and apprised of their good fortune.

The whole romance turned out to be a complete fabrication, but not until it had severely tried the patience of the executors.

This Foolish World a Dream

Harris Bletzer, who died on August 21, 1910, at his home, 35 Moore Street, Brooklyn, N.Y., worth about $10,000, had pretty definite ideas as to how he wanted his money to go after his death, and he also had come to the conclusion that, after all, this was a foolish world and a dream, so he wrote down in Hebrew his philosophical conclusions and had it properly attested as his last will and testament. This remarkable document has been translated for Surrogate Ketcham's benefit, and it has been offered for probate. Mr. Bletzer wants his wife to have all his money for her lifetime, and she isn't to be dictated to by anybody, either, as to what she does with it, the testator says, for she worked for it as hard as her husband did. But he says that when their two daughters, Sarah and Mazie, get married, their mother can spend $2000 upon each of them, and it shall be considered as their share of their father's estate. After the widow dies, then the money is to be divided among the sons. The reason for his opinion of life is given in language not quite grammatical, as follows:

"Lying in my bed, with my weak strength, and figured out with a clear mind and a clear conscience, man going through his life in this foolish world; so I have decided, with my full reason, that the entire world is a dream. The years run by and the day of leave-taking is expected, and I have decided to declare what shall be done with my little wealth which I have accumulated by my sweat through my hard work."

It paid to be Heavy

A Scotchman left to each of his daughters her weight in one-pound bank notes. By this provision, one daughter, being stouter than the other, received $30,000 more than her sister.

Opposed to Mustaches

Mr. Fleming, an upholsterer, of Pimlico, by his will, proved in 1869, left £10 each to the men in his employ — those who did not wear mustaches; those who persisted in wearing them to have £5 only.

Must be Tall

The county of Yorkshire in England is noted for its tall men, and a resident of that county left his entire estate to those of his descendants who were not less than six feet four inches in height.

Newspaper Reading Prohibited

A Vienna banker made a bequest to his nephew with the stipulation that "he shall never, on any occasion, read a newspaper, his favorite occupation."

A Beam and Bell

The will of Reginald atte Pette, of Stockbury, dated 12th of January, 1456, is in part as follows: "Item, I bequeath toward the making of a new beam in the Church of Stockbury, xiii *s.* iiii *d.*; towards a new bell called trebyll vi *s.* viii *d.*; towards the work of the new isle in the aforesaid Church iv marcs; and towards the making of a new window there xx *s.* Witnesses, John Petytt, Nich. Cowstede, Adomar atte Pette, Thomas atte Pette, Peter atte Pette, Christopher, Clerk of the Parish there, Vicar of Stockbury."

Must become an Actress

A maiden lady over fifty years of age, with a strong aversion to all theatrical amusements, was scandalized by being put down for a legacy in the will of a facetious friend, who attached the condition that within six months of the testator's death the legatee obtain an engagement at a theatre and must perform there for one whole week.

Will sustained, Codicil rejected

A Protestant clergyman, the Reverend John Markhouse, aged 70, bequeathed £12,000 for the purpose of establishing a school for illegitimate children only, at Bradchurch, Hants, England. He added a codicil providing for educational expenses by a further sum of £8000. The disappointed relatives appealed against the will; but the court, strangely enough, decided in favor of the will and against the codicil, on consideration of the plea that towards the close of his life he had appeared eccentric enough to justify the conclusion that he was not of sound mind when he wrote the latter. Nevertheless the sequitur seems logical enough.

Music

An Englishman, Richard Lane, otherwise Tomson, by his will, dated 24th of July, 1619, gave to one of the deacons of the Cathedral Church of Hereford 40*s.* yearly forever, to prick fairly into books, songs, and church service, for the use of the same church; and upon his coming every half-year for his wages, he should bring with him the sub-chanter of the choir, who would show to him who had the payment of the money, what he had done in that business the half-year last past; and if he should be found negligent therein, then the payment for that time should be given to twelve poor men the Saturday next following.

Repeat the Catechism on Christmas Day

Robert Barber, Cambridgeshire, England, by will, dated 21st of June, 1818, gave unto the minister of Haslingfield and the tenant of the farm, on which Mr. Wallace then lived, £20 in trust, to be placed out at interest, upon good security, and the interest thereof to be by them given every year after his decease unto that child under the age of thirteen years, who should most perfectly repeat the Catechism, on Christmas Day.

A Plain Case

The will of E. J. Halley was filed for probate in October last at Memphis, Tennessee. It would seem from attendant circumstances that Mr. Halley was not a teetotaler, and that prohibition is not entirely effective in Tennessee.

Mr. Halley was the foster son of a lady known as "Joanna Madden, the hermit": contrary to the rule in such matters, this hermit left a large estate, consisting of gold and silver snugly put away in her home; a squad of policemen escorted the money to a local bank; this Mr. Halley received, but he did not live long to enjoy it; but it is reported, however, that he did enjoy it while he lived. Death came, and by his will, duly executed, he left the estate to schoolmates, nurses, favorite baseball players, deputy sheriffs, and a few orphan asylums, for good measure; with some of the legatees he was not acquainted. Among other provisions in this highly interesting testament, may be recited the following:

"To the nurse who kindly removed a pink monkey from the foot of my bed, $5000."

"To the cook at the hospital who removed snakes from my broth, $5000."

The heirs at law reached the conclusion that too high a value had been put upon these services and temporary friendships, and filed a bill to enjoin the payment of the legacies.

Penchant for Paper-knives

M. Charles Asselineau, a well-known Frenchman, died in 1874. His estate appears to have consisted largely of books and paper-knives. These he disposed of by will in a bequest to a relative. He had as many paper-knives as Clapisson had whistles or Buffon butterflies, and they were all more or less remarkable by reason of the celebrity of the donors, or former owners, and the unique inscriptions they bore. Those who are interested may find amusement, if not recreation, in an attempt to ascertain the point and meaning of some of the phrases.

On one given him by Victor Hugo we read: "Madame, il fait grand vent et j'ai tué six loups."

On that of Ponsard: "Quand la borne est franchie, il n'y a plus de limites."

On that of Émile Augier: "Ce qui tombe au fossé, Madame, est au soldat." And so on.

In this collection are paper-knives that had belonged to Béranger, Bauville, Autran, Camille Doucet, and many other French writers of fame, each carefully enclosed in a case of its own and labelled.

An Odd Lot

There is a well-authenticated case of a wealthy man leaving his riches to deserving old maids, but he let his own daughters pine in single blessedness for want of portions. There was also an individual who desired to set up a lifeboat, compelling his boys to "paddle their own canoe," and there is yet another testator who, when death approached, bestowed his estate for the planting of a botanical garden, leaving his daughters to fade as wallflowers, and his sons to go to seed in penury; and these testamentary schemes were upheld, notwithstanding the adage that "Charity begins at home."

A Butcher made Happy

An old Parisian lady residing in the Rue Fontaine St. Georges, left by will the whole of her fortune to her butcher. Its amount was invested in rentes, and produced $7500 a year.

The butcher was in no way related to her, did not even know her by sight, neither had she ever seen him. As the testatrix had no heirs either direct or collateral, and no relations, the will was not disputed, and the butcher glided quite comfortably into his new position.

He used "Plain English"

The last will and testament of Mr. Daniel Martinett, of Calcutta, in the East Indies.

"In the name of God, I, Daniel Martinett, of the town of Calcutta, being in perfect mind and memory, though weak of body, make this my last Will and Testament in manner and form following. . . . To avoid Latin phrases, as it is a tongue I am not well versed in, 'I shall speak in plain English.'

"First. In the most submissive manner I recommend my soul to Almighty God, &c.

"Secondly. Now as to worldly concerns, in the following manner: — As to this fulsome carcase having already seen enough of worldly pomp, I desire nothing relative to it to be done, only its being stowed away in my old green chest, to avoid expense; for as I lived profusely, I die frugally.

"Thirdly. The undertaker's fees come to nothing, as I won them from him at a game of billiards, in the presence of Mr. Thomas Morrice and William Perkes, at the said William Perkes' house, in February last. I furthermore request, not only as it is customary, but as I sincerely believe the prayers of the good availeth, and are truly consistent with decency, that the Rev. Mr. Henry Butler read the prayers which are customary at burials, and also preach a sermon on Sunday next after my decease, taking his text from Solomon, "All is vanity." In consideration of which, over and above his fees, I bestow upon him all my hypocrisy, which he wants as a modern good man; but as my finances are low, and cannot conveniently discharge his fees, I hope he will please accept the will for the deed.

"Fourthly. To Henry Vansittart, Esq., Governor of Bengal, as an opulent man, I leave the discharge of all such sums of money (the whole not exceeding 300 rupees) that I shall stand indebted to indigent persons in the town of Calcutta.

"Fifthly. To Mr. George Grey, Secretary to the Presidency, I bequeath all my sincerity.

"Sixthly. To Mr. Simon Drose, Writer to the Secretary's office, all my modesty.

"Seventhly. To Mr. Henry Higgenson, also of the Secretary's office, all the thoughts I hope I shall die possessed of.

"Eighthly. To Mr. Thomas Forbes, all the worldly assurance which I had when I had taken a cheerful glass, though in fact a doleful cup.

"Ninthly. My wearing apparel, furniture, books, and everything else I die possessed of, I bequeath to them who stand most in need of them, leaving it to the discretion of my executor, Mr. Edward Gulston, excepting the things after mentioned: — Unto Capt. Edward Menzies, late commander of the ship *Hibernia*, I give my sea quadrant, invented by Hadley, and made by Howell, in the Strand; likewise my two-feet Gunter's scale. These I give him because I believe he knows the use of them better than any commander out of this port.

"My silver watch and buckles I give to Mr. Edward Gulston, in lieu of his sincere friendship to me during our acquaintance; and these I hope he will not part with, unless his necessities require it, which I sincerely hope will never be the case.

"Also to Mr. Thomas Forbes I give my gold ring with a blue stone set therein, which he may exchange for a mourning one if he pleases.

"I give my Bible and Prayer-book to the Rev. Mr. Henry Butler.

"My sword, with a cut-and-thrust blade, I give to Capt. Ransulie Knox, as I verily believe he not only knows how, but has courage to use it, and I hope only in a good cause.

"As I have lived the make-game of a modern gentleman, being a butt for envy and a mark for malice, by acting a little out of the common road, though, thank God, never in a base way, I hope I may die in sincere love and charity to all men, forgiving all my persecutors, as I hope for forgiveness from my Creator.

"As it lies not in my power to bequeath anything to my relations at home, I shall say nothing concerning them, as they have not for these six years past concerned themselves about me; excepting that I heartily wish them all well, and that my brothers and sisters may make a more prosperous voyage through this life than I have done.

"(Signed) DANIEL MARTINETT."

This original and singular will was deposited in the Registry Office at Calcutta, Bengal, after the death of the testator, which took place in 1825: the governor of Bengal generously accepted the equivocal legacy of debts and paid them. Mr. Martinett was an officer of the well-known East India Company.

HAD A CLAMOROUS TONGUE

Mr. Lewis Evan Morgan, an old Welsh gentleman, died at Gwyllgyth, in Glamorganshire, in the ninety-eighth year of his age. His will is neatly comprised in few words very much to the purpose: "I give to my old faithful servant, Ester Jones, the whole that I am possessed of either in personal property, land, or otherwise. She is a tolerable good woman, but would be much better if she had not so clamorous a tongue. She has, however, one great virtue, which is a veil to all her foibles — strict honesty."

ANCIENT, CURIOUS, AND FAMOUS WILLS 167

HATED LAWYERS

General Hawley, who drew up his own will "because of the hatred and suspicion with which I regard all lawyers," left "£100 to my servant Elizabeth Buskett because she has proved herself a useful and agreeable handmaid." The rest of his belongings he bequeathed to his adopted son, but provided that, if he should be foolish enough to marry the said Elizabeth, neither was to inherit a farthing.

He desired his executors to consign his "carcase" to any place they pleased, and if the parish priest should claim a burial fee, they were to "let the puppy have it."

A PEDLER AND HIS DOG

In the window at the west end of the nave at St. Mary's, Lambeth, in London, may be seen a singular group representing a pedler with a pack on his back followed by a dog. Its age is not known, but it was there at the end of the sixteenth century. It is connected with a piece of land called Pedler's Acre, anciently known as Church Hopys, which is entered in the parish register as bequeathed by a person unknown. A tradition preserved in the locality states that this isthmus was given to the parish to hold as long as the representation of himself and his dog was preserved in the church window.

HIS BROTHERS, WASHINGTON AND BONAPARTE

A resident of an Eastern State, who died recently, reflects in his will that he was shunned by his relatives, "who cannot, now that I am dying, do too much for my comfort." But the testator, one Dr. Wagner, takes on these relations a ghastly revenge. To his brother, Napoleon Bonaparte, he bequeathed his left arm and hand; to another brother, George Washington, his right arm and hand; and to others his legs, nose, ears, etc. Further, the testator leaves a thousand dollars for the dismembering of his body.

WILL WRITTEN ON A DOOR

An eccentric testator, having been told that so long as the proper formalities required by the law of wills were complied with it was immaterial whether the said will were written on paper, parchment, canvas, or wood, elected to write his on his door.

The executors had therefore no choice but to have the door unscrewed from its hinges and carried into court for probate before it could be administered. The author has not been able to locate the court in which this rather weighty will was probated, but its existence is well authenticated.

On a Card torn from a Freight Car

A strange document was recently filed as a will in Pittsburgh, Pennsylvania. Robert J. McElroy, after being fatally injured by a freight train, scribbled on a card torn from a freight car: "Mary, all that is mine is thine." The will left an estate of $5200 to his wife. After writing the will, McElroy signed the letter "R," but was unable to finish, and other trainmen completed the signature. McElroy died on June 12, 1910.

His Will on Wrapping-paper

Joseph Dwyer of Weymouth, Massachusetts, died in October, 1910. His will was probated in the Norfolk County Court at Dedham. This will was unusual in that it was written on a piece of grocer's brown wrapping-paper. Under it he gave to his wife an estate valued at $50,000. The will was held to be valid.

Will on a Collar Box

Nicholas Zimmer was a passenger on the steamer, *Kaiser Wilhelm der Grosse*, on a voyage from a European port to the United States, in October, 1910.

In mid-ocean, he mysteriously disappeared and undoubtedly jumped overboard. He was last seen on October 1, 1910, and his non-appearance at meals the following day led to a search of his cabin. Under a steamer rug was found a collar box, on the lid of which was written his last will and testament. A search of his papers disclosed that he was sixty years of age and an American.

During the voyage, he had spoken to many of his fellow-passengers, and had made friends with some of the stewards. He had in no wise acted strangely.

The will written on the lid of the collar box bequeathed seven hundred dollars in cash and ten thousand dollars in securities to his wife. This amount of cash, and the securities, were found in the box. When the steamer reached her dock, the government

ANCIENT, CURIOUS, AND FAMOUS WILLS 169

officials boarded the vessel, received the box and forwarded it to Mrs. Zimmer.

THREE-WORD WILL INVALID

Recently, the Supreme Court of Appeals of Virginia rejected the will of the late George T. Smith, of Richmond, which was composed of three words, "Everything is Lou's," in the suit of Samuel H. Smith, appellant, against Loula G. Smith.

These three words were written on a page of a book issued by the Southern Railroad Company to its employees for keeping records on trains.

The court held that such an instrument was not entitled to probate.

MAN MUST DRESS IN FEMALE ATTIRE

Money is so generally welcome that it is hardly conceivable that a legacy in cash would ever be refused. Occasionally, however, as a result of the absurdity or harshness of the conditions attached to legacies, substantial bequests of this kind have been declined. An Englishman refused a legacy of two hundred pounds because it was stipulated that before receiving it he must walk down the most important street of a fashionable summer resort (Brighton) "dressed in female attire."

A LION SERMON

Sir John Gayer, a citizen of London, and lord mayor upwards of 200 years ago, left by will some money to provide for a sermon, which is preached at the Church of St. Katharine Cree, Leadenhall Street, every October, in commemoration of his being saved from a lion on the coast of Africa, in answer to prayer.

WHAT'S IN A NAME

A gentleman named Furstone of Alton Hampshire, England, about to make his will, and having no family, left seven thousand pounds to any man legitimately bearing the name of Furstone, who should discover and marry a female Furstone. If the marriage should result in children, the sum was to descend to the male offspring, if any, or to any child or children of the opposite sex who should, after marriage, retain the name.

Would not speak to the Legatee

In 1772, John Edmunds, Esq., of Monmouth, England, bequeathed a fortune of upwards of twenty thousand pounds to one Mills, a day laborer, residing near Monmouth. Mr. Edmunds, who had so handsomely provided for this man, would not speak to or see him while he lived.

Only our Saviour could demand It

Recently a cynical old man in a Western town died, who in his will devised all his property to that man in the community who could prove that he was a Christian. Then a definition of a Christian was given, which would exclude every one who had lived on earth, except the Saviour himself: the will was promptly set aside and the property given to the legal heirs.

To throw Dice for Bibles

A dissenting minister bequeathed a sum of money to his chapel at St. Ives, to provide "six Bibles every year, for which six men and six women are to throw dice on Whit Tuesday after the morning service, the minister kneeling the while at the south end of the communion table, and praying God to direct the luck to His glory."

To a Hero or his Mistresses

A somewhat puzzling task devolved upon a real or imaginary body of men in Pennsylvania. A Mr. Smith Willie, in 1880, appointed as executors of his extraordinary will, a jury of honor consisting of all the householders in his native town, who could prove that they came honestly by their fortunes, each to receive for his trouble the sum of two hundred dollars. He computed that there could not be above twenty, and doubted whether that number would be reached.

The will itself is thus indited:

"Seeing that I have no direct descendants, and that I am wholly unacquainted with those I may possess collaterally, I bequeath my fortune to any one among them who, in the course of a twelvemonth from the date of my death, may distinguish himself by an act of heroism worthy of ancient times.

"In case none of my collateral descendants should be justified in making this claim, I then leave all I possess to be divided between all the women who can prove that they have been my mistresses, be it for ever so brief a period."

Imposed on the Nuns

A sick traveller once presented himself at the hospital of Auxerre, in France, where he was received and treated with the care and attention bestowed on all the sick who seek an asylum there. He expressed his gratitude for the kindness shown him, and his intention of testifying it in a more substantial manner, begging the nuns to let him see a notary.

This functionary having obeyed his summons, he informed him that, as an old soldier, he was in the enjoyment of a retiring-pension, and, having earned a medal, of a further allowance; that, in addition to this income, he owned a mortgage worth four thousand five hundred francs, of which the title, as well as his other papers, was deposited with the notary of the commune of the Département du Seine et Marne, where he had a settlement. Upon this he dictated to him a will, by which he bequeathed everything to the hospital, upon the sole condition that they should give him a decent and honorable burial.

At this time he appeared to be recovering, but suddenly his state became worse, and on the following day he died.

To fulfil the promise exacted from them, the administrators of the hospital, instead of supplying the simple funeral ordinarily accorded to the paupers who died there, responded liberally to the behest of their generous benefactor, and accompanied his interment with every mark of respect, after which they went to the office indicated to claim the inheritance bestowed on them. But here a new feature appeared in the case. The mayor and the notary of the parish indicated, expressed themselves entirely ignorant whether of the papers in question or of the singular testator, and on further inquiry they discovered him to be no more than a wretched cowherd, bearing in his neighborhood a very suspicious character. What his motive could have been in practising this deception in his dying moments it is difficult to guess, and his conduct remains an instance of one of those crookednesses of the human mind we often meet with, but do not understand.

Leaves Estate to Jesus

One of the most unique wills ever recorded, was filed recently in Worcester, Massachusetts. The testator, Charles Hastings, leaves several garden lots and buildings, valued at fifty thousand dollars, to the Lord Jesus, with the explanation that He is the rightful owner of all lands, according to the Bible, the first book of Laws.

The instrument is an odd mixture of a deed and a will, and was drawn twenty-five years ago. According to the probate records, the instrument was given in consideration of the love and goodwill of the Lord and one cent found in one of the buildings conveyed.

There was a reservation in the instrument, giving the grantor the right to use the lands for life, and to improve and repair the houses and to pay taxes and insurance.

It may be safely surmised that the title to this property will vest in the heirs of the testator.

Mr. Hastings was a resident of Ashburnham and a well-known citizen.

A Spirit Will

A spirit will was rejected in Washington, D.C., on August 12th, 1910, by Justice Barnard of the Supreme Court of the District of Columbia.

Mrs. Elida J. G. Crowell, widow of William H. Crowell, a clerk in the Treasury Department, applied to the court for the appointment of the deceased's brother as administrator of his estate and offered in evidence what purported to be a translation of an illegible message, which Crowell scribbled while on his deathbed, favoring his brother's appointment.

The court was unable to decipher the scrawl, but Mrs. Crowell said a "translation" had been made for her by a "slate-writing medium." The "translation" in part read:

"Dear Elida, —

"This is what I tried to write on a slip of paper: 'I want my brother, W. H. H. Crowell, Washington, U. S. A., if I should pass away with my sickness. I have perfect trust in him. I believe he will deal honestly with my children. I have set aside $5000 for the exclusive use of my wife. Give little Elizabeth and brother both $100 to put in the Savings Bank.' Ruby met me. I have seen many folk here. This is a beautiful world. Is better than the Sixth Auditor's office. They can't put me out here.

"Date, June 7, 1910." "W. H. Crowell."

ANCIENT, CURIOUS, AND FAMOUS WILLS

Mystery of a Little Trunk

On September 1st, 1910, Adolph Steinberg, an old German cobbler, died in Brooklyn, New York, at 36 Snyder Avenue. For a quarter of a century he had half-soled and mended shoes for those who lived in that section of the city. Mayor Gaynor was one of his customers, and many other prominent men used to go to his little shop to have their shoes repaired.

There always lay close to Steinberg's feet, as he stitched away, a little metal trunk that was never out of his sight a moment during the day. It was never open, and no one ever caught a glimpse of its contents. At night it was placed under Steinberg's bed, and in the morning he would pull it out and drag it over to his bench.

Steinberg's solicitude for the trunk finally caused comment among his customers, and the report got out that the old cobbler kept his money and valuables there, and that a snug fortune was locked up in the little box. It was known that Steinberg was well to do, and for many years he used to lend out money to people who were temporarily out of funds. In such cases, he would get them to leave a watch or some other article of value as security. When they called to repay, Steinberg would return their valuables, charging them no interest for the money loaned.

In the course of many years, Steinberg accumulated quite a collection of watches and trinkets, because many of those to whom he lent money never came back to claim their valuables. So the collection grew and grew.

By his will Steinberg directed that the trunk be not opened until thirty days after his death. His wife and children respected his wish, and much to their satisfaction found it contained securities and other property of considerable value, an accumulation of many years.

Dolly Varden Garters and other Matters

The following are extracts from some recent English wills: Thomas Blyth, after directing that no person was to wear mourning for him out of his money, goes on to say : "But I cannot forget the kindness of the ladies who have promised to wear Dolly Varden garters of black and white as a mark of respect for my memory." William Hampton, after leaving to his son Lawrie's "Interest Tables," says he does so, "not from its intrinsic value, but from the hope that so small an incident may be of use to him in future years. And I particularly recommend to him the study of the compound interest tables, as showing that from comparatively small investments, by patience, large sums may be realized." James Brown evidently believed in every man voting according to his own political convictions, for after leaving to a nephew two cottages, "for which he is to get his vote on," adds, "and to vote the way which he likes best." William Farren's statement as to the character of Cambridge undergraduates is, we hope and believe, unfounded: he hopes by his disposition of his property, "to save his family from keeping or living in an undergraduate lodging-house, as undergraduates are more like wolves and dogs than human beings."

OSTENTATION

Matthew Wall of Braughing, Hertfordshire, England, by will, in 1595, charged all his lands and tenements in the parish of Braughing with the yearly payment of twenty shillings, to be distributed by the minister and churchwardens on St. Matthew's Day, in the following manner:

To the sexton, to make up his grave yearly, and to ring the bell, 1s. 10d. To twenty boys, between the age of six and sixteen, twenty groats. To ten aged and impotent people of the parish, ten threepences. To sweep the path from his house to the churchgate every year, 1s. To the crier of Stortford, to make proclamation yearly, on Ascension and Michaelmas Day, that he left his estate to a Matthew, or William Wall, as long as the world should endure, 8d. To the parish clerk at Hallingbury for the same, 8d., and to the minister and churchwardens, to see his will performed, 5s.

POWDER PLOT AND SPANISH ARMADA

Robert Wilcox, of Alcester, Warwickshire, England, by will, dated 24th of December, 1627, gave a house and grounds to the town of Alcester, for the maintenance of three sermons in the year, viz.:

"One upon the 5th of November, in remembrance of our happy deliverance, with our king, nobles and states, from the pestilent design of the Papists in the Powder Plot; one on the 17th of November, in remembrance of that good Queen Elizabeth, her entrance unto the Crown; and the third upon the last day of July, in remembrance of the Lord's gracious deliverance from the Spanish Armada, in '88."

And whereas the rent was 20s. by the year then, and the goodwife, Lilly, having her life in it, after her decease no doubt the house and close would be worth 30s. by the year; then his will was that the said overplus should be given to the poor every year, as the rent should come in, forever.

More Generous than Polite

The will of Edward Wortley Montagu, son of Mr. Montagu, Ambassador to Constantinople in 1716, by Lady Mary Wortley Montagu, his wife, the supposed "Sappho" of Pope, is more than singular. After some bequest "to my noble and worthy relation, the Earl of ——," he adds, "I do not give his lordship any further part of my property because the best part of that he has contrived to take already. Item, to Sir Francis —— I give one word of mine, because he has never had the good fortune to keep his own. Item, to Lord M—— I give nothing, because I know he'll bestow it on the poor. Item, to —— the author, for putting me in his travels, I give five shillings for his wit, undeterred by the charge of extravagance, since friends who have read his book consider five shillings too much. Item, to Sir Robert W—— I leave my political opinions, never doubting he can well turn them into cash, who has always found such an excellent market in which to change his own. Item, my cast-off habit of swearing oaths I give to Sir Leopold D——, in consideration that no oaths have ever been able to find him yet."

From some quarrel with his family he advertised for some widow or single lady of good manners likely to bring him an heir in —— months. This treasure to his arms his valet brought by his desire to meet him at Venice, from England; but as the ship of Wortley Montagu was entering the Venetian lagunes, to wed the chaste bride on the following day, the eager and expectant bridegroom swallowed too hastily a chicken bone, which, sticking in his throat, suffocated him in a few minutes.

To encourage Matrimony and Horse-racing

By a deed, dated 12th of August, 1801, executed in pursuance of a decree in Chancery, relative to the will of John Perram of New Market, England, dated 30th of May, 1772, the trustees of a sum of £410 6s. 2d. Three Per Cent Consols and £21 Bank Long Annuities, being the original sum given by the will, together with such accumulations thereon which had accrued during the proceedings in Chancery, were declared; to hold them upon trust, six weeks at least before Easter, to cause notice to be given, as therein directed, that a marriage portion of £21 would be given to a parishioner of the said parish, who should, on Thursday in the Easter week, be married at the church to a woman belonging to it; neither party to be under twenty, nor to exceed twenty-five years of age, nor be worth £20; the trustees to attend in the vestry to receive claims, and pay the bequest to such couples as should be qualified to receive it. In case of two claims, the determination to be by ballot who should receive it. In case of no claimants, then the money, for that year only, to be paid by the trustees to the winner of the next town horse-race; the race course at New Market is four miles long and is regarded the finest in the world.

Bequests of the Human Brain

Both in France and the United States there exist medical societies which make a special study of the human brain. In the United States a regular blank form of testamentary bequest has been formulated, and the brains of a number of prominent persons, particularly those of doctors, have passed under its provisions; a form used is here given:

"I, ———, of ———, recognizing the need of studying the brains of educated and orderly persons rather than those of the ignorant, criminal or insane, in order to determine their weight, form, and fissural patterns, the correlations with bodily and mental powers of various kinds and degrees, and the influences of sex, age and inheritance, hereby declare my wish, that at my death, my brain shall be entrusted to the Cornell Brain Association, or to the Curator of the Collection of human brains, in the Museum of Cornell University, for scientific uses, and for preservation, as a whole or in part, as may be thought best. If my near relatives, by blood or marriage, object seriously to the fulfilment of this bequest, it shall be void. I earnestly hope that they may interpose neither objection nor obstacle.

Date ——— " ———.
Witnesses:
———————
——————— ."

Medical works state that college professors are among the individuals best adapted to subserve the purposes indicated, by reason of their sharply defined capacities and attainments; lawyers, doctors and preachers seem to come next in favor.

It will be recalled that the late Florence Nightingale by will left her body for dissection and the cause of medical science.

MUST SETTLE DISPUTES

Mrs. Susan M. Corning died recently at Rockaway Beach, New York, leaving an estate valued at several thousand dollars. By an unusual clause in her will she appointed an arbitration committee to pass upon any dispute which might arise in the distribution of her estate. The clause reads:

"It is my express will and wish and I hereby order and direct that if any differences shall arise concerning any gift, bequest or other thing in this will, no suit shall be brought over the same, but the said difference shall be referred wholly to George Bennett, Louis Kreusher and Albert Meisel, all of Rockaway Beach, and what they order and direct shall be binding and conclusive to all persons concerned."

There seems some reason to question the legality of such a provision.

LONG ON TROUSERS

A New Yorker dying in 1880 supposed to be sane, left this will:

"I bequeath all my fortune to my nephews and nieces, seven in number.

"They are to share it equally, and on no account to go to law about it, on pain of forfeiting their respective shares.

"I own seventy-one pairs of trousers, and I strictly enjoin my executors to hold a public sale at which these shall be sold to the highest bidder, and the proceeds distributed to the poor of the city.

"I desire that these garments shall in no way be examined or meddled with, but be disposed of as they are found at the time of my death; and no one purchaser is to buy more than one pair."

As the testator had always been more or less eccentric in his ways, no one was much surprised at these singular clauses, which were religiously observed. The sale was held, and the seventy-one pairs of trousers were sold to seventy-one different purchasers. One of these, in examining the pockets, discovered in the fob a packet of some sort, closely sewn up. He lost no time in cutting the thread, and was not a little surprised to find a bundle of banknotes representing a thousand dollars. The news soon spread, and each of the others found himself possessed of a similar amount.

As may be supposed, all were well satisfied except the heirs, who could not find redress in law, this recourse being prohibited.

Complication over Horses

In a celebrated case, frequently quoted, the testator bequeathed to the plaintiff, "all my black and white horses." Now the testator had six black horses, six white horses and six pied horses, and the question was whether the pied horses passed under the terms of the bequest. After elaborate argument, judgment was given for the plaintiff, and then it was moved in arrest of judgment that the pied horses were mares.

Must marry "Anton" or "Antonie"

An eccentric Frenchman left his estate to his six nephews and six nieces on the condition that "every one of my nephews marries a woman named Antonie and that every one of my nieces marries a man named Anton." They were further required to give the Christian name Antonie or Anton to every first-born child according to the sex. The marriage of each nephew was to be celebrated on one of the St. Anthony's Days, either January 17th, May 10th, or June 13th, and if, in any instance, this last provision was not complied with before July, 1896, one-half of the legacy was in that case to be forfeited.

Must sing Anthems

Elizabeth Townsend of Westbury, Wilts, England, widow, by her will, dated 11th of June, 1820, gave unto the churchwardens and overseers of the parish of Westbury as much money as should be sufficient, when invested in the stocks, to yield the yearly sum of £3 clear of all deductions, upon trust to pay the dividends thereof unto the vicar, organist, parish clerk, and choir of the parish church of Westbury, for the time being, upon special condition that the said choir should forever thereafter, in the morning and afternoon service, at the parish church, on the Sunday preceding the 24th of June in each year, sing the anthem composed by her late husband's grandfather, Roger Townsend, from the 150th Psalm, and also the 112th Psalm, for which the vicar was to have 4s., the organist 10s., the clerk 5s., and 4s. apiece to the choir singers, viz., two counter, two tenor, three treble, and three bass singers, and in default of their singing, then to divide such £3 amongst the poor at Christmas.

The same person made a similar bequest to the choir of the parish church of Warminster, Wilts.

Will of Dr. Dunlop

The humorous will of Dr. Dunlop of Upper Canada is worth recording, though there is a spice of malice in every bequest it contains.

To his five sisters he left the following bequests:

"To my eldest sister Joan, my five-acre field, to console her for being married to a man she is obliged to henpeck.

"To my second sister Sally, the cottage that stands beyond the said field with its garden, because as no one is likely to marry her it will be large enough to lodge her.

"To my third sister Kate, the family Bible, recommending her to learn as much of its spirit as she already knows of its letter, that she may become a better Christian.

"To my fourth sister Mary, my grandmother's silver snuff-box, that she may not be ashamed to take snuff before company.

"To my fifth sister, Lydia, my silver drinking-cup, for reasons known to herself.

"To my brother Ben, my books, that he may learn to read with them.

" To my brother James, my big silver watch, that he may know the hour at which men ought to rise from their beds.

"To my brother-in-law Jack, a punch-bowl, because he will do credit to it.

"To my brother-in-law Christopher, my best pipe, out of gratitude that he married my sister Maggie whom no man of taste would have taken.

"To my friend John Caddell, a silver teapot, that, being afflicted with a slatternly wife, he may therefrom drink tea to his comfort."

While "old John's" eldest son was made legatee of a silver tankard, which the testator objected to leave to old John himself, lest he should commit the sacrilege of melting it down to make temperance medals.

Vanity follows us to the Grave

John Troutbeck of Dacre, Cumberland, England, by will, dated 27th of October, 1787, gave to the poor of Dacre, the place of his nativity, £200, the interest thereof to be distributed every Easter Sunday on the family tombstone in Dacre churchyard, provided the day should be fine, by the hands and at the discretion of a Troutbeck of Blencowe, if there should be any living, those next in descent having prior right of distribution; and if none should be living that would distribute the same, then by a Troutbeck, as long as one could be found that would take the trouble of it; otherwise by the minister and churchwardens of the parish for the time being; that not less than five shillings should be given to any individual, and that none should be considered entitled to it that received alms, or any support from the parish.

Temperance and Early Rising enjoined

In the will of the late Mr. J. Sargeant, of Leicester, England, who died some forty years ago, is the following clause: "As my nephews are fond of indulging themselves in bed in the morning, and as I wish them to prove to the satisfaction of my executors that they have got out of bed in the morning, and either employed themselves in business or taken exercise in the open air, from five to eight o'clock every morning from the fifth of April to the 10th of October, being three hours every day, and from seven to nine o'clock in the morning from the 10th of October to the 5th of April, being two hours every morning; this is to be done for some years, during the first seven years to the satisfaction of my executors, who may excuse them in case of illness, but the task must be made up when they are well, and if they will not do this, they shall not receive any share of my property. Temperance makes the faculties clear, and exercise makes them vigorous. It is temperance and exercise that can alone ensure the fittest state for mental or bodily exertion."

Picture of a Viper as a Bequest

The following is an extract from the will of John Hylett Stow, proved in 1781:

"I hereby direct my executors to lay out five guineas in the purchase of a picture of the viper biting the benevolent hand of the person who saved him from perishing in the snow, if the same can be bought for the money; and that they do, in memory of me, present it to ――――, Esq., a king's counsel, whereby he may have frequent opportunities of contemplating it, and, by a comparison between that and his own virtue, be able to form a certain judgment which is best and most profitable, a grateful remembrance of past friendship and almost parental regard, or ingratitude and insolence. This I direct to be presented to him in lieu of a legacy of three thousand pounds I had by a former will, now revoked and burned, left him."

This will provoked a suit for libel, a proceeding not altogether unknown, for defamation contained in a testamentary document, though such proceedings are rare. Mr. John Marshall Gest of Philadelphia refers to this clause in his excellent address on "Practical Suggestions for Writing Wills." It is also to be found in the "Curiosities of the Search Room," an English work of the highest merit.

NO CRUELTY TO ANIMALS

Grates v. Fraser. This was a suit for the administration of the estate of the late Dr. Fraser, of Hampstead, England, who left a large amount of property to be distributed among various charities. The will, probated in 1878, contained several very singular clauses, one of which was to this effect: That he had previously left ten thousand pounds to the Senatus Academicus of the University of Edinburgh, for the purpose of founding certain bursaries connected with the medical profession, but having learnt that the horrible and atrocious practice prevailed there of performing unspeakably cruel operations and experiments on living animals, he now by his will cancelled the bequest, and desired to benefit the Scottish Society for Prevention of Cruelty to Animals to a similar extent, since he could not reconcile it with his feelings to encourage, however remotely, the barbarous practice of vivisection. The testator also directed that his funeral should be conducted with as little parade as possible, without cloaks, hatbands, or scarfs, and that no feathers, wands, or other absurdities should be used on the occasion, and that the ridiculous display of hired mourners, mutes, or attendants, be dispensed with. Most sensible people, he continued, condemn the above useless customs, but nevertheless, from vanity or in blind obedience to antiquated usages, perpetuate and encourage them. He then directed his body to be buried in any cemetery, without reference to its being what was called "consecrated" or "unconsecrated" ground, or whether any service should be repeated at the grave or not, as these were matters about which he was utterly indifferent; they could avail him nothing, but might, if the weather were cold, cause the health of some friend to suffer.

Whiskey to Exterminate the Irish

An English gentleman, who had from his earliest years been educated with the most violent prejudices against the Irish, came, when advanced in life, to inherit a considerable property in the county of Tipperary, but under the express condition that he should reside on the land. To this decree he very reluctantly conformed, but his feelings towards the natives only grew more bitter in consequence.

At his death some years after, on the 17th of March, 1791, his executors were extremely surprised on opening his will to find the following dispositions:

"I give and bequeath the annual sum of ten pounds, to be paid in perpetuity out of my estate, to the following purpose. It is my will and pleasure that this sum shall be spent in the purchase of a certain quantity of the liquor vulgarly called whisky, and it shall be publicly given out that a certain number of persons, Irish only, not to exceed twenty, who may choose to assemble in the cemetery in which I shall be interred, on the anniversary of my death, shall have the same distributed to them. Further, it is my desire that each shall receive it by half-a-pint at a time till the whole is consumed, each being likewise provided with a stout oaken stick and a knife, and that they shall drink it all on the spot. Knowing what I know of the Irish character, my conviction is, that with these materials given, they will not fail to destroy each other, and when in the course of time the race comes to be exterminated, this neighbourhood at least may, perhaps, be colonized by civilized and respectable Englishmen."

Must Wait One Hundred Years

A very curious will was that of a Polish landlord, M. Zalesky, who died in 1889, leaving property valued at one hundred thousand roubles. His will was enclosed in an envelope bearing the words: "To be opened after my death." Inside there was another envelope, "To be opened six weeks after my death." When this time had passed, the second envelope was opened, and a third uncovered, "To be opened one year after my death." At the end of the year, a fourth envelope was discovered, to be opened two years after the testator's death; and so the game went on until 1894, when the actual will was discovered and read. The contents of this will were quite as eccentric as the directions attached to its

ANCIENT, CURIOUS, AND FAMOUS WILLS

opening. The testator bequeathed half his fortune to such of his heirs as had the largest number of children. The rest of the property was to be placed in bank, and a hundred years after his death to be divided, with the accumulated interest, among the will-maker's descendants.

WILL OF AN IRISH MISER

An Irishman named Dennis Tolam, who died at Cork possessed of considerable wealth, in the year 1769, left a singular will, containing the following testamentary dispositions: "I leave to my sister-in-law four old stockings, which will be found under my mattress, to the right. Item: To my nephew, Michael Tarles, two odd socks and a green nightcap. Item: To Lieutenant John Stein, a blue stocking, with my red cloak. Item: To my cousin, Barbara Dolan, an old boot, with a red flannel pocket. Item: To Hannah, my housekeeper, my broken water-jug." After the death of the testator, the legatees having been convened by the notary to be present at the reading of the will, each, as he or she was named, shrugged their shoulders and otherwise expressed a contemptuous disappointment, while parties uninterested in the succession could not refrain from laughing at these ridiculous, not to say insulting, legacies. All were leaving the room, after signifying their intention of renouncing their bequests, when the last-named, Hannah, having testified her indignation by kicking away the broken pitcher, a number of coins rolled out of it; the other individuals, astonished at the unexpected incident, began to think better of their determination, and requested permission to examine the articles given to them. It is needless to say that, on proceeding to the search, the stockings, socks, pocket, etc., soon betrayed by their weight the value of their contents; and the hoard of the testator, thus fairly distributed, left on the minds of the legatees a very different impression of his *worth*.

MUST NOT MARRY A DOMESTIC SERVANT

A curious and peculiarly hard case came before a Vice-Chancellor in London in 1880. The facts are as follows: A Miss Turner devised a large amount of real estate to her father for life, and then to her brother on these conditions: "But if my brother shall marry during my life without my consent in writing, or if he shall already have married, or hereafter shall marry, a domestic servant," then such bequest to her brother was to be void. It appears the brother came into possession of the estate and died in 1898, leaving a widow and two children. Suit was instituted against the widow and children on the ground that the testatrix's brother had forfeited his title to the legacy by marrying a domestic servant. It was contended on behalf of the widow that she had been a housekeeper, and not a domestic servant. The Vice-Chancellor, however, was of the opinion that a housekeeper was a domestic servant, and thus the legacy was forfeited.

To Sing in Opera

Stanislas Poltzmarz, a Hungarian, possessed of considerable wealth, and residing at Pesth, died about 1835, bequeathing the larger part of his fortune, consisting of three million florins, to a notary named Lotz, but stipulated that before claiming it he should engage himself at the Scala at Milan, to perform in the operas of "Otello" and "La Sonnambula." The testator, who was eighty years of age, deprecates being considered in his dotage, and takes the trouble to explain that, having some few years before met the said Lotz at an evening party, where he had sung fragments of the parts of Elvino and Otello, he had admired the beauty of his tenor voice, and predicted that it only depended on himself to become the favorite of the whole musical world. "If, therefore," he concludes, "I am right, he will thank me, and so will all *dilettanti*, for my acumen; if, on the other hand, he should fail, he will have money enough to compensate for the hisses he may incur."

Hair of the Prophet's Beard

"The Prophet's Beard Case," which created a sensation among the followers of the Prophet at Madras, was called on for final disposal before Mr. Justice Innes, Acting Chief Justice, in August, 1879. The subject of dispute was a hair of the Prophet's beard, which is enclosed in a case and is called the "Aussaree Shareef," or sacred relic, and in connection with which the Government allows a monthly pension of Rs. 47–14–4, obtained from funds left by a late Nabob for the purpose of carrying out ceremonies in connection with the sacred relic. There were, when the case was first instituted, no less than six claimants, two by right of a will, the others claiming it in succession from generations. Two of the claimants and the plaintiff withdrew from the suit, leaving only four to establish their rights to the sacred heirloom. His lordship, in a lengthy judgment, decided that the first, third, and fourth defendants were entitled to the sacred relic; but as the first defendant was a woman she could not hold office in connection with it, and as No. 3 was the elder brother of No. 4, he directed that he should hold the "Aussaree Shareef," and perform all ceremonies in connection with it, making three equal shares of whatever remained from the allowance after their performance.

JOKE ON HIS FRIENDS

Mr. Arbirlot, a Scotch gentleman, left extremely handsome legacies to a number of his friends. The lawyer who wrote down his wishes, looked up from time to time to ascertain whether his client could be in earnest; at last he could not refrain from asking him whether he was sure his assets would cover all these bequests. At this the humorous testator burst out laughing, admitting that of course they wouldn't, only he didn't like to go out of the world without leaving the expression of his regard for these legatees, by showing what he *would* have done for them if he had *had* the means. No doubt the intention was a benevolent one; but we doubt whether the joke was one calculated to be received in a spirit of affectionate gratitude, especially by the executors, whose equanimity would have been put to a severe test had the puzzle not been explained before the testator's death.

A REMARKABLE ANNUITY

A county newspaper some years ago recorded the death of a Major Hook, and spoke of him as "a singular character." "He died," says the report, "on Monday sennight, at his house, Ham Street, Ham Common. He was an officer in the East India Company's service, and reached the age of seventy-five. His house was remarkable for its dingy and dilapidated condition."

His wife had become entitled to a life annuity, bequeathed to her in these ambiguous terms: "And the same shall be paid to her as long as she is above ground." When, therefore, the good lady died, her husband very naturally objected to forfeit this income by putting her *below* ground; and ingeniously devised a mode of keeping her in a room which he allotted "to her sole and separate use," placing a glass-case over her remains. For thirty years he thus prolonged his enjoyment, if not of his wife's society, at least of her income.

To help Young Newspaper Men

William J. Haskett, a lawyer, who died in New York in 1890, left a will containing this curiously worded clause: "I am informed that there is a society composed of young men connected with the public press; and as in early life I was connected with the papers, I have a keen recollection of the toils and troubles that bubbled then and ever will bubble for the toilers of the world in their pottage caldron; and as I desire to thicken with a little savory herb their thin broth in the shape of a legacy, I do hereby bequeath to the New York Press Club of the City of New York, $1000, payable on the death of Mrs. Haskett."

Angelic Virtue Required

Not long ago, a wealthy gentleman on Long Island died, who provided that none of his heirs should inherit, unless they could show that they had led a life of angelic virtue. Among the conditions mentioned, were these: That they should not smoke or drink; that they should rise every morning and breakfast at a certain hour; that they should be in the house every evening at a certain hour; that they should be industrious and strictly moral; that they should never enter a barroom, and should not get married before the age of twenty-five. It is stated that the heirs were practically disinherited, all but one having failed to live up to the conditions.

Bare Arms Immodest

A rector of a Yorkshire parish, who died in 1804, left a considerable property to his only daughter under the following conditions:

1st. That she should not marry unless with the consent of his two executors, and

2d. That she should dress with greater propriety than theretofore.

This clause was worded thus: "Seeing that my daughter Anna has not availed herself of my advice touching the objectionable practice of going about with her arms bare up to the elbows, my will is that, should she continue after my death in this violation of the modesty of her sex, all the goods, chattels, moneys, land, and other property that I have devised to her for the maintenance of her future life shall pass to the oldest of the sons of my sister Caroline. Should anyone take exception to this my wish as being too severe, I answer that license in dress in a woman is a mark of a depraved mind."

A Fanatical Baptist Minister

The will (dated March 26th, 1874) of the Rev. William Hill, late of Lansdowne Villas, Springfield Road, Cotham, Bristol, Baptist minister, who died on November 11, 1879, was proved at the district registry, Bristol, by Emerson Geerish and Thomas Bowbeer, the executors, under three thousand pounds. After the death of his wife he gives to the Society for the Relief of Aged and Infirm Baptist Ministers, instituted in Bath, 1816, and to the Baptist Foreign Missionary Society, each one hundred pounds. The testator directs "the payment of all my just debts, funeral and testamentary expenses, as soon as conveniently may be after my departure to heaven; but, as this is to be my final public document, I shall here record my detestation of all State establishments of religion, believing them to be anti-scriptural and soul-ruining. I have for years prayed the King of Zion to overthrow the politico-ecclesiastical establishment of the British Empire, and I leave the world with a full conviction that such prayer must ere long be answered. I thirst to see the Church brought down, the Church by man set up, for millions are by it led on to drink a bitter cup. I desire all posterity to know that William Hill was a conscientious Trinitarian Baptist Minister, and that he believed infant sprinkling to be from his Satanic Majesty, the keystone of Popery, therefore the parent of unnumbered terrible evils; this delusion must also pass away at the Divinely-appointed time, and the immersion of believers, as plainly taught by the Great Teacher, the Holy Ghost, and the Apostles, shall one day universally triumph. Man says, some water in the face, and that before the child has grace, is what is meant in Jesus' word, by being buried in the Lord. The deadly drinking customs of professors and non-professors are likewise doomed. Heaven dash all error, sin, and the devil from the earth, and cause truth, holiness, and Christ everywhere to prevail. Amen."

Three Testamentary Gems

The three testamentary gems following are to be found in one volume of the Pennsylvania State Reports:

NUMBER ONE

"February the 28, 1858.
"the requeste of tresse Carey i
want ransler Carey to hav my plase
as long as he shall live i want drusilla Carey
to stay and keepe house for hur father and
marten i want mr carey to give lovica shoop wone
shale wone pare of
stockings Rozanner clark wone coveled i want
cathern stanten
to hav my cloak and to Dresses
i want (erasure) mr carey to give
Won hundred Dolars two the methodus
Church I want drusila carey to hav
all my household property as soon as i am ded.
 and after mr carey is ded i
want drusila (erasure) (erasure)
carey two hav my farm.
                                        her
                            Tereisse X carey "
                                        mark

NUMBER TWO

"In the Name of god I Samull Eddinger
of Moore Township County of Northampton
State of Penn Do make this my Last will
and testament as follows
that is to Say my Disire
my son John he Shall have one
thousand Dollars in Advance before
any of the heirs Shall hav any money
from my Estate personal property
first my Son John Shall Settle up all
my Depts funeral Expace &c.
 till all is paid
my Son John he shall setle
my personal property as soon
 it is Posible
he shall pay the of the money from
my personal goods the half of
the money to my Daughter Margret and

what is Left from the Balence of
the Thousand Dollrs he tookt of for
himself
my Son John Shall pay to my
Daughter Margret an Annally one a
Hundred and twenty five Dollars for her
Natural Life time or as long she
will Liv in this World
and my Son John he shall have
all my Real Estate for his own
property as Soon my Daughter is Deased
my Son John Shall not pay any Longer
Not to her heirs and to nobody
it be Stopt."

NUMBER THREE

The third runs as follows: "it to be understood that any of my grandchildren who shall be guilty of having an illegitimate child, or of the sin of intemperance, or that do wickedly and illegitimately profane God's holy name, he, she, or they, to forever debar themselves from the benefit of any bequest," and that the shares of offending ones should be divided amongst their brothers and sisters, "whose life and conversation is free from reproach."

CLAIMING TO BE THE SON OF A KING

One of the most singular cases that ever came before a court of justice was the dispute as to the validity of the will of the late Mr. W. R. Smee, probated in 1880 in England. That the testator was a man of exceptional ability is beyond doubt. His powers of organization were so good that he was employed by the Post Office authorities to readjust several departments which had got into a state of disorder. A pamphlet of his, on the question of the "Repeal of the Malt Duties," attracted the attention of the acting Lord Chief Baron and Mr. Bass, who sought an interview with the writer; and after 1860 he wrote many able articles for various newspapers. At the same time, there is equally little doubt that Mr. Smee had insane delusions of the sort which most commonly afflict lunatics. He believed that he was a son of George IV, and rightful heir to the throne, and in 1859, before the composition of the articles just mentioned, he wrote a letter to the Prince Consort, enclosing a preposterous petition to the Queen on the subject of his "rights." This absurd document stated that when out walking with his nurse he had been recognized by a crowd as the Prince of Wales, and escorted home amid loud hurrahs. The king had taken him on his royal knee, and said to him, "Poor boy, poor boy, get on with your learning. A great destiny is preparing for you, though you do not know it." Every morning, he asserted, drugs were administered which took away his memory. The Duke of Wellington, disguised in a mechanic's dress, followed him round Finsbury Circus; and, during his last illness, Mr. William Smee, senior, had said: "Extraordinary and unheard of means have been adopted to keep him down, or he must have come to the throne." In his will the testator left his property to the corporation of Brighton, wishing to be associated with his supposed royal father as a benefactor to that town. As must have been generally expected, the Court pronounced against the will which benefited the popular seaside resort. "The fact that a man was capable of transacting business, to whatever extent that might go, however complicated the business might be, and however considerable the powers of intellect it might require, did not exclude the idea of his being of unsound mind," the president stated in the course of his interesting judgment. "A man might be a good carpenter and follow his calling, and yet his mind might be tainted with insanity to such an extent that he might he held irresponsible for a crime on the ground that he did not know the nature of the act he committed. Therefore, all the arguments addressed to the jury on the subject of the testator's capacity to deal with complex subjects, to write pamphlets, and to make calculations, had nothing to do with the question whether he was of unsound mind or not. He was admittedly of unsound mind, because shown by that which was the most conclusive symptom and evidence of unsoundness — namely, the presence of delusions — that was to say, ideas which they could not conceive any rational man entertaining." These arguments do not tend to simplify the difficult duties of those who have the misfortune to be called upon to give advice in cases of mental disease.

A Word Left Out

Mary Richardson, who died on the 28th of May, 1874, made, by her will, numerous charitable bequests, amongst which was £500 to the "London Church Building Society." There being no society in London bearing that title exactly, a petition was presented by the treasurers of the London Diocesan Church Building Society for the payment out of court of the bequest named. The Bishop of London's fund likewise presented its claim; as also did the Incorporated Society for Promoting the Enlargement Building, and Repairing of Churches in England and Wales, the latter supposing that it most exactly answered the description of a London church building society. The Vice-Chancellor, however, Sir C. Hall, decided in favor of the London Diocesan Church Building Society, because the words used most nearly approached those of the title given by the testatrix.

An Enigma

WILL OF ROSINE BARROT

I give to my sister	20	I give to Gustave		6
" Jeanne	10	" Eugénie		7
" Pauline	6	" Annie		14
" Marie	6			
" Julie	6			75

This is my last will and testament, made at Meude, 20th October, 1767. ROSINE BARROT.

As this was the entire will, without any clue whatever to its signification, the surviving relatives, for there were no executors appointed, set their wits to work to discover its enigmatic signification. At last they found that the testatrix's property amounted to 75,000 francs, and they therefore concluded that each unit represented 1000. Another difficulty arose from the fact that there were in the family several repetitions of some of the names mentioned in the will. The decision, however, was worked out by common sense, and, strange to say, two trials at law that followed, failed to overthrow it.

Body Bequeathed for Useful Purposes

A certain testator devised his property to a stranger, wholly disinheriting the heir or next of kin, and directed that his executors should "cause some part of his bowels to be converted into fiddle strings, and that others should be sublimed into smelling salts, and that the remainder of his body should be vitrified into lenses, for optical purposes." In a letter attached to this will the testator said, "The world may think this to be done in a spirit of singularity or whim, but I have a mortal aversion to funeral pomp, and I wish my body to be converted into purposes useful to mankind." The testator was shown to have conducted his affairs with great shrewdness and ability, and had been regarded by his associates through life as a person possessing high business qualifications, and the will was upheld.

WILL CONTAINED A SERMON

Another unusual will showing a strong religious belief and which incorporates a sermon to his heirs, is that of Elias Boudinot which was probated in Luzerne County, Pennsylvania, in 1821. The will contained twenty-six closely written pages of manuscript. The beginning of the will which contains the sermon is as follows:

"Know all men by these presents that I, Elias Boudinot, late of the city of Philadelphia, and director of the mint of the United States, but now of the city of Burlington, N.J., Doctor of Laws, being by the unmerited goodness of Almighty God, after great affliction, by a long series of bad health, and having passed my eighty-first year and returned to a tolerable state of bodily health, so as to possess a sound and disposing mind and memory; but being often reminded of the uncertainty of life and the propriety of settling the intended disposition of my property while free from the distresses of a sick bed, do make and publish this my last will and testament.

"And as this instrument cannot take effect till after my death, but must then be frequently resorted to by my representatives, I do therefore improve so good an opportunity of repeating the profession I have made for more than sixty years, and which by the free grace of God, through Jesus Christ, and by the continued influences of his Holy Spirit, has been strengthened and confirmed by the most happy experience, founded on solid ground and by a thorough examination and inquiry into the divine scriptures through that long period, and in which I hope under the same blessed influences to finish my mortal race, I mean that of a firm, unfeigned and prevailing belief in one sovereign, omnipotent and eternal Jehovah, a God of infinite love and mercy who hath delivered us from the powers of darkness and hath translated us into the kingdom of his dear Son, in whom we have redemption through his blood, even the forgiveness of sins, who is the image of the invincible God, the first born of every creature, and he is before all things and by him all things consist, and whoever has been and still is reconciled a guilty world unto himself by his righteousness and atonement, his death and his resurrection, through whom alone life and immortality have been brought to light in his gospel, and by the all-powerful influence of his daily spirit, is daily sanctifying, enlightening and leading his faithful people into all necessary truth.

"And as it has pleased a holy and sovereign God to favor me with the continuance of one only child, to whom I most cordially wish and pray for the best and greatest possible good in time and eternity, I do in the most solemn manner, as in the presence of the one only great and glorious God, the Father, the Son and the Holy Spirit, and in view of an approaching eternity, beseech and entreat her to make the fear and love of God the great objects of her constant attention and pursuit, and in a particular manner that she will by a persevering inquiry into, and a thorough knowledge of the spirit and power of the gospel of Jesus Christ, which she has been so long, and I trust through divine mercy savingly acquainted with, endeavor to cherish and increase the like temper, disposition and usefulness in life as are therein so clearly and plainly taught and enforced, and which, generally speaking, consist in an universal benevolence, meekness, self-denial, deep contrition for sin and unfeigned love to our brethren, with an habitual lively faith in and dependence upon our Lord Jesus Christ, as the only atonement for our sins, the source of every blessing, and when the gift of God will inevitably work by love, purify the heart and be productive of good works, aways remembering that however the profession of a particular denomination of our holy religion among men may be beneficial to herself and others in their state of imperfection in which every aid should be sought to support and manifest the Christian character, yet that the Church of Christ is one universal and Catholic Church, a communion of saints not confined to time or place, name or party of Christians, but that every one who exercises deep and sincere repentance towards God, unfeigned faith in his beloved Son and worketh righteousness, is born of God.

"And I do more expressly press it upon her under every circumstance of life, to consider that day as worse than lost, in which she does not seek earnestly communion with her Heavenly Father under the special influence of His Holy Spirit, and she may be positively assured that this may be done even amidst the common and ordinary business of life as in the most profound and secret retirements, assisted by the ordinances of his gospel; would also earnestly recommend her habitually living under prevailing sense of God's overruling providence, which, however wonderful, regards the smallest things of those who love and fear him, even to the numbering of the hairs of the heads.

"As to all and singular, the temporal estate wherewith it has pleased God in his undeserved mercy to amply reward my industry and application to business, for the use and enjoyment of which I do him my most grateful thanks, acknowledging his great goodness and beneficence to me therein, I do dispose of the same and all my estate therein in the following manner, wishing to do what I think by solemn and serious consideration, will not be contrary to his divine will, but in the end may advance the honor of his great name."

Thereafter follow the bequests.

A Partnership with God

We might head this paper "Why Paul Duhalde made his Will," for certainly no idea could be much more original than that on which its principal, and disputed, clause was founded.

A brief sketch of the history of Paul Duhalde cannot fail to interest our readers, and will best explain the peculiarity of this testamentary document.

This individual was born at Paris in 1691; he died in 1725; he was the son of a dealer in diamonds, and lost his father at the age of sixteen years, when he was sent to Spain by his mother to learn the arcana of the business. The lad had no success, and returned. He was then placed with a merchant at Rouen, but did not get on, and subsequently passed to America, but his restless disposition soon sent him back to France. This brought him to the year 1717, and he was now twenty-six years of age. He remained some months with his mother, and then, having contracted a partnership with two jewel merchants, set off a second time to Madrid; this enterprise was, however, not more successful than those preceding it, and he came back to Paris, in the month of February, 1719, profoundly discouraged, and not without reason.

Here the melancholy reflections consequent on his repeated and persistent failures suggested to him a very singular notion, that of contracting a partnership with God. He proceeded to enter seriously into this abnormal contract, and drew up an act in regular and technical form, which he transcribed into his day-book on September 24, 1719, in the following terms: "I have resolved to enter into a partnership with God, promising and undertaking to fulfil all the within-mentioned articles; and I enjoin my heirs, whoever they may be, to carry out these my intentions in case I should die before accomplishing them myself."

He then proceeds to declare that this association, the object of which is to deal in precious stones, shall hold good for five years, reckoning from October 2, 1719. He fixes his capital at 3000 Spanish piastres, about $3000, being all that remained to him of his patrimony. He binds himself not to enter into any other partnership during the five years, unless with a woman, by marriage. As soon as the five years shall have elapsed, he proposes to balance his accounts, to begin by withdrawing from the partnership the 3000 piastres with which he started; secondly, to take from it the dowry that his wife may have brought him; thirdly, any sum or sums that may have fallen in to him by succession or otherwise during the time; after which he adds, "And the surplus shall be equally divided between God and myself."

This unique partnership having been thus determined, Duhalde starts a third time for Spain, but the outset of this new attempt does not augur well for the partners. Two years after, however (1721), the project of a double marriage between the Courts of France and Spain gives a new impetus to the branch of commerce in which he is engaged, and he resolves to improve the opportunity. At last Fortune seems to smile upon his endeavors, and the ultimate results exceed his fondest hopes. He now returns to Paris, resolving to settle himself finally there.

In 1722 he married the daughter of De Hansy, a well-known bookseller, who brought him 30,000 livres, and from his mother, who died in September of the same year, he inherited 70,226 livres. On May 20, 1723, a son was born to him.

Meantime Dulhalde never loses sight of the obligations he has taken upon himself toward his partner. He draws, from time to time, from the common fund, sums which he distributes in the name of God, to the poor, and inscribes these with regularity and precision in his registers.

On October 1, 1724, the partnership expires. Duhalde strikes a balance of his accounts, and finds from the aggregate of the entries that he has already paid to the poor 13,684 livres; but this is not all. In the statement of account drawn up he has considered three classes of stones as constituting a portion of the profits: one of these lots is at Amsterdam, one at Madrid, and one at Paris;

these he shares equally, inscribing on the packets which contain them: "Half for the poor"; and at the foot of the statement of account he writes: "Misfortune and malediction upon my heirs, whoever they may be, if, under any pretext whatever, they should fail to distribute to the poor the half of whatever proceeds may come from the jewels now in my possession, if so be God should call me away before I shall have been able to satisfy their claims myself. Further, if by any extraordinary event it should appear at my death that no other amounts are forthcoming but those goods or sums which are virtually the property of the poor, let not a sacrilegious hand be laid upon them; they constitute a deposit which can under no circumstances be diverted from its just cause."

In addition to this precaution, and in order to secure to the poor the amounts he regarded as strictly their due, Duhalde drew up in the month of January, 1725, eight bills of 1000 livres each, payable to order from year to year, comprising the years 1725 to 1732, and placed these bills in the hands of the Vicar of St. Germain l'Auxerrois.

On January 14, 1725, he fell ill and made his will, by which he declares that: "In the books which contain the minutes of my affairs there are several articles touching matters that concern the poor; I beg my executor to examine these articles with the greatest accuracy, and to see they are carried out with the strictest attention."

Two months after, Duhalde dies, leaving a young widow, a minor, and an infant two years old. The schedule of property is called over, the administrators of the Hôpital Général are invited to attend. Among the effects of the deceased are found packets of precious stones, labelled "Half for the poor"; their portion is estimated at 18,188 livres. The administrators claim it, but offer to compromise for the sum of 15,900 ff. The young widow protests; the guardian contends that the will should be set aside on the ground that no sane men ever enter into partnership with God. The parties appeal to law, and, after a spirited altercation, a judgment is obtained, April 3, 1726, on the decision of D'Aguesseau (Avocat-Général), ordering that "The will of Duhalde and the acts and codicils dependent thereon shall be fulfilled according to the desire of the testator; he consequently condemns the guardian of the widow and her son to hand over to the administrators of the hospital funds the jewels constituting the legacy made by the testator to the poor, but leaving him the choice of paying the sum in

ANCIENT, CURIOUS, AND FAMOUS WILLS

money value, as estimated by experts to be provided by the Court; the course adopted by the said guardian to be decided on within a fortnight."

ECCENTRIC BUT CHARITABLE FRENCHMAN

A gentleman of French birth, named Pierre Henri Baume, died some years ago at Douglas, Isle of Man, leaving a large sum for charitable purposes. He was born at Marseilles in 1797, and at an early age was sent to a military college at Naples, where he became private secretary to King Ferdinand. About the year 1825 he came to London. At one time he was a preacher holding peculiar views on theology, then became manager of a theatrical company, and subsequently got up a scheme for the establishment of model gardens. He took a lively interest in various charitable institutions, and expressed a strong desire to accumulate a great fortune, with the object of eventually endowing or establishing an institution, on principles which he had himself drawn up, for the education and benefit of youth of the poorer classes. By great perseverance and industry, and by subjecting himself almost to privation, he at last succeeded in amassing a considerable fortune, and bought land at Colney-hatch, together with a small estate called Chifont, on Dibdin-hill, in Buckinghamshire. Several obstacles arose as to the fulfilment of his educational project, and he was ultimately induced to abandon this idea. After living about a quarter of a century in London, he went to Manchester and engaged vigorously in a movement "public-houses without drink." He also instituted Sunday afternoon lectures to working-men, which were carried on with varying success for several years. In 1857 he settled in the Isle of Man, purchased an estate there, and afterwards resided on the island. At Douglas he fitted up an odd kind of residence, the entrance to which he made almost inaccessible, and admission to which could only be obtained by those whom he had initiated into a peculiar knock. In this little den he lived like a hermit, sleeping in a hammock slung from the roof, for the room was so crowded with dusty books that there was no space for a bedstead or even for a table on which to take his food. He stated that his object in living in this condition and depriving himself of all comforts was to enable him to leave as much money as possible for charitable and educational purposes. He resided in this miserable place for several years; but his health failing him, he was induced, later, to remove, and died at a tradesman's house in Duke street,

Douglas. Public attention was directed to M. Baume's affairs in London, in consequence of proceedings taken by him to evict a number of squatters who had located themselves on his Colneyhatch property, which was popularly known as "The Frenchman's Farm." M. Baume took out letters of naturalization, which enabled him to enjoy the rights and privileges of an Englishman, and to dispose of his property as he thought best. He left the whole of his real and personal property, valued at £54,000, in trust for charitable purposes in the Isle of Man, on his death.

"Louis Agassiz, Teacher"

The will of Agassiz, probated in June, 1874, begins thus: "The last will and testament of Louis Agassiz, of Cambridge, in the County of Middlesex and Commonwealth of Massachusetts, teacher."

Of him the *Boston Globe* said: "We should think the heart of every schoolmaster and schoolmistress in the land should bound at reading this simple announcement. The great naturalist, the peer of Aristotle, Linnæus, Cuvier, and Von Baer, calls himself, in the most solemn of all documents, 'a teacher.' There is, to us, something inspiring in this designation. All teachers, whether they are professors in colleges or directors in the commonest village schools, must be thrilled and invigorated by the statement that Agassiz is proud to enroll himself in their ranks. The good, grand, noble man, the apostle of pure science, the investigator and discoverer, the person who was preëminently a scientific force as well as a scientific intelligence dies with the feeling that his occupation was that of a 'teacher.' He, of course, leaves little or no property to his family; the noble woman, the bereaved wife, the constant companion of his intellect as well as of his heart, she who followed him whithersoever he was led by the spirit of scientific research, is, we suppose, the executrix of little but his glory; but the will is sublime, because it records the fact that Louis Agassiz was 'a teacher.' That was his occupation on earth. What it may be above, we do not pretend to know. One thing we know is this, that the simple preamble to his will must kindle into a generous flame every soul engaged in the great cause of education. 'Louis Agassiz, teacher!' but what a teacher! We preserve many memories of precious conversations with him on this question of teaching. He considered that teaching was a communication of life as well as of knowledge. A lad of ten years once contrived to get into the State House when Agassiz was urging the incontrovertible arguments for his 'museum.' We happened to jostle against the lad as he was leaving the hall, and asked him, laughingly, his opinion of the performance. 'Well,' he said, 'I've been to many lectures, and have been tired to death, but Agassiz comes right up to my notion of the circus!' When we told Agassiz of this queer compliment, he was much pleased. He wanted to see the boy who had been so unconsciously appreciative of the spirit of his speech. He knew that he had magnetized grave and elderly men, and that what he asked for would be cheerfully granted; but he desired to shake hands with the lad who thought he was as good as 'a circus,' and sent out from his deep lungs great roars of laughter in welcoming the testimony of his juvenile admirer.

"It would be idle to multiply instances of the thorough humanity and geniality of Agassiz. Everybody who knew him can tell hundreds of anecdotes illustrative of his sympathy with all forms of life, whether in the jelly-fish, the human infant, the developing boy or girl, the mature man or woman. Still his conviction of the immateriality and personality of mind was something wonderful in so austere a naturalist. We happened once to please him by defining a jelly-fish as organized water. 'Now look at it through the microscope,' he said. 'But, Agassiz, the play of the organization is so wonderful that it seems to me that nothing but mind can account for it.' 'You are right,' was his answer; 'in some incomprehensible way, God Almighty has created these beings, and I cannot doubt of their immortality any more than I doubt of my own.' His fealty to the rights of animals exceeded that of any great naturalist who ever preceded him. Incompetent as we are to give him his due rank among the great naturalists of the world, we think he excelled every naturalist who has gone before him in striking at the soul and individuality of all animals below man. It is impossible to convey in words the peculiar feeling which Agassiz had on this matter. Doubtless this large and genial genius is now satisfied. We cannot penetrate beyond the veil.

"What we can do, however, is to celebrate Agassiz as a teacher, and try to send a new glow into the heart of every person engaged in the difficult art of teaching. How hard is their work! The present generation is brought up, as far as education is concerned, on the most economical principles. No consideration whatever is given to the point of the will of Agassiz. When he proudly calls himself 'a teacher,' he means that he is a radiator of heat as well as of light. A poet has well described the method of instruction adopted by Agassiz:

> "'He was like the sun giving me life;
> Pouring into the caves of my young brain
> Knowledge from his bright fountains.'"

Pipe, Tobacco and Matches in his Coffin

Mr. Klaës, who was known among his acquaintances by the name of the "King of Smokers," died some years ago near Rotterdam. According to the Belgian papers he had amassed a large fortune in the linen trade, and had erected near Rotterdam a mansion, one portion of which was devoted to the arrangement of a collection of pipes according to their nationality and chronological order. A few days before his death he summoned his lawyer, and made his will, in which he directed that all the smokers of the country should be invited to his funeral, that each should be presented with 10 lb. of tobacco and two Dutch pipes of the newest fashion, on which should be engraved the name, arms and date of the decease of the testator. He requested all his relatives, friends and funeral guests to be careful to keep their pipes alight during the funeral ceremonies, after which they should empty the ashes from their pipes on the coffin. The poor of the neighborhood who attended to his last wishes were to receive annually, on the anniversary of his death, 10 lb. of tobacco and a small cask of good beer. He desired that his oak coffin should be lined with the cedar of his old Havana cigar boxes, and that a box of French caporal and a packet of old Dutch tobacco should be placed at the foot of his coffin. His favorite pipe was to be placed by his side, along with a box of matches, a flint and steel, and some tinder, as he said there was no knowing what might happen. A clever calculator has made out that Mr. Klaës had, during his eighty years of life, smoked more than four tons of tobacco, and had drunk about 500,000 quarts of beer.

Thankfulness to God

In the codicil annexed to the last will of Robert North, Esq., of Scarborough, England, proved in October, 1765, the following occurs:

ANCIENT, CURIOUS, AND FAMOUS WILLS 201

"I give to Mrs. R. G. my English walnut bureau, made large to contain clothes, but hope she will not forget when she makes use of it that graces and virtues are a lady's most ornamental dress; and that that dress has this peculiar excellence, that it will last for ever and improve by wearing.

"I give to Lieutenant W. M., my godson, my sword, and hope he will (if ever occasion should require it) convince a rash world he has learnt to obey his God as well as his general, and that he entertains too true a sense of honour to admit anything into the character of a good soldier which is inconsistent with the duty of a good Christian.

"And now having, I hope, made a proper disposition of my lands and money, those pearls of great price in the present esteem of men, let me take this opportunity of expressing my gratitude to the grand original proprietor; and here I must direct my praises to that benign Being who through all the stages of my life hath encompassed me with a profusion of favours, and who by a wonderful and gracious Providence hath converted my very misfortunes and disappointments into blessings; nor let me omit, what the business just finished seems more particularly to require of me, to return Him my unfeigned thanks, who, to all the comforts and conveniences of life, hath superadded this also of being useful even in death, by thus enabling me to dispose of a double portion, namely, out of love to the poor, and another of gratitude to my friends.

"All my faults and follies, almost infinite as they have been, I leave behind me with wishes, that as here they had their birth and origin, they may here be buried in everlasting oblivion. My infant graces and little embryo virtues are, I trust, gone before me into heaven, and will, I hope, prove successful messengers to prepare my way. Thither, O Lord, let them mount up with unremitting constancy, while my soul in the meantime feasts itself with ecstatic reflections on that ravishing change when, from the nonsense and folly of an impertinent, vain, and wicked world, it shall be summoned to meet its kindred spirits, and admitted into the blissful society of angels and men made perfect; when, instead of sickness, gloominess, and sorrow (the melancholy retinue of sin and house of clay), glory and immortal youth shall be its attendants, and its habitation the palace of the King of Kings: this will be a life worth dying for indeed! thus to exist, tho' but in prospect, is at present joy, gladness, transport, ecstacy! Fired with the view of this transcendent happiness and triumphant in hope, these noble privileges of a Christian, how is it possible to forbear crying out O Death, why art thou so long in coming? why tarry the wheels of thy chariot?

"To that Supreme Being, whose treasures and goodness are thus infinite and inexhaustible, be all honour and glory for ever. Amen."

CHAPTER V

TESTAMENTARY AND KINDRED MISCELLANY

"Let the world slide, let the world go,
A fig for care, and a fig for woe!
If I can't pay, why I can owe,
And death makes equal the high and low."

TESTAMENTARY CAPACITY

THE following was copied a short time ago from a legal journal: a stranger on horseback was passing through a country village; a church was being moved, and he asked a resident the reason; the latter answered:

"Well, stranger, I'm mayor of these here diggin's, an' I'm fer law enforcement. We've got an ordenance what says no saloon shall be nearer than three hundred feet to a church. I give 'em jest three days to move the church."

I mean no disrespect in linking this decision of the Mayor with that of the Supreme Court of one of our great Western States.

That Supreme Court recently handed down a decision on testamentary capacity. It would seem that extreme mental obliquity is not a bar to will-making: here is the syllabus in the case:

"That where the testator used excessive amounts of a patent kidney medicine and recommended it to his friends for all kinds of diseases; manifested a hitherto unknown desire to make political speeches, and was positive in his utterances that certain candidates should not be permitted to run for office, and that Bryan was not honest and McKinley was not fit to be President, and that he could make a better President than McKinley; got up at night and sang Psalms; took his dogs and went hunting at night, though he got no game, and had not in former years been known to hunt; exhibited his stallion and other stock at church meetings, and failed to recognize acquaintances; carried on disconnected conversations, had a roaring in his head, used coal oil in his ears, and poured coal oil on trees and when it killed them said he had no sense, — neither these eccentricities nor other peculiarities like them show a want of capacity to make a will."

This testator was a being of a high order of reasoning as compared with many such cases to be met with. Old Diogenes said: "Most men are within a finger's breadth of being mad; for if a man walk with his middle finger pointing out, folk will think him mad, but not so if it be his forefinger."

Ordinary mortals are very strict in measuring craziness: even a slight divergence from the normal standard, or their standard of normality, causes them to adjudge their neighbors crazy: the courts are, however, much more lenient in their judgments in dealing with matters testamentary, and seem inclined to the view that all men are sane, only some are less so: or, as the Kentuckian says of a certain liquid produced in his State, "It's all good but some better than others"; in fact, that weird performances and peculiar actions are indications of individuality and not of mental incapacity. The Supreme Court of North Carolina has decided that while a failure to go to church is a moral delinquency, yet it does not unfit a man to make a will.

The Supreme Court of New York has decided that though one believe in all the abominations and wanton rites of ancient Greece and Rome, and in sincerity worship Egypt's wandering gods, disguised in brutish form, or, like the Hindoo, stand for a lifetime on one leg to secure salvation, or be yet a howling dervish, and rave and gash his naked body, thinking he is doing God service, yet he may be able to transact the affairs of life or dispose suitably of his property.

Any number of individuals have been accused of inability to make their last wills on account of an inclination to hunt for hidden treasures. One such in New York State took with her her nephew, and had him carry a red rooster under his arm for good luck, and they dug diligently, but found no gold. She left gold, however, but not so apportioned as to suit her relatives, and a will contest followed. Another person bandaged his face with handkerchiefs, to prevent false impressions being made on his mind: probably he did not succeed, yet his will was sustained. One gentleman charged his wife with putting tongs in his bed to make him uneasy. Whether hot or cold tongs, is not stated by the decision of the Supreme Court of Connecticut; but the Court did decide that such an offence was more often chargeable to the heart than to the head.

A belief in perpetual motion, and a denial of the revolution of the earth on its axis, and assertions that "the sun do move," have

ANCIENT, CURIOUS, AND FAMOUS WILLS 205

not been sufficient to undermine testamentary capacity, according to the Supreme Court of Wisconsin.

Frequent efforts have been made to show that marriage late in life was evidence of insanity, but always unsuccessfully.

The Supreme Court of Connecticut held that it was a perfectly natural trait for the aged to tell favorite stories and to embellish them a little more or less, as fancy prompted.

A woman's fondness for gossip, and the constant changing of her mind in regard to the arrangement of the house she was building and the color of paints used for it, were insufficient reasons for setting aside her will: on the contrary, the Court intimated that it was perfectly natural that she should change her mind and that the workmen should be scolded. Certain it is, that one feature of this decision has long been sustained by custom.

The same Court, the Supreme Court of Michigan, decided that a disposition on the part of an individual to give his services to the United States Government in the management of its financial affairs, did not necessarily show insanity, and added that if it did, most of us would not escape.

So, after contemplating some of these peculiar and generally uncomfortable departures from the straight line of human conduct, one feels that Dryden spoke by the card when he said, "There is a pleasure sure in being mad which none but madmen know."

PRACTICAL SUGGESTIONS FOR WRITING WILLS

Mr. John Marshall Gest, a prominent member of the Philadelphia Bar, delivered an address to the students of the Law School of the University of Pennsylvania, October 17th, 1907, on "Practical Suggestions for Writing Wills." It is by far the most entertaining and erudite composition the author has ever read on the subject. It can be found in the American Law Register for November, 1907, Volume 55, No. 8. Mr. Gest opens his address in the following words:

"Every man who knows how to write thinks he knows how to write a will, and long may this happy hallucination possess the minds of our lay brethren, for surely St. Ives, the Patron Saint of lawyers, extends to none a heartier welcome in the life beyond than to the Jolly Testator who makes his own Will."

Too little is recorded of this Patron Saint of the legal profession. The author offers the following information concerning him:

Over in France, on its western shore, is a peninsula, the province of Bretagne, or Brittany, and on its rock-bound coast the waves of the Atlantic forever beat; it derives its name from the fact that during early history, the inhabitants of Great Britain, in times of local strife, left their native country, and went to Brittany to reside. This province is one of the most interesting portions of Europe, being rich in history and Celtic ruins, and its landscapes are said to be surprisingly beautiful; its people still retain their ancient language and customs.

In the year 1253, there was born in Brittany, of a noble family, one Yves-Helori, who is recognized the world over as the Patron Saint of lawyers; he espoused the cause of the orphan, the widow, and the poor; he was greatly honored by his countrymen, and was canonized by Clement VI at Avignon; many monuments have been erected and hymns written to perpetuate his virtues and his memory; he died at the age of fifty years, and on a tablet in one of the churches of Brittany are these words in Latin:

"St. Ives was of Brittany;
He was a lawyer, and not a robber,
At which the people wondered."

Following the opening words of his address, Mr. Gest says: "But with deference to amateur lawyers, it is by no means easy to draw a proper will. Lord Coke said, in Butler and Baker's case, one which had been argued twenty-one times, "I find great doubts and controversies daily arise on devises made by last wills, in respect of obscure and insensible words and repugnant sentences, the will being made in haste, and some pretend that the testator in respect of extreme pain was not *compos mentis* and divers other scruples and questions are moved upon wills. But if you please to devise your lands by will, make it by good advice in your perfect memory and inform your Counsel truly of the estates and tenures of your land, and by God's Grace the resolution of the Judges in this case will be a good direction to learned counsel to make your will according to law and thereby prevent questions and controversies."

"For some three centuries," adds Mr. Gest, "this sound advice has been open to him who would read it, and yet testators have such a reluctance to pay a fee to a lawyer, that they will draw their wills themselves, sometimes with the assistance of Dunlap, or have them, as Lord Coke says in the preface to the second

ANCIENT, CURIOUS, AND FAMOUS WILLS

Volume of his Reports, 'Intricately, absurdly and repugnantly set down by parsons, scriveners and such other imperites.'"

Sir Edward Coke died in 1634; as is well known, he was one of the Chief Justices of England. His ardent support of liberal measures in Parliament, especially the right of Freedom of Debate, brought him into trouble, and he suffered nine months' imprisonment in the Tower of London. He had great popularity, and his utterances and courage did much to contribute to the final result in the struggle between the Crown and Commons. His books are still regarded as authoritative treatises on English Law.

A Last Will

The following prose poem was written by Mr. Williston Fish, a prominent lawyer of Chicago, Illinois: Mr. Fish still resides in Chicago. The will is a sentimental and purely fanciful creation: it first appeared in "Harper's Weekly" in 1898, and is reproduced here by permission of Messrs. Harper and Brothers. The will has become one of the classics of American literature, and has been published and republished by newspapers and magazines throughout the English-speaking world. The original from the pen of Mr. Fish varies slightly from the copy here given, this production having been embellished somewhat by various editors. It has sometimes been designated as the "Insane Man's Will," and Mr. Fish has been deluged with inquiries on the subject: the history given above, however, is based on personal investigation made by the author.

"He was stronger and cleverer, no doubt, than other men, and in many broad lines of business he had grown rich, until his wealth exceeded exaggeration. One morning, in his office, he directed a request to his confidential lawyer to come to him in the afternoon. He intended to have his will drawn. A will is a solemn matter, even with men whose lives are given up to business, and who are by habit mindful of the future. After giving this direction he took up no other matter, but sat at his desk alone and in silence.

"It was a day when summer was first new. The pale leaves upon the trees were starting forth upon the still unbending branches. The grass in the parks had a freshness in its green like the freshness of the blue in the sky and of the yellow of the sun — a freshness to make one wish that life might renew its youth. The clear breezes from the south wantoned about, and then were still, as if loath to go finally away. Half idly, half thoughtfully, the rich man wrote upon the white paper before him, beginning what he wrote with capital letters, such as he had not made since, as a boy in school, he had taken pride in his skill with the pen:

"I, Charles Lounsbury, being of sound mind and disposing memory, do hereby make and publish this my last will and testament, in order as justly as may be to distribute my interest in the world among succeeding men.

"That part of my interest which is known in law and recognized in the sheep-bound volumes as my property, being inconsiderable and of no account, I make no disposal of in this my will.

"My right to live, being but a life estate, is not at my disposal, but these things excepted all else in the world I now proceed to devise and bequeath:

"Item: I give to good fathers and mothers, in trust for their children, all good little words of praise and encouragement, and all quaint pet names and endearments, and I charge said parents to use them justly and generously, as the needs of their children may require.

"Item: I leave to children inclusively, but only for the term of their childhood, all and every, the flowers of the fields and the blossoms of the woods, with the right to play among them freely, according to the customs of children, warning them at the same time against thistles and thorns. And I devise to children the banks of the brooks, and the golden sands beneath the waters thereof, and the odors of the willows that dip therein, and the white clouds that float high over the giant trees. And I leave the children the long, long days to be merry in, in a thousand ways, and the night and the moon and the train of the Milky Way to wonder at, but subject nevertheless to the rights hereinafter given to lovers.

"Item: I devise to boys jointly all the useful idle fields and commons where ball may be played; all pleasant waters where one may swim; all snow-clad hills where one may coast and all streams and ponds where one may fish, or where, when grim Winter comes, one may skate; to have and to hold the same for the period of their boyhood. And all meadows with the clover blossoms and butterflies thereof, the woods and their appurtenances, the squirrels and birds, and echoes and strange noises, and all distant places which may be visited, together with the adventures there found, and I give to said boys each his own place at the fireside at night, with all pictures that may be seen in the burning wood, to enjoy without let or hindrance, and without any incumbrance of care.

"Item: I give and bequeath to girls all beauty and gentleness; and to them I give the crown of purity and innocence which is theirs by right of birth and sex; and also in due season the abiding love of brave and generous husbands, and the divine trust of motherhood.

"Item: To young men jointly I devise and bequeath all boisterous, inspiring sports of rivalry, and I give to them the disdain of weakness and undaunted confidence in their own strength, though they are rude. I give them the power to make lasting friendships and of possessing companions, and to them exclusively I give all merry songs and brave choruses, to sing with lusty voices.

"Item: To lovers, I devise their imaginary world, with whatever they may need, as the stars of the sky, the red roses by the wall, the bloom of the hawthorn, the sweet strains of music, and aught else by which they may desire to figure to each other the lastingness and beauty of their love.

"Item: And to those who are no longer children or youths or lovers, I leave memory, and I bequeath to them the volumes of the poems of Burns and Shakespeare and of other poets, if there be others, to the end that they may live over the old days again, freely and fully, without tithe or diminution.

"Item: To our loved ones with snowy crowns I bequeath the happiness of old age, the love and gratitude of their children, until they fall asleep."

THE LAWYER'S BEST FRIEND

A hundred years ago, English lawyers, when dining together, used to drink to the health of "The Schoolmaster," for schoolmasters then often drew up wills for people, and by their ignorance of legal technicalities gave the gentlemen of the long robe much remunerative business. "To the lawyers' best friend — the man who makes his own will," was also a regular toast at dinners of the Bar.

The following poem is inscribed to the legal profession:

THE JOLLY TESTATOR WHO MAKES HIS OWN WILL

"Ye lawyers who live upon litigants' fees,
And who need a good many to live at your ease;
Grave or gay, wise or witty, whate'er your degree,
Plain stuff or State's Counsel, take counsel of me: —
When a festive occasion your spirit unbends,
You should never forget the profession's best friends:

So we'll send round the wine, and a light bumper fill
To the jolly testator who makes his own will.

"He premises his wish and his purpose to save
All dispute among friends when he's laid in his grave;
Then he straightway proceeds more disputes to create
Than a long summer's day would give time to relate.
He writes and erases, he blunders and blots,
He produces such puzzles and Gordian knots,
That a lawyer intending to frame the thing ill,
Couldn't match the testator who makes his own will.

"Testators are good, but a feeling more tender
Springs up when I think of the feminine gender!
The testatrix for me, who, like Telemaque's mother,
Unweaves at one time what she wove at another.
She bequeathes, she repeats, she recalls a donation,
And ends by revoking her own revocation;
Still scribbling or scratching some new codicil,
Oh! success to the woman who makes her own will.

"'Tisn't easy to say, 'mid her varying vapors,
What scraps should be deemed testamentary papers.
'Tisn't easy from these her intention to find,
When perhaps she herself never knew her own mind.
Every step that we take, there arises fresh trouble:—
Is the legacy lapsed? Is it single or double?
No customer brings so much grist to the mill,
As the wealthy old woman who makes her own will.

"The law decides questions of *meum* and *tuum*,
By kindly consenting to make the thing *suum*,
The Æsopian fable instructively tells,
What becomes of the oysters, and who gets the shells.
The legatees starve, but the lawyers are fed;
The Seniors have riches, the Juniors have bread;
The available surplus of course will be *nil*,
From the worthy testator who makes his own will.

"You had better pay toll when you take to the road,
Than attempt by a by-way to reach your abode;
You had better employ a conveyancer's hand,
Than encounter the risk that your will shouldn't stand.
From the broad beaten track when the traveler strays,
He may land in a bog, or be lost in a maze;
And the law, when defied, will avenge itself still,
On the man and the woman who make their own will."

ANCIENT, CURIOUS, AND FAMOUS WILLS 211

INGERSOLL ON DECORATION DAY

Robert G. Ingersoll died at Dobbs Ferry, New York, July 21, 1899. He left no will. A number of his great speeches were funeral orations. The following extract from an address made on Decoration Day to the Soldiers at Indianapolis, Indiana, is regarded as the most touching example of imagery and vision to be found in English literature:

"The past rises before me like a dream. Again we are in the great struggle for national life. We hear the sound of preparation — the music of the boisterous drums, the silver voices of heroic bugles. We see thousands of assemblages, and hear the appeals of orators; we see the pale cheeks of women and the flushed faces of men; and in those assemblages we see all the dead whose dust we have covered with flowers. We lose sight of them no more. We are with them when they enlist in the great army of freedom. We see them part from those they love. Some are walking for the last time in quiet woody places with the maidens they adore. We hear the whisperings and the sweet vows of eternal love as they lingeringly part forever. Others are bending over cradles, kissing babies that are asleep. Some are receiving the blessings of old men. Some are parting who hold them and press them to their hearts again and again, and say nothing; and some are talking with wives, and endeavoring with brave words spoken in the old tones to drive from their hearts the awful fear. We see them part. We see the wife standing in the door, with the babe in her arms — standing in the sunlight sobbing; at the turn of the road a hand waves — she answers by holding high in her loving hands the child. He is gone — and forever."

ELEGY ON A WIFE

A tender and touching tribute to a deceased wife by Mr. Mitchell Kennerley, of New York, is contained in "Thysia, an Elegy"; this beautiful little volume was issued about a year ago, and is one of the profoundest utterances of grief appearing in print in recent years.

The lines below are taken from the poem "Alone," which is typical of the contents of the volume:

ALONE

"The bier, the bell, the grave, silence, and night;
  And you are laid in that cold ground, and gone.
I hardly missed my love till now; — O light
  Of my worn, weary life, dark, dark, alone,
Blindly I feel your empty pillowed place;
  O sacred head, luxuriant hair, and arm
Through the dim hours linked in some dear embrace,
  Lips pressed to mine, and bosom beating warm,
Breath, than the evening breath of heaven more sweet,
  Words faltering, passion-mixed, or sighed with prayer,
Shy, soft caresses of the hand, to greet
  Or tell some passing need, or gentle care —
O love, all these have been; ah, woe is me,
For you are gone, and these no more shall be.

A MEMORY

"I think the gentle soul of him
  Goes softly in some garden place,
With the old smile time may not dim
  Upon his face.

"He was a lover of the spring,
  With love that never quite forgets,
Surely sees roses blooming
  And violets.

"Now that his day of toil is through,
  I love to think he sits at ease,
With some old volume that he knows
  Upon his knees.

"Watching, perhaps, with quiet eyes
  The white clouds' drifting argosy;
Or twilight opening flower-wise
  On land and sea.

"He who so loved companionship
  I may not think walks quite alone,
Failing some friendly hand to slip
  Within his own.

"Those whom he loved aforetime, still,
  I doubt not, bear him company;
I think that laughter yet may thrill
  Where he may be.

"A thought, a fancy — who may tell?
　Yet I who ever pray it so
Feel through my tears that all is well
　And this I know.

"That God is gentle to His guest,
　And, therefore, may I gladly say,
Feel through my tears 'tis for the best,
　On this sad day."

WILL OF MARGARET HAUGHERY

The first monument erected to a woman in this country was that to the memory of Margaret Haughery.

The monument stands in Margaret Place, not far from Canal Street in the City of New Orleans. The figure is that of a woman sitting in a rustic chair, dressed in a plain skirt and loose sack, with a simple shawl thrown over her shoulders, her arm encircling a child.

Prior to her death and by her last will she gave to charitable institutions of the city of New Orleans about six hundred thousand dollars. She died in 1882.

Her parents were Irish immigrants, who died of yellow fever. When quite young she married an Irishman of her own rank, who also died shortly after the marriage, and a year thereafter she lost her only child. The childless widow became a laundress in the St. Charles Hotel, and afterward entered into the bakery business, in which she was eminently successful. Her whole life was devoted to charities, Catholic, Protestant, and Hebrew alike. She never learned to read or write, and could not distinguish one figure from another. Her will is signed with a mark.

The fund for the monument was obtained by popular subscription.

Her funeral sermon was preached by the Archbishop; the business of the city was stopped, and a thousand orphans representing every asylum occupied seats of honor.

WILL OF JOHN ERICSSON

John Ericsson built the *Monitor* and other engines of destruction, but the rattle of drays, the crowing of cocks, and the barking of dogs were too much for his nerves. There is in existence a receipt for five dollars paid to one Charles Herbert for the removal of a dog and the agreement not to keep one on his premises for a period of one year. And it is also a part of history that he bought up his neighbors' chickens to secure the privilege of wringing their necks.

Ericsson died March 8, 1889. His will is dated the 15th day of May, 1878.

On November 7, 1884, he wrote to a friend in Sweden as follows: "They imagine in Sweden that I now possess a large fortune, not considering what it has cost me to be useful to my fellow-men. They do not know that for twenty years, during which time I have spent a million crowns, I have not worked for money."

His fortune at the time of his death amounted to about one hundred thousand dollars, and his claims against the United States Government were required to make good the bequests in his will. These were distributed among his office assistants, female dependents, certain friends, Von Rosen, Adlersparre, the widow of his son Hjalmar, and his nephews and nieces.

The instrument is of considerable length, and he describes himself as John Ericsson, Civil Engineer, of the city of New York. In a codicil to his will, he mentions his share of the profits and emoluments that might arise from the manufacture and sale of his patents that might thereafter be granted by the United States for improvements in engines. These engines are described as two motive engines, designated as a solar engine and a sun motor.

"Men of genius," said Dean Stanley over the grave of Charles Dickens, "are different from what we suppose them to be. They have greater pleasures and greater pains, greater affections and greater temptations than the generality of mankind, and they can never be altogether understood by their fellowmen." "Genius implies always a certain fanaticism of temperament," says James Russell Lowell. Mr. William Conant Church, in his life of Ericsson, concludes his work with these words: "Let us, in spite of his own doubts, accept the cheerful faith of his friend Adlersparre, that assigns to him a kindlier sphere beyond, where just appreciation and intelligent sympathy may stimulate him to still higher efforts. So ends the story of John Ericsson, the son of Olaf, the son of Nils, the son of Eric, the son of Magnus Stadig, the miner."

The *Baltimore*, an American warship, under command of Captain Schley, conveyed the remains of Ericsson to Sweden, flying on her foremast a white, square flag with five blue crosses, indicating that she was on King's business and must not be halted or interfered with on her journey.

Henry Swinburne

Henry Swinburne was an ecclesiastical lawyer, born at York, England, in 1560, and died in 1623. He was educated at Oxford. He wrote "A briefe Treatise of Testaments and last Willes," which was first published in London in 1590 and passed through many editions, the last one appearing in three volumes in 1803. The book is a rare one at this time, being one of the earliest written on the subject of wills. It was formerly much consulted and greatly valued.

Swinburne was an entertaining writer; he mentions the case of a monk, who came to a dying gentleman to make his will. The monk asked the gentleman if he would give such a manor and lordship to his monastery; the gentleman answered yea: then if he would give such and such estates to such and such pious uses. The gentleman answered yea, again. The heir at law, observing the covetousness of the monk and that the estate would be taken from him, asked the testator if the monk was not a very knave, and he again answered yea: and this last answer having been reported to the Court, the instrument was adjudged no will.

A Friend of Charles Dickens

By his will, dated May 8th, 1868, Mr. H. F. Chorley, an English critic and author who died in 1872, bequeathed to his friend, Charles Dickens, of Gad's Hill place, £50 for a ring as a token from one greatly helped by him. An annuity of £200 he gave to Mary, the eldest daughter of Dickens.

A Place for Everything

Mr. Justice Dean once remarked in a will case before him: "In what particular or inappropriate place an elderly lady, or, for that matter, a young one, will put articles or writings of value, is hard to even guess."

Poverty and Riches

Of the poor man, it has been written: "He may make his will upon his nail for anything he has to give."

Bulwer says, "A will is wealth's last caprice."

The Legality of a Mass

In England, masses are held to be superstitious and unlawful: in the United States, opinions are divided: in most of the States of the Union, bequests for the purposes of masses are valid; in others, however, they are looked upon as an attempt to create a private trust for the benefit of the deceased, without any one to enforce it, and consequently invalid. It may be said that the decisions holding the latter view are not very numerous.

Religious Bequests Forbidden

The State of Mississippi has a statute which absolutely forbids bequests, legacies and devises to religious and ecclesiastical bodies; it reads:

"Every legacy, gift, or bequest, of money or personal property, or of any interest, benefit or use therein, either direct, implied, or otherwise, contained in any last will and testament, or codicil, in favor of any religious or ecclesiastical corporation, sole or aggregate, or any religious or ecclesiastical society, or to any religious denomination or association, either for its own use or benefit, or for the purpose of being given or appropriated to charitable uses, shall be null and void, and the distributees shall take the property as though no such testamentary disposition had been made."

Under the laws of the State of Ohio, testamentary gifts for benevolent, religious, educational or charitable purposes, as against issue, are void, unless the will be executed at least one year before the decease of the testator.

In the District of Columbia, and in the states of Georgia, Idaho, Maryland, Montana, Nevada, New Hampshire, New Mexico, New York, Pennsylvania and Washington, are also to be found laws restricting gifts for religious or charitable purposes.

In the Pocket of an Old Dress

Some five years ago, a young girl about seventeen years old came to a lawyer in a Western city and asked him if he had drawn her grandmother's will. She was a kittenish little person, such as one would think lived on cakes and chocolate. When told it had been drawn, she notified the lawyer that her grandmother had just died of apoplexy. He then informed her that her grandmother had called a few days before and taken the will with the avowed intention of cutting her off. The girl left, and the next day was back at the law office with the will, holding it tightly with both hands. She had found it in the pocket of an old dress; it had not been changed, and the young woman receives the revenue on $100,000 during her life. She has since married three times, yet retains much life and romance in her composition. Each yule-tide she sends the lawyer a book; the last one was "Fanchon the Cricket," which treats of how to rear twins. May she grow old gracefully, bless her!

From Father to Son

The late William E. Dodge, of New York, received by will from his grandfather a large sum to be invested and the income to be devoted to the spread of the Gospel and to promote the Redeemer's Kingdom on earth, and to be transmitted, unimpaired, to his descendants for the same purpose. By his will, Mr. Dodge bequeathed the sum to his eldest son to be by him invested and the income to be sacredly devoted, as indicated in the grandfather's will, and to be handed down to his descendants for a like purpose. With regard to charitable bequests, Mr. Dodge in his will said: "Acting from a judgment deliberately formed, based upon observation of the inexpediency of testamentary bequests to religious and charitable objects, and believing it better and wiser to give liberally during life to such objects, I make no bequests of that character."

Spoke from Experience

The late Rufus Hatch, of New York, in his will gave this advice to his children: "I do not wish my boys to go to college, but to receive a commercial education. Should any of them, however, wish to become lawyer, doctor or clergyman, then he may go to college. I most strongly warn my children not to use tobacco in any shape, or form: nor to touch, taste or use wine or liquor in any way. I earnestly desire that my children shall not gamble in any way for money, as *their father has had experience sufficient to serve for all posterity.*"

Will of Eugene Kelley

In the will of the late Eugene Kelley, of New York, is found this beautiful sentiment: "I desire to record in this solemn instrument, the expression of my respect and esteem of my friend, J. D., and the honor in which for many years past I have held him. During our long association, his upright and manly character has ever been the same, and has so endeared him to me, that I could not rest satisfied to part from him without giving utterance to this testimony. His ample fortune would make it idle for me to attest my feeling toward him by a legacy, but I trust he will receive from my wife some personal article of mine which will remain to him a reminder of his friend's affection." With reference to charitable bequests, he adds, "I make this expression of preference in favor of Catholic and Hebrew institutions, solely because other denominations are wealthier and better able to care for their poor."

Samuel J. Randall died Poor

The late Samuel J. Randall, an American political leader, left an estate valued at $789.74, which was not enough to pay the bills of the physicians who attended him in his last illness. Of this amount, $589.74 was due by the government for salary, leaving the total value of his property $200 at the time of his death. This is a remarkable showing for a man who spent thirty years of his life in the most responsible positions in the service of his country.

Will of James Smithson

The Smithsonian Institution in Washington was founded by James Smithson, an Englishman born in France. He was never in the United States, yet he left his fortune of half a million dollars to found at Washington, under the name of the Smithsonian Institution, "an establishment for the increase and diffusion of knowledge among men," provided a certain nephew died without issue, legitimate or illegitimate. The disposition of the fund was for ten years debated in Congress, but finally the trust was accepted, and a board of regents was appointed. Our Weather Bureau is one of the creations of the Institution.

Sailors' Snug Harbor

Robert Richard Randall, of New York, was the founder of the "Sailors' Snug Harbor" for the purpose of maintaining and supporting aged, decrepit and worn-out sailors. The will was attacked by the heirs, but was held valid by the United States Supreme Court.

Where to Invest

Collis P. Huntington, of New York, directed his executors to invest funds in bonds of the United States, or in bonds, stocks or securities of any state north of the Potomac and Ohio rivers, and east of the Mississippi.

A Big Undertaking

Amos R. Eno, late of Connecticut, made a bequest to the Chamber of Commerce, of New York, to provide for, and assist, such of its members as might be reduced to poverty, and their widows and children.

The Term "Miss Nancy"

The term "Miss Nancy" is applied to a man who is over-fastidious in his dress, or who has effeminate manners. The expression dates back to 1730. There was a celebrated actress known as Mrs. Anna Oldfield, and she was buried in Westminster Abbey: she was familiarly known as "Miss Nancy," and was noted for her extreme vanity and particularity in dress. Not only did she devote much thought to this during her life, but she was careful to provide for her proper attire after death, and, according to her instructions, she lay in state attired in elegant garments and the rarest of laces. She has had many eulogists; one poet says:

"Engaging Oldfield, who, with grace and ease,
Could join the arts to ruin and to please."

And the poet, Pope, also credits her with saying to her maid:

"One would not sure be frightful when one's dead,
And, — Betty, — give this cheek a little red."

She died in 1730 in London, and left the royalty and half the town in tears.

A Pew for a Sealskin Sack

A certain lady, dying in New York, was entitled to the use for several years to come of a pew in Grace Church, New York; she bequeathed its use to a female relative living in Johnstown, Pennsylvania; the donee, being unable to use the pew, transferred the right to one who could use it, and received in return a sealskin sack which is reported to have been of great length and beauty, thus showing like John Gilpin's wife that, though on comfort bent, "she had a frugal mind."

Found in a Note-book

Not known until recently to be in existence, because it was written faintly in pencil in an old pocket memorandum book, the will of Dr. John D. Potter, of Pittsburgh, who died July 22, 1906, was recently filed for probate by his brother, Robert J. Potter.

The will disposes of $5000 personal property and real estate of unestimated value situated in Pittsburgh and East Deer township. It reads:

"John D. Potter will, dated January 22, 1903. I bequeath to my mother all my property, both real and personal. I hereby appoint my brother, R. J. Potter, executor of my estate without bond. John D. Potter, M.D."

Working with a Will

"All lawyers like to take a rest,
Like most of us, and still
The average lawyer's happiest
When working with a will."

A Certain Pastor and Elder Debarred

There has just been filed at Pottsville, Pennsylvania, the oddest instrument ever recorded in that city: the document conveys land for the erection of a new church, but stipulates that when the church is erected, a certain pastor shall be forever debarred from holding an office or preaching a sermon in the building, and that a specified elder shall also be precluded from holding an office.

Accuracy in Writing

Few realize the value of accuracy in testamentary and other writings. The other day there appeared a decision by the Supreme Court of Missouri, upsetting a sale, where the judges gravely decided that "Mike" did not mean "Michael"; and one of the arguments in reaching this result was, that to have called Michael Angelo, "Mike" Angelo, would have been a sacrilege to the memory of the great painter.

A Will of the Future

If the late prevailing high prices for meat continue, *Puck* of New York suggests the following will:

"In the name of God, Amen! I, John Doe, in the City of Jersey,

ANCIENT, CURIOUS, AND FAMOUS WILLS

County of Hudson, State of New Jersey, being of sound mind and memory, do hereby make, publish, and declare this my Last Will and Testament in manner following, that is to say:

"FIRST, *I bequeath to my eldest son*, JOHN, *two juicy porterhouse steaks now in the custody of the Arctic Storage Company;*

"SECOND, *I leave to my son*, WILFRED, *a leg of spring lamb now stored with the Freezem Warehouse;*

"THIRD, *I leave to my daughter six pounds of veal chops locked in the refrigerator in the cellar beneath my residence, the combination for the lock of which is held by the Columbia Trust Company. It is also my desire that the executors have these chops frenched before turning same over to the legatee;*

"FOURTH, *I leave to my mother-in-law one haslet, which will be delivered to her upon application at either the Morris or Swift beef houses.*

"LASTLY, *I hereby nominate* RICHARD ROE, *the wholesale butcher,* MORRIS MOE, *the beef-trust magnate, and* PAUL POE, *meat manipulator, to be executors of this my last will and testament, hereby revoking all former wills by me made.*

"In Witness Whereof, I have hereunto set my hand and seal, the eighth day of May in the year of our Lord, Nineteen Hundred and Ten.

"F. P. PITZER."
[Seal]

DOING HIS DUTY

The farmer marched into the little grocer's shop with a firm step. "I want that tub of butter," he said, "and that lot of sugar, and all that other stuff."

"Good gracious!" said the widow who kept the shop. "Whatever do you want with all them goods?"

"I dunno," said the farmer, scratching his head; "but, you see, I'm the executor of your husband's will, and the lawyers told me I was to carry out the provisions."

MAJOR ANDRÉ'S REQUEST OF WASHINGTON

"Tappan, the 1st October, 1780.
"Sir.

"Buoy'd above the Terror of Death by the Consciousness of a Life devoted to honorable pursuits and stained with no Action that can give me Remorse, I trust the request I make to your Excellency at this serious period and which is to soften my last moments will not be rejected.

"Sympathy towards a Soldier will surely induce Your Excellency and a military Tribunal to adapt the mode of my death to the feelings of a Man of honour.

"Let me hope Sir, that if aught in my character impresses you with Esteem towards me, if aught in my misfortunes marks me as the victim of policy and not of resentment, I shall experience the operation of these Feelings in your Breast by being informed that I am not to die on a Gibbet.

"I have the honour to be
"Your Excellency's
"Most obedient and
"most humble Servant
"JOHN ANDRÉ
"Ad. Gen. to the Brit : : Army.

"His Excellency
"General Washington
"&ca. &ca. &ca."

PRESIDENT MCKINLEY'S LAST PRAYER

The last words of great men seem always to possess a peculiar value in the minds of the people; the following is a touching example:

In the afternoon of his last day on earth the President began to realize that his life was slipping away, and that the efforts of science could not save him. He asked Dr. Rixey to bring the surgeons in. One by one the surgeons entered and approached the bedside. When they gathered about him, the President opened his eyes and said:

"It is useless, gentlemen; I think we ought to have prayer."

The dying man crossed his hands on his breast and half closed his eyes. There was a beautiful smile on his countenance. The surgeons bowed their heads. Tears streamed from the eyes of the white-clad nurses on either side of the bed. The yellow radiance of the sun shone softly in the room.

"Our Father which art in Heaven," said the President in a clear, steady voice.

The lips of the surgeons moved.

"Hallowed be Thy name. Thy kingdom come. Thy will be done —"

The sobbing of a nurse disturbed the still air. The President opened his eyes and closed them again.

"Thy will be done in earth as it is in Heaven."

A long sigh. The sands of life were running swiftly. The sunlight died out; the raindrops dashed against the windows.

"Give us this day our daily bread; and forgive us our debts as we forgive our debtors: and lead us not into temptation, but deliver us from evil."

Another silence. The surgeons looked at the dying face and the friendly lips.

"For Thine is the kingdom, the power and the glory, forever, Amen."

"Amen," whispered the surgeons.

LAST WORDS OF COUNT LEO TOLSTOI

It was disclosed to the observant eye of Washington Irving that when the noble elk finds himself mortally wounded, he leaves his companions, and turning aside, seeks some out-of-the-way place to die; and his incomparable pen depicts such a scene in his "Tour of the Prairies," a book which is ever a delight to lovers of nature and outdoor life; and so when death was about to overtake him did Tolstoi, one of the Masters of the Old World, attempt to withdraw from mankind and quietly disappear, dying at a little railway station in Russia.

His valuable manuscripts passed by his last will to his daughter: by another testament, written at the Optina Monastery on November 11, 1910, a few days before his death, he left an address entitled "Effective Means." It says:

"I am naturally anxious to do all I can against evil, which tortures the best spirits of our time.

"I think the present effective war against capital punishment does not need forcing; there is no need for an expression of indignation against its immorality, cruelty and absurdity; every sincere, thinking person, everybody knowing from youth the sixth commandment, needs no explanation of its absurdity and immorality; there is no need for descriptions of the horrors of executions, as they only affect hangmen, so men will more unwillingly become executioners and governments will be obliged to compensate them more dearly for their services.

Knowledge Banishes Delusions

"Therefore, I think that neither the expression of indignation against the murder of our fellow-men, nor the suggestion of its horrors, is mainly needed; but something totally different.

"As Kant well says, there are delusions which cannot be disproved, and we must communicate to the deluded mind knowledge which will enlighten, and then the delusions will vanish by themselves.

"What knowledge need we communicate to the deluded human mind regarding the indispensableness, usefulness or justice of capital punishment in order that said delusion may destroy itself.

"Such knowledge in my opinion is this: The knowledge of what is man, what his surrounding world, what his destiny; hence, what man can and must do, and principally what he cannot and must not do.

"Therefore, we should oppose capital punishment by inculcating this knowledge to all men, especially to hangmen's managers and sympathizers who wrongfully think they are maintaining their position, thanks only to capital punishment.

"I know this is not an easy task. The employers and approvers of hangmen, with the instinct of self-preservation, feel that this knowledge will make impossible the maintenance of the position which they occupy; hence not only will they themselves not adopt it, but by all means in their power, by violence, deceit, lies and cruelty, they will try to hide from the people this knowledge, distorting it and exposing its disseminators to all kinds of privations and suffering.

"Therefore, if we readily wish to destroy the delusion of capital punishment, and if we possess the knowledge which destroys this delusion, let us, in spite of all menaces, deprivations and sufferings, teach the people this knowledge, because it is solely the effective means in the fight.

"Leo Tolstoi.

"Optina Monastery, November 11, 1910."

"Remember Crittenden"

If not a will, the last writing of William Logan Crittenden carried with it a wealth of sentiment and affection; he was a member of the celebrated Kentucky family, and a graduate of West Point. In the year 1851, he joined General Narcisso Lopez, who sought volunteers in the United States to aid in the struggle then going on for Cuban independence. The expedition had intended to land at some remote part of the island of Cuba, but a heavy gale drove the vessel to a small port barely twenty miles from the city of Havana. Crittenden and his party were captured: cruelly bound, he was taken to Havana and imprisoned in the grim Atares Castle; on the following day, he and his companions were shot. Shortly before his death, he was permitted to pen the following pathetic lines to a friend: "This is an incoherent letter, but the circumstances must excuse it. My hands are swollen to double their natural thickness, resulting from having been too tightly corded during the last eighteen hours. Write John (his brother), and let him write to my mother. I am afraid that the news will break her heart. My heart beats warmly for her now. Farewell. My love to all my friends." When one of the Kentucky regiments was in action during the Spanish-American War, their battle-cry was, "Remember Crittenden." At Santiago, Cuba, there is placed a commemorative tablet, which serves to recall another ill-fated attempt to aid in a Cuban insurrection, that of 1873. The *Virginius*, a steamer carrying the American flag, was captured by a Spanish man-of-war, the officers, crew and passengers were shot: the tablet reads: "Thou who passest this place, uncover thyself. This spot is consecrated earth. For thirty years it has been blessed with the blood of patriots immolated by tyranny."

CONFUCIUS

History does not record that the great Chinese philosopher and sage made a testamentary disposition of his worldly effects; but we find that just before his death in 478 B.C., with his hands behind his back, dragging his staff, he moved about his door reciting:

"The great mountain must crumble,
The strong beam must break,
The wise man must wither away like a plant."

The grave of Confucius is in Kung Cemetery near the city of Kiuh-Fow: a magnificent gate opens into a beautiful avenue which leads to his tomb, this avenue being shaded by cypresses and other fine old trees: the inscription on his tomb reads:

"The most sagely ancient Teacher,
The all-accomplished, all-informed King."

The great temple erected here in his honor is a splendid edifice.

Confucius enunciated the Golden Rule five hundred years before Christ, and although negatively put, it is to all intents and purposes the same as given by the Master:

"What ye would not, that others should do unto you, do ye not unto them."

Undertaker paid in Advance

The will of Elijah Bell was probated at Columbus, Ohio, on October 5, 1910. It disposes of an estate of twenty thousand dollars between his widow, children and grandchildren. In a codicil, he states that no changes have been made in his will, and that if any were found on opening that document, the court was to declare the instrument a forgery.

He also declared that he had paid the undertaker for his burial, the sum of one hundred and ninety-eight dollars; the items being, a casket one hundred and forty dollars, a vault fifty dollars, and a shroud eight dollars.

Sings at his Own Funeral

William Faxon died recently at Ovid, Michigan. When the mourners had gathered at the Faxon home, in which lay his open coffin, they were surprised to hear his voice in an anthem from behind a screen of flowers and palms.

Sometime before his death, Faxon conceived the idea of preserving his own voice by means of the phonograph, to be a part of the service when he died. He was a well-known choir singer, and possessed a rich tenor voice.

Heavenly Securities

An inventory recently filed in the County Court at Nashville, Tennessee, is probably the most unusual instrument of its kind ever admitted to probate. The document is signed by Mrs. Corra W. Harris, the author of a book of high merit, "A Circuit Rider's Wife"; her husband, the Reverend Lundy H. Harris, is reported to have died by his own hand; he is said to have been the real circuit rider of the story; his wife qualified as his administratrix. The inventory given below is embodied in a letter addressed to the Clerk of the County Court, which had jurisdiction of the estate of the deceased minister; it is a pathetic and touching tribute from an able pen.

"Mr. W. F. Hunt, City.

"Dear Sir:

"I have your card saying that if I do not furnish you an Inventory of the estate of Lundy H. Harris, of which I was appointed administratrix, within ten days from receipt of this notice, you will proceed as the law directs.

"I did not know it was my duty to furnish such an inventory and now you demand it I do not know how to do it. If the one I send you is not in proper form to be recorded upon your books, I enclose postage and request you to let me know wherein I have failed.

"It is not with the intention of showing an egregious sentimentality that I say I find it impossible to give you a complete and satisfactory inventory of the estate of Lundy H. Harris. The part that I give is so small that it is insignificant and misleading.

"At the time of his death he had $2.35 in his purse, $116.00 in the Union Bank & Trust Company of this city, about four hundred books, and the coffin in which he was buried, which cost $85.00.

"The major part of his estate was invested in heavenly securities, the values of which have been variously declared in this world, and highly taxed by the various churches, but never realized. He invested every year not less (usually more) than $1200. in charity, so secretly, so inoffensively and so honestly that he was never suspected of being a philanthropist, and never praised for his generosity. He pensioned an old outcast woman in Barton County, an old soldier in Nashville; he sent two little negro boys to school and supported for three years a family of five who could not support themselves. He contributed anonymously to every charity in Nashville, every old maid interested in a 'benevolent' object received his aid, every child he knew exacted and received penny tolls from his tenderness. He supported the heart of every man who confided in him with encouragement and affection. He literally did forgive his enemies and suffered martyrdom on Sept. 18th, 1910, after enduring three years of persecution without complaint. He considered himself one of the Chief of Survivors and was ever recognized as one of the largest bondholders in Heaven.

"You can see how large this estate was and how difficult it would be to compute its value so as to furnish you the inventory you require for record on your books. I have given you faithfully such items as have come within my knowledge.

"Sincerely yours,
"Corra W. Harris, Admx."

An Unusual Condition

On April 15, 1910, there was an announcement in the newspapers of how a wealthy and well-known lady in St. Louis died, leaving her entire fortune to her husband; the remainder to their children; but in the event he remarries, the estate to pass immediately to their children. This is the second instance we have known of such a provision in a will. A learned legal writer of San Francisco states in his work on wills that he had never met with such an instance.

Will of Earl of Pembroke

The will of William, Earl of Pembroke, written July 27, 1469, among other clauses, says: " . . . And wyfe ye remember your promise to me to take the ordre of wydowhood as ye may be the better mastre of your owne to performe my wylle. . . ." And in a codicil he adds: " . . . I will that Maud my daughter be wedded to the Lord Henry of Richmond; Ann to Lord Powys; and Jane to Edmund Malafaul."

To pay National Debts

In the year 1784 there was probated in England, the last will and testament of one, M. Fortune Ricard, a teacher of arithmetic. It seems that in his eighth year, his grandparent had given him a small sum of money, and directed him to add the interest to the principal each year, and at his death to employ the result in good works for the repose of their souls. The testator was in his seventy-first year at the time of his death. He divided the fund into five parts. At the end of one hundred years, one part was to be given for the best theological dissertation proving the lawfulness of putting money out at interest. At the end of two hundred years, the second part was to be expended for prizes for distinguished, virtuous actions, literature and other purposes. At the end of three hundred years, the third part was to be used in establishing five hundred patriotic banks in France, lending money without interest. At the end of four hundred years, the fourth part was to be expended in the building of a hundred towns to accommodate the people of France. At the end of five hundred years, the fifth part was to be used in paying off the national debts of England and France.

The will concludes with a hope for the success of these enterprises, above all, that his example would enkindle the emulation of patriots, princes and public bodies, and cause them to give attention to this new and most powerful and invaluable means of serving posterity.

THE NOBEL PRIZES

Alfred Bernard Nobel, a Swedish inventor and philanthropist, was born at Stockholm in 1833, and died in 1896. He was a student of the distinguished John Ericsson: he was educated in St. Petersburg, and studied mechanical engineering in the United States: he was granted patents by the United States on nitroglycerin and dynamite: his patents were very numerous, there being filed in Great Britain one hundred and twenty-nine. In 1875, he controlled fifteen dynamite factories in different parts of the world. He is best known by his will in which he founded the Nobel Prize Fund of $9,200,000, reduced by taxation to $8,400,000, the interest on which is annually divided into five equal parts, and awarded as prizes to the person who shall have made, (1) the most important invention or discovery in the domain of physics, (2) in chemistry, (3) in physiology or medicine, (4) who shall have produced in the field of literature the most distinguished work of an idealistic tendency, and, (5) who shall have most or best promoted the interest of universal peace.

The first four prizes are awarded by the academies of Sweden, and the fifth by the Norwegian Storthing (Parliament). The value of each prize is about $38,000; the right to make nominations is bestowed upon members of corresponding academies of other countries, professors holding proper chairs in Scandinavian and foreign universities, recipients of Nobel prizes, and other persons of distinction. The plan of award is that the prizes shall go to those persons who shall have contributed most materially to benefit mankind during the year immediately preceding. The stipulation that the award should be for achievements of the preceding year has been, to a large extent, disregarded, and in many instances the award is the result of the life work of the recipient.

SPITEFUL WILLS

Mr. Russell, in his work, "Seeing and Hearing," says: "Wills which, by rehearsing and revoking previous bequests, mortify the survivors when the testator is no longer in a position to do so *viva voce*, form a very curious branch of the subject. Lord Kew was a very wealthy peer of strict principles and peculiarly acrid temper, and, having no wife or children to annoy, he 'took it out,' as the saying is, on his brothers, nephews, and other expectant kinsfolk. One gem from his collection I recall, in some such words as these: 'By a previous will I had left fifty thousand pounds to my brother John; but, as he has sent his son to Oxford instead of Cambridge, contrary to my expressed wish, I reduce the legacy to five hundred pounds.' May the earth lie light on that benevolent old despot!"

A Jilted Lover's Will

Dr. Forbes (Benignus) Winslow, though of New England stock, was born in London. He studied medicine in New York and afterward at the Royal College of Surgeons. He made a specialty of the treatment of insanity after locating in London, and became noted as an alienist and was at one time President of the Medical Society of London. He reports the following very singular will:

"A certain individual, who having been crossed in love, concluded to end an unhappy and disappointing life, ordered his body to be boiled down, and all the fat to be extracted therefrom to be used in making a candle, which was to be presented to the object of his affections, together with a letter containing his adieus and expressions of undying love. The time chosen for the delivery of the candle and the letter was at night, in order that the lady might read the touching lines by this veritable 'Corpse Candle.'" The will, the learned Dr. Winslow tells us, was literally carried out.

Will of Frederic Gebhard

Frederic Gebhard, once the favorite of the stage and of society, with an income of $100,000 a year, a private car, and blooded horses and dogs, left an estate valued at less than $10,000. His will, making no mention of his widow, was filed September 21st, 1910, in the Surrogate's office of New York.

Gebhard died at Garden City on September 8th last. His will provides that his entire estate shall be given to his sister, Mrs. Mary Isabel Neilson, who is the mother-in-law of Reginald Vanderbilt.

The will is dated June 21, 1905, some time prior to his marriage to his last wife, formerly Marie Wilson, one of the original Florodora Sextette girls. They were wedded early in 1906, but were reported to have separated. Mrs. Gebhard returned to him some time before he died.

Gebhard attracted public attention over twenty years ago as an admirer of Lily Langtry, who came to this country as a stage beauty. Gebhard accompanied her about the country, and purchased a ranch adjoining her ranch in California. Later she returned to England to become Mrs. Hugo de Bathe, and Gebhard wedded Lulu Morris. She divorced him, and became Mrs. Henry Clews, Jr.

In Colonial Days

The will of William Farrar of colonial times, related to many St. Louisans, was probated in 1677 in Henrico County, Virginia. This document and the inventory portray the customs of those days. There passed under this will, "one Indian boy named Will, and another named Jack"; there is a recital that the "Hoggs being out and uncertain, and one young mare, are left undivided." The valuations are in tobacco, the Indian boys being worth 2800 pounds each. This is rather a novel association of the Indian with tobacco.

Five Drawers to be Opened

A few years ago, there died a wealthy English gentleman who directed that the five drawers in his desk be opened on the five consecutive anniversaries of his death. That was all; not a word about the disposition of his large fortune. When the fourth drawer was reached, a sealed letter contained this message: "Have faith and hope, and you will attain unto the fruition of all your desires." When on the fifth anniversary the last drawer was opened, a properly executed will was found, leaving the property to those who had expected it.

Anticipating Marriage

There is a strong tendency on the part of men to draw up their wills in favor of the ladies to whom they are affianced. By thus anticipating what they would probably do after marriage, they not only take duty by the forelock, so to speak, but reap a present reward in the increased ardor of the adored ones.

Difficult Task for the Judge

The will of Mrs. Sophia Striewe, of St. Louis, was filed in the Probate Court in November, 1910. Six-fourteenths of the residuary part of her estate, amounting to seven thousand dollars, it was directed should go the one who did the most for her during her last days. The Probate Judge will probably decline to pass on so delicate a matter.

Dental Safeguards

Quite recently, a Boston philanthropist provided a fund by means of which the school children of that city were insured the proper care of their teeth. Dental statistics show that this act must be considered as far more worthy than any gift of a like nature in the field of philanthropy for many years; it cannot be doubted that the state of the health depends to a very large degree on the condition of the teeth, and actual figures show that only one child in thirty-five has sound teeth, and much of the sickness of the country can be thus accounted for in this impairment of one of nature's equipments.

What Commodore Vanderbilt said

When Commodore Vanderbilt was on his death-bed, he was visited by his nephew, Samuel Barton. "Sammy," he said, "I've been thinking all day about Alexander Stewart's will. I can't explain it. I can't understand how the greatest merchant in this country, who began with nothing and made a fortune of millions, who was always clear-headed in business matters — how was it possible for a man of that kind to make such an utter damn fool of himself when he came to write his will?"

"One Clover Blossom"

A poetic nature and a love for clover blossoms are at once shown by a Michigan testator who devised land to his native village for park purposes; the only rental being "one clover blossom per annum," which is to be picked on the premises and delivered to his heirs or descendants. No provision seems to have been made for substitute rental in the event of a failure of the clover crop.

ANCIENT, CURIOUS, AND FAMOUS WILLS 233

"ONE RED ROSE IN THE MONTH OF JUNE"

Baron Heinrich Wilhelm Stiegel was born in Germany near Manheim, Baden, of a noble and wealthy family, in 1730. Before he was twenty years of age, he ventured into the New World with a fortune of $200,000: he located in Lancaster County, Pennsylvania, after having built a home in Philadelphia. He was a man of great note, establishing iron and glass works and other industries, and built an elegant mansion at Manheim, in Lancaster County; the old Lutheran Church in Manheim, built in 1770, was located on ground now occupied by a modern church of the same denomination, built in 1891. Stiegel, by will or an instrument of kindred nature, gave the lot on which the church stands, for a consideration of five shillings and "the annual rental of one red rose in the month of June forever." The payment of the rose occurs on the first Sunday in June, and is an annual ceremony of great interest; the church officers bear the rose to the altar on a costly tray, and a descendant of the testator comes forward at the request of the minister to receive it. An extended account of Stiegel appears in the proceedings of the Lancaster County Historical Association for September 4th, 1896.

DESIRED BURIAL ON MOUNTAINS

Robert Louis Stevenson, in his directions for his burial, selected the apex of a mountain in the Samoan Islands; it was necessary to employ a great many natives to clear the way to the mountain top. There, in the midst of singing birds, the blooming of flowers, and the tonic of the sea breeze, one may read his epitaph, written by himself, but for another:

> "Under the wide and starry sky,
> Dig my grave and let me lie.
> Glad did I live and gladly die,
> And I laid me down with a will.

> "This be the verse you grave for me,
> Here he lies where he longed to be,
> Home is the sailor, home from the sea,
> And the hunter home from the hill."

Cecil John Rhodes admired the grandeur of the Matoppo Hills in Rhodesia, and directed in his will that he be buried there in a square to be cut out of the rock on the top of a hill at a point which commanded a magnificent view of the surrounding country.

Helen Hunt Jackson, the authoress, was buried at her direction, on Cheyenne Mountain, near the top of Seven Falls, a short distance from Colorado Springs, Colorado; she desired this for her last resting place, on account of her love for the surroundings, which are of rare beauty, and which no doubt gave her inspiration for her literary productions.

Thomas Jefferson, his wife and two daughters are buried near the crest of Monticello, "Little Mountain."

Monticello, the home of Jefferson, is beautifully situated, and commands a view of the town of Charlottesville, the University of Virginia, and the neighboring country. It has long been known as one of the most picturesque spots in the South. For many years, a monument bearing the following inscription from his own pen marked Jefferson's grave:

> HERE WAS BURIED
> THOMAS JEFFERSON
> AUTHOR
> OF THE DECLARATION OF
> AMERICAN INDEPENDENCE
> OF
> THE STATUTE OF VIRGINIA
> FOR RELIGIOUS FREEDOM, AND
> FATHER OF THE UNIVERSITY
> OF VIRGINIA
> BORN APRIL 2D
> 1743 O.S.
> DIED [JULY 4]
> [1826]

The old monument was removed about fifteen years ago, and now stands on the campus of the University of Missouri, at Columbia, Missouri, and a more imposing one was erected in its place.

No Trips to Europe

Mr. Jefferson G. James, an old and prominent citizen of San Francisco, died in May, 1910; he was a pioneer cattle dealer and politician; he left a large estate to be disposed of under his will, which was written with his own hand and is an eccentric document. One provision in the nature of advice to the distributees reads as follows:

"Don't be mean. Don't pay my employes more than is being paid them now. No outside speculations. No expensive trips to Europe. Spend your money in this country. Buy or build nice residences and live and enjoy yourselves among people you know. The dividends to the small stockholders will assist in the support of a family."

In a codicil, he recurs to the subject of European travel, which seems to have been a pet aversion; he again says, "No trips to Europe."

Rights of an Uxoricide Denied

An appeal from a decision of Vice-Chancellor Malins, of London, questioning the rights of M. de Tourville to inherit under his wife's will, was decided against him.

M. de Tourville was found guilty of murdering his wife by flinging her down a precipice while travelling with her near Botzen, Austria, in July, 1876. The marriage took place in November, 1875, and the lady was a widow possessed of large property. The day after the marriage she made a will, leaving her property to trustees for the benefit of her children, should there be any, but in default of such, she gave the whole to her husband, the husband being cognizant of this arrangement, and thereby, as alleged by the wife's relations, instigated to commit the crime of which he was subsequently convicted and sentenced to death by the Austrian courts. Having appealed, however, his sentence was commuted to imprisonment for eighteen years.

Under these circumstances, the wife's relations claimed a declaration that De Tourville was incapable of taking any interest under his wife's will, and argued that the property belonged to Madame de Tourville's next of kin.

The Vice-Chancellor refused the application for a commission, on the ground that the question of law should first be determined whether, in his position, De Tourville should lose the benefits conferred on him by the will, and directed an amendment of the pleadings for that purpose.

The case was further complicated by the fact that, previous to his conviction, De Tourville had (not perhaps so cleverly as he thought) assigned his interest under the will to another person.

The Master of the Rolls and Lords Justices James and Bramwell, however, reversed the decision of the Vice-Chancellor, and granted the application for a commission, the Master of the Rolls remarking that he was at a loss to understand why the application should have been refused.

He answered the Questions

About the year 1875, "Scotch" John Wilson, a native of Scotland, then living near Tecumseh, Nebraska, drove from his home his son, John Wilson, and told him never to darken the doors again. The son had graduated from an Iowa law school and wanted to practise law; the father wanted the son to stay on the farm; they disagreed and this resulted in the son's being driven from home. He rode away on a circus train and never saw his parents again.

A few years ago, the elder Wilson died, leaving an estate valued at thirty thousand dollars. By his will, he directed that this estate be turned over to any claimant who might appear and say he was the missing son, and who could answer thirty questions. These thirty questions dealt largely with family history, dates, and other matters which were peculiarly within the knowledge of the son.

The son appeared, after an absence of thirty-five years, and answering satisfactorily the thirty questions before the Probate Court, was awarded the estate. After the decision in his favor, he began crying and remarked, "I would have preferred to have seen my mother rather than to take this money."

From under the Sea

On April 15th, 1910, while manœuvering off Kura in Hiroshima Bay, Submarine No. 6 of the Royal Japanese Navy was sunk: her commander, Lieutenant Saguma, and fourteen men were lost. When the vessel was raised two days after the catastrophe, a document written by him was discovered; it is a remarkable instrument and may be regarded as a testamentary log. This paper, written when the commander was slowly choking to death from the gases generated as the submarine lay helpless at the bottom of the sea, is a striking instance of the spirit of silent sacrifice and immolation found in the Japanese character. It reads as follows:

"I have no excuse or apology for having sunk His Majesty's No. 6 submarine by my carelessness, but the crew of the boat bravely and calmly discharged their duties. We now die for the sake of our country, but we regret that the future development of submarines will receive a heavy blow as the result of this disaster. It is, therefore, my hope that you will engage in deeper study of the submarine without any misapprehension of disasters. If you do this, we shall feel no regret at our deaths. We were making a gasoline dive when the submarine sank lower than was intended, and we tried to close the sluice valve, when the chain unfortunately snapped. I therefore closed the valve with my own hands, but it was too late to avert disaster, and the boat sank with a list of 25 degrees. The boat sank at 10 A.M., and it is now 11.45 A.M. The depth of the water is about ten fathoms. I always expect death when away from home. My will is therefore prepared and in the locker, and I hope Mr. Taguchi will send it with this paper to my father."

There were numerous other requests, one to the Emperor, an earnest appeal to supply the means of livelihood to the poor families of the crew.

WRITTEN BY ENTOMBED MINERS

In November, 1909, over three hundred miners were entombed for a period of ten days in a mine at Cherry, near Spring Valley, Illinois. The living were imprisoned with the dead. At the end of ten days, twenty-two miners were rescued; those saved had kept themselves free from fatal gas by building a barricade. Saved from death by suffocation, they were threatened with death by thirst. Two of these men, self-constituted leaders, gave orders for the protection of the community; they conducted religious services and cared for the sick and exhausted, and their directions were strictly carried out.

Two of the miners wrote wills while so imprisoned; they are pathetic documents. The writer of the following will, Joe Pegati, was rescued:

"This is the 4th day that we have been down here. That's what I think, but our watches stopped. I am writing this in the dark because we have been eating the wax from our safety lamps. I also have eaten a plug of tobacco, some bark and some of my shoe. I could only chew it. I hope you can read this. I am not afraid to die. O Holy Virgin, have mercy on me.

"I think my time has come. You know what my property is. We worked for it together and it is all yours. This is my will, and you must keep it. You have been a good wife. May the Holy Virgin guard you. I hope this reaches you some time, and you can read it. It has been very quiet down here and I wonder what has become of our comrades.

"Good-by until heaven shall bring us together.
"JOE PEGATI."

The writer of the second will, Samuel D. Howard, aged twenty-one, died in the mine; his will in part is in these words:

"Alive at 10.30 o'clock yet. Sam D. Howard and Brother Alfred is with me yet. A good many dead mules and men. I tried to save some, but came almost losing myself. If I am dead give my diamond ring to Mamie Robinson. The ring is coming to the Post Office. Henry can have the ring I have in my good clothes. The only thing I regret is that my brother could not help mother after I am dead and gone.

* * * * * * *

"To keep me from thinking I thought I would write these few lines. There is rock falling all over. We have our buckets full of water, seep water, and we drink it and bathe our heads in it.

* * * * * * *

"Seven fifty o'clock in the morning. This is Sunday. There is no air. We have fanned ourselves with the lids of our buckets. Twenty five after 9 and black damp coming both ways. Twenty five after 10 we gave up all hope. We have done all we could. The fan had better start above soon. Twenty five after 10 A.M. Sunday. We are still alive, the only hope is the fan.

"I think I won't have strength to write pretty soon. Fifteen after 12 o'clock Sunday. If they can't give us air, we will make fans ourselves. We take turns at the fan. We have three of them going. Twenty seven to 3 P.M. and the black damp is coming in on us.

"Only for the fans we would be dead. Eleven to 4 P.M. dying for want of air. We have six fans moving. One after another fifteen feet apart. We all had to come back. We can't move front or backward. We can stand it with our fans until Monday morning.

"Fifteen after 2 A.M. Monday. Am still alive. We are cold, hungry, weak, sick and everything else. Alfred Howard is still alive. 9.15 A.M.

"Monday morning, still breathing. Something better must turn up or we will soon be gone. Eleven fifteen A.M. still alive at this time. Sixteen to 1 P.M. Monday, we are still getting weak, Alfred Howard as well as the rest of us."

The Town Crier

Doctor Roland Williams was an author of considerable distinction; he was, at one time, professor in the College of St. David's, Lampeter, South Wales, but had difficulty with the faculty of that institution. He exiled himself to a neighboring town, where he died, leaving in his will fifty pounds to the town of Lampeter, one-third of the income of which is perpetually to be given to the town crier, "for making proclamation once a year, about midsummer, on a market day, that he, Roland Williams, never consented to the election of George Lewellin to a scholarship in this college, but in this and other things he was foully slandered by men in high places; because he loved righteousness and hated iniquity; therefore, he died in exile; but while unjust men permitted this, he both kept the needy student by his right, and defended the alms of the altar of God."

Curll's Collection of Wills

A very curious and now rare collection of wills was made about 1720, by Edmund Curll, who, according to Pope and Swift, possessed himself surreptitiously of these as well as of many anecdotes of the private lives of some of his contemporary celebrities, and published them anonymously, garbling and altering in a scurrilous manner many of the facts he had obtained, so that Arbuthnot observed to Swift that "Curll was one of the new terrors of death;" and the author of "The Man of Taste" wrote:

"Long live old Curll! he ne'er to publish fears,
The verses, speeches, and last wills of Peers."

Besides the memoirs and will of "Alderman John Barber," of "Peter Le Neve, Esq., Norroy King-at-Arms," and that of "Anthony Collins, Esq.," he issued thirty-one pamphlets containing the "Life, Correspondence, and last Will and Testament" of each of the following worthies. The list of them is to be found on the last leaf of the said life of Alderman Barber, and is as follows:

" 1. Archbishop Tillotson.
 2. Bishop Atterbury (Dean of Ch. Ch.).
 3. Bishop Barnes.
 4. Bishop Curll.
 5. Earl of Halifax.
 6. Lord Carpenter.
 7. Lord Chancellor Talbot.
 8. Lord Chancellor Pengelly.
 9. Judge Price.
10. Rev. Mr. George Kelly.
11. Mr. Wright of Newington.
12. Wm. Congreve, Esq.
13. Mr. Addison.
14. Mr. Prior.
15. Mr. Locke (with his letters and memoirs).
16. Matthew Tindall, LL.D.
17. Mr. Nelson.
18. Dr. Radcliffe.
19. Dr. Williams.
20. Dr. South (2 vols., with his posthumous works).
21. Dr. Hickes.
22. Dr. Burnet (of the Charterhouse).
23. Mr. W. Partridge (the Astrologer).
24. Mr. Mahomet (Servant to his late Majesty).
25. Mr. John Guy.
26. Mr. Wills (the Comedian).
27. Elias Ashmore, Esq.
28. Arthur Maynwaring, Esq.
29. Walter Moule, Esq.
30. Wm. King, LL.D.
31. Mr. Manley (Author of the 'Atlantis')."

Indeed, Curll seems to have had an itching hand for seizing on everybody's will; for, among other of the singular productions he put before the public, is a satirical work called "Pylades and Corinna: Memoirs of the Lives, Letters, and Adventures of two Lovers, Richard Grinnett, Esq., of Great Shurdington in Gloucestershire, and Mrs. Elizabeth Thomas Jenner of Great Russell Street, Bloomsbury, together with all the Incidents of their Sixteen Years' Courtship, and two complete Copies of their last Wills and Testaments;" and yet more extraordinary, he invented a will for the Evil One, which he styled: "Satan turned Moralist; or, The Devil's last Will and Testament. Price 1s." A copy of this rare book, worthless though it may be as far as it might afford entertainment to any reader of the present day, would, we fancy, command a good many shillings now.

Of these, fifteen are still extant, and in the library of the British Museum, viz.: those numbered, in our list of Curll's publications, respectively 2, 4, 9, 10, 12, 13, 14, 15, 18, 21, 22, 23, 25, 26, 29; but it is no easy task to find them, even in the Catalogue.

ANCIENT, CURIOUS, AND FAMOUS WILLS

A Weird Custom

In one of Balzac's best novels, "The Country Doctor," he tells of a strange custom which prevails in some of the mountainous districts of France. It will be recalled that the Country Doctor leaves Paris and takes up his abode in a remote country district, the purpose being to make amends for a life which at the outset had not been blameless and had brought about remorse and contrition. He devotes a long and useful life to the unsophisticated country people among whom he locates.

The custom referred to is that upon the death of a husband the neighbors surround the bier and at intervals wail, "The master is gone! The master is gone! The master is gone!" The widow with her own hands cuts off her hair and places it in the hands of the corpse, as an evidence of devotion and constancy.

To the Devil

There is perhaps no sentiment, grateful or spiteful, or any phase of humor, good or bad, which has not been illustrated in testamentary documents.

Probably the legatee who stood the least chance of realizing was the Devil; an attempt was made to make him a land owner in Finland: a few years ago, a queer old native of that country devised all his property to the Devil without attempting to establish the identity of the devisee. The Devil's claim was disregarded and the property went to the heirs of the testator. It was suggested by one writer that doubtless the testator desired to make a good impression on his Satanic Majesty with a view to conciliating him; another writer suggests that even the name of the Devil in a will is better than none, such omissions being frequently found in wills.

Devise to an Idol

Within recent years, the Judiciary Committee of the Privy Council of Great Britain was called upon to pass on the validity of a testamentary devise made four hundred years prior to that time by a resident of India, conveying by will certain lands to the use of an idol, and, strange to say, this gift was sustained.

Mr. Justice Riddell, of the Supreme Court of Canada, recently called attention to this remarkable devise, in an address before the State Bar Association of Missouri.

It appears that one of the descendants of the original testator, after the lapse of four centuries, by a subsequent will, attempted to devise the same property which was formerly conveyed to the use of the idol. The Privy Council upheld the original gift, and the lands are still devoted to the use of the idol.

The Lost Dauphin

It is said the Duchesse d'Angoulême, sister of the "Lost Dauphin," was a cold-hearted woman who preferred the prospect of a throne to the calls of family affection. She died childless and in exile at Prague in 1845.

There is a story that on her deathbed she called to her side General la Rochejacquelein and whispered:

"General, I have a fact, a very solemn fact, to reveal to you. It is the testament of a dying woman. My brother is not dead; it has been the nightmare of my life. Promise me to take the necessary steps to trace him. France will not be happy nor at peace till he is on the throne of his fathers."

The story is probably apocryphal; if true, it is a pity that the dying duchess left no documentary proof of her belief, even though it involved the awful confession that it was her selfishness that had cheated her brother out of a throne and rendered him a nameless outcast.

George Sand's Curiosity

George Sand married in early life a coarse type of man, Casimir Dudevant. Their union was not a happy one. It happened that she found a packet in her husband's desk, marked, "Not to be opened until after my death." She wrote of this in her correspondence:

"I had not the patience to wait till widowhood. No one can be sure of surviving anybody. I assumed that my husband had died, and I was very glad to learn what he thought of me while he was alive. Since the package was addressed to me, it was not dishonorable for me to open it."

And so she opened it. It proved to be his will, but containing, as a preamble, his curses on her, expressions of contempt, and all the vulgar outpouring of an evil temper and angry passion. At once she formed the great decision of her life.

She went to her husband as he was opening a bottle, and flung the document upon the table. He cowered at her glance, at her firmness, and at her cold hatred. He grumbled and argued and entreated; but all that his wife would say in answer was: "I must have an allowance. I am going to Paris, and my children are to remain here at Nohant."

She went into the Latin Quarter, and not only Paris but the world heard much of her. She wrote, "The proprieties are the guiding principle of people without soul or virtue," and, as is well known, her life was in accord with this sentiment.

CHARLES DICKENS ON ELDERLY TESTATORS

When Dickens came to America in 1842, he visited the charitable institutions of Boston, Massachusetts, and of them wrote in his "American Notes": "I sincerely believe that the Public Institutions and Charities of Boston are as nearly perfect, as the most considerate wisdom, benevolence, and humanity can make them. I never in my life was more affected by the contemplation of happiness, under circumstances of privation and bereavements, than in my visits to these establishments."

In this connection he writes of the creation of such institutions through wills:

"The maxim that 'out of evil cometh good,' is strongly illustrated by these establishments at home; as the records of the Prerogative Office in Doctors' Commons can abundantly prove. Some immensely rich old gentleman or lady, surrounded by needy relatives, makes, upon a low average, a will a-week. The old gentleman or lady, never very remarkable in the best of times for good temper, is full of aches and pains from head to foot; full of fancies and caprices; full of spleen, distrust, suspicion, and dislike. To cancel old wills, and invent new ones, is at last the sole business of such a testator's existence; and relations and friends (some of whom have been bred up distinctly to inherit a large share of the property and have been, from their cradles, especially disqualified from devoting themselves to any useful pursuit, on that account) are so often and so unexpectedly and summarily cut off, and reinstated, and cut off again, that the whole family, down to the remotest cousin, is kept in a perpetual fever. At length it becames plain that the old lady or gentleman has not long to live; and the plainer this becomes, the more clearly the old lady or gentleman perceives that everybody is in a conspiracy against their poor old dying relative; wherefore the old lady or gentleman makes another last will

— positively the last this time — conceals the same in a china teapot, and expires next day. Then it turns out, that the whole of the real and personal estate is divided between half-a-dozen charities; and that the dead and gone testator has in pure spite helped to do a great deal of good at the cost of an immense amount of evil passion and misery."

The Cloak and Earring of Charles I.

On the morning of January 30th, 1649, Charles I. rose early and for some time remained in prayer and meditation; he was then taken to Whitehall for execution, accompanied by his faithful Confessor, William Juxon, Bishop of London. On the scaffold with him were Colonel Hacker, another officer, and two men disguised with masks; though heard by few, the King addressed the vast crowd in the following words: "For the people, truly, I desire their liberty and freedom as much as any body whosoever, but I must tell you that their liberty and their freedom consists in having of government those laws by which their life and their goods may be most their own. It is not for having share in Government, Sirs; that is nothing pertaining to them; a subject and a sovereign are clean different things, and therefore until you do that, I mean that you do put the people in that liberty as I say, certainly they will never enjoy themselves."

He made a last profession of faith and gathered his hair under his cap; then took off his cloak and George and gave them to Bishop Juxon with one word, "Remember." He then took from his left ear a large pearl earring and formally bequeathed it to one of his faithful followers; it is still preserved and is now owned by the Duke of Portland. It is pear-shaped, about five-eighths of an inch long and mounted with a gold top, and has a hook to pass through the ear. He then laid himself down on the block, breathed a short prayer, and stretched forth his hands, the appointed signal for the executioner, who performed his duty well, for the head of the King was severed by one blow and it was held up to the view of the crowd, which answered with a fearful groan.

Masculine earrings were formerly quite common: Sir Walter Raleigh wore one, and so did Horace Walpole, and the Earl of Southampton; Shakespeare indulged the same taste. In modern times such male finery has been largely relegated to sailors, gypsies and negroes.

ANCIENT, CURIOUS, AND FAMOUS WILLS

EXHORTATION TO CONDEMNED PRISONERS

Robert Dowe of St. Sepulchre, London, in his lifetime, on the 8th of May, 1705, gave £50 to the end that the vicar and churchwardens of that parish should, forever, previously to every execution at Newgate, cause a bell to be tolled, and certain words to be delivered to the prisoners ordered for execution, in the form and manner specified in the terms of his gift, as set forth in the old will book.

An annual sum of £1 6s. 8d. in respect of this gift was charged upon the parish estate in West Smithfield; it was paid to the sexton, who employed a person to go to Newgate on the night previous to every execution, where he offered to perform the prescribed duty, which was always declined, as all needful services of that kind were performed within the prison.

Noorthouck, in his History of London, gives the words of the exhortation. He states that the sexton "comes at midnight, and after tolling his bell calls aloud,

'You prisoners that are within,
Who for wickedness and sin,

after many mercies shewn you, are now appointed to die to-morrow in the forenoon, give ear and understand, that to-morrow morning the greatest bell of St. Sepulchre's shall toll for you in form of and manner of a passing bell, as is used to be tolled for those that are at the point of death; to the end that all godly people hearing that bell, and knowing it is for you going to your deaths, may be stirred up heartily to pray to God to bestow his grace and mercy upon you whilst you live. I beseech you for Jesus Christ's sake to keep this night in watching and prayer, to the salvation of your own souls, while there is yet time and place for mercy; as knowing to-morrow you must appear before the judgment seat of your Creator, there to give an account of things done in this life, and to suffer eternal torments for your sins committed against Him, unless upon your hearty and unfeigned repentance you find mercy through the merits, death, and passion of your only mediator and advocate Jesus Christ, who now sits at the right hand of God to make intercession for as many of you as penitently return to him.'

"On the morning of execution, as the condemned criminals pass by St. Sepulchre's churchyard to Tyburn, he tolls his bell again and the cart stopping, he adds, 'All good people pray heartily unto God for these poor sinners, who are now going to their death, for whom this great bell doth toll. You that are condemned to die, repent with lamentable tears; ask mercy of the Lord for the salvation of your own souls, through the merits, death, and passion of Jesus Christ, who now sits at the right hand of God, to make intercession for as many of you as penitently return unto Him.

> 'Lord have mercy upon you!
> Christ have mercy upon you!
> Lord have mercy upon you!
> Christ have mercy upon you!'"

The Pardoned Poet's Farewell

"John Carter," the convict whose poems brought him pardon, did not leave his Minnesota prison without a farewell message to his friends within its walls. This "last will and testament" was first printed in the weekly *Prison Mirror*, published in the penitentiary. The St. Paul *Dispatch* quotes it as follows:

"This is the last will and testament of me, Anglicus. I hereby give and bequeath my collection of books (amounting to some 6000 volumes) to Mr. Van D., in memory of the not altogether unpleasant hours we spent together, hours marked by no shadow of animosity at any time. We could not be happy, but we were as happy as we could be. To Dr. Van D. I leave my mantle of originality, and what remains of the *veuve cliquot*, in memory of encouragement when I most needed it.

"To the editor I leave my space on this journal and the best of good wishes in memory of his unfailing courtesy and forbearance.

"To Uncle John and to Sinbad go my heartiest wishes that we may meet soon in some brighter clime.

"To Mr. Helgrams, my best dhudeen and the light of hope.

"To young Steady and to Mr. D. M., my poetic laurels, which they are to share in equal measure.

"To the boys in the printing-office, the consolation of not being obliged to set up my excruciating copy.

"To the tailors (and to the boss tailor in particular, 'Little Italy,') my very best pair of pants.

"To Jim of the laundry, — but nothing seems good enough for Jim, the best soul that ever walked.

"To Portfiro Alexio Gonzolio, a grip of the hand.

"To Davie, pie, pie again, and yet more pie.

ANCIENT, CURIOUS, AND FAMOUS WILLS

"To the band boys — why, here's to 'em! May they blow loose.

"To my fellow pedagogues, 'More light,' as Goethe put it, more fellowship; it would be impossible to wise them. They know where I stand and I know where they stand.

"Lawdy! lawdy! If I hadn't forgotten Otto and his assistant. Here's all kinds of luck to 'em, and no mistake about it.

"Finally to all those not included hereinbefore (for various reasons), here's to our next merry meeting. To those in authority, thanks for a square deal. To mine enemy — but I mustn't bulcon him.

"Gentlemen, I go, but I leave, I hope I leave my reputation behind me.

"ANGLICUS."

PROBATES HIS OWN WILL

Judge R. B. Tappan, of Alameda, California, in July, 1910, practically probated his own will. He filed in the Recorder's Office, of Alameda County, a document which makes the Alameda Lodge of Elks his beneficiary. He provides that if he dies or becomes insane his property is to go to the Elks. Throughout the legal phraseology of the instrument Judge Tappan has made many unique observations, among which he states that he trusts that no one will inspect him too closely for signs of dementia. He says:

"I hope that such things as leading a horse over a hill while I am hatless and coatless and wearing a bandana handkerchief over my head or wearing moccasins in the city will not be considered evidence of insanity sufficient to revoke the terms of this trust."

On Judge Tappan's death he directs that such property as he has transferred to the trust shall immediately be put to the uses of the Elks lodge after paying his funeral expenses, which, he says, should not be over $75. He remarks in the document that he has already paid $10 for a redwood box to convey his remains to the crematory. In regard to the document, Judge Tappan said:

"I have the consent of the directors of my lodge of Elks to keep for me in their possession during my life my property now in their possession, and any property which I may place in their custody hereafter will be similarly held. I have made provisions in the declaration which will pass the trust fund to the Elks lodge in the event of my death or in the event of my becoming insane. The question of insanity is left to the officers of my lodge. There may arise an occasion where some meddlesome person or persons would lodge a contest, and perhaps my wishes concerning the disposition of what belongs to R. B. Tappan would not be complied with. I have a right to do what I see fit with what is mine without consulting any one else, and it is a great satisfaction to me to-day to know just where my property will go in the event of the happening of either one of the conditions referred to. This proposition involves a large sum of money and securities which are as good as gold coin, and the matter is no joke. The officers realize this, or else they would not have accepted the trust. I never speculate or gamble in any form; hence my trust is not likely to shrink much."

Trust Companies as Executors

The Trust Companies of the United States and other countries have, in recent years, proved themselves the best mediums for administering wills; such an institution located in Melbourne, Australia, in pointing out its merits and stability, quite uniquely, we think, quoted Tennyson's lines:

" . . . Men may come,
And men may go,
But I go on for ever."

CHAPTER VI

WILLS OF FAMOUS FOREIGNERS

"Farewell! a long farewell, to all my greatness!"

WILL OF THE MARQUIS D'ALIGRE

BEFORE quoting the will of the Marquis d'Aligre, we will recall a little incident of his life, which, though it serves to show his character, does not prepare us for the various phases of his shrewd and humorous mind.

One day the marquis went to pay a visit to the Duc de X., one of his friends, a man of scrupulous propriety and a great stickler for etiquette. Hardly had he taken leave, after an hour's chat, before the duke perceived on the mantelpiece a pair of brown gloves; he looked at them and then drew back with horror; these gloves of an indescribable hue had evidently once been white! and it was actual wear that had tinted them. The tips of the fingers were twisted about and stiff, and the gaping buttonholes testified to their protracted and loyal service. No housemaid would have worn them to clean her stoves.

The duke took his tongs, seized the gloves, and laying them on a folded newspaper, rolled them up with precaution, and having written on a slip of paper, "Gloves belonging to a great nobleman, one of the largest landowners in France," he fixed it with a pin to this singular parcel. Not many minutes later arrives the valet of the marquis, who, presenting himself before the duke, begs to know, not without some embarrassment, and blushing up to his ears, whether his master had not forgotten his gloves. Needless to say they were forthwith handed to him.

We now proceed to the will of this gentleman, of which we propose to transcribe the most remarkable clauses, which, however, we must remark, seem to have been penned in a spirit of justice.

"Art. IV. — I leave to M. de Boissey, my blessing, to compensate him for the curses which M. Pasquier heaped upon him every day. May it be of use to him on the judgment-day."

"Art. VII. — I withdraw from M. A . . . , and M . . . x the

sums I had left them by a former will; they have so often proclaimed that I am a man who would cut a farthing in four, that I would on no account oblige them to change their opinion."

"Art. IX. — I advise Madame de Pomereu, or those she may authorize, to pay to the *charcutiers* of Paris the sum of 10,000 francs in remembrance of their predecessors, who before the Revolution dealt for their ham and other smoked meats at the Hôtel d'Aligre, Rue St. Honoré.

"Art. X. — I leave 20,000 francs a-year to the *invalide* who, being on guard on the Pont des Arts in 1839, and, judging from the shabbiness of my dress that I was in distress, paid for me the five centimes toll."

"Art. XIII. — Considering that virtue ought to be encouraged, I consecrate 100,000 francs yearly to the formation of fifty dowries of 2000 francs in favour of fifty *Rosières*. The Mayor of Nanterre, who finds these maidens every year, will be good enough to undertake the distribution. If by chance his commune should not furnish him the necessary contingent, he is authorized to address himself to the Gymnase Theatre.

"Art. XIV. — I leave 200,000 francs a-year to the 'Phalansterians'; but they are only to receive this sum on the day on which they shall have transformed the ocean into orangeade, and gratified mankind with that appendage he needs to make him equal to the gibbon."

"Art. XVI. — Taking compassion on the poor of the first arrondissement, I desire that the value of the cereals harvested on my land at the next harvest shall be distributed to them in its entirety.

"Art. XX. — Finally, I leave to my relatives, oblivion; to my friends, ingratitude; to God, my soul. As for my body, it belongs to my family vault."

The brother of the testator was put into the will for a legacy so absurdly disproportionate to what he considered he had a right to expect that the following not very maturely considered observation thereon appeared in a newspaper of the date (1847):

"The celebrated Crœsus who has just died has revealed in his will certain little peculiarities of which few suspected him. He was a great protector of rats; and on the day but one before that of his death he was at the races with four of these animals in his calêche. He had a brother who gave him very good advice on this subject, like the Cléante of 'Tartuffe,' to whom he replied by a little posthumous epigram, indicative of his churlish disposition; he has left him, out of his large fortune, a dole of 20,000 francs per annum. There is no revenge so hard and bitter as that of an old man. There are, we venture to think, many brothers, all the same, who would be very glad of a fraternal legacy of eight hundred a-year, and, moreover, we know nothing of the provocation that may have been given; like Lord Campbell, 'we should like to hear the dog's story.'"

Possibly the old Marquis felt the separation he contemplated between himself and the fortune he had amassed, but if he entertained any malicious sentiments against those to whom he was obliged to leave what he could not take away with him, he seems to have been fully justified in the somewhat severe animadversions he has passed on some of his legatees.

To a lady relative, who had been full of attentions for him, he left a broken cup, jeering her with the taunt that while she thought she was taking him in he was laughing in his sleeve at the grimace she would make when she found that it was he who had got all her little gifts, her smiles and favors out of her, knowing all the while that he had no intention of repaying them as she expected.

"As for you," he says at the end of the will, "you, my good and admirable valet, who have so long taken me for your dupe, you will now learn that it is you who have been mine; when at the conclusion of my dinner you thought I was applauding your economy and your zeal, in carefully putting together the remains of bottles of wine and keeping them for the next meal, it never occurred to you that I was well aware you took for your own use whole bottles. When you came with tearful eyes and coaxing voice to wait on me the moment I was suffering from any trifling indisposition, presenting to me my *tisanes* with an assumed air of condolence and anxiety, you little thought how my instinct, following you into the servants' hall, guessed the language in which you expressed yourself there. 'The old fellow,' you used to say, ' can't last much longer, and then I shall come in for my hard-earned legacy.'

"Well, my dear fellow, I am sorry to tell you this was all a mistake, and you have got to learn that masters are not always so much stupider as you suppose than their servants.

"As for you, my relatives, who have been so long spelling upon this fortune, on which ' I had concentrated all my affections,' you are not going to touch a penny of it, and not one of you will be able to boast that you have squandered the millions which the old Marquis d'Aligre had taken so many years to hoard up."

CARDINAL ANTONELLI'S WILL

The great wealth Cardinal Antonelli, who died in 1876, is reported to have left, has aroused special interest with regard to his will, and given rise to endless gossip, not only as to its contents, but concerning the document itself. At first it was reported that it could not be found; then, that it had disappeared in some remarkable manner; that it had been purposely destroyed; that the cardinal had made no will; and many other *canards* were circulated. Later, however, the *Libertà* announced that it was in the hands of the public notary in the Piazza San Claudio, where it could be seen, but that only those having a direct interest in its contents could be permitted to examine it. Subsequently the *Popolo Romano* published the document *in extenso*, together with the notary's statement concerning it, as follows:

"REPERTORY NO. 187

"Reigning His Majesty Victor Emmanuel II., by the grace of God and the will of the nation, King of Italy.

"I, the undersigned, public notary, certify that among my acts under the hereafter-inscribed day is to be found the registered report of the deposit of the holograph testament of the defunct Most Eminent Cardinal Giacomo Antonelli, made at the instance of the illustrious advocate, Signor Antonio Bachetoni, to the following effect:

"The year one thousand eight hundred and seventy-six on Thursday, the twenty-third day of the month of November, in Rome. Before me, Scipione Vici, public notary, having my office upon the Piazza San Claudio, No. 93, and inscribed in the Council of Notaries of the district of the Collegio di Roma, assisted by the undersigned witnesses, qualified according to law, and in the presence of the illustrious advocate Signor Enrico Simonetti, Prætor of my mandament, duly executed at his residence, situated in Via Gesù e Maria, No. 28, and of the Signori Jacopini Torollo, son of the late Giovanni Batta, of Arcidosso, in the Province of Grosseto, domiciled Via Orsoline No. 2, and Filippo Ciavambini, son of the late Petito, of Ascoli, domiciled Via de' Specchi No. 3, both *employés*, has personally appeared the illustrious advocate Antonio Bachetoni, son of the late Giovanni, native of Spoleto, domiciled in Rome, in Via del Corso No. 509, of full age, being juridically qualified, and known to me, notary, who, in consequence of express instructions received from the noble Signori Conti Gregorio, Angelo, and Luigi Antonelli, brothers german, has applied to me to deposit with me notary, certain papers, which they assert contain the last testamentary dispositions of the aforesaid defunct Most Eminent and Most Reverend Signor Cardinal Giacomo Antonelli, who passed from among the living on the sixth day of the current November, as results from the certificate of the Board of Health, given the 22nd day of November, 1876, and which I insert (Appendix No. 1). Wherefore, in presence of the aforesaid Signor Prætor and of the aforesaid witnesses, he has consigned to me an open envelope, on the outside of which was found written, ' Testament of Cardinal Giacomo Antonelli,' and having examined the contents of the same, they were found to consist of two sheets of paper folded in quarto, and another small envelope, of which the requisite description will be made in its proper place. Opening the two sheets, it was found that they were in one handwriting and consisted of six pages written throughout, and the seventh upon the half only, followed by the date 'Rome, January 18, 1871,' and by the signature ' G. Card. Antonelli.' On the third page an interlineation of fifteen words was observed, and on the fifth and seventh pages the insertion of a word in each without any marginal note or erasure, as follows:

"' WILL OF CARDINAL GIACOMO ANTONELLI

"' Desiring to dispose of my property now that, by the grace of God, I find myself sane in mind and body, using the faculties which I have as Cardinal of the Holy Roman Church, with this document, by me written and subscribed, I make herewith my last will and testament. Before everything else I recommend my poor soul to the infinite mercy of God, trusting that through the intercession of the Most Holy Immaculate Mary, and of my patron saints, St. Peter, St. Paul, St. James, and St. Louis, He may grant me remission of my sins, and make me worthy of the eternal glory of Paradise. I forbid the dissecting or embalming of my body after death in any way or for whatsoever motive, and order that it be interred in the burying-place of my chapel in the Church of Sta. Agata alla Suburra, near my good mother.

"' The funeral shall be made according to custom in the church which it shall please the Holy Father to appoint. During the eight days following my death I order that a hundred masses a day be celebrated, with the alms of thirty sous for each mass.

"' A part of these masses shall be caused to be celebrated by the

Mendicant Friars. I humbly beg the Holy Father to accept the respectful offering I make him of the crucifix standing on my writing-table, having the cross inlaid with lapis-lazuli, and at the base the kneeling Magdalene, within the centre of said base a bas-relief, representing the Addolorata, and other ornaments in silver. I pray him to accept with paternal goodness this object as a homage from the most devoted and faithful of his subjects, who dies tranquil in the conscience of never having failed in duty towards his sacred person, and the conviction of having always with all earnestness and honesty served him in the true interests of the Church and of the State. Before proceeding to dispose of my private fortune, I declare that I do not possess any other capital beyond that which came from the heritage of my excellent father, or which I have been able to acquire through the means left me by him. I protest, therefore, against all the calumnies which on that and on any other account whatsoever have been in so many ways circulated through the world, before God who is to judge me, and before Him I forgive from my heart all those who have tried to do me evil.

"'If, in doing my duty, I may have caused displeasure to anyone, I have the conscience of never having had even the intention of injuring anyone whomsoever. I direct my heirs to consign to the persons whom I have thought it my duty to remember some memoranda which I shall leave written in a sealed paper by me subscribed.

"'I leave to the Hospital of Santo Spirito, for one time only, twenty-five francs, and other twenty-five francs to the Holy Places of Jerusalem.

"'To my Titular Church of Santa Maria in Via Lata, I leave my white *tonacella*. The red one I leave to the Church of Sta. Agata alla Suburra, the *commenda* of which I hold. The violet *pianeta* I leave to the monastery of St. Marta, of which I am protector.

"'The sacred hangings and altar-plate of my private chapel I desire may be preserved for the chapel of my house on the Quirinal, and they shall belong to the heir to whom I assign the said house.

"'I institute as universal proprietary heirs my dearest brothers, Filippo, Gregorio, Luigi, and Angelo, my nephew, Agostino, son of Gregory, and my other nephew, Paolo, son of Luigi, to each of whom, as I shall say afterwards, I assign and determine such portion of the property and of the objects as I will they may possess, and I will that each of them may bear the respective legacy-duty according to the value of the share falling to him.

"'All my possessions, furniture, gold, silver, precious objects, titles, and effects whatsoever, the credits, and the little money that may be found in my possession at the time of my death, except the collection of stones and other things of which I shall dispose hereinafter, I assign to my brothers as above, Filippo, Gregorio, Luigi, and Angelo, and I pray them to accept this my disposition as a proof of the sincere affection which I have always borne them equally, and as an attestation of the gratitude I have always entertained towards them for the affection which they have shown me under all circumstances.

"'I assign to my nephew Agostino, heir as above, my house in Rome, situate near the Quirinal, bought from Conte Vimercati, with everything which is in the said house at the moment of writing this present will; so that, if at the moment of my death any objects of whatsoever kind be found there which are now in my apartment at the Vatican these I declare to belong to my brothers as above. I assign also to my aforesaid nephew the altar-furniture of my private chapel at the Vatican. I assign him also the collection of marbles, with the cabinets containing them, exactly as they are in my apartment at the Vatican.

"'I declare, however, that in the aforesaid collection I do not mean to comprehend the rock crystals and other objects which are kept in three other separate cabinets, one of which contains medals, which I declare to belong to my brothers as above. I assign to my nephew, Paolo, son of my brother, Luigi, heir as above, all the property I possess in the territory of Ceccano and adjoining territories, with all that is to be found in it, nothing excluded, with the following conditions — that is, that my brother, Angelo, having had the patience to occupy himself always with the administration of my possessions in Ceccano and adjoining territories, I ordain that neither my said nephew nor any other person have any right or title whatsoever to take him to account for the aforesaid administration, he having always done everything with my full understanding and having always regularly transmitted to me all the rents of the aforesaid properties.

"'I dispose, moreover, that all that shall exist at the time of my death of products or rents, as well natural as civil, from the said properties as above, for two seasons following the same, including that in which my death shall happen, shall be freely enjoyed by him as legatee, continuing to hold the administration as he did during my lifetime, exonerating him again from any rendering of account whatsoever. I dispose also that the heir shall not enter into possession of the aforesaid property until after two seasons as aforesaid after my death.

"'I leave besides, as a legacy to my said brother, Angelo, the two large silver vases with bas-reliefs on their bowls which are to be found in my writing-room of my apartment in the Vatican, and I request my said brother to accept and preserve them as an attestation of my affection and a recognition of all the affectionate regards he has shown towards me during my life. And I also request of all my heirs that all the legacies of furniture, pictures, and other objects may be preserved and used in their respective families, avoiding under any circumstances that any portion of them be sold by public auction.

"'Finally, I direct that all my said heirs shall amicably divide my heritage among themselves in the portions according as I have assigned them, making of them a simple familiar description for their own guidance. I also leave to all my servants for their natural lives; to those in my service at the time of my death, and who have served me for more than twenty-five years, the full monthly wages they received when I was alive; to those who have served me for more than fifteen years I leave two-thirds of their monthly wages; and to those who have served me for less than ten years, one-third of their monthly wages. In the enjoyment of this disposition, notwithstanding that it is unnecessary to declare it, I intend that the two ecclesiastics who form part of my household shall be comprised. I expressly prohibit that any of the aforesaid shall, for whatsoever reason, effect mortgages upon the property which constitutes my heritage or upon that of my heirs for the purpose of securing any assignments I have left them, and I declare that I have made the said assignments solely under the express condition that they do not affect any such mortgage; and if any or all of them should think fit to do so, then I declare that *ipso facto* they are excluded from the prescription of the said assignment, which is none other than a gratuitous liberality, and I give them instead one hundred scudi for once only.

"'G. CARDINALE ANTONELLI.

"'Rome, 18th January, 1871.'

"The small envelope enclosed with the above bears on the outside the following inscription: 'For my heirs.' The contents, being taken out, consisted of a small sheet of paper written evenly

in the same handwriting, on the first two pages throughout, and a part of the third, and at bottom the date — Rome, 18th of January, 1871, and the signature, 'G. Card. Antonelli.' There are neither erasures nor marginal notes, interlineations nor additions. The tenor of this little sheet is as follows:
"' My heirs are to pay the following legacies:
"' To my good sister Rosalia, married Sanguigni, 5000 francs.
"' To my niece Anna Sanguigni, married to Count Pocci, 5000 francs.
"' To my niece Lucia Antonelli, 5000 francs.
"' To my niece Teresa Antonelli, 5000 francs.
"' To my niece Innocenza, married Bornana, the *bénitier* with silver bas-relief representing the Nativity, which stands near my bed.
"' To my nephew Agostino, the watch which stands on the little table, with the arms of the Holy Father, given me by His Holiness on occasion of the Centenary of St. Peter.
"' To my nephew Domenico, the other pocket-watch, with my arms.
"' To my nephew Paolo, the watch, with gold chain, which I wear every day, with my arms on one side and my cipher on the other.
"' To my nephew Pietro, twelve silver *couverts* of those which I use daily.
"' To my sister-in-law Mariana, one of my pair of great silver lamps, whichever she chooses. The other I leave to my sister-in-law Peppina.
"' To my sister-in-law Mimma, I leave my triangular silver inkstand which stands upon my best writing-table, together with one of the two little boxes of Florentine mosaic which are in the same room.
"' To my sister-in-law Vittoria, I leave the silver basin and vase of English work which are in the case. To my niece Emma, wife of Agostino, I leave all my lace. To her good mother, Contessa Garcia, I leave the little service of silver-gilt, consisting of tray, coffee-pot, cream-jug, sugar-bowl, and cups, with spoons, requesting her to accept them as a remembrance of one who is grateful to her for all the kindness she used towards him while he was in this world, and who prays her to make use of the said objects for her *déjeûner*.
"'G. CARD. ANTONELLI.
"' Rome, January 18th, 1871.' "

Then follow the attestation of the notary and the signatures of Cardinal Antonelli's lawyer, of the Prætor, and of the witnesses, and the note of expenses of registration.

WILL OF MATTHEW ARNOLD

The estate of Matthew Arnold amounted to £1041. His will is in his own handwriting, and is one of the shortest that ever came under probate: " I leave everything of which I die possessed to my wife, Frances."

WILL OF JEAN BAPTISTE ROBERT AUGER

Jean Baptiste Robert Auger, Baron de Montyon, was born in 1733 and died in 1820; he was a French economist and philanthropist, and a friend of Franklin. The Baron was a member of the King's Government just before the Revolution. Although by birth and social position an aristocrat, all his heart was with the poor and suffering of the land.

In 1783 he founded several prizes, the chief one being a prize for the most remarkably virtuous act on the part of any poor French citizen. By his will he left a large sum of money for the purpose of "aiding virtue," as he said. "The doers of the actions honored," the will stipulated, "shall not be of a station above the middle classes of humanity." The annual award of these prizes is made by the French Academy.

As years have passed, other rich philanthropists have added to the original sum, until to-day the income is sufficient to award every year a large number of prizes that are really of substantial aid to those who receive them.

For a number of years after the Government had received the bequest, it did not make any awards. During the Revolution the convention voted that it did not approve of awarding any such prizes; so the principal was allowed to accumulate. But during the reign of Napoleon it was turned over to the newly restored Academy as the most capable and impartial tribunal in the land, and the Academy, which is composed of forty foremost men of letters in France, has had charge of the constantly increasing fund ever since.

The award of prizes is made with much ceremony at a public meeting of the Academy on a certain fixed day every year. One of the most eloquent members of the Academy is chosen to tell in an "oration" to whom, and why, the prizes for that year have been awarded. If all these "orations" could be collected and published, they would make one of the most inspiring books ever written.

Part of each bequest is set aside to employ investigators to make thorough inquiries about each request for a reward. Such requests are never permitted to come from the person to be rewarded, nor from his family. Generally, the people in a small town or village send a joint petition to the Academy, requesting the reward for one of their members.

Among the recent rewards is the characteristic case of Laurentine Armenjon, a girl from the mountains of Savoy. She is eighth in a family of fifteen children. When nine years old, her youngest sister was carried away by gypsies, and from grief and distress over this, the mother lost her reason. Ever since, now ten years ago, Laurentine has had charge of the brothers and sisters, older as well as younger; and of the bedridden demented mother besides, while the father is away in the fields toiling for his scanty living.

A gift of one thousand francs was sent to one of the most remote islands of the South Pacific, to three nuns who are surely among the most heroic of living creatures. The Island of Mangareva, where they live, is a leper colony. It is not likely that one of these women will ever leave this lonely desolate spot, so far away from the land of their families and friends that news from home comes only once in six months. The nearest civilization lies forty days' journey over the ocean. Many nuns have gone before these three to voluntary exile on this island, but they have all succumbed within a few years; one or two were driven insane by the very loneliness and desolation of the life. Though they knew this in advance, yet these three women from Brittany have consecrated the rest of their lives, be they long or short, to God's service there.

No prize is ever granted for one act of heroism; but every award is made to a person who has devoted years of patient service to some good cause. Moreover, the awards are rather aids than prizes, granted in order to enable the person awarded to carry on some good work to even greater usefulness.

WILL OF LORD BACON

Lord Bacon in 1625, bequeathed his soul and body to God, while his name and memory he left to men's charitable speeches and to foreign nations and the next ages.

Will of the Duke of Brunswick

"To-day, the 5th of March, 1871, Hôtel de la Metropole, Geneva.

"This is our Will or Testament, — We, Charles Frederic Auguste William, by the Grace of God Duke Sovereign of Brunswick and of Luneburg, &c., being in good health of body and mind, declare —
"1. That we revoke by the present all testaments or writings prior to this one. 2. We wish that after our death our executors here named shall cause our body to be examined by five of the most celebrated physicians and surgeons in order to make sure that we have not been poisoned, and to make an exact report in writing, signed by them, of the cause of our death. 3. We wish that our body be embalmed, and if better for its preservation, petrified, according to the printed method adjoined. We wish our funeral to be conducted with all the ceremony and splendour due to our rank of Sovereign Duke. 4. We wish our body to be deposed in a mausoleum above the ground, which shall be erected by our executors at Geneva, in a dignified and prominent position. The monument shall be surmounted by an equestrian statue and surrounded by those of our father and grandfather of glorious memory, after the design attached to this testament in imitation of that of the Scaglieri at Verona; our executors shall construct the said monument ad libitum of the millions of our succession, in bronze and marble, by the most celebrated artists. 5. We make the condition that our testamentary executors shall not enter into any sort of compromise with our unnatural relations — Prince William of Brunswick, the ex-King of Hanover, his son, the Duke of Cambridge, or any one else of our pretended family, their servitors, their agents, or any other person whatever. 6. We wish our testamentary executors to use every means to put themselves in possession of our fortune remaining in our Duchy of Brunswick, in Hanover, in Prussia, in America, or elsewhere. 7. We make as a condition that our executors respect and execute all the codicils and legacies which we have the intention to make in favour of our surroundings. 8. We declare that we leave and bequeath our fortune — that is, our chateaux, domains, forests, estates, mines, saltworks, hotels, houses, parks, libraries, gardens, quarries, diamonds, jewels, silver, pictures, horses, carriages, porcelain, furniture, cash, bonds, public funds, bank-notes, and particularly that important part of our fortune which has been taken from us by force and kept since 1830, with all the interests in our Duchy of

Brunswick, to the city of Geneva. 9. We leave to Mr. George Thomas Smith, of No. 228, King's Road, Chelsea, in England, administrator-general, grand treasurer of our fortune, 1,000,000f., and we nominate him executor in chief of this testament. We likewise appoint M. Ferdininant Cherbuliez, advocate at Genoa. This testament is entirely written and signed by our hand, and sealed with our arms.

"DUKE OF BRUNSWICK."

WILL OF LORD BULWER-LYTTON

The will of the late Lord Bulwer-Lytton, who died in 1873, contained special directions as to the examination of his body, in order to provide against the possibility of his being buried whilst in a trance, which appeared to be an apprehension of his. The will further provided that the funeral expenses should be limited to what was usual, simply, in the interment of a private gentleman; and that any epitaph which might be intended for his tomb should be written in the English language.

WILL OF EDMUND BURKE

Edmund Burke is believed to have been born in Dublin on the 12th day of January, 1729; he died on the 8th day of July, 1797. His gifts of oratory impressed the people of his time, and have remained models ever since; he must ever be held in affectionate esteem by Americans, for his speeches on "American Taxation" and "Conciliation with America" are regarded as the most brilliant examples of his eloquence and statesmanship. Had his counsels been adopted, the War of Independence would have been averted. Burke left strict injunctions that his burial should be private, and in spite of a great demand for his interment in Westminster Abbey, he was laid to rest in the little church at Beaconsfield, a few miles from Windsor.

His will remains on file at Somerset House, London, and the testament is here given as it there literally appears:

" If my dear Son & friend had survived me, any Will would have been unnecessary but since it has pleased God to call him to himself before his Father, my duty calls upon me to make such a disposition of my worldly affairs as seems to my best Judgment most Equitable and reasonable; therefore, I, Edmund Burke, of the parish of Saint James, Westminster, though suffering under sore and inexpressible affliction being of sound and disposing Mind and not affected by any bodily infirmity, do make my last will and Testament, in manner following; First, according to the Ancient good and laudable Custom of which my Heart & understanding recognizes the propriety, I bequeath my soul to God, hoping for his Mercy thro' the only Merits of our Lord and Saviour Jesus Christ; my Body I desire, if I should die in any place very convenient for its Transport thither (but not otherwise), to be buried in the Church at Beaconsfield near to the Bodies of my dearest Brother & my dearest Son, in all Humility praying that as we have lived in perfect Amity together we may together have a part in the Resurrection of the Just; I wish my Funeral to be (without any Punctiliousness in that respect) the same as that of my brother and to exceed it as little as possible in point of Charge, whether on Account of my Family or of any others who would go to a greater expence, & I desire in the same manner and with the same Qualifications that no Monument beyond a Middle sized Tablet with a small and simple inscription on the Church Wall or on the Flagstone be erected; I say this because I know the Partial kindness to me of some of my Friends, but I have had in my life time but too much of noise and compliment: as to the rest it is uncertain what I shall leave after the Discharge of my Debts which when I write this are very great. Be that as it may, my Will concerning my worldly substance is short. As my entirely beloved, Faithful & affectionate Wife did during the whole time in which I lived most happily with her take on her the charge & Management of my affairs, assisted by her son, whilst God was pleased to lend him to us, did conduct them (often in a state of much derangement and embarrassment) with a patience and prudence which probably have no example, & thereby left my Mind free to prosecute my publick duty or my Studies or to indulge in my relaxations or to cultivate my friends at my pleasure; so on my Death I wish things to continue as substantially they have always been. I therefore by this my last and only Will devise, leave & bequeath to my entirely beloved and incomparable Wife, Jane Mary Burke, the whole real Estate of which I shall die seized, whether Lands, Rents or Houses, in absolute Fee simple; as also all my Personal Estate, whether Stock, Furniture, Plate, Money or Securities for Money Annuities for lives or Years, be the said Estate of what nature, Quality, extent or description it may be, to her sole uncontrolled Possession & disposal, as her property in any manner which may seem proper to her to possess or to dispose of the same (whether it be real Estate or Personal Estate) by her last will or otherwise; it being my intention that she may have as clear and uncontrolled a right and Title thereto and therein as I possess myself as to the use, expenditure, Sale or devise. I hope these Words are sufficient to express the absolute and unconditioned, unlimited right of compleat Ownership. I mean to give to her the said Lands and Goods and I trust that no words of surplusage or ambiguity may vitiate this my clear intention; there are no persons who have a right or I believe a disposition to complain of this bequest which I have only weighed and made on a proper consideration of my Duties and the relations in which I stand. I also make my wife, Jane Mary Burke, aforesaid, my sole Executrix of this my last Will, knowing that she will receive advice and assistance from her and my excellent Friends D[r] Walker King & D[r] Lawrence, to whom I recommend her & her concerns, though that perhaps is needless, as they are as much attached to her as they are to me. I do it only to mark my special Confidence in their affection, Skill and Industry. I wish that my Dear Wife may, as soon after my Decease as Possible (which after what has happened she will see with Constancy and resignation), make her last will with the advice and assistance of the two persons I have named; but it is my wish also that she will not think herself so bound up by any bequests she may make in the said Will & which whilst she lives can be only intentions, as not during her life to use her property with all the Liberty I have given her over it, just as if she had written no Will at all but in everything to follow the directions of her own Equitable and Charitable Mind and her own prudent and measured understanding. Having thus committed every thing to her Discretion I recommend (subject always to that Discretion) that if I should not during my life give or secure to my Dear Niece, Mary C. Hairland, wife of my worthy Friend, Capt[n] Hairland, the sum of a thousand pound or an Annuity equivalent to it, that she would bestow upon her that Sum of Money or Annuity Conditioned and limited in such manner as she, my Wife aforesaid, may think proper by a Devise in her Will or otherwise, as she may find most convenient to the situation of her affairs without pressure upon her during her life; my Wife put me in Mind of this which I now recommend to her; I certainly some years ago gave my

Niece reason to expect it but I was not able to execute my intentions. If I do this in my life time this recommendation goes for nothing. As to my other Friends, Relations, and Companions through Life, and especially to the Friends and Companions of my Son, who were the dearest of mine, I am not unmindful of what I owe them, if I do not name them all here and mark them with tokens of my Remembrance I hope they will not attribute it to unkindness or to a want of a due Sense of their Merits towards me. My old Friend and Faithful Companion, Will. Burke, knows his place in my heart. I do not mention him as Executor or Assistant. I know that he will attend to my Wife, but I chose the two I have mentioned as from their time of Life of greater activity. I recommend him to them. In the Political World I have made many connections and some of them amongst persons of high rank; their Friendship from political became personal to me and they have shewn it in a manner more than to satisfie the utmost demands that could be made from my love & sincere attachment to them. They are the worthiest people in the Kingdom; their intentions are excellent, and I wish them every kind of success. I bequeath my brother in law, John Nugent, & the friends in my poor Sons list, which is in his Mother's hands, to their protection as to them & to the rest of my Companions who constantly Honoured and Cheered our House as our Inmates I have put down their names in a list that my Wife should send them the usual remembrance of little Mourning Rings as a token of my remembrance. In speaking of my Friends to whom I owe so many obligations I ought to name specially Lord Fitzwilliam, the Duke of Portland and the Lord Cavendishes with the D. of Devonshire the worthy head of that Family. If the intimacy which I have had with others has been broken off by a Political Difference on great Questions concerning the State of things existing and impending, I hope they will forgive whatever of general human Infirmity or of my own particular Infirmity has entered into that contention. I heartily entreat their forgiveness. I have nothing Further to say. Signed & Sealed as my last Will and Testament this 11th day of August, 1794 being written all with my own hand. Edm. Burke — in the presence of — Dupont — William — Webster — Walker & King.

"In reading over the above Will I have nothing to add or essentially to alter but one point may want to be perfected & explained. In leaving my Lands and Heredits to my wife I find that I have omitted the Words which in Deeds Create an Inheritance in Law.

Now tho' I think them hardly necessary in a Will yet to obviate all doubts I explain the matter in a Codicil which is annexed to this — (sic) 22 1797. — Edm. Burke.

"I Edm. Burke of the parish of Beaconsfield, in the county of Bucks, being of sound and disposing Judgment and Memory, make this my last will and testament, in no sort revoking but explaining & confirming a Will made by me and dated the eleventh of August, in which will I have left, Devised and Bequeathed all my estate of whatever nature and Quality the same may be, Whether lands, Tenements, Houses, Freehold or Leasehold, Interests, Pensions for lives or years, Arrears of the same, Legacies or other debts due to me; Plate, Household Stuff, Books, Stock in Cattle & Horses & utensils of Farming & all other my Goods and Chattels to my dear Wife I: M: Burke in as full & perfect manner as the same might be Devised, Conveyed or transferred to her by any Act or Instrument whatsoever; with such recommendations as in my Will aforesaid are made & with a wish that in the discharge of my Debts the course hitherto pursued may be as nearly as possible observed, Sensible however that in payment of Debt no exact rule can be preserved; the same is therefore left to her Discretion, with the advice of our Friends whom she will naturally Consult. The reason of my making this will or Codicil to my former Will is from my having omitted in devising by that Will my Lands and Heredits to my Wife aforesaid, the full and absolute Property thereof & therein I have omitted the legal Words of Inheritance. Now tho' I think those words however necessary in a Deed are not so in a Will, yet to prevent all Question, I do hereby devise all my Lands Tenements and Heredits as well as all other property that may be subject to a strict Rule of Law in Deeds & which would pass if left undevised to my Heirs. I say I do devise the same Lands tenements and Hereditaments to my Wife, Jane Mary Burke, and her Heirs for ever in pure absolute and unconditional Fee simple. I have now only to recommend to the kindness of my Lord Chancellor L^d. Loughborough, to his Grace the Duke of Portland, to the most Honorable the Marquiss of Buckingham, to the R^t Honble Wm Windham & to Dr Lawrence of the Commons and Member of Parliament, that they will after my death continue their Protection and favour to the Emigrant School at Penn & will entreat, with a weight on which I dare not presume, the R^t Hon. Wm Pitt to continue the necessary allowances which he has so generously and charitably Provided for those unhappy Children of Meritorious Parents; that they will superintend the same, which I wish to be under the more Immediate care and direction of Dr King and Dr Lawrence, & that they will be pleased to exert their influence to place the said young Persons in some Military Corps or other Service as may best suit their dispositions & Capacities, Praying God to bless their endeavours. Signed and sealed as a Codicil to my Will or a Confirmation and Explanation thereof agreeably to the Note which some days ago I put to the end of it. This 29th January 1797. Edm: Burke, in the presence of — Walker King — Richd Bourke — Ed: Nagle."

WILL OF QUEEN CAROLINE

The will of Queen Caroline was drawn up by her directions on Sunday, the 5th day of August, 1821, within a few days of her death. It appears that on this same day she sent for the undertaker, by name Busch, to measure her for her coffin. Finding he did not come, she, a second time, ordered a servant to go for him, and then gave precise orders desiring it might be made of cedarwood, and that it should bear this inscription:

CAROLINE OF BRUNSWICK,
Born 17th May, 1768,
Died 7th August, 1821.
Aged 54.
The outraged Queen of England.

This desire she again mentioned by a special codicil to her will.

As the remains of this princess were to be buried at Brunswick, on the arrival of the coffin at Colchester, it was deposited in the chapel for the night, with a guard of honor to watch it. During this time, it appears, the executors, and some others who formed the *cortège* in attendance — Lord Hood, Sir Robert Wilson, Count Vassali, Messrs. Lushington, Wilde, and others — managed to introduce themselves into the chapel by night, and caused the plate in question to be nailed on.

On the following morning, however, much to the discomfiture of these gentlemen, and notwithstanding their protestations, this was removed and was replaced by the following, drawn up by an heraldic council and approved by the Government:

"Depositum serenissimæ principissæ Carolinæ Ameliæ Elizabethæ, Dei gratiâ reginæ consortis augustissimæ, potentissimi

monarchæ Georgii quarti, Dei gratiâ Britanniarum regis, fidei defensoris, regis Hanovriæ ac Brunsvici et Luneburgi ducis. Obiit vii. die mensis Augusti, Anno Domini mdcccxxi. ætatis liv."
And it so remains.

WILL OF LORD CHESTERFIELD

One of the most prominent of those whose wills were proved in 1773 was the "great" Lord Chesterfield, the arbiter on all matters of politeness, whose famous "Advice to his Son" was so summarily criticised by Dr. Johnson. This "first gentleman in Europe" of his day, left the bulk of his property to his godson, Philip Stanhope, with a very unfashionable and unpalatable restriction: "The several devises and bequests hereinbefore and hereinafter given by me to and in favour of my said godson Philip Stanhope, shall be subject to the condition and restriction hereinafter mentioned; that is to say, that, in case my said godson Philip Stanhope shall at any time hereafter keep, or be concerned in the keeping of, any race-horse or race-horses, or pack or packs of hounds, or reside one night at Newmarket, that infamous seminary of iniquity and ill-manners during the course of the races there, or shall resort to the said races, or shall lose in any one day at any game or bet whatsoever the sum of £500, then, and in any of the cases aforesaid, it is my express Will, that he my said godson shall forfeit and pay out of my estate the sum of £5000 to and for the use of the Dean and Chapter of Westminster, for every such offence or misdemeanour as is above specified, to be recovered by action for debt in any of his Majesty's Courts of Record at Westminster."

WILL OF JOHN DRYDEN

John Dryden, of Ashbye, Northampton, died in 1684. He left the following curious preamble to his will:
"I, John Dryden, of Ashbye, in the county of Northampton, gentleman, doe make and ordeyne my last will and testament in manner following: First, I bequeathe my soule to Almightie God my Creator, by the merits of whose son Jesus Christe, my Savior and Redeemer, I doe believe to be saved, the Holy Ghost assuring my spirit that I am the elect of God. My bodie to be buried in the church of Ashbye, and although I doe not allow of pompe in burialls, yet, for some reasonable considerations, I will that the stone I have allready prepared shall be layde upon my grave, and

my arms and my wyve's graven in brass thereupon. Notwithstanding, if God call mee far from Ashbye, then should it yet be thought necessary to my executors to bring me hither, I refer that to their discressions, and soe doe I the place of my buriall, whether in the place aforesaiyde or in the churchyard, or els in the church."

Will of Edward IV

It is almost certain that Edward IV left a will, but it has never been discovered. The editors of the royal wills rationally conjecture that it was destroyed during the usurpation of his brother, Richard III, as it has never been found.

Will of Sir Charles Fellowes

Sir Charles Fellowes, the author and antiquarian, died in 1860. He left by his will Milton's watch to the British Museum. His wife, who died in March, 1874, left her collection of watches (many of which had belonged to celebrities) to the same institution.

Will of Lord Edward Fitzgerald

The will of this unfortunate nobleman was made under very singular circumstances, after he was mortally wounded in the desperate struggle with Major Sirr, and while in confinement in Newgate, Dublin, where, whatever his political errors, he seems to have been treated with needless severity.

"Even for the purpose of drawing up his will, which he wrote on the 26th May, 1798," says Moore, "no person at all connected with his own family was allowed to have access to him, and Mr. John Leeson, who executed the instrument, sat in a carriage at the door of the prison, while Mr. Stewart, the government surgeon, communicated between him and the prisoner during the transaction."

"I, Lord Edward Fitzgerald, do make this as my last will and testament, hereby revoking all others; that is to say, I leave all estates, of whatever sort I may die possessed of, to my wife, Lady (Pamela) Fitzgerald, as a mark of my esteem, love, and confidence in her, for and during her natural life, and on her death to descend, share and share alike, to my children, or the survivors of them; she maintaining and educating the children according to her discretion; and I constitute her the executrix of this my last will and testament.

"Signed, sealed, and delivered, May the 26, 1798.
"In presence of . . . . . ALEXANDER LINDSAY.
"GEORGE STEWART.
"SAMUEL STONE."

WILL OF GARRICK

David Garrick, who was born at Hereford in 1716, was originally intended for business, and consequently was sent to an uncle settled at Lisbon as a merchant, but showing no aptitude for this calling nor yet for the law, to which he applied himself subsequently, he plunged into the life of a comedian, and first appeared at Ipswich in 1741. In October of the same year, however, he came out in London, and obtained great success at one of the small theaters in the character of Richard III. In 1742 he went to Dublin, where he was enthusiastically received, and thence returned to London, where his fame and fortune were shortly made. At length, in 1747, he was able to purchase Drury Lane Theatre, obtained a renewal of its privileges, and retained the management for nearly twenty years; for on the 10th of June, 1776, he took leave of the public, and retired after obtaining £2200 for what had originally cost him £320. His withdrawal from the stage was universally and profoundly deplored; he only survived his retirement three years, but he died full of honors and possessed of considerable wealth. His death took place in London on Wednesday, 20th of January, 1779.

The stir made by his funeral was surprising, but scarcely greater than that produced in Paris a century later, at the interment of Déjazet: the procession was formed by seventy mourning-coaches, twenty-four of which were filled by the *élite* of English society. Arrived at Westminster Abbey, the corpse was met by the Chapter; the Bishop of Rochester officiated, and the remains of Garrick were interred close to the monument of Shakespeare.

There is nothing remarkable in his will, which disposes of his fortune in a spirit of fairness, liberality, and benevolence. It was made the year previous to his death:

"I, David Garrick, at this present occupying my house in the Adelphi, do deposit in the hands of Lord Camden, of the Right Hon. Richard Rigby, of John Patterson, and of Albany Wallis, Esquires, my house at Hampton-on-the-Thames, in the county of

Middlesex, with the two islands dependent thereon, the temple and the statue of Shakespeare, my house in the Adelphi, with the furniture and pictures contained in the two said houses, to be delivered up to Eva Maria Garrick, my wife, in order that she may enjoy the same during her natural life, and that she may reside there.

"I give and bequeath to my said wife all my linen, plate, china, horses, carriages, and wine that may be contained in my cellars in both my houses.

"I give her furthermore £1000, payable immediately after my decease, and £5000 payable a year after.

"I give and bequeath to my said wife £1500 per annum during the term of her natural life, and as long as she shall reside in either of my before-mentioned houses, and £1000 should she quit England and settle whether in Scotland or Ireland.

"I give and bequeath to my nephew, David Garrick, the dwelling-house, farms, garden, and tenements and lands situated at Hampton, save and except that bequeathed to my wife.

"I deposit in the hands of my said executors the freehold of Hendon, with my right and patronage over the church of the said freehold, with directions to sell it, and to employ the produce according to my hereinafter-mentioned desires.

"I give, after the decease of my wife, the statue of Shakespeare and my collection of old plays to the British Museum.

"I give to my nephew, Carrington Garrick, the rest of my library, with the exception of books to the value of £100 in favour of my wife and at her choice.

"I give to the institution established for the relief of impoverished actors, the houses I bought along with Drury Lane Theatre.

"I give to my brother, George Garrick, £10,000; to my brother Peter, £3000; to my nephew Carrington Garrick, £6000; to my nephew David Garrick, besides the dowry I agreed to pay him on the day of his marriage, the sum of £5000.

"I deposit in the hands of my executors the sum of £6000 in favour of my niece Arabella Shaw, wife of Captain Shaw.

"I give to my niece, Catherine Garrick, the sum of £6000, to be paid to her on the day on which she shall marry or attain her majority.

"I give to my sister, Mercia Doxey, the sum of £5000; and to the niece of my wife actually residing with us at Hampton, the sum of £1000.

"Should the above-named legacies exceed the fund assigned to their payment, each legatee shall submit to a reduction in his legacy, proportioned to its amount, until the death of my wife; after that event, and on the sale of Hampton, the sums thus withheld shall be made up out of the amount produced by that sale.

"Should there, on the other hand, be more than sufficient to cover these legacies, I will that such surplus be divided in equal portions among my nearest relations according to the order observed with those who die intestate.

"In pursuance of this my last will, I name the within-mentioned my executors, and in token thereof I here sign and seal this document with my arms this 24th day of September, 1778.

"(Signed)   DAVID GARRICK.
"Sic transit gloria mundi."

By this testament it appears that David Garrick, the portionless son of a half-pay captain, had earned by his own unaided talents a fortune amounting in money to nearly £50,000, besides his superb estate at Hampton, with its islands, farms, orchards, and appurtenances; his property at Hendon; his houses in London; the theatre at Drury Lane; his costly furniture, valuable plate, china, wines, library, statues, pictures, and other works of art, horses, carriages, etc.

When we compare this splendid fortune with that of Shakespeare, who could only leave to his wife his "second best bed, with the furniture," we are tempted to wonder why the fickle goddess should have so much more highly favored him who exhibited the fruits of genius than him who produced them.

WILL OF LORD HAILES

Lord Hailes (Sir David Dalrymple), a Lord of Session, appointed in 1766, died in 1792, apparently without a will. Great search was made, no testamentary paper could be discovered, the heir-at-law was about to take possession of his estates, to the exclusion of his daughter and only child, and Miss Dalrymple prepared to retire from New Hailes, and from the mansion-house in New Street. Some of her domestics, however, were sent to lock up the house in New Street, and, in closing the window-shutters, there dropped out upon the floor, from behind a panel, Lord Hailes' will, which was found to secure her in the possession of his estates.

Will of Thomas Hood, the Poet

"Devonshire Lodge, New Finchley Road,
"St. John's Wood, February 7th, 1845.

"It is my last Will and desire that 'Nash's Hall's' be given, in my name, to my dear William and Georgiana Elliot, in recognition of their brotherly and sisterly affection and kindness.

"My 'Knight's Shakspeare's,' for a like reason, to dear Robert Elliot.

"'Chaucer or Froissart,' as he may prefer, to F. Reseigh Ward, Harvey, Phillips, and Hardman, to select a book apiece for remembrance.

"'Nimrod's Sporting' to Philip de Franck.

"All else that I possess, I give and bequeath to my dear wife, to be used for her benefit and that of our dear children, whom God bless, guide and preserve.

"With my farewell love and blessing,
"To all friends,
"Thomas Hood."

Will of Lord Howden

Hamilton v. Dellas. — Before Vice-Chancellor Sir James Bacon. — The loss, vexation, and complexity so frequently occasioned by intestacy, was in a partial measure manifested by the lapse in the will of the late Lord Howden, and serves in good stead to show how guarded persons should be to see, not only that they leave a properly prepared and executed will, but likewise that no lapse is left unsupplied. In the case of Lord Howden, although the lapse was only trifling, considering the vast wealth of his lordship, yet it was represented by a considerable amount. The case is a very curious one, as Lord Howden held a very high status in England, being a peer of the realm, and had taken the oath and his seat in the House of Lords; he was also a G.C.B., lieutenant-general in the army, and Deputy-Lieutenant for the County of York. Notwithstanding all these ties, in 1850 he sold his estate at Grimston Park, in Yorkshire, and all his real estate in England, and went to Spain as Minister Plenipotentiary, in which position he continued till 1857, when he went to France, and resided on an estate near Bayonne, which he acquired about that time, and where he built a château called "Casa Caradoc," in which he generally resided up to the date of his death. In 1863 he visited Scotland, and then

ANCIENT, CURIOUS, AND FAMOUS WILLS 273

wrote a letter declining to come to England, and expressing his intention of never doing so again; he likewise, in certain legal proceedings taken in England, claimed to be domiciled in France, *sine animo revertendi*. Lord Howden had made separate wills relating to his personal property in England and in France, and the confusion arose respecting one-fourth of that in England, the person to whom it had been bequeathed having died during his lordship's lifetime. The question was to whom this undisposed of personalty should belong, as by English law the whole of it would pass to Lady Rose Meade, as his lordship's nearest relation and sole next-of-kin, while, according to French law, a moiety only would pass to Lady Rose Meade, who was his lordship's nearest relation on the father's side, and the other moiety amongst his lordship's nearest relations on the mother's side. The case therefore rested on the point, whether Lord Howden's domicile was English or French at the time of his death, and the Vice-Chancellor said that, in the absence of authority, he should be sorry at this time of day to decide that a peer could not take up his permanent residence abroad. There was nothing to prevent any one, be he peer or peasant, from leaving the country to reside abroad. He then distinguished the cases of persons actually officers in the army, and the cases known of an Anglo-Indian domicile. On the facts, he said, it was clear that Lord Howden had acted so as to acquire a French domicile. There was only the question of the article in the Code Napoleon, which clearly only related to the acquisition of civil rights, and not the question of domicile at all. He therefore declared the domicile of Lord Howden to have been French.

WILL OF DR. SAMUEL JOHNSON

Dr. Samuel Johnson is one of the foremost figures in English literature; his will, copied by Boswell, is an interesing document:
"In the name of God, Amen! I, Samuel Johnson, being in full possession of my faculties, but fearing this night may put an end to my life, do ordain this my last will and testament."
This will was written the 8 day of December, 1784. Sir John Hawkins and the distinguished painter, Sir Joshua Reynolds, were executors. A codicil written on December 9, 1784, is several times the length of the will written the day before. Both in the will and in the codicil, Francis Barber, a negro man-servant, is made the chief beneficiary. It is said that the amount received by Barber

under this will, exclusive of an annuity on the sum of $3750, was about ten thousand dollars. A copy of his great French dictionary, as well as a copy of his own dictionary, were given to Sir Joshua Reynolds. A striking provision in Johnson's will, is the following clause:

"I bequeath to God, a soul polluted by many sins, but I hope purified by Jesus Christ."

The celebrated letter written by Dr. Johnson to Lord Chesterfield, from a point of combined politeness, satire, and irony, has probably never been surpassed, and was doubtless a just resentment of the treatment he had received from his patron. The date of this letter is given by Boswell and other authorities, as February 7, 1775; the true date is 1755, for it was in that year that his Dictionary was completed. A brief history of this letter is as follows:

Boswell in his "Life of Johnson," says the story was current that the great philosopher was kept waiting in Lord Chesterfield's antechamber upon the occasion of a visit to him; that Dr. Johnson was violently provoked when the door finally opened, and out walked Colley Cibber, an English actor and dramatist. Johnson himself, however, told Boswell that there was no truth in this story, but that during his years of struggle, Lord Chesterfield had studiously neglected him. When the Dictionary was on the eve of publication, Lord Chesterfield attempted, in a courtly manner, to conciliate Dr. Johnson by writing two articles in *The World*, a leading London paper, in commendation of the work; the courtly device failed of its effect.

Johnson said to Boswell, "Sir, after making great professions, he had, for many years, taken no notice of me; but when my Dictionary was coming out, he fell a scribbling in *The World* about it. Upon which I wrote him a letter expressed in civil terms, but such as might show him that I did not mind what he said or wrote, and that I had done with him." And, he added, "This man, I thought had been a lord among wits, but I find, he is only a wit among lords." The letter follows:

"To the Right Honourable the Earl of Chesterfield

"February 7, 1755.

"My Lord,

"I have been lately informed, by the proprietor of *The World*, that two papers, in which my Dictionary is recommended to the public, were written by your lordship. To be so distinguished is an honour, which, being very little accustomed to favours from the great, I know not well how to receive, or in what terms to acknowledge.

"When, upon some slight encouragement, I first visited your lordship, I was overpowered, like the rest of mankind, by the enchantment of your address, and could not forbear to wish that I might boast myself *Le vainqueur du vainqueur de la terre;* — that I might obtain that regard for which I saw the world contending; but I found my attendance so little encouraged, that neither pride nor modesty would suffer me to continue it. When I had once addressed your lordship in public, I had exhausted all the art of pleasing which a retired and uncourtly scholar can possess. I had done all that I could; and no man is well pleased to have his all neglected, be it ever so little.

"Seven years, my lord, have now passed, since I waited in your outward rooms, or was repulsed from your door; during which time I have been pushing on my work through difficulties, of which it is useless to complain, and have brought it, at last, to the verge of publication, without one act of assistance, one word of encouragement, or one smile of favour. Such treatment I did not expect, for I never had a patron before.

"The shepherd in 'Virgil' grew at last acquainted with Love, and found him a native of the rocks.

"Is not a patron, my lord, one who looks with unconcern on a man struggling for life in the water, and, when he has reached ground, encumbers him with help? The notice which you have been pleased to take of my labours, had it been early, had been kind; but it has been delayed till I am indifferent, and cannot enjoy it; till I am solitary, and cannot impart it; till I am known, and do not want it. I hope it is no very cynical asperity, not to confess obligations where no benefit has been received, or to be unwilling that the public should consider me as owing that to a patron, which Providence has enabled me to do for myself.

"Having carried on my work thus far with so little obligation to any favourer of learning, I shall not be disappointed though I shall conclude it, if less be possible, with less; for I have been long wakened from that dream of hope, in which I once boasted myself with so much exultation,

"My Lord, your lordship's most humble,
"Most obedient servant,
"SAM. JOHNSON."

Will of Mr. George Henry Lewes

The will, dated November 21, 1859, of Mr. George Henry Lewes, the celebrated author, formerly of Holly Lodge, South Fields, Wandsworth, but late of The Priory, North Bank, Regent's Park, who died on November 20, 1879, was proved by Mary Ann Evans, the sole executrix, the personal estate being sworn under £2000. The testator gives to his three sons, Charles Lee, Thornton Arnott, and Herbert Arthur, all his copyright and interest of every description in all his literary and dramatic works, and the residue of his real and personal estate to his executrix.

Will of Maria Cristina, Queen Dowager of Spain

The will (dated 1874), with a codicil (dated 1875), both made in Paris, of her Majesty the Queen Doña Maria Cristina de Borbon y Borbon, who died on August 22, 1879, in France, was proved in London. The personal estate in England is sworn under £6000. The testatrix directs that 5000 recited masses shall be performed for her soul, 5000 for the soul of her late husband, 1000 for the souls of her deceased children, and 500 for the souls of her deceased grandchildren, to be performed by poor priests in churches to be selected by her executors, the alms for each mass to be ten reals. She bequeaths money to the needy poor and sick of several towns. Special directions are given as to her numerous papers; they are divided into four classes, viz. her business papers, political papers, confidential papers, and intimate private papers; her secretary, Don Antonio Maria Rubio, is charged with the arranging of them, and he is to deliver the papers of the first three categories, sealed up, to her son, Don Fernando, and the papers of the last-named category to her daughter, Doña Maria Cristina, also sealed up; they are not to be opened until the expiration of forty years from her decease, and the testatrix states that she so orders not for her own sake or from any want of confidence in her children, but with views of delicacy towards the many persons she has had political relationship with during her long and checkered career. If upon examination any papers are found among her own property belonging to her first husband, or the Government of Spain, they are to be delivered to her august daughter, the Queen Isabella, for eventual transmission to the successor of her first husband in the crown of Spain, "say her grandson King Alfonso."

WILL OF MICHAEL EYQUEM DE MONTAIGNE

Montaigne, the celebrated essayist and philosopher, is stated to have got over any difficulties in the way of carrying out his testamentary intentions by the happy expedient of calling all the persons named in his will around his deathbed, and counting out to them severally the bequests he had made them. Any doubtful testator might usefully follow Montaigne's example, but there is always the risk of the donor getting better, and finding himself penniless. A small farmer in Suffolk, England, being very ill, was advised by his affectionate relatives to distribute his money, and thus save legacy duty. He did so, but got well again; he did not, however, recover the amount he had distributed, and the poor old farmer had to seek relief from the parish.

WILL OF NAPOLEON

In Scott's "Life of Napoleon Buonaparte," published in 1828, is a complete copy of this celebrated document, the first division of which is as follows:

"Napoleon.

"This 15th April, 1821, at Longwood, Island of St. Helena. This is my Testament, or act of my last Will.

I

"1. I die in the apostolical Roman religion, in the bosom of which I was born, more than fifty years since.

" 2. It is my wish that my ashes may repose on the banks of the Seine, in the midst of the French people, whom I have loved so well.

" 3. I have always had reason to be pleased with my dearest wife, Marie Louise. I retain for her to my last moment, the most tender sentiments — I beseech her to watch, in order to preserve my son from the snares which yet environ his infancy.

" 4. I recommend to my son, never to forget that he was born a French prince, and never to allow himself to become an instrument in the hands of the triumvirs who oppress the nations of Europe; he ought never to fight against France, or to injure her in any manner; he ought to adopt my motto — ' Everything for the French people.'

" 5. I die prematurely, assassinated by the English oligarchy.. . . . The English nation will not be slow in avenging me.

"6. The two unfortunate results of the invasions of France when she had still so many resources, are to be attributed to the treason of Marmont, Augerau, Talleyrand and La Fayette.

"I forgive them — may the posterity of France forgive them like me!

"7. I thank my good and most excellent mother, the Cardinal, my brothers Joseph, Lucien, Jerome, Pauline, Caroline, Julie, Hortense, Catarine, Eugénie, for the interest which they have continued to feel for me. I pardon Louis for the libel which he published in 1820; it is replete with false assertions and falsified documents.

"8. I disavow the 'Manuscript of St. Helena,' and other works, under the title of Maxims, Sayings, &c., which persons have been pleased to publish for the last six years. These are not the rules which have guided my life. I caused the Duc d'Enghien to be arrested and tried, because that step was essential to the safety, interest, and honor of the French people, when the Count d'Artois was maintaining, by his confession, sixty assassins at Paris. Under similar circumstances, I would act in the same way."

In the second division of the will are thirty-five bequests to Buonaparte's generals and others who had been associated with him the whole amounting to five million six hundred thousand francs. He says, "These sums will be raised from the six millions which I deposited on leaving Paris in 1815; and from the interest, at the rate of five per cent, since July, 1815." He further directs that the excess of five million six hundred thousand francs shall be distributed as a gratuity amongst the wounded at the battle of Waterloo, and others of his soldiers; the amounts to be paid, in case of death, to the widows and children of the legatees.

In the third division, he speaks of his "private domain of which no French law can deprive me." This "private domain," he estimates to exceed 200,000,000 of francs. This amount, together with his plate, jewels and other property, he bequeaths, one-half to the surviving officers and soldiers of the French army who had fought for the glory and independence of the nation; the distribution to be made in proportion to their appointments in active service. He appoints Counts Montholon, Bertrand and Marchand the executors of his will.

The instrument concludes: "This present will, wholly written with my own hand, is signed, and sealed with my own arms."

Affixed to this will is a codicil consisting of many parts and numerous items, such as would well befit the great Emperor to possess. The minutest detail is shown in an itemized statement of these articles. Among others, might be mentioned, medals, watches, gold ornaments, spurs, libraries, cravats, daggers, and hundreds of other articles. He directed Marchand to preserve his hair, from which bracelets were to be made, to be sent to the Empress Marie Louise, to his mother, brothers, sisters, nephews, nieces, to the Cardinal, and one of larger size to his son. In this codicil he again expresses the wish that his ashes should repose on the banks of the Seine in the midst of the French people whom he loved so well.

In the fourth codicil, Napoleon gives ten thousand francs to the subaltern officer Cantillon, who had undergone a trial on the charge of having endeavored to assassinate the Duke of Wellington, of which he was pronounced innocent. Napoleon writes, "Cantillon had as much right to assassinate that oligarchist, as the latter had to send me to perish upon the rock of St. Helena."

In the fifth codicil to the will is a reference to Empress Marie Louise, "my very dear and well beloved spouse." He adds, "This is my codicil, or act of my last will, the execution of which I recommend to my dearest wife, the Empress Marie Louise."

There are seven codicils to this will, all written at Longwood, by his own hand, the last being dated the 25th day of April, 1821. Ten days after writing this codicil, he died, May 5, 1821.

Napoleon's deep affection for his son, François Charles, is evidenced throughout the will by numerous bequests, comprising the greater part of his personal belongings and articles that he most prized.

He also evinced great solicitude for his generals and those who were with him in his many campaigns, which is manifested by the gifts to them, not only in his will, but in several of the codicils thereto.

The instrument, though of the very greatest interest, is too lengthy to be fully set out. The reader is referred to Scott's "Life of Napoleon Buonaparte" for the details of this famous will. The death of the Duke of Reichstadt, July 22, 1832, only son of the first Napoleon, left Louis Napoleon the representative of his family. He was elected President of France in 1848 and promised to restore its glories. It is said that many of the legacies mentioned in his uncle's will were paid by him.

Will of Lord Nelson

The battle of Trafalgar was fought October 21, 1805. At daylight Nelson hoisted the signal, "England expects every man to do his duty," and gave the order to close in and the game of death began. Each side had made a move. Nelson retired to his cabin and wrote the following codicil to his will:

"October 21st, 1805.—In sight of the combined fleets of France and Spain, distance about ten miles. Whereas the eminent services of Emma Hamilton, widow of the Right Honourable Sir William Hamilton, have been of the very greatest service to my king and country, to my knowledge, without ever receiving any reward from either our king or country. *First:* That she obtained the King of Spain's letter, in 1796, to his brother, the King of Naples, acquainting him of his intention to declare war against England: from which letter the ministry sent out orders to the then Sir John Jervis to strike a stroke, if the opportunity offered, against either the arsenals of Spain or her fleets. That neither of these was done is not the fault of Lady Hamilton: the opportunity might have been offered.

"*Secondly:* The British fleet under my command could never have returned the second time in Egypt, had not Lady Hamilton's influence with the Queen of Naples caused a letter to be written to the Governor of Syracuse, that he was to encourage the fleet being supplied with everything, should they put into any port in Sicily. We put into Syracuse, and received every supply; went to Egypt and destroyed the French fleet. Could I have rewarded these services, I would not now call upon my country; but as that has not been in my power, I leave Emma, Lady Hamilton, therefore, a legacy to my king and country, that they will give her an ample provision to maintain her rank in life.

"I also leave to the beneficence of my country my daughter, Horatia Nelson Thompson; and I desire she will use in future the name of Nelson only.

"These are the only favours I ask of my king and country, at this moment when I am going to fight their battle. May God bless my king, and country, and all those I hold dear!   "Nelson.

"Witness { Henry Blockwood.
T. M. Hardy."

Shortly after, while his ship, the *Victory*, was grappled with the *Redoubtable* and chained fast to her, Nelson was struck by a musket ball fired from the yards of the *Redoubtable*. He called for his trusted captain, Hardy, and said: "They have done for me now, Hardy — my back is broken." And soon after, he died; but not before adding, "I would like to live one hour, just to know that my plans were right — we must capture or destroy twenty of them."

There is a splendid monument to Nelson in Trafalgar Square, London, but the English did not respect his wishes with reference to Lady Hamilton. As a matter of fact, she was arrested on a charge of debt and imprisoned, and practically driven out of England, although the sisters of Lord Nelson believed in her and respected her to the last. She died in France in 1813. The daughter, Horatia Nelson, lived until 1881. She was a strong and excellent woman; she married the Reverend Philip Ward, of Teventer, Kent, and raised a family of nine children. One of her sons moved to America and made his mark upon the stage and also in letters.

WILL OF FLORENCE NIGHTINGALE

"Rich in honors," says the *New York World*, Florence Nightingale died "leaving the world, which had paid tribute to her as it has to few women, her debtor." She was known by the various names of "The Lady-in-Chief," "The Lady with the Lamp," "The Lady of the Crimea," in reference to the service she rendered Great Britain and the world on the battle-fields of the Crimean War.

Longfellow wrote of her:

> "On England's annals through the long
> Hereafter of her speech and song
> That light its rays shall cast
> From portals of the past.
> A lady with a lamp shall stand
> In the great history of the land
> A noble type of good,
> Heroic womanhood."

The lamp referred to is the nurse's lamp with which she used to make her nocturnal rounds of the hospitals when all was silent.

She was born in Florence, Italy, May 12, 1820, of wealthy, English parents, and died at her home in England, August 14, 1910. She was given the name of the place of her birth.

Her will, recently taken from the Records of Somerset House, London, is in the following words:

"I, Florence Nightingale, Spinster, declare this to be my last Will, revoking all wills by me heretofore executed.

"1. I appoint my Cousins, Henry Bonham Carter, Esquire, Samuel Shore Nightingale and Louis Hilary Shore Nightingale, Esquires (sons of my late Cousin, William Shore Nightingale), and Arthur Hugh Clough, Esquire, to be the EXECUTORS of this my Will.

"2. I give my executors all my books, papers (whether manuscripts or printed) and letters relating to my Indian work (together with the two stones for Irrigation maps of India at Mr. Stanford's, Charing Cross, and also the woodcut blocks for illustrations of those works at Messrs. Spottiswoodes), upon trust, in their absolute discretion or in that of the survivors or survivor of them to publish or prepare for publication such part, if any, as they or the majority of them for the time being may think fit, and I give them a sum of two hundred and fifty pounds for those purposes. And without limiting the exercise of such discretion I should wish my executors to consult my friend, Sir William Wedderburn, in the matter of such publication. And I declare that if my executors, within three years from my death, have taken no, or only partial, steps to publish or before that time have decided not to publish anything, the said sum of two hundred and fifty pounds, or any unexpended part thereof, shall fall into the residue of my estate. And subject to the foregoing, I authorize my executors to destroy all or any of the above mentioned books and papers, stones and blocks or otherwise to dispose of the same as they may think fit.

"3. I bequeath to the children of my late dear friend, Arthur Hugh Clough and his widow, my Cousin, Blanch Mary Shore Clough, the sum of seven thousand pounds to be divided between them in the following proportions:

"To the said Arthur Hugh Clough two thousand pounds;

"To Blanch Athena Clough two thousand five hundred pounds, and to Florence Anne Mary Clough two thousand five hundred pounds. I bequeath to each of them, the said Samuel Shore Nightingale and Louis Hilary Shore Nightingale, the sum of three thousand five hundred pounds. To each of them, Rosalind Frances Mary Nash and Margaret Thyra Barbara Shore Nightingale (daughters of my said late Cousin, William Shore Nightingale) the sum of one thousand five hundred pounds. I bequeath five hundred pounds to the said Henry Bonham Carter as a tiny sign of my gratitude for his wise and unfailing exertions in connection with our Training Schools for Nurses, and also the portraits of Sir Bartle Frere Mohl Hallam Bunsen and the Sidney Herberts. And I also give to him a further legacy of one thousand three hundred pounds for his objects, and to Joanna Frances Bonham Carter a legacy of one hundred pounds. I give to Francis Galton two thousand pounds for certain purposes and I declare that the same shall be paid in priority to all other bequests given by my Will for charitable or other purposes. I give one hundred pounds to Mary Ureth Frederica, the daughter of William Bacheler Coltman and Bertha Elizabeth Shore Coltman, his wife, and fifty pounds to each of their sons, William Hew Coltman and Thomas Lister Coltman. I bequeath th ee hundred pounds to J. I. Frederick, Esquire, Secretary of the Army Sanitary Commission, three hundred pounds to Sir Douglas Galton of Chester Street, London. I bequeath one hundred pounds each to Mary and Emily, daughters of the late Dr. William Farr of the General Register Office; two hundred and fifty pounds to Mother Stanislaus, Reverend Mother of the Hospital Sisters in Great Ormond Street, for her objects; one hundred pounds to John Croft, Esquire, late Instructor of the Nightingale Training School at St. Thomas' Hospital, and two hundred and fifty pounds to the Mother Superior at the time of my death of the Devonport Sisters of Mercy. I direct my executors to purchase out of my estate an annuity of sixty pounds on the life of Miss Crossland, late 'Home Sister' of the Nightingale Training School at St. Thomas' Hospital. And also an annuity of thirty pounds on the life of Miss Vincent, now Matron of St. Marylebone Infirmary. And I bequeath to each of those ladies respectively the annuity so purchased on her life absolutely : each annuity to commence from the date of my decease. I bequeath one hundred pounds to Miss Styring, now Matron of Paddington Infirmary; one hundred pounds to Miss Spencer, now Lady Superintendent of Edinburgh Royal Infirmary; one hundred pounds to Madame Caroline Werckner, who nursed the French Prisoners in the Franco-German War at Breslau (now at Lymington); one hundred pounds to the daughters of Margaret, wife of Sir Edmund Verney, in equal shares; one hundred pounds to the daughters of Frederick W. Verney (youngest son of the late Sir Harry Verney) in equal shares; Five hundred pounds to Paulina Irby of Serajevo, Bosnia, for her objects; One hundred and fifty pounds to Peter Grillage (from Balaclava) and Temperance, his wife, whose maiden name was Hatcher, now at Ridgway, Plympton, Devon, to be equally divided between them and in case one of them should predecease me the survivor to take the whole; Fifty pounds to Fanny Dowding now McCarthy, formerly in my service; One hundred pounds to Robert Robinson now residing at 101 West Street, Grimsbury, Banbury; One hundred and seventy five pounds to my servant, Elizabeth Mary Coleman, if living with me at the time of my decease, and to Ellen Pearce twenty five pounds under the same condition; One hundred pounds to William Rathbone, Esquire, M.P. as a feeble sign of heartfelt gratitude for his unbounded goodness to the cause of Trained Nursing and to me; Two hundred and fifty pounds to the said Sir William Wedderburn for certain purposes; One hundred pounds to each of my executors as an acknowledgment of his trouble in executing the provisions of my Will, in addition to any other legacy left to him. I bequeath one hundred pounds to Mr. William Yeomans of Holloway House, with thanks for his kindness to the people of Holloway for me; I leave twenty pounds for a small gold cross or crucifix to be chosen by the said Henry Bonham Carter for Miss Pringle, formerly Matron of St. Thomas' Hospital.

"4. I give and bequeath the following specific legacies (namely), the jewels from the Queen and the bracelet from the Sultan and the other medals and Orders, together with my engraving of the ground round Sebastopol, to the Managers for the time being of the Reading Room at Herbert Hospital, or at Netley or at Aldershot or at some other place where soldiers may see them, as my executors may in their absolute discretion decide. All my prints, framed or otherwise (except those that I may otherwise dispose of), and including those of the Queen and Prince Albert given me by the Queen at Balmoral, in one thousand eight hundred and fifty six, and of Landseer's 'Highland Nurses' to my executors to be distributed by them amongst the Nightingale Training Schools for Nurses and those connected with us, in such manner in all respects as my executors may in their absolute discretion decide. The framed Michael Angelo photographs, the portfolio of Venice photographs from Mrs. Bracebridge, the two lovely water colour sketches of Embley, and the copy of Turner's 'Rock' by Louisa Elenor Shore Nightingale, my father's watch and spectacles, the book case in the drawing room given me by the said William Shore Nightingale and Louisa Eleanor, his wife, the portrait of Sir John McNeill, the little Soutari clock and the box (Miss Coape's) with all the 'stuff' in it, *i.e.* annotated in pencil by Mr. Stuart Mill and

Mr. Jowett, with their letters, et cetera, upon it, to the children of the said William Shore Nightingale, living at my death, to be divided amongst them in such manner as they shall agree upon, and in default of agreement as my executors, other than the said Samuel Shore Nightingale and Louis Hilary Shore Nightingale, shall determine. The cutlery given me by the town of Sheffield and any Tallboy or book case or tall stand for papers he may choose to the said Samuel Shore Nightingale. The 'Colas' bronze of Sophocles, all copies of the printed three volumes entitled 'Suggestions for Thought,' the three volumes of Quetelet given me by Mr. Quetelet with my M. S. papers in the same parcel, and my Dante in three volumes quarto with illustrations, to the said Rosalind Frances Mary Nash. The sketch of the older Parthe to Mrs. Hawthorn, a bookcase or tallboy and the picture of the head of Christ with the Crown of Thorns (Nazarene), in my room, to the said Louis Hilary Shore Nightingale. The Titian 'Virgin' with the two sides of Angioletti and the (rare) cast of the Avignon Crucifix to the said Margaret Thyra Barbara Shore Nightingale. To each of them, the said Samuel Shore Nightingale and Louis Hilary Shore Nightingale, Rosalind Frances Mary Nash and Margaret Thyra Barbara Shore Nightingale, such six of my books as they shall select. The picture of Gordon in 'The last Watch' to the said Louisa Eleanor Shore Nightingale. The Bible given me by Pleasley to the said Frederick W. Verney. The Michael Angelo Sistine Chapel ceiling, stretched on two screen poles, and my chatelain with the blue seal ring, etc. upon it to the said Bertha Elizabeth Shore Coltman. The desk given me by Lea to Beatrice Lushington during her life, and after her death to the said Louis Hilary Shore Nightingale. The framed 'Nile' given me by the said Henry Bonham Carter and the Models of Highgate Infirmary and Chapel made by Patients there to Sibella, the wife of the said Henry Bonham Carter. The prints which belonged to dear Hilary, namely the Correggio 'Magdalen' and 'Christ in the Garden,' the large Michael Angelo of Isaiah (all framed), also a packet of papers of Hilary's (in my despatch box) to be divided between Alice Bonham Carter and her sister, Elinor Dicey, or if either of them should die before me, all the said articles to the survivor, but if neither of them should survive me I direct that the said papers shall be burnt. The large framed photograph of her father, Sidney Herbert, given me by his wife, to Mary Herbert, now Baroness Hugel. The large framed Madonna di San Sisto (with a little secret between us about Gwendolen's likeness) to Maude, wife of the said Frederick W. Verney; such of my blue books, War Office, India and Statistical and Hospital Reports and Books as he shall choose to the said J. J. Frederick, and the remainder of them to the said Sir Douglas. The volume of Prince Albert's speeches given me by the Queen, with her autograph in the book, to the said Henry Bonham Carter. The life of the Prince Consort given me by the Queen, with her autograph in it, and the Athens photograph book given me by Emily Verney to the said Margaret Verney. The Illustrated New Testament and Prayer Book to my two little Goddaughters, Ruth, child of the said Margaret Verney, and Kathleen, child of the said Frederick W. Verney. The Roman Catholic books in English or French, some of which were given me by the Reverend Mother Clare of Bermondsey, who died in one thousand eight hundred and seventy four, to the said Mother Stanislaus; my Schiller to Miss Shalders, formerly Governess to the children of Mrs. Frederick Verney, and to Blanch Mary Shore Clough some article to be selected by her out of my personal chattels, not subject to other destinations.

"5. I give and bequeath all my remaining books, clothes, furniture, trinkets and personal chattels to my executors, requesting them thereout to give some remembrance of me to their children and to the children of my deceased friend, the said Arthur Hugh Clough the elder, and Blanch Shore Clough, his widow; the children of the said Bertha Elizabeth Shore Coltman, of the said Sir Edmund Verney, of the said Frederick W. Verney, of George Lloyd Verney and of Henry Bonham Carter and Sibella, his wife; to the widow of the said George Lloyd Verney and to Mr. Burton of Lea School. To my beloved and reverend friends, Mr. Charles H. Bracebridge and his wife, my more than mother, without whom Scutari and my life could not have been and to whom nothing that I could ever say or do would in the least express my thankfulness, I should have left some token of my remembrance had they, as I expected, survived me. I further request my executors to distribute the whole of the remainder of the said articles, including the useful furniture and books, amongst the Matrons Home Sisters, Ward Sisters, Nurses and Probationers trained by us for whom they know me to have a regard, particularly remembering the hospital of St. Thomas and of Edinburgh and the Infirmaries of St. Marylebone and Paddington, and including the successor of Miss Jones, formerly Superior of St. John's, now at 30 Kensington Square. And I declare that the gifts hereinbefore directed or authorized to be made by my executors out of the articles aforesaid shall be entirely in the uncontrolled discretion of my executors, both as to selection of the gifts and of the donees, other than those mentioned by name.

"6. I request that all my letters, papers and manuscripts (with the exception of the papers relating to India and the other exceptions hereinbefore contained) may be destroyed without examination; also that the pencil notes in the pages of any religious books may be destroyed with the books, and I appeal to the love and feeling of my cherished friends and executors and earnestly entreat of them entirely to fulfil these my last wishes.

"7. I declare that every legacy hereinbefore given to a legatee for his (or her) objects, or for certain purposes, shall be considered in law as an absolute gift to such legatee and that every power of appropriation, user or application, hereinbefore contained shall be exercisible by the legatee on whom the same is conferred without any liability to account for its exercise.

"8. I direct that all legacies, annuities and bequests given by this my Will or any Codicil thereto, whether pecuniary or specific, shall be free from duty, which shall be paid out of my residuary personal estate.

"9. In case any of the children of the said Arthur Hugh Clough, the father, or of the said William Shore Nightingale shall die in my lifetime, then I give and bequeath the legacy, or legacies (specific or pecuniary) herein before given to such child, to his or her children (if any) who shall be living at my death and if more than one in equal shares.

"10. I devise and bequeath all the residue of my personal estate and effects whatsoever and wheresoever and all my real estate of every tenure and wheresoever situate unto and to the use of the children of the said William Shore Nightingale who shall be living at my death, and the child or children then living of any deceased child of his absolutely, and if more than one in equal shares, but so that the children of any deceased child of his shall take equally between them only the share which their parent would have taken had he or she survived me.

"11. I authorize my executors to determine what articles pass under any specific bequest contained in this my Will or any Codicil hereto and to determine all questions and matters of doubt arising under this my Will or any Codicil hereto. And I declare that every such determination, whether made upon a question actually raised or implied in the acts or proceedings of my executors, shall be conclusive and binding on all persons interested under this my Will. And I declare that all powers, authorities and discretions thereby expressed to be vested in or given to my executors shall be vested in and exercisible by the acting executors or executor for the time being of this my Will. And I declare that my executors may employ the said Louis Hilary Shore Nightingale professionally, if they think proper, and that if so employed he shall be entitled to charge and be paid all usual professional or other charges for any business done by him and whether in the ordinary course of his profession or business or not.

"12. I give my body for dissection or postmortem examination for the purposes of Medical Science and I request that the directions about my funeral given by me to my uncle, the late Samuel Smith, be observed; my original request was that no memorial whatever should mark the place where lies my 'Mortal Coil.' I much desire this but should the expression of such wish render invalid my other wishes, I limit myself to the above mentioned directions, praying that my body may be carried to the nearest convenient burial ground, accompanied by not more than two persons without trappings and that a simple cross, with only my initials, date of birth and of death, mark the spot.

"In witness whereof I have to this my last will and testament contained in six sheets of paper set my hand this twenty eighth day of July, one thousand eight hundred and ninety six.

"FLORENCE NIGHTINGALE."

Then follows the attestation clause. There are three codicils to this unusual will; the first making slight changes in legacies, but of no particular interest to the general reader.

There are two items in the second codicil worthy of reproduction and they are here given:

"4. I revoke the paragraph numbered 6 of my said will and bequeath the letters, papers, manuscripts and books which I thereby requested might be destroyed and the majority of which I believe should be destroyed, to my said cousin, Henry Bonham Carter.

"5. I bequeath to Elizabeth Mary Wiggins the sum of twenty pounds and my cats; and to my maid Ellen Kate Tugby, if she shall be in my service at the time of my death, my parrot and the sum of two hundred and five pounds with my best thanks for her loving service; and to my messenger, William Magee, if he shall be in my service at the time of my death, the sum of forty five pounds with my best thanks for his faithful service."

The third and last codicil contains nothing which is of special importance.

WILL OF PHILIP, FIFTH EARL OF PEMBROKE

Those who possess leisure and patience for the research might find in the pigeon holes of will offices some remarkable evidences of human malignity.

Among the most capricious, perhaps, is the specimen we subjoin, penned by an Earl of Pembroke, who lived during the political turmoils of the seventeenth century; it testifies to a shrewd knowledge of character, and is expressed with a considerable amount of dry humor which considerably softens its severity.

The copy from which this is taken bears the signature of the then keeper of these records — Nathaniel Brind — beneath the words "Concordat cum originali."

"I, Philip, V Earl of Pembroke and Montgomery, being, as I am assured, of unsound health, but of sound memory — as I well remember me that five years ago I did give my vote for the despatching of old Canterbury, neither have I forgotten that I did see my King upon the scaffold — yet as it is said that Death doth even now pursue me, and, moreover, as it is yet further said that it is my practice to yield under coercion, I do now make my last will and testament.

"Imprimis: As for my soul, I do confess I have often heard men speak of the soul, but what may be these same souls, or what their destination, God knoweth; for myself, I know not. Men have likewise talked to me of another world, which I have never visited, nor do I even know an inch of the ground that leadeth thereto. When the King was reigning, I did make my son wear a surplice, being desirous that he should become a Bishop, and for myself I did follow the religion of my master: then came the Scotch, who made me a Presbyterian, but since the time of Cromwell, I have become an Independent. These are, methinks, the three principal religions of the kingdom — if any one of the three can save a soul, to that I claim to belong: if, therefore, my executors can find my soul, I desire they will return it to Him who gave it to me.

"Item: I give my body, for it is plain I cannot keep it; as you see, the chirurgeons are tearing it in pieces. Bury me, therefore; I hold lands and churches enough for that. Above all, put not my body beneath the church-porch, for I am, after all, a man of birth, and I would not that I should be interred there, where Colonel Pride was born.

"Item: I will have no monument, for then I must needs have an epitaph, and verses over my carcase: during my life I have had enough of these.

"Item: I desire that my dogs may be shared among all the members of the Council of State. With regard to them, I have been all things to all men; sometimes went I with the Peers, sometimes with the Commons. I hope, therefore, they will not suffer my poor curs to want.

"Item: I give my two best saddle-horses to the Earl of Denbigh whose legs, methinks, must soon begin to fail him. As regardeth my other horses, I bequeath them to Lord Fairfax, that when Cromwell and his council take away his commission he may still have some *horse* to command.

"Item: I give all my wild beasts to the Earl of Salisbury, being very sure he will preserve them, seeing that he refused the King a doe out of his park.

"Item: I bequeath my chaplains to the Earl of Stanford, seeing he has never had one in his employ; having never known any other than his son, My Lord Grey, who, being at the same time spiritual and carnal, will engender more than one monster.

"Item: I give *nothing* to my Lord Saye, and I do make him this legacy willingly, because I know that he will faithfully distribute it unto the poor.

"Item: Seeing that I did menace a certain Henry Mildmay, but did not thrash him, I do leave the sum of fifty pounds sterling to the lacquey that shall pay unto him my debt.

"Item: I bequeath to Thomas May, whose nose I did break at a mascarade, five shillings. My intention had been to give him more; but all who shall have seen his 'History of the Parliament' will consider that even this sum is too large.

"Item: I should have given to the author of the libel on women, entitled 'News of the Exchange,' three pence to invent a yet more scurrilous mode of maligning; but, seeing that he insulteth and slandereth I know not how many honest persons, I commit the office of paying him to the same lacquey who undertaketh the arrears of Henry Mildmay; he will teach him to distinguish between honourable women and disreputable.

"Item: I give to the Lieutenant-General Cromwell one of my words, the which he must want, seeing that he hath never kept any of his own.

"Item: I give to the wealthy citizens of London, and likewise to the Presbyterians and the nobility, notice to look to their skins; for, by the order of the State, the garrison of Whitehall hath provided itself with poniards, and useth dark lanterns in the place of candles.

"Item: I give up the ghost."

WILL OF WILLIAM PENN

William Penn died in 1718. His will, which follows, and the comments concerning it, are copied from an excellent little booklet issued by the Chelten Trust Company of Germantown, Pennsylvania:

"I William Penn Esqr so called Cheife proprietor & Govenour of the Pennsilvania and the Territoryes thereunto belonging, being of sound mind and understanding, for which I bless God, doe make and declare this my last Will and Testament.

"My Eldest Son being well provided for by a Settlement of his Mothers and my ffathers Estate I give and devise the Rest of my Estate in manner following

"The Government of my Province of Pennsylvania and Territories thereunto belonging and all powers relateing thereunto I give and devise to the most Hono'ble the Earle of Oxford and Earl Mortimer, and to William Earle Powelett, so called, and their Heires, upon trust to dispose thereof to the Queen or any other Person to the best advantage they can to be applyed in such a manner as I shall herein after direct.

"I give and devise to my dear Wife Hannah Penn and her ffather Thomas Callowhill and to my good ffriends Margarett Lowther my dear Sister, and to Gilbert Heathcote Physitian, Samuel Waldenfield, John ffield, Henry Gouldney, all liveing in England, and to my friends Samuel Carpenter, Richard Hill, Isaac Norris, Samuel Preston, and James Logan, liveing in or near Pensilvania and their heires all my lands Tenements and Hereditamts whatsoever rents and other profitts scituate lyeing and being in Pensilvania and the Territores thereunto belonging, or else where in America, upon Trust that they shall sell and dispose of so much thereof as shall be sufficient to pay all my just debts, and from and after paymt thereof shall convey unto each of the three Children of my son Willm Penn, Gulielma-Maria, Springett, and William respectively and to their respective heires 10,000 acres of land in some proper and beneficiall places to be sett out by my Trustees aforesaid. All the rest of my lands and Hereditamts whatsoever, scituate lyeing and being in America, I will that my said Trustees shall convey to and amongst Children which I have by my present Wife, in such proporcon and for such estates as my said Wife shall think fit, but before such Conveyance shall be made to my Children I will that my said Trustees shall convey to my daughter Aubrey whom I omitted to name before 10,000 acres of my said Lands in such places as my said Trustees shall think fitt.

"All my P'sonall estate in Pennsilvania and elsewhere and arreares of rent due there I give to my said dear Wife, whom I make my sole Executrix for the equall benefitt of her and her Children.

"In Testimony whereof I have sett my hand and seal to this my Will, which I declare to be my last Will, revoking all others formerly made by me.

"Signed Sealed and Published by the Testator William Penn in the presence of us who sett our names as Witnesses thereof in the P'sence of the said Testator after the Interlineacon of the Words above Vizt whom I make my sole Executrix.

WILLIAM PENN.

(Five Witnesses)

"This Will I made when ill of a feavour at London with a Clear understanding of what I did then, but because of some unworthy Expressions belying Gods goodness to me as if I knew not what I did, doe now that I am recovered through Gods goodness hereby declare that it is my last Will and Testament at Ruscomb, in Berkshire, this 27th of the 5th Month, called May, 1712.

"WM. PENN.

(Seven Witnesses)
"Postcript in my own hand

"As a further Testimony of my love to my dear Wife I of my own mind give unto her out of the rents of America vizt Pennsilvania 300 pounds a year for her naturall life and for her care and charge over my Children in their Education of which she knows my mind as also that I desire they may settle at least in good part in America where I leave them so good an Interest to be for their Inheritance from Generacon to Generacon which the Lord p'serve and prosper. Amen. WM. PENN."

COMMENTS ON THE WILL

This will, of interest to all Americans, has been quoted, not as showing how to prepare a will, but how *not* to do it.

James Logan, man of affairs, Secretary of the Province and the business representative of the Penn family in Pennsylvania, was dismayed when a copy was placed in his hands He wrote to Hannah Penn, the widow, November 4, 1718:

"The sloop 'Dolphin' arrived from London, bringing us divers letters and among ye rest one from Jno Page to me with a copy of our late Proprietor's will wch gives me some uneasiness as being Drawn in hast I believe by himself only, when such a settlement required a hand better acquainted with affairs of that Nature.

"The Estate in these parts is vested in so many without impowering any P'ticular or a suitable number to grant and Convey, that I fear we shall be puzzled. I hope that you will take advice there what methods must be pursued in ye Case."

James Logan, with his clear mind, saw at once the difficulties which would surround the execution of such a will, and regretted that Penn had not employed some competent person to draw up this important document for him. Such a will, disposing of so many and varied interests, as Logan quaintly expressed it, "required a hand better acquainted with affairs of that Nature."

Logan's criticism and fears were well grounded as the litigation over the Founder's will extended over a period of nine years.

The life of Penn reveals him as gifted with extraordinary wisdom, prudence, and forethought. In the ordinary as well as the trying and unusual crises of his eventful life, these qualities stood him in good stead, but when he came to draw up his own will they failed him, as they have failed so many men who have tried in vain to draw a valid will.

It is a wise provision of the religious society of which Penn was one of the founders, by which it annually recommends to its members:

"Friends are earnestly advised to inspect the state of their outward affairs at least once in a year and to consider carefully, whilst in health, the just disposition of their estates by will or otherwise."

Will of Samuel Pepys

Samuel Pepys was an interesting figure in England in the latter part of the seventeenth century. We know him chiefly as the well-known diarist, though he did work of high order in connection with the British navy. He died on May 26, 1703. Of his diary, the London *Athenæum* has said: "It is the best book of its kind in the English language."

By his will, he left to Magdalene College, Cambridge, the Pepysian Library of some three thousand volumes. This collection is kept in a separate building, and contains manuscript of his celebrated diary, together with many rare and curious documents, including the love letters of Henry VIII to Anne Boleyn, a collection of Scottish poetry and ancient English ballads. The diary, which was deciphered from the author's shorthand notes, is yet a popular book and is of standard importance to English literature, reflecting, as it does, the court, times, characters, and peculiarities of the age of Charles II.

Will of Cecil John Rhodes

Cecil John Rhodes, of Cape Town, South Africa, who died in 1902, was a South African statesman and financier; an affection of the lungs necessitated his leaving England when a young man, and he acquired fame and wealth in the home of his adoption. Rhodes's mode of life was the subject of diverse criticism; he was regarded as a man actuated by selfish motives, and preëminently, a man of money, but by his will, he left nearly his entire fortune to educational purposes; his scholarships have commanded the admiration of the world, and former estimates of his character were modified. Certain portions of this remarkable will, taken from Mr. Remsen's excellent work, follow:

"I, The Right Honourable Cecil John Rhodes of Cape Town in the Colony of the Cape of Good Hope, hereby revoke all testamentary dispositions heretofore made by me and declare this to be my last Will which I make this first day of July 1899.

"1. I am a natural-born British subject and I now declare that I have adopted and acquired and hereby adopt and acquire and intend to retain Rhodesia as my domicile.

"2. I appoint (naming seven persons) to be the Executors and Trustees of my Will and they and the survivors of them or other the Trustees for the time being of my Will are hereinafter called 'My Trustees.'

"3. I admire the grandeur and loneliness of the Matoppos in Rhodesia and therefore I desire to be buried in the Matoppos on the hill which I used to visit and which I called the 'View of the World' in a square to be cut in the rock on the top of the hill covered with a plain brass plate these words thereon — 'Here lie the remains of Cecil John Rhodes' and accordingly I direct my Executors at the expense of my estate to take steps and do all things necessary or proper to give effect to this my desire and afterwards to keep my grave in order at the expense of the Matoppos and Bulawayo fund hereinafter mentioned."

The testator gives certain pecuniary legacies, directs the erection or completion of a monument on the said hill in memory of certain dead, and provides for interments thereon. He provides for the cultivation of certain of his lands "for the instruction of the people of Rhodesia," the establishment of a park, "planted with every possible tree," with funds for their maintenance.

He places in trust certain property for the use of his brothers and sisters with gift over. He gives his college in the University of Oxford a sum of money for the erection of new college buildings and other purposes. He provides, by means of a trust, for the use of his residence and grounds at Cape Town as a public park until the Federal Government of the State of South Africa shall be founded, and thereafter as the residence of the Prime Minister in that government.

After reciting his educational views and desire to promote unity among the English-speaking people throughout the world, the testator provides for the establishment of certain scholarships at the University of Oxford, for the benefit of students for British Colonies and the United States of America. To this, by codicil, he subsequently added certain scholarships for the benefit of German students. He also prescribes certain rules and regulations for the election of students to such scholarships.

"36. My trustees shall invest the scholarship fund and the other funds hereinbefore established or any part thereof respectively in such investments in any part of the world, as they shall in their uncontrolled discretion think fit and that without regard to any rules of equity governing investments by trustees and without any responsibility or liability should they commit any breach of any such rule, with power to vary any such investments for others of a like nature."

"37. Investments to bearer held as an investment, may be deposited by my Trustees for safe custody in their names with any banker or banking company or with any company whose business it is to take charge of investments of that nature and my trustees shall not be responsible for any loss incurred in consequence of such deposit."

"40. I give the residue of my real and personal estate unto such of them the said (persons who are named as Executors and Trustees,) as shall be living at my death absolutely and if more than one as joint tenants."

"41. My Trustees in the administration of the trust business may instead of acting personally, employ and pay a Secretary or Agent to transact all business and do all acts required to be done in the trust including the receipt and payment of money."

"42. My intention is that there shall be always at least three Trustees of my Will so far as it relates to the Scholarship Trusts and therefore I direct that whenever there shall be less than three Trustees, a new Trustee or new Trustees shall be forthwith appointed."

"In witness whereof I have hereunto set my hand the day and year first above written.

"C. J. Rhodes."

(Subscribed by three witnesses.)

CODICIL

There is a long codicil to the will wherein the testator devises in tail his palatial home, known as "The Delham Hall Estate" and makes disposition of his great treasures in heirlooms, in and about Delham Hall.

Will of Cardinal Richelieu

This very interesting and remarkable will is extremely rare to find, although the copy from which we take it was in print, having been preserved, among many other curious papers, by M. Bourée, of Châtillon; docketed along with it was a collection of isolated papers, all more or less *piquants*, relating to the famous and formidable cardinal, and consisting of satirical verses, epitaphs, lampoons, parasitical flatteries, apologies, etc. There is also a rough copy of a *billet d'enterrement*, apparently drawn up with the intention of being distributed to the court to invite them to the funeral.

Our readers will no doubt peruse with curiosity the last wishes of this pompous and magnificent minister, who contrived to rehabilitate himself after an early disgrace, to maintain his proud supremacy to the last, and to die bequeathing gifts to his sovereign and master.

Of his luxury and extravagance, his nepotism so costly to the country, his assumption of power, and the art with which he knew how to make himself obeyed and feared by all classes and conditions of men, history amply informs us in details scarcely credible at the present day; and that it was he who by his despotism and tyranny laid the foundations of that terrible revolution, which blasted the face of the country and cast its fatal blight, more or less fatally, over the whole civilized world, none are likely to forget.

If we wanted an instance of pomp, unexampled even in the history of the Roman Empire, of uncompromising consideration as claimed by and accorded to this *parvenu* prince, whose personal expenses are estimated at more than a thousand crowns a day — considerably more than the monarch he served had at his private disposal — we may find it in the narrative of his (happily) last journey from Tarascon to Paris. It is to be regretted the famous Tarasque had not broken loose that day and devoured him before he started on his egotistical expedition.

Pronouncing himself unable to bear the fatigue of saddle, carriage, or litter, he ordered a room to be built of light boards covered with crimson satin damask, which was to be furnished with a bed, two chairs, and a table for his secretary; this movable house was hoisted on the shoulders of eighteen of the cardinal's guards, to be relieved at stated distances; they were to walk on bareheaded, no matter what weather, and it was during the month of August, or about the hottest season in France.

When this singular *cortège* — for the cardinal was followed by carriages containing his numerous suite — arrived at the towns he had to pass through, they found the walls and gates already demolished and cleared away by the direction of a vanguard of attendants sent on before to see that room was made for his Eminence to pass without delay or interruption.

When he reached Paris, chains were stretched along both sides of the streets to keep back the people who crowded them to contemplate in wonder and silent awe the despot, who a few days before, had hurried to the scaffold the youthful Cinq-Mars and his virtuous friend De Thou.

This sight made a profound and lasting impression on the youthful Bossuet, who, being on that day fifteen years of age, arrived in Paris for the first time.

It would be superfluous to cite this will in its entirety; we therefore only transcribe such passages as we feel will be of general interest, and these we give verbatim.

It is dated Narbonne, 23d of May, 1642, and bears the signature of Pierre Falconis, notaire royal. It is contained in twelve quarto pages of very close printing.

After two paragraphs of pious preamble and directions for his funeral, it proceeds to appoint to his *niessce*, Madame la Duchesse d'Eguillon (*sic*), all the cash in gold and silver he might possess at his decease, except a sum of 1,500,000 livres to be placed in the hands of his Majesty immediately on his death for a purpose he will explain farther on. It then goes on to declare that by contract he had given to the Crown ". . . Mon grand hostel que j'ai basti sous le nom de Palais Cardinal, ma chapelle d'or enrichie de diamans, mon buffet d'argent ciselé, et un grand diamant que j'ai acheté a Lopez, toutes lesquelles choses le roi a eu agréable par sa bonté d'accepter à ma trez humble et très instante supplication. . . .

"Je supplie S. M. d'avoir agréables huit tentures de tapisserie et trois lits que je prie Madame la Duchesse d'Eguillon, ma niessce, et M. de Noyers de choisir entre mes meubles, pour servir à une partie de l'ameublement des principaux appartemens du dit Palais Cardinal.

"Comme aussi je la supplie d'agréer la donation que je lui fais en outre de l'hostel qui est devant le Palais Cardinal, lequel j'ai acquis de feu M. le Commandeur de Sillery, pour au lieu d'icelui faire une place au devant du dit palais.

"Je supplie aussi très humblement S. M. de trouver bon que l'on lui mette entre les mains la somme de 1,500,000 livres dont j'ay fait mention cy-dessus, de laquelle somme je puis dire avec vérité de m'estre servi très utilement aux plus grandes affaires de son estat, en sort que si je n'eusse eu cet argent à ma disposition quelques affaires qui ont bien succédé eussent apparemment mal réussi, ce qui me donne sujet d'oser supplier S. M. de destiner ceste somme que je lui laisse, pour employer en diverses occasions, qui ne peuvent souffrir la longueur des formes de finance."

He then orders all his property, whether *in esse* or *in posse*, to be distributed as follows. The list supplies some idea of the shameless extent to which this man, who began life without any kind of fortune, enriched himself at the expense of the State.

"Je donne et lègue à Armand de Maillé, mon nepveu et fileul, fils d'Arban de Maillé, Marquis de Brézé, Mareschal de France, et de Nicole du Plessis, ma seconde sœur, et en ce je l'institue mon héritier pour les droicts qu'il pourrait prendre en toutes les terres et autres qui se trouveront en ma succession ainsi que s'ensuit."

These *biens* consisted of (for the share of this nephew alone) the *duché et pairie* of Fronsac et Caumont; of the lands and Marquisate of Graville; of the county of Beaufort en Vallée; of the lands and barony of Fresne; of 300,000 livres deposited at the Château de Saumur; and of the *ferme des poids de Normandie*, the returns from which amount to 50,000 livres annually.

Next comes the before-named niece who, over and above the *biens* settled on her at her marriage, was to have ". . . la maison où elle loge à present, nommé le Petit Luxembourg, joignant le palais de la reine, mère du roi; ma maison et ma terre de Ruel; le domaine de Pontoise; la rente que j'ay à prendre sur les cinq grosses fermes de France qui monte à 60,000 livres par an.

"Item: A ma dite niessce, tous les cristaux, tableaux, et autres pièces qui sont dans le cabinet principal de la dite maison le Petit Luxembourg, sans y comprendre l'argenterie du buffet dont j'ay dejà disposé.

"Item: Je lui donne aussi toutes mes bagues et pierreries à l'exception seulement de ce que j'ay laissé à la Couronne, ensemble un buffet d'argent vermeil doré neuf, pesant 535 marcs 4 gros, contenu en deux coffres faits exprez."

The next legatee is his nephew, François de Vignerot, to whom he leaves first the sum of 200,000 livres on condition that he shall lay it out in the purchase of an estate, to enjoy it during his lifetime, and after his decease to go to Armand, his eldest son, or to whichever of his sons succeeds to the title of Duc de Richelieu. He leaves him further his *duché-pairie* de Richelieu with the appurtenances, dependencies, and lands thereto belonging.

Item: The lands and barony of Barbézieux;

Item: The lands and principality of Mortagne;

Item: The county of Cosnac, the baronies of Coze, Laugeon and d'Alvas, the domain of Hiers en Brouage, the hostel of Richelieu planned and ordered to be built adjoining the Palais Cardinal.

Item: The tapestries representing the history of Lucretia, bought of M. le Duc de Chevreuse, with all the figures, statues, busts, pictures, crystals, cabinets, tables, and other furniture at present in the *conciergerie* of the Palais Cardinal, in order worthily to furnish and adorn the said Hostel de Richelieu, when it shall be completed; and besides these all other movables or immovables, claims upon the king or his domains, and generally all property not as yet disposed of by this will; but all and only on the condition that he shall assume the sole name of Du Plessis Richelieu, and that neither he nor his descendants shall ever be known by any other, or quarter any other arms, under the following penalties. . . .

To this nephew, the cardinal also leaves his library, but with the proviso that it is to be at the service of all members of the family, and also of the public; and he desires, therefore, that on his decease, a full and complete catalogue be made under the directions of his executors, who are to call to their assistance two Doctors of the Sorbonne, who shall be present during the making of the said inventory; which, being made in duplicate, one copy was to be deposited in his own library, signed by his executors and by the said Doctors of the Sorbonne; and the other copy, similarly signed, in the Sorbonne itself.

There are further conditions attached to the ownership of the library, viz., that a librarian shall be appointed at a salary of one thousand livres per annum; three candidates having first been chosen by the Sorbonne and nominated by his successors. He desires further that a person shall be kept to sweep out the library every day, and to beat, dust, and wipe the books at stated and frequent intervals, at a yearly wage of four hundred livres. He also stipulates that one thousand livres shall be put by every year for the purchase of additional books.

He explains that his "niessce la Duchesse d'Enghien" having displeased him by her marriage, he leaves her nothing, "moyennant ce que je lui ai donné en dot, dont je veux et ordonne qu'elle se contente."

After several clauses relating to the edifice of the Sorbonne, to his burial, to several constructions to be added to the Hostel de Richelieu, and to a legacy of sixty thousand livres to the "vingt pères de la mission établie à Richelieu," he adds a very characteristic clause as follows:

"Et d'autant plus qu'il a plu à Dieu benir mes travaux et les faire considérer par le roy mon bon maistre, en les reconnoissant par sa munificence royale, audessus de ce que je pouvoir espérer, j'ay estimé, en faisant ma disposition présente, devoir obliger mes héritiers à conserver l'établissement que j'ay fait en ma famille, en sorte qu'elle se puisse maintenir longuement en la dignité et splendeur qu'il a plu au roi lui donner, afin que la posterité connoisse que si je l'ay servi fidellement, il a sçu par une vertu toute royale m'aymer et me combler de ses bienfaits." And here follow certain conditions which need not be detailed.

In the next clause the pride of family crops up again: "Je defends à mes héritiers de prendre alliance en des maisons qui ne soient pas vrayement nobles, les laissant assez à leurs aise pour avoir plus d'égards à la naissance et à la vertu qu'aux commodités et aux biens."

The clause relating to servants and their bequests is worth quoting, as testimony to the magnificence of his Eminence's retinue:

"Pour marque de la satisfaction que j'ay des services qui m'ont esté rendus par mes domestiques et serviteurs je donne au Sieur Didier, mon aumosnier, 1500 liv.; au Sieur de Bar, 10,000 liv.; au Sieur de Manse, 6000 liv.; au Sieur de Belesbat, parceque je ne lui ay encore rien donné, 10,000 liv.; à Beaugensi, 3000 liv.; à Estoublon, 3000 liv.; au Sieur de Marsal, 3000 liv.; au Sieur de Palvoisin, parceque je ne lui ay jusques icy rien donné, 12,000 liv.; à Grenillé, 2000 liv.; à Blouin, 6000 liv.; au Sieur Cytois, 6000 liv.; au Sieur Renaudot, 2000 liv.; à Bertereau, 6000 liv.; à Des Bornais, mon valet de chambre, 6000 liv., et je desire qu'il demeure concierge, soutz mon petit neveu, du Pont de Courlay, dans le Palais Cardinal; au Cousin, 6000 liv.; à l'Espolette et à Prevost, chacun 3000 liv.; à Picot, 6000 liv.; à Robert, 3000 liv.; au Sieur de Graves et de Saint-Leger, mes escuyers, chacun 3000 liv.; et en outre, mes deux carosses avec leurs deux attelages de chevaux, ma litière et les trois mulets qui y servent, pour estre également partagés entre mes dits deux escuyers; à Chamarante et Du Plessis, chacun 3000 liv.; à Vilandry, 1500 liv.; à De Roques, dixhuit chevaux d'escole, après que les douze meilleurs de mon escurie auront esté choisies par mes parents; au Sieur de Fortes Cuieres, 6000 liv.; à Grandpré, capitaine de Richelieu, 3000 liv.; à la Jeunesse, concierge de Richelieu, 5000 liv.; au petit Mulat, qui escrit soutz le Sieur Charpentier, mon secrétaire, 1500 liv.; à la Garde, 3000 liv.; á mon premier cuisinier, 2000 liv.; à mon credencier, 2000 liv.; à mon premier cocher, 1500 liv.; à mon premier muletier, 1200 liv.; à chacun de mes valets de pied,

600 liv.; et généralement à tous les autres officiers de ma maison scavoir: de la cuisine sommeliers et escuyers, chacun six années de leurs gages outre ce qui leur sera deu jusques au jour de mon decez.

"Je ne donne rien au Sieur Charpentier, mon secrétaire, parceque j'ay eu soin de lui faire du bien pendant ma vie; mais je veux rendre ce temoignage de luy, que durant le longtemps qu'il m'a servy, je n'ay poinct connu de plus homme de bien, ny de plus loyal et plus sincère serviteur.

"Je ne donne rien aussi au Sieur Cherré, mon autre secrétaire, parceque je le laisse assez accommodé, estant néanmoins satisfait des services qu'il m'a rendus.

"Je donne au baron de Broye, héritier du feu Sieur Barbin, que j'ay sceu estre en nécessité, la somme de 30,000 livres."

The remainder of the will consists of various, and we may add very numerous, formalities, signatures of witnesses, etc.

It is a curious fact that, on the death of the last surviving descendant of the Du Plessis family, 17th of May, 1822 — a man, be it observed, of singular probity and true grandeur of character — the colossal fortune amassed by the cardinal had dwindled down to such small proportions that all that remained of it was swallowed up in paying off the debts of his profligate father, and of his grandfather, the notorious Duc de Richelieu who figures so largely in the "Chronique Scandaleuse" of his day.

Will of Jean Jacques Rousseau

Although Rousseau's will was made in 1737, it remained unknown to the world until 1820. It never was executed, nor ever became an effectual or a legal document; but it is, nevertheless, curious as testifying to the state of mind of the writer and the fervent sentiments of piety he entertained at the age of twenty-five.

The original, which is well authenticated, was found in the garret of an old house at Chambéry. It was among the forgotten minutes of a former notary of that town, named Rivoire, and occupied pages 104, 105, and 106 of the minute. It is dated June 7, 1737 — a day on which, as stated in the will, Rousseau met with an accident which obliged him to keep his bed, and having a bandage on his forehead covering his eyes, was thus prevented signing his will; though, says the notary, "sain de ses sens ainsi qu'il a paru par la suite et solidité de ses raisonnements." It seems to have been a case of "The devil was sick," etc., and the will appears to be such as Rousseau was not likely to have written at any other moment. The deed was received at the house of M. Le Comte de St. Laurent, Contrôleur-général des finances de S. M. le Roi de Sardaigne, inhabited at the time by Madame Warens, who afterwards occupied so large a place in the life of Rousseau.

The testator, after making the sign of the Cross, recommending his soul to God, and begging the intercession of the holy Virgin and of SS. John and James, his patrons, professes his intention of living and dying in the faith of the Catholic apostolic and Roman Church. He leaves his obsequies to the discretion of his heiress, and charges her to see that prayers are offered for the repose of his soul.

After these preliminaries he bequeaths 16 livres to each of the Convents of the Capuchins, the Augustinians, and the Clares of Chambéry, that they may celebrate masses for the repose of his soul.

He bequeaths his patrimony to his father, praying him to be content therewith as gratitude renders it his duty to dispose of his other possessions in favor of his benefactors.

He leaves 100 livres to the Sieur Jacques Barillot of Geneva; he appoints as his heir Madame Françoise-Louise de la Tour Comtesse de Warens, to whom he declares it his wish to pay over and above this, the sum of 2000 livres to cover the expenses of his board during ten years. Finally he recognizes a debt of 700 livres in favor of the Sieur Charbonnel, a tradesman of Chambéry, for goods delivered and money lent.

The will is signed by Claude Morel (procureur au sénat), Antoine Bonne des Echelles, Jacques Gros de Vanzy, Antoine Bouvard, Pierre Catagnole and Pierre Cordonnier. The seventh witness, Antoine Forraz de Bissy, is declared "illitéré." This act was registered 22d of July, 1737, in fol. 662 of the second book of the year 1737.

According to all appearance this will was not engrossed, and Rousseau, whose life was so checkered, and who so often changed his domicile, probably forgot all about it, and about the accident which occasioned it, when he drew up his Confessions.

The *Journal de Savoie*, under date 7th of April, 1820, supplies some curious particulars as to the minutes of the above-named notary, Rivoire, among which were found a power of attorney to Jacques Barillot by Rousseau, to withdraw at Geneva the rights of his mother Suzanne Bernard. This document is dated 12th of July, 1737, and registered on the 15th of the same month.

Rousseau, born at Geneva, 28th of June, 1712, died at Ermenonville, 2d of July, 1778.

Will of Lord St. Leonards

The necessity that there should be some better fashion for the safe keeping of wills, during the lifetime of testators, than at present exists, is, perhaps, more vividly portrayed in the case of the late Lord St. Leonards than in any other on record. In this case we have the loss of the will, not only, of one of the astutest of lawyers, the most orthodox of conveyancers, but of a man who had made it his chief pleasure and study during the last four years of his life to provide for the disposition of his worldly wealth, when his Creator should summon away his spirit from earth, and return his mortal frame to the dust from which He had made it. Moreover, the testator is no less a person than the very ingenious conveyancer, Lord Chancellor of England, and author himself of that famous "Handy-book," in which men are exhorted in the most convincing manner to make due and thorough disposition of their earthly possessions. Here, during the years he had been engaged in making his will, the greatest care was evinced for the preservation of the precious document, as it was not only kept locked up in a box, but during his Lordship's illness the Honorable Miss Charlotte Sugden, his daughter, took charge of the box and retained it in her custody until her father should be able to leave his room, when it was replaced by her in its ordinary position, and where it remained until his last illness, when she again took charge of it, and in whose custody it continued until his Lordship's death in January, 1875. After the solemn ceremony of the funeral this well-cared-for box was opened, but, alas! the will was not there. How this strange circumstance occurred no one has been able to furnish any information; but the loss gave rise to litigation of the most serious character in the Court of Probate. The triumph gained in that court by Miss Sugden in establishing a will, carrying out the wishes of her father, on the simple basis of her recollection of the contents of the lost document, is as wondrous an achievement as any one well could imagine, and testifies to the grave respect with which her evidence must have been regarded by the searching judgment and scrutinizing eye of the learned judge.

ANCIENT, CURIOUS, AND FAMOUS WILLS

Notwithstanding all this, the loss of the will has not escaped the attendance of great and grievous evils, unnecessary to be related. The judge having in a most eloquent manner reviewed the case, as elucidated by the pleadings of the very learned counsel engaged on the trial, most admirably concluded his summing-up with the following remarks:

"Now let me call attention to a passage in one of Lord St. Leonards' own works which has a bearing upon this subject, and it shows how the wisest of men may be mistaken, as I think, in the advice which they give to others. And I may say this case illustrates the false security in which Lord St. Leonards lived, and in which I dare say we all of us live. With the other members of his family, he lived in the belief that his Will was secure from the hands and eyes of either the curious or the dishonest. It was thought that the only means of access to it was by the only key which Lord St. Leonards carried about him; and that there was no means of access to the duplicate key, which would open the Will-box, and yet it turned out that there were no less than four keys in the house by which anybody might have opened the escritoire in which the duplicate key was kept, and so have obtained possession of it. Believing as I do that this Will has been lost, and not destroyed by the testator, and that the loss has arisen from its insecure custody, though that custody seemed to all concerned to be perfectly safe, it is well that it should be known and I particularly desire that it should be known to the public, that the law has provided a means of obtaining as nearly a certainty as can be obtained in human affairs that a Will will be forthcoming at the death of the testator. . . .

"The result is that I find as a fact, that the Will of 1870 was duly executed and attested; that the several codicils also were duly executed and attested; that the Will was not revoked by the testator; and I further find that the contents of the Will were, with the exception I have mentioned, as set out in the declaration."

WILL OF WILLIAM SHAKESPERE

"Vicesimo quinto die Martii, Anno Regni Domini nostri Jacobi nunc Regis Angliæ, &c., decimo quarto, et Scotiæ quadragesimo nono. Anno Domini 1616.

"In the name of God, Amen. I, William Shakespere, of Stratford-upon-Avon, in the county of Warwick, gent., in perfect health and memory, (God be praised!) do make and ordain this my last Will and testament in manner and form following; that is to say:

"First, I commend my soul into the hands of God my creator, hoping, and assuredly believing through the only merits of Jesus Christ my Saviour, to be made partaker of life everlasting; and my body to the earth whereof it is made.

"Item: I give and bequeath unto my daughter Judith one hundred and fifty pounds of lawful English money, to be paid unto her in manner and form following; that is to say, one hundred pounds in discharge of her marriage portion within one year after my decease, with consideration after the rate of two shillings in the pound for so long time as the same shall be unpaid unto her after my decease; and the fifty pounds residue thereof, upon her surrendering of, or giving of such sufficient security as the overseers of this my Will shall like of, to surrender or grant, all her estate and right that shall descend or come unto her after my decease, or that she now hath, of, in, or to, one copyhold tenement, with the appurtenances, lying and being in Stratford-upon-Avon aforesaid, in the said county of Warwick, being parcel or holden of the manor of Rowington, unto my daughter Susanna Hall, and her heirs for ever.

"Item: I give and bequeath unto my said daughter Judith one hundred and fifty pounds more, if she, or any issue of her body, be living at the end of three years next ensuing the day of the date of this my Will, during which time my executors to pay her consideration from my decease according to the rate aforesaid: and if she die within the said term without issue of her body, then my Will is, and I do give and bequeath one hundred pounds thereof to my niece Elizabeth Hall, and the fifty pounds to be set forth by my executors during the life of my sister Joan Hart, and the use and profit thereof coming, shall be paid to my said sister Joan, and after her decease the said fifty pounds shall remain amongst the children of my said sister, equally to be divided amongst them; but if my said daughter Judith be living at the end of the said three years, or any issue of her body, then my Will is, and so I devise and bequeath, the said hundred and fifty pounds to be set out by my executors and overseers for the best benefit of her and her issue, and the stock not to be paid unto her so long as she shall be married and covert baron; but my Will is, that she shall have the consideration yearly paid unto her during her life, and after her decease the said stock and consideration to be paid to her children, if she have any, and if not, to her executors or assigns, she living the said term after my decease: provided that if such husband as she shall at the end of the said three years be married unto, or at any (time) after, do sufficiently assure unto her, and the issue of her body, lands answerable to the portion by this my will given unto her, and to be adjudged so by my executors and overseers, then my Will is, that the said hundred and fifty pounds shall be paid to such husband as shall make such assurance, to his own use.

"Item: I give and bequeath unto my said sister Joan twenty pounds, and all my wearing apparel, to be paid and delivered within one year after my decease; and I do Will and devise unto her the house, with the appurtenances, in Stratford, wherein she dwelleth, for her natural life, under the yearly rent of twelve-pence.

"Item: I give and bequeath unto her three sons, William Hart, —— Hart, and Michael Hart, five pounds a-piece, to be paid within one year after my decease.

"Item: I give and bequeath unto the said Elizabeth Hall all my plate (except my broad silver and gilt bowl) that I now have at the date of this my Will.

"Item: I give and bequeath unto the poor of Stratford aforesaid ten pounds; to Mr. Thomas Combe my sword; to Thomas Russel, esq., five pounds; and to Francis Collins of the borough of Warwick, in the county of Warwick, gent., thirteen pounds six shillings and eight-pence, to be paid within one year after my decease.

"Item: I give and bequeath to Hamlet (Hamnet) Sadler twenty-six shillings eight-pence, to buy him a ring; to William Reynolds, gent., twenty-six shillings eight-pence, to buy him a ring; to my godson William Walker, twenty shillings in gold; to Anthony Nash, gent., twenty-six shillings eight-pence; and to Mr. John Nash, twenty-six shillings eight-pence; and to my fellows, John Hemynge, Richard Burbage, and Henry Cundell, twenty-six shillings eight-pence a-piece, to buy them rings.

"Item: I give, Will, bequeath, and devise, unto my daughter Susanna Hall, for better enabling of her to perform this my Will, and towards the performance thereof, all that capital messuage or tenement, with the appurtenances, in Stratford aforesaid, called the New Place, wherein I now dwell, and two messuages or tenements, with the appurtenances, situate, lying, and being in Henley

Street, within the borough of Stratford aforesaid; and all my barns, stables, orchards, gardens, lands, tenements and hereditaments whatsoever, situate, lying, and being, or to be had, received perceived, or taken, within the towns, hamlets, villages, fields, and grounds of Stratford-upon-Avon, Old Stratford, Bishopton, and Welcombe, or in any of them, in the said county of Warwick; and also all that messuage or tenement, with the appurtenances, wherein one John Robinson dwelleth, situate, lying, and being, in the Blackfriars in London, near the Wardrobe; and all other my lands, tenements, and hereditaments whatsoever; to have and to hold all and singular the said premises, with their appurtenances, unto the said Susanna Hall, for and during the term of her natural life; and after her decease to the first son of her body lawfully issuing, and to the heirs males of the body of the said first son lawfully issuing; and for default of such issue, to the second son of her body lawfully issuing, and to the heirs males of the body of the said second son lawfully issuing; and for default of such heirs, to the third son of the body of the said Susanna lawfully issuing, and to the heirs males of the body of the said third son lawfully issuing; and for default of such issue, the same to be and remain to the fourth, fifth, sixth, and seventh sons of her body, lawfully issuing one after another, and to the heirs males of the bodies of the said fourth, fifth, sixth, and seventh sons lawfully issuing, in such manner as it is before limited to be and remain to the first, second, and third sons of her body, and to their heirs males: and for default of such issue, the said premises to be and remain to my said niece Hall, and the heirs males of her body lawfully issuing; and for default of such issue, to my daughter Judith, and the heirs males of her body lawfully issuing; and for default of such issue, to the right heirs of me the said William Shakespere for ever.

"Item: I give unto my wife my second best bed, with the furniture.

"Item: I give and bequeath to my said daughter Judith my broad silver gilt bowl. All the rest of my goods, chattels, leases, plate, jewels, and household-stuff whatsoever, after my debts and legacies paid, and my funeral expenses discharged, I give, devise and bequeath to my son-in-law, John Hall, gent., and my daughter Susanna his wife, whom I ordain and make executors of this my last Will and testament. And I do entreat and appoint the said Thomas Russel, esq., and Francis Collins, gent., to be overseers hereof. And do revoke all former Wills, and publish this to be my last Will and testament. In witness whereof I have hereunto put my hand, the day and year first above written.

"By me,
"William Shakespere.

"Witness to the publishing hereof,
Fra. Collyns,
Julius Shaw,
John Robinson,
Hamnet Sadler,
Robert Whattcoat."

WILL OF M. SILHOUETTE

M. Silhouette died in 1767 in Paris. His will is as dry as the political and financial details of a period of history insipid in itself could make it; but the history of the man who wrote it is singular and suggestive, and shows how greatly the success of a public functionary depends on the circumstances in which he is placed, and far less than we are apt to suppose on his genius or skill.

Etienne Silhouette, Contrôleur-général and Minister of State, only held office during nine months, but at a time when the Treasury was already in an exhausted state in consequence of ruinous wars and the lavish expenditure of his predecessors. He had no choice but to replenish the coffers of the State by the imposition of new taxes, as economy alone would not have sufficed, though it might have aided to fill the alarming void. So far, however, from commending this needful, if not indispensable measure, his policy was turned into ridicule; and the people whom he did his best to serve and to save, heaped upon him every kind of obloquy. Among other insults they changed the name of a street issuing from the Place des Victoires, which had been styled after him La Rue Silhouette, into La Rue Vide Gousset, which it retains to this day; and as among other articles, he had imposed a tax upon likenesses taken in black paper, cut out, and pasted on a white card, which were then extremely popular, not only these portraits, but thence all black outlines received the name of *silhouettes*, which has adhered to them ever since.

WILL OF DEAN SWIFT

Dean Swift died October 19, 1745. The "Last Will of Jonathan Swift, D.D., taken out of the Prerogative Court of Dublin" in book form, neatly rebound and covering twenty-seven pages of written matter can yet be found in the bookstores of London. The instrument is dated the third day of May, 1740, and the document itself was printed a few years later. In turning its pages, a feeling of awe and reverence is experienced by the reader as he reviews the last words of the noted Irish clergyman, satirist and author of "Gulliver's Travels." Several important items of the Will follow:

"In the Name of God, Amen. I, Jonathan Swift, Doctor in Divinity, and Dean of the Cathedral Church of St. Patrick, Dublin, being at this Present of sound Mind, although weak in Body, do here make my last Will and Testament, hereby revoking all my former Wills.

"*Imprimis*, I bequeath my Soul to God, (in humble Hopes of his Mercy through Jesus Christ) and my Body to the Earth. And I desire that my Body may be buried in the great Isle of the said Cathedral, on the South Side, under the Pillar next to the Monument of Primate Narcissus Marsh, three Days after my Decease, as privately as possible, and at Twelve o'Clock at Night: And, that a Black Marble of —— Feet square, and seven Feet from the Ground, fixed to the Wall, may be erected, with the following Inscription in large Letters, deeply cut, and strongly gilded."

HIC DEPOSITUM EST CORPUS
JONATHAN SWIFT, S. T. P.
HUJUS ECCLESIÆ CATHEDRALIS
DECANI,
UBI SÆVA INDIGNATIO
ULTERIUS COR LACERARE NE-
QUIT.
ABI, VIATOR,
ET IMITARE, SI POTERIS,
STRENUUM PRO VIRILI LIBER-
TATIS VINDICEM.
OBIIT ANNO [MDCCXLV.]
MENSIS [OCTOBRIS] DIE [19.]
ÆTATIS ANNO [LXXVIII.]

"Item: I give and bequeath to my Executors all my worldly Substance, of what Nature or Kind soever (excepting such Part thereof as is herein after particularly devised) for the following Uses and Purposes, that is to say, to the Intent that they, or the Survivors or Survivor of them, his Executors, or Administrators, as soon as conveniently may be after my Death, shall turn it all into ready Money, and lay out the same in purchasing Lands of Inheritance in Fee simple, situate in any Province of Ireland, except Connaught, but as near to the City of Dublin, as conveniently can be found, and not incumbered with, or subject to any Leases for Lives renewable, or any Terms for Years longer than Thirty-one:"

He provides that a considerable sum be laid out in the purchase of lands near Dublin and a building be erected thereon "An Hospital for the Reception of as many Idiots and Lunaticks as the annual income of the said lands and worldly Substance shall be sufficient to maintain: And, I desire said Hospital may be called St. Patrick's Hospital."

He then goes into great detail as to the management of the Hospital.

"Item: Whereas I purchased the Inheritance of the Tythes of the Parish of Essernock near Trim in the County of Meath, for Two Hundred and Sixty Pounds Sterling, I bequeath the said Tythes to the Vicars of Laracor for the Time being, that is to say, so long as the present Episcopal Religion shall continue to be the National Established Faith and Profession in this Kingdom: But whenever any other Form of Christian Religion shall become the Established Faith in this Kingdom, I leave the said Tythes of Essernock to be bestowed, as the Profits come in, to the Poor of the said Parish of Laracor, by a weekly Proportion, and by such Officers as may then have the Power of distributing Charities to the Poor of the said Parish, while Christianity under any Shape shall be tolerated among us, still excepting professed Jews, Atheists, and Infidels.

"Item: I bequeath also to the said Martha, the Sum of Three Hundred Pounds Sterling, to be paid her by my Executors out of my ready Money, or Bank Bills, immediately after my Death, as soon as the Executors meet. I leave, moreover, to the said Martha, my repeating Gold Watch, my yellow Tortoise Shell Snuff Box, and her Choice of four Gold Rings, out of seven which I now possess.

"Item: I bequeath to Mrs. Mary Swift alias Harrison, Daughter of the said Martha, my plain Gold Watch made by Quare; to whom also I give my Japan Writing Desk, bestowed to me by Lady Worseley, my square Tortoise Shell Snuff Box, richly lined and inlaid with Gold, given to me by the Right Honourable Henrietta now Countess of Oxford, and the Seal with a Pegasus, given to me by the Countess of Granville.

"Item: I bequeath to Mr. Ffolliott Whiteway, eldest Son of the aforesaid Martha, who is bred to be an Attorney, the Sum of Sixty Pounds; as also Five Pounds to be laid out in the Purchase of such Law Books as the Honourable Mr. Justice Lyndsay, Mr. Stannard, or Mr. McAullay shall judge proper for him.

"Item: I bequeath to my dearest Friend Alexander Pope of Twittenham, Esq., my Picture in Miniature, drawn by Zinck, of Robert late Earl of Oxford.

"Item: I leave to Edward now Earl of Oxford, my Seal of Julius Cæsar, as also another Seal, supposed to be a young Hercules, both very choice Antiques, and set in Gold: Both which I chuse to bestow to the said Earl, because they belonged to her late Most Excellent Majesty Queen Anne, of ever Glorious, Immortal, and truly Pious Memory, the real nursing Mother of all her Kingdoms.

"Item: I leave to the Reverend Mr. James Stopford, Vicar of Finglass, my Picture of King Charles, the First, drawn by Vandyke, which was given to me by the said James; as also my large Picture of Birds, which was given to me by Thomas, Earl of Pembroke.

"Item: I bequeath to the Reverend Mr. Robert Grattan, Prebendary of St. Audeon's, my Gold Bottle Screw, which he gave me, and my strong Box, on Condition of his giving the sole Use of the said Box to his Brother Dr. James Grattan, during the Life of the said Doctor, who hath more Occasion for it, and the second best Beaver Hat I shall die possessed of.

"Item: I bequeath to Mr. John Grattan, Prebendary of Clonmethan, my Silver Box in which the Freedom of the City of Cork was presented to me; in which I desire the said John to keep the Tobacco he usually cheweth, called Pigtail.

"Item: I bequeath all my Horses and Mares to the Reverend Mr. John Jackson, Vicar of Santry, together with all my Horse Furniture: Lamenting that I had not Credit enough with any chief Governor (since the Change of Times) to get some additional Church Preferment for so virtuous and worthy a Gentleman. I also leave him my third best Beaver Hat.

"Item: I bequeath to the Reverend Doctor Francis Wilson, the Works of Plato in three Folio Volumes, the Earl of Clarendon's History in the three Folio Volumes, and my best Bible; together with thirteen small Persian Pictures in the Drawing Room, and the small Silver Tankard given to me by the Contribution of some Friends, whose Names are engraved at the Bottom of the said Tankard.

"Item: I bequeath to the Earl of Orrery the enamelled Silver Plates to distinguish Bottles of Wine by, given to me by his excellent Lady, and the Half-length Picture of the late Countess of Orkney in the Drawing Room.

"Item: I bequeath to Alexander McAullay, Esq., the Gold Box in which the Freedom of the City of Dublin was presented to me, as a Testimony of the Esteem and Love I have for him, on Account of his great Learning, fine natural Parts, unaffected Piety and Benevolence, and his truly honourable Zeal in Defence of the legal Rights of the Clergy, in Opposition to all their unprovoked Oppressors.

"Item: I bequeath to Deane Swift, Esq., my large Silver Standish, consisting of a large Silver Plate, an Ink Pot, a Sand Box and a Bell of the same Metal.

"Item: I bequeath to Mrs. Mary Barber the Medal of Queen Anne and Prince George, which she formerly gave me.

"Item: I leave to the Reverend Mr. John Worrall my best Beaver Hat.

"Item: I bequeath to the Reverend Doctor Patrick Delany my Medal of Queen Anne in Silver, and on the Reverse the Bishops of England kneeling before her Most Sacred Majesty.

"Item: I bequeath to the Reverend Mr. James King, Prebendary of Tipper, my large gilded Medal of King Charles the First, and on the Reverse a Crown of Martyrdom, with other Devices. My Will, nevertheless, is, that if any of the above named Legatees should die before me, that then, and in that Case, the respective Legacies to them bequeathed, shall revert to myself, and become again subject to my Disposal.

"In witness whereof, I have hereunto set my Hand and Seal, and published and declared this as my last Will and Testament, this Third Day of May, 1740.

"JONATHAN SWIFT."

Will of J. M. W. Turner, R.A.

The great painter, J. M. W. Turner, R.A., died in 1851. It is unnecessary to quote this lengthy and well-known document; indeed, we might speak of the unfortunate will and its numerous codicils in the plural.

It was dated June 10, 1831, and was attested by George Cobb, John Saxon, and Charles Tall. It is written in various legal hands, all except the first codicil, the whole of which is in autograph.

After legacies to private friends and servants, and to various charities, and the bequests of his valuable works to the nation, under very special and stringent conditions, this eccentric, wealthy, and benevolent artist ordered that the residue of his estate should be devoted to the founding and maintaining of an "institution for the support of poor and decayed male artists, born in England and of English parents only, and lawful issue."

"Unfortunately for the poor artists of England," says Turner's biographer, "the will being a most cloudy document, full of confusions and interpolations, it was disputed by the next of kin, who endeavoured to establish that the testator was of unsound mind. But this effort to annihilate its validity failed, the testator being held to be of sound mind and capable of making a legal disposition of his estate.

"The trustees and executors thereupon filed a bill in Chancery on the 25th of April, 1852, praying the court to construe the will, and enable them to administer the estate. The next of kin, by their answer, contended that since it was impossible to place any construction upon the will at all, it was necessarily void."

The testator's property, we may remark, was sworn under £140,000.

The documents in this Chancery suit, which extended to four years, are of several tons weight. The bills of costs alone would fill a butcher's cart. How Turner would have groaned to see the lawyers fattening on his hard-earned savings!

A compromise was eventually effected between all parties to the suit, and on March 19, 1856, a decree was pronounced, with their consent, to the following effect:

1. The real estate to go to the heir-at-law.
2. The pictures, etc., to the National Gallery.

3. £1000 for the erection of the monument in St. Paul's Cathedral.
4. £20,000 to the Royal Academy, free of legacy duty.
5. Remainder to be divided among next of kin.

WILL OF VAUGELAS

Claude Favre de Vaugelas the French Grammarian, one of the lights of the "Salon Bleu," and honored by the friendship of Madame de Rambouillet, was born at Bourg en Bresse in 1585, and after making an illustrious name in the annals of literature, and being rewarded by several pensions, died in a condition of abject poverty in Paris, in 1650. It is difficult to account for the sad circumstances under which he ended his days, unless, like many of the literary characters found in history, he led a life of reckless expenditure, possibly good-naturedly lending to those who never repaid him, and generally neglected to keep any kind of order in his affairs.

Fréron, in his "Année Littéraire," reports a singular clause in his will, but one which does honor to his sense of rectitude and his conscientiousness.

"Vaugelas," says he, "died, so to speak, in penury; he was so deeply in debt that he was obliged to remain all day at home (a single room), and could only go out at night for fear he should fall into the hands of his creditors. On this account he was named the 'Hibou.' His will was remarkable: after having ordered his little all to be sold for the payment of his debts, he adds, 'But as, after all has been distributed, there may remain some creditors whose claims will not be satisfied, my last will is that my body be sold to the surgeons for the highest price that can be obtained, and the product applied to the liquidation of the debts I may still owe, so that, if I have been unable to be of any use during my life, I may at least serve some purpose after my death.'"

WILL OF VOLTAIRE

Among Voltaire's papers was found a note, endorsed "Mon Testament," which, on being opened, exhibited these lines in his own hand:

"Je meurs en adorant Dieu,
En aimant mes amis,
En ne haissant point mes ennemis,
En detestant la superstition."

Voltaire spent his last days in Paris, dying there in 1778. It was there Benjamin Franklin took to him his grandson on whom he asked Voltaire to pronounce a blessing. Voltaire placed his hand upon the young man's head, uttering at the same time in English, "God and liberty."

WILL OF IZAAK WALTON

"Simon Peter saith unto them, I go a fishing. They say unto him, we also go with thee."

Izaak Walton died December 15, 1683, at the age of ninety, and was buried in the north transept of Winchester Cathedral. He is best known and loved by his work, "The Compleat Angler, or Contemplative Man's Recreation;" for quaintness and pastoral freshness it has never been excelled and has passed through more than a hundred editions. Of the book Charles Lamb said: "It would sweeten a man's temper at any time to read it." The following verses in praise of tobacco, are taken from a poem of considerable length, Gosden's edition of the "Journey to Beresford Hall."

"Me thinks I see Charles Cotton, and his friend,
The modest Walton, from Augusta's town,
Enter the Fishing-house an hour to spend,
And by the marble table set them down.

"'Boy, bring me in the jug of Derby Ale,
My best tobacco, and my smoking tray;'
The boy, obedient, brings the rich regale,
And each assumes his pipe of polished clay.

. . . .

"Now cloud on cloud pervades the fishers' room,
The Moreland Ale rich sparkles to the sight;
They draw fresh wisdom from the circling gloom,
And deal a converse pregnant with delight.

. . . .

"Me thinks I see them with the mental eye,
I hear their lessons with attentive ear,
Of early fishing with the summer fly,
And many a pleasing tale to Anglers dear."

The Fishing-house of Charles Cotton, where Walton visited and where Piscator and Viator communed, stood "in a kind of peninsula," as Cotton describes it, "with a delicate clear river about it;" this "little house" was on the river Dove in Staffordshire: over the arched door were the words "Piscatoribus Sacrum" and on the Key-stone the Cypher of Cotton and Walton. In 1835 this venerable and historic building was restored to nearly the same state as when originally built, by its owner, the Marquis of Beresford.

The will of Walton is deposited in the great registry of English wills at Somerset House, London, and may there be seen by the visitor. An exact copy recently taken from the original is here given, word for word:

"In the name of God, Amen: I, Izaak Walton, the elder, of Winchester, being the present day in the ninetyeth yeare of my age and in perfect memory, for which praysed be God, but considering how suddainly I may be deprived of both, doe therefore make this my last will and testament as followeth; and first, I doe declare my beleife to be that their is only one God who hath made the whole world and mee and all mankind, to whome I shall give an account of all my actions which are not to be justified but I hope pardoned for all the merrets of my saviour Jesus, and because the profession of Christianity does at this time seeme to be subdivided into papist and protestant I take it at least to be convenient to declare my beleife to be in all points of ffaith as the Church of England now professeth and this I doe, the rather because of a very long and a very true friendship with some of the Roman Church and for my worldly estate (which I have neither got by falsehood or flattery or the extreame Cruelty of the law of this nation) I doe hereby give and bequeath it as followeth: first I give my sonne in law Doc! Hawkins and to his wife to them I give all my title and right of or in a part of a house and shop in Pater noster rowe in London which I hold by lease from the Lord Bishop of London for about ffifty years to come, and I doe alsoe give to them all my right and title of or to a house in Chansery Lane London wherein M! Greinwood now dwelleth in which is now about sixteene yeares to come I give these two leases to them they saving my Executor from all damage concerning the same; and I give to my sonne Izaak all my right and title to a lease of Norington Farme which I hold from the Lord Bishop of Winton and I doe also give him all my right and title to a Farme or land neare to Stafford which I bought of Mr. Walter Noell; I say I give it to him and his heires for ever but upon the condicon following namely; if my sonne shall not marry before he shall be of the age of forty and one yeare, or being married shall dye before the said age and leave noe sonne to inherit the said Farme or Land, or if his sonne or sonns shall not live to obtaine the age of twenty and one yeares, to dispose otherwayes of it then I give the said Farme or land to the Towne or Corporation of Stafford (in which I was borne) for the good and benefit of some of the said towne as I shall direct and as followeth, but first note that it is at this present time rented for twenty one pounds tenn shillings a yeare (and is like to hold the said rent if care be taken to keepe the barne and houseing in repair) and I wood have and doe give ten pound of the said rent to bind out yearly two boyes, the sonns of honest and poore parents, to be aprentizes to some Tradesmen or handycraft men to the intent the said boyes may the better afterward get their owne liveing; and I doe alsoe give five pound yearly out of the said rent to be given to some maide Servant that hath attained the age of twenty and one yeare (not lesse) and dwelt long in one service or to some honest poore mans daughter that hath attained to that age, to be paid her at or on the day of her marriage and this being done my will is that what rent shall remaine of the said Farme or land shall be disposed of as Followeth: first I doe give twenty shillings yearly to be spent by the Mayor of Stafford and those that shall collect the said rent and dispose of it as I have and shall hereafter direct, and that what mony or rent shall remaine undisposed off shall be imployed to buy Coales for some poore people that shall most need them in the said towne, the said Coales to be delivered the first weeke in January or in every first weeke in February; I say then because I take that time to be the hardest and most pinching times with poore people and God reward those that shall doe this without partialitie and with honestie and a good conscience; and if the said Mayor and others of the said towne of Stafford shall prove so negligent or dishonest as not to imploy the rent by mee given as intended and exprest in this my will (which God forbid) then I give the said rents and profitts of the said Farme or land to the Towne and cheife magastraits or governers of Ecles-hall to be disposed by them in such manner as I have ordered the disposall of it by the towne of Stafford, the said Farme or land being near the Towne of Ecles-hall; and I give to my sonne in Law Doctor Hawkins (whome I love as my owne sonn) and to my daughter, his wife, and my sonne Izaak to each of them a ring with these words or motto — "love my memory I: W. obiet;" to the Lord Bishop of Winton a ring with this motto "a mitt for a million I: W. obiet;" and to the friends hereafter named I give to each of them a ring with this motto "A friend's farewell I: W. obiet;" and my will is the said rings be delivered within forty dayes after my death, and that the price or value of all the said rings shall be thirteen shillings and four pence a peece. I give to Doctor Hawkins Doctor Donn's Sermons, which I have heard preacht and read with much content; to my sonn Izaak I give Doctor Sibbs his Soules conflict, and to my daughter his brused reed desireing them to read them for as to be well acquainted with them; and I alsoe give unto her all my bookes at Winchester and Droxford and whatever in those two places are or I can call mine except a Trunck of Linnen which I give to my sonne Izaak; but if he doe not live to Marry or make use of it then I give the same to my Granddaughter, Anne Hawkins, and I give my daughter Doctor Halls works which be now at Farnham: to my sonn Izaak I give all my bookes (not yet given) at Farnham Castell and a deske of prints and pictures, alsoe a Cabinet nere my bedshead in which are some little things that he will value, tho of noe great worth. and my will and desire is that he will be kind to his Aunt Beachame and his Aunt Rose Ken by allowing the first about fifty shillings a yeare in or for Bacon and Cheese (not more) and paying four pound a yeare toward the boarding of her sonnes dyet to M̃ John Whitehead; for his Aunt Ken I desire him to be kind to her according to her necessity and his own abilitie and I commend one of her children to breed up (as I have said I intend to do) if he shall be able to doe it, as I know he will, for they be good folke. I give — to M̃ John Darbishire the Sermons of M̃ Anthony Faringdon or of Do̅: Sunderson, which my Executor thinks fitt: to my servant, Thomas Edghill, I give five pound in mony and all my Clothes linnen and wollen (except one sute of Clothes which I give to M̃ Holinshed and forty shillings) if the said Thomas be my servant at my death, if not my Clothes only; and I give my old friend, M̃ Richard Marriot, tenn pound, in mony to be paid him within three Months after my death, and I desire my sonne to shew kindness to him if he shall neede and my son can spare it; and I doe hereby will and declare my sonn Izaak to be my sole Executor of of this my last will and testament and doctor Hawkins to see that he performes it, which I doubt

not but he will. I desire my burial may be neare the place of my death and free from any ostentation or charge but privately: this I make to be my last will (to which I shall only add the Codicell for rings) this sixteenth day of August, One Thousand Six hundred eighty three. Izaak Walton. Witnesse to this will
"The Rings I give are as on the other side.

"To my brother, Jon Ken; to my sister, his wife; to my brother, Doctor Ken; to my Sister Pye; to Mr Francis Morley; to Mr George Vernon; to his wife; to his three daughter; to Mristris Nelson; to Mr Richard Walton; to Mr Palmer; to Mr Taylor; to Mr Tho Garrard; to the Lord Bp of Sarum; to Mr Rede, his servant; to my cozen Dorothy Kenrick; to my Cozen Lewin; to Mr Walter Higgs; to Mr Charles Cotton; to Mr Rich: Marryot 22; to my brother Beacham; to my Sister, his wife; to the Lady Anne How; to Mrs King Doctor Philips wife; to Mr Valentine Harecourt; to Mrs Eliza: Johnson; to Mrs Mary Rogers; to Mrs Eliza: Milward; to Mrs Dorothy Wallop; to Mr Will Milward of Christ church, Oxford; to Mr John Darbesheire; to Mrs Unedvill; to Mrs Rock; to Mr Peter White; to Mr John Lloyde; to my Cozen Greinsells widdow, Mrs Dalbin, must not be forgotten 16; Izaak Walton note that severall lines are blotted out of this will for they were twice repeated and that this will is now Signed and Sealed this twenty and fourth day of October, One thousand Six hundred eighty three, in the presence of us Witnesse Abra: Markland, Jos: Taylor, Thomas Crawley."

Will of Duke of Wellington

Arthur Wellesley, first Duke of Wellington, died September 14, 1852: he was probably born in Dublin, though both the place and date of birth are uncertain. He is buried in St. Paul's Cathedral, London.

His will, taken from the original on file at Somerset House, London, is as follows:

"An attempt having been made to assassinate me on the night of the 10th instant, which may be repeated with success, and being desirous of settling my worldly affairs and there being no professional person at Paris to whom I can entrust the task of drawing my Will, I now draw it in my own hand writing, hereby revoking all former Wills particularly one likewise in my own hand writing made in the year 1807 previous to the Expedition to Copenhagen.

"I hereby leave to the trustees appointed by Act of Par^t to carry into execution the objects of the various Grants to me, my house in Piccadilly London with its furniture and all I possess in money and other valuables in the funds in Exchequer Bills and elsewhere according to the schedule annexed in trust for the following purposes:

"*First:* To carry into execution my Marriage Settlement with the Duchess of Wellington.

"*Secondly:* To pay to all my servants one year's wages beyond what may be due to each on the day of my death.

"*Thirdly:* To pay all my just debts.

"*Fourthly:* To pay to my second son, Lord Charles Wellesley, the sum of one thousand pounds per annum for his life, besides what he will be entitled to under my Marriage Settlement and by the operation of the Acts conveying the Parliamentary Grants to my family. In case he should marry or when he will be thirty years of age, he is to have the option of continuing to receive this annuity or the sum of twenty thousand pounds sterling which is to be paid to him out of the funds aforesaid.

"*Fifthly:* To purchase a freehold estate in England with the whole money aforesaid or such part thereof as they the said trustees may think proper, charging it with the provisions above specified for the Duchess of Wellington and Lord Charles Wellesley.

"*Sixthly:* To give to my eldest son Arthur, Marquis of Douro, and the heirs male of his body the use of the House in Piccadilly, of the furniture thereto belonging, and to pay him and the heirs male of his body the annual interest which may be received for such money in the funds in Exchequer Bills or wherever it may be and the rent arising from any estate which the trustees may think proper to purchase with the said money. In case of the death without heirs male of my eldest son Arthur, Marquis of Douro,

"*Seventhly:* I give to my second, The Lord Charles Wellesley, and the heirs male of his body the use of the said house in Piccadilly and of the furniture thereunto belonging, and to pay him The Lord Charles Wellesley and the heirs male of his body the annual interest which may be received for such money in the funds in Exchequer Bills or wherever it may be and the rent arising from any estate which the trustees may think proper to purchase with the said money. In case of the death without heirs male of my sons, Arthur, Marquis of Douro and Lord Charles Wellesley,

"*Eighthly:* To give my nephew, Arthur Wellesley, the eldest son of my brother The Hble. and Revd. Gerald Wellesley, by Lady Emily his wife, and the heirs male of his body, the use of my house in Piccadilly and the furniture thereunto belonging, and to pay him the said Arthur Wellesley and the heirs male of his body the annual interest which may be received for such money in the funds in Exchequer Bills or wherever it may be and the rent arising from any estate which may be purchased by the trustees with the said money. In case of the death of both my sons Arthur, Marquis of Douro, and Lord Charles Wellesley and of my nephew, Arthur Wellesley, aforesaid all without heirs male,

"*Ninthly:* To give to my nephew, Gerald Wellesley, the third son of my brother, The Honble. Henry Wellesley, by Lady Charlotte his wife, and the heirs male of his body, the use of my house in Piccadilly and the furniture thereunto belonging, and to pay him the said Gerald Wellesley and the heirs male of his body the annual interest which may be received for such money in the funds in Exchequer Bills or wherever it may be and the rent arising from any estate which may be purchased by the trustees with the said money. In case of the death without heirs male of both my sons and both my nephews aforesaid Arthur Wellesley and Gerald Wellesley,

"*Tenthly:* To give to my nephew Henry Wellesley, the eldest son of my brother, the Honble. Henry Wellesley, by Lady Charlotte his first wife, and the heirs male of his body, the use of my house in Piccadilly and the furniture thereunto belonging, and to pay him the said Henry Wellesley and the heirs male of his body the annual interest which may be received for such money in the funds in Exchequer Bills or wherever it may be and the rent arising from any estate which may be purchased by the trustees with the said money. My son Arthur, Marquis of Douro, will have all that has been granted to me by Parl^t, the Estate granted to me by the Cortes and King of Spain, the Pension granted to me by the King of Portugal and the Estate granted to me by the King of the Netherlands, and in case of his death without heirs male, my second son, Lord Charles Wellesley, will succeed to the same. In case of the death without heirs male of my two sons above mentioned, I leave and bequeath to my nephew Arthur Wellesley, the eldest son of my brother Gerald Wellesley, by

Lady Emily his wife, and the heirs male of his body all the money which has been granted to me by Parl^t and the estates purchased with the said money. In case of the death without heirs male of my sons aforesaid and of my nephew, the said Arthur Wellesley, I leave and bequeath to my nephew Gerald Wellesley, the third son of my brother Henry Wellesley, by Lady Charlotte his first wife, and the heirs male of his body all the money which has been granted to me by Parl^t and the estates purchased with the said money. In case of the death without heirs male of both my sons and nephews aforesaid, I leave and bequeath to my nephew, Henry Wellesley the eldest son of my brother Henry Wellesley, by Lady Charlotte his wife, and the heirs male of his body all the money which has been granted to me by Parl^t and the estates purchased with the said money.

"I request the trustees appointed by Parl^t to carry into execution the objects of the different Grants made to me, to be the Guardians of my sons. I wish them both, as well as my nephews above mentioned, to serve the King in his Army and that they should receive the best education which can be given to them in order to qualify them to do so with advantage to the King and honour to themselves. They should therefore finish their studies at Eton and at one of the Universities, besides obtaining a knowledge of the Sciences necessary for those who enter the Military Profession.

"I wish my Secretary, Col. Hervey, to take charge of my Private papers at Paris and to burn such as he may think proper.

"WELLINGTON (LS).

"Signed and Sealed at Paris on the 17th of February, 1818, in the presence of — C. Campbell, Col. and Capt. Ad Guards — Geo. Cathcart 6th D.G. — Arthur Hill Capt. 2nd Drag^{ns}."

CHAPTER VII

WILLS OF FAMOUS AMERICANS

"... The past is all holy to us;
Sad and soft in the moonlight of memory."

WILL OF JOHN QUINCY ADAMS

JOHN QUINCY ADAMS died February 23, 1848. His will is in part as follows:

"Know all men by these presents,

"that I, John Quincy Adams, of Quincy in the County of Norfolk and Commonwealth of Massachusetts, Doctor of Laws, do make, ordain, publish and declare this to be my last will and testament hereby revoking all wills by me heretofore made and particularly one made on or about the 30th day of October, 1832, the last will made by me preceding the present, which has become mislaid among my papers so that I cannot find it; I therefore revoke and annul the same in all and every particular of the same; of which said will, as far as my memory retains it, Joseph Hall, Edward Cruft and James H. Foster were subscribing witnesses.

"1st. I do hereby constitute and appoint my only surviving son Charles Francis Adams of Boston Esquire, my sole Executor for all my property in this Commonwealth or in the District of Columbia or elsewhere; and I direct him hereby to take out Letters of Administration as well in the County of Norfolk in this Commonwealth as in the County of Washington in the District of Columbia, and if necessary in the State of Pennsylvania, so that he may administer upon any property, real, personal or mixed pertaining to me in any part of the United States at the time of my decease, and I hereby constitute my said son residuary Legatee of all property, real, personal and mixed belonging to me, not otherwise disposed of by this will.

"2nd. But in the event of the decease of my said Son, which God forbid, my beloved wife still surviving, I do hereby constitute her the Sole Executrix of all my goods, estate and property not previously administered, with such assistants as she may name and as may be assented to by the Judge of Probate of the County wherein my said will may be proved and approved."

He gives and bequeaths to his beloved wife Louisa Catherine Adams, his dwelling house and lot in the city of Washington, and the dwelling house and farm at Quincy "including the lots of Salt Marsh heretofore leased in Connexion therewith."

He also gives to his wife the dwelling-house and land situated on F. Street in the city of Washington, being his residence in the capital.

He gives to his said wife the furniture in the dwelling-house at Quincy, with the exception of such articles as are specifically otherwise bequeathed, also all carriages and horses, china, plate and plated ware, as well at Quincy as at Washington, excepting such articles thereinafter otherwise bequeathed, and all the wines in the cellars and closets in dwelling-houses in both places.

He gives to his said wife in lieu and as a full equivalent for her right of dower in all the rest and residue of his real estate, whether in Massachusetts or in Washington, or elsewhere, provided she consent to renounce the same, the sum of $2000 per annum, to be paid to her during her natural life, constituting the same a charge upon his estate, to be paid to her in cash every year she may live.

To his son, Charles Francis Adams, he gives all shares and certificates of stocks in the Middlesex & Quincy Canals, Braintree and Weymouth Turnpike, Banks, Insurance Companies, Markets and Hotels; also all interest in mortgages upon real estate and city stocks, and generally all and singular the personal property of every description, not otherwise bequeathed, in trust upon the following conditions and for the following purposes : That he shall, " during the natural life of my said wife, Louisa Catherine Adams, pay over to her one entire third part of the revenue in each and every year; and of the remaining two-thirds of said revenue, he shall reserve one-half to himself and his own use and behoof, and of the other half he shall pay over to my daughter-in-law, Mrs. Mary Catherine Adams one moiety thereof during her natural life, and the remaining moiety to my granddaughter, Mary Louisa Adams, daughter of my son John Adams, deceased, and said Mary Catherine."

Upon the death of his wife, Louisa Catherine Adams, a division is to be made of the principal of the personal property thus held by his son and executor, by which one-half is to be given to his said son Charles Francis Adams, and of the income arising from the other half of the same, the sum of $6000 is to be paid to his daughter-in-law, Mary Catherine Adams, and the remainder of said income and proceeds shall be paid to his granddaughter, Mary L. Adams, during the natural life of her mother, and "upon the decease of her mother the whole of said half part of said property as well as all other personal property held in trust by said executor for the benefit of said Mary L. Adams" is to be settled upon said Mary L. Adams by said executor.

He gives to his son, Charles Francis Adams, his estate at Mount Wollaston in the town of Quincy, with the dwelling-house and barns thereon situated.

He gives to his son, Charles Francis Adams, and the heirs of his body all the rest and residue of real estate, including all wood lots, quarry lands and salt marsh, of which he shall die seized within the limits of the towns of Quincy, Braintree or Milton: "Provided there be secured to be paid by said son, the principal sum of $20,000, said sum to be a capital for the benefit of my granddaughter, Mary L. Adams."

He gives to his son, Charles Francis Adams, realty situated in Fremont Street and in Court Street, city of Boston, and county of Suffolk.

He gives and bequeaths to his granddaughter, Mary L. Adams, the estate in Beach Street, city of Boston, and also the estate of which he stands possessed under breach of condition of mortgage in Curve Street in Boston, "should the same become mine, as is probable, by foreclosure, in regular course of law," also all right, title and interest he has or may have in two stores on Eastern Railway Avenue, in said Boston, over and above amounts for which they are respectively mortgaged, to her and her heirs and assigns forever.

He gives to his son, Charles Francis Adams, the estate in Weston, in this commonwealth, bequeathed to him by his friend Ward Nicholas Boylston, Esq., and the whole of his estate situated in city and county of Washington, D.C., consisting of house in F. Street, and the land appertaining, subject to life estate already granted to his wife, also store and house situated in Pennsylvania Avenue, also estate known under name of Columbia Mills, also Square numbered 592 and all other lands of which he may die seized and possessed in the District of Columbia, to have and to hold to him, his heirs and assigns, in trust, however, for the benefit of his granddaughter, Mary L. Adams.

ANCIENT, CURIOUS, AND FAMOUS WILLS 327

He constitutes and creates a charge upon all various devises of real estate made for the benefit of his granddaughter, Mary L. Adams; that out of the annual proceeds, rents and profits of same there be paid during the life or widowhood of his mother, Mary Catherine Adams, the sum of $600 in each and every year to the said Mary Catherine Adams.

He gives to Elizabeth C. Adams, Isaac H. Adams, John Quincy Adams and Joseph H. Adams, surviving children of his brother, the late Thos. B. Adams, of Quincy, the house and farm in Braintree and house and farm in Medford, which were mortgaged to him by said brother, and of which he had taken legal possession for breach of condition of said mortgage.

He gives his library of books, manuscript books and papers and those of his father and all his family pictures, except such as may be therein otherwise specifically devised to his son, Charles Francis Adams, "trusting that his mother shall at all times have the use of any of the books in the library at her discretion"; and recommends that his said son, as soon as suits his own convenience, shall "cause a building to be erected, made fireproof, in which to keep the said library, books, documents and manuscripts safe, but always to be subject to his convenience," and especially recommends to his care the said library, manuscripts, books and papers, and that he will as far as may be in his power keep them together as one library to be transmitted to his eldest son as one property to remain in the family, and not to be sold or disposed of as long as may be practicable, being always confided to the faithful custody of the person holding the legal title in the same.

He gives to his granddaughter Mary L. Adams, "Portrait of my father, painted by Stewart and all the other family portraits now in house in F. Street which I occupy."

He gives to the people of the U.S. of America an ivory cane presented to him by Julius Pratt of Meriden in Connecticut and by him deposited in the custody of the Commissioner of Patents at Washington to remain in his custody until called for by him, the said cane bearing on it an inscription in honor of the repeal by the House of Representatives of a bill prohibiting the reception of petitions on the subject of slavery, December 3, 1844.

He gives to his grandson, John Quincy Adams, son of Charles Francis Adams, "a gold-headed cane cut from the timbers of the frigate Constitution and presented to me by Minot Thayer, Samuel A. Turner, Ebenezer T. Fogg, Solomon Richards and

Harvey Field, Committee, April 1st, 1837, on the head of which is engraved the members of the House of Representatives of Massachusetts from the several towns of my District in the year 1837, in token of their sense of my public services in defending in the Congress of the United States the right of petition of the people of the U.S. in that body; and I request my son to have the custody of this bequest until his said son John Quincy shall come of age."

"20th. I give and bequeath to my grandson Charles Francis Adams second son of my son, aforesaid, a cane also cut from the timbers of the frigate Constitution, and given to me by its Commander Commodore Isaac Hull in the year 1836, which is marked upon a silver ring immediately under the head of said cane.

"21st. I give to my grandson Henry Brooks Adams, third son of my son aforesaid, a cane made of olive from Mount Olivet in Jerusalem, given to me by my nephew Joseph Harrod Adams by whom it was caused to be cut on the spot, he being personally there as an officer of the United States.

"22nd. I have given to my daughter A. B. Adams, wife of my son Charles Francis Adams, the portfolio of engravings of pictures of Colonel Trumbull, presented to me by him. I now give to her a silver tankard which was my mother's, from her grandfather John Quincy — also the portrait of the said John Quincy at two years of age now in her house at Quincy, and that of his mother, being Anna Shepard, daughter of the celebrated Thomas Shepard, minister of Charleston, by whom the estate at Mount Wollaston was bequeathed by will to the said John Quincy. These pictures were given to me by will of Norton Quincy, only son of the said John Quincy.

"23rd. I give and bequeath to my friend the Reverend Dr. Nathaniel L. Frothingham, a seal with a device of an oak acorn, and the motto 'alteri seculo' as a small token of my personal esteem and friendship for him.

"24th. I give and bequeath to my friend Dr. George Parkman of Boston a seal enchased with the image of General George Washington as a small token of the esteem and affection which I bear to him.

"25th. I give and bequeath to my grandson John Quincy Adams my Chronometer made by French, bearing his initials, being the same as my own, to be kept by his father until he shall think proper to deliver it to him.

"26th. I give to my granddaughter Mary Louisa Adams, my

seal bearing a Lion engraved upon a Silesian stone, which I had engraved there at the time of my tour through that country; the gold medal presented to me by the Corporation of the City of New York struck on the opening of the Grand Canal, the silver cup with the inscription 'Circes pocula nosti' — and the seal engraved on a Sardonyx with my cipher on one side and the Boylston arms on the other. I give all other medals, coins, or presents of small value which I have received, a silver wafer box, and pair of portable candlesticks, my own cushion, seal at arms on a cornelian and my seal with the device of the Eagle and Lyre to my son Charles Francis Adams. Also a bronze medal given to me by Commodore Jesse D. Elliot struck by his order in honor of Thomas Cooper Esqr. and also another medal in silver which he directed to be given to the historical society of Rhode Island, refused by that society shortly before his death and held by me subject to their order. Also the history of the Croton Aqueduct a present from the City of New York.

"27th. I give to my daughters in law Mary Catharine Adams, widow of my son John Adams, and to Abigail Brown Adams, wife of my son Charles Francis Adams, one hundred dollars each to purchase some permanent token of remembrance of me which they may leave to their daughters; and I further give to my said daughter Mary Catherine Adams the clock with the device of Penelope in my chamber at Washington.

"28th. I give to my nephew and namesake John Quincy Adams my small seal with my cipher engraved upon a cornelian; and a pair of gold sleeve buttons, with the motto 'aequam memento servare memtem' which I wore when I was President of the United States."

He gives to each of his two granddaughters, Mary Louise Adams, daughter of his son, John Adams, deceased, and to Louisa Catherine Adams, daughter of his son, Charles Francis Adams, one-half of the sums deposited in his name in the Institution for Savings in the City of Boston, the said sums to remain on deposit there until the thirteenth day of August 1852, when the younger of the two would, if living, attain the age of twenty-one years.

"30th. I also give to my son Charles Francis Adams and to his heirs and assigns the Pew numbered Fifty four in the Stone Meeting house at Quincy, also the Pew in the Gallery Numbered Five, and the family tomb in the grave yard opposite the said meeting house.

"31st. I also give to my wife Louisa Catherine Adams the pew which I own in St. Johns Church at Washington, and also the pew which I own in Christ Church at Quincy.

"32nd. I give and devise to the supervisors of the Adams Temple and school fund at Quincy all the remaining pews in the Stone Meeting house at Quincy of which I retain the property to be by them held or sold as in their judgment shall be deemed best; and the proceeds of the same shall be applied to the erection of a stone school house over the cellar which was under the house formerly built by the Reverend John Hancock, conformably to the deed of gift of my deceased father John Adams, of the twenty fifth of July in the year eighteen hundred and twenty two to the Inhabitants of the Town of Quincy.

"33rd. I give and bequeath to my cousin Louisa Catherine Smith the sum of fifty dollars per annum as an annuity to be paid by my Executor during her life and as a slight token of my regard for her.

"In testimony whereof I have hereunto set my hand and seal at the City of Boston this Eighteenth day of January in the year of our Lord eighteen hundred and forty seven.

"JOHN QUINCY ADAMS."

WILL OF CAPTAIN JOHN ALDEN

The gravestone of Captain John Alden, who died at Boston, Massachusetts, on the 14th day of March, 1702, at 5 o'clock in the afternoon, at the age of seventy-five, is now in the porch of the New Old South Church. He was the son of John Alden who was engaged in making repairs on the *Mayflower* at Southampton, and sailed in her with the Pilgrim Fathers, afterwards marrying Priscilla Mullens, whose name is familiarized by Longfellow's poem, "The Courtship of Myles Standish."

Captain John Alden's will is dated the seventeenth day of February, 1701. He directed that his body should be decently buried, at the discretion of his executors in said will named. After the payment of his just debts and funeral expenses and legacies, the remainder of his estate in "housing, lands, money, plate, debts, goods & moveables wheresoever lying or to be found," was to be divided into five equal parts or shares: one part was to be given to his son, John Alden, and the remaining fifths divided among other children and grandchildren. And his children are given the liberty of using his kitchen "for washing, brewing and baking" and all his garden "for the hanging and drying of their cloathes."

WILL OF BENEDICT ARNOLD

Benedict Arnold, the traitor of his country, died in London, June 14, 1801. Any one interested in seeing the original of his will can find it in the Recorder's Office at Somerset House, London. As many of our readers will be interested in knowing how he ended his days, his last will is here given in full:

"I, Benedict Arnold of the city of London, being of sound mind and memory, do make and constitute this my last will and testament in manner following:

"Imprimis. It is my will that all my just debts and funeral expenses be first paid, the latter I request may be only decent, but by no means attended with any expense that can be possibly avoided.

"Item. I give to my sister Hannah Arnold forty pounds sterling per annum during her natural life, to be paid to her annually out of the interest of such monies or income of such estate as I may die possessed of, provided she shall and does give up to my heirs or executors all obligations that she may have against me and also does relinquish all claims against my estate except for the annuity before mentioned.

"Item. I give and bequeath to my sons Richard and Henry all sums of money that they are in anywise indebted to me and having in the course of the last and present year written to them to draw Bills of Exchange upon me in London for the following sums of money, vizt: one hundred and eighty pounds sterling (to make up a sum of three hundred pounds part of which I have paid to them) to enable them to build and stock their farm in Canada, also two hundred and thirty pounds sterling to enable them to pay two protested Bills as also three hundred and sixty pounds sterling to enable them to pay all their debts due in January 1801, to the total amount adding these sums, of seven hundred and seventy pounds sterling. I give and bequeath the before mentioned sums of money to my sons Richard and Henry equally, and it is my will and pleasure that their Bills of Exchange for the before mentioned sums be honored by my executors and paid out of the estate I may die possessed of.

"Item. I give, devise and bequeath to my beloved wife, heirs, executors and administrators all my estate both real and personal that I may die possessed of, after paying my debts and legacies as before and hereinafter mentioned, for her own use and benefit during her continuing a widow and to be disposed of among all my children at her death, as she may think proper not doubting her doing them all equal justice; but should she marry again, then it is in that case my will and pleasure that all my property shall be divided among my children upon her second marriage, and in that case I do hereby give, devise and bequeath all my estate both real and personal that I now have or may die possessed of to my children to be divided among them in such equal proportions as my beloved wife shall think just and proper, consideration being had for the sums of money that they have already received and that have been expended upon them for their education &c; and consideration being also had to their respective ages and situations in life not doubting that she will do them all equal justice as she well knows it is and has always been my intention (as my affection has been equally divided amongst them) to make an equal provision for them all.

"Item. I give, devise and bequeath to John Sage, now in Canada living with my sons there (being about fourteen years of age) twelve hundred acres of land being part of a Grant of thirteen thousand four hundred acres of land made to me as an half-pay Officer for myself and family by Order of the Duke of Portland by his letter directed to Peter Russel Esquire President of the Council in Upper Canada, dated the 12 June 1798, which said 1200 acres of land I give to him to be counted altogether in one place out of the before mentioned grant as my executrix may judge equal and fair. I also do hereby give and bequeath to the said John Sage twenty pounds per annum to be paid to my sons Richard and Henry for his use for board cloathing and education until he shall be of the age of twenty-one years, to be paid out of the estate I may die possessed of. I also give and bequeath to the said John Sage fifty pounds, to be paid to him when he shall attain the age of twenty one years. I do hereby constitute and appoint my beloved wife sole Executrix to this my last will and testament and in case my wife should marry again or die intestate I do hereby constitute and appoint Miss Ann Fitch and Miss Sarah Fitch of Devonshire Street joint trustees to manage my estate and carry this my will into execution, and they are hereby authorised (should it be necessary to sell any part of my real estate for that purpose) to give receipts to the purchasers for the purchase money, which shall be considered as good and valid; but should my wife die intestate I do hereby give, devise and bequeath to all my children all my estate both real and personal that I may die possessed of, after paying my legacies &c to be divided among them in the following manner, vizt: the whole to be divided into twelve equal shares & to Sophia I give four shares, to William I give two shares, to George I give two shares, and to Richard, Henry, Edward and James I give each one share, and I do hereby appoint the before named trustees to see the same carried into execution, and I do hereby constitute and appoint my beloved wife sole Executrix of this my last will and testament, in witness whereof, I have hereunto set my hand and seal in London this 30th day of August in the year of our Lord one thousand eight hundred.

"BENEDICT ARNOLD."

WILL OF JOHN JAMES AUDUBON

John James Audubon died January 27, 1851. His will is a short document and is as follows:

"In the Name of God Amen.

"I, John James Audubon of the City and State of New York do make and publish this my last Will and Testament as follows:

"1st. First: I order and direct that all my just debts and funeral expenses be paid as soon after my decease as conveniently can be done.

"2d. Second: I give devise and bequeath to my wife Lucy Audubon and to my two sons Victor Gifford Audubon and John Woodhouse Audubon all my real and personal property of whatever nature or kind soever excepting my household furniture articles of silver and silver plate share and share alike.

"3rd. Thirdly: I give, devise and bequeath to my wife all my household furniture articles of silver and silver plate.

"Lastly. I nominate, constitute and appoint my said two sons Executors and my wife Executrix of this my last Will and Testament hereby revoking and annulling all other and former Wills by me made.

"In witness whereof I have hereunto signed my name and affixed my seal this nineteenth day of April in the year of our Lord one thousand eight hundred and forty one.

"JOHN JAMES AUDUBON."

Will of Phineas Taylor Barnum

Phineas Taylor Barnum died April 7, 1891. The Probate Court of Bridgeport, Connecticut, will, on request, furnish you with a copy of his will; it would seem that printer's ink is used by Barnum's executors, following the testator's example, for the will is in the shape of a booklet containing fifty-three pages, and is the most lengthy testamentary document which has come under our observation. The legacies and gifts under it exceed one hundred and fifty in number and several million dollars in amount. Then are added to the will, eight codicils of unusual length and of great particularity. The will itself is dated the 30th day of January, 1882, the last codicil, the year in which he died, 1891.

By the will, the testator gives an annuity of $9000 to his wife, Nancy, together with the use of certain personal property; there is also given her, the use for life of his residence, "Waldemere," which was a villa in imitation of the Brighton Pavilion. He says: "I love the pleasant city of my adoption (Bridgeport), and ardently hope for its moral and material improvement; a large share of my income, during my residence here of nearly forty years, has been devoted to its public and private charities, and to improving and developing its parks, avenues, and its waste places, erecting houses, factories, &c. Having thus preferred to see my money used here, under my own eyes, rather than to leave it to be used by others." There is an annuity of $1500 given a daughter, Helen, during her natural life, subject to certain legacies and annuities; the residue of his estate is placed in the hands of trustees to be divided equally between a daughter, Caroline C. Thompson, the children of a deceased daughter, Pauline T. Seeley, and the children of a daughter, Helen M. Buchtel. The old family Bible, the bust of Jenny Lind, and the contract with Jenny Lind, are given to his daughter, Caroline: seven gifts of books are made to publishers, "as a faint recognition of the Public Press, to which I am so much indebted."

From the profits of the "show business," the executors are directed to reserve a fund of $200,000, "to meet the outlays yearly required for the successful prosecution of said business in an honorable, respectable and strictly moral manner with a view to refine and elevate such recreations and to edify and instruct as well as innocently amuse those who attend them; and the agents employed for the purpose must be qualified and of temperate habits, and undoubted integrity."

By the first codicil, a diamond stud is given to his wife, Nancy, to be hers absolutely: numerous bequests are made, many of them for charitable purposes, including an endowment fund for "Barnum Institute" for scientific purposes. The testator states, that having no son, the name Barnum will not be continued, and on condition that his grandson, Clinton H. Seeley, will call himself Barnum Seeley, and take legal steps to change his name, he is to receive $25,000.

In codicil number two, numerous bequests and legacies are made, and an estimated value of three million dollars is placed on his estate. Reference is made to a gift of $2500 for "preaching the Gospel and distributing Universalist Literature."

Codicil number three revokes certain provisions of codicil number one.

Codicil number four contains legacies to Tufts College, the Barnum Museum of Natural History, Bridgeport Scientific Society, and other institutions, including the "Boys' Club" and "Girls' Club" of Bridgeport.

Codicil number five gives to the city of Bridgeport $1000 for the erection of a statue of Henry Bergh, the founder of the society for the prevention of cruelty to animals. To his wife, Nancy, he gives, absolutely, $100,000 and $40,000 a year during her natural life, these in lieu of the legacies and annuities given her by the will and former codicils.

Codicil number six directs that Thomas Ball, a sculptor, of Florence, Italy, be consulted with reference to a piece of ornamental statuary to be placed on the testator's burial lot, not to exceed in cost $8000.

Codicil number seven gives $500 to his family physician, as a mark of gratitude.

Codicil number eight mentions the erection of a building in Bridgeport, to be known as "The Barnum Institute of Science and History."

WILL OF HENRY WARD BEECHER

Henry Ward Beecher died March 8, 1887. His will is as follows:
"In the Name of God, Amen.
"I, Henry Ward Beecher, of the City of Brooklyn, and State of New York, hereby revoking all, other and former Wills by me heretofore made, do make, publish and declare this to be my last Will and Testament.

"I. I hereby authorize and direct my Executors, or such of them as shall qualify, upon my death to collect and receive the amount of my life insurance, to invest the same, and to pay the proceeds of such investment to my wife during her life, in equal quarter yearly payments.

"II. I hereby give, bequeath and devise unto my executors, or such of them as shall qualify, the rest, residue and remainder of my estate, both real and personal, of every kind, in trust for the benefit of my children. And I hereby direct that my said Executors, distribute and apportion my said estate, among my said children, in such manner and form, and at such time or times, as shall in their Judgment be for the best interest of my said children; giving unto my said Executors full powers to sell and Mortgage such and so much of my real and personal property, as they shall deem best, and to invest or distribute the proceeds of such sale or sales, as herein provided.

"III. It is my Will, that, if any of my said children should die, before the complete distribution of my estate as above provided, leaving issue them surviving, that such issue shall stand and take in the place and stead of their parent, taking *per stirpes*, and not *per capita*.

"IV. I hereby nominate, constitute and appoint my sons, Henry B. Beecher, William C. Beecher and Herbert F. Beecher, all of Brooklyn, New York, and my son-in-law, Rev. Samuel Scoville, of Norwich, New York, the Executors and Trustees of this my will, and it is my will that no bonds shall be required of them or either of them.

" July 11th 1878. "Henry Ward Beecher."

Will of Thomas H. Benton

Thomas H. Benton died April 10, 1858. His will is as follows:

"I, Thomas H. Benton of the State of Missouri, now in the City of Washington in the District of Columbia, do make and publish this my last will and testament, hereby revoking any and all wills made by me at any time heretofore.

"I hereby constitute and appoint my sons in law William Carvey Jones, John C. Fremont and Richard Taylor Jacob, and my friends Montgomery Blair and Samuel Phillips Lee, to be executors of this my last will and testament.

"After the payment of my just debts and charges, should there be any such at the time of my death, I dispose of my estate as follows:

"I give, devise and bequeath to my said executors and the survivor of them, and the heirs, executors, administrators and assigns of such survivor, my house and lot on C Street in said Washington city, now occupied by me, with all my furniture and other personal property, except my books, in trust to hold the same to the sole and separate use of my daughter Mrs. Eliza P. C. Jones, free from any control by, or liability for or on account of, her present or any future husband, and subject to such direction as to the disposition of the same as she may at any time give in writing to my said executors and trustees or to any of them; and should she in writing direct the said property, or any part thereof, to be commuted for other property, then to hold the property so received in commutation on the same trust as aforesaid. It is my intention and will that my said daughter Mrs. Eliza P. C. Jones may, if she be so pleased, direct the property hereby devised in trust for her, or any part thereof, to be sold, and receive and enjoy the proceeds of such sale.

"I give and bequeath all my library of books to my said son-in-law William Carvey Jones.

"I hereby will and direct that out of the first moneys which may be paid to my estate under subsisting contracts for a certain number of years with Messrs. Appleton & Co. of New York, publishers of my literary works, and out of the first proceeds of the sale thereof, my said executors shall pay to my daughter Mrs. Eliza P. C. Jones the sum of ten thousand dollars, and to my daughter Mrs. Susan T. Boileau the sum of five thousand dollars, or invest the same in trust for their sole and separate use respectively, as they may respectively direct,—and that my said executors shall divide the residue of the moneys which may arise, as the same shall be received from my literary works, equally among my four daughters Mrs. Eliza P. C. Jones, Mrs. Jessie Ann Fremont, Mrs. Sarah McD. Jacob and Mrs. Susan T. Boileau, or invest the same in trust for their sole and separate use respectively, as they may respectively direct.

"And I hereby will and direct that it shall be competent for any two of my aforesaid Executors and Trustees, to do any act in relation to the premises which the whole five could do. In witness whereof I have hereto set my hand and seal this thirteenth day of September in the year eighteen hundred and fifty-seven.

"THOMAS H. BENTON."

Will of James G. Blaine

James G. Blaine died January 27, 1893. His will is a brief instrument, and is as follows:

"I, James G. Blaine of Augusta in the State of Maine, at present residing in the City of Washington, D.C., being of sound and disposing mind and memory do make, publish and declare this to be my last will and testament hereby revoking all former wills by me at any time made.

"1. I direct my executor hereinafter named to pay my just debts and funeral expenses.

"2. I give and bequeath to my daughter Margaret, to my son James, and to my daughter Harriet, to each the sum of fifty dollars:

"3. I give and bequeath to my grandchildren Emmons Blaine, Blaine Coppinger and Conor Coppinger, to each the sum of twenty five dollars:

"4. All the rest and residue of my property, real, personal or mixed wheresoever situate which I now own or may hereafter acquire and of which I shall die seized or possessed I give, devise and bequeath absolutely and in fee simple to my wife Harriet S. Blaine, her heirs and assigns forever:

"5. I name, constitute and appoint my said wife Harriet S. Blaine, Executrix of this my last will and testament, and I request that my Executrix be not required to give bond for the performance of her duty as such.

"Witness my hand this seventh day of January A.D. 1892.

"JAMES G. BLAINE."

Will of Edwin T. Booth

Edwin T. Booth died June 7, 1893. His will is as follows:

"I, Edwin Thomas Booth, Actor, do make, publish and declare this my last Will and Testament.

"First: I order and direct that all my just debts be paid as soon after my decease as may be practicable.

"Second: I give and bequeath to my Brother Joseph A. Booth, Ten thousand ($10,000) dollars.

"To my niece Marie Booth Douglass, Ten thousand ($10,000) dollars.

"To my nieces and nephews Asia, Clarke Morgan, Andrienne Clarke, Junius B. Booth, Sidney Booth, Creston Clarke and Wilped Clarke, to each Five thousand ($5000) dollars.

"To my Cousins Charlotte Mitchell of Baltimore and Robert

Mitchell of North Carolina, to each, Twenty-five hundred ($2500) dollars.

"To my friend Mrs. Maria Anderson, Five thousand ($5000), dollars.

"To my friends John H. Magonigle and his wife Catherine, to each Ten thousand ($10,000) dollars.

"To my friend Mrs. Margaret Devlin, a sister of Mrs. Catherine Magonigle Five thousand ($5000) dollars.

"To the 'Actors Fund,' the 'Actors Order of Friendship,' both of the City of New York, the 'Actors Order of Friendship' of Philadelphia, the 'Trustees of the Masonic Hall and Asylum Fund of New York' and the 'Home for Incurables' at West Farms, New York, to each, Five thousand ($5000) dollars.

"Third. I order and direct that my Executors transfer and convey all the rest, residue and remainder of my estate, real and personal to the Central Trust Company of New York, as Trustee for the following uses and purposes: That said Trustee invest and re-invest the same and pay the income thereof to my daughter Edwina Booth Grossmann during her natural life and upon her sole and separate receipt, and that upon her decease the said Trustee divide the said principal of said Trust together with the income accrued thereon into as many parts as my said daughter shall leave children her surviving, the issue of any deceased child of my said daughter counting one in making such division and pay the income of one of such portions to each of her said children until he or she shall attain the age of twenty one years, in which event, the principal of such portion shall be paid to him or her.

"In the event any of her children shall die before attaining the age of twenty one years without leaving issue the portion which he or she would have received if living at that age, shall be divided, added to and disposed of as part of the portions of the other children surviving or of their issue if deceased.

"The issue of any deceased child of my said daughter shall in every event take what its parent would have taken if living at the time of the decease of my daughter.

"Fourth: I authorize and empower my Executors or any of them who may qualify as such Executors their survivor or survivors, successor or successors to sell and convey at Public Auction or private sale and upon such terms as they may approve any or all of the real or personal estate of which I shall die possessed wheresoever the same may be situate.

"Fifth: I authorize and empower my Trustee hereinbefore named or its successor in said Trust, to hold and retain any security, bonds, stocks or investments of which I shall die possessed as part of the said Trust fund to be held by it under this my Will.

"Sixth: I hereby nominate and appoint my friends Elias C. Benedict, William Bispham and John H. Magonigle, all of New York City, Executors of this my last Will and Testament hereby revoking all other and former Wills by me made and I request that no bond or other security be required from my said Executors for the faithful performance of their trust.

"In Witness Whereof I have hereunto signed my name and affixed my seal this Fifteenth day of June A.D. 1892.

"EDWIN T. BOOTH."

WILL OF DAVID J. BREWER

David J. Brewer, late Chief Justice of the United States, died on March 29, 1910.

His will, together with a codicil thereto, is as follows:

"In the name of God; Amen —

"I David J. Brewer being of sound mind & memory do make publish & declare the following to be my last will & testament—

"Item First —

"I give & devise my home No. 1923 — 16th Str. N. W. Washington D.C. to my wife Emma M. Brewer — the legal title is now in her — Probably this is sufficient, but as most of the cost was paid by me, I make this devise to avoid all question —

"Item Second —

"I give devise & bequeath to my daughters Harriet B. Jetmore, Henrietta B. Karrick & Elizabeth B. Wells, share & share alike, my cottage at Thompson's Point with all the personal property in or connected with it — On the 35th anniversary of my marriage to my then wife Louise L. Brewer I deeded this property to her — whether such a deed from husband to wife is good under the laws of Vermont I do not know & so make this devise & bequest to avoid all question of our children's full title —

"Item Third —

"I have $30,000 life insurance which was made payable to my wife Louise L. Brewer — I find in the several policies different provisions respecting the beneficiaries in case of her death — To carry out the intent with which these policies were taken out I give & bequeath to my said daughters, share and share alike, those policies & all sums which may be due thereon — The policy in the N. Y. Mutual provides for a 20 year 5 per ct. gold bond — I desire that this be taken out in the name of Harriet B. Jetmore & be her share in said life insurance — I prefer a registered bond if obtainable —

"Item Fourth —

"I give & bequeath to my wife Emma M. Brewer all the furniture, including therein pictures, in my home, which has been purchased since our marriage —

"Item Fifth —

"I give & bequeath all other personal property to my said daughters share & share alike —

"I appoint my wife Emma M. Brewer & my son in law James L. Karrick to execute this my will & desire that no bonds be required of them.

"In witness whereof I have hereto signed my name this 25th day of Oct., 1906.   "DAVID J. BREWER."

CODICIL TO THE FOREGOING WILL

"I David J. Brewer the testator in said will attach thereto & make the following additional provisions —

"Item (1) The gold watch given me by the lawyers of Leavenworth County, I give unto my grandson David Brewer Karrick — the watch given me by my wife Emma M. Brewer I give to her grandnephew David Brewer Hall — the ring I wear on the little finger of my left hand given me by my wife Louise L. Brewer I give to my grandson David Brewer Jetmore — my scrap books & the books edited by me as well as the bound volumes of my talks & writings I give to my daughter Etta B. Karrick — the Bible given me by my wife Louise L. Brewer I give to my granddaughter Harriet Louise Jetmore — Out of my other personal property I wish my executor & executrix to select for each of my grandchildren not specifically named herein some suitable article as a special gift from grandfather —

"Item (2) I wish to be buried in Leavenworth by the side of my wife Louise L. Brewer —

"Item (3) In case of the death of my wife Emma M. Brewer before my own death then I direct that all the gifts to her are annulled & revoked & my entire property with the special bequests excepted I give devise & bequeath to my daughters share & share alike — In witness whereof I have hereto set my hand & seal this 7th day of March 1908. "DAVID J. BREWER."

WILL OF AARON BURR

Aaron Burr died September 14, 1836. His will is in part as follows:

"I, Aaron Burr, of the City of New York, now residing at number 23 Nassau Street, do make and publish this my Last Will and Testament as follows: I appoint Matthew L. Davis, Peter Townsend, and Henry P. Edwards, Attorney and Counsellor at Law, my Executors. I give the charge and custody of my private papers to the said M. L. Davis, to be disposed of at his discretion. I propose in a Codicil to be hereunto annexed to give a list of my debts, and to point out the resources from which they are to be paid, and I authorize my said Executors to settle all suits and claims which I may have against any person whatsoever, and to give receipts and acquittances thereupon, and to sell any land or real estate to which I may be entitled at the time of my death, and to give deeds therefor. And I do hereby revoke and annul all former and other Wills and Testaments by me made. In Testimony whereof I have hereunto subscribed my name, this twenty-first day of April, in the year of our Lord one thousand eight hundred and thirty four.

"Witnesses: "A. BURR."
"CHARLES F. HILL,
"HENRY OSCAR TAYLOR." p 342

There are three codicils of considerable length to this will. A part of one codicil reads as follows:

"I direct that all my private papers, except my law papers appertaining to suits now depending, be delivered to my friend, Matthew L. Davis, Esq., to be disposed of at his discretion, directing him nevertheless to destroy or to deliver to the parties interested, all such as may in his estimation be calculated to affect injuriously the feelings of individuals against whom I have no complaint."

Another item reads:

"I give to my friend and kinsman, Theodosia Provost, the picture of my daughter, which is enamelled on a china cup, which is believed to be in the upper drawer of my yellow desk."

WILL OF BENJAMIN F. BUTLER

Benjamin F. Butler died January 11, 1893. A copy of his will, together with a codicil thereto, is as follows:

"In the Name of God Amen. I, Benjamin F. Butler of Lowell, Esquire, being of sound and disposing mind and memory do make and publish this my last will and testament.

"First. After payment of all my just debts and liens — upon my estate I direct as much thereof as will raise the sum of one hundred and forty dollars nett income to be securely invested and said amount paid semi-annually to my Mother Charlotte Butler, which with the Estate upon Willow Street, of which I have given her a life lease upon a nominal Rent is all that I feel myself able to secure to my Mother for her declining years, and I hope and trust that my brother Andrew will add enough to make her independent as I have endeavored to relieve her from want. This sum to be paid her during her natural life or untill she shall recieve a pension from Government equal at least to such sum during her said life.

"Second. All the rest and residue of my estate real personal or mixed, saving some specific legacies I bequeath and devise as follows: The use and improvement of one entire and just third thereof to my wife Sarah H. Butler during her natural life whether she shall remain sole after my decease or marry again. But in case of her marriage then to be her seperate estate free from all control of her husband.

"Third. The remainder of my estate is to be equally divided between the children of myself and wife *in esse* at the time of my decease. The portion thereof which may go to any female child of mine to be her own seperate estate and free from all control of her husband whensoever she may marry.

"Fourth. To my Br ther Andrew my seal ring with my love in token of affection.

"Fifth. To F. A. Hildreth my watch & chain and I commend to his care my wife and children; he knows my affairs and will deal justly by them; and,

"Lastly, I appoint my beloved wife sole executrix of this my last will & testament with full faith that right will be done to all.

"Signed, sealed and published as my last will and testament in presence of the witness whose names are hereto affixed this third day of July in the year one thousand eight hundred and fifty four.

"BENJ. F. BUTLER."

"Be it remembered that I, Benj. F. Butler, the above named testator being about to depart upon a dangerous service do alter this my last will and testament in this. Having sold the estate on Willow Street herein spoken of and bought another whereon my mother now lives, consisting of two houses one of which is now rented, I devise and bequeath to my Mother the use and improvement of all said estate during her natural life instead of the estate sold. This with the sum of money bequeathed to her or her pension will take care of her in comfort during her life.

"Witness my hand and seal, published as my last will and codicil this twentieth day of February in the year one thousand eight hundred and sixty two.
"BENJ. F. BUTLER."

WILL OF SALMON P. CHASE

Salmon P. Chase died May 7, 1873. A copy of his will is as follows:

"I appoint Henry D. Cooke of Washington, sole Executor of this my last Will and Testament.

"I require that all my just debts be paid and discharged from the assets which will come into his hands.

"Of the residue it is my will that an income at Seven per cent on Six Thousand Dollars be paid to my Niece, Jane Auld, during her life, and that if her daughters survive her that the principal thereof be paid to them equally.

"It is my further will that of the residue of my Estate there be transferred to the Wilberforce University, Nine Thousand Dollars, in a bond or bonds of the Western Union Telegraph Company, and One Thousand Dollars in a bond of the Cleveland and Pittsburg Railroad Company; and to Dartmouth College Three Thousand Dollars in the bonds of the Washington and Georgetown Railroad Company, and Seven Thousand Dollars in the bonds of the Warren and Franklin Railroad Company.

"It is my will that whatever sum may be due to me from my late brother Edward I. Chase, may be wholly remitted to his widow and administratrix, of Lockport, N.Y.

"I bequeath the picture of Chief Justice Marshall, presented to me by the members of the Bar and other citizens of New York, to the United States for the use of the Supreme Court.

"It is my will that the remainder of my Estate be distributed in equal parts to my two dear Children, Katharine Chase Sprague and Janet Ralston Chase.

"I commit my Soul to the mercies of God, in Christ Jesus our Saviour, through the Holy Spirit.

"Signed and sealed in the presence of Jacobs W. Schuckers and R. C. Parsons as my last Will and Testament this 19th day of November in the year of Our Lord One Thousand Eight Hundred and Seventy.

"S. P. CHASE."

WILL OF HENRY CLAY

Henry Clay died June 29, 1852. After the usual formal opening, his will has the following provision:

"I give and devise to my wife during her life, the use and occupation of Ashland, with the exception of the piece thereof hereinafter devised to my son John, and also during her life all my slaves except those heretofore or hereinafter otherwise disposed of without her being liable to any account for the profits thereof. I also give to her in fee all my furniture, plate, paintings, library, carriages and Horses, and such of my other horses, mules, working beasts, Milch Cows and other live stock as she may select and choose to retain but upon this condition nevertheless, that either during her life, or by her last Will and Testament she dispose of the same among our children and our other descendants in such way as she may think proper according to her own sense of their kindness, affection and obedience to her. If she die without making such disposition the same is to be considered as part of my residuary estate.

"Should my wife not desire to reside at Ashland after my death I will and direct that a house and lot be purchased, built, or rented for her wherever she may prefer to dwell."

The next provision invests his executors with full power and authority to sell and convey any part of his estate wherever situated, which is not in the will specifically devised or bequeathed. He next directs that in the event of the sale of his Ashland property, the proceeds shall be loaned out upon good and sufficient security, and that the interest accruing thereon be regularly paid to his wife during her life, and upon her death, the property in trust should pass into his residuary estate after the payment of the legacies mentioned in the will.

Unto his son Thomas, he devises the place known as Mansfield, where the son resided, in trust, however, that it should be retained free from all debts or encumbrances as a residence for the son and his wife and children.

There is given to the son, Thomas, the sum of five thousand dollars, and he was acquitted from any debts which he owed the testator.

Unto his son John, he gives two hundred acres of the Ashland estate, to be taken off the south side thereof. He also gives to his son John, certain slaves, Harvey, Milton, Henry and Bob. There is also a gift to the son John, of certain horses, particularly "Margaret Woods and her Harold filly."

The next reference is to his son Theodore, and he directs that "during his unhappy alienation of mind, he shall be decently and comfortably supported in whatever situation it may be deemed best to place him. If it should please God to restore him to reason, I will and direct that after the death of my wife, out of the proceeds of the sale of Ashland and other property herein directed to be sold the sum of ten thousand dollars be paid to him without interest."

Unto the children "of my lamented Daughter Anne," he gives the sum of seven thousand five hundred dollars, to be equally divided between them to be paid without interest after the death of his wife.

Unto the children of his son Henry, he gives the sum of seven thousand five hundred dollars, in addition to what had been given their father, to be equally divided between them.

Certain general provisions of the will are as follows:

"I give to my son Thomas my stock in the Lexington and Richmond Turnpike Road Company.

"I give to my grandson Henry, son of Henry, my breast pin containing his Father's hair.

"I give to my grandson Henry Boyle, son of my son Thomas, the gold watch which I wear presented to me by my friend Dr. Mercer.

"I give to my friend Dr. B. W. Dudley the gold snuff box presented to me by Dr. Huntt late of Washington City.

"I give to my friend Dr. W. N. Mercer my snuff box inlaid with gold said to have belonged to Peter, the great Emperor of Russia.

"I give to my friend Henry T. Duncan my ring containing a piece of the Coffin of General Washington.

"I give to my granddaughter Lucy my diamond gold ring.

"I give to each of my sons Thomas, James and John one of my walking canes to be chosen by them in the order in which I have named them; my wife may distribute the residue of my walking canes and snuff boxes among such of our descendants or friends as she may think proper."

The next item of interest in the will is with reference to the slaves owned by Mr. Clay, and as it reflects his views upon the subject of slavery, we quote it in full:

"In the sale of any of my slaves I direct that the members of families shall not be separated without their consent.

"My will is and I accordingly direct that the issue of all my female slaves, which may be born after the first day of January, 1850 shall be free at the respective ages of the males at twenty eight and of the females at twenty five and that the three years next preceding their arrival at the age of freedom, they shall be entitled to their hire or wages for those years or the fair value of their services to defray the expense of transporting them to One of the African Colonies and of furnishing them with an outfit on their arrival there. And I further direct that they be taught to read, to write and to Cipher, and that they be sent to Africa. I further will and direct that the issue of any of the females who are so to be entitled to their freedom at the age of twenty five shall be deemed free from their birth, and that they be bound out as apprentices to learn farming or some useful trade upon the condition also of being taught to read, to write and to Cipher. And I direct also that the age of twenty one having been attained, they shall be sent to one of the African Colonies; to raise the necessary funds for which purpose, if they shall not have previously earned them, they must be hired out a sufficient length of time.

"I request and enjoin my Executors and descendants to pay particular attention to the execution of this provision of my will, and if they should sell any of the females who or whose issue are to be free I especially desire them to guard carefully the rights of such issue by all suitable stipulations and sanctions in the contract of sale. But I hope that it may not be necessary to sell any such persons who are to be entitled to their freedom but that they may be retained in the possession of some of my descendants."

All the rest, residue and remainder of his estate, after the death of his wife, and which is not needed to pay the legacies mentioned, nor for debts,— and he states, "I hope to leave none,"— he directs shall create a trust fund, a portion of the revenue from which shall be used for the comfortable support of his son Theodore; the remainder to be divided in equal portions between the sons Thomas and James during their lives, and to their respective heirs upon their deaths. He directs that the trust fund shall be invested in loans upon good security, so that the interest may be collected annually, and the sons Thomas and James are permitted to borrow the trust fund upon proper security. The sons Thomas and James are given the power to dispose of the trust fund by will, but in default of wills, the same shall pass to their heirs, under the Kentucky law.

Within five years after the death of the testator, the Trustees are directed to place in the residuary estate the sum of ten thousand dollars, given to the son Theodore, if he fails to be restored to reason.

A codicil to the will is in the following words:

"I give to my grandson Harry Clay, son of James B. Clay my Scotch pebble seal which has on it the initials of my name."

WILL OF SAMUEL L. CLEMENS (Mark Twain)

Samuel L. Clemens died April 21, 1910; his will is dated August 17, 1909. He directs the payment of his just debts and obligations, and his funeral expenses. Article Second reads:

"I give and bequeath to my daughter Clara Langdon Clemens, her heirs, executors, administrators and assigns absolutely, five per cent (5%) of any and all moneys which at the time of my death, may be on deposit to my credit, and subject to withdrawal on demand in any bank or trust company, or in any banking institution."

Article Third is identical, except his daughter Jean Lampton Clemens is named.

Article Fourth provides that all the rest, residue and remainder of the estate shall vest in three trustees for certain trust purposes. The Executors and Trustees named are Jervis Langdon, of Elmira, New York, Edward E. Loomis and Zoheth S. Freeman, both of New York City, and no bond is to be required of them as Executors or Trustees.

The residuary estate is divided into two equal parts for the benefit of the daughters, they to receive respectively, one-half of the income as long as they live: each daughter is given the right to dispose of her part of the estate, but failing to do so, and leaving issue, then such issue to take the mother's share: but either dying without issue surviving, without leaving a last will, then that share to be held by the trustees for the other daughter: and should either daughter become entitled to the whole estate by the death of the other, then the trustees, at her death, are to convey the whole trust estate to such persons as she may by will direct, but in the event the estate is not disposed of by will, then the trustees are to convey it to the next of kin of the surviving daughter.

Each executor and trustee is given one vote in determining questions of administration, and full power is given them in the management, control and disposition of the estate.

The last article of the will reads in part as follows:

"As I have expressed to my daughter Clara Langdon Clemens, and to my Associate, Albert Bigelow Paine, my ideas and desires regarding the administration of my literary productions, and as they are especially familiar with my wishes in that respect, I request that my executors and trustees above named confer and advise with my said daughter Clara Langdon Clemens, and the said Albert Bigelow Paine, as to all matters relating in any way to the control, management and disposition of my literary productions, published and unpublished, and all my literary articles and memoranda of every kind and description, and generally as to all matters which pertain to copyrights and such other literary property as I may leave at the time of my decease."

The testator then states that the foregoing suggestion as to consultation is subject to a contract with Albert Bigelow Paine for the publication of his letters and in full recognition thereof, and also subject to a contract with Albert Bigelow Paine and Harper Brothers with reference to his biography.

The testator's daughters are the sole beneficiaries under the will.

WILL OF GROVER CLEVELAND

Ex-President Grover Cleveland died June 24, 1908. The following is an abstract of the copy of his will, dated at Princeton, New Jersey, February 21, 1906, which is on file in the Office of the Register of Wills, Washington, D.C.

He directs that after the payment of all debts and funeral expenses, an appropriate monument with brief inscription, and only moderately expensive, be erected at his grave and paid for out of his estate. "I desire to be buried wherever I may reside at the time of my death, and that my body shall always remain where it shall be at first buried — subject to its removal only if it shall be absolutely necessary in order that it shall repose by the side of my wife and in accordance with her desire."

He gives to his niece Mary Hastings, daughter of his sister Anna Hastings, the sum of three thousand dollars to be paid to her as soon as practicable after his death; and to each of the four daughters of his nephew Richard Hastings, then or lately living with his sister Anna Hastings, the sum of two thousand dollars each.

"*Third.* I give to my friend Richard Watson Gilder, the watch given to me in 1893 by the said Gilder and E. C. Benedict and J. J. Sinclair — and also the chain attached to the same when last worn by me."

"*Fifth.* I give to Frank S. Hastings, my good friend and Executor of this will, as the most personal memento I can leave to him, the seal ring I have worn for many years, which was given to me by my dear wife, and with whose hearty concurrence this gift is made."

To his two daughters Esther and Marion, and his two sons, Richard F. and Francis G., he bequeaths the sum of two thousand dollars each, to be paid to them respectively as they each arrive at the age of twenty-one years, and until these legacies are paid, or shall lapse, they shall be kept invested, and the income derived therefrom shall be paid to his wife, and the aggregate of said income, shall be applied by her to the support, maintenance and education of the said children in such manner and in such proportions as she shall deem best, without any liability to any of said children on account thereof. If any of the said daughters, shall before her legacy becomes payable, cease for any reason to reside with her mother, then and from that time, the income arising from the investment of her legacy, shall be paid to said daughter. In case any of the said children shall die before his or her legacy shall be actually paid, leaving a child or children, then said legacy shall be paid to said child or children, but otherwise the said legacy shall lapse and become a part of the residuary estate disposed of by the instrument.

All the rest and residue of his estate and property he gives to his dear wife Frances F. Cleveland and to her heirs and assigns forever; and he appoints her guardian of all his children during their minority.

"*Eighth.* I hereby appoint my wife Frances F. Cleveland Executrix, and Frank S. Hastings Executor of this my last will and testament."

ANCIENT, CURIOUS, AND FAMOUS WILLS 351

WILL OF ROSCOE CONKLING

Roscoe Conkling died April 18, 1888. His will is as follows:
"I, Roscoe Conkling of Utica, N.Y., do make, publish and declare my last Will and Testament as follows:

"I give, devise and bequeath to my wife Julia, and to her heirs and assigns forever, all my property and estate whether real, personal or mixed, and I constitute and appoint my said wife sole executrix of this my Will.

"In Testimony whereof, I hereto sign my name this 21st of June, A.D. 1867.

"ROSCOE CONKLING."

WILL OF WILLIAM W. CORCORAN

William W. Corcoran died February 24, 1888. By his will, after numerous bequests and legacies to friends and relatives, he gives the sum of seventeen thousand dollars to charitable institutions in the City of Washington, D.C., and adds, "All these sums to be held and invested by the institutions to which they are severally given, and a sufficient part of the income therefrom used to furnish the inmates with the usual Christmas and strawberry festivals and feasts, commenced by my daughter about forty years ago, and continued by me to the present time."

A cane given to the testator by the widow of General Robert E. Lee, he gives to his eldest grandson, William Corcoran Eustis, as well as his diamond shirt studs and his library.

To his grandson, George Peabody Eustis, he gives his Palmetto cane, presented to him by the citizens of South Carolina in 1874.

The celebrated Corcoran Gallery of Art in Washington, is remembered in the following language:

"In addition to the gifts heretofore made by me to 'The Trustees of the Corcoran Gallery of Art' in the City of Washington, and now being enjoyed by said Gallery, and which amount to about the sum of $1,500,000, I give and bequeath to 'The Trustees of the Corcoran Gallery of Art,' in the District of Columbia, the sum of One Hundred Thousand Dollars to be applied by said Trustees, for the purposes of said Gallery, according to a request which I shall make in writing to said Trustees."

To the Trustees of the Louise Home of the City of Washington, D.C., he gives the sum of fifty thousand dollars, which he states is in addition to the sum of five hundred thousand dollars, already given to said institution.

To his grandson, William Corcoran Eustis, he gives "the old brick house on Bridge Street in Georgetown, D.C., built in the year 1791 by my father, and in which I was born," with the request that the same be not sold, but that the devisee pass it by will to his eldest son.

The rest of his estate he directs shall, from time to time, be divided between his grandchildren.

The will concludes with the following items:

"I give and bequeath to my barber George Gray, the sum of One Hundred Dollars."

"I hereby direct that all my horsehaired furniture shall be equally divided between my said grandchildren."

WILL OF JEFFERSON DAVIS

Jefferson Davis died at New Orleans, Louisiana, December 6, 1889. His will is as follows:

"I, Jefferson Davis, of the County of Harrison and State of Mississippi, being of sound and disposing mind, but of such advanced age, as to suggest a near approach of death, do make this my last Will and Testament, written with my own hand and signed in the presence of three competent witnesses.

"1. I give and bequeath to my wife Varina Davis, all of my personal belongings, including library, furniture, correspondence and the Brierfield plantation (proper) with all its appurtenances, being and situated in the County of Warren, State of Mississippi, and being the same on which we lived and toiled together for many years from the time of our marriage.

"2. I give and bequeath to Mary Routh Ellis of Philadelphia, Penn., all of my right, title and interest in and to the 'Elliston' plantation, being and situated in the Parish of Tensas, State of Louisiana, the same being the place on which her Father resided.

"3. I give and bequeath to Mary Ridgely Dorsey, eldest daughter of William H. G. Dorsey, of Howard County, State of Maryland, all of my right, title and interest in and to the 'Limerick' plantation, being and situated in the Parish of Tensas, State of Louisiana, viz. the interest in and to so much of said plantation as was the property of the late Mrs. Sarah A. Dorsey.

"4. I give and bequeath to my daughter Varina Anne Davis,

all the other property, real, personal and mixed, which was inherited by me from Mrs. Sarah A. Dorsey, deceased, and of which I may die seized and possessed.

"5. To my wife, Varina Davis, and to my daughters Margaret Davis Hayes, and Varina Anne Davis, as residuary Legatees, I give and bequeath all the property real, personal and mixed of which I may die seized and possessed, and which has not been disposed of by the preceding articles.

"6. I appoint my tried and true friend Jacob U. Payne, of New Orleans, La. and my son in law, J. Addison Hayes, Jr., of Memphis, Tenn. Executors of this my last Will and Testament, they to serve without bond, and to have immediate seizure and possession of all my property cotemporaneously with the happening of my death, and to each I delegate the power to select and appoint his successor, to take effect in the contingency of the death of either, before the affairs of the estate have been finally settled.

"In testimony whereof this Will written by my own hand is signed on the day and date below written, and in the presence of Frank Kennedy, R. W. Foster and A. Evans.

"JEFFERSON DAVIS.

"Saturday 20th Feb. 1886."

WILL OF STEPHEN A. DOUGLAS

Stephen A. Douglas died June 11, 1861. A copy of his will, together with a codicil thereto, is as follows:

"Know all men by these presents that I, Stephen A. Douglas of the City of Chicago and State of Illinois, in view of the uncertainty of life and the certainty of death at such time as an all wise Providence shall ordain, do hereby declare and subscribe the following as my will which I desire all persons to respect after my death, to wit:

"It is also my will after my said debts shall be paid, all the residue of my property, personal and real shall be divided by my executors into two equal parts, and that one part thereof shall belong to my two children, Robert M. Douglas and Stephen Douglas, and that the other part thereof, that is to say, one-half of all my property real and personal and of all moneys or debts due me shall belong to and is hereby declared to belong to my dear and beloved wife, Adele Cutts Douglas.

"It is also my will and positive direction that my said wife shall be and she is hereby declared to be the sole guardian of my said children, and that she shall have the possession, control and education of them until they shall respectively arrive at the age of twenty-one years, knowing her to be the best person in the world to perform this sacred trust.

"It is also my will that my said wife, Adele Cutts Douglas and my friend and relative, Daniel P. Rhodes, of Cleveland, Ohio, be and they are hereby declared my executors to carry this will into effect, and to that end I do hereby waive all legal process and letters of administration and dispense with any and all security on the part of my said executors and direct that they may proceed and execute this will the same that I could do were I alive.

"Having thus provided for all my worldly affairs, I commit my soul to God and ask the prayers of the good for His divine blessing.

"In testimony whereof I have hereunto set my hand and seal this 4th day of September A.D. 1857.

"S. A. DOUGLAS."

CODICIL ADDED JULY 30, 1859

"Be it known that I, Stephen A. Douglas, do hereby add the following supplement to the above as my last will and testament, to wit: that in event that my said wife shall have any child or children by me, whether born before or after my death, it is my will and direction that in the distribution of my estate an amount of property shall first be set apart and allotted to said child or children equal to the amount which my other children will receive from their mother's estate, and that the residue of my property after paying all just debts shall be divided into two equal parts and one of said parts shall belong to my said wife, to her sole use and benefit and the other to my said children, born or to be born as aforesaid, in equal proportions, it being my wish and intention that such children should inherit an equal amount of property with reference to the estate from which it shall be derived.

"In witness whereof I have hereunto set my hand and seal at the City of Washington, this 30th day of July, A.D. 1859.

"STEPHEN A. DOUGLAS."

WILL OF MARY BAKER G. EDDY

Mary Baker G. Eddy died December 3, 1910. Up to the age of fifty, her life had been a complete failure, filled with domestic

ANCIENT, CURIOUS, AND FAMOUS WILLS 355

misfortunes and discouraging experiences. She was an exception to the rule, that the leaders of great religious systems and reforms have been men. That late in life she exerted an astonishing influence, both in spiritual and material affairs, gained a prodigious success, and developed a wonderful personality, the world is willing to admit. Her recent death, and the popular interest in her life work and leadership in the Christian Science Church, justify the insertion of her will in full. This document is duly attested by four witnesses, the two codicils thereto each having three.

"Be it known that I, Mary Baker G. Eddy, of Concord, New Hampshire, being of sound and disposing mind and memory, do make, publish and declare this to be my last will and testament in manner and form following, that is to say;

"1. I hereby nominate and appoint Honorable Henry M. Baker, of Bow, New Hampshire, sole executor of this my last will and testament; and, having ample confidence in his ability and integrity, I desire that he shall not be required to furnish sureties on his official bond.

"2. Having already transferred and given to my son, George W. Glover, of Lead City, South Dakota, four certain mortgage deeds bought of the Farmers' Loan and Trust Company, of the State of Kansas, and having already given him a house and lot located in Lead City, South Dakota, and monies at various times, I hereby confirm and ratify said transfers and gifts, and, in addition thereto, I give and bequeath to my said son, George W. Glover, the sum of ten thousand dollars.

"3. I give and bequeath to George H. Moore, of Concord, New Hampshire, the sum of one thousand dollars; to each of the five children of my son, George W. Glover, the sum of ten thousand dollars; to Mrs. Mary A. Baker, of Boston, Massachusetts, widow of my late brother, the sum of five thousand dollars; to Frances A. Baker, of Concord, New Hampshire, the sum of one thousand dollars; to Henrietta E. Chanfrau, of Philadelphia, Penn., the sum of one thousand dollars; to Fred N. Ladd, of Concord, New Hampshire, the sum of three thousand dollars; to my adopted son, Benjamin J. Foster, M.D., the sum of five thousand dollars; to Calvin A. Frye, of Concord, New Hampshire, the sum of ten thousand dollars, provided he continues in my service to the date of my decease; to Pauline Mann, of Concord, New Hampshire, the sum of one thousand dollars, provided she continues in my service to the date of my decease; to Joseph G. Mann, of Concord, New

Hampshire, three thousand dollars, provided he continues in my service to the date of my decease; to Laura E. Sargent, of Concord, New Hampshire, three thousand dollars, provided she continues in my service to the date of my decease.

"4. I give and bequeath to the Mother Church — First Church of Christ, Scientist, in Boston, Massachusetts, the sum of fifty thousand dollars.

"5. I give and devise to Calvin A. Frye and Joseph G. Mann, above named, provided they shall respectively remain in my service to the date of my decease, the right, during the term of their respective natural lives, to occupy and use my homestead and grounds called 'Pleasant View,' in Concord, New Hampshire, as their residence and home, but the rights hereby conditionally granted to said Frye and Mann shall not be assignable to any other person. Said homestead and grounds connected therewith shall not be leased to, or occupied by, any persons, except as herein provided. No part of said homestead, or lands connected therewith, shall be devoted to any other uses or purposes than those of a home for said Frye and Mann during their respective lives (provided they respectively remain in my service to the date of my decease) and a home for my grandchildren according to the terms of this will and, after the termination of the rights of said Frye and Mann and my grandchildren as herein provided, as a place for the reception, entertainment, and care of Christian Science visitors and their friends, and to such other purposes looking to the general advancement of the Christian Science religion as may be deemed best by the residuary legatee. All the personal property, except my jewelry, in and about said homestead and lands shall be kept and carefully used on said premises.

"In my contract with Edward A. Kimball of Chicago, dated October 9, 1899, provision is made for the creation of a trust fund for the purpose of procuring an annual revenue or income which shall be used for maintaining in a perpetual state of repair my said homestead. A further provision is also made for that purpose in said contract. If, for any reason, sufficient funds for such purposes shall not be provided from the sources named in said contract, then I direct that my residuary legatee shall provide and expend such sums, from time to time, as may be necessary for the purpose of maintaining said homestead and grounds in a perpetual state of repair and cultivation.

"I hereby give and devise to my grandson, George W. Glover, Jr., the right and privilege of living and having a home at Pleasant View and of being supported therein in a reasonable manner at the expense of my estate while he is obtaining his education preparatory to admission to Dartmouth College, provided he shall select and choose to obtain his education at that institution. I also direct my executor to pay all of said George W. Glover, Jr.'s, reasonable expenses while at said college, giving him, in the meantime, the privilege of a home at Pleasant View.

"I also give and devise to my granddaughters the right and privilege of living and having a home at Pleasant View, and of being supported therein in a reasonable manner at the expense of my estate, while they, or either of them, are obtaining a high school education, provided they, or either of them, desire the advantages of such course.

"6. I give and bequeath to the Christian Science Board of Directors of the Mother Church — The First Church of Christ, Scientist, in Boston, Massachusetts — and their successors in office, the sum of one hundred thousand dollars, but, nevertheless, in trust for the following purposes, namely; said trustees shall hold, invest, and reinvest the principal of said fund and conservatively manage the same, and shall use the income and such portion of the principal, from time to t me, as they may deem best, for the purpose of providing free instruction for indigent, well-educated, worthy Christian Scientists at the Massachusetts Metaphysical College and to aid them thereafter until they can maintain themselves in some department of Christian Science.

"I desire that the instruction for which provision is hereby made shall be at the said College, but my said trustees are hereby authorized to provide said instruction elsewhere, if, in the unanimous judgment of all said trustees for the time being, such course shall seem best. The judgment and discretion of said trustees with reference to the persons to be aided as herein provided and the amount of aid furnished to each of said persons shall be final and conclusive.

"7. I hereby ratify and confirm the following trust agreements and declarations, viz.

"(1) The deed of trust dated September 1, 1892, conveying land for church edifice in Boston and on which the building of the First Church of Christ, Scientist, now stands.

"(2) The trust agreement dated January 25, 1898, conveying to Edward P. Bates, James A. Neal, and William P. McKenzie, and their successors, the property conveyed to me by the Christian

Science Publishing Society, by bill of sale dated January 21, 1898, the said trust being created for the purpose of more effectually promoting and extending the religion of Christian Science as taught by me.

"(3) The trust agreement dated February 12, 1898, specifying the objects, purposes, terms, and conditions on which the First Church of Christ, Scientist, in Boston, Massachusetts, shall hold the real estate situated at #385 Commonwealth Avenue, in Boston, Massachusetts, which was conveyed by me to said church on said February 12, 1898.

"(4) The trust agreement dated January 31, 1898, whereby certain real estate was conveyed to George H. Moore, Calvin A. Frye, and Ezra M. Buswell, and their successors, and, in addition thereto, the sum of one hundred thousand dollars, for the purpose of a Christian Science church to be erected on said real estate.

"(5) The trust agreement dated May 20, 1898, under which the sum of four thousand dollars was transferred to The First Church of Christ, Scientist, in Boston, for the benefit of the children contributors of the Mother's room in said church.

"(6) The deed of trust dated December 21, 1895, transferring five hundred dollars to the trustees of Park Cemetery Association of Tilton, New Hampshire.

"8. I give, bequeath and devise all the rest, residue and remainder of my estate, of every kind and description, to the Mother Church — The First Church of Christ, Scientist, in Boston, Massachusetts, in trust for the following general purposes; I desire that such portion of the income of my residuary estate as may be necessary shall be used for the purpose of keeping in repair the church building and my former house at #385 Commonwealth Avenue in said Boston, which has been transferred to said Mother Church, and any building or buildings which may be, by necessity or convenience, substituted therefor; and, so far as may be necessary, to maintain my said homestead and grounds ('Pleasant View' in Concord, New Hampshire) in a perpetual state of repair and cultivation for the uses and purposes heretofore in this will expressed; and I desire that the balance of said income, and such portion of the principal as may be deemed wise, shall be devoted and used by said residuary legatee for the purpose of more effectually promoting and extending the religion of Christian Science as taught by me.

"Witness my hand and seal this thirteenth day of September, A.D. 1901.   "MARY B. G. EDDY."

"Be it known that I, Mary Baker G. Eddy, of Concord, New Hampshire, do hereby make, publish and declare a codicil to my last will and testament, originally dated September 13, 1901, a duplicate of said will having been this day reëxecuted by me upon the discovery of the loss of the original, dated September 13, 1901, as aforesaid, in manner following, namely;

"1. I hereby revoke the bequest, in paragraph numbered 5 of my said will, to Joseph G. Mann, of the right to occupy with Calvin A. Frye my homestead premises known as 'Pleasant View,' during the lifetime of the said Mann, and I hereby bequeath unto Irving C. Tomlinson, of Concord, New Hampshire, and to his sister Mary E. Tomlinson the right during the term of their respective lives to occupy and use as a home said premises known as 'Pleasant View,' said occupancy and use by them to be personal to them and not assignable to any other person by them or either of them and shall be exercised with due regard to the rights of other persons named in said will, excepting said Mann, to occupy and enjoy said premises.

"2. I give and bequeath to Laura E. Sargent the sum of five thousand dollars ($5000), this legacy to be in lieu of the legacy provided for her in paragraph numbered 3 of my said will, and to be unconditional.

"3. I give, devise and bequeath to the Second Church of Christ, Scientist, in New York City, a sum not exceeding one hundred and seventy-five thousand dollars ($175,000) sufficient to pay the indebtedness which may exist at the time of my decease upon the church edifice of said Second Church of Christ, Scientist, and direct that said sum of one hundred and seventy-five thousand dollars ($175,000), or so much thereof as may be necessary for the purpose, shall be applied as soon as may be after my decease to or towards the extinguishment of said indebtedness; if the amount required for this purpose shall not be as much as one hundred and seventy-five thousand dollars ($175,000), then this legacy shall be limited to the amount actually required.

"4. I give and bequeath to Mrs. Pamelia J. Leonard, of Brooklyn, New York, the sum of three thousand dollars ($3000); to Mrs. Augusta E. Stetson, of New York City, my "crown of diamonds" breastpin; to Mrs. Laura Lathrop, of New York City, my diamond cross; to Mrs. Rose Kent, of Jamestown, New York, my gold watch and chain; and to Henry M. Baker, of Bow, New Hampshire, my portrait set in diamonds.

"5. Mrs. Mary A. Baker, to whom I have bequeathed five thousand dollars (5000), by my will, having deceased since the original execution of said will on September, 13, 1901, I hereby revoke the legacy therein provided for her.

"6. The bequest in my will to Calvin A. Frye is hereby increased to twenty thousand dollars, but subject to the same condition as therein provided.

"I hereby ratify and reaffirm my will as originally executed on September 13, 1901, and as again executed this day, in all respects except as herein modified.

"In witness whereof I have hereunto set my hand and seal at Concord, New Hampshire, this seventh day of November, A.D. 1903.

"MARY BAKER G. EDDY."

"Be it known that I, Mary Baker G. Eddy, of Concord, New Hampshire, do hereby make, publish, and declare this second codicil to my last will and testament originally dated September 13, 1901, a duplicate of said will having been reëxecuted by me on November 7, 1903, in manner following, namely;

"1. I hereby direct and require that the executor of my will shall sell, within three months after his appointment, at public auction or, if he sees fit, at private sale, for such price as he may determine upon and to such purchaser as he may see fit, my real estate in said Concord known as 'Pleasant View,' consisting of my homestead and the grounds occupied in connection therewith, and I hereby direct that the proceeds of such sale shall be forthwith paid over to the Directors of the First Church of Christ, Scientist, in Boston, Massachusetts, to be used for such purposes in connection with said Church as said Directors may determine. Nothing contained in my will or codicils thereto shall be considered inconsistent with said Church purchasing said real estate, if the Directors may consider it desirable so to do.

"I hereby revoke the provisions of my will and first codicil providing for the occupancy of said real estate by various persons, the preservation and maintenance thereof at the expense of my estate, and all other provisions of my will and codicil inconsistent with the foregoing direction to my executor to sell said real estate.

"2. I hereby give and bequeath to The First Church of Christ, Scientist, in Boston, Massachusetts, all the contents of my said homestead and of the other buildings at 'Pleasant View,' — except so far as any of the same may be specifically bequeathed in my will and codicils thereto, which specific bequests I do not modify by this provision, — the same to be kept or disposed of as may be determined by the Directors of said Church; but I direct that Calvin A. Frye shall have the privilege of selecting from said articles such keepsakes or mementos, not exceeding in intrinsic value the sum of five hundred dollars, as he may desire, and I give and bequeath the same to him when so selected.

"3. I hereby direct that said Calvin A. Frye shall be provided with a suitable home in my house at No. 385 Commonwealth Avenue, Boston, if he so desires, he to have the exclusive occupancy of two furnished rooms therein, to be designated by my executor, and to have his board, suitable heat, light, and all other things necessary for his comfortable occupancy of said premises during his natural life, the expense thereof to be provided out of the income from the residue of my estate which I have left to said The First Church of Christ, Scientist, in Boston, Massachusetts.

"4. I give and bequeath to Lydia B. Hall, of Brockton, Massachusetts, the sum of one thousand dollars.

"5. I give and bequeath to Irving C. Tomlinson, of said Concord, the note which I hold signed by him, it being my intention hereby to release him from said indebtedness.

"In all other respects except as herein specified, I hereby ratify and reaffirm my will and codicil above mentioned.

"In witness whereof I have hereunto set my hand and seal at Concord, New Hampshire, this fourteenth day of May, A.D. 1904.

"MARY BAKER G. EDDY."

BURIAL OF MRS. MARY BAKER G. EDDY

On January 26, 1911, at Boston, in a concrete grave on the shores of Lake Halcyon, in Mount Auburn Cemetery, was deposited a bronze coffin containing the body of Mrs. Mary Baker G. Eddy, the founder of Christian Science.

On the coffin rested a bronze box inclosing a complete set of the works of Mrs. Eddy, together with all recent Christian Science publications, while the silver plate beneath gave her name and the dates of her birth and death.

The ceremony was attended by the directors of the church and a score of its strongest supports. Judge Clifford P. Smith, the first reader of the First Church, read the ninety-first Psalm and the last two verses in Jude which were read at the funeral December 8, 1910.

Then the grave was sealed. Later, the spot will be marked by a mausoleum.

Since the funeral service of Mrs. Eddy the bronze coffin had reposed in the receiving tomb at Mount Auburn, with a guard beside it day and night.

That guard was relieved shortly after noon Jan. 26, when half a dozen carriages rolled up to the door of the tomb, and an hour later the coffin was drawn out and placed on the bier.

The bronze plate covering the features of Mrs. Eddy was pushed back, and one by one the little party gazed for the last time on her face. It had changed but little in the seven weeks.

In the construction of the grave the skill of engineers was invoked to make it impervious to desecration, or even to decay. The coffin rests on four feet of concrete and is incased in steel uprights.

Upon it rests the copper box with the Christian Science literature, and above are alternate layers of concrete and steel network to the level of the turf.

Will of Ralph Waldo Emerson

Ralph Waldo Emerson died at Concord, Massachusetts, April 27, 1882. His will is as follows:

"I, Ralph Waldo Emerson, of Concord, in the County of Middlesex and Commonwealth of Massachusetts, make this as my last will and testament, hereby revoking all other wills by me at any time made.

"First. (1) I give all my real estate, wherever situated, excepting only my house and homestead estate in Concord, equally to my three children Edward Waldo Emerson, Ellen Tucker Emerson and Edith Emerson Forbes, wife of William Hathaway Forbes of Milton, and their heirs. But the pasture land and wood land in Concord is given, subject to certain rights reserved for the benefit of my wife and my daughter Ellen, as hereinafter named.

"(2) I give my library to my three children equally. All my manuscripts and unpublished writings I give to my three children and the survivors and survivor of them in joint tenancy.

"(3) The copyright and plates and ownership of all my published writings I give to my son Edward; and I also assign to him for his own benefit all my contracts for the publication of said writings.

"(4) I give to my daughter Edith the book of selections known in my family as the 'Black Anthology;' and to the five children of my daughter Edith I give as follows: — to Ralph my watch, to Edith my bronze image of Goethe, to Cameron the cane cut at the Grotto of Egeria and given to me by my valued friend, Judge Hoar, to John my cane of teak wood, and to Edward my small brass candle-sticks and Roman lamp.

"(5) To the oldest child of my son Edward I give my sole leather trunk.

"(6) I give to my son Edward the sum of thirteen hundred dollars ($1300) and to my daughter Ellen the sum of twenty-three hundred dollars ($2300). In naming these sums and in not here giving any sum to my daughter Edith I am influenced by the fact that I have heretofore made certain advancements to Edith and to Edward at the time when they were married.

"Second. — As to all the residue and remainder of my property of every kind whatever, I give it as follows:

"(1) In case my wife should survive me (a) I give to my daughter Ellen the sum of three thousand dollars ($3000); and while I do not in this place give a like sum to Edward and my daughter Edith, because the immediate enjoyment of the property is likely to be of less importance to them, I nevertheless direct that in the final division of my property the share of Ellen shall contribute to each of the shares of Edward and Edith the sum of one thousand dollars as of the date of the payment of this legacy to Ellen; and (b) all the rest of said residue I give to my son Edward to hold it during his mother's lifetime in trust for her benefit, to keep the income-bearing part of the property well invested, to pay all taxes and to make all necessary or proper repairs, and to pay over the net income and proceeds of the property, quarterly or oftener as may be convenient to my wife, during her life. As to the house and homestead estate in Concord and all the furniture, plate, pictures and other articles of household use or ornament therein, except what is herein otherwise disposed of, the trustee is to take care that my wife has the full use and enjoyment thereof during her life, and he shall also provide wood for her use at the house from the Concord woodlots and pasturage on the Concord farm for the cows.

"(2) In case my wife should not survive me, and also in the event of her death, if she should survive me, I give all the said residue of my property not otherwise disposed of, as aforesaid, equally to my three children and their heirs, executors and administrators. But I qualify this division in two particulars: first, the share of my daughter Ellen shall contribute to the shares of Edward and Edith in case of the payment of said legacy of three thousand dollars ($3000); and second, in addition to her one-third of the said residue of my property, I direct that my daughter Ellen shall have the right, during her lifetime and free from all charge or payment therefor, to occupy my said house and homestead estate and to have, from my other land in Concord, wood for her use at the house and pasturage for her cows; and also that if she should prefer not to occupy said house she shall have the right to take for her use elsewhere and as her own property, such part as she may select of the furniture, plate, pictures and other articles of household use or ornament in my house, not herein otherwise disposed of.

"Third. — I appoint my friend James Elliot Cabot to be my literary executor, giving him authority, acting in coöperation with my children or the survivors or survivor of them, to publish or to withhold from publication any of my unpublished papers.

"Fourth. — I appoint my son Edward Waldo Emerson and my son-in-law William A. Forbes to be the executors of my will; and in case of the death of either of them, whether before or after my death, I appoint my daughter Ellen to be executrix in his place.

"Fifth. — I request that neither of my executors or my trustee, herein named, shall be required to give surety on his official bond.

"In witness whereof I have hereunto set my hand and seal this fourteenth day of April in the year eighteen hundred and seventy-six.

"R. WALDO EMERSON."

WILL OF EDWIN FORREST

Edwin Forrest died December 12, 1872, at his home in Philadelphia. He was regarded one of the ablest representatives of Shakespearian characters of the age in which he lived nd died; he accumulated a large fortune. It will be recalled that his unfortunate quarrel with Macready resulted in 1849 in a riot in New York, which was accompanied by a serious loss of life. His will is dated April 5, 1866; there are two codicils, but they are of no very great importance. After making numerous bequests to friends and servants, the bulk of his large estate was directed to be placed in the hands of trustees, under an elaborate scheme "for the support and maintenance of actors and actresses decayed by age or disabled by infirmity." The institution was to be known as "The

Edwin Forrest Home." His will is a most interesting and unique document, and for this reason the whole of that portion which created "The Edwin Forrest Home" is here exactly copied from the original.

"The following is an outline of my plan for said Home, which may be filled out in more detail by the charter and by-laws:

"ARTICLE I

"The said Institution shall be for the support and maintenance of actors and actresses decayed by age or disabled by infirmity, who, if natives of the United States, shall have served at least five years in the theatrical profession, and if of foreign birth shall have served in that profession at least ten years, whereof three years next previous to the app ication shall have been in the United States, and who shall in all things comply with the laws and regulations of the Home, otherwise be subject to be discharged by the Managers, whose decision shall be final.

"ARTICLE II

"The number of inmates in the Home shall never exceed the annual net rent and revenue of the Institution, and after the number of inmates therein shall exceed twelve, others to be admitted shall be such only as shall receive the approval of the majority of the inmates, as well as of the Managers.

"ARTICLE III

"The said Corporation shall be managed by a Board of Managers, seven in number, who shall in the first instance be chosen by the said Trustees and hall include themselves, so long as any of them shall be living, and also the Mayor of the City of Philadephia for the time being, and as vacancies shall occur the existing Managers shall from time to time fill them, so that, if practicable, only one vacancy shall ever exist at a time.

"ARTICLE IV

"The Managers shall elect one of their number to be the President of the Institution, appoint a Treasurer and Secretary, Steward and Matron, and, if needed, a Clerk; the said Treasurer, Secretary, Steward, Matron and Clerk subject to be at any time discharged by the Managers. Except the Treasurer, the said officers may be chosen from the inmates of the Home, and the Treasurer shall not be a Manager, nor either of his sureties. The Managers shall also appoint a physician for the Home.

"ARTICLE V

"Should there be any failure of the Managers to fill any vacancy which may occur in their Board for three months, or should they in any respect fail to fulfill their trust according to the intent of my will and the charter of the Institution, it is my will that upon the petition of any two or more of said Managers, or of the Mayor of the City, the Orphans' Court of Philadelphia County shall make such appointments to fill any vacancy or vacancies and all orders and decrees necessary to correct any failure or breach of trust which shall appear to said Court to be required, as in case of any other testamentary trust, so that the purposes of this charity may never fail or be abused.

"ARTICLE VI

"The purposes of the said 'Edwin Forrest Home' are intended to be partly educational and self-sustaining, as well as eleemosynary, and never to encourage idleness or thriftlessness in any who are capable of any useful exertion. My library shall be placed therein in precise manner as now it exists in my house in Broad street, Philadelphia. There shall be a neat and pleasant theatre for private exhibitions and histrionic culture. There shall be a picture gallery for the preservation and exhibition of my collection of engravings, pictures, statuary and other works of art, to which additions may be made from time to time, if the revenues of the Institution shall suffice. These objects are not only intended to improve the taste, but to promote the health and happiness of the inmates and such visitors as may be admitted.

"ARTICLE VII

"Also, as a means of preserving health and, consequently, the happiness of the inmates, as well as to aid in sustaining the Home, there shall be lectures and readings therein upon oratory and histrionic art, to which pupils shall be admitted, upon such terms and under such regulations as the Managers may prescribe. The garden and grounds are to be made productive of profit, as well as of health and pleasure, and, so far as capable, the inmates, not otherwise profitably occupied, shall assist in farming, horticulture and the cultivation of flowers in the garden and conservatory.

"ARTICLE VIII

"'The Edwin Forrest Home' may also, if the revenue shall suffice, embrace in its plan lectures on science, literature and the arts, but preferably oratory and the histrionic art, in manner to prepare the American citizen for the more creditable and effective discharge of his public duties, and to raise the education and intellectual and moral tone and character of actors, that thereby they may elevate the drama and cause it to subserve its true and great mission to mankind, as their profoundest teacher of virtue and morality.

"ARTICLE IX

"'The Edwin Forrest Home' shall also be made to promote the love of liberty, our country and her institutions, to hold in honor the name of the great dramatic Bard, as well as to cultivate a taste and afford opportunity for the enjoyment of social rural pleasures. Therefore, there shall be read therein to the inmates and public, by an inmate or pupil thereof, the immortal Declaration of Independence, as written by Thomas Jefferson, without expurgation, on every Fourth Day of July, to be followed by an oration under the folds of our national flag. There shall be prepared and read therein before the like assemblage, on the birthday of Shakespeare, the twenty-third of April, in every year, an eulogy upon his character and writings, and one of his plays, or scenes from his plays, shall on that day be represented in the theatre. And on the first Mondays of every June and October 'The Edwin Forrest Home,' and grounds shall be opened for the admission of ladies and gentlemen of the theatrical profession and their friends, in the manner of social picnics, when all provide their own entertainments.

"The foregoing general outline of my plan of the Institution I desire to establish has been sketched during my preparations for a long voyage by sea and land, and, should God spare my life, it is my purpose to be more full and definite; but should I leave no later will or codicil, my friends who sympathize in my purposes will execute them in the best and fullest manner possible, understanding that they have been long meditated by me, and are very dear to my heart. They will also remember that my professional brothers and sisters are often unfortunate, and that little has been done for them, either to elevate them in their profession or to provide for their necessities under sickness or other misfortunes. God has favored my efforts and given me great success, and I would make my fortune the means to elevate the education of others and promote their success, and to alleviate their sufferings and smooth the pillows of the unfortuate, in sickness or other disability, or the decay of declining years.

"These are the grounds upon which I would appeal to the Legislature of my native State, to the Chief Magistrate of my native city, to the Courts and my fellow-citizens, to assist my purposes, which I believe to be demanded by the just claims of humanity, and by that civilization and refinement which springs from intellectual and moral culture.

"I, therefore, lay it as a duty upon my Trustees to frame a bill which the Legislature may enact, as and for the charter of said Institution, which shall ratify the articles in said outline of plan; shall authorize the Mayor of the city to act as one of its Managers, and the said Court to exercise the visitatorial jurisdiction invoked, and prevent streets from being run through so much of the Springbrook grounds as shall include the buildings and sixty acres of ground. Such a charter being obtained, the Corporation shall be authorized, at a future period, to sell the grounds outside said space, the proceeds to be applied to increase the endowment and usefulness of the Home. And so far as I shall not have built to carry out my views, I authorize the said Managers, with consent of my sisters, or survivor of them, having a right to reside at Springbrook, to proceed to erect and build the buildings required by my outline of plan, and towards their erection apply the income accumulated or current of my estate, and should my sisters consent, or the survivor of them consent, in case of readiness to open the Home, to remove therefrom, a comfortable house shall be procured for them elsewhere, furnished and rent and taxes paid, as required in respect to Springbrook, at the cost and charge of my estate or of the said Corporation, if then in possession thereof. Whensoever the requisite charter shall be obtained and the Corporation be organized and ready to proceed to carry out its design, then it shall be the duty of said Trustees to assign and convey all my said property and estate unto the said 'Edwin Forrest Home,' their successors and assigns forever, and for the latter to execute and deliver, under the corporate seal, a full and absolute discharge and acquittance forever, — with or without auditing of accounts by an auditor of the Court, as they may think proper, — unto the said Executors and Trustees.

"In testimony whereof, I have hereunto set my hand and seal this fifth day of April, eighteen hundred and sixty-six.

"Edwin Forrest."

The State of Pennsylvania heartily coöperated with the Trustees, but they found themselves powerless to realize fully the hopes and wishes of the testator. It was necessary to make a settlement with the divorced wife of the testator, whose legal claims had been entirely overlooked by him. This and other legal complications hampered the Trustees, and the amounts of money necessarily expended seriously crippled the estate. The Home, however, was established upon his beautiful property known as "Springbrook," where it yet exists under excellent management, and its doors are still open to those who are entitled to enter under the conditions fixed by the testator.

WILL OF BENJAMIN FRANKLIN

In the "Life of Benjamin Franklin," by Jared Sparks, is to be found Franklin's will, a document of great length and unusual interest. Franklin died in 1790: the will is dated July 17, 1788; a codicil of almost equal length is dated June 23, 1789. The will in part reads:

"I, Benjamin Franklin, of Philadelphia, printer, late Minister Plenipotentiary from the United States of America to the Court of France, now President of the State of Pennsylvania, do make and declare my last will and testament as follows:

"To my son, William Franklin, late Governor of the Jerseys, I give and devise all the lands I hold or have a right to in the Province of Nova Scotia, to hold to him, his heirs and assigns forever. I also give to him all my books and papers which he has in his possession, and all debts standing against him on my account books, willing that no payment for, nor restitution of the same be required of him by my Executors. The part he acted against me in the late war, which is of public notoriety, will account for my leaving him no more of an estate he endeavored to deprive me of.

"I give and devise my dwelling house, my said three new houses, my printing office and also my silver plate, pictures and household goods of every kind, now in my said dwelling house, to my daughter, Sarah Bache, and to her husband, Richard Bache, to hold to them for and during their natural lives, and the life of the longest liver of them: and from and after the death of the survivor of them, I do give, devise and bequeath the same to all children already born or to be born of my said daughter, and to their heirs and assigns forever, as tenants in common and not as joint tenants.

"All lands near the Ohio and the lots near the centre of Philadelphia, which I lately purchased from the State, I give to my son-in-law, Richard Bache, his heirs and assigns forever: I also give him the bond I have against him of 2072 pounds 5 shillings and direct the same to be delivered up to him by my Executors cancelled, requesting that in consideration thereof, he would immediately after my decease manumit and set free his negro man, Bob: I leave to him also the money due me from the State of Virginia for types: I also discharge him, my son-in-law, from all claims of rent and moneys due to me, on book account or otherwise. I also give him all my musical instruments.

"The King of France's picture, set with four hundred and eight diamonds, I give to my daughter, Sarah Bache, requesting, however, that she would not form any of those diamonds into ornaments, either for herself or daughters, and thereby introduce or countenance the expensive, vain and useless pastime of wearing jewels in this country.

"The philosophical instruments I have in Philadelphia, I give to my ingenious friend, Francis Hopkinson.

"I was born in Boston, New England, and owe my first instructions in literature to the free grammar schools established there: I therefore give 100 pounds sterling to my Executors to be by them paid over to the managers or directors of the free schools in my native town of Boston."

The fund has been successfully applied and is or was formerly employed in purchasing medals for distribution in the schools of Boston.

There is a gift to the State of Pennsylvania of 2000 pounds to be employed in making the Schuylkill River navigable.

He concludes with this clause: "I would have my body buried with as little expense or ceremony as may be."

In the codicil to the will are found these expressions and gifts:

"It has been my opinion, that he who receives an estate from his ancestors is under some kind of obligation to transmit the same to their posterity: this obligation does not lie on me, who never inherited a shilling from any ancestor or relation."

One thousand pounds was given to Boston and another thousand to Philadelphia, to be held by trustees, which sums he directed should be "let out on interest at 5 per cent per annum to young married artificers under the age of twenty-five years." These cities accepted the sums, and they have been wisely used.

"I wish to be buried by the side of my wife, if it may be, and that a marble stone be made by Chambers, six feet long, four feet wide, plain, with only a small moulding around the upper edge, with this inscription,

BENJAMIN
DEBORAH } FRANKLIN

to be placed over us both."

This request was carried out.

"My fine crabtree walking-stick, with gold head curiously wrought in the form of the cap of liberty, I give to my friend, and the friend of mankind, General Washington. If it were a sceptre, he has merited it and would become it. It was a present to me from that excellent woman, Madame de Forbach, the Dowager Duchess of Deux Ponts, connected with some verses, which should go with it."

"I give my gold watch to my son-in-law, Richard Bache, and also the gold watch-chain of the thirteen United States, which I have not yet worn. My time-piece that stands in my library, I give to my grandson, William Temple Franklin. I give him also my Chinese gong. To my dear old friend, Mrs. Mary Hemson, I give one of my silver tankards marked, for her use during her life, and after her decease, I give it to her daughter, Eliza. I give to her son, William Hemson, who is my godson, my new quarto Bible, Oxford edition, to be for his family Bible, and also the botanic description of the plants in the Emperor's garden at Vienna, in folio, with colored cuts. And to her son, Thomas Hemson, I give a set of *Spectators*, *Tatlers*, and *Guardians*, handsomely bound.

"I give twenty guineas to my good friend and physician, Dr. John Jones.

"I request my friend, Mr. Duffield, to accept my French Way-weiser, a piece of clockwork in brass, to be fixed on the wheel of any carriage.

"My picture drawn by Martin in 1767, I give to the Supreme Executive Council of Pennsylvania, if they shall be pleased to do me the honor of accepting it and placing it in their chamber.

"I give to my Executors, to be divided equally among those that act, the sum of sixty pounds sterling as some compensation for their trouble in the execution of my will."

Will of Melville W. Fuller

The late Chief Justice Melville W. Fuller of the United States Supreme Court died at his summer home near Bar Harbor, Maine, July 4, 1910. By his last will and testament, he disposed of an estate of nearly one million dollars. The estate is to be held in trust for the daughters and the son of the Chief Justice, and their heirs. Nothing was left to charity or to parties other than the direct descendants of the testator. The will was signed at Washington, February 23, 1910. In substance it is as follows:

"I devise to the Merchants' Loan and Trust Company and my old friend Stephen S. Gregory, or their survivors, or such successors as may be appointed for them, in case of both of them becoming unable to act, all of my property, real, personal and mixed, to be held in trust until the decease of the last survivor of my children, to pay and discharge my just debts and obligations, and to collect and to pay over the net revenue of the property in such reasonable allowances as shall from time to time be determined by them in view of the existing circumstances; but each of the children, or their children, in case of my death, shall receive finally an equal share.

"I empower my said trustees to sell any of the property, if and as deemed by them or their survivors or successors advisable, and to reinvest and hold the proceeds upon the same trust, to make and to renew loans and secure the same by trust deed or mortgages; to lease and to build or rebuild. In short, I impart to my said trustees the same powers I myself possess, subject to effectuating the foregoing trust."

Will of Stephen Girard

Stephen Girard was born in Bordeaux, France, the son of a sea captain. He died December 26, 1831. His immense wealth was accumulated in Philadelph a, where he spent the greater part of his life.

It was during the financial panic of 1810, that Girard loaned the government of the United States five million dollars, when it could not be had elsewhere; this, it is said, exhausted his entire fortune.

Girard was also something of a farmer, and Girard College is located on what was formerly his farm; it was there that he labored with his trees and his flowers. History says that a large, shaggy dog followed him in his travels, and that each of his ships which went to sea, carried one.

By his will, he left large sums for the betterment of humanity; it is stated that up to that time, it was the largest amount ever given away by an individual philanthropist in the history of this country, if not of the world. While his gifts to charitable and other institutions in the City of Philadelphia and the State of Pennsylvania were numerous and large, he is best known by a bequest of two million dollars for the founding of Girard College; besides this sum, there was a residue of a large amount which also went to this college. This endowment fund now amounts to sixteen million dollars, and the income is over one million dollars a year.

That famous section of this famous will, with reference to clergymen, which has produced so much discussion, is set out in full below. The injunction with reference to ministers and ecclesiastics holding office or entering the premises is still at least outwardly respected.

The heirs of Girard attempted to break his will; their argument was partly based on the provision with reference to religion: the Supreme Court of the United States upheld the will, notwithstanding the contestants had the assistance of Daniel Webster.

Girard College has an attendance of over two thousand boys: the scope and plan of the Institution has been greatly enlarged, and it has met with marked success in its ability to place many of its students in permanent and often valuable commercial positions.

The section in question is as follows:

"ARTICLE XXI. Section 9. Those scholars, who shall merit it, shall remain in the College until they shall respectively arrive at between fourteen and eighteen years of age; they shall then be bound out by the Mayor, Aldermen and Citizens of Philadelphia, or under their direction, to suitable occupations, as those of agriculture, navigation, arts, mechanical trades, and manufactures, according to the capacities and acquirements of the scholars respectively, consulting, as far as prudence shall justify it, the inclinations of the several scholars, as to the occupation, art or trade, to be learned.

"In relation to the organization of the College and its appendages, I leave, necessarily, many details to the Mayor, Aldermen, and Citizens of Philadelphia, and their successors; and I do so with the more confidence, as, from the nature of my bequests, and the benefits to result from them, I trust that my fellow-citizens of Philadelphia will observe and evince especial care and anxiety in selecting members for their City Councils, and other agents.

"There are, however, some restrictions, which I consider it my duty to prescribe, and to be, amongst others, conditions on which my bequest for said College is made, and to be enjoyed, namely; *first*, I enjoin and require, that if at the close of any year, the income of the fund devoted to the purposes of the said College shall be more than sufficient for the maintenance of the Institution during that year, then the balance of the said income, after defraying such maintenance, shall be forthwith invested in good securities, thereafter to be and remain a part of the capital; but in no event, shall any part of the said capital be sold, disposed of, or pledged, to meet the current expenses of the said Institution, to which I devote the interest, income and dividends thereof, exclusively: *Secondly*, I enjoin and require that *no ecclesiastic, missionary, or minister of any sect whatsoever, shall ever hold or exercise any station or duty whatever in the said College; nor shall any such person ever be admitted for any purpose, or as a visitor, within the premises appropriated to the purposes of the said college:* — In making this restriction, I do not mean to cast any reflection upon any sect or person whatsoever; but as there is such a multitude of sects, and such a diversity of opinion amongst them, I desire to keep the tender minds of the orphans, who are to derive advantage from this bequest, free from the excitement which clashing doctrines and sectarian controversy are so apt to produce; my desire is, that all the instructors and teachers in the College, shall take pains to instil into the minds of the scholars, *the purest principles of morality*, so that, on their entrance into active life, they may *from inclination and habit*, evince *benevolence toward their fellow creatures*, and *a love of truth, sobriety, and industry*, adopting at the same time, such religious tenets as their *matured reason* may enable them to prefer. If the income, arising from that part of the said sum of two millions of dollars, remaining after the construction and furnishing of the College and out-buildings, shall, owing to the increase of the number of orphans applying for admission, or other cause, be inadequate to the construction of new buildings, or the maintenance and education of as many orphans as may apply for admission, then such further sum as may be necessary for the construction of new buildings and the maintenance and education of such further number of orphans, as can be maintained and instructed within such buildings as the said square of ground shall be adequate to, shall be taken from the final residuary fund hereinafter expressly referred to for the purpose, comprehending the income of my real estate in the city and county of Philadelphia, and the dividends of my stock in the Schuylkill Navigation Company — my design and desire being, that the benefits of said institution shall be extended to as great a number of orphans, as the limits of the said square and buildings therein can accommodate."

WILL OF JAY GOULD

Jay Gould died December 2, 1892. By his will, he transferred, as is well known, an immense fortune. After giving certain legacies to his children, relatives and friends, including one to a son for services rendered, and establishing a trust for the benefit of a grandson, he gives his residuary estate to trustees for the benefit of his children for life in equal separate trusts with gifts over to their issue as appointed by the beneficiaries, and in default thereof "in the proportions provided in and by the statutes of this State in the case of intestacy," and if no issue then "to my surviving children and to the issue of any deceased child share and share alike *per stirpes* and not *per capita.*"

The testator directs that the securities of each trust be separately invested, and that the accounts thereof shall be separately kept.

A son and daughter are appointed guardians of his minor children.

The seventh item in his will reads as follows:

"Seventh. I hereby declare and provide that if any of my children shall marry without my consent during my lifetime, or thereafter without the consent of a majority of the then executors and trustees under this will, then and in that event the share allotted to the child so marrying in and by said will and codicil, shall be reduced one-half, and the principal of the other half of the said share shall be paid, assigned, transferred or set over to such persons as under the laws of the State of New York would take the same if I had died intestate."

There is a marked similarity in many of the provisions of this will to those of the late William H. Vanderbilt.

Will of Horace Greeley

Horace Greeley died at Pleasantville, New York, November 29, 1872. His will is as follows:

"I, Horace Greeley, being nearly sixty years old and in medium health but admonished by recent illness of the uncertainty of life, do make and publish this my last will and testament superseding and revoking all of earlier date which may be found or exist.

"Item: I will and bequeath to my daughter, Ida Lillian Greeley, requesting her to share the proceeds therefrom with her sister Gabrielle Miriam Greeley all my books, copyrights and sums which may be due and owing me from publishers, at the time of my decease naming especially my 'American Conflict,' 'Recollections of a Busy Life,' 'Political Economy,' and 'What I Know of Farming,' as works wherefrom some income may accrue from copyrights after my decease.

"Item: I will and bequeath to my two daughters aforesaid all the real estate whereof I may die possessed or be entitled to, except the farm on which my brother Nathan Barnes Greeley lives, in Wayne Township, Erie County, Pennsylvania, directing that my daughter Ida Lillian aforesaid be and hereby is authorized and empowered during the minority of her sister Gabrielle Miriam to manage, let, improve, lease or sell the whole or any portion of the same as she shall judge expedient and advantageous to herself and her sister aforesaid, the same to be subject to the right of dower inhering in my wife Mary Young Greeley unless and until she shall see fit to release the same to my two daughters aforesaid.

"Item: I bequeath to my brother Nathan Barnes Greeley aforesaid and his wife Ruhanna the full and uninterrupted use for life of either of them of my farm lying in the Township of Wayne, Erie County, Pennsylvania, aforesaid. And I further bequeath to whichever of his sons the said Nathan Barnes Greeley may designate the reversion or remainder of one-half of said farm, it being my understanding and purpose that said son shall live with and take care of said Nathan Barnes and Ruhanna Greeley to the end of their several lives.

"Item: I direct that if any share or shares in the Tribune Association shall remain to me at my decease one of them shall be sold under the rules of said association to the highest bidder and the proceeds without deduction or abatement be paid over as my bequest to the Childrens Aid Society, whereof New York City is the focus of operations, to be invested or disbursed as its proper authorities shall direct. If more than one share of stock in the Tribune Association shall remain to me at my death and if my wife, Mary Young Greeley, shall survive me, I bequeath to her one-half of such remaining shares of stock in lieu of all other dower, except those reserved to her as aforesaid, and I hereby renounce and disclaim in favor of my said wife all claim on my part or on that of my heirs to the real estate once mine but now wholly hers near the Village of Chappaqua in the Township of New Castle, Westchester County, New York, as also to the two shares of Tribune stock now standing in her name and which were never mine but wholly purchased by her money, and I further renounce and disclaim in her favor all right to the stock and funds of the Northern Pacific Rail Road which I have paid for with her money and which now stands in her name on the books of the Company and I give and bequeath unto my said wife all the animals, implements, machinery, crops, products and materials which may at the time of my death exist upon or pertain to her farm and buildings in New Castle township aforesaid:

"Item: I direct that whatever stock in the Tribune Association may remain to me at the time of my death after fulfilling and satisfying the foregoing bequests be sold in accordance with the rules of said association and that from the proceeds thereof and from the proceeds of such portions of the debts due or owing to me from all persons whatever as may at anytime be collected, there be paid the following bequests in their order namely:

"1. Two thousand dollars to my sister Margaret Greeley Bush, in case she survive me, and in case she should not but her daughter Evangeline Bush shall survive me then the said sum of two thousand dollars shall be paid to her my said sister's daughter Evangeline Bush.

"2. One thousand dollars each to my sister Arminda, wife of Lovewell Greeley and Esther, wife of John F. Cleveland or to their surviving children respectively in case they or either of them shall die before I do.

"3. I give or bequeath all the residue or remainder of my property of whatever name or nature to my daughters Ida Lillian and Gabrielle Miriam Greeley and to the survivor in case but one of them shall survive me.

"I hereby appoint Samuel Sinclair, Publisher Tribune, Charles Storrs, merchant now of 73 Worth Street, New York City and

Richard C. Manning now residing in Clinton Avenue, Brooklyn or any two of them who may survive me and accept the trusts, executors of this my last will and testament.

"In witness whereof, I have hereunto set my hand and seal this ninth day of January in the year of our Lord one thousand eight hundred and seventy-one.

"Horace Greeley."

Will of Alexander Hamilton

"In the name of God, Amen. I, Alexander Hamilton, of the City of New-York, Counsellor at Law, do make this my last Will and Testament as follows:

"First. I appoint John B. Church, Nicholas Fish, and Nathaniel Pendleton, of the city aforesaid, Esquires, to be Executors and Trustees of this my Will; and I devise to them, their heirs and assigns, as joint tenants and not as tenants in common, all my estate real and personal whatsoever, and wheresoever, upon trust at their discretion to sell and dispose of the same, at such time and times, in such manner, and upon such terms, as they, the survivors and survivor, shall think fit; and out of the proceeds to pay all the debts which I shall owe at the time of my decease; in whole, if the fund be sufficient; proportionably, if it shall be insufficient; and the residue, if any there shall be, to pay and deliver to my excellent and dear wife Elizabeth Hamilton.

"Though, if it should please God to spare my life, I may look for a considerable surplus out of my present property; yet, if He should speedily call me to the eternal world, a forced sale, as is usual, may possibly render it insufficient to satisfy my debts. I pray God that something may remain for the maintenance and education of my dear wife and children. But should it on the contrary happen, that there is not enough for the payment of my debts, I entreat my dear children, if they, or any of them, should ever be able, to make up the deficiency. I, without hesitation, commit to their delicacy a wish which is dictated by my own. — Though conscious that I have too far sacrificed the interests of my family to public avocations, and on this account have the less claim to burthen my children, yet I trust in their magnanimity to appreciate as they ought, this my request. In so unfavourable an event of things, the support of their dear mother, with the most respectful and tender attention, is a duty, all the sacredness of which they will feel. Probably her own patrimonial resources will preserve her from indigence. But in all situations they are charged to bear in mind, that she has been to them the most devoted and best of mothers."

Alexander Hamilton was, perhaps, the most finished character in the history of the United States, and the value of his services to this country cannot be overestimated: after the lapse of more than a hundred years, his greatness and usefulness are still revered, and his untimely death lamented.

On June 18, 1804, Aaron Burr addressed to Hamilton, a communication calling attention to a letter published by Charles B. Cooper, wherein he said, "I could detail to you a still more despicable opinion which General Hamilton has expressed of Mr. Burr," together with a further statement that Burr was "a dangerous man and one who ought not to be trusted with the reins of government:" the lengthy and dignified answer of Hamilton was not satisfactory to Burr, and again on June 21st, he wrote, "Political opposition can never absolve gentlemen from a rigid adherence to the laws of honour and rules of decorum." Further unsatisfactory correspondence followed, with the result that the two met at seven o'clock A.M., July 11th, 1804, at Weehawken, New Jersey, opposite New York, and fought a duel; Hamilton fell at Burr's first shot, mortally wounded, dying the next day at two o'clock: on the day before the duel, Hamilton wrote Nathaniel Pendleton, who accompanied him to the field, a letter containing his motives for accepting the challenge, and his reflections on the situation, which is in part as follows:

"On my expected interview with Col. Burr, I think it proper to make some remarks explanatory of my conduct, motives, and views.

"I was certainly desirous of avoiding this interview for the most cogent reasons.

"1. My religious and moral principles are strongly opposed to the practice of duelling, and it would ever give me pain to be obliged to shed the blood of a fellow creature in a private combat forbidden by the laws.

"2. My wife and children are extremely dear to me, and my life is of the utmost importance to them, in various views.

"3. I feel a sense of obligation towards my creditors; who in case of accident to me, by the forced sale of my property, may be in some degree sufferers. I did not think myself at liberty as a man of probity, lightly to expose them to this hazard.

"4. I am conscious of no *ill will* to Col. Burr, distinct from political opposition, which, as I trust, has proceeded from pure and upright motives.

"Lastly, I shall hazard much, and can possibly gain nothing by the issue of the interview.

"But it was, as I conceive, impossible for me to avoid it. There were *intrinsic* difficulties in the thing, and *artificial* embarrassments from the manner of proceeding on the part of Col. Burr.

". . . I have resolved, if our interview is conducted in the usual manner, and it pleases God to give me the opportunity, to *reserve* and *throw away* my first fire, and I *have thoughts* even of *reserving* my second fire — and thus giving a double opportunity to Col. Burr to pause and to reflect.

. . . .

"To those who, with me, abhorring the practice of duelling, may think that I ought on no account to have added to the number of bad examples, I answer, that my *relative* situation, as well in public as private, enforcing all the considerations which constitute what men of the world denominate honour, imposed on me (as I thought) a peculiar necessity not to decline the call.

. . . .

"A. H."

Hamilton was buried on the following Saturday with every possible evidence of respect and sorrow; in the funeral procession his gray horse dressed in mourning was led by two black servants dressed in white; the streets of New York were lined with people, and doors and windows were filled, and housetops occupied, and every civic and military organization was represented. Gouverneur Morris delivered the funeral oration from a stage erected in the portico of Trinity Church to an immense concourse. When Hamilton's distracted wife and children, seven in number, were brought to his bedside, shortly before his death, he said to her, "Remember, my Eliza, you are a Christian."

General Hamilton married Elizabeth Schuyler, a daughter of General Philip Schuyler, thus allying himself with one of the most distinguished founders of New York.

Aaron Burr lived to be eighty years old. The loss of his only daughter, Theodosia Alston, at sea, left him without family ties. There is a tradition that Burr, a broken and sorrowing man, watched the sea ever afterward, hoping that the lost Theodosia might be returned to him. At the age of seventy-eight he married the second time; he and this wife separated, but were never divorced.

WILL OF EDWARD H. HARRIMAN

This will is unique in its brevity, containing only ninety-nine words, and has been criticised for its omissions: it will be seen that there is no mention of the testator's children, and that the will has but two witnesses, which is unusual where so vast an estate is disposed of and the property located in many states. It will also be noted that the testator's wife, who is made executrix, is not exempted from giving bond as such. Mr. Harriman, at the time of his death, controlled perhaps the largest corporate interests of any person in the United States, particularly those of railways. He died in September, 1909. His will is as follows:

"I, Edward H. Harriman of Arden in the State of New York, do make, publish and declare this as and for my last will and testament that is to say:

"I give, devise and bequeath all of my property real and personal of every kind and nature to my wife, Mary W. Harriman to be hers absolutely and forever and I do hereby nominate and appoint the said Mary W. Harriman to be executrix in this my will.

"In witness whereof, I have hereunto set my hand and seal this 8th day of June in the year 1903.

"EDWARD H. HARRIMAN."

WILL OF PATRICK HENRY

"There is no retreat but in submission and slavery. Our chains are already forged. Their clanking may be heard on the plains of Boston. The next gale that sweeps from the north will bring the clash of resounding arms. Our brethren are already in the field. Why stand we here idle? What is it that gentlemen wish? What would they have? Is life so dear or peace so sweet as to be purchased at the price of chains and slavery? Forbid it, Almighty God! I know not what course others may take, but as for me, give me liberty or give me death!"

Patrick Henry was born in Hanover County, Virginia, on May

29, 1736; he died at his county seat, Red Hill, in Charlotte County, Virginia, on June 6, 1799. The will of this distinguished orator and statesman is given at length; notwithstanding the conditions imposed in restraint of marriage, his widow took unto herself another spouse, Judge Edmund Winston, who was Patrick Henry's cousin.

"In The Name of God, Amen:— I, Patrick Henry, of Charlotte County, at my leisure and in my health do make this my last Will and Testament in manner following, and do write it throughout with my own hand. I, knowing my ever dear wife Dorethea to be worthy of the most full and entire confidence, I do will and devise to her the Guardianship of my children, and do direct and order that she shall not in any manner be accountable to any person for her management therein. I do give to my said wife Dorethea all my Lands at and adjoining my dwelling place called Red Hill, purchased from Fuqua, Booker, Watkins, & others, out of the tract called Watkins's Order, to hold during her life, together with twenty of my slaves, her choice of them all, and at her death the said Lands are to be equally divided in value in fee simple between two of my sons by her; and she is to name and point out the two Sons that are to take the said Lands in fee simple at her discretion. I will and direct all my Lands in my Long Island estate in Campbell County to be divided into two parts by Randolph's old road, till you come along it to the place where the new road going from the Overseer's house to Davis's mill crosses it at two white oaks and the stump of a third, from thence by a straight line a few hundreds yards to Potts's Spring at the old Quarter place, from thence as the water runs to the river which is near to the upper part where Mr. Philip Payne lives is to be added the Long Island and other Islands, to the lower part the Overseer's residence and also one hundred and fifty acres of the back land out of the upper part most convenient for both parts for Timbers to the lower. These two estates to be in fee simple to two of my other sons by my said wife, whom she is also to name and point out. I will and direct that there be raised towards paying my debts one thousand pounds by sale in fee simple, out of my following Lands, viz. — Leatherwood, Prince Edward Lands, Kentucky Lands, Seven Island Lands, and those lately purchased of Marshall Mason, Nowell, Wimbush, Massy, and Prewett, or such parts thereof as my Executors may direct, and the residue thereof I will and direct to be allotted equally in value into two parts for a provision for other two of my sons in fee simple by my said wife, which sons she shall in like manner name and point out. But if the payment of my debts is or can be accomplished without selling any of my slaves or personal estate, then I desire none of these Lands to be sold, but they are to be allotted as the provision aforesaid for two of my sons. Thus I have endeavored to provide for my six sons by my dear Dorethea; their names are Patrick, Fayette, Alexander Spotswood, Nathaniel, Edward Winston, and John. I will my slaves to be equally divided amongst my children by my present wife except my daughter Winston, who has received hers, or nearly so; but the twenty slaves given to my said wife for her life, I desire she may give as she pleases amongst her children by me. I will that my wife have power to execute Deeds for any Lands I have agreed to sell, in the most ample manner. I give to my Grandson Edmund Henry, when he arrives to the age of twenty-one years and not before, in fee simple, the thousand acres of Land where his father died, joining Perego's line, Cole's line, and the line of the land intended for my son Edward, dec'd., together with the negroes and other property on the said one thousand acres of Land. But in case the said Edmund shall die under the age of twenty-one years, and without Issue then alive, I will the said Land, Slaves, and other property to my six sons above mentioned equally in fee simple. I have heretofore provided for the children of my first marriage, but I will to my daughters, Roane and Aylett, two hundred pounds each of them as soon as my estate can conveniently pay it by cropping. In case either of my six sons, viz. — Patrick, Fayette, Alexander Spotswood, Nathaniel, Edward Winston, or John, shall die under the age of twenty-one, unmarried and without Issue then living, I will that the estate of such decedent be divided among the Survivors of them in such manner as my said wife shall direct.

"All the rest and residue of my estate, whether Lands, Slaves, personal estate, Debts and rights of every kind, I give to my ever dear and beloved wife Dorethea, the better to enable her to educate and bring up my Children by her, and in particular I desire she may at her discretion collect, accommodate, manage, and dispose of the debt due to me from the late Judge Wilson in such manner as she thinks best, without being accountable to any person, but so as that the produce, whether in Lands, Slaves, or other effects, be by her given amongst her children by me, as I do hereby direct all the said residue to be given by her after her decease. If the said debt from the said Wilson cannot be recovered, then I give the Lands I covenanted to sell to him, the said Wilson, lying in Virginia and North Carolina, to my said wife in fee simple to make the most of and apply for the benefit of her children by me as aforesaid. But in case my said wife shall marry again, in that case I revoke and make void every gift, legacy, authority, or power herein mentioned, and order, will, and direct, She, my said wife, shall have no more of my estate than she can recover by Law; nor shall she be Guardian to any of my children, or Executrix of this my Will.

"I will that my daughters, Dorethea S. Winston, M. Catharine Henry, and Sarah Butler Henry, be made equal in their negroes. In case the debt from Judge Wilson's estate be recovered, I do desire and will that five hundred dollars each be paid to my dear Daughters, Anne Roane & Elizabeth Aylett, and Martha Fontaine.

"This is all the inheritance I can give to my dear family. The religion of Christ can give them one which will make them rich indeed.

"I appoint my dear wife Dorethea, Executrix, my friends Edmund Winston, Philip Payne, and George D. Winston, Executors, of this my last Will, revoking all others. In witness whereof I have hereunto set my hand and seal this 20th November, 1798.

"P. HENRY, L. S."

"Codicil to my Will, written by myself throughout, and by me annexed and added to the said Will and made part thereof in manner following, that is to say: Whereas, since the making of my said Will, I have covenanted to sell my Lands on Leatherwood to George Hairston, including the 1000 acres intended for my Grandson Edmund Henry, and have agreed to purchase from General Henry Lee two shares of the Saura Town Lands, amounting to about 6,314 acres certain, and the debt due me from Wilson's estate is agreed to go in payment for the said purchase, whereby there will exist no necessity to sell any of my estate for payment of my debts, I do therefore give the said Saura Town Lands in fee simple equally to be divided in value to two of my sons by my dear wife Dorethea, and desire her to name the sons who are to take that estate, and it is to be in Lieu and place of the Leatherwood, Prince Edward, Kentucky, and Seven Islands, and other lands allotted for two of my sons in my said Will, so that the Red

Hill estate, Long Island estate, and the Saura Town estate will furnish seats for my six sons by my wife.

"In case any part of my Lands be evicted or lost for want of title, I will that a contribution of my other sons make good such loss in Lands of equal value.

"I give to my Daughter Fontaine five hundred dollars; to each of my Daughters, Anne Roane and Elizabeth Aylett, one thousand dollars; to my Daughter Dorethea S. Winston, one thousand dollars, as soon as my estate can conveniently raise these sums. To my Daughters, Martha Catharine and Sarah Butler, I give one thousand pounds each, and these legacies to all and each of my daughters are to be in Lieu and place of everything before intended for them, and if it is not in the power of my Executors to pay my said Daughters their legacies in money from my estate, then and in that case all my said Daughters are to take property, real or personal, at fair valuation, for their legacies respectively. And to this end I give my Lands in Kentucky, Prince Edward, at the Seven Islands, all my Lands lately purchased near Falling River and its waters, containing about 17 or 1800 acres, and all others not mentioned herein, to my Executors for the aforesaid purpose of paying Legacies and for allowing my Grandson Edmund Henry eight hundred pounds in Lieu of the Leatherwood Lands in case he shall attain the age of twenty one years or marries, but not otherwise. His Land, if he has it at all, is to be in fee simple, as also all the Lands that may be allotted in Lieu of money are to go in fee simple.

"I also will that my said Dear wife shall at her discretion dispose of three hundred pounds worth of the said last mentioned Lands to any of her children by me, and finally of whatsoever residue there may happen to be after satisfying the foregoing demands, and that she shall have in fee simple all the residue of my estate, real or personal, not disposed of for the intent and purpose of giving the same amongst her children by me. If she chooses to set free one or two of my slaves, she is to have full power to do so. In case Judge Wilson's debt is lost by General Lee not taking it in payment, whereby the contract for Saura Town Lands becomes void, this Codicil is to become of no effect, and is to be void and null, and my Executors are to compensate the two of my sons to whom my Leatherwood Lands were to go, by the Lands sold to Judge Wilson, and they are in that case to have all the Lands directed to be joined with the Leatherwood, and so much money as will make their Lotts equal in value with the Lotts of my other sons by my present wife.

"In witness whereof I have hereunto set my hand and seal this 12th day of February, 1799.

"P. Henry, L. S.

"Indorsements: The within is my Will written throughout by my own hand this 20th November, 1798.

"P. Henry.

"The Codicil also written by myself, February 12th, 1799.

"P. Henry."

Will of Oliver Wendell Holmes

Oliver Wendell Holmes died October 7, 1894. His will is as follows:

"Know all men by these presents, that, I Oliver Wendell Holmes of Boston, in the County of Suffolk and Commonwealth of Massachusetts, being of sound and disposing mind and memory, do make this my last will and testament, hereby revoking all former wills and codicils by me at any time made.

"Imprimis. I direct my executor hereinafter named to pay all my just debts and funeral expenses as soon as may be after my decease.

"Item. I give to my grandson Edward Jackson Holmes, son of my youngest child Edward Jackson Holmes, five thousand dollars.

"Item. All the rest and residue of the property, real and personal, of which I shall die seized or possessed, or to which I shall be in any way entitled or over which I shall have any power of appointment at the time of my decease, I give, devise, bequeath and appoint to my son Oliver Wendell Holmes junior, to his own use, absolutely and in fee simple.

"Item. I appoint said Oliver Wendell Holmes junior, executor of this my will and request that no surety be required on his official bond.

"In witness whereof I hereto set my hand and seal, and declare this to be my last will and testament, this first day of June, A.D., eighteen hundred and eighty nine.

"Oliver W. Holmes."

ANCIENT, CURIOUS, AND FAMOUS WILLS

WILL OF JOHNS HOPKINS

Johns Hopkins, an American financier and philanthropist, and the founder of the Hospital and University which bear his name, died in Baltimore, Maryland, December 24, 1873.

The first item in his will is as follows:

"First and principally, I commit, with humble reverence, my soul to the keeping of Almighty God."

Then follows in great detail, the provisions for the establishment of the Johns Hopkins University and the Johns Hopkins Hospital. It was directed that the Hospital should have buildings, not only for the whites, but for the sick, poor colored people, and also a building for the reception and care of colored orphans and destitute children. Both the University and the Hospital were corporations which the will declares had been already created at the instance of the testator. The hopes of the testator with reference to the success of these institutions, has been fully realized, for they are recognized throughout the country as models of their kind.

The amount given to these two institutions was approximately seven and one-half million dollars.

WILL OF STEPHEN HOPKINS

Stephen Hopkins, a passenger of the voyage of the *Mayflower* died at Plymouth on or about June 6, 1644; his will in part is as follows:

"The sixt of June 1644 I Stephen Hopkins of Plymouth in New England being weake yet in good and prfect memory blessed be God yet considering the fraile estate of all men I do ordaine and make this to be my last will and testament in manner and forme following. . . . I do bequeath by this my will to my sonn Giles Hopkins my great Bull wch is now in the hands of Mrs Warren Also I do give to Stephen Hopkins my sonn Giles his sonne twenty shillings in Mrs Warrens hands for the hire of the said Bull Also I give and bequeath to my daughter Constanc Snow the wyfe of Nicholas Snow my mare also I give unto my daughter Deborah Hopkins the brodhorned black cowe and her calf and half the Cowe called Motley Also I doe give and bequeath unto my daughter Damaris Hopkins the Cowe called Damaris heiffer and the white faced calf and half the cowe called Mottley Also I give to my daughter Ruth the Cowe called Red Cole and her calfe and a Bull at Yarmouth wch is in the keepeing of Giles Hopkins wch is an yeare and advantage old and half the curld Cowe   Also I give and bequeath to my daughter Elizabeth the Cowe called Smykins and her calf and thother half of the Curld Cowe wth Ruth and an yearelinge heiffer wthout a tayle in the keepeing of Gyles Hopkins at Yarmouth.   Also I do give and bequeath unto my foure daughters . . . all the mooveable goods the wch do belong to my house, as linnen woollen beds bed-cloathes pott kettles pewter or whatsoev^r are moveable . . . and foure silver spoones that is to say to eich of them. . . ."

The inventory shows a long list of personal property, including the bulls, cows, the "heiffer without a tayle," spoons and other household goods.

Will of Sam Houston

Sam Houston died July 25, 1863; here is his will:

"In the name of God, the Father, the Son and Holy Spirit, I, Sam Houston, of the County of Walker and State of Texas, being fully aware of the uncertainty of life, and the certainty of death, do ordain and declare this my last Will and Testament.

"First: I will that all my just debts be paid out of my personal effects, as I think them sufficient without disposing of any of the family servants.

"Second: I bequeath my entire remaining estate to my beloved wife, Margaret and our children, and I desire that they may remain with her so long as she may remain in widowhood, and should she at any time marry, I desire that my daughters should be subject to her control, so long as their minority lasts.

"Third: My will is that my sons should receive solid and useful education, and that no portion of their time may be devoted to the study of abstract science. I greatly desire that they may possess a thorough knowledge of the English language, with a good knowledge of the Latin language. I also request that they be instructed in the knowledge of the Holy Scripture, and next to these that they may be rendered thorough in a knowledge of Geography & History. I wish my sons early taught an utter contempt for novels & light reading. In all that pertains to my sons I wish particular regard paid to their morals as well as to the character and morals of those with whom they may be associated or instructed.

"Fourth: I leave to my wife, as Executrix, and to the following gentlemen as my Executors, Thomas Gibbs, Thomas Carothers,

J. Carroll Smith, and Anthony M. Branch, my much beloved friends in whom I place my entire confidence, to make such disposition of my personal and real estate as may seem to them best for the necessities and interests and welfare of my family.

"Fifth: To my dearly beloved wife, Margaret, I confide the rearing, education and moral training of our sons and daughters.

"Sixth: To my eldest son, Sam Houston, Jr., I bequeath my sword, worn in the battle of San Jacinto, never to be drawn only in defense of the constitution, the laws and liberties of his country. If any attempt should ever be made to assail one of these, I wish it to be used in its vindication.

"Seventh: It is my will that my library should be left at the disposition of my dear wife.

"Eighth: To my dearly beloved wife I bequeath my watch, and all my jewelry, subject to her disposition.

"Ninth: I hereby appoint my dearly beloved wife, Margaret, Testamentary Guardian of my children, their persons and estates during minority. But should a wise Providence, through its inscrutable decrees see fit to deprive our offspring of both parents and make them orphans indeed, it is hereby delegated to my Executors who are hereby confirmed, J. Carroll Smith, Thomas Carothers, Thomas Gibbs, and Anthony M. Branch, to make such disposition in regard to their welfare as they may think best calculated to carry out the designs as expressed in this my last Will and Testament.

"Tenth: And I direct and enjoin my Executrix and Executors that after the probate and registry of this my last Will, and return of Inventory of my estate, the County or other Court of Probate, have no further control over my Executors or Testamentary Guardian or of my estate.

"Done at Huntsville the second day of April, 1863.

"SAM HOUSTON."

WILL OF JULIA WARD HOWE

Julia Ward Howe, poet, philanthropist and advocate of abolition and of the legal and political rights of women, died October 17, 1910, at the age of ninety-one.

The "Battle Hymn of the Republic," her most famous creation, was written in 1861; inspired, it is said, by the sight of troops marching to the tune of "John Brown's Body."

Her will was filed for probate in November 1910; it is in these words:

"I, Julia Ward Howe, of Boston, in the County of Suffolk and Commonwealth of Massachusetts, widow, do make this my last will and testament.

"I give and devise to George H. Richards, of Boston aforesaid, counsellor at law, and to his heirs, all my real estate in Tumwater, Thurston County, in the State of Washington, but in trust nevertheless, for the benefit of my grandchildren, Samuel P. Hall and Alice M. Richards and their heirs, with power to sell the same or any portion or portions thereof and to invest and re-invest the proceeds of any such sales in either real estate or personal property, and in trust to pay the net income of this trust equally to my said grandchildren or their heirs, and at the end of five years from the time of my death to sell all property, both real and personal, then held in this trust and pay over the proceeds of the same equally to my said grandchildren or their heirs, unless by their joint written request they shall name a later date for the termination of this trust.

"All the rest and residue of my property, real and personal, I give, devise and bequeath to my four children, Florence M. Hall, Henry M. Howe, Laura E. Richards and Maud H. Elliott, and to the issue of any that may have deceased by right of representation.

"I appoint the said George H. Richards, executor of this my will and I request that no sureties be required on his official bond either as executor or trustee.

"In witness whereof, I, the said Julia Ward Howe, have hereunto set my hand and seal this eleventh day of November, A.D. 1897.

"JULIA WARD HOWE. (Seal)

"Signed, sealed and published by the said Julia Ward Howe, as and for her last will and testament, in the presence of us, who at her request, in her presence and in the presence of each other have hereunto subscribed our names as witnesses.

"MARGARET LIVINGSTON CHANLER
"HENRY JAQUES
"HANNAH MCRAE"

WILL OF JOHN JAMES INGALLS

John J. Ingalls died August 16, 1900. His will was dated August 24, 1889, and is as follows:

"In the Name of God, Amen.

ANCIENT, CURIOUS, AND FAMOUS WILLS

"I, John James Ingalls, of the City and County of Atchison in the State of Kansas, Gentleman, mindful of the uncertainty of life and the certainty of death, do make, publish and declare this my last Will and Testament.

"I give, bequeath and devise unto my beloved wife, Anna Louisa, all my property and estate, real, personal and mixed of every description and wherever situated, and appoint her the sole executrix hereof without bond, surety or undertaking.

"In witness whereof, I have hereunto set my hand this 24th day of August, 1889.

"JOHN J. INGALLS."

WILL OF WASHINGTON IRVING

Washington Irving died November 28, 1859.

The following is an abstract of his will, which was drawn by himself. It bears date the 3rd day of December, 1858, not quite a year before his death. He declared his general intention to be, to dispose of all his estate so that it might be, as far as possible, kept together as a maintenance for his brother Ebenezer and his daughters, who had been accustomed to reside with him, to enable them to live with the same degree of comfort and in the same respectable style they had been accustomed to under his roof.

He gives to his nephew, Pierre Munro Irving, the copyright of his "Life of Washington," with the stereotype and electrotype plates which had been executed for the same, and the plates engraved for its illustration, together with the printed copies of the work that might have been stricken off, leaving him to do with the copyright, types, etc., what he might think proper for his pecuniary benefit. He bequeaths to him, also, all his letters and unpublished manuscripts.

All the rest of his personal estate, he gives to his brother Ebenezer for his life; and, on his death, to his daughters, then surviving him and unmarried. The will then proceeds:

"*Second*. I give and devise my land and dwelling house in Westchester County, which I have called 'Sunnyside,' to my brother, Ebenezer Irving, for his life. On his death, I give the same in fee to his daughters or daughter surviving him, and unmarried; trusting they will endeavor, as I have endeavored, to make this homestead a rallying point, where the various branches of the family connection may always be sure of a cordial welcome.

"I trust, also, they will never sell nor devise this particular property out of the family — though circumstances may render it expedient or necessary for them to rent it out or lease it for a term; but it is my wish that the last survivor of those to whom I thus bequeath my estate will, in turn, bequeath it entire to some meritorious member of the family bearing the family name, so that 'Sunnyside' may continue to be, as long as possible, an *Irving homestead.*

"I give all the residue of my estate, real and personal, to accompany the devise of 'Sunnyside' to the same persons, for the like interests, and subject to the like contingencies and power.

"*Third.* I authorize my executors to make sale of, or otherwise convert into money or productive funds, all other lands and tenements I may own, wheresoever situated.

"*Last.* I appoint my brother, Ebenezer Irving, and my nephew Pierre M. Irving, executors of this my will. I revoke all other and former wills."

*   *   *   *   *   *   *

"WASHINGTON IRVING."

WILL OF ANDREW JACKSON

Andrew Jackson died June 8, 1845. Extracts from his will, together with a synopsis of its interesting provisions, are here given:

"And whereas since executing my will of the 30th of September, 1833, my estate has become greatly involved by my liabilities for the debts of my well beloved and adopted son Andrew Jackson Jnr., which makes it necessary to alter the same."

"First. I bequeath my body to the dust whence it came, and my soul to God who gave it: hoping for a happy immortality through the atoning merits of our Lord Jesus Christ, the Saviour of the World."

He desires that his body be buried by the side of his wife in the garden at the Hermitage, in the vault prepared in the garden.

He desires that all of his just debts be paid out of his personal and real estate by his Executor, including the debt of "my good friends Gen'l J. B. Planche & Co. of New Orleans, for the sum of six thousand dollars with the interest accruing thereon, loaned to me to meet the debts due by A. Jackson Jnr., for the purchase of the Plantation, from Hiram G. Runnels, lying on the East bank of the River Mississippi in the State of Mississippi. Also a debt due by me of ten thousand dollars borrowed of my friends Blair and Rives, of the City of Washington and District of Columbia, with the interest accruing thereon being applied to the payment of the land bot. of Hiram G. Runnels as aforesaid, and for the faithful payment of the aforesaid recited debts, I hereby bequeath all my real and personal estate. After those debts are fully paid &c."

After the before recited debts are fully paid, he gives to his adopted son Andrew Jackson, Junier, the tract of land "whereon I now live, known by the Hermitage, with all my negroes that I may die possessed of, with the except on hereinafter named, with all their increase, all household furniture, farming tools, stock of all kind, both on the Hermitage tract farms as well as those on the Mississippi plantation, and his heirs forever."

To his beloved granddaughter, Rachel Jackson, daughter of A. Jackson, Jr., and Sarah, his wife, he gives several negroes (conveyance theretofore deposited with wife of Andrew Jackson, Jr.), and to his beloved grandson Andrew Jackson, son of A. Jackson, Jr., he gives a negro boy named "Ned, son of Blacksmith Aaron and Hannah his wife"; to his grandson, Samuel Jackson, he gives "one negro boy Davy or George, son of Squire and his wife Gincy."

To Sarah Jackson, wife of his adopted son, Andrew Jackson, of whom he speaks in very affectionate terms, "I hereby recognize by this bequest, the gift I made her on her marriage, of the negro girl Gracy which I bought for her, . . . as her maid and seamster with her increase, and my house servant Hannah, and her two daughters, . . . to her and her heirs forever." "This gift and bequest is made for my great affection for her; as a memento of her uniform attention to me, and kindness on all occasions, and particularly when worn down with sickness, pain and debility, she has been more than a daughter to me and I hope she will never be disturbed in the enjoyment of this gift, and bequest by any one."

To his nephew, Andrew J. Donelson, he gives "the elegant sword presented to me by the State of Tennessee," with an injunction.

To his grandnephew, Andrew Jackson Coffee, "I bequeath the elegant sword presented to me by the Rifle Company of New Orleans, commanded by Capt Beal, as a memento of my regard and to bring to his recollection the gallant services of his deceased father Genl. John Coffee in the late Indian and British war under my command, and his gallant conduct in defence of New Orleans in 1814 and 1815, with this injunction, that he wield it in the protection of the rights secured to the American citizen under our glorious constitution, against all invaders whether foreign foes or intestine traitors."

To his grandson, Andrew Jackson, "the sword presented to me by the citizens of Philadelphia, with this injunction, that he will always use it in defence of the constitution of our glorious union, and the perpetuation of our republican system — remembering the motto 'draw me not without occasion nor sheath me without honor!'"

"The pistols of Genl. Lafayette which was presented by him to Genl. George Washington and by Col. Wm. Robertson presented to me, I bequeath to George Washington Lafayette as a memento of the illustrious personages thro whose hands they have passed, his *father and the father of his Country.*"

"The gold box presented to me by the Corporation of the City of New York — the large silver vase presented to me by the Ladies of Charleston, South Carolina, my native State, with the large picture representing the unfurling of the American banner, presented to me by the Citizens of South Carolina, when it was refused to be accepted by the United States Senate, I leave in trust to my son A. Jackson Jnr. with directions that should our happy Country not be blessed with peace, an event not always to be expected, he will at the close of the war or end of the conflict, present each of said articles of inestimable value, to that patriot residing in the City or State from which they were presented who shall be adjudged by his Countrymen, or the Ladies, to have been the most valient in defence of his Country and our Country's rights."

To General Robert Armstrong he bequeaths his case of pistols and sword worn by himself throughout his military career.

To his son he leaves all his walking canes, and other relics, to be distributed amongst his young relatives, namesakes — first, to his namesake, Andrew J. Donelson, son of his nephew, A. J. Donelson, first choice, and then to be distributed as his son may think proper.

"Lastly, I appoint my adopted son Andrew Jackson Jnr., my whole and sole Executor of this my last will and testament."

WILL OF JOHN JAY

The will of Mr. John Jay, who died at his residence, Bedford, Westchester County, New York, May 17, 1829, in the eighty-fourth year of his age, is as follows:

"I, John Jay, of Bedford, in the county of Westchester, and State of New York, being sensible of the importance and duty of so ordering my affairs as to be prepared for death, do make and declare my last will and testament in manner and form following, viz.: — Unto Him Who is the author and giver of all good, I tender sincere and humble thanks for His manifold and unmerited blessings, and especially for our redemption and salvation by His beloved Son. He has been pleased to bless me with excellent parents, with a virtuous wife, and with worthy children. His protection has accompanied me through many eventful years, faithfully employed in the service of my country; and His providence has not only conducted me to this tranquil situation, but also given me abundant reason to be contented and thankful. Blessed be His holy name. While my children lament my departure, let them recollect that in doing them good, I was only the agent of their Heavenly Father, and that He never withdraws His care and consolations from those who diligently seek Him.

"I would have my funeral decent, but not ostentatious. No scarfs — no rings. Instead thereof, I give two hundred dollars to any one poor deserving widow or orphan of this town, whom my children shall select."

* * * * * * *

"I appoint all my children, and the survivors or survivor of them, executors of this my last will and testament. I wish that the disposition which I have therein made of my property, may meet with their approbation, and the more so, as their conduct relative to it, has always been perfectly proper, reserved, and delicate. I cannot conclude this interesting act, without expressing the satisfaction I have constantly derived from their virtuous and amiable behavior. I thank them for having largely contributed to my happiness by their affectionate attachment and attention to me, and to each other. To the Almighty and Beneficent Father of us all, to His kind providence, guidance, and blessing, I leave and commend them."

Will of Joseph Jefferson

Joseph Jefferson, the distinguished American comedian, died in 1905, in his seventy-sixth year. Aside from his reputation as a great actor, he was a landscape painter of considerable ability. His will, executed in duplicate, is dated the 27th day of October, 1899, and is signed "Joseph Jefferson" and "J. Jefferson." To certain friends, he bequeaths the sum of twenty-three thousand dollars ($23,000), one of whom was Joseph Sefton, of Fitzroy, Melbourne, Australia.

Unto his wife, Sarah Jefferson, he gives his books, pictures, horses, carriages and other personal property in and about his residence at Buzzards Bay; he also gives her his residence and lands constituting said estate, together with one-third of his bonds, stocks, mortgages and money, as well as one-half of the proceeds of his real estate in Louisiana, and one-third of the proceeds of all other real estate.

His oil paintings, painted by himself, he directed should be equally divided among his wife and children, in the following manner: "My wife shall first choose such paintings as she prefers to an extent equalling her share thereof: then my eldest child shall make a like selection; and my other children shall then in turn make their several selections."

All the rest of his estate, real and personal, he directs shall be sold and equally divided among his children. The will concludes:

"I desire that my remains shall be deposited in such burial plot or place as shall be selected by my family, and that my funeral shall be strictly private and without show or ostentation of any kind."

A codicil written at "The Reefe," Palm Beach, Florida, December 14th, 1904, is in the following words:

"To my Wife and to my Executor:

"I, Joseph Jefferson, being sound of mind, do make and authorize this document as a codicil to my last will and testament.

"I bequeath to my faithful attendant, Carl Kettler, if in my employ at the time of my death, the sum of $1000.00.

"Also I bequeath to George McQueen if in my employ at the time of my death, the sum of $500.00.

"I bequeath to the Actors' Home $1000.00; to the actors and actresses who are inmates of said Home $500.00; to be equally divided between them.

"I bequeath to the Theatrical Woman's League $500.00.
"I bequeath to the Actors' Fund $500.00.
"To my old friend, William Winter, Sr. the sum of $500.00 and one of my pictures painted by myself.
"To my friend, Honorable Grover Cleveland, my best Kentucky reel.
"My fishing and sporting tackle to be divided between my five sons.
"To my friend, Earnest Gittings of Baltimore, one of my own paintings to be selected by my wife.

"J. JEFFERSON."

WILL OF THOMAS JEFFERSON

Thomas Jefferson, the author of the Declaration of Independence, and the third President of the United States, died on July 4, 1826, the same day that his predecessor in office, John Adams, passed away.

His will is dated the 16th day of March, 1826, and on the following day a codicil of equal length was added. Both the will and the codicil will be found attractive and entertaining, and are here fully transcribed.

"I, Thomas Jefferson, of Monticello, in Albemarle, being of sound mind and in my ordinary state of health, make my last will and testament in manner and form as follows:

"I give to my grandson Francis Eppes, son of my dear deceased daughter Mary Eppes, in fee simple, all that part of my lands at Poplar Forest lying west of the following lines, to wit: beginning at Radford's upper corner near the double branches of Bear Creek and the public road, and running thence in a straight line to the fork of my private road, near the barn; thence along that private road (as it was changed in 1817), to its crossing of the main branch of North Tomahawk Creek; and from that crossing, in a direct line over the main ridge which divides the North and South Tomahawk, to the South Tomahawk, at the confluence of two branches where the old road to the Waterlick crossed it, and from that confluence up the northermost branch, (which separate M'Daniels' and Perry's fields) to its source; and thence by the shortest line to my western boundary. And having, in a former correspondence with my deceased son-in-law, John W. Eppes, contemplated laying off for him, with remainder to my grandson

Francis, a certain portion in the southern part of my lands in Bedford and Campbell, which I afterwards found to be generally more indifferent than I had supposed, and therefore determined to change its location for the better; now to remove all doubt, if any could arise on a purpose merely voluntary and unexecuted, I hereby declare that what I have herein given to my said grandson, Francis, is instead of, and not additional to, what I had formerly contemplated. I subject all my other property to the payment of my debts in the first place. Considering the insolvent state of the affairs of my friend and son-in-law, Thomas Mann Randolph, and that what will remain of my property will be the only resource against the want in which his family would otherwise be left, it must be his wish, as it is my duty, to guard that resource against all liability for his debts, engagements or purposes whatsoever, and to preclude the rights, powers, and authorities over it, which might result to him by operation of law, and which might, independently of his will, bring it within the power of his creditors, I do hereby devise and bequeath all the residue of my property, real and personal, in possession or in action, whether held in my own right, or in that of my dear deceased wife, according to the powers vested in me by deed of settlement for that purpose, to my grandson, Thomas J. Randolph, and my friends Nicholas P. Trist and Alexander Garrett, and their heirs, during the life of my said son-in-law, Thomas M. Randolph, to be held and administered by them, in trust, for the sole and separate use and behoof of my dear daughter, Martha Randolph, and her heirs; and aware of the nice and difficult distinction of the law in these cases, I will further explain by saying, that I understand and intend the effect of these limitations to be, that the legal estate and actual occupation shall be vested in my said trustees, and held by them in base fee, determinable on the death of my said son-in-law, and the remainder during the same time be vested in my said daughter and her heirs and of course disposable by her last will, and that at the death of my said son-in-law the particular estate of the trustees shall be determined, and the remainder in legal estate, possession, and use, become vested in my said daughter and her heirs, in absolute property forever. In consequence of the variety and indescribableness of the articles of property within the house at Monticello, and the difficulty of inventorying and appraising them separately and specifically, and its inutility, I dispense with having them inventoried and appraised; and it is my will that my executors be not held to give any security for the administration of my estate. I appoint my grandson Thomas Jefferson Randolph, my sole executor during his life, and after his death, I constitute executors my friends Nicholas P. Trist and Alexander Garrett, joining to them my daughter Martha Randolph, after the death of my said son-in-law Thomas M. Randolph. Lastly, I revoke all former wills by me heretofore made; and in witness that this is my will, I have written the whole with my own hand on two pages, and have subscribed my name to each of them this sixteenth day of March, one thousand eight hundred and twenty-six.

"THOMAS JEFFERSON."

"I, Thomas Jefferson, of Monticello, in Albemarle, make and add the following codicil to my will, controlling the same so far as its provisions go:

"I recommend to my daughter Martha Randolph, the maintenance and care of my well beloved sister Anne Scott, and trust confidently that from affection to her, as well as for my sake, she will never let her want a comfort. I have made no specific provision for the comfortable maintenance of my son-in-law Thomas M. Randolph, because of the difficulty and uncertainty of devising terms which shall vest any beneficial interest in him, which the law will not transfer to the benefit of his creditors, to the destitution of my daughter and her family, and disablement of her to supply him: whereas, property placed under the exclusive control of my daughter and her independent will, as if she were a feme sole, considering the relation in which she stands both to him and his children, will be a certain resource against want for all.

"I give to my friend James Madison, of Montpelier, my gold-mounted walking staff of animal horn, as a token of the cordial and affectionate friendship which for nearly now an half century, has united us in the same principles and pursuits of what we have deemed for the greatest good of our country.

"I give to the University of Virginia my library, except such particular books only, and of the same edition, as it may already possess, when this legacy shall take effect: the rest of my said library, remaining after those given to the University shall have been taken out, I give to my two grandsons-in-law Nicholas P. Trist and Joseph Coolidge. To my grandson Thomas Jefferson

Randolph, I give my silver watch in preference of the golden one, because of its superior excellence. My papers of business going of course to him, as my executor, all others of a literary or other character I give to him as of his own property.

"I give a gold watch to each of my grandchildren, who shall not have already received one from me, to be purchased and delivered by my executors to my grandsons, at the age of twenty-one, and granddaughters at that of sixteen.

"I give to my good, affectionate, and faithful servant Burwell, his freedom, and the sum of three hundred dollars, to buy necessaries to commence his trade of glazier, or to use otherwise, as he pleases.

"I give also to my good servants John Hemings and Joe Fosset, their freedom at the end of one year after my death; and to each of them respectively, all the tools of their respective shops or callings; and it is my will that a comfortable log-house be built for each of the three servants so emancipated, on some part of my lands convenient to them with respect to the residence of their wives, and to Charlottesville and the University, where they will be mostly employed, and reasonably convenient also to the interests of the proprietor of the lands, of which houses I give the use of one, with a curtilage of an acre to each, during his life or personal occupation thereof.

"I give also to John Hemings the service of his two apprentices Madison and Eston Hemings, until their respective ages of twenty-one years, at which period respectively, I give them their freedom; and I humbly and earnestly request of the legislature of Virginia a confirmation of the bequest of freedom to these servants, with permission to remain in this State, where their families and connections are, as an additional instance of the favor, of which I have received so many other manifestations in the course of my life, and for which I now give them my last solemn, and dutiful thanks.

"In testimony that this is a codicil to my will of yesterday's date, and that it is to modify so far the provisions of that will, I have written it all with my own hand in two pages, to each of which I subscribe my name, this seventeenth day of March, one thousand eight hundred and twenty-six.

"**Thomas Jefferson.**"

ANCIENT, CURIOUS, AND FAMOUS WILLS

WILL OF ROBERT E. LEE

General Robert E. Lee died October 12, 1870. The following is a literal copy of his will, together with a schedule of his property:

"I, Robert E. Lee of the U. S. Army, do make ordain & declare this instrument to be my last will & testament revoking all others.

"1. All my debts, whatever they may be, & of which there are but few, are to be punctually, & speedily paid.

"2. To my dearly beloved wife *Mary Custis Lee* I give & bequeath the use profit & benefit of my whole Estate real & personal, for the term of her natural life, in full confidence that she will use it to the best advantage in the education & care of my children.

"3. Upon the decease of my wife it is my will & desire that my Estate be divided among my children, in such proportions to each, as their situations & necessities in life may require; and as may be designated by her; & I particularly request that my second daughter Anne Carter, who from an accident she has recd. in one of her eyes, may be more in want of aid than the rest, may if necessary be particularly provided for.

"Lastly I constitute & appoint my dearly beloved wife *Mary Custis Lee* & my eldest son *George Washington Custis Lee* (when he shall have arrived at the age of twenty one years) executrix & executor of this my last will & testament, in the construction of which I hope & trust no dispute will arise.

"In witness of which I have set my hand & seal this thirty first day of August in the year one thousand eight hundred & forty six.   "R. E. LEE."

"SCHEDULE OF PROPERTY

" 100 Shares of the Stock of the Bank of Virginia Richmond	$10,000.00
39 Shares of the Stock of the Valley of Virginia Winchester	3,900.00
$6,100. of Jas. R. & Kanawha Compy Bonds	6,100.00
$2,000. Virginia 6 per ct State Bonds	2,000.00
$2,000. Phil: Wil: & Baltimore R. R. 6 per ct loan	2,000.00
$2,000. Bonds of Kentucky 6 pr cts	2,000.00
6 per cts Bonds of the State of Ohio	5,000.00
Bond of John Lloyd & wife	3,000.00
Bonds of Workner & Rice & of Louis Engel, St. Louis, Mo:	4,500.00
1 Share of Nat: theatre, Washington City	250.00
	$38,750.00

Nancy & her children at the White House New Kent all of whom I wish liberated, so soon as it can be done to their advantage & that of others. An undivided third part of the tract of land in Floyd Va. devised to me by my mother, of which I am negotiating a sale with M. N. Burwell for $2,500. My share of property in Hardy Va belonging to the estate of my father. My share of a claim of the property leased to the Government by my father at Harpers Ferry & believed to belong to his estate. My share or ⅓ of 200 acres of land in Fairfax Co: Va:

"R. E. LEE."

WILL OF JAMES LICK

James Lick was born at Fredericksburg, Lebanon County, Pennsylvania, on August 25, 1796. He began life as an organ and piano maker, first at Hanover, Pennsylvania, and afterwards at Baltimore, Maryland. In 1820, he started business on his own account in Philadelphia, and shortly afterward emigrated to Buenos Ayres, where for ten years he successfully prosecuted his trade; subsequently, he moved to Valparaiso and later to California, where he arrived with a moderate fortune in 1847. He spent his remaining days in California, dying there October 1, 1876, leaving an estate valued at about $4,000,000. He is said to have been of an unlovable, eccentric, solitary and avaricious character. Had it not been for his last will and testament, he would have died "unwept, unhonored, and unsung." This one act of his life was a contradiction of the whole. By a trust deed, which was to be fully effective at his death, after bequeathing a number of small legacies to friends and relatives, and reserving for his own use $25,000 per year during his life, he provided for the expenditure of $700,000 for the construction and equipment of an astronomical observatory for the University of California; $25,000 was bequeathed to the San Francisco Protestant Asylum; $10,000 to the California Society for the Prevention of Cruelty to Animals: he also set aside an amount equal to $20,000 for monuments to be erected to the memory of his father, mother, grandfather and sister; $100,000 for the founding of the Old Ladies' Home of San Francisco; $150,000 for the erection and maintenance of free public baths in San Francisco; $60,000 for the erection of a bronze monument in Golden Gate Park, San Francisco, "to the memory of Francis Scott Key, author of the song, 'The Star-Spangled Banner;'" $100,000 for a group of bronze statuary representing in three periods the history of California; $540,000 for the founding and erection of a California School of Mechanical Arts: the residue of his estate, he directed should be equally divided between the California Academy of Sciences and the Society of California Pioneers.

The observatory constitutes the astronomical department of the University of California, and was the most cherished of all Mr. Lick's schemes of public benefaction; it is claimed that he had nursed the idea for many years before he began to put it into practical shape; he directed that the telescope should be superior and more powerful than any yet made, and it was such at the time of its erection; it is now the second largest refracting telescope in the world, being surpassed only by that of the Yerkes Observatory of the University of Chicago, located at Williams Bay, Wisconsin. The situation on Mount Hamilton is particularly advantageous, giving, as it does, an unobstructed view for a radius of one hundred miles, and an opportunity for observation during the greater part of the year, — clear nights occurring regularly for six or seven months out of the year. In its construction, the wishes and hopes of the testator were fully carried out, for, up to that time, no such instrument had ever been cast or attempted.

WILL OF HENRY WADSWORTH LONGFELLOW

Longfellow, probably the most popular of American poets, died March 24, 1882.

Certain words were erased in his will, as indicated by the dashes; the instrument follows:

"The last will and testament of Henry Wadsworth Longfellow of Cambridge, in the County of Middlesex and State of Massachusetts, gentleman.

"I devise to my sister Mrs. Anna L. Pierce the sum of Five hundred dollars annually, during her life; and I direct my Executor hereinafter named, to retain in his hands an amount of property sufficient to yield the above sum in each and every year; the principal to be finally distributed among my heirs at law, as hereinafter provided.

"I also give the following sums as legacies to and among my relatives and friends.

"Five ———— to my brother Samuel Longfellow. ———— the

children of my brother Stephen Longfellow. Five Thousand dollars to my brother Alexander Wadsworth Longfellow. ——— the children of George W. Greene of East Greenwich, Rhode Island.

"The residue of my property I give to my children, in the same manner, as the same would have descended to them by the statutes of distribution in this Commonwealth, had I died intestate.

"I appoint my friend Richard H. Dana, Sr., Esquire of Cambridge, Executor of this my last will and testament.

"In witness whereof I have hereto set my hand and seal this twenty fifth day of May in the year eighteen hundred and sixty eight.

"HENRY W. LONGFELLOW."

WILL OF WILLIAM MCKINLEY

William McKinley died at Buffalo, New York, September 14, 1901. His will is as follows:

"EXECUTIVE MANSION, WASHINGTON.

"I publish the following as my latest will and testament, hereby revoking all former wills.

"To my beloved wife Ida S. McKinley I bequeathe all of my real estate wherever situate, and the income of any personal property of which I may be possessed at death, and during her natural life.

"I make the following charge upon all of my property both real and personal. To pay my Mother during her life One thousand dollars a year, and at her death said sum to be paid to my sister Helen McKinley.

"If the income from property be insufficient to keep my wife in great comfort, & pay the anuity above provided, then I direct that such of my property be sold so as to make a sum adequate for both purposes. Whatever property remains at the death of my wife I give to my brothers & sisters share & share alike. My chief concern is that my wife from my estate shall have all she requires for her comfort & pleasure, & that my Mother shall be provided with whatever money she requires, to make her old age comfortable and happy.

"Witness my hand and seal this 22ond day of October 1897, to my last will and testament made at the City of Washington Dist. of Columbia.

"WILLIAM MCKINLEY."

WILL OF DOLLY P. MADISON

The will of Dolly P. Madison, Washington's first social queen, wife of President James Madison, is as follows:

"In the name of God, Amen.

"I, Dolly P. Madison, widow of the late James Madison of Virginia, being of sound & disposing mind and memory but feeble in body having in view the uncertainty of life & the rapid approach of death do make publish and declare the following to be my last will and testament: That is to say I hereby give and bequeath to my dear son John Payne Todd the sum of ten thousand dollars being the one half of the sum appropriated by the Congress of the United States for the purchase of my husbands papers, which sum stands invested in the names of James Buchanan, John G. Mason & Richard Smith as trustees:

"Secondly I give and bequeath to my adopted daughter Annie Payne ten thousand dollars, the remaining half of the said sum of twenty thousand dollars, appropriated as aforesaid by Congress and standing in the names of said trustees, for her lifetime; hereby directing the said sum of ten thousand dollars to remain in the names of the said trustees for the use of my said adopted daughter for her life and that they the said trustees pay the interest as it becomes due on the same, to her, during her life.

"And I further will & devise that should my said son John Payne Todd survive my said daughter that upon her death the sum so devised to her shall be paid over to him & his executors; but in the event of my said adopted daughter Annie Payne, surviving the said John Payne Todd that the sum above devised to her for life shall be held by the said trustees for her & her executors forever free from all condition; leaving all the rest and residue of my property to be administered and distributed according to law.

"D. P. MADISON."

WILL OF JAMES MADISON

Ex-President James Madison, fourth President of the United States, died on June 28, 1836. By his will, he devises unto his wife, during her life, the tract of land whereon he lived; provided that within three years after his death, she would pay the sum of Nine Thousand Dollars for certain lands, but in the event she should not pay said sum, then the land should be sold for cash and divided as afterwards directed in the will.

Unto his wife, he devises his grist-mill with the land attached thereto, for her use during her life, to be sold at her death, and the purchase money to be divided between his nephews and nieces.

Unto his wife, he devises his house and lots in the city of Washington. He likewise gives unto his wife, the negroes owned by him, with the request, however, that none of them should be sold without their consent, unless for misbehavior; except that infant children might be sold with their parents, who would consent for them.

All his personal estate of every description, ornamental, as well as useful, except as otherwise bequeathed, is given to his wife, together with all manuscript papers, with the statement that the testator has entire confidence in her discreet and proper use of them.

He suggests that the report made by him of the Convention at Philadelphia in 1787, would be particularly gratifying to the people of the United States and to all who take an interest in the progress of political science and the cause of true liberty. This report he desires to be published under the authority of his wife and by her direction; the proceeds to be paid out as follows: Two Thousand Dollars to Mr. Gurley, Secretary of the Colonization Society; Fifteen Hundred Dollars to the University of Virginia; One Thousand Dollars to the College of Nassau Hall at Princeton, New Jersey; and One Thousand Dollars to the College of Uniontown, Pennsylvania, for the benefit of their respective libraries. This fund is also to embrace a trust created for the education of the sons of two deceased nephews, Robert S. Madison and Ambrose Madison.

Unto the University of Virginia, the testator gives all that portion of his library which is not possessed by the University and which the board of visitors might deem worthy of a place therein, reserving, however, to his wife, the right to select such books and pamphlets as she should choose, not exceeding three hundred volumes.

To his brother-in-law, John C. Payne, he devises two hundred and forty acres of land on which the said John C. Payne was living.

Unto his stepson, John Payne Todd, he gives the case of medals presented by George W. Erving, and the walking staff made from a timber of the frigate, *Constitution*, which was presented to the testator by Commodore Elliot, her commander.

His mounted walking staff, bequeathed to the testator by Thomas Jefferson, he directs shall be delivered to Thomas J. Randolph.

There is a codicil to this will, wherein the testator directs that the proceeds of the sale of the grist-mill, upon the death of his wife, shall be paid to the American Colonization Society. The codicil is written with the hand of the testator.

WILL OF CHIEF JUSTICE MARSHALL

The will of the great expounder of the Constitution of the United States is on file in Richmond, Virginia. Included in its provisions is the forest home of Lord Fairfax, Greenway Court, that George Washington surveyed, and where he was frequently a guest. The Chief Justice bought a portion of this land, and received the rest as a fee for arranging the disputed questions between the State of Virginia and the heirs of Lord Fairfax.

The will is dated April 9, 1832, and has five codicils, the last written a short time before his death. The will begins:

"I, John Marshall, do make this my last will and testament entirely in my own handwriting this ninth day of April, 1832. I owe nothing on my own account."

He mentions a suit for some property he had purchased, and some paper he was on, as surety for a friend. The suit mentioned in the will was one that was not settled until forty years after his decease, and his heirs were so numerous at that time that each received only eleven dollars out of a considerable sum.

The estate is divided equally between an only daughter and five sons, the wife having predeceased him. The share of the daughter is left in trust, and the testator states that common prudence dictates that a daughter should be protected from distress whatever casualties might happen.

His great affection for his wife is evidenced throughout the instrument. In carrying out some of her wishes, he spoke of her as one "whose sainted spirit has fled from the sufferings inflicted on her in this life." He also requests his daughter to remember that the departed wife "was the most affectionate of mothers." Accompanying the will was a beautiful eulogy to his wife, which he had written on the first anniversary of her death.

To each of his grandsons named John he gave one thousand acres of land.

The will concludes with the statement that, having prior to that time appointed his sons and son-in-law executors, but fearing so many executors would produce confusion in the management of the estate, he selected for this duty only one, namely, James Keith Marshall, directing that no surety be required of him as such, and allowing him a thousand dollars for his care and pains.

The favorite servant Robin it was directed should be emancipated, and if he desired to go to Liberia, he was to have a hundred dollars for that purpose. If he did not go, he was to receive fifty dollars. If under the law he could not be consistently emancipated, then he was to choose his own master among the sons, or, if he preferred, the daughter of the testator.

Will of James Monroe

James Monroe died July 4, 1831. His will, dated the sixteenth day of May, 1831, is in part as follows:

"Having given my estate called Ashfield to my daughter Elizabeth, which estate cost me about six thousand dollars, it is my will and intention to pay my daughter Maria that sum, to put them on an equality in the first instance; and then divide my property remaining after paying my just debts equally between them, my said daughters; with respect to the works in which I am engaged and leave behind, I commit the care and publication of them to my son in law Samuel L. Gouvernieur, giving to him one third of the profits arising therefrom for his trouble in preparing them for publication, one third to my daughter Maria and one third to my daughter Elizabeth.

"I appoint and constitute my son in law Samuel L. Gouvernieur my sole and exclusive executor of this my last will and testament, hereby revoking all others, giving him full powers to carry it into effect. I recommend my daughter E. K. Hay to the fraternal care and protection of my son in law Samuel L. Gouvernieur.

"James Monroe."

A codicil to the will is as follows:

"My very infirm and weak state of health, having rendered it altogether impossible for me to manage my own concerns in any one circumstance, I have committed them to Mr. Gouvernieur, in whose integrity I have perfect confidence. This has been extended to the grant lately made me by Congress, which I have authorized him, to enter and dispose of, in his own name, well knowing that he will apply it in that way, with more advantage than if entered in mine — I mention this, as a particular & interesting example, with which I wish my family, as well as he and myself to be acquainted. The whole will be under the operation after my departure of my present testament. He will, of course, pay particular attention to my other debts, as well as to that which I owe to himself, and I further request Captain James Monroe & William M. Price, to adjust and settle my account between Mr. Gouvernieur & myself — this request having been made at his suggestion. Signed sealed published and declared in the presence of ——— this seventeenth day of June in the year of our Lord one thousand eight hundred and thirty one.

"JAMES MONROE."

WILL OF GOUVERNEUR MORRIS

Gouverneur Morris, the celebrated orator and statesman of New York, died in 1816. He had great affection for his wife, whom he married late in life. This lady was Miss Ann Randolph, a cousin of John Randolph of Roanoke, and was much younger than himself; their married life was one of great happiness. He bequeathed to her a very handsome income and then provided that in case she remarried the income should be doubled. It must be noted that such cases are rare.

It was Gouverneur Morris who delivered funeral orations on Washington, Hamilton and Clinton, and these addresses are masterpieces in composition and literary finish.

WILL OF GEORGE PEABODY

George Peabody died in London, November 4, 1869. He was born in the parish of Danvers, Massachusetts, in 1795: twice during the War of 1812 he was a volunteer in defence of the United States.

He established the house of Peabody & Company in London, and died there, but ever maintained the liveliest interest in his native land; he remained unmarried; during his lifetime, he gave away nearly ten millions of dollars, largely for the betterment of society; the objects of his bounty are too well known to be stated;

the most influential during his life being three millions for the promotion of education in the Southern States, and three millions to erect model tenements for the poor of London.

When he died, the Queen attended his funeral in person, accompanied by the Royal Guard, and ordered that his body be placed in Westminster Abbey; Gladstone was one of his pall-bearers; by his will, however, he had directed that his body should rest in Harmony Grove in his native village, by the side of his father and mother and in a spot known to his boyish feet. The body was removed from the Abbey and placed on board the British man-of-war, *Monarch*, in the presence of the Prime Minister, the Secretary of Foreign Affairs and many distinguished citizens; the *Monarch* was convoyed to America by a French and an American man-of-war.

The Rev. Newman Hall said, in his funeral oration: "George Peabody waged a war against want and woe. He created homes — he never desolated one. He sided with the friendless, the houseless, and his life was guided by a law of love which none could ever wish to repeal. His was the task of cementing the hearts of Briton and American, pointing both to their duty to God and to Humankind."

The philanthropy of Peabody was not in secret, or posthumous; he did not clutch his treasures until death should release the grasp; he parted with his millions in his lifetime. Mr. Moody, the Evangelist, relates this incident:

"I was a guest of John Garrett once, and he told me that his father used to entertain George Peabody and Johns Hopkins. Peabody went to England, and Hopkins stayed in Baltimore. They both became immensely wealthy; Garrett tried to get Hopkins to make his will, but he wouldn't. Finally, Garrett invited both to dinner and afterward asked Peabody which he enjoyed most, the making of money or giving it away. Hopkins cocked up his ears, and then Peabody told him that he had a struggle at first, and it lasted until he went into his model London houses, and saw the little children so happy. 'Then,' said Peabody, 'I began to find out it was pleasanter to give money away than it was to make it.' Forty-eight hours later Hopkins was making out his will, founding the University and Hospital which bear his name."

WILL OF JAMES K. POLK

Mr. Polk had held distinguished positions in the State of Tennessee, but he was in no sense a national figure at the time of his nomination by the Democratic party. His will was written with his own hand at the Executive Mansion in Washington, at a time when he was President of the United States; he was a lawyer of recognized ability, and his will was witnessed by one who had been his law partner, but who was then a senator of the United States. It was evidently the result of much careful deliberation on his part. He died at Nashville on June 15, 1849, comparatively a young man, not long after quitting the office of President of the United States. His widow continued to reside on the Polk place in the City of Nashville, and she survived him some forty years. This venerable lady became one of the most unique social characters in America. An annual pension of five thousand dollars voted by Congress, maintained her in a position of ease and comfort, if not of retired elegance. The legislature of Tennessee, at every one of its sessions, adjourned and paid a ceremonial visit to her at her residence.

The life estate in the home place, which was devised to her by the will of her husband, terminated at her death, some years ago.

President Polk had seven brothers and sisters now dead, but all of whom left numerous children. Many of them joined together in a chancery suit to set aside his will on the ground that it was void as being contrary to the provision of the constitution of the State of Tennessee against perpetuities. It has been suggested that the meanness of these persons was extreme, as the estate was not large, and their action served to upset Mr. Polk's attempt to perpetuate his memory. The court did set aside the will.

The heirs claimed that the State of Tennessee had no power to accept the trust; that the trust was too vague and uncertain; that it created a perpetuity; that it established a house of nobility, and secured through the instrumentality of the State, a succession to persons related in blood, privileges and honors inconsistent with the laws of the State. The State of Tennessee affirmed that the main object of the testator was to set aside a small lot of land for a tomb for himself and his wife, and that the other matters devised were but incidents.

It was the desire of Polk that his homestead should never pass into the hands of strangers, and also that the most worthy of his name and blood might occupy it from generation to generation. The will also provided that the tomb should be kept in repair forever by the tenant, as a small return for the privilege of being permitted to occupy the home.

Will of George M. Pullman

George M. Pullman, of Pullman Palace Car fame, died October 19, 1897. The will opens with the statement that his wife is not appointed executrix or trustee, because the testator wishes to relieve her of the labors, cares and responsibilities of these positions. Certain friends are appointed executors of the will.

He directs his executors to set aside certain securities of great value, which he gives to a trustee, and directs the income therefrom to be paid to his wife during her life, and upon her death, the principal becomes a part of the residuary estate. A similar provision is made for his daughters. Upon the death of the daughters, however, leaving issue, the property held in trust shall become absolutely the property of such issue in equal shares. Upon the death of either daughter, leaving no issue, but leaving a husband, one-half of the property then held in trust for such daughter shall become absolutely the property of such husband, and the other half shall pass into the residuary estate, as shall all property so held in trust for either daughter dying without having issue or husband.

The eighth item of the will reads as follows:

"Inasmuch as neither of my sons has developed such a sense of responsibility as in my judgment is requisite for the wise use of large properties and considerable sums of money, I am painfully compelled, as I have explicitly stated to them, to limit my testamentary provisions for their benefit to trusts producing only such income as I deem reasonable for their support." Accordingly he established trusts for their benefit sufficient in the judgment of his executors to yield a fixed income for each with capital over to their issue.

Out of the remainder of his estate, after satisfying the provisions mentioned, the testator provides for his brothers and sisters by pecuniary legacies or trust provisions. In like manner, he also provides for other relatives, friends and employees, including household servants. A number of charitable corporations are also given legacies.

To a daughter, he gives an island in the St. Lawrence River, one of "The Thousand Islands," on which the testator had erected an edifice known as "Castle Rest," which was intended for a summer home for his mother, and which was used by her as such until the time of her death. This island and the castle, with all its appurtenances, furniture and pictures, is given to the daughter, as stated. The will then recites:

"It is my special wish that my said daughter shall each year keep open said island and Castle Rest from not later than the 26th day of July, which was my father's birthday, until after the 14th day of August, which was my mother's birthday, for the accommodation and enjoyment of all the descendants of my parents who may wish to visit and remain at said Castle Rest for the period during which it is so opened, or for any shorter time within said period."

The power is given the daughter to dispose of this property by her last will and testament, and if this right is not exercised, the property is to pass to her issue in equal shares.

Full power is given the executors to sell or dispose of the estate at their discretion. He directs that if any residue of the estate remain after the devises, trusts and legacies specifically set forth, have been satisfied, that such excess be divided into two equal shares and held as a trust fund for his daughters.

WILL OF JOHN RANDOLPH

John Randolph — of Roanoke, as he styled himself — was born at Cawsons, near the mouth of the Appomattox River, on the 3rd of June, 1773. He died of consumption at Philadelphia on the 24th of June, 1833, at the age of sixty years.

He was one of the most remarkable characters that this country has ever produced. As is well known, he was noted both for his brilliancy and his eccentricity; he was repeatedly elected to Congress, served a short time as Minister to Russia, and was also a United States senator.

After his death, it was ascertained that he had left several wills: one was written in 1819; another, without date, though written in 1821, had four codicils, and still another was dated the first day of January, 1832. The first will was not admitted to probate; the last one was set aside, because he was not considered of sound mind at the time he wrote it. The will of 1821, however, after a long contest, was finally upheld; by this instrument, he freed over three hundred slaves. This will and the four codicils are here given literally.

"In the name of God, Amen.

"I, John Randolph, of Roanoke, do ordain this my last will and testament, hereby revoking all other wills whatsoever.

"1. I give and bequeath all my slaves their freedom, heartily regretting that I have ever been the owner of one.

"2. I give to my ex'or a sum not exceeding eight thousand dollars, or so much thereof as may be necessary to transport and settle said slaves to and in some other State or territory of the U.S., giving to all above the age of forty not less than ten acres of land each.

"To my old and faithful servants, Essex and his wife Hetty, who, I trust, may be suffered to remain in the State, I give and bequeath three-and-a-half barrels of corn, two hundred weight of pork, a pair of strong shoes, a suit of clothes, and a blanket each, to be paid them annually; also, an annual hat to Essex, and ten pounds of coffee and twenty of brown sugar.

"To my woman servant Nancy, the like allowance as to her mother. To Juba (alias Jupiter) the same; to Queen the same; to Johnny, my body servant, the same, during their respective lives.

"I confirm to my brother, Beverly, the slaves I gave him, and for which I have a reconveyance.

"I bequeath to John Randolph Clay four hundred dollars annually to complete his education, until he shall have arrived at the age of twenty-four years, earnestly exhorting him never to eat the bread of idleness or dependence.

"I bequeath to my namesake, John Randolph Bryan, my gold watch, chain and seals, and the choice of my horses.

"I bequeath to his brother, Thomas, the choice of two of my horses.

"To William Leigh, of Halifax, I bequeath to him and his heirs forever all the land on which I live, lying between the Owen's ferry road and Carrington's, Cooke's, Lipscomb's and Morton's lines. Also, the books, plate, linen, household and kitchen furniture, liquors, stock, tools, and everything as it now stands, hereby appointing him my sole executor. And I do desire that he may not be required to give security, or to make any inventory of anything here; that is, at my mansion-house or the middle-quarter."

[Cut out in the original.]

"B. Dudley, all the interest I have under the will of Mrs. Martha Corran.

"My interest, under the will of Mrs. Judith Randolph, I desire my executor to sell if he shall see fit, but not otherwise.

"The land above the Owen's ferry road and the lower quarter, and the land I bought of the Reads, to be sold at my said executor's discretion, and whatever m[cut out in the original]y debts I give and bequeath to Francis Scott Key and the Rev. Wm. Meade, to be disposed of towards bettering the condition of my manumitted slaves.

"I have not included my mother's descendants in my will, because her husband, besides the whole profits of my father's estate during the minority of my brother and myself, has contrived to get to himself the slaves given by my grandfather Bland, as her marriage portion when my father married her, which slaves were inventoried at my father's death as part of his estate, and were as much his as any that he had. One-half of them, now scattered from Maryland to Mississippi, were entitled to freedom at my brother Richard's death, as the other would have been at mine.

"Witness my hand and seal."

The name [cut out in the original]. (SEAL.)

"In the presence of
   "RICHARD RANDOLPH, JR."

"Codicil to this my will, made the 5th day of December, 1821. I revoke the bequest to T. B. Dudley, and bequeath the same to my executor, to whom also I give in fee simple all my lots and houses in Farmville, and every other species of property whatever that I die possessed of, saving the aforesaid specifications in my will."

[The name cut out of the original.]

" Amelia County.

"The reason of the above revocation I have communicated to Wm. J. Barksdale, Esq."

The codicil of 1826.

"In the name of God, Amen. I, John Randolph, of Roanoke, being of sound mind and memory, but of infirm health, do ordain this codicil to my last will and testament, now in the possession of Wm. Leigh, Esquire, of Halifax county, Virginia, executor thereof, which said appointment I do hereby confirm, with all the bequests made to him therein, and bequests to or for the benefit of all, each and every of my slaves, whether by name or otherwise, and all bequests to him and them which may be contained in my codicil to my last will. I make the same provision for my body servant John that I made in my will for his father Essex, and the same provision for the said John's wife Betsy that I made for Hetty, the wife of Essex aforesaid, and similar provision for my man servant Juba, and his wife Celia, and the same for mulatto Nancy at the Lower Quarter, Archer's wife. And I humbly request the General Assembly (the only request that I ever preferred to them) to let the above named, and such other of my old and faithful slaves as desire it, to remain in Virginia, recommending them, each and all, to the care of my said ex'or, who I know is too wise, just and humane, to send them to Liberia, or any other place in Africa, or the West Indies.

"I revoke all and every bequest in my said will, or in any former codicil thereto (except as aforesaid, to my executor Wm. Leigh, and my slaves, whether by name or otherwise), of every description whatsoever, whether of my own proper estate or in expectancy or reversion from the Bland and Bizaree estate, or from any other contingency or source whatsoever. These reversions or remainders, or executor's devises, or whatsoever the law chooses to call them, I bequeath to my said executor, as a fund to be used at his discretion for the benefit of my slaves aforesaid, the surplus, if any, to be his own.

"I also give and bequeath to the said Wm. Leigh, my executor, the land that I bought of Pleasant Lipscomb's estate, to him and his heirs forever.

"I also give and bequeath to my said executor and his heirs forever the lot of fifty-three acres of land lying at the deep gut on Staunton river, in Halifax county, that I bought of Wm. Sims Daniel, and I request my said executor not to sell or lease the same, but to work it in three shifts, and to enable him to do so, I give and bequeath to him the lot of one hundred and seventy-five acres of land in Halifax county, which I also bought of Wm. Sims Daniel, to have and to hold during his natural life, and at his decease to that one of his children to whom he shall bequeath the aforesaid lot of fifty-three acres at the deep gut.

"I give and bequeath to my friend, Thomas H. Benton, all that part of the tract of land that I bought of Jonathan Read's heirs, that lies on the south-eastern side of Little Roanoke, containing about six hundred acres, as a mark of my regard to one whose friendship toward me was not expressed merely in words. I also give him my large pistols, made by Woydon & Burton.

"To my friend, Doctor John Brokenbough, I leave all my plate made by Rundle, Bridge & Rundle, viz. : 1 tea pot, one coffee pot, 1 sugar dish and tongs, two tureens, 4 sauce dishes. All the rest and residue of my plate, furniture of every sort, plantation utensils, &c., I give to my said executor, Wm. Leigh, and all my books, maps, charts, pictures, prints, and &c., except three folio manuscript volumes, bound in parchment, which I bequeath to the master and fellows (and their successors) of Trinity College, Cambridge, Old England, the first college of the first University of the world.

"To my friend Wm. J. Barksdale, of Haw Branch, Esquire, I bequeath my new English saddle and bridle, my silver spurs, my new English boots, and shoes, two pair each, my gold watch made by Baiwese, with the chain and seals, except the oldest seal with the Randolph arms and motto *nil admirari*, which I leave to R. Kidder Randolph, of Rhode Island.

"I also leave to the said W. J. Barksdale the choice of any of my mares or fillies.

"I leave to Edmond Irby, of Nottoway, the next choice of my mares or fillies, and any one of my horses or colts, to be selected by himself; also, my double barrel gun.

"To Peyton Randolph, of Buck river, Prince Edward, I leave my small cockney gun by Mortimer.

"All the rest and residue of my estate, real or personal, I leave to my executor, Wm. Leigh, hereby directing that no inventory or appraisement be made of my estate, and that no security shall be required of my said executor for the faithful discharge of the trust reposed in him — his own character being the best security, and where that is wanting, all other is unavailing.

"In witness whereof I have hereunto set my hand and affixed my seal (the following interlineation and expungings being first made; in the second paragraph the word 'Essex' interlined; in the third paragraph the word 'former' interlined, and the word 'or' expunged; and in the 7th paragraph the words 'and tongs' interlined) this thirty-first day of January, one thousand eight hundred and twenty-six (the whole of this codicil being written in my own hand).

       "JOHN RANDOLPH, of Roanoke, (SEAL).

"In presence of
 " M. ALEXANDER,
 " NATH. MACON.

"MEMORANDUM. — The folio volumes of Ms. bound in parchment, containing the records, &c., of the old London company."
The Codicil of 1828.

"Being in great extremity, but in my perfect senses, I write this codicil to my will in the possession of my friend Wm. Leigh, of Halifax county, Esquire, to declare that will is my sole last will and testament, and that if any other be found of subsequent date whether will or codicil, I do hereby revoke the same.

"Witness my hand and seal.

"JOHN RANDOLPH, of Roanoke, (SEAL.)
"May 6, 1828.
"Witness,
"EDMUND MORGAN,
"JO. M. DANIEL,
"ROBERT CARRINGTON.

"N.B. — When I was about to embark for Europe, in 1822, I did write a codicil on board the steamboat that was carrying me to the packet ship *Amity*, which codicil by my direction, Mr. Leigh destroyed.

"Since writing the above, it has occurred to me that the will referred to, as being in Mr. Leigh's possession, makes no disposition of the land that I purchased of Walter Coles and Letty his wife; also the land I bought of . . . Daniel, consisting of two small tracts in Halifax; also, of the land purchased of Pleasant Lipscomb's heirs. Now this writing witnesseth, that I give and bequeath the whole of the above recited lands, purchased since the date of my will aforesaid, to William Leigh, Esquire, my faithful friend, who has given me aid and comfort, not with words only, but by deeds.

"I also give and bequeath to him and his heirs forever, not each and every of the aforesaid tracts of land, but all the property of every description and kind whatsoever that I may have acquired since the date of that will aforesaid.

"Witness my hand and seal this same sixth day of May, 1828.

"JOHN RANDOLPH, of Roanoke, (SEAL.)
"EDMUND MORGAN,
"JO. M. DANIEL,
"ROBT. CARRINGTON.

"In the will above recited, I give to my said ex'or, Wm. Leigh, the refusal of the land above Owen's (now Clark's) ferry road, at a price that I then thought very moderate, but which a change in the times has rendered too high to answer my friendly intentions towards my said executor in giving him that refusal. I do, therefore, so far, but so far only, modify my said will as to reduce that price 50 per cent.; in other words, one-half, at which he may take all the land above the ferry road that I inherited from my father, all that I bought of the late John Daniel, deceased, and of Tom Beaseley, Charles Beaseley, and others of that name and family, this last being the land that Gabriel Beaseley used to have in possession, and whereon Beverly Tucker lived, and which I hold by deed from him and his wife, of record in Charlotte county court.

"Witness my hand and seal —— day and year aforesaid.
"JOHN RANDOLPH, of Roanoke, (SEAL.)
(The words 'but so far only,' and the word 'from' in the preceding page, first interlined.)
"Witness,
"EDMUND MORGAN,
"Jo. M. DANIEL,
"ROBT. CARRINGTON."

"As lawyers and courts of law are extremely addicted to making wills for dead men, which they never made when living, it is my will and desire that no person who shall set aside, or attempt to set aside, the will above referred to, shall ever inherit, possess, or enjoy any part of my estate, real or personal.
"JOHN RANDOLPH, of Roanoke, (SEAL.)
"Teste,
"ROBT. CARRINGTON,
"EDMUND MORGAN,
"Jo. M. DANIEL."
Codicil of 1831.

"On the eve of embarking for the U.S., considering my very feeble health, to say nothing of the dangers of the seas, I add this codicil to my last will and testament and the codicils thereto, affirming them all, except so far as they may be inconsistent with the following disposition of my estate:

"1. It is my will and desire that my dear niece, Elizabeth Tucker Bryan, shall have my lower quarter, with the lands purchased of Coles and wife and of Allen Gilliam's estate, with the mill; and I do hereby bequeath the same to her and her heirs forever.

"2. To my brother, Henry St. George Tucker, I give and

bequeath all my Bushy Forrest estate, on both sides of Little Roanoke, bought of the Reads, and all my interest in the estate of Mrs. Martha Corran, and my lots and houses in Farmville.

"3. I have upwards of two thousand pounds sterling in the hands of Barring Brothers & Co., of London, and upwards of one thousand pounds of like money in the hands of Gowane Marx; this money I leave to my ex'r, Wm. Leigh, as a fund for carrying into execution my will respecting my slaves. And in addition to the provision which I have made for my faithful servant John, sometimes called John White, I charge my whole estate with an annuity to him during his life of fifty dollars; and, as the only favor that I ever asked of any government, I do entreat the Assembly of Virginia to permit the said John and his family to remain in Virginia; and I do earnestly recommend him and them to my executor aforesaid and to my dear brother and niece aforesaid.

"4. My plate and library I leave to my dear niece, E. T. Bryan.

"Witness my hand, in Warwick street, Charing Cross, London, this twenty-ninth day of August, one thousand eight hundred and thirty-two, to which I have also appended my seal.

"JOHN RANDOLPH, of Roanoke, (L. S.)"

[Endorsement on the envelope,]

" J. R., of R.

In case of accident, to be sent to the U.S."

WILL OF PAUL REVERE

"Listen, my children, and you shall hear
Of the midnight ride of Paul Revere."

Paul Revere died May 10, 1818; his will is dated the 15th day of November, 1816, and a codicil, the 14th day of March, 1818.

"In the name of God, Amen. I, Paul Revere of Boston in the County of Suffolk and Commonwealth of Massachusetts, Esquire, being in good health and of sound memory, but knowing that all men must die, do make and declare this to be my last will and testament."

The payment of his just debts is directed, and the executor is to sell the real estate, if the personal property is not sufficient for that purpose.

"Item. I give, bequeath and devise unto my five children hereafter named, Mary Lincoln, wife of Jedediah Lincoln, Joseph

Warren Revere, John Revere, Harriet Revere, Marie, wife of Joseph Balestier, each and every of them four thousand dollars."

Item. Unto each of certain grandchildren, eighteen in number, the children of his deceased daughters, Deborah, Frances and Elizabeth, and a deceased son, Paul, he gives the sum of five hundred dollars.

"Item. It is my will that my grandson Frank (who now writes his name Francis) Lincoln, eldest son of my late daughter Deborah, shall have no part of my estate, except one dollar, which is here bequeathed to him."

Item. He desired that Joseph Warren Revere, his son, should be appointed guardian of the children of his deceased daughters, who should be under age at the time of the division of his estate. Joseph Warren, who had been of great assistance to his father in bringing the "copper business to the state in which it now is," is given the right to take, at a certain valuation, "all my real estate in the town of Canton, and County of Norfolk, whether lands, houses, mills, furnaces, together with the tools and instruments thereunto belonging, with all my stock, manufactured and unmanufactured, in Canton, Boston, or elsewhere."

Item. A preference of five hundred dollars over other heirs is given his grandson, Frederick Walker Lincoln, and to Joseph Eayres, another grandson, a preference of two hundred and fifty dollars.

Item. Unto his daughter, Harriet, should she be unmarried at the time of his death, he gives and bequeaths all household furniture for her sole use forever.

Item. John Revere, his son, was appointed sole executor.

"Item. I give the residue of my estate, real and personal, if any remain, after the payment of my debts and the legacies herein given, to my son, Joseph Warren, and his heirs forever." All former wills were revoked.

By a codicil, the amount given Mary Lincoln, Harriet Revere, and Marie Balestier, twelve thousand dollars, is annulled, and that sum is given in trust to his son, Joseph W. Revere, for the benefit of said daughters, the interest to be paid them during their natural lives, and after their deaths, respectively, the said fund is to be paid to their heirs (if the beneficiaries had not disposed of the same by will).

Will of Russell Sage

Russell Sage died July 21, 1906. His will is a clear, concise and pointed document, and might well serve as a model of its kind. Under it, safely passed one of the largest fortunes ever accumulated in the United States. It reads:

"I, Russell Sage, of the City and State of New York, do hereby make, publish and declare this my last Will and Testament, in manner and form following:

"*First:* I direct that all my just debts and funeral expenses be paid as soon after my decease as conveniently can be done.

"*Second:* I give and bequeath to my sister, Fanny Chapin, wife of Samuel Chapin, of Oneida, New York, should she survive me, the sum of Ten thousand ($10,000) dollars.

"*Third:* I give and bequeath to each and every of my nephews and nieces of my own blood me surviving, the sum of Twenty five thousand ($25,000) dollars; and in the event that any of such nephews or nieces shall have died before me, leaving lawful issue him or her surviving, then I give and bequeath a like sum of Twenty five thousand ($25,000) dollars to the surviving lawful issue of each nephew or niece so dying before me, the same to be distributed among such issue share and share alike, *per stirpes* and not *per capita.*

"*Fourth:* All the rest, residue, and remainder of my estate, real, personal and mixed, wheresoever situate, of which I may die seized or possessed, or to which I may be entitled at the time of my decease, I give, devise and bequeath to my wife, Margaret Olivia Sage, to have and to hold the same to her, absolutely and forever.

"*Fifth:* This provision for my wife is to be in lieu of all right of dower in my estate.

"*Sixth:* I authorize and empower my executors hereinafter named, and the survivors and survivor of them, to sell and dispose of all or any of the real estate of which I shall die seized or possessed, at public or private sale, at such times and on such terms and conditions as they, the survivors or survivor of them shall deem meet or proper, and to execute, acknowledge and deliver all proper writings, deeds of conveyance and transfers therefor.

"*Seventh:* Should any of the gifts and bequests made by me in the second and third paragraphs of this my will lapse or fail for any reason, I direct that the bequests so lapsing or failing shall go to and form part of my residuary estate, and be disposed of under and in accordance with the provisions of the fourth paragraph of this my will.

"*Eighth:* I nominate, constitute and appoint my wife, Margaret Olivia Sage; Dr. John P. Munn, of the City of New York; Almon Goodwin of said City, and Charles W. Osborne long my confidential and trusted assistant, the survivors and survivor of them, executrix and executors of this my last Will and Testament.

"In the event of the death, refusal or inability to act of said Charles W. Osborne, I hereby nominate and appoint Edward C. Osborne, also for some years past in my employment, as Executor in his place and stead. I further direct that none of the persons above named as executors shall be required to give any bond or security for the proper discharge of their duties.

"*Ninth:* I hereby authorize and direct my said executors to rent a suitable office for the transaction of the business of my estate, and to employ and pay out of the funds of my estate all the clerks and bookkeepers that may be necessary for the proper care and management thereof.

"*Tenth:* I hereby revoke all former or other wills and testamentary dispositions by me at any time heretofore made.

"*Eleventh:* Should any of the beneficiaries under this my will, other than my said wife, object to the probate thereof, or in any wise, directly or indirectly, contest or aid in contesting the same, or any of the provisions thereof, or the distribution of my estate thereunder, then and in that event I annul any bequest herein made to such beneficiary, and it is my will that such beneficiary shall be absolutely barred and cut off from any share in my estate.

"In witness whereof I have hereunto subscribed my name and affixed my seal at No. 2 Wall Street, New York City, Borough of Manhattan, this eleventh day of February, 1901, in the presence of Edward Townsend and Richard W. Freedman, whom I have requested to become attesting witnesses hereto.

"RUSSELL SAGE. (SEAL.)

"The foregoing instrument was subscribed, sealed, published and declared by Russell Sage as and for his last Will and Testament, in our presence and in the presence of each of us, and we, at the same time, at his request, in his presence and in the presence of each other, hereunto subscribe our names and residences as attesting witnesses this 11th day of February, 1901.

"EDWARD TOWNSEND, 130 West 121st St., New York.
"R. W. FREEDMAN, 32 West 123rd St., N. Y. City."

Will of John Sherman

John Sherman died Oct. 22, 1900. His will is as follows:

"Impressed with the uncertainty of human life I, John Sherman now a Senator of the United States and from the State of Ohio and a Citizen of Mansfield, do make and declare and publish this as my last will and testament.

"ARTICLE ONE. As the property I own has been mainly acquired since my marriage with Cecilia Stewart Sherman and my highest obligation is to her, I wish to secure her an ample provision during her life with reasonable means of bequest at her death; Therefore I hereby give, devise and bequeath to her as follows:

"FIRST. All my furniture, books, clothing, chattels and live stock and carriages wherever they may be at my Death (except such Books and papers as may be herein otherwise disposed of) to have and to hold in her own right without inventory and with power to dispose of as she deems proper.

"SECOND. I give and devise to her in fee simple all that part of the South east quarter of section Twenty (20) in Madison Township, Richland County, Ohio: Known as the Stewart farm and not disposed of at my death, my interest being three parts thereof and her interest by inheritance being one fourth, this is to include all sums due or accruing at the time of my death on contracts for the sale of any part of said farm.

"THIRD. I give and devise to her for and during her natural life, and for one year after her Death the use and occupation of my residence in Mansfield, Ohio, including all the lands and lots I now own, or may hereafter acquire, lying between West Market and Fourth Streets and Penn Avenue and Sycamore Street. And I give and devise to her for and during her Natural life and for One year after Death any House and the lot or lots on which it stands in the City of Washington then belonging to my estate which she may select and I direct my executors to pay all taxes General or special on the property described in his clause, and to keep it in good repair out of my General estate.

"FOURTH. I give and bequeath to her for and during her natural life an annuity of Twelve Thousand dollars payable monthly or one thousand Dollars a month at the beginning of each month, and in addition I bequeath to her the sum of five thousand dollars payable Promptly at my Death and the further sum of Twenty Thousand dollars to be disposed of by her will or other gift after her death and to secure the prompt and certain payment of this annuity I charge it upon all my property or the proceeds of it, not required to meet the other provisions of this will, and I direct my executors within six months after my death to set aside as a special Fund enough income producing property to yield without reasonable doubt the said sum of Twelve Thousand Dollars a year free from all Taxes and repairs to be selected by her, one half or more of which shall be rentable real estate, and such property and the income thereof shall be held to secure the payment of said annuity and any deficiency shall be made good from my general estate, a descriptive inventory of the property so set aside shall be delivered to her, and no part of it shall be sold or disposed of without her written consent.

"At her death the said property shall revert to my estate. This provision for my wife shall be in full for her dower, her year's allowance and any other allowance or provision provided by law for a widow, and I trust will be accepted by her as a just and ample one made with an earnest desire for her ease and comfort.

"ARTICLE SECOND. I give, devise and bequeath to my adopted Daughter, Mary Stewart Sherman the sum of One Hundred Thousand dollars as follows: I hereby direct my Executors within six months after my death with the consent and approval of my Daughter to set aside dedicate and designate as Mary's separate property so much of my estate as is equal in Cash value to the said sum of One Hundred Thousand dollars, one half or more of which shall be productive real estate and the remainder in good income producing Stocks, Bonds and Mortgages and the said property shall be held by my wife as long as she lives, as trustee for Mary, with power to re-invest and change security; the income and rents of said property or so much thereof as is necessary for the support and maintenance of Mary shall be paid to her as needed. Upon the death of my wife the principal whether in real estate or securities shall be conveyed transferred and delivered to Mary or to her issue n full ownership. If Mary should die without issue before the Death of my wife this devise and bequest shall revert to my estate."

Then follow legacies to brothers and sisters, amounting to $90,000.

"I give and bequeath to Kate Willock the only child of my sister Julia Willock (deceased) the sum of $600.00 a year (in lieu of an annuity I am now paying her) payable quarterly until the death of my wife, and if she survives my wife I give her five thousand dollars. The several bequests made in the third article are made (the 4th clause excepted) with the distinct condition that at the discretion of my executors they may be paid any time within two years after my death and either of them in whole or in part in any real estate of which I die seized at its fair market value.

"ARTICLE FOUR. I hereby constitute and appoint my wife Cecelia Stewart Sherman and my Nephew Henry Stoddart Sherman as the Executors of this my will and testament.

"I hereby will and direct that within two years after my Death my books and papers so far as needed shall be placed in the possession of some competent person and he shall prepare and publish an impartial Biography of me with selections of my speeches and writings and I appropriate for that purpose the sum of Ten Thousand dollars to be paid by my Executors as needed. This provision is made not to secure a eulogy for I am conscious of many faults, but I claim that in my duty to the public I have been honest, faithful and true. I hereby allow to Henry S. Sherman Two Thousand dollars a year commencing at the date of my death and continuing as long as he lives and my wife survives me, as full compensation for his services as executor and his acceptance of this trust shall be considered as his agreement to this rate of compensation. I trust my wife will take an active part as executrix for which I wish her paid liberally.

"After the death of my wife when the special fund provided for her support lapses to my estate I hereby give and bequeath:

"1st. To the President and Faculty of Kenyon College Ohio Five Thousand dollars. 2nd. To the president and Faculty of Oberlin College Ohio five Thousand dollars. 3rd. To the City of Mansfield, Ohio, Five Thousand dollars for the Improvement of the Sherman-Heineman Park each to be paid within one year after the Death of my wife.

* * * * * * *

"ARTICLE SIX. The rest and residue of my property and the accretion thereto after the death of my wife and the full execution of all the foregoing provisions of this will I hereby give, devise and bequeath in equal parts share and share alike to my Daughter Mary Stewart Sherman to Henry S. Sherman (son of my Brother Charles) to Hoyt Sherman (son of my Brother James) To Philemon Tecumseh Sherman (son of my Brother William T.) to Charles H. Sherman (son of my Brother Lampson) and to Charles M. Sherman (son of my Brother Hoyt) to be divided if practicable among the Six by amicable partition. In case of the Death of either of said residuary Legatees before this bequest accrues then his or her Share is hereby granted to his or her heirs at Law.

"Having made and declared this will after full consideration not in view of Death but of its ever constant possibility I appeal to my relatives to aid my Executors in a spirit of forbearance to carry it into full effect. I allow my Executors two years without interest to pay the legacies in article three of this will.

"I hope to live long enough to execute many provisions of this will, when they Shall cease and terminate. Any person contesting this will shall receive no gift or devise or legacy under it and my Executors are authorized and enjoined not to pay any such nor shall such person receive any portion of my estate by inheritance.

"JOHN SHERMAN."

There is a codicil to this will, dated the 15th day of January, 1900; in it two executors are named, one of those mentioned in the will having died: provision is made for the compensation of the executors, and other matters of minor importance are set forth.

WILL OF MYLES STANDISH

Captain Myles Standish, Longfellow's hero, died at Duxbury, Massachusetts, on Friday, October 3, 1656; his will was made March 7, 1656.

"1 my will is that out of my whole estate my funerall charges be taken out & my bod[y] to bee buried in Decent manor and if I Die att Duxburrow my body to bee layed as neare as Conveniently may bee to my two Daughters Lora Standish my daughter and Mary Standish my Daughterinlaw

" 2 my will is that out of the remaining prte of my whole estate that all my Jus[t] and lawfull Debts which I now owe or att the Day of my Death may owe bee paied

" 3 out of what remaines according to the order of this Govr-ment: my will is that my Dear and loveing wife Barbara Standish shall have the third prte

" 4 I have given to my son Josias Standish upon his marriage one young horse five sheep and two heiffers which I must upon that contract of marriage make forty pounds yett not knowing whether the estate will bear it att p^{r}sent; my will is that the resedue remaine in the whole stocke that every one of my four sons viz

Allexander Standish Myles Standish Josias Standish and Charles Standish may have forty pounds appeec; if not that they may have proportionable to ye remaining prte bee it more or lesse

"5 my will is that my eldest son Allexander shall have a Doubble share in land

"6 my will is that soe long as they live single that the whole bee in prtenership betwix[t] them

"7 I Doe ordaine and make my Dearly beloved wife Barbara Standish Allexander Standish Myles Standish and Josias Standish Joynt Exequitors of this my last will and Testament

"8 I Doe by this will make and appoint my loveing frinds Mr Timothy hatherly and Capt: James Cudworth Supervissors of this my last will and that they wilbee pleased to Doe the office of Christian love to bee healpfull to my poor wife and Children by theire Christian Counsell and advisse . . .

"By mee MYLES STANDISH"

WILL OF JANE LATHROP STANFORD

Jane Lathrop Stanford, late of San Francisco, California, together with her husband, Leland Stanford, founded the Leland Stanford Junior University. By her will, which is dated the 28th day of July, 1903, she gives many pecuniary legacies to relatives, friends and charitable institutions. Item XXII of her will reads as follows:

"All the rest, residue and remainder of my property and estate, of every kind and nature and wheresoever situated, not hereinbefore disposed of, I give, devise and bequeath to the Board of Trustees of the Leland Stanford Junior University as founded and endowed by my husband and myself by our joint grant of November eleventh, 1885, . . . to have and to hold to the said Trustees and to their successors forever as an integral part of the endowment of the said University, upon the trust that the principal thereof shall forever remain intact, and that the rents, issues and profits thereof shall be devoted to the maintenance of said University."

The will concludes with a beautiful expression of her faith in God and of her belief in a future life, in these words:

"I wish thus publicly to acknowledge my great gratitude to an allwise, loving Heavenly Father for His sustaining grace through the past ten years of bereavement, trial and disappointments. In all I have leaned hard on this Great Comforter and found rest and peace. I have no doubt about a future life beyond this; a fair land where no more tears will be shed and no more partings had."

WILL OF ALEXANDER STEPHENS

Alexander H. Stephens died March 4, 1883. His will is as follows:

" Georgia, Taliaferro County.

"In the name of God, Amen: I, Alexander H. Stephens, of the State and County aforesaid, being of sound mind and disposing memory, do make and declare the following to be my last will and testament hereby revoking and annulling all other wills heretofore made by me, and codicils thereto:

"Item First: It is my will and desire that my friend Quinea O. Neal shall have a home at 'Liberty Hall' and comfortable support out of my estate as long as he lives:

"Item 2nd: Eliza Stephens widow of Harry Stephens is to have a home in the house she now occupies as long as she may feel disposed to, free from rent or charge:

"Item 3rd: I will and bequeath to the children of my deceased Brother Linton Stephens the sum of Ten thousand dollars in money the same to be divided into six equal shares of Sixteen hundred and Sixty six dollars and sixty six cents each; the share which would go to Rebecca Salter, daughter of my said Brother were she in life, I bequeath to her two children to wit: John and Agnes Emiline Salter: the share which would go to Emiline Stephens, daughter of my said Brother, I bequeath also to the said John and Agnes Salter. The other four shares I bequeath to Claude, Nora, Alexander and Rose Mary Stephens, children of my said Brother Linton, each separately and severally.

"Item 4th. I hereby constitute my sister in law, Mary W. Stephens testamentary guardian of the property herein bequeathed to John and Agnes Emiline Salter and also of the property in like manner bequeathed to Nora, Alexander and Rose Mary Stephens.

"Item 5th: The share given to my niece Claude Stephens, I wish to go in any way she may by written instructions, direct, by will or otherwise even if made before my death.

"Item 6th: The portrait of my brother Linton, by Healy, I leave to sister Mary W. Stephens his widow, to dispose of as she sees proper; and if she dies without disposing of it, then to the State Library at Atlanta.

"Item 7th: The portrait by the same artist of my said Brothers first wife which I intended for Emma Stephens, her daughter, I wish if she shall so direct, to go to Agnes Emiline Salter:

"Item 8th: I wish sister Mary W. Stephens, widow of my said Brother Linton to have all his letters, which are in my possession except such as she may agree to let my Executor have:

"Item 9th: If my Nephew Alexander Stephens son of my Brother Linton, lives to the age of Twenty one years, I wish him to have if he desires them, all the letters in my possession, which passed between his father and myself, which run through a period of nearly forty years.

"Item 10th: According to a promise made to Micajah L. Jones, the house and lot which he occupied at the time of his death, and whereon his widow now lives, I bequeath to his said widow Minervia Jones for and during her natural life, and at her death to her children by the said Micajah L. Jones. And if her said children shall die without issue living at the r death then the remainder to go to my Nephew, Clarence Stephens. Provided further that if her son Carey Jones shall pay to my Executor the sum of two hundred dollars, then he is to have said lot after the death of his mother, and full titles to this effect shall be made to him the said Carey by my Executor: and my Executor shall pay over said sum of two hundred dollars to the said Clarence Stephens:

"Item 11th: To my nephew Linton A. Stephens I bequeath my Baptist Church, Atlanta fair Gold headed cane, besides what I have given him:

"Item 12th: To my Nephew Alexander Stephens, son of my Brother Linton, I give my Gold headed Oglethorpe County cane.

"Item 13th: To my Niece Mary S. Carey, I give my marble top centre table, which belongs to my parlor:

"Item 14th: To my faithful servant, Alexander Kent, I give the sum of two hundred dollars for his kind attention to me.

"Item 15th: To Jane Moore, daughter of Harry Stephens, and Quinea and Fanny Stephens, I give the sum of Ten dollars each.

"Item 16th: To Dora Stephens I give the gold watch which she now has in her possession.

"Item 17th: To all the other of my old servants, I wish my Executor to give such articles of furniture or other things, as mementos he may see fit and proper:

"Item 18th: My property I think upon a fair valuation is worth twelve thousand dollars. All this after payment of the foregoing

specific legacies and charges, I give to my Nephew John
A. Stephens, who is hereby constituted Executor of this will.
All the remainder of my Estate, consisting of real and personal property, and everything of value I may die possessed of,
including my Library, Manuscripts, &c. I bequeath to him on
condition that he shall pay all my debts : and the foregoing specific
legacies. The payment of the legacies to the minor children of my
Brother Linton, and Rebecca Salters two children, I wish to be
in three annual installments if my Executor shall desire: the interest on all legacies to commence one year after my death at the
rate of seven per cent per annum : In this way, the minor children
will have plenty to pay their annual school bills: And my said
Executor may be able, by sale if necessary, to raise the funds to
meet his engagements without embarrassment: I will also add
that I have never before given to my brother Lintons children
anything but a few small presents; while I have given to my
brother John and his children quite as much, perhaps, if not more
than I now leave to Lintons children: And I with my brother
Linton have also given to the children of our sister Catherine Grier
several thousand dollars, the exact amount I do not now remember,
nor is it material, but quite as much as I feel able to give them :
The foregoing four pages penned by John A. Stephens, my Executor
and written at my dictation, I have carefully read, with the three
interlineations on the third page and the erasure of the word in the
second line from the bottom on same page; and pronounce the
whole, as the 18 items now stand to be correct and as I wish and
will it.

"In witness whereof I have hereto set my hand and seal, this
15th day of July, 1881.

"ALEXANDER H. STEPHENS."

WILL OF HARRIET BEECHER STOWE

Harriet Beecher Stowe died at Hartford, Connecticut, July 1,
1896. Her will is as follows:

"I, Harriet Beecher Stowe of Hartford Conn. being of sound and
disposing mind and memory do make and ordain this my last will
and testament.

"1. I direct that all my just debts and funeral charges be first
paid.

"2. I give and devise to my son Charles the large silver inkstand given me by the women of England, also the cabinet of signatures standing in the hall. I give to my daughter Harriet the large silver waiter given to me by the women of England, and to my daughter Eliza the silver cake basket given to me by the women of England, and I give to my daughter Georgiana the gold bracelet given to me by the Duchess of Sutherland.

"3. I give all my pictures to my children to be divided among them by each choosing one beginning with the oldest and so in succession until they are all chosen.

"4. All the rest and residue of my property I give and devise as follows:

I give one third thereof to my son Charles, to him and his heirs for ever.

The remaining two thirds I give to John C. Parsons of the City of Hartford, as Trustee for the following purposes.

To safely invest and hold the same, and pay over half the income thereof quarterly to each of my two daughters Harriet and Eliza, so long as they both live, upon the death of either, said Trustee shall pay the whole of said income to the survivor so long as she shall live. If it shall become necessary, I authorize said trustee to expend from the principal such sums as shall be needed for the support of my said two daughters, if for any reason the income thereof shall not be sufficient for their support, but not otherwise. Upon the death of both my said daughters said trust shall cease, and the principal then in the hands of said Trustee or his successor I give to my son Charles, or his descendants if he should then be deceased. I make no provision out of my estate for my daughter Georgiana at her special request alone.

"5. I direct my executor to sell all my real estate as soon as practicable, and turn the same into personal property before the above division is made.

"6. I revoke all former wills and testaments and appoint my son Charles E. Stowe as executor of this will, and direct that he be required to give only the smallest bond as executor which the law will admit.

"In witness whereof I have hereunto set my hand and seal on this 3rd day of November A.D. 1885.

"HARRIET BEECHER STOWE."

Will of Samuel J. Tilden

Samuel J. Tilden died August 4, 1886. The failure of the trust created by his will has been extensively commented on by the lay and legal journals of the United States.

By a decision of the New York Court of Appeals, in the case of Tilden *v.* Green, the trust provision was overthrown. The late Professor J. B. Ames remarked: "Melancholy the spectacle must always be when covetous relatives seek to convert to their own use the fortune which a testator has devoted to a great public benefaction."

The learned author then, without quoting the exact provisions of the will creating what is known as the "Tilden Trust," transcribes as substantially correct, the summary of the same made by a majority of the judges of the New York Court of Appeals in the case in which the will was overthrown: "I request you (the executors) to cause to be incorporated an institution to be called the 'Tilden Trust,' with capacity to maintain a free library and reading-room in the city of New York, and such other educational and scientific objects as you shall designate; and if you deem it expedient — that is, if you think it advisable and the fit and proper thing to do — convey to that institution all or such part of my residuary estate as you choose; and if you do not think that course advisable, then apply it to such charitable, educational, and scientific purposes as, in your judgment, will most substantially benefit mankind." "The trustees," continues the learned commentator, "procured the incorporation of the 'Tilden Trust,' and elected to convey the entire residue to that institution. An admirable will and willing trustees — and yet the bequest was not sustained. If the trustees had not elected to give the property to the 'Tilden Trust,' that institution would have had no claim, nor would there have been, under the law of New York, any means of compelling them to apply it to the alternative charitable purposes. Therefore, the Court of Appeals decided, the trustees could not dispose of the property in either of the two modes indicated in the will, and the entire residue, amounting to some $5,000,000, must be distributed among the heirs and next of kin."

Will of Martin Van Buren

Martin Van Buren, Governor of New York, United States Senator and eighth President of the United States, was born at

Kinderhook, New York, on December 5, 1782, and died there on July 24, 1862. He attained eminence at the bar and as a politician was surpassed by few, if any, men of his day.

His will deals largely with domestic affairs, yet it is a carefully conceived and well drawn document:

"I, Martin Van Buren of the Town of Kinderhook, County of Columbia, and State of New York, heretofore Governor of the State, and more recently President of the United States, but for the last and happiest years of my life, a farmer in my native Town, do make & declare the following to be my last will & testament.

"First. I direct my Executors hereinafter named, to pay without delay, my funeral expenses, & all outstanding bills. Debts, in the ordinary acceptation of that term I owe none, & hope to leave none.

"Secondly. I direct that no account shall be taken of advances by me heretofore made to either of my sons, and that they shall be considered as settled, with the exceptions of a bond I hold against my son Abraham for two thousand dollars, and also a note against my son John for four thousand eight hundred and fifteen dollars, which were agreed to be considered as business transactions strictly, the amount due on each at my death (the interest having been punctually paid to the present year) is to be charged to them respectively, and deducted from their share of my estate. The like charge and deduction shall be made in respect to any future payments by me or by my estate in cases where I have made myself liable as surety for either of my sons, but in which nothing has yet been paid by me.

"Thirdly. In consideration of advances which I have made to my sons Abraham & John, whilst none have been made to my son Smith Thompson, I bequeath to the latter all my personal chattels and effects, excepting therefrom all the debts that may be due to me, and stocks that I may own at my death, and also my wine & stock on my farm. My miscellaneous library is intended to be included in this bequest, but not my law library, which I bequeath to my son John.

"Fourthly. I give to my grandson Singleton Van Buren a gold snuff box, presented to me with the Freedom of the City, by the corporation of the City of New York and to my grandson Martin, son of Abraham, the marble bust made of me by Powers, which I had previously presented to his mother, & now transfer to the son by her direction. I give to my grandson Martin, Son of my son Smith

Thompson, a silver pitcher presented to me, some years since by my old and always sincere friend Benjamin F. Butler.

"Fifthly. I direct my executors to expend four hundred dollars, or so much thereof as may be necessary, in obtaining a copy of the bust of me by Powers, which copy I give to my grandson Edward Livingston Van Buren.

"Sixthly. I direct my executors to lay out five hundred dollars for keep sakes for my grand son Travis Van Buren, and for my grand daughters Anna, Ellen, Catharine & Eliza Van Buren.

"Seventhly. I request my executors to regard themselves as standing towards my best of sisters Dirike Van Buren, if she shall survive me, in the relation I occupied when living, & to omit nothing in the way of pecuniary advances that may contribute to her comfort, out of my estate.

"Eighthly. I direct my executors to pay to my niece Christina Cantine two hundred dollars & to each of my nieces Lucretia Van Buren & Jane Ann Van Buren the sum of one hundred dollars: and I give and devise to my nephew Martin Van Buren son of my brother Lawrence, & to his heirs and assigns forever, all my interest in a small dwelling with the lot on which it stands adjoining his father's house conveyed to me by the latter as security for money lent, but the latter devise is upon condition that his father relieves me or my estate from my remaining securityship to the State of New York.

"Ninthly. I hereby appoint my three sons Abraham, John & Smith Thompson executors of my last & only will; and I do hereby authorize & empower them, or such of them as shall take upon themselves the execution thereof, and the survivors & survivor of them, to fulfill by the execution of conveyances and otherwise, as may be proper, any contracts for the sale of lands, made by me, which shall be outstanding at the time of my death.

"Lastly. I hereby give, devise & bequeath to my three sons Abraham, John & Smith Thompson all the remainder & residue of my personal estate not required for the purposes of my will under the provisions above made & all my real estate wheresoever situated, to be equally divided between them, To have & to hold their respective shares thereof to them, their heirs & assigns forever, subject to the following conditions & reservations, viz.; first that out of the avails of the sale of Lindenwald there shall be reserved & paid over to my son Smith Thompson, his heirs or assigns the sum of seven thousand five hundred dollars in full satisfaction for his advances towards the expenses incurred by the additions to and improvements upon the dwelling house & outbuildings with the expectation that the place would be devised to him upon terms that would be equitable in respect to his brothers, the payment to be without interest during my lifetime. Secondly that upon the sale of Lindenwald the preference shall be offered in succession to my sons, beginning for the reason above assigned & no other, with the youngest, if the son accepting the same is willing to pay therefor as much as the place can be sold for on the market.

"The three pieces of plate last presented to me by my deceased friend Benjamin F. Butler, I bequeath to my three sons Abraham, John & Smith Thompson to be equally divided between them.

"In Witness Whereof I have to this instrument set my hand & seal this eighteenth day of Janu^y in the year of our Lord one thousand eight hundred and sixty.
"M. VAN BUREN." (SEAL.)

"Subscribed, sealed, published and declared by the said testator Martin Van Buren to be his last will & testament in the presence of us the undersigned, who at his request & in his presence and in the presence of each other have hereunto subscribed our names as witnesses & affixed our respective places of residence this 18' of Jany 1860.

"JOHN M. PRUYN, M.D. of Kinderhook.
"LAURA COLLINS of Albany.

"If my faithful James remains with me until my death I wish my executors to make him a present of one hundred dollars.
"M. VAN BUREN."

WILL OF MATTHEW VASSAR

Matthew Vassar was an Englishman by birth: he accumulated his wealth as a brewer at Poughkeepsie, New York: he died in 1868, and was the founder of Vassar College: he gave to the Institution 200 acres of land and $788,000 by gift and bequest, and further sums have been contributed by members of the Vassar family: the student attendance numbers about one thousand.

By his will, he gives directions as to his burial, then gives to his nephews and other relatives certain real estate and personal property; the residue he gives to Vassar College.

He established a "Lecture Fund" "to defray the expenses of having lectures on Literature, and the Arts and Sciences, to be delivered at said college by distinguished persons, not officers therein."

There is also an "Auxiliary Fund," established to assist students of "superior mind and high scholarship."

There is the "Library, Art and Cabinet Fund " "to keep in good repair and condition, the library, cabinets and art gallery"; a "Repair Fund " for "making repairs, alterations and improvements." On the repair fund there is a charge for the board and tuition of the daughters of a certain friend, for four years each, as well as not more than four of his own female blood relatives, living at the time of his decease, who might wish to attend the college. He also provided that any lapsed legacies should pass to the college.

The testator left with his will a letter of advice to the trustees of the college.

Mr. Remsen, in his excellent work on Wills, recommends the course pursued by Mr. Vassar in securing the incorporation of charitable institutions in advance of the death of the testator, and in making testamentary gifts to them for maintenance. He states that this is a favorite method, and was pursued by the founders of the Corcoran Gallery of Art, Cooper Institute, Johns Hopkins University, Leland Stanford Junior University, and many other well-known institutions; this plan giving the institution the benefit, in its early stages, of the guiding hand of its founder.

WILL OF GEORGE G. VEST

George G. Vest was one of Missouri's most distinguished senators, a lawyer of great ability, and an orator of national fame. He died August 9, 1904.

By his will, which is dated March 25, 1903, he gave to his wife the sum of Five Thousand Dollars, also his residence and the sum of Two Thousand Dollars a year for her life; then appears this provision: "The acceptance by my wife of the provisions for her benefit contained in this will shall bar all claims by her of dower in any real estate heretofore or hereafter conveyed by me to any one"; this provision has occasioned much comment in view of the fact that it does not accomplish the purpose intended, as it does not preclude dower in realty owned at the time of his death. A few personal effects were given to friends, among them a cane "on which is a silver snake," to Adolphus Busch of St. Louis.

The giving of canes and walking-sticks by distinguished men has always been a marked feature in wills.

The balance of the estate was to be equally divided among three children, the portions for the sons in trust, and that for the daughter absolutely, less an advancement.

Senator Vest had few equals as a brilliant orator; perhaps no speech ever made by him at the bar or in the Senate will be longer remembered than the one given below. It was an address to a jury, delivered at Warrensburg, Missouri, about the year 1870. Senator Vest was then about forty years of age. A farmer had sued a neighbor for killing his dog, an ordinary fox hound, and Senator Vest was asked to assist the plaintiff. He made a brief address, and the jury gave a verdict for the full amount claimed. The case finally reached the Supreme Court of Missouri, and the finding of the lower court was upheld:

"Gentlemen of the Jury: —

"The best friend a man has in this world, may turn against him and become his enemy.

"His son or daughter that he has reared with loving care may prove ungrateful. Those who are nearest and dearest to us, those whom we trust with our happiness and our good name, may become traitors to their faith.

"The money that a man has, he may lose. It flies away from him, perhaps when he needs it most.

"A man's reputation may be sacrificed in a moment of ill-considered action. The people who are prone to fall on their knees to do us honor, when success is with us, may be the first to throw the stone of malice, when failure settles its cloud upon our heads.

"The one absolutely unselfish friend that man can have in this selfish world, — the one that never deserts him, — the one that never proves ungrateful or treacherous is the dog.

"Gentlemen of the jury, a man's dog stands by him in prosperity and in poverty, in health and in sickness. He will sleep on the cold ground, where the wintry winds blow and the snow drives fiercely, if only he may be near his master's side. He will kiss the hand that has no food to offer, and he will lick the wounds and sores that come in encounter with the roughness of the world.

"He guards the sleep of his pauper master, as if he were a prince. Whenever all other friends desert, he remains.

"When riches take wings, and reputation falls to pieces, he is as constant, in his love, as the sun in its journey through the heavens.

"If fortune drives the master forth, an outcast, in the world, friendless and homeless, the faithful dog asks no higher privilege than that of accompanying him to guard against danger, to fight against his enemies, and, when the last scene of all comes, and death takes the master in its embrace, and his body is laid away in the cold ground, no matter if all other friends pursue their way, there by the grave side will be found the noble dog, his head between his paws, his eyes sad, but open in alert watchfulness, faithful and true even in death."

WILL OF GEORGE WASHINGTON

George Washington died December 14, 1799. His original will is on file somewhere in Virginia. A copy thereof is on file in the Office of the Register of Wills at Washington, D.C., having been recorded there on November 15, 1802: the instrument is voluminous, but by reason of its interesting nature and the greatness and fame of the testator, the document is here given in full, omitting only a few inconsequential details:

"IN THE NAME OF GOD, AMEN

"I, GEORGE WASHINGTON, of Mount Vernon, a Citizen of the United States, and lately President of the same, Do make, ordain, and declare this Instrument which is written with my own Hand, and every page thereof subscribed with my Name, to be my last WILL and TESTAMENT, revoking all others, Imprimis.

"All my debts, of which there are but few, and none of magnitude, are to be punctually and speedily paid, and the Legacies herein after bequeathed, are to be discharged as soon as circumstances will permit, and in the manner directed.

"ITEM. To my dearly beloved wife MARTHA WASHINGTON, I give and bequeath the use, profit, and benefit of my whole estate, real and personal, for the term of her natural life, except such parts thereof as are specially disposed of hereafter. — My improved Lot in the town of Alexandria, situated on Pitt and Cameron Streets, I give to her and her heirs for ever; as I also do my Houshold and Kitchen Furniture of every sort and kind with the Liquors and Groceries which may be on hand at the time of my decease, to be used and disposed of as she may think proper.

"ITEM. Upon the decease of my wife, it is my will and desire that all the Slaves which I hold in my own right shall receive their freedom. To emancipate them during her life, would, though earnestly wished by me, be attended with such insuferable difficulties on account of their intermixture by marriages with the dower Negroes, as to excite the most painful sensations, if not disagreeable consequences from the latter while both descriptions are in the occupancy of the same proprietor; it not being in my power, under the tenure by which the dower Negroes are held, to manumit them. And Whereas, among those who will receive freedom according to this devise, there may be some who from old age or bodily infirmities, and others who, on account of their infancy, that will be unable to support themselves, it is my will and desire that all who come under the first and second description, shall be comfortably clothed and fed by my heirs while they live; and that such of the latter description as have no parents living, or, if living, are unable or unwilling to provide for them, shall be bound by the court until they shall arrive at the age of twenty five years; and in cases where no record can be produced, whereby their ages can be ascertained, the judgment of the court upon its own view of the subject, shall be adequate and final. The Negroes thus bound, are (by their masters or mistresses) to be taught to read & write & to be bro't up to some useful occupation, agreeably to the laws of the commonwealth of Virginia, providing for the support of orphan and other poor children. — And I do hereby expressly forbid the sale or transportation out of the said commonwealth of any Slave I may die possessed of under any pretence whatsoever. And I do moreover, most pointedly and most solemnly enjoin it upon my Executors hereafter named or the survivor of them to see that this clause respecting Slaves and every part thereof, be religiously fulfilled at the epoch at which it is directed to take place, without evasion, neglect, or delay, after the crops which may then be on the ground are harvested, particularly as it respects the aged and infirm; seeing that a regular and permanent fund be established for their support so long as there are subjects requiring it; not trusting to the uncertain provision to be made by individuals; — And to my mulatto man William (calling himself William Lee) I give immediate freedom, or if he should prefer it (on account of the accidents which have befallen him and which have rendered him incapable of walking or of any active employment) to remain in the situation he now is, it shall be optional in him to do so,

in either case however, I allow him an annuity of Thirty Dollars
during his natural life, which shall be independent of the victuals
and cloaths he has been accustomed to receive if he chuses the last
alternative; but in full with his freedom, if he prefers the first;
and this I give him as a testimony of my sense of his attachment
to me, and for his faithful services during the Revolutionary War.

"ITEM. To the Trustees (Governors, or by whatsoever other
name they may be designated) of the Academy, in the Town of
Alexandria, I give and bequeath, in trust, Four Thousand Dollars,
or, in other words, twenty of the Shares which I hold in the Bank
of Alexandria, towards the support of a Free School, established at,
and annexed to, the said Academy, for the purpose of educating
such Orphan Children, or the Children of such other poor and
indigent persons as are unable to accomplish it with their own
means; and who, in the judgment of the Trustees of the said
Seminary, are best entitled to the benefit of this donation.

"ITEM. WHEREAS by a law of the commonwealth of Virginia,
enacted in the year 1785, the legislature thereof was pleased (as an
evidence of its approbation of the services I had rendered the public
during the Revolution, and partly I believe, in consideration of
my having suggested the vast advantages which the community
would derive from the extension of its inland navigation under
legislative patronage) to present me with one hundred Shares of
one hundred Dollars each, in the incorporated company established for the purpose of extending the navigation of James River
from tide water to the mountains; — and also with Fifty Shares of
one hundred Pounds Sterling each, in the corporation of another
company likewise established for the similar purpose of opening
the navigation of the river Potomac from tide water to Fort
Cumberland; the acceptance of which, although the offer was
highly honourable and grateful to my feelings, was refused as inconsistent with a principle which I had adopted, and had never
departed from — Namely — not to receive pecuniary compensation for any services I could render my country in its ardious
struggle with Great Britain for its rights; and because I had evaded
similar propositions from other States in the Union. Adding to
this refusal, however, an intimation that, if it should be the
pleasure of the legislature to permit me to appropriate the said
Shares to public uses, I would receive them on those terms with
due sensibility; and this it having consented to, in flattering terms,
as will appear by a subsequent law and sundry resolutions, in the

most ample and honourable manner, I proceed after this recital for the more correct understanding of the case, to declare — That as it has always been a source of serious regret with me to see the Youth of these United States sent to Foreign countries for the purpose of Education, often before their minds were formed, or they had imbibed any adequate ideas of the happiness of their own; contracting too frequently, not only habits of dissipation and extravagance, but principles unfriendly to Republican government, and to the true and genuine liberties of mankind; which, thereafter are rarely overcome. — For these reasons, it has been my ardent wish to see a plan devised on a liberal scale which would have a tendency to spread systematic ideas through all parts of this rising empire, thereby to do away local attachments and state prejudices, as far as the nature of things would, or indeed ought to admit, from our National Councils. — Looking anxiously forward to the accomplishment of so desirable an object as this is (in my estimation) my mind has not been able to contemplate any plan more likely to effect the measure than the establishment of a UNIVERSITY in a central part of the United States, to which the Youths of fortune and talents from all parts thereof might be sent for the completion of their Education in all the branches of polite literature; in arts and sciences, in acquiring knowledge in the principles of politics and good government, and (as a matter of infinite importance in my judgment) by associating with each other and forming friendships in Juvenile years, be enabled to free themselves in a proper degree from those local prejudices and habitual jealousies which have just been mentioned; and which, when carried to excess, are never failing sources of disquietude to the public mind, and pregnant of <u>mischevious</u> consequences to this country; under these impressions, so fully dilated.

"ITEM. I give and bequeath in perpetuity the Fifty Shares which I hold in the Potomac Company (under the aforesaid acts of the legislature of Virginia) towards the endowment of a UNIVERSITY to be established within the limits of the District of Columbia, under the auspices of the general government, if that government should incline to extend a fostering hand towards it.

"ITEM. The hundred Shares which I hold in the James River Company, I have given, and now confirm in perpetuity, to and for the use and benefit of Liberty Hall Academy, in the county of Rockbridge, in the Commonwealth of Virginia.

"ITEM. I release, exonerate and discharge the estate of my

deceased Brother, Samuel Washington, from the payment of the money which is due to me for the land I sold to Philip Pendleton (lying in the county of Berkeley) who assigned the same to him, the said Samuel, who, by agreement, was to pay me therefor: AND WHEREAS, by some contract (the purport of which was never communicated to me) between the said Samuel and his Son, Thornton Washington, the latter became possessed of the aforesaid land, without any conveyance having passed from me, either to the said Pendleton, the said Samuel, or the said Thornton, and without any consideration having been made, by which neglect neither the legal nor equitable title has been alienated; it rests therefore with me to declare my intentions concerning the premises; and these are to give and bequeath the said land to whomsoever the said Thornton Washington (who is also dead) devised the same, or to his heirs forever, if he died intestate; exonerating the estate of the said Thornton, equally with that of the said Samuel, from payment of the purchase money, which, with interest, agreeably to the original contract with the said Pendleton, would amount to more than a thousand pounds; AND WHEREAS two other Sons of my deceased Brother, Samuel, namely, George Steptoe Washington, and Lawrence Augustine Washington, were by the decease of those, to whose care they were committed, brought under my protection, and in consequence have occasioned advances on my part for their education at College and other schools, for their board, clothing, and other incidental expenses, to the amount of near five thousand dollars over and above the sums furnished by their estate, which sum it may be inconvenient for them or their father's estate to refund — I do, for these reasons, acquit them and the said estate from the payment thereof — my intention being that all accounts between them and me, and their father's estate and me, shall stand balanced.

"ITEM. To my Nephew, Bushrod Washington, I give and bequeath all the Papers in my possession, which relate to my civil and military administration of the affairs of this country — I leave to him also, such of my private Papers as are worth preserving; and at the decease of my Wife, and before, if she is not inclined to retain them, I give and bequeath my Library of Books and Pamphlets of every kind.

"ITEM. To the Earl of Beuban I recommit 'the Box made of the Oak that sheltered the great Sir William Wallace after the Battle of Falkirk' — presented to me by his Lordship, in terms too flattering for me to repeat, with a request 'to pass it, on the event of my decease, to the man in my country, who should appear to merit it best, upon the same conditions that have induced him to send it to me.' Whether easy or not, to select the Man who might comport with his Lordship's opinion in this respect, is not for me to say; but conceiving that no disposition of this valuable curiosity can be more eligible than the recommitment of it to his own cabinet, agreeably to the original design of the Goldsmiths' Company of Edinburg, who presented it to him, and, at his request, consented that it should be transferred to me — I do give and bequeath the same to his Lordship; and, in case of his decease, to his heir, with my grateful thanks for the distinguished honour of presenting it to me, and more especially for the favorable sentiments with which he accompanied it.

"ITEM. To my Brother, Charles Washington, I give and bequeath the Gold headed Cane left me by Dr. Franklin, in his will. I add nothing to it, because of the ample provision I have made for his issue. To the acquaintances and friends of my juvenile years, Lawrence Washington and Robert Washington, of Chotanck, I give my other two Gold headed Canes, having my arms engraved on them; and to each (as they will be useful where they live) I leave one of the Spyglasses, which constituted part of my equipage, during the late war. To my Compatriot in arms and old and intimate Friend, Dr. Craik, I give my Bureau (or, as the Cabinet Makers call it, Tambour Secretary) and the circular Chair, an appendage of my Study. To Dr. David Stuart I give my Large Shaving and Dressing Table, and my Telescope. To the Reverend, now Bryan Lord Fairfax, I give a Bible, in three large folio volumes, with notes, — presented to me by the Rt. Rev. Thomas Wilson, Bishop of Sodor and Man. To General De la Fayette I give a a Pair of finely wrought Steel Pistols, taken from the enemy in the revolutionary war. To my Sisters-in-Law, Hannah Washington and Mildred Washington — to my friends Eleanor Stuart, Hannah Washington, of Fairfield, and Elizabeth Washington of Hayfield, I give, each, a Mourning Ring, of the value of one hundred Dollars. These bequests are not made for the intrinsic value of them, but as mementos of my esteem and regard. To Tobias Lear I give the use of the farm which he now holds, in virtue of a lease from me to him and his deceased wife (for and during their natural lives) free from rent during his life; at the expiration of which, it is to be disposed of as is herein after directed. To Sally

B. Haynie (a distant relation of mine) I give and bequeath three hundred Dollars. To Sarah Green, daughter of the deceased Thomas Bishop, and to Ann Walker, daughter of John Alton, also deceased, I give each one hundred Dollars, in consideration of the attachment of their fathers to me; each of whom having lived nearly forty years in my family. To each of my Nephews, William Augustine Washington, George Lewis, George Steptoe Washington, Bushrod Washington, and Samuel Washington, I give one of the swords or Cutteaux of which I may die possessed; and they are to choose in the order they are named. — These swords are accompanied with an injunction not to unsheath them for the purpose of shedding blood, except it be for self-defence, or in defence of their country and its rights; and in the latter case, to keep them unsheathed, and prefer falling with them in their hands to the Relinquishment thereof.

"And Now, having gone through these specific Devises, with explanations for the more correct understanding of the meaning and design of them, I proceed to the distribution of the more important parts of my Estate, in manner following:

"FIRST. To my Nephew, Bushrod Washington, and his heirs (partly in consideration of an intimation to his deceased Father, while we were Bachelors, and he had kindly undertaken to superintend my estate during my military services in the former war between Great Britain and France) that if I should fall therein, Mount Vernon (then less extensive in domain than at present) should become his property. I give and bequeath all that part thereof, which is comprehended within the following limits, Viz: —

"FIFTH. — All the rest and residue of my estate, real and personal, not disposed of in manner aforesaid, in whatsoever consisting, — wheresoever lying — and whensoever found — a Schedule of which as far as is recollected, with a reasonable estimate of its value, is hereunto annexed — I desire may be sold by my Executors at such times — in such manner, and on such credits (if an equal, valid, and satisfactory distribution of the specific property cannot be made without) as in their judgment shall be most conducive to the interest of the parties concerned, and the monies arising therefrom to be divided into twenty-three equal parts, and applied as follows:" (Here follows the list of beneficiaries and description of property); "and by way of advice I recommend it to my Executors not to be precipitate in disposing of the landed property (herein directed to be sold) if from temporary causes the sale thereof would be dull; experience having fully evinced that the price of land (especially above the falls of the rivers and on the western waters) have been progressively rising and cannot be long checked in its encreasing value.

"The Family Vault at Mount Vernon, requiring repairs, and being improperly situated besides, I desire that a new one of brick, and upon a larger scale, may be built at the foot of what is commonly called the Vineyard Inclosure, on the ground which is marked out — In which my Remains, with those of my deceased Relations (now in the old Vault) and such others of my Family as may chuse to be entombed there, may be deposited. And it is my express desire, that my Corpse may be interred in a private manner, without parade or funeral Oration.

"LASTLY, I constitute and appoint my dearly beloved Wife Martha Washington, my Nephews William Augustine Washington, Bushrod Washington, George Steptoe Washington, Samuel Washington, and Lawrence Lewis, and my Ward George Washington Parke Custis (when he shall have arrived at the age of Twenty Years) Executrix and Executors of this WILL and TESTAMENT — In the construction of which, it will readily be perceived that no professional character has been consulted, or has had any agency in the draught, and that although it has occupied many of my leisure hours to digest, and to throw it into its present form, it may, notwithstanding, appear crude and incorrect — but having endeavored to be plain and explicit in all the devises, even at the expence of prolixity, perhaps of tautology, I hope and trust that no disputes will arise concerning them; but if, contrary to expectation, the case should be otherwise from the want of legal expression, or the usual technical terms, or because too much or too little has been said on any of the devises to be consonant with law, my Will and Direction expressly is, that all disputes (if unhappily any should arise) shall be decided by three impartial and intelligent men, known for their probity and good understanding — two to be chosen by the disputants, each having the choice of one, and the third by those two — which three men thus chosen shall, unfettered by law or legal constructions, declare their sense of the Testator's intentions; and such decision is, to all intents and purposes, to be as binding on the parties as if it had been given in the Supreme Court of the United States.

"IN WITNESS of all, and of each of the things herein contained, I have set my Hand and Seal, this Ninth Day of July, in the Year

One Thousand, Seven Hundred and Ninety ——— [1] and of the Independence of the United States the Twenty-Fourth.

"GEORGE WASHINGTON."

WILL OF MARY WASHINGTON

Mary Washington, mother of George Washington, died August 25, 1789. Her will, registered in the clerk's office at Fredericksburg, Virginia, is a peculiarly interesting document, and is here given in full.

"In the name of God, Amen, I, Mary Washington, of Fredericksburg, in the County of Spotsylvania, being in good health, but calling to mind the uncertainty of this life, and willing to dispose of what remains of my worldly estate, do make and publish this, my last will, recommending my soul into the hands of my Creator, hoping for a remission of all my sins through the merits and mediation of Jesus Christ, the Saviour of mankind; I dispose of my worldly esate as follows: —

"Imprimis — I give to my son, General George Washington, all my land in Accokeek Run, in the County of Stafford, and also my negro boy George, to him and his heirs forever. Also my best bed, bedstead, and Virginia cloth curtains (the same that stands in my best bedroom) my quilted blue and white quilt and my best dressing glass.

"Item — I give and devise to my son, Charles Washington, my negro man Tom, to him and his assigns forever.

"Item — I give and devise to my daughter, Bettie Lewis, my phaeton and my bay horse.

"Item — I give and devise to my daughter-in-law, Hannah Washington, my purple cloth cloak lined with shag.

"Item — I give and devise to my grandson, Corbin Washington, my negro wench old Bet, my riding chair, and two black horses, to him and his assigns forever.

"Item — I give and devise to my grandson, Fielding Lewis, my negro man, Frederick, to him and his assigns forever, also eight silver tablespoons, half of my crockery ware and the blue and white tea china, with book case, oval table, one bedstead, one pair sheets, one pair blankets and white cotton counterpain, two table cloths, six red leather chairs, half my peuter and one-half of my kitchen furniture.

[1] It appears that the testator omitted the word "nine."

"Item — I give and devise to my grandson, Lawrence Lewis, my negro wench Lydia, to him and his assigns forever.

"Item. — I give and devise to my granddaughter, Bettie Carter, my negro woman, little Bet, and her future increase, to her and her assigns forever. Also my largest looking glass, my walnut writing desk and drawers, a square dining table, one bed, bedstead, bolster, one pillow, one blanket and pair sheets, white Virginia cloth counterpains and purple curtains, my red and white tea china, teaspoons, and the other half of my peuter and crockery ware, and the remainder of my iron kitchen furniture.

"Item — I give and devise to my grandson, George Washington, my next best glass, one bed, bedstead, bolster, one pillow, one pair sheets, one blanket and counterpain.

"Item — I devise all my wearing apparel to be equally divided between my granddaughters, Bettie Carter, Fannie Ball, and Milly Washington, but should my daughter, Bettie Lewis, fancy any one, two or three articles, she is to have them before a division thereof.

"Lastly, I nominate and appoint my said son, General George Washington executor of this, my Will, and as I owe few or no debts, I direct my executor to give no security or appraise my estate, but desire the same may be allotted to my devisees, with as little trouble and delay as may be desiring their acceptance thereof as all the token I now have to give them of my love for them.

"In witness thereof, I have hereunto set my hand and seal the 20th day of May, 1788.

"MARY WASHINGTON."

WILL OF DANIEL WEBSTER

Daniel Webster died October 24, 1852. His will is a lengthy document, and its chief features are here set out:

"In the name of Almighty God! I, Daniel Webster of Marshfield in the County of Plymouth and Commonwealth of Massachusetts, Esquire, now being confined at my house with a serious illness which, considering my time of life, is undoubtedly critical, but being nevertheless in the full possession of all my mental faculties, do make and publish this my last will and testament.

"I commit my soul into the hands of my heavenly Father, trusting in his infinite goodness and mercy.

"I direct that my mortal remains be buried in the family vault at Marshfield, where monuments are already erected to my deceased children and their mother. Two places are marked for other monuments, of exactly the same size and form. One of these, in proper time, is to be for me, and perhaps I may leave an epitaph. The other is for Mrs. Webster. Her ancestors and all her deceased kindred lie in a far distant city. My hope is, that after many years, she may come to my side, and join me and others whom God hath given me. I wish to be buried without the least show or ostentation, but in a manner respectful to my neighbors, whose kindness has contributed so much to the happiness of me and mine, and for whose prosperity I offer sincere prayers to God.

"Concerning my worldly estate, my will must be anomalous and out of the common form, on account of the state of my affairs. I have two large real estates. By marriage settlement, Mrs. Webster is entitled to a life estate in each, and after her death they belong to my heirs. On the Franklin estate, so far as I know, there is no encumbrance except Mrs. Webster's life-estate. On Marshfield, Mr. Samuel Frothingham has an unpaid balance of a mortgage, now amounting to twenty five hundred dollars. My great and leading wish is, to preserve Marshfield, if I can, in the blood and name of my own family. To this end, it must go in the first place to my son, Fletcher Webster, who is hereafter to be the immediate prop of my house, and the general representative of my name and character."

Then follow certain suggestions with reference to trustees, by which they are given the right to dispose of the estate as exigencies may require. Mrs. Webster, by marriage settlement, was entitled to a life-estate in certain valuable real estate owned by the testator, and he indicated his desire that this life-estate should be purchased as being the best means to provide for her welfare. He then appointed his wife, Caroline LeRoy Webster, his son, Fletcher Webster, and R. M. Blatchford of New York, to be his executors. He then named James W. Paige, Franklin Haven of Boston, and Edward Curtis of New York, Trustees of all the real estate in the town of Marshfield, in the State of Massachusetts, and the town of Franklin in the State of New Hampshire, being his two principal estates, upon certain trusts: First, to pay to his wife, Caroline LeRoy Webster, the estimated value of her life interest: Secondly, to pay to said wife from the rents, profits and income of said two estates, the sum of five hundred dollars per annum during her natural life, and so much of the revenue not needed for the purposes aforesaid for the use of his son, Fletcher Webster, during his natural life; and after the decease of said son, to convey the same in fee to such of his male descendants as a majority of said Trustees might elect. He expressed the desire that his grandson, Ashburton Webster, take one, and his grandson, Daniel Webster, Jr., take the other of said estates.

He directed that his wife, Caroline LeRoy Webster, should have the right, at all times during her life, to reside in the mansion he had at Marshfield.

Unto his Executors, he gave all the books, plate, pictures, statuary, furniture and other personal property in the mansion at Marshfield, except such articles as were given to others in a latter portion of his will, in trust, to preserve the same in the mansion house for the use of his son, Fletcher Webster, during his natural life, and after his death, to make over and deliver the same to the person who would then become owner of the estate of Marshfield; the testator expressing his intention that they remain attached to the house while it was occupied by any of his name and blood.

Unto his son, Fletcher Webster, he gave all his law books, wherever situated, for his own use. To his son-in-law, Samuel A. Appleton, he gave his California watch and chain. The picture of himself by Healy he gave to his granddaughter, Caroline LeRoy Appleton. His gold snuff-box with the head of General Washington, together with all his fishing-tackle and his Selden and Wilmot guns, he gave to his grandson, Samuel Appleton; to his grandson, Daniel Webster Appleton, his Washington medals; to his granddaughter, Julia Webster Appleton, he gave a clock presented to her grandmother by the Honorable George Blake.

An item of general interest in the will is as follows:

"I appoint Edward Everett, George Ticknor, Cornelius Conway Felton, and George Ticknor Curtis, to be my literary executors; and I direct my son, Fletcher Webster to seal up all my letters, manuscripts and papers, and at a proper time to select those relating to my personal history and my professional and public life, which in his judgment should be placed at their disposal, and to transfer the same to them, to be used by them in such manner as they may think fit. They may receive valuable aid from my friend George J. Abbot Esq. now of the State Department."

The following provisions conclude the document:

"Item. My servant William Johnson is a freeman. I bought his freedom not long ago for six hundred dollars. No demand is to be made upon him for any portion of this sum, but so long as is agreeable, I hope he will remain with the family."

"Item. Monicha McCarty, Sarah Smith and Ann Bean, colored persons now also, and for a long time in my service, are all free. They are very well deserving, and whoever comes after me must be kind to them."

"Item. I request that my executors and trustees be not required to give bonds for the performance of their respective duties under this will."

WILL OF JOHN G. WHITTIER

The poet Whittier died September 7, 1892.

Omitting pecuniary legacies to various friends and relatives, amounting to $40,000, his Will is in the following words:

"Know all men by these Presents, That I, John G. Whittier of Amesbury in the County of Essex and Commonwealth of Massachusetts, being of sound mind and memory, but in enfeebled bodily health, do make this my last will and testament, hereby revoking any and all former wills by me before made.

"After the payment of all my just debts and funeral charges I give, bequeath and devise as follows:

"1st. I give, bequeath and devise to my niece Lizzie W. Pickard my homestead place in Amesbury, with all the books, pictures and furniture therein. I also give, bequeath and devise to my said niece my dwelling house known as the 'Gove Place' on the corner of Friend and Pleasant Streets in said Amesbury. I also give and bequeath to my said niece Fifteen Thousand dollars. . . ."

"9th. I give and bequeath to the Haverhill City Hospital One thousand dollars. . . ."

"14th. I give and bequeath to Caroline Johnson, Mary Johnson and Abby J. Woodman, my furniture, books and pictures at Oak Knoll, Danvers, not otherwise disposed of, to be equally divided among them. I also give and bequeath to each of them Five Hundred dollars. . . ."

"18th. I give and bequeath to Lucy Larcom, Five hundred dollars; also the copyright of 'Child Life,' 'Child Life in Prose' and 'Songs of Three Centuries.' . . ."

"22nd. I give and bequeath to my niece Lizzie W. Pickard before named, the Portrait of myself by Hoyt, at Oak Knoll, Danvers.

"23rd. I give and bequeath to Sarah O. Jewett of So. Berwick, Lanman's picture of the Sea and its marshes at the mouth of the Merrimac River, also at Oak Knoll, Danvers.

"24th. I give and bequeath to Annie Fields the Picture of Venice, also at Oak Knoll, Danvers.

"25th. I give and bequeath to the American Peace Society, Five hundred dollars.

"26th. I give and bequeath to the Amesbury Charitable Society, Five hundred dollars.

"27th. I give and bequeath to the Friends in Amesbury, Two hundred dollars, for the care of their burial ground. . . . "

"29th. The copyrights of my writings, with the exception of those given as aforesaid to Lucy Larcom, I place in the hands of my Executors, whom I hereby constitute and appoint as Trustees of the same; the income of which (as stipulated in an agreement with my publishers, Houghton, Mifflin & Co., dated August 12, 1883, to continue until ten years from that date) I hereby direct them to pay annually to Lizzie W. Pickard, Alice G. Berry, Charles F. Whittier, Louis H. Caldwell, Phebe J. Woodman and Addie P. Cammett, in the ratio and proportion of the cash legacies made to the above named persons in this Instrument: Nevertheless if in the judgment of my said Executors and Trustees it is deemed advisable, they are at liberty to dispose of said copyrights and divide the proceeds among the above named persons, in the proportion above named.

"30th. I give, bequeath and devise one half of the rest and residue of my estate, be it real, personal, or mixed, to Lizzie W. Pickard, Alice G. Berry, Charles F. Whittier, Louis H. Caldwell, Phebe J. Woodman, Addie P. Cammett and Adelaide G. Caldwell in the same ratio and proportion as mentioned in item 29th.

"31st. I give, bequeath and devise the remaining one half of the rest and residue of my estate, be it real, personal or mixed, in equal shares, to the Amesbury and Salisbury Home for Aged Women, The Anna Jaques Hospital in the City of Newburyport and the Normal and Agricultural Institute for Colored and Indian Pupils at Hampton, Va.

"32nd. I entrust my manuscripts, letters and papers to Samuel T. Pickard of Portland, Me., and request all who have letters of mine to refrain from publishing them, unless with his consent. It is my wish that my funeral may be conducted in the plain and quiet way of the Society of Friends with which I am connected, not only by birthright, but also by a settled conviction of the truth of its principles, and the importance of its testimonies.

"33rd. I hereby constitute and appoint George F. Bagley and George W. Cate both of Amesbury as Executors and Trustees of this my last Will and testament, and hereby request that they may be exempt from giving any surety or sureties on their bond as Executors or Trustees.

"In testimony whereof I hereunto set my hand, and in the presence of the three witnesses named below, declare this to be my last will and testament this eleventh day of February, in the year of our Lord one thousand eight hundred and ninety.

"JOHN G. WHITTIER."

WILL OF MARY CHILTON WINSLOW

In the files of Suffolk County Registry of Probate at Boston, there are still preserved a number of wills of members of the Plymouth Colony, of Mayflower fame, which are both quaint and interesting. Among these is the original will of Mary Chilton Winslow, together with a bond of the administrators, signed by her son, John Winslow, and son-in-law, Richard Middlecott.

This will is written on one side of a sheet of paper, a little over eighteen by fourteen inches in size, and is in excellent condition, except in some of the creases made by folding. The instrument is dated July 31, 1676. It recites:

"I, Mary Winslow of Boston in New England Widdow being weake of Body but of Sound and perfect memory praysed be almighty God for the same Knowing the uncertainety of this present life and being desirous to settle that outward Estate the Lord hath Lent me. I doe make this my last Will and Testam^t in manner and forme following:"

The bequests are very numerous: she gives to her son, John Winslow, her "great Square table." Unto her daughter, Sarah Middlecott, her "Best gowne and Pettecoat" and her "Silver beare bowle," and to each of her children, "a Silver Cup with a handle." Unto her daughter, Susanna Latham, one "long Table and one great Cupboard"; and unto her grandchild, Susanna Latham, one "Pette Coat with the silke Lace." To Mary Winslow, daughter of her "sone," Joseph Winslow, the "sume of twenty pounds in money to be paid unto said Mary when she attains the age of eighteen years or day of Marriage which of them should first happen." Unto "Thomas Thacher paster of the third Church in Boston," the sum of five pounds was given. The inventory attached to this will is an exceedingly interesting document, dealing as it does with the articles of dress and household use of those days.

Will of Brigham Young

It does not fall to the lot of many men to make such a testamentary disposition as that of Brigham Young. He died on August 29, 1877.

He provided for the payment of his debts and the current expenses of his numerous families: the bulk of his fortune of the estimated value of Two Million Five Hundred Thousand Dollars, was left in trust for his families; the trustees being George Q. Cannon, Brigham Young, Jr., and Albert Carrington.

His families were divided into classes, each class being represented by a wife and children, or a wife without children, or the children of a deceased wife. There were nineteen classes in all. At the time of his death, his living wives numbered eighteen, and there were three deceased: he was also "sealed" to a number of other women, in accordance with the ritual of the Mormon Church. The authorities vary as to the number of these spiritual wives. However, no mention is made of them in the will. He had forty-eight children, including an adopted child.

The estate was divided into nineteen parts, as stated; upon the death of the mother, the children taking the mother's share, which was to be held in trust until they became of age, respectively.

Though Mr. Young is said to have given largely to charities during his life, no such bequests are included in his will.

INDEX

INDEX

Accuracy, in writing of wills necessary, 220.
Acorns, to be planted on grave of Sir Charles Hastings, 155.
Actors, benefited by the will of Garrick, 270; by the will of Booth, 339; by the will of Forrest, 364–369; by the will of Jefferson, 396.
Actors' Fund, the, 339, 397.
Actors' Home, the, 396.
Actress, beneficiary must become an, 162.
Adam, said to have left a will, xii, 10.
Adams, John Quincy, will of, 324–330.
Agassiz, Louis, preamble to will of, 198; his pride in vocation of teacher, 198; *Boston Globe* editorial on, 198–200.
Alcott, Louisa M., will of a child in "Little Women," 58.
Alden, Captain John, will of, 330, 331.
Alienation of land, forbidden in will of Plato, 14.
Aligre, Marquis d', will of, 249–251.
Americans, famous wills of, 324–454.
Ancient Wills, 10–48; Barnabé Brisson an authority on, xii.
André, John, Major, his last request to General Washington, 221, 222.
"Anglicus," the pardoned poet, will of, 246, 247.
Anglo-Saxon Wills, made in triplicate, xii.
Angoulême, Duchesse d', her remorse for the "Lost Dauphin," 242.
Animals, *see* Dumb Animals.
Annuity, a prolonged, 185.
Anthems, bequest for singing of favorite, 178.
"Anticipating the past," 90.
Antonelli, Cardinal Giacomo, will of, 252–258.
Aram, Eugene, skull of, in York Castle, 135.
Arbilot, Mr., the humorous will of an eccentric Scotchman, 185.
Arbitration, disputes over estate of Susan M. Corning to be settled by, 177.
Archer, Henry, bequest for benefit of poor in gratitude for honors conferred, 117.

Aristotle, will of, 14–16.
"Arlotto, the Parson," will of, 35.
Armada, The Spanish, bequest for sermon on deliverance from, 174.
Armenjon, Laurentine, 259.
Arms, bare, considered immodest by Yorkshire rector, 186.
Arnold, Benedict, will of, 331–333.
Arnold, Matthew, will of, 258.
Artists, poor, provided for in the will of Turner, 314.
Ashes, cast into the sea, 127, 144.
Ashes, cast to the four winds from Eads Bridge, St. Louis, 157.
Asselineau, Charles, his unique collection of paper-knives, 163.
Astronomical observatory, of Lick, 402, 403.
Audubon, John James, will of, 333.
Auger, Jean Baptiste Robert, will of, 258, 259.
Augustus Cæsar, will of, 17–20.
Aunt Lunky, will of a negro servant, 81.
Autopsy, Duchess of Northumberland prohibits, 132.

Bacon, Lord, will of, 259.
Bakhuysen, Ludolf, gold coins and wine distributed at his funeral, 133.
Baliol, John, of Barnard Castle, heart disposed of by widow, 21.
Balliston, John, devise to provide bread, beer, beef, and broth for poor, 120.
Balls, Elizabeth, her charitable will, 95; provision for her horse and greyhound, 95.
Balzac, Honoré de, quotation from, 7; describes a weird custom in "The Country Doctor," 241.
Banks, bequest for founding patriotic, 228.
Banquet-table, a strange guest at, 138.
Barber, Robert, bequest for best recital of catechism, 163.
Bardsey Island, to be reinterred in, 132.
Barefooted, must walk, on anniversary of husband's death, 89.
Baring-Gould, S., comments on the will of a pig, 20.

458 INDEX

Barn, coffin to hang from beam in, for thirty years, 143.
Barnum, Phineas Taylor, will of, 334, 335.
Barnum Institute, the, 335.
Barrot, Rosine, enigmatical will of, 191.
Bastian, Elizabeth, provides for a costly mausoleum at expense of relatives, 135.
Battle, bequest as memorial of gratitude for preservation in, 116.
Baume, Pierre Henri, his frugal life, 197; his fortune for charity, 197, 198.
Beauchamp, Guy de, Earl of Warwick, will of, 24.
Beauchamp, William de, will of, 22.
Beauchamp, William de, Earl of Warwick, will of, 23.
Beaumont sur Vingeanne, Seigneur de, François de la Palu Varembon, his desire for bright colors, 152; his heirs to wear white at his funeral, 152.
Bed, M. Helloin buried in his, as Death found him, 143; Langton Freeman buried in his, in summer-house, 144.
Beecher, Henry Ward, will of, 335, 336.
Beer, provided for in will of eccentric German, 106.
Bell, bequest for tolling of the, 116.
Bell, Elijah, will of, 226; his undertaker paid in advance, 226.
Benoît, Sieur, desired to be buried in a leather trunk, 138.
Bentham, Jeremy, strange will of, 138; his body preserved and placed at banquet-table, 138; now in possession of University College, 138; description of Dr. Smith regarding, 139.
Benton, Thomas H., will of, 336, 337.
Beresford Hall, 316, 317.
Bergavenny, Joan, Lady, desired to be buried without pomp or vainglory, 151.
Berkeley, Mr., leaves pension for four dogs, 99; his gratitude to, 99.
Berne, will of citizen of, to fix price of corn and wine, 118.
Berne, Richard, will of, 32; bequest to prisoners, 32; for repair of highways, 32.
Bevill, Sir Robert, vindictive will of, 86.
Bibles, bequest of, 170; possession of decided by throwing dice, 170.
Bigsby, James, will of, in rhyme, 70.
Birkbeck, Anna Margaret, directs that family letters be placed in coffin, 140.
Bizony, Emile von, bequest to his twelve horses, 94.
Blaine, James G., will of, 338.
Bletzer, Harris, his view of the world, 161.
Blyth, Thomas, directs that no mourning be worn for him, 173; his appreciation of Dolly Varden garters, 173.
Boby, Sieur, eccentric will of, 128; his heart to be removed, 129; his epitaph, 129.
Body, Jeremy Taylor's, preserved and seated at banquet-table on great occasions, 138|; to be dismembered and given to relatives, 167; bequeathed for useful purposes, 191; to be sold for liquidation of debts, 315.
Books, an early bequest of, 31; in the coffin of John Underwood, 151.
Booth, Edwin T., will of, 338–340.
Boston, Mass., Charles Dickens's views on charitable institutions of, 243; benefited by the will of Benjamin Franklin, 370, 371.
Boston Globe, the, editorial on Louis Agassiz, 198–200.
Boudinot, Elias, a lengthy sermon in will of, 192.
Bouton, Charles, simplicity marked obsequies of, 142.
Bouton, Philippe, fourteen girls dressed in green to attend his obsequies, 142.
Brain, of Dr. Ellerby to be preserved, 129; blank form for bequest of, 176.
Braunmiller, Joel, directs that his body be cremated and his ashes cast to the four winds, 157; to be done from Eads Bridge, St. Louis, 157.
Bread, bequest for, for poor, 116, 118, 121; in honor of John Bunyan, 117.
Bread, beer, beef, and broth, devise to provide, for poor, 120.
Bretagne, François, Duc de, bequest for masses and instructions for bell ringing, 133.
Bretagne, Marguérite de, bequest for masses, 134.
Brewer, David J., will of, 340–342.
Brisson, Barnabé, authority on ancient wills, xii; works of, 134.
Brotherly love, bequest for promotion of, 114.
Brown, James, his views on political independence, 174.
Brunswick, Duke of, will of, 260, 261.
Budd, Henry, antipathy to mustaches shown in will of, 87.
Budgell, Eustace, account of, 58.
Bull Baiting, provided for in will of George Staverton, 110; since discontinued, 111.
Bulwer-Lytton, Edward, quotation from, 215; will of, 261.
Bunyan, John, bequest for bread in honor of, 117.
Burial, provision for, in will of Virgil,

INDEX 459

16; instructions of Augustus, 18; of William de Beauchamp, 23; of Dukes of Lancaster, 25; of Lady Joan De Cobham, 25; instructions for in various wills, 122-158; customs in Austria, 138.
Buried alive, fear of being, 25, 130.
Burke, Edmund, will of, xiii, 261-266.
Burney, Frances, the will in "Memoirs of an Heiress," 56.
Burns, Peter, philanthropic bequest in will of, 103.
Burr, Aaron, will of, 342; duel with Alexander Hamilton, 379, 380; later life, 380, 381.
Butcher, unexpected good fortune of a, 164.
Butler, Benjamin F., will of, 343, 344.
Butler, George, devise of land and buildings for a Travellers' Rest, 107.
Butler and Baker's Case, 206.

CAFÉ, testator desired his body carried to favorite, on day of his funeral, 152, 153.
Camelford, Lord, desired to be buried in a beautiful country, 152.
Capacity, comment on testamentary, 203-205.
Carey, Tereisse, unique and illiterate will of, 188.
Caroline, Queen, will of, 266, 267.
Carp, bequests to, 91.
Carriages, to be burned on the day of owner's funeral, 131.
Carrington, Richard Christopher, ordered a deep grave, 153; no service to be read over, 153; not to be shaved, 153.
Cartault, Madame Jeanne, bequest for marriage portion to most deserving poor working girls, 113; requirements for naming the first-born, 113; the first beneficiary of, 114.
Cartouche, bequest of his skull to Genovevan Monastery at Paris, 135.
Cassiday, Joseph Johnson, will of, in rhyme, 71.
"Castle Rest," summer home of Pullman's mother, 413.
Cat, bequests to, 100, 101, 102; instructions for feeding, 101.
Cat and Dog Money, provided in certain parts of England, 100.
Catechism, bequest for best recital of, 163.
Cats' home, bequest for, by Jonathan Jackson, 101.
Cayuga Lake, heir must not go to or upon, 80.
Cecilia, in "Memoirs of an Heiress," 56; restrictions on marriage of, 56.

Cervantes, Saavedra, will of "Don Quixote," 60.
Character, wills a reflection of, xi.
Charitable and kindred institutions, gifts to, 7.
Charity, 102-122.
Charles I., last moments of, 244; his cloak and earring, 244.
Chase, Salmon P., will of, 344, 345.
Chesterfield, Lord, bequest for pet cat, 102; will of, 267; letter to Dr. Johnson, 274, 275.
Cheyenne Mountain, the burial place of Helen Hunt Jackson, 234.
Child, will of a, in "Little Women," 58.
Children, provision for, 8; one hundred at *monethe's minde*, 33; dislike of, 88; one half of estate to heirs who had the most, 183.
Chinaman, unique will of a, 78.
Chorley, H. F., bequests to Charles Dickens and his daughter Mary, 215.
Christian Science Church, benefited by will of Mrs. Eddy, 356-361.
Christiano, Dr., bequest for benefit of three dogs, 98.
Christmas dinner, bequest for, for almshouse women, 116.
Christ's Hospital, bequest for raisins for boys of, 118.
Chudleigh, Elizabeth, Duchess of Kingston, remarkable will of, 134.
Church, bequest to poor who attend, on stated days, 111; bequest to encourage attendance at, 115; body of donor mixed in mortar of, 144.
Cicero, mentions wills, xii.
Clay, Henry, will of, 345-348.
Clegg, a conjurer, humorous will of, 141; music and drinking a feature of his funeral, 141; to be dressed in his "roast-meat" clothes for burial, 141.
Clemens, Samuel L., will of, 348, 349.
Clergy, executors of early French wills, xii.
Clergymen, as affected by the will of Stephen Girard, 373, 374.
Cleveland, Grover, will of, 349, 350.
Clover blossom, yearly rental of a town park to be one, 232.
Cobham, Lady Joan De, will of, 25; directions for burial, 25; provision for seven thousand masses, 26.
Codicil, to will, 9.
Coffin, of plain boards covered with black calico, 128; to hang for thirty years from beam in barn, 143; and vault to be lighted by electricity, 149.
Cogan, John, bequest for encouragement to long service by maid-servants, 110.

Coke, Lord, comment on wills, vii, 6; in *Butler and Baker's Case*, 206.
Cold World, A, pathetic will so states, 82.
Collar box, a valid will on a, 168.
Columbus, Christopher, will of, 36; a mere codicil, 36; written in Latin, 36; peculiar signature to, 36; provides for an hospital, 36.
Confucius, quotation from, 225; tomb of, 225; Golden Rule of, 226.
"Coningsby," will of Lord Monmouth in, 52.
Conjurer, humorous will of a, 141.
Conkling, Roscoe, will of, 351.
Cooke, John, provides for sweeping aisle of church, 106; for a lantern to burn all night, 106.
Cooper, Edward, bequest of "a drinking," 115.
Cooper, Ellen H., pathetic will of, 82.
Corcoran, William W., will of, 351, 352.
Corcoran Gallery of Art in Washington, bequest to, 351.
Corn, will of citizen of Berne to control price of, 118.
Cornfield, to be buried in a ploughed, 148.
Corning, Susan M., disputes over estate of, to be settled by arbitration, 177.
Cortusio, Lodovico, desired a gay funeral, 140; disinherits those who weep and rewards laughter, 140; a dowry for twelve girls who carried his body, 141; his wishes observed to the least detail, 141.
Costs, in suit over Turner's will, 314.
Cotton, Charles, and Izaak Walton, 316, 317.
"Count of Monte Cristo, The," Old Noitier's will in, 51.
"Country Doctor, The," a weird custom described in, 241.
Court, requested not to make another will, 54.
Cows, bequest to provide, for use of the poor, 120.
Cremation, William Kinsett an early believer in, 127; account of an early, in Dodsley's *Annual Register*, 127.
Crittenden, William Logan, last lines from, 224, 225.
Cross, wood from the true, 23.
Crowell, W. H., spirit will of, 172.
Cumming, Dr. F. W., bequest for snuff and tobacco for poor, 116.
Cup, broken, bequest of, by Marquis d' Aligre, 251.
Curious Wills, 73-202.

Curll, Edmund, rare and curious collection of wills of, 239, 240; a list of those he published, 240.
Cynical will, a, 170.

DALRYMPLE, Sir David — see Hailes, Lord.
Darkness, a horror of, 149; provision against, 149.
Daughter, bequest of, by Eudamidas, 11.
Daughter, restrictions on marriage of, 23, 52.
Davis, Jefferson, will of, 352, 353.
Davis, Mary, ordered that she be dressed in cambric for burial, 124.
Davis, Mr., a bequest for liquor, 160.
Dean, Mr. Justice, remarks in a will case, 215.
Death, figure of on tombstone, 65.
Debts, strange clause in a will to provide for payment of, 315.
Decoration Day, Robert G. Ingersoll's address on, 211.
Denny, Sir Thomas, will of, 65; directions for tombstone and epitaph, 65.
De Ovies, Count Julian S., directs that his body be cremated and his heart sent to Spain, 123.
Desbillons, François J. T., will of, in Latin, 65.
Desertion, by wife rewarded, 88.
Desk, a novel way of secreting will in a, 231.
Destroyed will, in "The Thunderbolt," by Pinero, 55.
Devil, attempts to bequeath property to, 241.
Dice, bequest of Bibles decided by throwing, 170.
Dickens, Charles, a great will-maker, 55; his views of the charitable institutions of Boston, 243; of elderly testators, 243.
Dickinson, Charles C., eccentric will of, 80; disliked Cayuga Lake, 80.
Dijon, Viscomte de, desired to be buried where people could walk over his body, 123.
Dilke, Fisher, a miserly husband, 157.
Dispatch, the St. Paul, quotes will of the pardoned poet, 246, 247.
Disraeli, Benjamin, will of Lord Monmouth in "Coningsby," 52.
Dodge, William E., bequest to eldest son for spread of the Gospel, 217; views on charitable bequests, 217.
Dodsley's *Annual Register*, 1769, an early account of a cremation, 128.
Dog, Mother Hubbard's, will of, 62; income from bank stock for a, 95; for the care of a favorite, 95; an-

INDEX   461

nuities for a, 96, 98; suit to obtain damages for the killing of a, 438.
Dogs, hospital for, in Marseilles, 97; bequest for three, 98; pensioned by Mr. Berkeley, 99.
Domicile, place of, England or France, as affecting a will, 273.
Don Quixote, will of, 60.
Door, will written on a, 167.
Douglas, Stephen A., will of, 353, 354.
Dowe, Robert, bequest for exhortation to condemned prisoners in Newgate, 245; the form of, 245, 246.
Dower, clause with regard to, in will of George G. Vest, 437.
Dowry, bequest of annual, for young girl of testator's native village, 133; conditional on beneficiaries dancing on his grave annually, 133.
Dress, will in the pocket of an old, 216.
Drinking, a bequest for, 115; a feature at funeral of a conjurer, 142.
Drinking fountains, established by will of Phoebe Deliah Nye, in St. Louis, 97.
Dryden, John, will of, 267, 268.
Dryenforth, Robert G., exacting and peculiar will of, 146; his heir in a difficult position, 147.
Du Cange, Charles Dufresne, mentions wills on bark, xii.
Du Châtelet, desired to be buried standing, 123.
Duhalde, Paul, his partnership with God, 194; the sincerity of his intentions, 195; justified by his will, 196.
Dumas, Alexandre, Old Noitier's will in "The Count of Monte Cristo," 51.
Dumb Animals, bequests to, 90–102.
Dunlop, Dr., his humorous will not unmixed with malice, 179.
Duplicate, wills should be in, 9.
Dupuis, Madame, bequest for pet cats, 101; instructions for feeding cats, 101.
Dwyer, Joseph, a valid will on wrapping-paper, 168.

EADS BRIDGE, St. Louis, ashes cast to the four winds from, 157.
Earle, William Benson, bequest for food for poor, and for flowers on grave, 118.
Early Rising, bequests contingent on, 180.
Early Wills, in France, xii.
Earring, of Charles I, 244.
Earthly happiness, insured by refusal of proposals to marriage, 160.
Easter, love-feast, bequest to provide turkeys for, 120.
Eccentricities, wills a reflection of, xi.

Ecles-hall, England, in Izaak Walton's will, 318.
Eddinger, Samuel, unique and illiterate will of, 188.
Eddy, Mary Baker G., will of, 354–361; burial of, 361, 362.
Edmett, Thomas, annuity for favorite dog, 98.
Edmunds, John, unusual bequest of, 170.
Education, clauses relating to, in will of Cecil John Rhodes, 295; in will of Sam Houston, 388; in will of George Washington, 442.
Edward I, will of in French, 24; his body to be boiled in a caldron, 24; Edward II ignores request, 24.
Edward IV, will of, 268.
Edwin Forrest Home, The, 364–369.
Egypt, wills in, xii.
Elder, a certain, debarred from holding office in testator's church, 220.
Eldon, Lord, annuity to his dog, 96; Lord Campbell's account of, 96; his dog painted by Landseer, 96.
Elegy on a wife, 211, 212.
Eliot, George, Mr. Casaubon's will in "Middlemarch," 52.
Elizabeth, Queen, bequest for sermon in remembrance of, 174.
Elks, Alameda Lodge of, beneficiary under will of R. B. Tappan, 247.
Ellerby, Dr., bequeaths his heart, brain, and lungs to friends, 129.
Embalmed, body not to be, 25.
Emerson, Ralph Waldo, will of, 362–364.
England, wills known in, before Conquest, xii; forbidden by law in, xii.
Engler, Lawrence, will of, 84; peculiar provision in, 84.
Enigmatical will, of Rosine Barrot, 191.
Eno, Amos R., bequest to New York Chamber of Commerce for impoverished members, 219.
Epitaph, instructions for, 65; a unique, 125, 134; of Robert Louis Stevenson, 233; of Thomas Jefferson, 234; of Queen Caroline, 266; of Dean Swift, 310.
Erasmus, Dedidierius, will of, 37; in Latin, 37; bequest to industrious young people, 38.
Ericsson, John, his nervousness, 213, 214; will of, 214; his remains sent to Sweden on U. S. S. *Baltimore*, 214.
Eudamidas of Corinth, will of, 11; filial and parental affection shown by, 11.
Executor, a farmer's idea of the duty of an, 221.
Executors, of wills, 9; trust companies as, 248.

462 INDEX

FABYAN, Robert, curious will of, 145; detailed instructions for tomb of, 145.
Fanatical will, of Rev. William Hill, 187.
Fanciful will, "A Last Will," 207–209.
Fane, John, bequest for prayers for his soul, 132.
Farrar, William, will of, 231.
Farren, William, his opinion of undergraduates, 174.
Faxon, William, phonograph reproduces his singing at his funeral, 226.
Fellowes, Sir Charles, will of, 268.
Female attire, a bequest contingent on a man wearing, 169.
Fiction and Poetry, wills in, 49–72.
Fish, bequest for, for poor in Lent, 120; annuity for poor for, 121.
Fish, Williston, author of "A Last Will," 207–209; beautiful sentiment expressed by, 207.
Fitzgerald, Lord Edward, will of, 268, 269.
Fleming, Mr., was opposed to mustaches, 161.
Food, bequest of, for poor, 118.
Foreigners, wills of famous, 249–323.
Forgotten, John Underwood desired to be, 151.
Forrest, Edwin, will of, 364–369.
Fortunes, bequests for, honestly acquired, 170.
France, early wills in, xii; executed by the clergy, xii.
François II., Duke of Brittany, bequest for masses, 134.
Franklin, Benjamin, will of, 369–371; and Voltaire, 316.
Fraser, Dr., his bequest to the S. S. P. C. A., 181; his opposition to vivisection, 181; his dislike for funeral display, 181.
Freeman, Langton, buried in his bed in summer-house, 144; his body mummified, 144.
Frenchman, eccentric will of a, 156; devised fortune to people of London, 156; desired new cooking recipes, 156; makes restitution through insane asylum, 156; peculiar clause in will of, regarding names of Anton and Antonie, 178.
Froissard, records will of Edward I., 24.
Fuller, Melville W., will of, 372.
Funeral, provision for, by William de Beauchamp, 23; a pauper's, for a wealthy man, 131; to be "third class," 137; to be gay and mirthful, 140; elaborate and costly, 149.
Funeral expenses, his, bequeathed to nephew by wealthy aunt, 124.
Furstone, Mr., bequest to any man of same name under certain conditions, 169.

GARASSE'S "DOCTRINE CURIEUSE," mentions will of Lodovico Cortusio, 140.
Garrick, David, will of, 269–271.
Garters, black and white, as a mark of respect, 173.
Gayer, John, Sir, bequest for a sermon on being saved from a lion, 169.
Gazetta del Popolo (Turin), account of will for benefit of dogs, 98.
Gebhard, Frederic, will of, 230.
Generous bequests, made with a small estate, 159.
Geneva, benefited by will of Duke of Brunswick, 260, 261.
George, Mr., makes imaginary children residuary legatees, 160.
German, peculiar request of eccentric, 156; his ashes scattered to the four winds of heaven, 156.
Germans, wills not recognized by ancient, xii.
Gest, John M., address on "Practical Suggestions for Writing Wills," 205–207.
Gifts, *causa mortis*, 8.
Gilwee, James, provides trust fund for a favorite horse, 95.
Gimcrack, Nicholas, a virtuoso, will of, 56.
Girard, Stephen, will of, 372–375.
Girard College, 372–375.
Gloves, story of the Marquis d'Aligre's, 249.
God, Paul Duhalde's partnership with, 194; thankfulness to, as expressed in will of Robert North, 200–202.
Gold coins and wine, distributed at funeral of Bakhuysen, 133.
Goldfish, legacy to, 91; flowers for their graves, 91.
Goodaker, James, bequest to provide cows for use of poor of parish, 120.
Goodman, Valentine, bequest for most indigent paupers, 111; or for redemption of Turkish captives, 112.
Gosden, his edition of the "Journey to Beresford Hall," quoted, 316.
Gospel, bequest for spread of the, 217.
Gossip, Duchesse D'Olonne afraid of, 150.
Gould, Jay, will of, 375.
Grainger, Robert, bequest for bread for poor, 121.
Granary Burying-Ground (Boston), last resting place of "Mother Goose," 63.
Grant, Ulysses S., died intestate, vii.
Grates v. *Fraser*, 181.
Grave, bequest for flowers on, 118; Du Châtelet desired perpendicular, 123;

INDEX 463

Viscomte de Dijon desired people to walk over his, 123; beneficiaries to dance on, 133; a deep, 136; tobacco to be planted on, 150; acorns on, 155.
"Greater Testament, The," by François Villon, will in, 64.
Greece, wills introduced into, by Solon, xii.
Greeley, Horace, will of, 376–378.
Green Bag, The, on wills of the novelists, 51; account of "Mr. Meeson's Will," 53.
Green, Henry, four green waistcoats to be given yearly by beneficiary of, 111.
Greftulke, John Louis, fear of being buried alive, 148; orders body embalmed and not buried, 148.
Gregory, James J. H., bequest for benefit of twins born in Marblehead, 109.
Griffen, Jesse H., desired no display at his funeral, 142; his will written on a bill-head, 142.
Guardian, earliest known mention of, in a will, 13.

HAGGARD, H. Rider, "Mr. Meeson's Will," 53.
Hailes, Lord (Sir David Dalrymple), will of, 271.
Hair, weird custom relating to, of widow, 241.
Hall, John, bequest to provide turkeys for Easter love-feast, 120.
Halley, E. J., his will full of unique bequests, 163.
Halliday, Robert, bequest for promotion of brotherly love, 114.
Hamerton, Sir Richard, will of, 33.
Hamilton, Alexander, will of, 378, 379; duel with Aaron Burr, 379, 380.
Hamilton, Lady, and Lord Nelson's will, 280, 281.
Hampton, William, bequest of Interest Tables, 173.
Hand, Countess of Loudoun directs that her, be cut off, 125.
Harding, Robert, annuity for poor to buy cuttings of fish in Lent, 121.
Harper, Frederic, bequest for pet cat, 102.
Harper's Weekly, on property rights of women, 75–78.
Harriman, Edward H., will of, 381.
Harris, Lundy H., unusual inventory filed by wife of, 226, 227.
Haskett, William J., his bequest to the New York Press Club, 186.
Hastings, Charles, the unique will of, 172.
Hastings, Charles, Sir, desired no coffin, 155; his grave to be planted with acorns, 155.

Hatch, Rufus, advice to children in will of, 217.
Hatch, Thomas, bequest for marriage fees of poor couples, 113.
Haughery, Margaret, monument to, 213; her work for charity, 213.
Hawley, General, drafted his own will out of hatred for lawyers, 167.
Hazlitt, William, on will making, in "Table Talk or Original Essays," 49–51.
Heart, disposition and bequests of, 21, 23; of Count De Ovies to be sent to Spain, 123; of Sieur Boby to be removed and buried, 129; of Dr. Ellerby to be preserved, 129.
Hedges, John, will of, in rhyme, 65.
Heemskirk, Martin, bequest for annual dowry for a young girl of his native village, 133; conditional on beneficiaries dancing on his grave annually, 133.
Heidelberg Library, Luther's will in, 42.
Height, beneficiaries must be tall in, 161.
Helloin, M., buried in his bed as Death found him, 143.
Henry II. (England), will of, in "Testamenta Vetusta," 43.
Henry III. (England), will of, in "Testamenta Vetusta," 43.
Henry IV. (England), will of, in "Testamenta Vetusta," 43.
Henry V. (England), will of, in "Testamenta Vetusta," 43.
Henry VI. (England), will of, in "Testamenta Vetusta," 43.
Henry VII. (England), will of, 37; opposed to pomp and ceremonial, 37; will in "Testamenta Vetusta," 43.
Henry VIII. (England), will of, 43; great testamentary powers conferred on, 43; found in Nicholas's "Testamenta Vetusta," 43.
Henry, Patrick, will of, 381–386.
Henterus, his exact copy of Luther's will, 42.
Heviant, Thomas, singular bequest for prizes for riding pigs, 102.
Hickington, William, will of, in rhyme, 66.
Highway, bequest for repair of, 31, 32.
Hill, William, fanatical will of, 187; his religious belief, 187.
History of wills, 1; a Roman invention, 2; difficulty of making proper, 2; making of, an important act, 2; defects in, 2; legality of, important, 3; fallacies regarding, 3; distinction between words in, 3; illustration of improper phrasing, 4; general framework of, 5; proper time to make, 6;

INDEX

gifts to charitable and kindred institutions in, 7; legal advice in making, 8; witnesses to, 8; provision for children in, 8; trust provisions in, 9; executors of, 9; codicils to, 9; planning of, 9; duplicates of, 9.
Holbein, Hans, will of, 42; found in St. Paul's Cathedral archives, 43.
Hollis, Thomas, peculiar instructions for burial of, 148.
Holmes, Oliver Wendell, will of, 386.
Holybrande, William, kindness to widow enjoined by, 83.
Home, heirs must remain at, 84.
Homer, cites will of Telemachus, 11.
Hood, Thomas, will of, 272.
Hook, Major, his original method of prolonging an annuity, 185.
Hopkins, Johns, will of, 387; anecdote of, 410.
Hopkins, Stephen, will of, 387, 388.
Horace, mentions wills, xii.
Horse, will in favor of a, 94.
Horse-racing, contingent bequest for, 176.
Horses, testators, to be shot, 93; bequest to twelve, 94; hospital for, in Marseilles, 97; to be shot the day after owner's funeral, 131; complication over bequest of black and white, 178.
Hospital, for Idiots, money bequeathed for, by Dean Swift, 311.
Houston, Sam, will of, 388, 389.
Howard, Samuel D., will of an entombed miner, 238, 239.
Howden, Lord, will of, 272, 273.
Howe, Julia Ward, will of, 389, 390.
Humorous will, not without malice, 179; suggested by *Puck*, 220, 221.
Hungerford, Lady Joane, will of, 31; provides for three thousand masses, 31; torches to be held by poor women suitably clothed, 32; provides for mourning for her family, 32.
Hunnis, William, will of, in rhyme, 70.
Hunter, Caroline, legacy to a parrot, 93.
Hunter, Elizabeth, annuity to pet parrot, 92.
Huntingdon, John, devise to provide white peas for poor, 122.
Huntington, Collis P., his directions as to investments, 219.
Hurst, Edward, peculiar requirement as to marriage of son, 89.
Husband, two hundred dollars for a, 78; a contrite, 81; must not remarry, 228.
Husbands, duty of, to make wills, 75.
Husbands, wives, and children, 73–90.

IDIOTS, Hospital for, *see* Insane Asylum.
Idol, devise of lands to an, held valid, 241, 242.

Illegitimate children, school for, 162; having, a bar to inheritance, 189.
Illiterate wills, 188.
Imber, Luke, directs that he be buried in an old chest, 124.
Indian slaves, valuation of, in tobacco in colonial times, 231.
Infidel, wishes of an, ignored by relatives, 132.
Ingalls, John James, will of, 390, 391.
Ingersoll, Robert G., address on Decoration Day, 211.
Insane Asylum, French lawyer makes restitution through, 156; provided for in will of Swift, 311.
Inscription, *see* Epitaph.
Interest, bequest for best dissertation on putting money out at, 228.
Interest Tables, bequest of, as incentive to economy, 173.
Interment, *see* Burial.
Inventory, an unusual, 226, 227.
"Iris," by Pinero, will in, 54; widow forbidden to remarry, 54.
Irish, an Englishman's bequest for whiskey for the extermination of the, 182.
Irish Law Times, comments on oldest written will, 12.
Irving, Washington, will of, 391, 392.
Italian nobleman, revengeful will of, 81.

JACKETT, Will, will of, in rhyme, 67.
Jackson, Andrew, will of, 392–394.
Jackson, Helen Hunt, her desire to be buried on Cheyenne Mountain, 234.
Jackson, Jonathan, bequest for cats' home, 101.
Jackson, Luke, devise for the preaching of sermons, and for the poor, 109.
Jacob, makes earliest known reference to testamentary disposition, 10; will of, 11.
James, Jefferson G., eccentric will of, 235; his aversion to European travel, 235.
Jay, John, will of, 395.
Jefferson, Joseph, will of, 396, 397.
Jefferson, Thomas, his grave on the crest of Monticello ("Little Mountain"), 234; his epitaph, 234; monument to, 234; will of, 397–400.
Jekyll, Dr., *see* "Strange Case of Dr. Jekyll and Mr. Hyde."
Jerome, Jerome K., humorous description of wills, 54.
Jewelry, bequest of, by Sennacherib, 13.
Jewess, will of rich, provided that her body be taken to Jerusalem for interment, 144.
Jilted lover, unique will of a, 230.

INDEX 465

Job, said to have left a will, xii; will of, 10.
Johns Hopkins Hospital, 387.
Johns Hopkins University, 387.
Johnson, Cora, had a small estate, but made generous bequests, 159.
Johnson, Dr. Samuel, will of, xiii, 273, 274; letter of, to Lord Chesterfield, 274, 275.
Johnston-Wood, Harriette M., on property rights of women, in *Harper's Weekly*, 75-78.
Jolly Testator Who Makes His Own Will, The, 209, 210.
Jones, Charles, bequest for an hospital for 12 poor men of Pullhelly, 105.

KATHERINE OF ARAGON, will of, 39.
Kelley, Eugene, tribute to his friend in will of, 217, 218; preferences in charitable bequests, 218.
Kennerley, Mitchell, his tribute to his deceased wife, 211, 212.
King, W. R. Smee's delusion that he was the son of a, 190.
Kingston, Duchess of, *see* Chudleigh.
Kinsett, William, an early believer in cremation, 127.
Klaës, Mr., known as the "King of Smokers," 200; his bequests of pipes and tobacco, 200; tobacco and smoking utensils in his coffin, 200.

LALANNE, M., a pauper's funeral for a wealthy man, 131.
Lamb, Charles, quoted on Izaak Walton, 316.
Lancaster, Dukes of, wills of, 25.
Lane, Richard, bequest for church music, 162.
Langland, William, the will in "Vision of Piers Plowman," 63.
Lantern, to be lighted all night, 105, 106.
Last Will and Testament, Importance of the, 1-9.
Laughter, the heartiest, to indicate the principal heir, 140.
Launde, Sir Robert, will of, 25.
Laurens de la Barre, du, Adolphe-Théodore-Ange, bequest for marriage portion to girls of republican opinions, 108.
Law-suit, as affecting the heirs of Chief Justice Marshall, 407.
Lawyers, General Hawley's dislike for, 167.
Lawyer's Best Friend, 209.
L. C., annuity in will of, for stray dogs, 98; annuity for favorite dog, 98.
Lee, Robert E., will of, 401, 402.
Legal advice, desirability of, 8.

Leland Stanford Junior University, 428.
Lent, bequest for fish for poor in, 120; annuity for fish for poor in, 121.
"Lesser Testament, The," by François Villon, will in, 64.
Letters, of husband and children to be placed in coffin of Anna Margaret Birkbeck, 140.
Lewes, George Henry, will of, 276.
Libel, an instance of testamentary, 181.
Library, the Pepysian, 294; of Richelieu, 300; of Izaak Walton, 319; of John Quincy Adams, 327; of Thomas H. Benton, 337; of Ralph Waldo Emerson, 362; of Edwin Forrest, 366; of Thomas Jefferson, 399; of James Madison, 406; of Alexander Stephens, 431; of Martin Van Buren, 434.
Lick, James, will of, 402, 403.
Lincoln, Abraham, died intestate, vii.
Ling, John, unique will of, 78.
Lion, bequest for a sermon in gratitude for being saved from a, 169.
Literary works, clauses in wills referring to: in will of Florence Nightingale, 282, 287; in will of Mark Twain, 349; in will of Ralph Waldo Emerson, 362; in will of Horace Greeley, 376; in will of Washington Irving, 391; in will of James Madison, 406; in will of James Monroe, 408; in will of Daniel Webster, 450; in will of J. G. Whittier, 451, 452.
Loans, to poor people provided by will of Peter Burns, 103.
Logan, James, on William Penn's will, 293.
London, people of, heirs of eccentric Frenchman, 156.
Longfellow, Henry Wadsworth, quoted, on Florence Nightingale, 281; will of, 403, 404.
Loss of wills, 252, 268, 271, 302, 304, 305.
"Lost Dauphin," remorse of Duchesse d'Angoulême for the, 242.
Loudoun, Countess of, directs that her hand be cut off and buried, 125.
Love, Alice, will of, 35; bequest of her wardrobe, 35.
Lungs, of Dr. Ellerby to be preserved, 129.
Luther, John B., "anticipating the past" in his will, 90.
Luther, Martin, will of, 41; uncertainty concerning authenticity of, 41; Van Proet's comment concerning, 41; Seckendorff's remarks on, 41; copy of, by Henterus, 42; Ranke's researches regarding, 42; original in Heidelberg Library, 42; his confidence in his wife, 41.

INDEX

McElroy, Robert J., pathetic will of, 168.
McKinley, William, last prayer of, 222, 223; will of, 404.
Madison, Dolly P., will of, 405.
Madison, James, will of, 405–407.
Mai, Cardinal, discovers and publishes will of Job, 10.
Maid-servants, bequest to encourage long service by, 110.
Malevolent will, a, 88.
Malicious will, of Dr. Dunlop, but with much humor, 179.
Maliciousness, in wills, 251, 289–291.
Manney, Sir Walter, will of, 29; a penny for the poor at his funeral, 29.
Manuscript, disposition of, by Virgil, 16.
March, Amy Curtis, will of, in "Little Women," 58.
Maria Cristina, Queen Dowager of Spain, will of, 276.
Markhouse, John, his will allowed, its codicil rejected, 162; founds school for illegitimate children, 162.
Mark Twain, see Clemens, Samuel L.
Marriage, peculiar requirement as to, 89.
Marriage, restrictions on, of daughter, in will of William de Beauchamp, 23.
Marriage fees, bequests for, of poor couples, 113.
Marriage portion, bequest for, with conditions, 175.
Married, must be, within a week, 79.
Marseilles, hospital for dogs and horses in, 97.
Marshall, ———, will for charitable purposes disallowed as perpetuity was involved, 102.
Marshall, Isabella, daughter of Earl of Pembroke, wills heart to her brother, 21.
Marshall, John, chief justice, will of, 407, 408.
Martin, Francis Offley, his desire to curtail funeral expenses, 154.
Martinett, Daniel, unique will of, 164; his use of plain English, 165.
Mary Queen of Scots (Mary Stuart), will of, 44; written on eve of execution, 44; provides for prayers in perpetuity, 45.
Mary Stuart, see Mary Queen of Scots.
Mass, the legality of a, 216.
Masses, seven thousand, 26; three thousand, 32; bequest for foundation of, and instructions for bell ringing, 133, 134.
Mausoleum, a costly, for a New York spinster, 135.

Meat, bequest for, for poor, 115.
Mellent, Earl of, will of the, 21.
"Memoirs of an Heiress," the will in, 56.
"Memorabilia Judaica," contains will of Pinedo, the Portuguese Jew, 104.
Memory, A, 212.
Menial service, required by rich testator of his heirs, 87.
"Merchant of Venice," will of Portia's father in, 56.
"Middlemarch," Mr. Casaubon's will in, 52.
Milk, devise to provide, for poor, 122.
Miners, wills of entombed, 237–239.
Minta, William, bequest for bread for poor, and for tolling the bell, 116.
Mirandola, Count of, annuity to a pet carp, 92.
Miscellaneous wills, 158–202.
Mississippi, religious bequests forbidden by laws of State of, 216.
"Miss Nancy," origin of the term, 219.
Mr. Casaubon's will, in "Middlemarch," 52; codicil to prevent wife marrying Ladislaw, 52.
"Mr. Meeson's Will," by H. Rider Haggard, 53; tattooed on back of heroine, 53; probated by photographic copy, 54.
Modesty, views of a Yorkshire rector on, 186.
Monmouth, Lord, will of, in "Coningsby," 52.
Monroe, James, will of, 408, 409.
Montagu, Edward Wortley, his will more generous than polite, 175.
Montaigne, Michel Eyquem de, will of, 277.
Morgan, Lewis Evan, his fortune to his servant with a "clamorous tongue," 166.
Morlet, Professor, bequest of his skull to the anatomical museum of Berne, 135; his name to be engraved on it, 136.
Morris, Gouverneur, will of, 409.
Mother, bequest of, by Eudamidas, 11; pathetic affection of a, 148.
Mother Hubbard's Dog, will of, 62.
Mountain, Robert Louis Stevenson's desire to be buried on a, 233.
Mourning, provided by Lady Hungerford for her family, 32; opposition to, 127, 154, 155, 173; desire for, 155.
Music, at funeral of Cortusio to be light and joyful, 140.
Mustaches, antipathy to wearing of, 87, 161.
Mutual Wills, danger in, 85.

NAME, bequests by John Nicholson to poor of same, 112; bequest designed to perpetuate a, 169; eccentric will of a Frenchman regarding, 178.
Napoleon, will of, formerly at Doctors' Commons, xiii; restored to French nation, xiii; will of, 277–279.
Nash, Ezekiel, bequest for bread for poor, 116; a memorial of his gratitude to God, 116.
National Debt, bequest for paying, of England and France, 228.
Nelson, Horatio, Lord, will of, xiii, 280, 281.
Newborough, Lord, curious provision in will of, regarding reinterment, 132.
Newspaper reading, enjoined by Vienna banker in bequest to nephew, 161.
New York Press Club, bequest to, by William J. Haskett, 186.
Nicholas's "Testamenta Vetusta," contains wills of many sovereigns, 43.
Nicholson, John, bequests to poor of same name, 112.
Nightingale, Florence, her body left for dissection, 177; will of, 281–289.
Noah, said to have left a will, xii; reputed will of, 10.
Nobel, Alfred Bernard, will of, establishing the Nobel Prizes, 229.
Nobel Prizes, foundation of, 229.
Noitier's will, in "The Count of Monte Cristo," 51.
Norman Conquest, wills known in England before the, xii.
Normandy, Duke of (Richard-sans-Peur), desired the utmost simplicity in his burial, 152.
North, Robert, his thankfulness to God, as expressed in his will, 200–202.
North American Review, editorial on wills, 1.
Northumberland, Duchess of, desired no autopsy, 132.
Nose, bequest to Miss B., in admiration of her adorable, 158.
Note-book, will of John D. Potter written in an old, 220.
Nouilles, Countess Anna Maria Helena de, peculiar stipulations in will of, 103.
Novelist, Wills of the, 51–62; the *Green Bag* on, 51.
Nuns, how a sick traveller imposed on the, of Auxerre, 171.
Nye, Phoebe Deliah, provides for chloroforming her favorite dog, 97; establishes drinking fountains in St. Louis for animals, 97.

OBELISK, to be buried in the shadow of an, 134.
Offe, Robert, kindness to widow enjoined by, 83.
O'Kelly, Pat, will of, in rhyme, 68.
Oldest Written Will, the, 12.
Oldfield, Anna, original of "Miss Nancy," 219.
Olivia, will of, in "Twelfth Night," 56.
Olonne, Duchesse D', eccentric will of, 149; exacting requirements regarding funeral of, 149, 150; her servants exiled, 150.
Opera, heir of Stanislas Poltzmarz must appear in, 184.
Oral bequests, Biblical tradition of, 11.
Oral will, probably delivered on deathbed, 13.
Original will, an, 87.
"Orley Farm," the will in, 52; forgery of codicil to, 52; widow convicted of perjury, 53.
Ostentatious will, of Matthew Wall, 174.
Oxford University, scholarships established at, by Cecil John Rhodes, 295.

PALMERSTON, Lady, tribute to husband in will of, 89.
Paper-knives, Charles Asselineau's unique collection of, 163.
Parker, John, will of, 86.
Parker, William, kindness to widow enjoined by, 83.
Parren, Ellen Elizabeth, her obsequies of a bright character, 153; a unique funeral cortège, 154.
Parrot, life of, depends on contest of will, 92; annuity for, 92, 93; must have handsome cage, 93.
Pastor, a certain, debarred from preaching in testator's church, 220.
Pathetic will, 82; of entombed miners, 237–239.
Paupers, bequest to most indigent, 111.
Peabody, George, philanthropy of, 409, 410; will of, 410.
Peas, devise to provide white, for poor, 122.
Pedler and his Dog, A, statue of, 167; ownership of Pedler's Acre contingent on preservation of, 167.
Pedler's Acre, contingent on preservation of a statue, 167.
Pegati, Joe, the will of an entombed miner, 237, 238.
Pelham, Sir William, will of, 40; sermons to be preached for, 40.
Pembroke, Philip, Earl of, will of, 289–291.
Pembroke, William, Earl of, his widow must not remarry, 228.
Penn, William, will of, 291–293.

Peoples Pulpit, the, quotation from, 90.
Pepys, Samuel, will of, 294.
Pepysian Library, the, 294.
Perpetuities, rule against, 3.
Perpetuity, a gift in, 35.
Perram, John, bequest for a marriage portion with conditions, 175; contingent bequest for horse-racing, 176.
Perren, Madame Veuve, bequest to Marseilles for hospital for dogs and horses, 97.
Petrarch, will of, 26; selects place of burial, 27; bequest to Boccaccio, 27.
Petrie, William M. P., discovers oldest written will, 12.
Pette, Reginald atte, an early bequest for church improvements, 162.
Pew, use of a, exchanged for sealskin sack, 219.
Philadelphia, Penn., benefited by the will of Benjamin Franklin, 370, 371; by the will of Stephen Girard, 373–375.
Phonograph, voice of William Faxon reproduced at his funeral by, 226.
Pierre II, Duke of Brittany, bequest for masses, 133.
Piers Plowman, *see* "Vision of Piers Plowman."
Pig, will of a, 21.
Pigs, singular bequest for prizes for riding, 102.
"Pincher," Lord Eldon's dog, receives annuity, 96; painted by Landseer, 96.
Pinedo, the Portuguese Jew, munificent bequests in will of, 104.
Pinero, Arthur W., will in "Iris," 54; "The Thunderbolt" based on a will, 55.
Piper, Mary Thomas, bequeaths his funeral expenses to nephew, 124.
Pipes, the "King of Smokers'" collection of, 200; bequests of, 200.
Pitt, Rev. Mr., bequest for bread for poor, 118.
Pitt, William, will of, xiii.
"Plain English," use of, in will of Daniel Martinett, 165.
Plan, general, for making a will, 5.
Plato, will of, 14.
Playing cards, directions that a pack be placed in the coffin, 128.
Pocket, will in the, of an old dress, 216.
Poet, will of the pardoned, 246, 247.
Poetry or Rhyme, Wills in, 49–72.
Police Station, generous bequest to a, 158.
Polk, James K., will of, 411, 412.
Poltzmarz, Stanislas, stipulation that his heir must appear in opera, 184.
Poor, at burial of Sir Walter Manney to receive one penny, 29.
Poor man, quotation on a, 215.

Pope, Alexander, satire on Eustace Budgell, 58.
Porter, Edmund, devise for milk for poor, 122; since commuted for bread, 122.
Portrait, of favorite brother to be placed in coffin, 140.
Potter, John D., his will written in an old note-book, 220.
Powder Plot, bequest for sermon on deliverance from, 174.
Powell, Byrd, bequest of his skull to a pupil, 136.
"Practical Suggestions for Writing Wills," by John M. Gest, in *American Law Register*, 205.
Praslin, Duchesse de, will of, 81.
Prayer, widow to spend life in, 81.
Primitive Belief, A, regarding the spirit, 122.
Prisoners, bequest for exhortation to condemned, in Newgate, 245.
Prison Mirror, will of the pardoned poet "Anglicus," 246, 247.
Probates, R. B. Tappan, his own will, 247.
Profanity, a bar to inheritance, 189.
Property rights of women, 75–78.
Prophet's Beard Case, The, sensation caused by, 184.
Puck, humorous will suggested by, 220, 221.
Pullman, George M., will of, 412, 413.
Pym, William, will of, 87.

QUESTIONS, claimant of estate must answer thirty, 236.

R., MR., fear of being buried alive and precautions against, 130.
Rabelais, will of, 43.
Radier's, "Recréations Historiques," mentions will of Lodovico Cortusio, 140.
Raisins, bequest for, to boys of Christ's Hospital, 118.
Ralli, Theodore James, bequests to art institutions, 126; wanted no mourning, 127.
Randall, Robert Richard, founder of the "Sailors' Snug Harbor," 218.
Randall, Samuel J., small estate of, 218.
Randolph, John, will of, 413–420.
Ranke, Leopold von, researches regarding Luther's will, 42.
Reading of will, stipulation regarding, 104.
Recipes, eccentric Frenchman desired new cooking, 156.
Redding, Maria, curious instructions in will of, 149; an economical provision, 149.

INDEX 469

Redman, John, peculiar will of, 136; a deep grave, 136; codicil to will of, 137; wine for his executors, 137.
Reed, John, bequest of his skull to the "properties" of Walnut Street Theatre (Philadelphia), 136; to represent the skull of "Yorick," 136.
Registry of Wills, London, wills of famous personages in, xiii.
Registry of Wills, Washington, contains wills of famous Americans, xiii.
Religious bequests, restrictions on, in United States, 216.
Remarriage, of husband, forbidden, 228.
Remarriage, of widow, restrictions on, 5, 15, 54, 228.
Remsen, Daniel S., comments on making of wills, 2.
Residuary legatees, Mr. George makes imaginary children, 160.
Revenge, will made in, 81.
Revere, Paul, will of, 420, 421.
Rhodes, Cecil John, directs that he be buried in the Mattopo Hills, 233; will of, 294–296.
Rhyme, Wills in, 49–72.
Ricard, Fortune, will of, 228; the five funds established by, 228.
Richard-sans-Peur, *see* Normandy, Duke of.
Richardson, Mary, an important word omitted in will of, 190.
Richelieu, Cardinal, will of, 296–302; the extravagance and pompousness of, 297; his library, 300.
Riedel, Robert, a veteran's bequest to his old comrades, 123.
Rigid conditions, in bequest to poor, 112.
Rings, bequeathed by Izaak Walton, 319.
Roe, T. P., provides by will for her pet dog, 95.
Roman Law, origin of testamentary disposition in, xii, 2.
Romans, will-makesque invention of, 2.
Roman Wills, sealing of, xii.
Rose, yearly tribute of one red, 233.
Rosebery, Lord, address on Byron, xi.
Rosière of Puteaux, establishment of, 114; first beneficiary of, 114.
Rousseau, Jean Jacques, will of, 302–304.
Ruffell, William, will of, in rhyme, 68.

SACRILEGIOUS WILL, in rhyme, 68.
Sage, Russell, will of, 422, 423.
Saguma, Lieutenant, letter of, written in destroyed submarine, 236, 237.
"Sailors' Snug Harbor," founded by Robert Richard Randall, 218.
St. Jerome, mentions the will of a pig, 20.
St. Leonards, Lord, will of, 304, 305.

St. Louis Times, the, comments on the "Two-hundred-dollar Husband," 79.
St. Patrick's Hospital, provided for, in Swift's will, 311.
Saints, desired the company of the, 132.
Saladin, will of, 21.
Salter, John, Sir, a salutation required by, 158.
Salutation, a yearly, required by Sir John Salter, 158.
Sand, George, her curiosity regarding a mysterious packet, 242; its result, 242, 243.
Sandwich, Dowager Countess of, desired no display at her funeral, 149.
Sarcastic Will, of a British sailor, 80; of Edward Wortley Montagu, 175.
Sargeant, J., his bequests contingent on early rising and temperance, 180.
Satirical will, of Rabelais, 43.
Say, Maud De, her request for a simple burial, 148.
Scardeon's "Vies des Jurisconsultes de Padoue," mention will of Lodovico Cortusio, 140.
Scarron, Paul, will of, in verse, 63.
Scenery, Lord Camelford desired beautiful, 152.
Scholarships, established by Cecil John Rhodes, 295.
Schumann, Carl, directs that his body be cremated and his ashes tossed to the winds, 127.
Sealskin sack, use of a pew exchanged for a, 219.
Sennacherib, will of, 13.
Sermon, will of Elias Boudinot contained a lengthy, 192.
Sermons, twenty to be preached for Sir William Pelham, 40; devise for the preaching of, 109.
Servant, unfortunate result of beneficiary marrying a domestic, 183.
Shakespeare, William, will of, xiii, 305–309; Olivia's will in "Twelfth Night," 56; will of Portia's father in "Merchant of Venice," 56.
Shelley, Phillip, devise for benefit of maimed soldiers, 107.
Sherman, John, will of, 424–427.
Shirt, mentioned in will of Saladin, 22.
Silhouette, Etienne, will of, 309; history of, 309.
Silhouette, origin of the word, 309.
Sixpences, peculiar bequest of, 139.
Skulls, various bequests of, 135, 136.
Slavery, release from, by will, 14, 15, 16.
Slaves, clauses in will concerning: in will of Henry Clay, 345, 347; in will of Patrick Henry, 383; in will of Andrew Jackson, 393; in will of Thomas

Jefferson, 400; in will of R. E. Lee, 402; in will of James Madison, 406; in will of Chief Justice Marshall, 408; in will of John Randolph, 414–416; in will of George Washington, 440; in will of Mary Washington, 447, 448.
Smee, W. R., his will disallowed, 190; his delusion that he was the son of a king, 190.
Smiles, bequest to young lady who, so sweetly, 158.
Smith, George T., the three-word will of, held invalid, 169.
Smithers, his brief will in rhyme, 62.
Smithson, James, his foundation of the Smithsonian Institution, 218.
Smithsonian Institution, foundation of, 218.
Smoking, wonderful record of Mr. Klaës in, 200.
Snuff, bequest for, for poor, 116.
Soldiers, devise for benefit of maimed, 107.
Solon, said to have introduced wills in Greece, xii.
South, Sir James, annuity for favorite dog, 98.
Spackman, Thomas, bequest to poor who attend church on stated days, 111.
Spanish Armada, *see* Armada, The Spanish.
Spirit will, of W. H. Crowell, 172.
Spiteful wills, 229, 230.
Stafford, England, in Izaak Walton's will, 318.
Stafford, Henry, Earl of, will of, 85; unhappy marriage of, 85.
Standish, Myles, will of, 427, 428.
Stanford, Jane Lathrop, will of, 427, 428.
Starkey, John, tribute to wife in will of, 82.
Staverton, George, provides by will for bull-baiting, 110; since discontinued, 111.
Steinberg, Adolph, will of, in mysterious trunk, 173.
Stephens, Alexander, will of, 429–431.
Stevenson, Robert Louis, will of Dr. Jekyll, 52; the directions for his burial, 233; his epitaph, 233.
Steward, testator's opinion of his, 87.
Stiegel, Heinrich Wilhelm, unique rental for a church lot, 233.
Stock, Ottilie, will of, 92; contest over, 92.
Stow, John Hylett, his bequest of the picture of a viper, 180; the suit for libel which resulted, 181.
Stowe, Harriet Beecher, will of, 431, 432.
"Strange Case of Dr. Jekyll and Mr. Hyde," will of Dr. Jekyll, 52.
Stray Dogs, annuity for benefit of, 98.

Striewe, Sophia, peculiar clause in will of, 232.
Study, restrictions on hours of, 103.
Submarine, letter written in destroyed Japanese, 236, 237.
Sugden, the Honorable Miss Charlotte, daughter of Lord St. Leonards, 304.
Sun, The (New York), account of an unusual marriage, 78.
"Sunnyside," Washington Irving's estate, 391, 392.
Swift, Jonathan, will of, 309–313.
Swinburne, Henry, author of "A briefe Treatise of Testaments and Last Willes," 215; story told by, 215.
Symonds, Peter, bequest to boys of Christ's Hospital, for raisins, 118.

"TABLE TALK OR ORIGINAL ESSAYS," Hazlitt on will making in, 49–51.
Tacitus, mentions wills, xii.
Tageblatt, the, account of a peculiar provision for beer, 106.
Tapley, Valentine, his pride in his whiskers, 156; a strong tomb to protect, 156.
Tappan, R. B., probates his own will, 247, 248.
Tassoni, Alessandro, will of, 47, 48.
Tatler, the, will of Nicholas Gimcrack in, 56.
Taylor, William, bequest for Christmas dinner to almshouse women, 116.
Teacher, vocation of, ennobled by Louis Agassiz, 198.
Teeth, fund created to care for, of Boston (Mass.) school children, 232.
Telemachus, will of, cited by Homer, 11.
Temperance, bequests contingent on, 180.
Terral, E. Y., provides for no funeral services and a simple burial, 128.
"Testamenta Vetusta," ii, will of Robert Fabyan, 145.
Testamentary and kindred miscellany, 203–248.
Testamentary capacity, 203–205.
Testators, Charles Dickens's views on elderly, 243.
Thake, John, bequest for fish for poor in Lent, 120.
Theatrical Woman's League, the, 397.
Three-word will, not valid, 169.
"Thunderbolt, The," by Pinero, based on a will, 55.
Tilden, Samuel J., will of, 433.
"Tilden Trust, The," 433.
Tobacco, bequest for, for poor, 116; to be planted on grave, 150.
Tolam, Dennis, singular will of, 183; original method of paying bequests, 183.

Tolerant nature, a, shown in will of William Wilson, 108.
Tolstoi, Leo, Count, last words of, 223.
Tombstone, dropping money on, for the poor, 109.
Torches, to be held by poor women suitably clothed, 32; of sixteen pounds' weight, held by poor men, 32.
Toste, Robert, directs that his body be buried under step of altar, 124.
Tourville, M. de., right to estate of wife whom he murdered denied, 235, 236.
Town crier, bequest for, in will of Roland Williams, 239.
Towns, bequest for building, in France, 228.
Townsend, Elizabeth, bequest for singing of favorite anthems, 178.
Travel, aversion to European, 235.
Travellers' Rest, devise of land and buildings for, 107.
Trollope, Anthony, the will in "Orley Farm," 52.
Trousers, eccentric manner of distributing money by means of, 177.
Troutbeck, John, his vainglorious will, 179.
Trunk, Sieur Benoît desired to be buried in a leather, 138; will of Adolph Steinberg in mysterious, 173.
Truro, Lady, simplicity in obsequies of, 155.
Trust, provision for, 9.
Trust Companies, as executors, 248.
Tuke, M., bequeaths one penny to each child attending his funeral, 125; an annuity to woman who tucked him up in bed, 125; bread to be thrown to poor on Christmas Day, from church roof, 125.
Turkeys, bequest to provide, for Easter love-feast, 120.
Turkish captives, conditional bequest to, 112.
Turner, J. M. W., will of, 314, 315.
Turner, Miss, peculiar restrictions in will of, 183; unfortunate result of, 183.
Turner, Sharon, tribute to wife in will of, 83.
Turvyle, John, will of, 35; a gift in perpetuity, 35.
"Twelfth Night," Olivia's will in, 56.
Twins, bequest for benefit of, born in Marblehead (Mass.), 109.

UNDERCLOTHES, beneficiary not to wear, in winter, 159.
Undergraduates, poor opinion of, held by William Farren, 174.
Undertaker, paid in advance, 226.
Underwood, John, his epitaph, 150;
unique funeral of, 150, 151; the books placed in his coffin, 151; his desire to be forgotten, 151.
University, George Washington's bequest for the establishment of, 442.
Uxoricide, rights of an, denied, 235.

VAINGLORIOUS WILL, the, of John Troutbeck, 179.
Valet, bequest of Marquis d'Aligre to his, 251.
Van Bunschooten, Rev. Dr., will to be read by Church at all official meetings, 104.
Van Buren, Martin, will of, 433–436.
Van Proet, M., comment on Luther's will, 41.
Vanderbilt, ——, bequest to Miss B., in admiration of her adorable nose, 158.
Vanderbilt, Cornelius, Commodore, his view of Alexander Stewart's will, 232.
Vandyck, Anthony, will of, xiii.
Vangelas, Claude Favre de, will of, 315.
Varembon, François de la Palu, see Beaumont sur Vingeanne, Seigneur de.
Vassar, Matthew, will of, 436, 437.
Vassar College, 436, 437.
Vest, George G., will of, 437–439; extract from speech of, on dog, 438, 439.
Villon, François, wills in verse in his "The Lesser Testament," and "The Greater Testament," 64.
Vindictive Will, 86.
Viper, bequest of a picture of a, 180.
Virgil, will of, 16; disposition of Æneid, 16; directions for burial, 16.
Virtue, rewarded by will of wealthy New Yorker, 186; bequests for the purpose of aiding, 250, 258, 259.
Virtuoso, will of a, 56.
"Vision of Piers Plowman," will in, 63.
Vivisection, Dr. Fraser's opposition to, 181.
Voltaire, F. M. A. de, will of, 315; and Benjamin Franklin, 316.

WAGNER, DR., grewsome bequests of, 167.
Waistcoats, four green, to be given yearly to poor women, 111.
Wales, Prince of, Edward (1376), will of, 30.
Walker, Thomas, bequest to encourage attendance at church, 115.
Wall, Matthew, ostentatious will of, 174.
Wallace, John W., directions for a simple funeral and for cremation, 130.
Walpole, Horace, account of peculiar preamble to a will, 54.
Walton, Izaak, will of, xiii, 316–320.

Wardall, John, provides for lantern to be lighted all night, 105.
Washington, George, will of, xiii, 439–447.
Washington, Mary, will of, 447, 448.
Webster, Daniel, will of, 448–451.
Weeping, the relative found, to be disinherited, 140.
Weight, a bequest to daughters by, 161.
Wellesley, Arthur, *see* Wellington, Duke of.
Wellington, Duke of, will of, xiii, 320, 323.
West, Joshua, will of, in rhyme, 69.
West, Lady Alice, will of, 30; bequest of her books, 31.
Western Reserve Law Journal, editorial on testamentary habits, 73–75.
Whiskers, Valentine Tapley's pride in his, 156.
Whisky, bequest for, for extermination of the Irish, 182.
Whitbread, Samuel, bequest in honor of John Bunyan for bread for poor, 117.
White, desired, to be worn at funeral, 152.
White, Dr. Thomas, bequest to poor with rigid conditions, 112.
Whittier, John G., will of, 451–453.
Widow, legacy to, doubled if she married, 80; kindness to, enjoined by testator, 83.
Widow, restrictions on marriage of, 15, 54.
Widow's cap, legacy depending upon wearing of, 88.
Wife, would not be good, 84; desertion by, rewarded, 88; curious revenge on a nagging, 89; elegy on a, 211, 212.
Wilcocks, John, ambiguous wording in will of, 126.
Wilcox, Robert, bequests for three sermons on the Powder Plot, Queen Elizabeth, and deliverance from the Spanish Armada, 174.
Williams, Roland, peculiar bequest in will of, 239.
Williamson, Thomas, bequest for meat for poor for stormy weather, 115.
Willie, Smith, extraordinary will of, 170.
Will-making, on, 49–51.
Wilson, John, unique method of finding missing son, 236.

Wilson, William, bequest for sick poor, 108.
Windsor, Thomas, will of, 32; torches to be held by poor men at his burying and *monethe's minde,* 32; one hundred children at his *monethe's minde,* 33; priests to sing at his *monethe's minde,* 33.
Wine, will of citizen of Berne to control price of, 118.
Winslow, Frederick Christian, singular provision regarding his horses, 93.
Winslow, Mary Chilton, will of, 453.
Winter, beneficiary not to wear underclothes in, 159.
Withipol, J., will of, 81; a contrite spirit, 81.
Witnesses, importance of, 4; not interested in the instrument, 8.
Wives, beautiful sentiments to, 82, 83; desired to be buried between his two, 132.
Woeltge, Albert, makes mutual will with wife, 85.
Woeltge, Mary Louise, makes mutual will with husband, 85.
Woman, not to be buried near a, 131; first monument in United States to a, 213.
Woman Hater, a, 131.
Women, property rights of, 75–78.
Word, omission of important, 190.
Words, legal distinction between, in wills, 3.
"Working with a Will," 220.
Wrapping-paper, a valid will on, 168.
Wyatt, Surgeon-Major, buried in full-dress uniform, 154; no mourning to be used, 154, 155.
Wyndsore, Lady Alice, will of, 31; provides for funeral and burial, 31; gift to poor on day of her sepulture, 31; for repairing highways, 31.

YOUNG, Brigham, will of, 454.
Ysabeau of Scotland, Duke of Brittany, bequest for masses, 134.

ZABRISKIE, Sarah Titus, bequest to pet cat, 100.
Zalesky, M., eccentric will of, 182.
Zimmer, Nicholas, a valid will on a collar-box, 168.

Printed in the United States
1310600002B/211